Feasting on the Word®

Feasting on the Word®

Preaching the
Revised Common Lectionary

Year C, Volume 1

DAVID L. BARTLETT and BARBARA BROWN TAYLOR

General Editors

WJK WESTMINSTER
JOHN KNOX PRESS
LOUISVILLE · KENTUCKY

Book design by Drew Stevens
Cover design by Lisa Buckley

First edition
Published by Westminster John Knox Press
Louisville, Kentucky

This book is printed on acid-free paper that meets the American National Standards Institute Z39.48 standard. ♾

PRINTED IN THE UNITED STATES OF AMERICA

12 13 14 15 16 17 18 — 10 9 8 7 6 5 4 3

Library of Congress Cataloging-in-Publication Data

Feasting on the Word : preaching the revised common lectionary / David L. Bartlett and Barbara Brown Taylor, general editors.
      p. cm.
   Includes index.
   ISBN 978-0-664-23100-2 (v. 5 alk. paper)
   ISBN 978-0-664-23099-9 (v. 4 alk. paper)
   ISBN 978-0-664-23098-2 (v. 3 alk. paper)
   ISBN 978-0-664-23097-5 (v. 2 alk. paper)
   ISBN 978-0-664-23096-8 (v. 1 alk. paper)
   1. Lectionary preaching.   2. Common lectionary (1992)   I. Bartlett, David Lyon, 1941–
II. Taylor, Barbara Brown.
   BV4235.L43F43   2008
   251'.6—dc22

                                                                      2007047534

Contents

Publisher's Note

Feasting on the Word: Preaching the Revised Common Lectionary is an ambitious project that is offered to the Christian church as a resource for preaching and teaching.

The uniqueness of this approach in providing four perspectives on each preaching occasion from the Revised Common Lectionary sets this work apart from other lectionary materials. The theological, pastoral, exegetical, and homiletical dimensions of each biblical passage are explored with the hope that preachers will find much to inform and stimulate their preparations for preaching from this rich "feast" of materials.

This work could not have been undertaken without the deep commitments of those who have devoted countless hours to working on these tasks. Westminster John Knox Press would like to acknowledge the magnificent work of our general editors, David L. Bartlett and Barbara Brown Taylor. They are both gifted preachers with passionate concerns for the quality of preaching. They are also wonderful colleagues who embraced this huge task with vigor, excellence, and unfailing good humor. Our debt of gratitude to Barbara and David is great.

The fine support staff, project manager Joan Murchison and compiler Mary Lynn Darden, enabled all the thousands of "pieces" of the project to come together and form this impressive series. Without their strong competence and abiding persistence, these volumes could not have emerged.

The volume editors for this series are to be thanked as well. They used their superb skills as pastors and professors and ministers to work with writers and help craft their valuable insights into the highly useful entries that comprise this work.

The hundreds of writers who shared their expertise and insights to make this series possible are ones who deserve deep thanks indeed. They come from wide varieties of ministries. They have given their labors to provide a gift to benefit the whole church and to enrich preaching in our time.

Westminster John Knox would also like to express our appreciation to Columbia Theological Seminary for strong cooperation in enabling this work to begin and proceed. Dean of Faculty and Executive Vice President D. Cameron Murchison welcomed the project from the start and drew together everything we needed. His continuing efforts have been very valuable. Former President Laura S. Mendenhall provided splendid help as well. She made seminary resources and personnel available and encouraged us in this partnership with enthusiasm and all good grace. We thank her, and look forward to working with Columbia's new president, Stephen Hayner.

It is a joy for Westminster John Knox Press to present *Feasting on the Word: Preaching the Revised Common Lectionary* to the church, its preachers, and its teachers. We believe rich resources can assist the church's ministries as the Word is proclaimed. We believe the varieties of insights found in these pages will nourish preachers who will "feast on the Word" and who will share its blessings with those who hear.

Westminster John Knox Press

Series Introduction

A preacher's work is never done. Teaching, offering pastoral care, leading worship, and administering congregational life are only a few of the responsibilities that can turn preaching into just one more task of pastoral ministry. Yet the Sunday sermon is how the preacher ministers to most of the people most of the time. The majority of those who listen are not in crisis. They live such busy lives that few take part in the church's educational programs. They wish they had more time to reflect on their faith, but they do not. Whether the sermon is five minutes long or forty-five, it is the congregation's one opportunity to hear directly from their pastor about what life in Christ means and why it matters.

Feasting on the Word offers pastors focused resources for sermon preparation, written by companions on the way. With four different essays on each of the four biblical texts assigned by the Revised Common Lectionary, this series offers preachers sixteen different ways into the proclamation of God's Word on any given occasion. For each reading, preachers will find brief essays on the exegetical, theological, homiletical, and pastoral challenges of the text. The page layout is unusual. By setting the biblical passage at the top of the page and placing the essays beneath it, we mean to suggest the interdependence of the four approaches without granting priority to any one of them. Some readers may decide to focus on the Gospel passage, for instance, by reading all four essays provided for that text. Others may decide to look for connections between the Hebrew Bible, Psalm, Gospel, and Epistle texts by reading the theological essays on each one.

Wherever they begin, preachers will find what they need in a single volume produced by writers from a wide variety of disciplines and religious traditions. These authors teach in colleges and seminaries. They lead congregations. They write scholarly books as well as columns for the local newspaper. They oversee denominations. In all of these capacities and more, they serve God's Word, joining the preacher in the ongoing challenge of bringing that Word to life.

We offer this print resource for the mainline church in full recognition that we do so in the digital age of the emerging church. Like our page layout, this decision honors the authority of the biblical text, which thrives on the page as well as in the ear. While the twelve volumes of this series follow the pattern of the Revised Common Lectionary, each volume contains an index of biblical passages so that all preachers may make full use of its contents.

We also recognize that this new series appears in a post-9/11, post-Katrina world. For this reason, we provide no shortcuts for those committed to the proclamation of God's Word. Among preachers, there are books known as "Monday books" because they need to be read thoughtfully at least a week ahead of time. There are also "Saturday books," so called because they supply sermon ideas on short notice. The books in this series are not Saturday books. Our aim is to help preachers go deeper, not faster, in a world that is in need of saving words.

A series of this scope calls forth the gifts of a great many people. We are grateful first of all to the staff of Westminster John Knox Press: Don McKim, Jack Keller, and Jon Berquist, who conceived this project; David Dobson, who worked diligently to bring the project to completion, with publisher Marc Lewis's strong support; and Julie Tonini, who has painstakingly guided each volume through the production process. We thank former President Laura Mendenhall and former Dean Cameron Murchison of Columbia Theological Seminary, who made our participation in this work possible. We thank President Steve Hayner and Dean Deborah Mullen for their continuing encouragement and support. Our editorial board is a hardworking board, without whose patient labor and good humor this series would not exist. From the start, Joan Murchison has been the brains of the operation, managing details of epic proportions with great human kindness. Mary Lynn Darden, Dilu Nicholas, Megan Hackler Denton, and John Shillingburg have supported both her and us with their administrative skills.

We have been honored to work with a multitude of gifted thinkers, writers, and editors. We present these essays as their offering—and ours—to the blessed ministry of preaching.

David L. Bartlett
Barbara Brown Taylor

A Note about the Lectionary

Feasting on the Word follows the Revised Common Lectionary (RCL) as developed by the Consultation on Common Texts, an ecumenical consultation of liturgical scholars and denominational representatives from the United States and Canada. The RCL provides a collection of readings from Scripture to be used during worship in a schedule that follows the seasons of the church year. In addition, it provides for a uniform set of readings to be used across denominations or other church bodies.

The RCL provides a reading from the Old Testament, a Psalm response to that reading, a Gospel, and an Epistle for each preaching occasion of the year. It is presented in a three-year cycle, with each year centered around one of the Synoptic Gospels. Year A is the year of Matthew, Year B is the year of Mark, and Year C is the year of Luke. John is read each year, especially during Advent, Lent, and Easter.

The RCL offers two tracks of Old Testament texts for the Season after Pentecost or Ordinary Time: a semicontinuous track, which moves through stories and characters in the Old Testament, and a complementary track, which ties the Old Testament texts to the theme of the Gospel texts for that day. Some denominational traditions favor one over the other. For instance, Presbyterians and Methodists generally follow the semicontinuous track, while Lutherans and Episcopalians generally follow the complementary track.

The print volumes of *Feasting on the Word* follow the complementary track for Year A, are split between the complementary and semicontinuous tracks for Year B, and cover the semicontinuous stream for Year C. Essays for Pentecost and the Season after Pentecost that are not covered in the print volumes are available on the *Feasting on the Word* Web site, www.feastingontheword.net.

For more information about the Revised Common Lectionary, visit the official RCL Web site at http://lectionary.library.vanderbilt.edu/ or see *The Revised Common Lectionary: The Consultation on Common Texts* (Nashville: Abingdon Press, 1992).

Feasting on the Word®

Jeremiah 33:14-16

¹⁴The days are surely coming, says the LORD, when I will fulfill the promise I made to the house of Israel and the house of Judah. ¹⁵In those days and at that time I will cause a righteous Branch to spring up for David; and he shall execute justice and righteousness in the land. ¹⁶In those days Judah will be saved and Jerusalem will live in safety. And this is the name by which it will be called: "The LORD is our righteousness."

Theological Perspective

This brief essay will attend to the continuing theological significance of (1) the reality of human despair, (2) a reading of the promise in light of both the experience of exile and the practice of waiting in Advent, and (3) the collective and sociopolitical aspects of the promise.

The Reality of Human Despair. Much of the story told in Jeremiah has to do with the threat and fulfillment of the destruction of Judah and, in particular, Jerusalem. The people have been violating their covenantal relationship with God, and the subsequent Babylonian control would serve as punishment for their infidelity. The complete sacking of Jerusalem, however, is more horrific and absolute than the people might have imagined. The destruction is so severe that God's voice, through the prophet, also wails in lamentation.

In view of the devastation that characterizes the sociohistorical context of the "Book of Consolation," Kathleen O'Connor describes the situation of the people in this way: "The people . . . are taken captive, dragged from their land, and deprived of their Temple. They are beaten, imprisoned, and face death as a people, and, like Jeremiah, they cry out to God

Pastoral Perspective

"In those days . . ." On Christmas Eve Luke will turn the church back to a historical context of Jesus' birth, anchoring the event in time with persons and places, in a world of Caesar and census: "In those days a decree went out from Emperor Augustus that all the world should be registered" (Luke 2:1). But on the First Sunday of Advent, Jeremiah turns us forward to the future: "In those days and at that time . . ." In these days before Christmas the future is not where our culture encourages us to go; it fosters a holiday experience that is nostalgic and immediate. "In those days and at that time" God will decree justice and righteousness. Seasonal traditions dictate charity. "The days are surely coming" when God will fulfill the promise. We are sure that consumerism will deliver our fulfillment. The church is called to hear the prophets in this season, not for "once upon a time" background music, but for an overture playing in real time, sounding themes to be developed going forward. "In those days" there will be "justice and righteousness," peace and security. Next week Zechariah will pick up the tune of righteousness and peace (Luke 1:68–79), and Advent will end with Mary singing of God's justice. The church may light its Advent candles for preparation, hope, joy, and love, but the prophets sound justice and righteousness.

Exegetical Perspective

Part of the climactic verses of the Little Book of Comfort, as chapters 30–33 in the book of Jeremiah have been called since Martin Luther, the lectionary passage Jeremiah 33:14–16 proclaims salvation in the form of restoration of the Davidic monarchy and pronounces a new name for Jerusalem after the Babylonian exile. The subsequent verses also promise the revival of the Levitical priesthood. Set in a part of the book of Jeremiah where destruction of the Holy City and deportation of the people to Babylon has been threatened numerous times and already taken place for the royal court and the upper classes (see the cycles of judgment oracles in Jer. 1–25 and throughout the remainder of the book), these eschatological promises of a different historical reality are spoken to give hope to a crushed people and inspire faithful endurance of the present circumstances.

How one understands what is meant by the present time and realities for Jeremiah depends on which hypothesis of composition of the book one accepts. Most biblical scholars locate the passage in exilic or postexilic writings of members of the Deuteronomistic school, who are generally considered the authors and editors of the prose sections of the book of Jeremiah during the later sixth century

Homiletical Perspective

The season of Advent is puzzling to many Christians. The stories read during this season are, by and large, not childhood favorites. They have no star in the east guiding devout magi, no soliloquy of angels stirring shepherds to go and see the babe, no harried innkeeper, no touching moment when Mary ponders these things in her heart.

The stories of Advent are dug from the harsh soil of human struggle and the littered landscape of dashed dreams. They are told from the vista where sin still reigns supreme and hope has gone on vacation. Many prefer the major notes of joy and gladness in the Christmas stories to the minor keys of Advent.

Advent also leaves us dizzy over time. Advent is not a steady, constant, "time marches on" kind of time, a persistent drumbeat of day after day, year after year. Advent is unpredictable time, unsteady time. In this time-tumbling season, we look for a baby to be born while we know that the baby has already been born, and still is being born in us—this Emmanuel who came and is coming and is among us right now. Not only is Advent not well behaved, neat, and orderly; it contorts time. Given the nature of Advent, it is no surprise that Jeremiah is its herald.

Jeremiah speaks to hostages being seduced to start a new life in balmy Babylon. He tells a tough audience

Jeremiah 33:14-16

Theological Perspective

in anger and despair."[1] John Calvin imagined the context in even more explicit terms: "As they were then exposed to slaughter, . . . the children of God saw thousand deaths; so that it could not be but that terror almost drove them to despair; and in their exile they saw that they were far removed from their own country, without any hope of a return."[2]

When faced with such death, slaughter, and imprisonment in a strange place, who would not despair? While despair is among the most human of human conditions, it cannot be fully understood apart from its theological implications. In a number of his writings, Reinhold Niebuhr associated despair with our failed attempts to procure security for ourselves, optimistically pretending that we are not subject to the vicissitudes of creatureliness. Despair is characterized primarily by the conspicuous absence of theological hope. Humans meet despair when they cannot imagine God's promised alternative future.

God's Promise to a People Waiting. The writer recounts the promises made to "the house of Israel and the house of Judah," that God would provide the people a safe, just, and peaceful future under a justly appointed and righteous ruler. This week's reading is addressed to a people in exile. God's promise, in this case, is meant to be a comfort and source of hope to the exiled, rather than a foretelling of the faithful remnant that appears between Jeremiah's condemnations of unjust rulers. Here we meet the God who promises to protect and restore the people, even as they are in the midst of great suffering and at the edge of despair. It is in precisely this context that God speaks the promise, and it is in precisely this context that despair opens the door to creativity and hope. Calvin acknowledged that the promises of God seem to disappear, but that with faith and patience, we look forward to their fulfillment.

In part, this is the theological significance of Advent too. The inclusion of prophetic literature in the Advent lections points to the importance of waiting, anticipating, and trusting in a promised future that seems very removed from our current circumstance. And it is in the season of Advent that we engage in the strenuous and crucial Christian

1. Kathleen O'Connor, "Jeremiah," in *The Women's Bible Commentary*, ed. Carol A. Newsom and Sharon H. Ringe (Louisville, KY: Westminster John Knox Press, 2002), 174.
2. John Calvin, *Commentaries on the Book of the Prophet Jeremiah and the Lamentations*, vol. 4, ed. and trans. John Owen (Grand Rapids: Eerdmans, 1950), 247. http://www.ccel.org/ccel/calvin/calcom20.i.html (accessed from Christian Classics Ethereal Library, March 17, 2008).

Pastoral Perspective

A pastoral perspective on Advent is attuned to the yearnings of our day for a different day, and aware of both the temptation to look backward for God and good and the trepidation in looking forward. The prophet Jeremiah speaks a pastoral word, assuring the people of his time and ours that what is coming is of God. He is adamant about the things that we are tentative about: "The days are surely coming . . ." (here and in 23:5–6; see also 31:27, 31, 38); "I have . . . plans for your welfare and not for harm, to give you a future with hope" (29:11). There will be a future in God's time and fulfillment on God's terms. This particular text envisions not a day to come at Advent's end, but days to come that will inaugurate a new beginning.

The congregation that observes Advent will mark time differently from those people who live December as a countdown to Christmas and the end of the year. The Sundays of Advent count forward to a time that begins with the birth of Christ. The First Sunday of Advent is for Christians the first Sunday of the year, a new year in sacred time, opening to the mystery and certainty of God's presence. Worship that celebrates an alternative New Year's Day affirms time as God's home and workplace, not as a calendar of accumulating years but as a movement toward fulfillment, not a day for self-improvement resolutions but for community reaffirmation of trust in God's promises, past, present, and future. "With grateful hearts the past we own; The future, all to us unknown, We to your guardian care commit." Philip Doddridge wrote on the manuscript of his hymn, "For the New Year."[1]

Jeremiah 33:14–16 preached on the First Sunday in Advent rightly leads to the Eucharist; in this sacrament believers are nourished by the hope of God's coming and participate in God's future. An Advent liturgy recalls that through the words of the prophets God promised the Redeemer, "and gave hope for the day when justice shall roll down like waters, and righteousness like an ever rolling stream."[2] Prayers that are evoked by this text will acknowledge God as the One who lives and moves and comes to us in time and who works justice and righteousness in all times; they will express gratitude for time as God's good gift; they will confess our preoccupation with the immediate and our fear of the future; they will ask for our confidence in God's

1. Philip Doddridge (1702–51), "Great God, We Sing That Mighty Hand," in *The Presbyterian Hymnal* (Louisville, KY: Westminster/John Knox Press, 1990).
2. *The Book of Common Worship* (Louisville, KY: Westminster/John Knox Press, 1993), 133.

Exegetical Perspective

BCE.[1] Thus, the passage represents a vision of a radically new future added in retrospect with a postexilic audience in view. When read, however, from a literary canonical perspective,[2] the Little Book of Comfort and verses 14–16 of chapter 33 therein function as a temporary reprieve from an onslaught of judgment oracles leading up to the precise event of the destruction of the temple in Jerusalem on a particular day, the ninth of Ab in the year 587 BCE.

Opening with a formula typical of salvation oracles, "the days are surely coming," verse 14 introduces divine first-person speech. God is assuring the audience that God will fulfill "the promise," literally "the good word" with a definite article—not "a" promise, one of many, but a particular one made to both the house of Israel and the house of Judah. Harkening back to Jeremiah 23:5–6, another eschatological interlude, verse 15 reiterates what was promised there, namely, that God will birth a "righteous" (*tsedaqah*) offspring of the Davidic monarchy, who will act in ways that will promote "justice and righteousness" (*mishpat* and *tsedaqah*). While some will read this as a contradiction in terms—the Davidic monarchy has been blamed throughout the book of Jeremiah for exploitation and unfaithfulness (see Jer. 2:4–8, 26–28; 3:6–10; 7:1–15; 21:11–12)—the focus on qualities associated with the Sinai covenant, justice, and righteousness, so central to the theology and worldview of Jeremiah, does constitute something radically new in light of the present realities of destruction and impending exile.

What was promised to both Israel and Judah narrows to a promise to Judah and Jerusalem in what follows in verse 16. Both in historical and in literary terms, this makes historical sense. The Babylonian exile occurs well after the fall of the northern kingdom, so Judah and Jerusalem are at the center of the events leading up to it. Literarily, paralleling the house of Israel and the house of Judah with Judah and Jerusalem serves the movement from the bigger picture to what is at hand, the giving of a new name to the people, personified in Jerusalem. This new name is a confession of faith "YHWH is our righteousness (*tsedaqah*)." So whenever anybody utters the name of the Holy City, the person confesses his faith in the God of the covenant at Sinai. The proclamation goes even further. Given the power associated with naming in ancient Israel, giving

1. See, e.g., Walter Brueggemann, *A Commentary on Jeremiah: Exile and Homecoming* (Grand Rapids: Eerdmans, 1998).
2. See Angela Bauer, *Gender in the Book of Jeremiah: A Feminist-Literary Reading* (New York: Peter Lang, 1999).

Homiletical Perspective

that, despite every sign to the contrary, "days are coming," days when God's promises will be fulfilled. Jeremiah tells his kin that God's future will come not by giving up on God's promises and making the best of a bad situation—after all, "when in Babylon"—but by trusting in the creative and redemptive and sure purposes of God: "Days are coming!"

With the world that he has known crumbling around him, Jeremiah pushes his people to see a future, God's future, which seems laughable given the current circumstances. No wonder Jeremiah is the church's usher into Advent. Later in the season, Mary will sing about God's future, despite her own laughable circumstance.

Along with Jeremiah and Mary, preachers would do well to consider another Advent singer. Heidi Neumark is a Lutheran pastor who writes about this holy season amid her ministry in the roughest part of the Bronx:

> Probably the reason I love Advent so much is that it is a reflection of how I feel most of the time. I might not feel sorry during Lent, when the liturgical calendar begs repentance. I might not feel victorious, even though it is Easter morning. I might not feel full of the Spirit, even though it is Pentecost and the liturgy spins out fiery gusts of ecstasy. But during Advent, I am always in sync with the season.
>
> Advent unfailingly embraces and comprehends my reality. And what is that? I think of the Spanish word *anhelo*, or longing. Advent is when the church can no longer contain its unfulfilled desire and the cry of *anhelo* bursts forth: Maranatha! Come Lord Jesus! O Come, O Come, Emmanuel![1]

As the first, lone candle of Advent wreath burns, Jeremiah recalls his own city burning, and yet he speaks not of destruction but of God's future as he offers his cry of longing, of *anhelo*. Like Jeremiah, most preachers have their own list for which they cry *anhelo*, and they serve people with their own lists of longings, for which they cry *anhelo*.

As I listen to the cries of Jeremiah throughout the scope of his prophecy, I long for the day that is surely coming when God's future will be a reality beyond the violent boastings of the ruling Babylon of the day. I long for the day that is surely coming when in God's future the poor are not sent to shelters or forced to sleep on the streets. I long for the day that is surely coming when God's future has no space for violence, when we will stop producing

1. Heidi Neumark, *Breathing Space* (Boston: Beacon Press, 2004), 211.

Jeremiah 33:14-16

Theological Perspective

task of *imagination.* Together with the prophet, we are called not only to name suffering and injustice, but to lean into God's promised alternative future.

Theological imagination is not speculative, but relies on God's continuous presence and acts on behalf of creation over time. Trusting in God's provision for us in the past, we imagine what shape God's fulfillment of promises will take in the future. Although we do not bring about God's intended alternative future through sheer force of will, in our waiting we do try to place ourselves in a posture so that we might become partners with God in the advent of a new reality.

The Collective and Sociopolitical Aspects of God's Promise. The promise Jeremiah recalls is not an otherworldly, escapist spirituality that encourages us merely to "wait it out." Particularly in the prophetic literature, and echoed in Gospel texts like the Magnificat (Luke 1:46–55), we find repeated affirmations that God's promise includes a transvaluation of social, economic, and political relationships. In this particular lection, the prophet anticipates a time in which even the failed leadership will be made aright and "do what kings are supposed to do, namely, practice justice and righteousness. . . . When the king practices justice and righteousness, the city and the land will be healed and saved."[3] In the creative moment of near-despair, the prophet calls us to imagine a new social context in which we live together in safety, peace, and righteousness. God will do this, as promised, and even bring about new life for the city.

JENNIFER RYAN AYRES

Pastoral Perspective

tomorrow and pray for those who yearn for the justice and righteousness that they will not know in their days.

Congregational life during Advent that is faithful to the prophetic vision of "the days . . . surely coming" emphasizes political as well as personal relationships. This text insists that covenantal life in all its expressions is characterized by justice and righteousness, allowing no dichotomy of "prophetic" and "pastoral." Life together is to embody the nature of God, "The Lord is our righteousness." Jeremiah uses the name first for a promised person (23:6) and again here, intentionally, for a promised place (33:16). The vision of the time to come impugns the time at hand. What leader and what community could claim "The Lord is our righteousness"? The promise challenges our reality, and drives a reappropriation of "righteousness." The word is uncommon, if not pejorative, in common parlance and unwelcome in the lexicon of many faithful because of its frequent companionship with "self."

One of the pastoral tasks is to teach the vocabulary of faith, and "righteousness" is one of the first words of the language of Advent. In Matthew's Gospel, "righteousness" is Jesus' first word, spoken to John the Baptist: "Let it be so now . . . in this way to fulfill all righteousness" (Matt. 3:15). Righteousness is not an attitude or an absolute standard. It refers to conduct in accord with God's purposes. It is doing the good thing and the God thing: right doing as opposed to wrongdoing, and doing as opposed to being. Self-righteousness is the inflated ego of self-approval; righteousness is the humble ethic of living toward others in just and loving relationships. A congregation will be edified by preaching and teaching that brings righteousness into its language and life. It will be challenged to reflect on the integrity of its witness in the world. *Is* the Lord our righteousness? *Are we ready* to be named and claimed by that kind of God? *Are we willing* to welcome the day when God's justice and righteousness will be fulfilled?

DEBORAH A. BLOCK

3. Walter Brueggemann, *A Commentary on Jeremiah: Exile and Homecoming,* 2nd ed. (Grand Rapids: Eerdmans, 1998), 318.

Exegetical Perspective

someone or something a new name means changing them existentially. That is to say, a radical new reality is here proclaimed: the city and its people will live faithfully within the Sinai covenant by embodying its fundamental principles, justice and righteousness.

As a theological claim, such a promise goes even deeper as the new reality of a just, fair, and righteous government embraces competing theological trajectories in the First Testament—integrating the Zion covenant within the Sinai covenant.[3] This promise also fits with the more orthodox Jeremianic prophecies in particular (see Jer. 16:14–21; 23:5–8; 30:2–9; 31:1–6, 21–26, 31–34). At the same time, it joins the visions of a different way of living together as a divided people after the exile, beyond former allegiances and worldviews (see, e.g., Isa. 51:19; 54:1–17; 56:1–8; 61:1–11; Zech. 6:9–15).

By focusing on these three verses during the First Sunday of Advent, the lectionary invites the preacher and congregation to draw analogies between Jeremiah's world and contemporary dynamics locally and globally. Instances of death, destruction, and exile abound, yet particularity is encouraged. The preacher who follows the assigned text and stops with verse 16, not including the remainder of chapter 33, will want to use caution not to forget Judah's concrete historical circumstances. Jeremiah's audience is a people facing impending exile or already suffering in it. Jeremiah offers that people a vision of a radically new way their political and religious institutions may work in the future. The new generation of Davidic kings will act in ways that promote justice and righteousness, rather than exploitation, self-promotion, and violence. Further, even the Levitical priesthood will live according to the Sinai covenant, rather than continue their insistence on their own orthodoxies at the expense of inclusion, justice, and righteousness in faith and religious observance. Both king and priest someday may embody and lead the way into God's bright new reality.

Leaving out the grim present reality of soon-to-be exiles allows for a too facile connection of the passage with the New Testament readings, which, while also eschatological in nature, presuppose a different historical context. The challenge and promise of grappling with this passage in the book of Jeremiah on the First Sunday of Advent lies in its contemporary echoes in the power structures of our time.

ANGELA BAUER-LEVESQUE

Homiletical Perspective

body bags—because there are no dead soldiers to fill them. I long for the day that is surely coming when God's future affords no room for rancor, a day when our world is no longer torn asunder by racism and sexism and homophobia.

Preaching Advent from the perspective of Jeremiah, I long for the confidence of the prophet's words about the righteous future of our God. I long for people to know the God whom Jeremiah heralds and whom Jesus will incarnate, not a hidden God who refuses to traffic in the human enterprise, but a God who hears God's people when they cry *anhelo*. I long for people to know, not the God of religious fanatics or bigots, not a God who enjoys seeing Jerusalem set afire, but the God who, in God's own time, will bring more mercy and justice than we will ever grasp.

As preachers consider the prophecy from Jeremiah, maybe there is no more important homiletical clue to preaching this text than to pay attention to the *anhelo* within them and around them. Maybe, then, Jeremiah is the best biblical voice to lead us into Advent, the season that brings *anhelo* to expression.

In many liturgical traditions, the First Sunday of Advent brings the community to the holy Table. In many ways, Jeremiah's promise that "days are coming" finds its most poignant meaning at this table of *anhelo*. Just look at it. This meal does not point to magi and a star, but to a world gone mad. It is a table not cloaked in romance and sweet memories, but set with food paid for at a price way too dear. It is not just a table of *anhelo*, it is *the* table of *anhelo* for all with deep longings, people who pray with Jeremiah for the days that are surely coming.

Maybe Advent is not so puzzling after all.

GARY W. CHARLES

---

3. See Jon D. Levenson, *Sinai and Zion: An Entry into the Jewish Bible* (San Francisco: Harper & Row, 1985).

Psalm 25:1-10

¹To you, O Lᴏʀᴅ, I lift up my soul.
²O my God, in you I trust;
    do not let me be put to shame;
    do not let my enemies exult over me.
³Do not let those who wait for you be put to shame;
    let them be ashamed who are wantonly treacherous.

⁴Make me to know your ways, O Lᴏʀᴅ;
    teach me your paths.
⁵Lead me in your truth, and teach me,
    for you are the God of my salvation;
    for you I wait all day long.

Theological Perspective

The beginning of Advent may be just the right time to consider the ten verses of petition, praise, and promise in this lection from Psalm 25. Emphasis in the first portion of the passage on the writer's needs—for deliverance, for guidance, and for forgiveness—presents a lens for reflecting on how the Advent gift to come may respond to these specific needs as well as to the needs of many, many others. Lament, honesty, and hope form the progression through the text and are interrelated elements of the response to needs included there.

Lament. Two categories—poems of praise and poems of lament—are generally accepted as a way interpreters classify the majority of chapters in the book of Psalms. Because of its petitionary nature and its focus on the requirement for help, this psalm is identified as a lament. In the liturgical tradition from which these poems arose, a lament is a deep expression of individual or communal grief in the presence of and directed to God. Some interpreters further assert that lament includes three elements: petition, praise, and assurance. A close look at the passage at hand reveals that it is not only a text that expresses the psalmist's particular needs, but also a meditation about God's goodness, which the writer trusts, hopes in, and depends on for deliverance.

Pastoral Perspective

One of the fundamental questions of life is this: in whom or what can we trust? It is a question about people, politics, the economy, and ultimately about life itself. The question of trust is certainly relevant to the question of truth in advertising and political speech. Can I trust the advertisements that I read in magazines or view on TV? Can I trust our elected leaders to tell the truth about what is happening?

The term "spin" is relevant for both of these arenas. In public relations, "spin" is a pejorative term signifying a biased report—one that exaggerates a truth or downplays a failure. The term evokes a spinning basketball atop someone's finger. You can see the ball spinning, but you can't read the label, for to do so would leave your head spinning. People who are particularly good at "spin" are called "spin doctors." We have grown accustomed to believing that advertisements and political speech will often downplay failures or exaggerate truths by spinning the facts. Yet in spite of spinning truths, it is ironic how we continue to place an enormous amount of trust in politicians and advertising.

The question of trust is also about life itself. To what extent can I trust that I am secure in life, amid terrorist threats, tsunamis and earthquakes, and news of shootings at places thought to be peaceful, like college campuses? In light of these threats,

^{6}Be mindful of your mercy, O LORD, and of your steadfast love,
    for they have been from of old.
^{7}Do not remember the sins of my youth or my transgressions;
    according to your steadfast love remember me,
    for your goodness' sake, O LORD!

^{8}Good and upright is the LORD;
    therefore he instructs sinners in the way.
^{9}He leads the humble in what is right,
    and teaches the humble his way.
^{10}All the paths of the LORD are steadfast love and faithfulness,
    for those who keep his covenant and his decrees.

Exegetical Perspective

The First Sunday of Advent offers us a psalm of lament and Torah—complaint and a desire to learn. Lament psalms, the most common type in the psalter, express the distress of an individual or community, invoke God, state a complaint, present a petition, and usually end with an exclamation of praise and thanksgiving. As a psalm of Torah, Psalm 25 speaks one side of a deeper, ongoing educational conversation between friends. The psalmist approaches God amid the turmoil of life and asks for help. Their covenantal friendship inclines the psalmist to expect that the Lord's ways are mercy and truth, loving and sure.

Psalm 25 addresses God as a teacher. The psalmist, caught in the laboratory of life, commands, begs, and demands to be taught. What an excited student! This student intends to learn God's guidance. He knows the outcomes of the course: walking with God in faithfulness and love.

Psalm 25 somewhat faithfully follows an acrostic model; acrostic designates a structure facilitating memorization in Hebrew, because the first letter of each verse is a consecutive letter of the alphabet. The first half of the psalm, verses 1–10, contains nine commands; these include do not let me be ashamed, and show, teach, and guide me (vv. 2, 4–5a). Verses 7b–10 explain aspects of God's character. Repeated

Homiletical Perspective

Advent comes, sneaking up on us, often with surprising speed that catches us unaware and unprepared. Is it Advent already? In four short weeks we are expected to make time and space to prepare our lives for God's indwelling *and* lead our congregations through a similar time of preparation. All the while, everyone everywhere wants to break out the carols to accompany the dizzying whirl of parties and purchasing that precede Christmas, or actually is Christmas for many.

In much of the Northern Hemisphere Advent comes in the "bleak midwinter." No wonder people want to party. Still, at a deeper level, it is also possible that this may be experienced as the time of year when, as the earth lies fallow, we dwell in expectancy of the new life we hope spring will bring. This mind-set shapes the way the church in this hemisphere observes Advent. In a cold and fallow season, a season characterized by waiting and watching and wondering, it is not surprising that one might find oneself reflecting on the past and looking to the future, taking stock and hoping for something better in the springtime to come.

When we purchase those special, colorful bulletin covers for Advent, they almost always trumpet hope as the theme for the First Sunday of Advent. Hope is clearly a focus of these opening verses of Psalm 25.

Psalm 25:1-10

Theological Perspective

Historically, psalms of lament (and praise) arose in response to particular events that persons encountered. The relationship to specific incidents is indicated through the immediacy of the emotional reaction and the spontaneity of the verbal response captured in the language about the event. Reflecting the original emergence of the psalms in patriarchal family histories, the poems also relate a remarkable depth of feeling about what has just occurred. As Israel grew into a nation, however, worship practices became more communal, more formal, and less spontaneous. Some of the depth evident in earlier prayers is lost as later psalms reflect a more settled national culture and a more ceremonial worship life. The specific event prompting this text is uncertain, though some interpreters believe it to be a psalm of reflection during David's old age. Regardless of the chronology of a psalm's origin, however, scholars generally agree that the Psalms persist as an important element of individual and communal worship because they capture common human reactions to life events and invite us honestly to confront our own experiences as they are reflected there.

Progression to Self-Reflection. The honest expression of need in this psalm points to an opportunity to enter the Advent season with new openness to what is about to unfold and the help it will bring. The writer's need is evident at the start of the text, as indicated by the opening assertion of dependence: "To you, O LORD, I lift up my soul" (v. 1). Need becomes even more explicit and intimate in verses immediately following the opening, as the poem moves through the first petition (vv. 2–3), for deliverance from one identified as an enemy, to a second petition (vv. 4–5), for direction in life, to a final petition (vv. 6–7), for forgiveness of the failures of youth. Progression of the three petitions goes from focus on the other as the source of the lament to a focus on self-identity, as the writer moves from the circumstantial challenge of needing to be saved from persons called enemies to personal recognition of a need to be taught and finally to repent. The progression ultimately reflects the honesty required to confront the lack and inadequacy that abounds in even the most accomplished individual life, if growth is to occur. The progression also suggests a need for reconciliation and communal well-being, since personal challenges such as need for direction and need for forgiveness may both cause alienation and prompt a plea for resolution of conflict.

Pastoral Perspective

science has become a trusted resource for sorting out how to secure our families and ourselves. For many, science has become a savior.

Thus, closely related to the question of trust is the question of salvation. Amid the anxieties, insecurities, and threats of life, in whom or what is my salvation? People often use the language of salvation when referring to politicians. In the United States, Roosevelt was considered by many a savior amid the Great Depression and World War II; both Kennedy and Reagan were in different ways considered saviors amid the Cold War; and as I write these words both Democrats and Republicans seem to be looking for a savior amid the tragedy of Iraq. Long before Jesus Christ was called Savior, the Roman emperors had adopted the title for themselves. In fact, Luke's Gospel draws a polemical contrast between Jesus as Savior and Augustus Caesar as savior.

So it is rather striking to read Psalm 25 and note the utter confidence and trust that the psalmist places in God for his or her salvation: "To you, O LORD, I lift up my soul. O my God, in you I trust. . . . Lead me in your truth, and teach me, for you are the God of my salvation; for you I wait all day long" (vv. 1, 5). What is astounding about these affirmations is that the psalmist seems to know all about the threats that life can bring, yet nonetheless places utter trust in God. Indeed, the psalmist bares the soul, saying, "Do not let me be put to shame; do not let my enemies exult over me" (v. 2). In the Psalms we never get a clear idea about the identity of the enemy. The most helpful suggestion is that the identity of the "enemy" is open ended so that the reader can adopt the psalm to his or her own circumstance.[1] The enemy could be a badly performing economy that has left him destitute and shamed because of poverty, or a friend who has betrayed her or abandoned and failed her, or a political leader who has been a bitter disappointment or who has become a political foe; or perhaps he or she has been the victim of malpractice of some sort. Whatever the circumstance, the psalmist knows threat. Yet in spite of the threat, the focus of the psalmist is on God, in whose hands alone is the ground of his salvation.

By contrast, our attention is often diffused. Our confidence and hope for salvation may be in money, friends, family, politics, or some medical cure. While many of these resources are undoubtedly

1. See J. Clinton McCann, *A Theological Introduction to the Book of Psalms: The Psalm as Torah* (Nashville: Abingdon Press, 1993), 91–92.

Exegetical Perspective

words give an indication of the text's direction. They include "shame" (three times, vv. 2, 3, 20), "way/s" (four times, always referring to God's way/s, vv. 4, 8, 9, 12), "hope" (twice, vv. 3, 5), and "good" (twice, vv. 7–8). The psalm lingers on certain characteristics of God. God is good (vv. 7b, 8) and upright (v. 8). In addition, God guides and teaches the humble (v. 9). God also instructs sinners in his way; finally, all God's paths are loving and faithful (vv. 8b, 10).

David begins by lifting up his soul, the essence of who he is, to his God (v. 1). In Israelite culture, this meant lifting up one's hands. The hands are empty—without weapons, without even gifts. Vulnerable, exposed, and urgently needy, David courageously invites God's scrutiny. The psalmist beckons as one accustomed to hearing from God. The psalmist prophesies that no one who hopes in God (himself included!) will be put to shame (v. 3). The psalmist draws on his rank as a covenant person. As such, he has rights and responsibilities. God has promised: "I . . . will be your God, and you shall be my people" (Lev. 26:12). The covenant was put in place for a time like this. The covenant has to hold.

The friendship is covenantal because the psalmist (David, according to the tradition of the superscript) keeps God's commandments (v. 10). The friendship is personal because God is personal. God is *my* God (v. 2), *my* Savior (v. 5), who guides *me* (v. 5), teaches *me* (v. 5). The Lord is the depository of *my* hope throughout the entire day (v. 5), has a short memory about *my* sins (v. 7), and demands accountability from someone like *me*, for *we* are in covenant together. God rewards someone like *me* with a loving and even delightful way for keeping the covenant (v. 10, all italics obviously added!).

Because the psalmist already has kept to God's ways, he expects God to deliver him from any shame his enemies plot, and he also asks for the same blessings on the rest of Israel (v. 22). The psalmist does not request a removal of his troubles but instead demands guidance and instruction to meet them. However, he wants to get through them without shame. Shame in the psalms is associated with mockery and humiliation and is therefore an appropriate punishment for enemies—not for a covenant believer! The lives of the psalmist and God are so entwined that the enemies' triumph would bring shame upon them both.

The psalmist next calls upon God to have a selective memory. He asks God to forget his youthful sins and instead to remember God's own good qualities of mercy and love. The sins remain

Homiletical Perspective

This is a psalm of confident hope. It is the song of one who has known the complexities, the downs and ups, of life and still maintains a steadfast trust that God will provide for him, that God will care for him, that the future is ultimately in God's hands. This is the song of one who has escaped the exile, who is at home, sitting in her chair, thinking over how her life has been both challenged and blessed.

The verses we are given to consider alternate between the writer's penitence for sin committed and confidence that God will restore the writer to wholeness. Hope is always situated between the world gone wrong, life off track, tasks undone, and expectations of the world righted, life moving steadily ahead on God's mainline, work well done. It is the human condition to live in the tension between failure and fulfillment, sin and salvation, trouble and hope. This psalm shows the very human tendency to mix concerns and expectations, reality and dreams, as the stream of consciousness flows through the mind. One may be aware of having strayed from faithfulness to God at the same time one holds hope for restored relationship. Many in our congregations will identify with this kind of careful reflection that acknowledges limitations at the same time it holds hope for future fulfillment.

In this psalm, apparently written after the time of exile for the Hebrew people, the hope for return to the land of promise does not infuse the text with the anguish of exile or a desperate desire to return home. Nor, on a personal level, does the writer seem to be weighed down with guilt and shame over some great unresolved sin. This does not seem to be a *de profundis* hymn. Though there is reference to the sins of youth, the confession of this writer seems to be the confession of one who ruminates toward the end of a relatively full and decent life. This is the prayer of one whose sin consists mostly of youthful indiscretion and small transgressions that separate one from the fullness of life that is possible while living in complete obedience to God and God's law.

Old Testament theologian Walter Brueggemann, in reflecting on this psalm, says that "humanness is pervasively hope-filled, not in the sense of buoyant, unreflective optimism, but in a conviction that individual human destiny is powerfully presided over by this One who wills good and works that good. . . . Yahweh is not *instrumental* to the hope of Israel, but Yahweh is in fact the very *substance* of that hope."[1]

1. Walter Brueggemann, *Theology of the Old Testament: Testimony, Dispute, Advocacy* (Minneapolis: Fortress Press, 1997), 497.

Psalm 25:1-10

Theological Perspective

Old Testament interpreter Walter Brueggemann identifies recognition of the need for self-reflection as disorientation that makes way for new orientation, saying the Psalms invite us "into the wholeness that comes in embraced brokenness."[1] In the fragile grace that emerges in moments of brokenness when we really see ourselves, the disorientation of confronting personal imperfections may indeed open a possibility for reconciled relationship. Reconciliation as a response to petitions (such as those of this psalm) can be anticipated among many other possibilities as Advent begins, but this reconciliation becomes possible only as a result of honesty about dependence and spiritual challenges. In a global culture that often demonizes both combatants and national leaders during times of war, and at a time when social cultures seem to celebrate incivility and hostility, reconciliation as the final resolution of conflict truly is a new orientation.

Hope and God. The final section of the passage (vv. 8–10) reflects hope for a satisfactory resolution of the issue presented in the initial verses. The hope expressed in this final section is implied throughout the passage as praise for "the God of my salvation" (v. 5) and appeal to the divine nature as merciful, loving, and good (vv. 6–7). Praise intensifies as the text closes, with the writer celebrating divine work. The psalmist's praise of God points especially to divine justice, which suggests that hope exists even for one engaged in a conflict and in need of guidance and forgiveness.

Many will see the praises in these final verses as signaling the promise of forgiveness and new beginnings anticipated in Advent. The psalm pictures a listening and trustworthy God. Christians entering the Advent season may join the psalmist in celebrating the hope that emerges from the divine nature and from divine past action in faithfully leading and teaching those who come looking for and anticipating a new beginning.

ROSETTA E. ROSS

Pastoral Perspective

helpful, they can be theologically dangerous. We are easily led to believe that they are our ultimate source of salvation.

In another mistake, just as dangerous, we let ourselves believe that we are a savior of others. In a short story by Flannery O'Connor entitled "The Lame Shall Enter First," a recreation director named Shepherd tries to help a physically disabled juvenile delinquent named Johnson. In a pointed exchange, when Johnson has refused Shepherd's help, Shepherd says: "I'm stronger than you are and I'm going to save you. The good will triumph." Johnson, however, replies: "Not when you ain't true. . . . Not when it ain't right." "My resolve isn't shaken . . . I'm going to save you," Shepherd repeats. Johnson thrusts his head forward and hisses: "Save yourself. . . . Nobody can save me but Jesus."[2]

This story reminds us how our attention is easily deflected from God as the ultimate object of trust and ground of salvation. Amid spinning truths and impending threats, our confidence wavers, and we trust in that which is less than God. Economic policies, political parties and ideologies, and science are often wedged into the place of God. Sometimes we even lapse into trusting ourselves. In the ministry of the church, it is common for pastors and lay leaders to think of themselves as saviors for their people. The church's social ministries, however noble, are falsely embraced as the saving media of God.

Our psalm, however, points us to the God in whom alone is our help and salvation. The implication of the psalm is clear. We are not God. We are not saviors. Neither does our salvation rest in economics or politics. Indeed, the psalm offers the only sane affirmation amid a world in which we often trust in other saviors or believe ourselves to be saviors of others. The psalmist directs us to a practice that can be called "soul lifting," that is, the practice of placing ourselves, our families, friends— and, indeed, the world—into the very hands of God.

ROGER J. GENCH

---

1. Walter Brueggemann, *The Spirituality of the Psalms* (Minneapolis: Augsburg Fortress, 2001), xv. See also *The Message of the Psalms: A Theological Commentary* (Minneapolis: Augsburg, 1984).

2. Quoted in McCann, 81–82.

Exegetical Perspective

unspecified, as do the ways God will shower God's own great mercy and love on the psalmist. In order to pursue the friendship, the psalmist realizes forgiveness must occur.

God's remembrances are among the sweetest words in Scripture, and the psalmist calls upon this record. For example, Genesis 8:1: God remembered Noah and all that were with him in the ark—and sent a wind over the earth. Genesis 30:22: God remembered Rachel—and opened her womb. Exodus 2:24: God remembered the covenant with Abraham, Isaac, and Jacob—and started the deliverance of the Hebrews from Egyptian slavery. 1 Samuel 1:19: God remembered Hannah—and gave her a son. In the Psalms, God remembers God's mercy and truth (98:3); God's eternal covenant (105:8); and our low estate (136:23).

Derek, another significant word meaning way or journey, occurs four times in the text (vv. 4, 8, 9, 12). It carries covenantal aspects, for the canon consistently says the spiritual journey is a choice between the way of death and the way of life (see Prov. 4:14; 6:23). The psalmist knows this and cries out to be instructed, guided, and led by God. The whole course of life is to be lived in conformity with ever-present, ever-renewing covenant obligations (Exod. 18:20).

As a student favoring a repetitive learning technique, David signs up for a refresher course in the loving and faithful ways of the covenant. David commands God to repeat the instruction he already knows and to continue leading him in the new ways opening up. It is not remiss to ask for clarity and continued instruction of God's principles to meet new situations.

The psalm mentions God's lovingkindness (*hesed*) twice (vv. 7, 10). This wonderful word, which is not easily translated into English, denotes the constant love and help offered by one of superior rank toward one of lesser rank; if the help does not come, the one of lesser rank probably will perish. Often *hesed* pairs poetically with words like "covenant" (Deut. 7:9), "faithfulness" (Pss. 36:5, 57:10); "compassion" (103:4), and "pity" (109:12). God's *hesed* shows God's unceasingly generous nature in forgiving, blessing, and having compassion on God's covenant followers, and on this psalmist in particular.

ROBIN GALLAHER BRANCH

Homiletical Perspective

This is indeed the hope into which Advent invites us to enter fully, the fulfillment of the promise that, in all our living, God will provide for us, take care of us, save us.

As an Advent text that is meant to prepare us for the coming of Christ, the messianic promise is not presented directly here. Still, the implication can be drawn as the preacher encourages the congregation to look to the "God of . . . salvation." The hope of salvation is the hope for fulfillment of the messianic promise; it is the coming Christ who will bring God's redemption to God's people. One might wonder if Anna and Simeon did not chant this psalm as they waited patiently in the temple for just such a fulfillment of God's promise.

Barbara Brown Taylor writes movingly of living with such a promise: "The promise may not be fully in hand. It may still be on the way, but to live reverently, deliberately and fully awake—that is what it means to live in the promise, where the wait itself is as rich as its end. All it takes are some regular reminders, because as long as the promise is renewed, the promise is alive, as vivid as a rainbow, as real as the million stars overhead."[2]

Regardless of one's social situation, words of hope carry meaning. Of course, socioeconomic standing will affect how one understands and relies on hope. Preaching on this text to people of privilege and affluence may take more creative work than preaching it for those who depend on hope for a different future to see them through their daily lives. This text presents an opportunity to expand a congregation's understanding of hope beyond the familiar; or it may be an opportunity to stress hope for those who struggle with daily existence. Surely, confident hope is crucial to the good news that Advent promises will soon burst upon the world: good news that carries the promise of transformation of life from sin to salvation, from oppression to liberation, from injustice to wholeness, from life to death.

RANDLE R. MIXON

2. Barbara Brown Taylor, *Gospel Medicine* (Cambridge: Cowley Publications, 1995), 41.

1 Thessalonians 3:9-13

[9]How can we thank God enough for you in return for all the joy that we feel before our God because of you? [10]Night and day we pray most earnestly that we may see you face to face and restore whatever is lacking in your faith.

[11]Now may our God and Father himself and our Lord Jesus direct our way to you. [12]And may the Lord make you increase and abound in love for one another and for all, just as we abound in love for you. [13]And may he so strengthen your hearts in holiness that you may be blameless before our God and Father at the coming of our Lord Jesus with all his saints.

Theological Perspective

This passage from the apostle Paul's First Letter to the Thessalonians provides an important window on one early Christian church as it struggled to grasp the wonderful and bewildering future inaugurated by the risen Christ. This letter is almost unanimously affirmed as the apostle's first letter. As such it provides a view into the witness, proclamation, and practice of the nascent Christian church. According to Abraham Malherbe, in 49 CE the apostle Paul journeyed to Thessalonica to proclaim the gospel. A group of day laborers heard and received his message, and from these humble beginnings a church was formed.[1] This particular passage reveals a fundamental tension and ambiguity most clearly visible in this letter, whose traces are intermittently apparent throughout the Pauline corpus.

The Coming of Christ. There is evidence that this community was confused about and therefore focused on the coming of Christ (1 Thess. 5:1–11). This focus allows Paul not only to tolerate but to embrace the embryonic faith of the Thessalonians. Indeed, the incompleteness of their faith is a reason for rejoicing. "For what thanks can we render to God

Pastoral Perspective

There may be no more difficult day for the preacher than the First Sunday of Advent. It poses a number of challenges that upon closer examination might prove to be pastoral opportunities.

In the first instance, this is the first Sunday of the New Year on the Christian liturgical calendar, but in many settings there is scant opportunity to reflect on this significance. There is little about late November or early December that easily fosters a New-Year mood. Consider, however, the pastoral possibilities of engaging in New-Year resolution making before Christmas observances that leave many exhausted, overextended, emotionally drained, and financially debt ridden.

A congregation I served for sixteen years shared its building with a Reformed Jewish congregation that used the church's sanctuary for its High Holiday services. Celebrated in the Jewish month of Tishri, the holidays fall on the secular calendar in September or October and begin with Rosh Hashanah, the Jewish New Year. Observing the religious New Year at a time other than January 1 affords Jews the occasion to focus on change and renewal and on learning from the past and recommitting the future, at a time unencumbered by the folderol of secular New Year's celebrations. The Rosh Hashanah greeting is "Le Shana Tova Teekataivu," which means, "May you be

---

1. See Abraham Malherbe, *Letters to the Thessalonians,* Anchor Bible Commentary (Garden City, NY: Doubleday, 2000).

Exegetical Perspective

What's in a benediction? For Christians accustomed to hearing one spoken at the end of Sunday services, the benediction performs a key transition, sending us with God's blessing from the ordered communal intimacy of divine worship out to the more chaotic improvisational demands of faithfully lived lives in the world. The benediction in 1 Thessalonians 3:11–13 also effects a transition—from a celebration of intimate Christian friendship between Paul and this fledgling church (1:2–3:10) to their training in intimate Christian living with one another (4:1–12; 5:11–22) and in faithful Christian dying (4:13–5:10). This transitional purpose impacts the shape of Paul's prayer: for reunion with one another (3:11) and for the Thessalonians' growth in communal love (3:12), which is sound preparation for the coming Christ (3:13). In the Thessalonian community we have the youngest church that Paul addresses in any of his letters. Circumstances abruptly ended Paul's time with them early. It is appropriate, then, that the entire letter is summed up simply in the brief epitome of 3:11–13.

Now may our God and Father himself, and our Lord Jesus, direct our way to you.[1] Paul prays first that

1. Translations in italics by the author.

Homiletical Perspective

In our text, appropriate to the central action of Advent, Paul is waiting. And waiting. He is worried about the fledgling church at Thessalonica, especially since his first visit there (Acts 17) was less than a spectacular success. So he sends Timothy to visit the church and report back to him. Timothy returns with very positive news that warms the heart of the anxious, waiting Paul. This story resembles the mission of the seventy (Luke 10), where Jesus waits for their report and rejoices when they return successful. Jesus tells the seventy not to rejoice in their success, but then tells them privately that they have achieved what prophets and kings could not.

Paul similarly praises the Thessalonians: "How can we thank God enough for you in return for all the joy that we feel before our God because of you?" (v. 9). But then he also says: "May [God] so strengthen your hearts in holiness that you may be blameless before our God and Father at the coming of our Lord Jesus with all his saints" (v. 13). Praise is followed by a prayer close to reproof. The Thessalonians were not blameless yet, but Paul asked God to make them so before the return of Jesus.

Since the season of Advent cannot escape the pull from both past and future, a good use of this strain in Paul's message might move like this. After reading the first part of the text and setting it in its context,

1 Thessalonians 3:9-13

Theological Perspective

again for you, for all the joy wherewith we joy for your sakes before our God; Night and day praying exceedingly that we might see your face, and might perfect that which is lacking in your faith?" (1 Thess. 3:9–10 KJV). The fact that Paul can give thanks for a faith that is to come reveals, for our time, the ambiguity of Advent. This ambiguity is evident in our seasonal celebrations focused on an event that happened more than 2,000 years ago, while the message of Advent is focused on a reality that is yet to come. Part of the reason for this ambiguity is that we tend to view Advent through the lens of Good Friday and Easter.

Theological Tensions. There are several theological tensions presented by this text. First, any theological appropriation of it is immediately caught in the tension of living in the *now* versus living in the *then*. Second, the background of the text suggests that the adversary of this early Christian community is the Jewish community, and not, as would come to be the case, Judaizing Christians. This means that this text presents a Christianity not yet ensconced in internecine conflicts. This is a Christianity that is engaged, for better or for worse, in a genuine interreligious exchange. Third, the theological focus is on the coming of Christ and not the cross of Christ. The theological center is on what Christ will do or is doing, rather than on what Christ has done. Terms like "salvation" must be understood in this context. Salvation, as understood in this letter, is a continuing and future act, rather than a past and accomplished one. Fourth, at the time that this letter was written, the appellation "lord" indicated the head of the Roman Empire. Here the early church engaged an early hermeneutical tension: the emperor as lord and Christ as Lord. The juxtaposition of the "lord" and the "Lord" provided the occasion for both political persecution and prophetic proclamation. The fact that four times in this short pericope the term *kyrios*, Lord, is used with reference to Jesus suggests that this Christian community was determined to wrest this name from the imperial lexicon.

The Hope of the Kingdom. The major Christian doctrine illuminated by this text is Christian hope. It is significant that this earliest of Paul's letters would center on hope. As the church dealt with the delayed Parousia, the notion of hope moved from the foreground to the background in doctrinal reflection. It was not until Jürgen Moltmann recovered this emphasis in his *Theology of Hope* that this theme

Pastoral Perspective

inscribed for a good year." The emphasis is on having a *good* rather than a *happy* year. Purposeful, sober reflection is required. Rosh Hashanah, like Advent, is not about "don't worry, be happy" revelry; it is, rather, a recommitment, as a new year unfolds, to live toward the good, the just, and the true. Christian observance of the New Year at the First Sunday of Advent can help congregants embrace more fully the New Year's resolution-like dimension of Paul's prayer to "restore whatever is lacking in your faith."

A second challenge/opportunity is the timing of the First Sunday of Advent shortly after the U.S. observance of Thanksgiving and long after the consumer world has already decorated for Christmas. As the liturgical season of preparation commences, instead of decrying the secular rush to Christmas, we might admire the diligence with which secular preparation has been undertaken. A neighbor of mine in retail sales works through the night the day before Halloween to ready his store for Christmas—a secular analogy to Paul's earnestly praying "night and day" that he might see his congregation "face to face." We might also invite spiritual preparedness at least equal to the physical preparation that accompanies making ready for the holidays. Amid frenzied buying sprees and endless party going, Advent can be refocused as a time to "increase and abound in love," thus reaffirming H. Richard Niebuhr's assertion, rooted in the Great Commandment, that "the purpose of the church [is] the increase of the love of God and neighbor."[1] There is neither a simpler nor a more demanding depiction of faithful living than this.

A third challenge of Advent's First Sunday that can be an opportunity is its emphasis on the second coming rather than the first. The challenges of staying in preparation mode rather than succumbing to premature celebration are complicated when invitation is to make ready not for the birth of God's Anointed One, but for the Anointed One's return. In the first century of the Common Era, faith was bolstered by the assumption that the second coming was imminent. Paul preached with certainty about the "parousia's [second coming's] power to unite the people of God."[2] It is because of this expectant certainty of reunion with the "Lord Jesus . . . [and] all his saints" that Thessalonian hearts are strengthened in holiness.

---

1. H. Richard Niebuhr, *The Purpose of the Church and Its Ministry* (New York: Harper & Row, 1956), 27.
2. Abraham Smith, "First Letter to the Thessalonians," in *The New Interpreter's Bible*, vol. 11 (Nashville: Abingdon Press, 2004), 714.

apostle and church might see one another again soon. By this point in the letter, we have already heard much of this longing in Paul (2:17–18; 3:1–5) and of Paul's new assurance that the Thessalonians share it (3:6). We have also heard the intimate language of family, in which Paul understands himself to be both their brother (1:4; 2:1, 17) and their father (2:11), as well as their nurturing nurse (2:7). This close relationship makes a desire to reunite natural. It would be a reduction, though, to see in chapters 1–3 a mere stoking of relational fires. Paul has already commended this church for the way they "became imitators of us and of the Lord" (1:6; see 1 Cor. 11:1) while Paul's team was ministering among them. Personal example was a central feature in the moral formation of ancient popular philosophy. Now, even at a letter-writer's distance, Paul hopes that the active love he describes having for them while he was among them will be a model for their own love toward one another. Thus, while some see in the strikingly intimate language of the letter's first part (e.g., of 2:1–8, 17–18; 3:1–2) the anxious attempt of an insecure apostle to regain his audience, Paul's assurance about Thessalonian allegiance to him (3:6) suggests that it is more than that. The second part of our First Advent lection suggests that he offers his passion and compassion for them as a model.

. . . and may the Lord make you increase and abound in love to one another and to all people, as we do to you. Paul has offered the template: love others as we love you. And so after three chapters celebrating the mutual love between himself and the Thessalonians, Paul calls them to widen that circle and practice mutual love for one another in Christian community and even beyond that for all people. In this middle clause of the prayer, he sets the pattern for half of what is yet to come in the letter. Chapter 4 begins with the general summons: follow Paul's lead by walking (*peripateō*) in a way that pleases God. This will involve their not wronging a brother or sister in matters sexual (4:3–6) and generally loving their Christian brothers and sisters in a God-taught way that will even catch the outsider's eye (4:9–12). All of this they "learned from" Paul and his team in the first encounter (4:1a) but should do "more and more" (4:1b, 10). To these daily-life instructions, Paul adds seventeen discrete commands that paint a beautiful portrait of "love to one another" lived out in the worshiping community (5:12–22).

let the congregation feel the warmth of Paul's praise and then, in a kind of encomium, praise the congregation for what "we" ("we" is important here) have accomplished this year. It is encouraging for people occasionally to hear that they have done good things for God and God's people and done them well.

Then read the second part of the text. There's the rub. Paul prays that we might be holy in heart and blameless when Jesus comes with all the saints. Is that encouraging? The very idea that we could ever be called to blamelessness makes many want to give up without even trying. Can we imagine living a blameless day, much less a blameless life?

Just as our heads are spinning, we hear rumbles from the apocalyptic language that follows. When Jesus returns, he will bring with him those who have died. And we will go to meet them. And what else will Jesus bring? Not blame, but mercy. Not judgment, but grace. Not condemnation, but forgiveness. Not wrath, but salvation! Did Jesus condemn Peter who denied him? No. Did Jesus condemn the sinful woman? No. Did Jesus condemn Paul, who persecuted his followers? No. And Jesus does not condemn us. The news, after all, is good.

Writer and teacher Reynolds Price developed a spinal tumor that was not only deadly but incredibly painful. He tells us that he was not an especially religious person. But very early one morning he had a vision that transported him to the shore of the Sea of Galilee. He saw twelve persons that he knew were the disciples and a sleeping man that he knew was Jesus. Jesus then stood up and walked toward him. Taking his hand, he led Price into the water. He took handfuls of water and poured them on Price's head and damaged back. Then Jesus said: "Your sins are forgiven." Price asked, "Am I also cured?" And Jesus said, "That too."[1]

We are called to do the best we can to live lives pleasing to God. Though we will surely fail to live up to the high standards of perfection, we can be grateful for those things we have done for God and live in hopeful confidence that the love and mercy of the risen Christ will not let us go. As Tennyson wrote of his faith, "Not one life shall be destroyed, or cast as rubbish to the void."[2]

And there is more. Remember, when Jesus comes, he will bring with him those who have gone before, those whom we have loved and lost a while, and they will stand up for us before the throne of

1. Reynolds Price, *A Whole New Life* (New York: Atheneum, 1994), 43.
2. Alfred, Lord Tennyson, *In Memoriam* 54:5, in *The Literature of England*, ed. George B. Woods et al. (Chicago: Scott, Foresman & Co., 1958), 2:631.

1 Thessalonians 3:9-13

Theological Perspective

regained prominence. In the introduction to his watershed work, Moltmann observes that "the more Christianity became an organization for discipleship under the auspices of the Roman state religion and persistently upheld the claims of that religion, the more eschatology and its mobilizing, revolutionizing, and critical effects upon history as it has now to be lived were left to fanatical sects and revolutionary groups.... From first to last, and not merely in the epilogue, Christianity is eschatology, is hope, forward looking and forward moving, and therefore also revolutionizing and transforming the present."[2]

It is hope that draws both love and faith into maturity. Because this text rests on the foundation of hope, Paul's prayer in verse 12—"And may the Lord make you increase and abound in love for one another and for all, just as we abound in love for you"—can be understood as an exhortation and testimony to imperfect people pursuing a perfect love.

The Work of the Kingdom. Malherbe's observation that this letter was originally addressed to a group of laborers suggests that there may be a theological connection between the ideas of work and hope. The group of day laborers whom Malherbe mentioned at the beginning of this reflection was the locus of the meeting of the Word and the human need that gave rise to the church in Thessalonica. Their experience as workers provided a hermeneutic lens through which they viewed the gospel message. This word was one of hope as we noted above, but it was also a word that revalorized their labor.

According to some scholars, religious instructors of the day had the options of supporting themselves through the patronage of the wealthy, asking for alms, and working. Common work was denigrated because professional people of the day despised physical labor. However, the apostle Paul chose to work as a tentmaker, and according to tradition every Jew was expected to have a trade, including rabbis. Therefore, it is not surprising that theologies of hope are closely connected with theologies of work. Moltmann suggests that the hope which calls us into the future is one that requires work. That work painstakingly shapes the promise into the reality. It may well have been this realization that struck a redemptive chord in that now hopeful group of workers.

JAMES H. EVANS JR.

Pastoral Perspective

How do we access the insights of the Thessalonian correspondence from a postmillennial perspective? How do we ready ourselves for "the coming of our Lord Jesus" if, unlike Paul, we do not believe in the Parousia's imminence? Can we find value in the text's expectancy without embracing its time line? Pastorally, the answer is surely yes. Life is full of endings and beginnings. There are crossroads moments in each life when an accounting is demanded and transformed living is called for, regardless of *when* the end will come; what we know is that it will eventually come. There comes a time when there is no time left and "there is such a thing as being too late.... There is an invisible book of life that faithfully records our vigilance or our neglect."[3]

Living with a posture of expectancy is the antidote to being "too late." Such living entails a commitment to faithfulness and diligent preparation that results in an "increase . . . in love for one another and for all" and is not dependent on the Parousia's time line. One need not embrace a notion of the Parousia's proximity to live expectantly, for "about that day or hour no one knows" (Mark 13:32). The time to live with purpose is ever present. Abounding love and strengthened hearts produce faithful living, not just amid the anticipation of the Parousia, but "in season and out of season" (2 Tim. 4:2 RSV), while we wait and however long we wait.

On the First Sunday of Advent many congregations light the hope candle. A vision of "the coming of our Lord Jesus with all his saints" can encourage hope, regardless of how or when it occurs, whether the hearer conceives of this coming literally in history or metaphorically in the experiences of individuals and communities. To be ready for the "coming of our Lord Jesus" is a faithful way of living not dependent on predictions as to when. Endings and beginnings abound. Personal tragedy or world calamity can intrude at any time. Faithful preparation and expectant living can help us face whatever comes. Paul's words of assurance that were intended to "restore whatever is lacking" in the faith of the Thessalonians can bolster the faith of contemporary hearers as well and can be the impetus for all to "increase and abound in love."

PHILIP E. CAMPBELL

2. Jürgen Moltmann, *Theology of Hope: On the Ground and Implications of a Christian Eschatology*, trans. James W. Leitch (Minneapolis: Augsburg Fortress, 1993), 15–16.

3. Martin Luther King Jr., *Where Do We Go from Here: Chaos or Community?* (Boston: Beacon Press, 1968), 191.

Exegetical Perspective

. . . so that he may establish your hearts unblamable in holiness before our God and Father at the coming of our Lord Jesus with all his holy ones. The single greatest anxiety among the Thessalonian Christians concerns the shape of God's future for the dead. One or some of their number have apparently died since Paul's time in town, and the church is at a loss to understand what has become of them. During his visit, Paul had taught them that God's Son would return "from heaven . . . and [rescue] us from the wrath that is coming" (1:10; see also 5:1–2). What they clearly did not hear from Paul, or have forgotten, is what happens to Christians who don't live until that time.

To offer comfort (4:18), Paul supplies a brief but reassuring schedule of the end times, in which the dead in Christ precede even those who are alive at his coming. Paul uses the Greek phrase *hama syn autois* to describe the gathering of the dead and the living at that time: the living shall be caught up "together with them" in clouds. Thus, if Paul and the Thessalonians are anticipating their own earthly reunion at some time soon (3:11), the apostle here gives these grieving brothers and sisters the even brighter hope that they will be reunited with dear ones who are "asleep."

Consolation does not exhaust Paul's purpose for his eschatological moment. He will not have these Thessalonians sitting on their rooftops. Rather, he chases his words of assurance with a strong call to vigilance and right living in the meantime. Because the longed-for Son will come "like a thief in the night" the Thessalonians should be constantly ready for his coming—by living as children of light, embodying faith and love. This watchful, awake way of living is not a private or isolated undertaking, but involves the work of mutual edification. The day of reunion will come. The meantime is full of mundane preparations for it.

An Appropriate Prayer. Uneasy is the preacher called to hold forth on Christ's second advent. The mystery of the eschaton eludes us, leaving us and our congregations at least as confused as our ancient Thessalonian brothers and sisters. But on this First Sunday of Advent Paul's brief benediction advocates neither hopelessness nor idle cloud watching. Rather, it invites us into the uneasy tension of 1 Thessalonians: the call to live lovingly in God's present, even as we await God's brilliant someday.

ALLEN HILTON

Homiletical Perspective

grace. In a brief tribute to the great preacher Carlyle Marney after his death, the editors of *Theology Today* said: "Isn't it wonderful to dream that he has his foot in the door for us [when we come to the gates of heaven]."[3] I live and will die in the hope that Frank Mabee, Ronald Osborn, Elizabeth Redwood, Ambrose Edens, and perhaps a few others will stand up for me when the time comes. I promise that I will stand up for you. Will I put my foot in the door if need be? That too.

Another theme that might be pursued emerges from the structure of this little text. In the first section, Timothy brings a good report to Paul, who rejoices in it. The next section contains Paul's ethical message to the church. Paul moves from praise to paraenesis by way of prayer. His prayer provides not only the transitional words that carry the text from the past to the future, but also the key word "now." I have a friend who moves regularly from one meeting to another. She frequently cannot find a nearby parking place, but that does not bother her. As she said once with a smile, "I got to pray for six blocks today." This Advent, as we wait in line at the checkout stand, get tired telephone ears from being on hold, and wonder how long we must wait to get out of this traffic jam, our daily devotions can be enriched by those open-eyed transitional prayers that join the past and future of our faith story with a blessed "God is Now."

JOSEPH R. JETER

---

3. *Theology Today* 35, no. 4 (January 1979): 450.

Luke 21:25-36

[25]"There will be signs in the sun, the moon, and the stars, and on the earth distress among nations confused by the roaring of the sea and the waves. [26]People will faint from fear and foreboding of what is coming upon the world, for the powers of the heavens will be shaken. [27]Then they will see 'the Son of Man coming in a cloud' with power and great glory. [28]Now when these things begin to take place, stand up and raise your heads, because your redemption is drawing near."

[29]Then he told them a parable: "Look at the fig tree and all the trees; [30]as soon as they sprout leaves you can see for yourselves and know that summer is already near. [31]So also, when you see these things taking place, you know that the kingdom of God is near. [32]Truly I tell you, this generation will not pass away until all things have taken place. [33]Heaven and earth will pass away, but my words will not pass away.

[34]"Be on guard so that your hearts are not weighed down with dissipation and drunkenness and the worries of this life, and that day does not catch you unexpectedly, [35]like a trap. For it will come upon all who live on the face of the whole earth. [36]Be alert at all times, praying that you may have the strength to escape all these things that will take place, and to stand before the Son of Man."

Theological Perspective

Ordinary Bible readers are at times provided with instructions that are *almost* true, such as, "When reading the text, always look for promises," and "Read the Bible like a love letter." When it comes to reading Advent texts, an added *almost*-true piece of advice says, "Relate the text to Christmas"; after all, aren't Advent texts announcing the *advent* of the birth of the Savior? As half-truths these guidelines are just that, *half*-truths; as much as they help the reader, they also may misguide the reader. What I mean is this: There are Bible texts such as the Gospel text for the First Sunday of Advent for which neither promise nor love-letter hunting does any good. This text—a heavily loaded apocalyptic and eschatological text that comes within the larger unit continuing the narrative from the first verse of the chapter—has as its message anything but sentimental feelings of love. Its promise nature is a bit more "promising" as a hermeneutical aid, but even that can be appropriated only after one hears the forceful apocalyptic nature of the text in its radical and almost fearful strangeness.

When it comes to the relation of Advent Sundays to Christmas, even that is an issue that has to be framed widely enough: while this Advent text of course speaks of the coming of the Messiah, it speaks of it in relation to the final eschatological advent of

Pastoral Perspective

Why such apocalyptic imagery of endings and great calamities on the First Sunday of Advent? It feels indecorous at the opening of "the Christmas season." Even if one brackets an expectation that this be a time of happy socializing, in order to begin the church year with contemplation, repentance, preparation, remembering Christ's birth—even then, one may be left wondering what the strident imagery of this passage might be saying pastorally. In a second view, the confusion of endings and beginnings is characteristic of biblical witness, as though a dimension of the life of faith can be imagined in that moment at the top of the swing when the one swinging doesn't know whether she is completing one sweep, beginning another, or is just *still*, present to that pregnant instant in between that doesn't really exist except as a sort of moment out of time. The Bible and the life it imagines plays with time in instructive ways.

This sense is heightened when the Jeremiah passage for this day is also brought into view (33:14–16). This passage is easier for Advent, as the prophet proclaims his vision of a reunified, prosperous people. In a time of political intrigue and changing fortunes, Jeremiah resisted those who counseled expediency. God promised faithfulness to the people from the first, and God's promise is sure. Even in a time of material defeat, God's faithfulness

Exegetical Perspective

The First Sunday of Advent might seem an odd time to read about the end "drawing near," and yet it is traditional because it is appropriate, as the church reflects on Christ's first coming, to reflect also on his return. Earlier in chapter 21, Jesus describes signs of the impending doom of Jerusalem. Now, however, the language shifts to apocalyptic drama, with nature in turmoil and humanity on alert. It raises a key question: Does Jesus here refer to the end times? Or does he continue his discussion about Jerusalem's destruction? While Tom Wright opts for the latter in his approachable *Luke for Everyone* commentary, most scholars see a shift at verse 26 to the end times, Christ's return, and the consummation of the kingdom.[1] This commentator agrees with the latter interpretation, for the imagery presents the completion of all that has been promised. This text does allow dual levels of interpretation, however, so it could apply to the events of 70 CE while also intimating a grander, final fulfillment.

Nature will violently mark the coming of the Son of Man (vv. 25–28). The sea shakes and the sky fills with portents, leaving people terrified and confused.

1. Tom Wright, *Luke for Everyone* (Louisville, KY: Westminster John Knox Press, 2004), 249–56; in contrast with Darrell L. Bock, *Luke*, vol. 2, *9:51–24:53* (Grand Rapids: Baker, 1996), 1688–92; Joel B. Green, *The Gospel of Luke* (Grand Rapids: Eerdmans, 1997), 739–42.

Homiletical Perspective

It's the First Sunday of Advent. The shopping malls have been displaying Christmas decorations and playing carols since just after Halloween. Children have already watched the Christmas parade. Parents and grandparents have been stocking up on the perfect Christmas gifts for months. And now these folks come to church to experience Advent worship. If they come expecting more of what their culture offers, they are certainly in for a rude awakening! In worship they won't find Santa, nor will they encounter a smiling young Mary, a cooing baby Jesus, inquisitive shepherds, or singing angels. They may be both disappointed and dismayed by the Gospel text.

This section of Jesus' speech from the temple in Jerusalem is full of frightening images, confusing metaphors, and shocking admonitions. We do not encounter the sweet baby Jesus people wait for during Advent this first Sunday, but the stern, adult Jesus, picturing the whole universe being shaken and turned upside down. It is not a text most preachers are thrilled to explore in congregations full of people who don't understand why the church "can not just get on to Christmas already!"

The season of Advent demands a very different kind of preparation than the shopping malls and glitzy catalogs recommend. And on this First Sunday

Luke 21:25-36

Theological Perspective

God's salvific work, the coming of God's kingdom. That is the whole point of having the lectionaries guide preachers to the eschatological texts of the New Testament (as well as the Old Testament in terms of other readings for this season).

At the same time, there is the true other half: the Gospel text also ties the coming of the Christmas child to the whole history of Israel's expectations. This text does announce Jesus. The title "Son of Man"—a nomenclature subject to misinterpretation based on older exegesis that equated it merely with the human nature of the Savior—speaks volumes to ears tuned in to Old Testament theology. The one "like a son of man" in the apocalyptic vision of Daniel 7:13–14 (RSV) was given dominion and authority over nations and rulers. While the title Son of Man of course may at times speak of the humanity of the God-Man, its main New Testament theological meaning is the opposite: it is the highest christological title. To add to the complexity of this title, exegetes are telling us that "Son of Man" is also widely used in New Testament passages that speak of suffering. It other words, perhaps the best way to try to capture what the Lukan text is telling those who are preparing their hearts for the coming of the child is to refer to the imagery of the last New Testament book, appropriately called Apocalypse, with its picture of the Lamb who had been slain sitting on the throne and to whom were given the keys of "reading the future" of the scroll.

The task of the preacher in every generation is to study carefully the "theological geography" of salvation history and help Advent Sunday worshipers make these connections between the past promises, Advent Sunday, Christmas, and the eschaton. Preparing the homily for the First Sunday of Advent's Gospel text is not the place to engage in the (speculative) guesswork of end-time time lines or charts. Luke and other evangelists drew the apocalyptic materials from the rich Old Testament (and intertestamental) reservoir without any interest—as far as I can tell—in juggling with the order of events. The message of the pericope for the Christian expositor and theologian is simply this: a transformative chain of events was launched at the announcement of the coming of the infant, God-incarnate, the strangeness and peculiarity of which can be proclaimed only with the help of this frightening apocalyptic imagery.

Once the apocalyptic force of the text is heard in all its oddity, the congregation is ready to appreciate the hope-filled message of Luke. As exegetes remind

Pastoral Perspective

will yet be written *within*, in the *hearts* of God's people. As they redirect themselves and their community toward the ways of life that God has given them, a new covenant will be written on their hearts, despite desolation and fear. And the memory of their leader David will one day be recovered as a son of David's line will be restored to the throne. Here God is relentlessly faithful, carrying and chastening hearts through all things.

And so the church turns to Luke on the First Sunday of Advent, perhaps expecting to hear another origin story of Jesus, from David's line. But this doesn't come. In earshot of Jeremiah's faith, the church has not made it so easy. We are taken, instead, to the *end*, right before the plot to kill Jesus unfolds. We're taken to a passage in which Jesus speaks not of his *first*, but of his anticipated *second* coming at the end of the age. And we're told not just to prepare, but to *beware*.

No "city sidewalks, busy sidewalks, dressed in holiday style" here. We hear Jesus tell of more ominous signs and portents: "distress among nations confused by the roaring of the sea and the waves"; the powers even of the heavens to be "shaken" and people to be fainting "from fear and foreboding." It is then that his hearers will see the Son of Man coming in a cloud. And this will mark the beginning of the end and the end of the beginning.

Luke wrote with a deep and growing sense that Christian discipleship is a kind of *living in between*— aware of Jesus, waiting for Jesus, and coming to know this Jesus for whom we wait in the midst of an eventful, unpredictable, even tumultuous world, waiting to stand before him, yet not always knowing where he is.

"Look at the fig tree. It tells you when summer is coming. Read the times as you read a fig tree. Stay awake. Do not let your hearts be weighed down with things distracting from the truth of it." This Jesus taught as a second Jeremiah. "The world's a scary place, but don't let your hearts be troubled. I have overcome the world. So wait in the midst of it all, just before the dawn, for in the midst of the night there are strange and redeeming events afoot."

And with this the church begins a new year, asked to begin afresh, not just on a calendar, but in individual hearts, in relationships, in congregations, and in our yearning for a promise worth living for. Hearers of this passage are bidden to live lives of faithful, active waiting in the *meantime* because they hear again the name of the One who holds them in the *ending* time.

Exegetical Perspective

Earlier prophets identified the arrival of God's judgment in similar language (e.g., Isa. 13:6–11; Ezek. 32:7–8; Joel 2:30–31), and this may be understood as nature literally descending into chaos or as the complete overturning of earthly political and military domination. The latter would have been apparent not only in the destruction of Jerusalem but also in the political chaos of the first-century Roman Empire. The nature images, however, remind us of the sheer power and unexpected nature of a tsunami or an earthquake and the helplessness of all humanity in the face of such destruction. These descriptions portend a catastrophe greater than even the worst political disaster.

Within this first section are two exegetical cruxes: the identity of the Son of Man in verse 27 and the definition of "redemption" in verse 28. Parallels to Daniel 7:13 suggest interpreting this passage in light of Daniel's vision. While Daniel 7:13–14 depicts a single figure, the interpretation of the dream in Daniel 7:18, 22, and 27 identifies "one like a son of man" as a group given the power to reign. Throughout Luke, however, Jesus consistently uses the title "Son of Man" self-referentially; so within this context Luke's Jesus functions as the representative saint, one truly righteous who will bring about God's kingdom and, together with the saints, rule. Regarding the term "redemption," Luke describes liberation from the fallen world and its corruption, not the Pauline sense of forgiveness of sin and deliverance from its just penalty. Those who trust in God and live faithfully need not fear when the world collapses around them. Rather, they should stand confidently, trusting in God's faithfulness to bring about their emancipation from a world hostile to Christians.

In the next section (vv. 29–31), Jesus uses a nature illustration to clarify that his audience ought to discern the meaning of the signs here described. The fig tree loses its leaves each winter but regains them in the spring. The signs, Jesus states, will be clearly identifiable. Every person in history who has predicted an exact date for the final return of Christ has been wrong, so it would behoove believers to live in expectation of Christ's return as wars and natural disasters pile up, but also to live in humility, realizing Christ's return will be like a thief in the night (cf. Luke 12:33). Finally, Jesus maintains that these signs indicate that the end is "near," not necessarily "arrived." Christians ought to remain alert, careful to stay faithful despite upheaval or persecution.

Verses 32–33 give two brief, proverbial statements, the first about "this generation" not passing away

Homiletical Perspective

of Advent the Gospel text sets a very different tone than the cultural Christmas season that surrounds worshipers outside the church. Vincent van Gogh captures the mood of this Advent text in his most famous painting, *The Starry Night* (1889). The painting exhibits the bold colors that van Gogh is known for and the postimpressionist style that he helped to make famous. Van Gogh was the son of a Dutch pastor and for a time an evangelist to the poor himself, so he was likely familiar with texts such as this one from Luke 21. The painting depicts an apocalyptic sky, like that described by Jesus. There are swirling clouds in bold yellows and white on deep, dark blue and black. There is a bold and bright yellow moon and very bright stars, described by one art critic as "rockets of burning yellow."[1] In the background is a small town, with the church steeple as its most prominent feature. In the foreground, a foreboding flamelike image connects earth and sky. Art historians take it to be a cypress tree, which in van Gogh's time would have been associated with graveyards and mourning. The famous painting elicits differing reactions from those who admire it. Some see it as a daunting image of a frightening sky, others as something bold and beautiful, others as a glimpse of God.

Like van Gogh's great painting, Luke's apocalypse elicits different reactions from those who admire it. Frightening, bold, and beautiful glimpses of God— this is what Jesus offers on this First Sunday of Advent. As difficult as it is to hear, as troubled as the text may make listeners feel, in it are treasures that help focus us on the true meaning and purpose of Advent. In it, Jesus challenges us, as he did his original hearers in the Jerusalem temple, to look up, pay attention, and be ready. Advent means "coming" or "arrival," and this apocalyptic text from Luke offers the preacher the opportunity to remind worshipers that Advent involves preparing for two comings: God coming to earth in the infant Jesus whom we await at Christmas, and Christ returning to earth at a time we do not know. With this second Advent, it is not a matter of if, but of when, and Jesus wants us to be ready. We do so, Jesus says, by keeping alert, constantly preparing, and continuing to put our hope in our loving God, who comes to us in Jesus Christ.

Some preachers and worshipers in our time emphasize its fearful tones, others its encouragement

---

1. Nicholas Pioch, "Gogh, Vincent van, The Starry Night" (Webmuseum Paris, 2002), http:// www.ibiblio.org (accessed October 2, 2007).

Theological Perspective

us, Luke relates the frightening future to his readers more directly than other evangelists and adds the remark on the coming of the Son of Man with a promise. Furthermore, Luke ends this pericope with an encouragement and exhortation. While heavens and earth may pass away in the final eschatological transformation, the word of God stays firm, Luke reminds us. While judgment seems evident, "redemption is drawing near."

The Gospel text for the First Sunday of Advent, cast in the form and using the content of apocalyptic eschatology, is neither a world-renouncing fatalism or despair nor an escapist withdrawal or paralysis, but rather a "theology of hope." The church father Tertullian put it this way: "The kingdom of God, beloved brethren, is beginning to be at hand; the reward of life, and the rejoicing of eternal salvation, and the perpetual gladness and possession lately lost of paradise, are now coming, with the passing away of the world; already heavenly things are taking the place of earthly, and great things of small, and eternal things of things that fade away. What room is there here for anxiety and solicitude?"[1] The Reformed theologian Jürgen Moltmann makes a similar statement, with reference to the telling title of his first landmark book: "With *Theology of Hope* . . . I tried to present the Christian hope no longer as such an 'opium of the beyond' but rather as the divine power that makes us alive in this world."[2]

The preacher, having opened this eschatological horizon to her or his listeners, may be in a better place to help the congregation see the wider historical and sociopolitical context of this Gospel as a frame for the text of the Second Sunday of Advent and the strongly ethical and eschatological text for the Third Sunday of Advent.

VELI-MATTI KÄRKKÄINEN

Pastoral Perspective

Harbingers of both progress and doom would give time differently. They would say that the future comes only when the hands of our clocks have moved to the right, and that the past is little more than fodder for a sense of superiority or fuel for hurt feelings—but there is a different story of time told here. It's a story of a time bigger than our own life stories, and of a time that gives lives a meaning full of a promise that neither optimism nor pessimism can even begin to comprehend. It's an *eschatology of eventfulness*—if one wants to name it—in which we live our lives, and see all creation alive, in a rhythm of reality and promise.

The reality is this: anything can happen at any moment—and in one way or another everything *is* happening in every moment. There is no present moment to which one can cling, and change is not limited by predictability and control. Here is an opportunity gently to challenge the kind of religion that turns faith into a sort of fee-for-service arrangement with the Divine. Yet, even as we *do* participate in our happiness, and even as there *are* indefinable connections between how we live and *what* we live, these connections are never exact. There are other realities at work that sometimes overwhelm—realities of brokenness and evil, of serendipity and grace—and so the present moment is itself an event *for* us, worth loving and worth living, because it is a *gift*. One can only accept it with thanksgiving, trust the promise that lies behind it, and pray for the strength to do what is necessary to fill it with faithfulness—waiting for God. No nostalgia here, and no pie-in-the-sky dreaming. No resignation to oppression or failure, either, and no overestimation of powers or virtues. *Real* hope, *real* knowledge, *real* love in Jesus. Faith is living in the *reality*, by virtue of the *promise*. There may lie the pastoral word.

WESLEY D. AVRAM

1. Tertullian, *The Treatises, 7: On the Mortality* in *Ante-Nicene Fathers*, 10 vols. (Grand Rapids: Eerdmans, 1988), 5:64, 69.
2. Jürgen Moltmann et al., *Love: The Foundation of Hope; The Theology of Jürgen Moltmann and Elisabeth Moltmann-Wendel*, 1st ed. (San Francisco: Harper & Row, 1988), 4.

Exegetical Perspective

before Jesus' words are fulfilled, the latter about the eternal nature of his words. Scholarly discussion concerning what Jesus meant by "this generation" is multifaceted, but this essay will consider two main solutions. The first holds that the "generation" means "those who oppose Jesus and his message," a meaning consistent in Luke and still available to our observation today. The second posits that "generation" refers to the generation in which the signs first appear, to whom the end also will be revealed, within one generation and not extending over decades or centuries. The term remains ambiguous. In contrast, however, in verse 33 Jesus equates his words to authoritative, enduring Scripture. Despite delay or confusion, Jesus' followers are not to doubt his words: things *will* come to pass as he has described. This affirmation grounds the injunctions of the final section, because the confidence to "stand" and "lift your heads" comes from trust in God's faithfulness to God's promises.

This last section resembles the practical injunctions ending Paul's letters, commands given based on the theology already presented. Jesus warns his hearers to "be careful" so that they are not surprised on the day of judgment. A favorable judgment is not guaranteed to all who claim to be followers of Jesus. Instead, while judgment happens to all, only those who have remained faithful and lived obediently—not becoming enamored with the world and all that is in it—will stand before Jesus. Here "to stand before" seems to indicate the same thing as "eternal life." Those who "make it" through judgment are those who remained faithful. This obedient living, however, is not done independently, as a "works-righteousness" to earn salvation. Instead, verse 36 reveals that it is done prayerfully, depending upon God to give strength to persevere despite temptation or persecution. This, indeed, is the point of the whole passage, which is as relevant to our latter-day selves and congregations as it was to our first-century brothers and sisters: be watchful and alert, prayerful and humble, trusting in God and awaiting redemption from the world's systems that only God can, and will, bring.

MARIAM J. KAMELL

Homiletical Perspective

and consolation. For over a decade at the turn of the twenty-first century, the bestselling fiction series *Left Behind* has captured readers all over the globe. The focus of the series is on the end times and the great turmoil that exists in the world as the forces of good and evil face off in preparation for Christ's second coming. The books foster fear and desperation for those who may get "left behind," and many pulpits feature this message.

Luke's painting of the apocalypse resists this fearful interpretation. Despite some frightening images, the Advent text from Luke offers not fear and damnation, but hope and expectation. God in Christ is coming because God loves us—because God wants to redeem us (v. 28). In the midst of the fearful specter, Jesus calls us to "stand up and raise [our] heads, because [our] redemption is drawing near." We may not live as the Lukan community, on the margins of society, in a world riddled with disease and drought and despair. Nevertheless, we too find hope in apocalyptic writing about a better world that can break forth at any time. Famine, drought, war, disease, still plague our world, and closer to home people struggle with greed, addiction, mental illness, and misplaced priorities. Christ's call to be alert and constantly praying for God's kingdom to break through into our world is as pertinent a call for us this Advent as it ever has been. Our broken and hurting selves and world need Christ to come, and we must take time this Advent to prepare to receive him.

The good news of Advent is not simply that Christ is coming, but that his coming means we can hope, despite all that is falling apart in our lives, our communities, and the world around us. Just as the leaves on the fig tree offer hope in late winter that summer is coming again, so God's word, in Jesus, promises us new life. Advent offers us expectation and hope for something new. "Stand up and raise your heads, because your redemption is drawing near" (v. 28). "Be alert at all times" (v. 36). May those who come to Advent worship leave with a commitment to use this season of Advent to prepare for God's kingdom breaking forth, as we await the radical, earth-shattering welcome of the Prince of Peace—the little baby, and the risen Lord.

KATHY BEACH-VERHEY

Malachi 3:1-4

¹See, I am sending my messenger to prepare the way before me, and the Lord whom you seek will suddenly come to his temple. The messenger of the covenant in whom you delight—indeed, he is coming, says the LORD of hosts. ²But who can endure the day of his coming, and who can stand when he appears?

For he is like a refiner's fire and like fullers' soap; ³he will sit as a refiner and purifier of silver, and he will purify the descendants of Levi and refine them like gold and silver, until they present offerings to the LORD in righteousness. ⁴Then the offering of Judah and Jerusalem will be pleasing to the LORD as in the days of old and as in former years.

Theological Perspective

Despite all of the ambiguities regarding the date and authorship of Malachi, most scholars agree that this minor prophet was speaking to a postexilic community of Jews who had returned to Judah. Much of the book is written as a series of *disputations*, and the prophet serves as an arbiter in these conflicts between the people and God. In response to complaints that God has failed to exercise divine judgment, the prophet delivers an eschatological rebuttal, which raises several points with significant theological import. This essay will address two broad themes, which the reader finds woven together throughout the lection: (1) divine judgment, the Day of the Lord, and the character of God's justice, and (2) the purification of the people.

Divine Judgment, the Day of the Lord, and the Character of God's Justice. The people, newly restored in Judah, are skeptical of God's justice, because their practices of piety have yielded neither divine retributive judgment against "evildoers" nor prosperity for the restoration community. Their challenges to the prophet smack of self-righteousness, and they seemingly have failed to notice that their compromised worship practices, marital infidelity, and social injustice dishonor God. They seek and desire the coming of the Lord,

Pastoral Perspective

Years ago I heard Elie Weisel, the Jewish writer and Nobel Prize winner, recall a childhood story. When he was a boy, his mother would greet him every day when he returned from school. Every day she would ask him the same question. She did not ask, "What did you do today?" or "Whom did you talk to today?" or even "What did you learn today?" She would ask, "Did you have a good question today?"

Malachi had some good questions for his day. How has God loved us? (1:2) "Has not one God created us?" (2:10) "Where is the God of justice?" (2:17) How shall we return to God? (3:7) Malachi poses twenty-two questions in just fifty-five verses. God's questions to the priests and the people are articulated; their responses to God are anticipated. Rhetorical questions emphasize the prophetic passion for integrity; direct inquiries evoke the people's questions and provoke impassioned response. The question-and-answer style opens prophetic deliverance to more of a prophet-and-people deliberation, edgy but candid, confrontational and engaging. They are now partners in critical reflection on the nature of God and self-critical reflection on the conduct of Israel.

Malachi has some good questions for our day. His very use of questions as a means of prophetic revelation counters the unthinking certitude of much

Exegetical Perspective

The short biblical book of Malachi hails from the Second Temple period, also known as postexilic times, and was written clearly after the dedication of the Second Temple in 515 BCE (see Ezra 6:15). Lamenting the corruption of the priesthood, its author must have lived long enough after the initial celebration and dedication to allow for the witness of discontent and questionable ritual practices (Mal. 1:6–14), somewhere in the first half of the fifth century BCE. Malachi, the Hebrew word for "my messenger," may be the self-designation of a priest disgruntled with the practices of his colleagues and congregation, rather than a personal name; alternatively, it may be a pun on such a name. While some ancient sources assume that the messenger is Ezra (see Targum; also *b. Meg.* 15a), others have identified him as Mordecai (Rabbi Nachman). Yet others wonder whether this was a reference to the prophet Elijah (see Mal. 4:5–6). Prophesying from the center of religious (and by extension some social) power, this temple prophet identifies with divine first-person speech, calling other priests and the people to account.[1]

1. See for example, Eileen M. Schuller, OSU, "The Book of Malachi: Introduction, Commentary, and Reflections," in *The New Interpreter's Bible,* vol. 7 (Nashville: Abingdon Press, 1996), 841–77.

Homiletical Perspective

The word of the Lord came to Malachi as a word of promise. That promise comes as good news to us; but there is also at least a degree of uneasiness in the promise. There are some elements of the promise that we would love to have fulfilled and other elements that we would just as soon leave unfulfilled.

This blend of joy and apprehension at the prospect of promise fulfillment is most clearly reflected in verse 2: "But who can endure the day of his coming, and who can stand when he appears? For he is like a refiner's fire and like fullers' soap." The believer responds to this promise by wondering exactly what is meant by the refining. What exactly in my life is in need of refining? And how much will it hurt? What might I have to give up (or what might be taken from me) before I would be refined like gold and silver?

In many ways, our response to this text is probably not that much different from the response of Malachi's original audience. Like them, we want to stand and see that day. We want our offerings to be pleasing to the Lord. We want to see the restoration of the covenant. We want to see things made right, the way God intended—and yet . . . and yet we are not so sure. We do not want to go through too much change or pain to see it happen.

This tension between joy and apprehension could provide great fodder for preaching, as we try to hear

Malachi 3:1-4

Theological Perspective

imagining that it will be favorable for them. The prophet, however, reminds the people that the arrival of divine judgment rarely meets human expectations—it is sudden, surprising, and often as much a judgment against the ones yearning for it as it is a judgment against their enemies (Amos 5:18). When the Day of the Lord arrives, the prophet warns, all will be found guilty and all will be deserving of punishment. In particular, in verse 5 (curiously, not part of this lection), the prophet warns that God's swift judgment will be executed upon the perpetrators of social injustice.

God's judgment should not, however, be understood as solely punitive, even though the people seem to deserve punishment. God's justice is not the justice expected by the restoration community. Instead, in this text we find that the divine judgment to be exercised on the Day of the Lord has a more long-range telos, in that it will issue in a process of purification that makes a place hospitable for the abiding presence of God. In the end, God's schema of justice is restorative rather than retributive.

The Purification of the People. In two places in this short lection, we find references to the ways in which purifying preparations are made for God's presence with the people. In verse 1, the prophet points to the coming of a messenger who would clear or "prepare the way of the Lord." In verses 2–3, the prophet describes the Lord's coming as like the refiner's fire, whose purpose is to remove impurities and strengthen the substance being refined. John Calvin wrote this about the refiner's fire: "The power of the fire, we know, is twofold: for it burns and it purifies; it burns what is corrupt; but it purifies gold and silver from their dross."

The refiner's fire has made a number of appearances in theological discourse over time. What is it that stands in need of purification? And what will be consumed by flames in the process? After purification, what is it that God reckons as precious metal? Calvin thought that the refiner's fire would serve to correct the corruption not only of the people, but of the Levitical priests also: "Such then was the contagion, that not only the common people became corrupt, but even the Levites themselves, who ought to have been guides to others, and who were to be in the Church as it were the pattern of holiness. God however promises that such would be the purifying which Christ would effect, and so regulated, that it would consume the whole people,

Pastoral Perspective

so-called religious conviction. "Who can endure the day of his coming?" (3:2) Who will be "pure and blameless" in the day of Christ? (Phil. 1:10) Who will prepare the way by repentance and forgiveness? (Luke 3:1–6) Advent questions! Advent questions our worthiness, readiness, and willingness for Christ's coming. "The descendants of Levi" are called to new "integrity and uprightness," a turning "from iniquity," and a renewed "reverence" for God's "covenant of life and well-being" with us (Mal. 2:5–6). Like the ancient priesthood, the contemporary priesthood of believers opens its life to the refining presence of God and offers its life in righteous practice.

A faithful hearing of this text will turn the church to some good questions about its worship life during Advent: Are prayers prophetic as well as personal, directed to injustice and corruption as well as seasonal anxiety and individual omissions? A prayer of confession for Advent admits, "We live casual lives, ignoring your promised judgment. We accept lies as truth, exploit neighbors, abuse the earth, and refuse your justice and peace." A prayer for the Second Sunday of Advent addresses the God of mercy: "You sent your messengers the prophets to preach repentance and prepare the way for our salvation. Give us grace to heed their warnings and forsake our sins."[1]

Is the Word proclaimed through the sacrament of baptism? The baptismal liturgy poses some good questions. Malachi's indictment that "you have turned aside from the way" (2:8) and John's "baptism of repentance for the forgiveness of sins" (Luke 3:3) are echoed in the profession of faith. "Trusting in the gracious mercy of God, do you turn from the ways of sin and renounce evil and its power in the world?" Malachi's image of God's messenger as "fullers' soap" who "will purify the descendants of Levi" (3:2b–3) is reflected in the Thanksgiving over the Water when we praise God for giving us a "cleansing and rebirth . . . that we might . . . serve you as a royal priesthood."[2] The communal significance of baptism involves the entire congregation in reaffirming God's "covenant of life and well-being" in Jesus Christ. Baptism prepares the way, and it answers one of Malachi's most pressing questions: "Where is the God of justice?" (2:17). Today's text begins an answer. "See, I am sending my messenger to prepare the way." The sacrament of baptism is a sign that God is here, with us, in the world.

1. *Book of Common Worship* (Louisville, KY: Westminster/John Knox Press, 1993), 133.
2. Ibid., 407, 411.

Exegetical Perspective

This lection follows Malachi's poignant questions of dysfunctional religion by means of rhetorical questions about the people's accountability to the covenant and the implied lack thereof, which ignorantly ask where to find the God of justice (Mal. 2:17). The prophet switches his tone in 3:1–4 while continuing the judgment oracle, which is the fourth of six oracles in the book (1:2–5; 1:6–2:9; 2:10–16; 2:17–3:5; 3:6–12; 3:13–4:3). Alternating between first- and third-person divine speech, the passage talks about a future time, characterized as a day of judgment (Mal. 3:5). Language reminiscent of Second Isaiah (see Isa. 40:3) proclaims the commission of God's messenger "to prepare the way before me" to usher in the sudden arrival of God in the temple. This staging of a grand entrance for YHWH at a time of discontent and disappointment, in the midst of struggles for direction among those who find themselves back in Judah, utilizes the memory of comfort and liberation from a century earlier to invoke the possibility of another change in direction.

The passage continues with *YHWH Zebaoth*, the God of hosts, promising the arrival of "the messenger of the covenant" with the attribute "in whom you delight" (Mal. 3:1b). This attribute is a formula used for both God and human beings throughout the First Testament (see Deut. 10:15; Gen. 34:19; 1 Sam. 18:22; Pss. 5:5; 34:13; etc.). While much more prevalent in its absence, its presence indicates a specially sanctioned event. So what is going on in this grand entrance, and who is really arriving? The text remains ambiguous as to whether the reference is to a messenger, who may or may not be identical with the messenger of the covenant mentioned in the following sentence, or to God, or to the "great king" promised in Malachi 1:14. Commentators through the ages have debated the identity of this messenger, including the possibility of a priestly messiah figure. Centuries later, in the New Testament the Malachi verse is merged with the verse in Second Isaiah to identify the messenger with John the Baptizer (Matt. 11:10; Mark 1:2; Luke 7:27).

While the actual identity of this ominous figure remains vague, its impact is not. This messenger is to enforce the covenant with powerful means, "like a refiner's fire and like fullers' soap" (Mal. 3:2). It is not just any fire and any soap, but very particular ones, resulting in a particular process of cleansing. Such purification will be characterized by extreme heat and strong lye; all possible uncleanliness will be burned and washed away from the Levitical priesthood until the ideal of covenant faithfulness is

Homiletical Perspective

this promise anew and to reflect on our relationship to it. From a homiletical perspective, we ask how we can best approach the tension and gain some understanding. Two approaches lend themselves readily to addressing the tension in the promise of something new: we can reflect on the anticipation of a couple expecting a child, and we can reflect socially and culturally on what might really be changed when God's promised messenger of the covenant does come.

The culture of every people has stories about the anticipation involved in those nine months of waiting for a child to be born. Whether you retell a story from film or television or you tell your own story, the important point to make is that major events in life often come with very mixed emotions and mixed feelings. Even in the midst of joy at the prospect of this new life, this new person to love, there is often fear about the unknowns involved.

One story that reflects these ambivalences appears in the acclaimed 2007 film *Juno*. The title character in the film, a pregnant high-school student, wrestles throughout the movie, whose time frame is the nine-month pregnancy, with what this pregnancy and child mean for her relationship with friends, family, the baby's father, prospective adoptive parents, and herself. This story may help our parishioners reflect on our own feelings at hearing Malachi's promise. Juno wants to see this baby born and be healthy and have a good life. But what exactly does that mean for her? What does she have to sacrifice to get there? What will be changed in her life, regardless of the choices she makes going forward?

Another interesting layer of *Juno* for this text is the degree to which events are outside of Juno's control during the pregnancy. There are some choices she can make and some ways that she can affect outcomes, but there are many ways that she cannot. After hand-selecting adoptive parents for her as-yet unborn child, Juno comes to discover that nothing is guaranteed and people sometimes turn out to be different from what you at first may have thought. Events that have deep meaning for Juno and her child happen outside of her effective control. In the same way, God's promise of covenant restoration happens outside of our control. It is God's promise and God's restoration. It will happen, in God's way and whether we are ready for it or not.

Another approach to the same themes may come from some quite honest reflection on our church and our broader society. What might be refined and purified in God's promised refining fire? When

Malachi 3:1-4

Theological Perspective

and yet purify the elect, and purify them like silver, that they may be saved."[1]

Two things should be said about Calvin's interpretation of verse 3 and the association he makes with the *doctrine of election*. First, Calvin's commentaries on the prophets, not surprisingly, have a christocentric focus that sometimes crosses over into a supersessionist interpretation. We must always exercise a bit of caution, then, when consulting these texts, even when we do so in the context of Advent, a time in the liturgical year particularly set aside for the anticipation of the coming Messiah. Second, even as Calvin derives support for the doctrine of election in the Malachi passage, he also reminds the reader that election is not for privilege, but for a purpose. Once again, proper temple worship would be restored, and the people (Levitical priests, in particular) would make offerings acceptable to God.

Purification has another possible purpose, as well, in addition to the removal of impurities. When silver is refined, it is treated with carbon or charcoal, preventing the absorption of oxygen and resulting in its sheen and purity. One writer has suggested that a silversmith knows that the refining process is complete only when she observes her "own image reflected in the mirror-like surface of the metal."[2] If this is the case, does the prophet also suggest that the *imago Dei* is restored in this process? Is humanity deemed good and righteous when once again the divine image is reflected in the human heart?[3]

JENNIFER RYAN AYRES

Pastoral Perspective

Do hymns and choral music express the messenger's judgment as well as the joy? While many are eager to sing and hear the familiar Christmas carols, Advent hymn themes are discordant, unsung, and unpopular in many congregations. The notes of today's lectionary texts are sounded in hymns like "O Day of God, Draw Near," which sings of judgment and faithfulness, justice and security.[3]

The text of Malachi 3:1–3 appears in one of the signature choral works of this season, George Frideric Handel's *Messiah*. With his libretto, Charles Jennens raised Malachi's faithful question about the nature of God's love. He answered it with a catena of powerful Scriptures. A congregation blessed with the choral acumen to offer this masterpiece should hear the Malachi text in context. The recitative ("The Lord, whom ye seek shall suddenly come"), air for bass ("But who may abide the day of his coming?") and chorus ("He shall purify the sons of Levi") is answered by an alto, "Behold, a virgin shall conceive, and bear a Son, and shall call his name Emmanuel, God with us." Music can sing the Word and proclaim the good news.

On this Second Sunday of Advent, music can sing the Word, proclaim the good news, and challenge both preacher and congregation. After the first presentation of *Messiah* in London in 1741, Handel wrote to a friend: "I should be sorry if I only entertained them. I wished to make them better." The composer challenges the preacher to go beyond feeling good to doing good. At issue are some good questions about worship in our day: Entertainment or edification? Diversion or direction? Amusement or awareness? Handel himself provided an answer. Although by 1751 he was blind, until his death he conducted *Messiah* as an annual benefit for the Foundling Hospital in London, which served mostly widows and orphans of the clergy. The intent was not just to entertain; Handel's hope was to make them just and better. His ear was open to the prophetic word: "Present offerings to the LORD in righteousness" (Mal. 3:3).

Malachi opens the church to some good questions for today.

DEBORAH A. BLOCK

1. John Calvin, *Commentaries on the Twelve Minor Prophets*, ed. and trans. John Owen (Grand Rapids: Eerdmans, 1950), 5:573.

2. Ralph L. Smith, *Micah-Malachi*, Word Bible Commentary 32 (Waco, TX: Word Books, 1984), 329.

3. Calvin famously likened the *imago Dei* to a mirror within the human soul, which is meant to reflect God's glory (*Institutes of the Christian Religion*, ed. John McNeil, trans. Ford Lewis Battles [Philadelphia: Westminster Press, 1960], 1.15.4).

3. *The New Century Hymnal* (Cleveland: The Pilgrim Press, 1995), 611; *The Presbyterian Hymnal* (Louisville, KY: Westminster/John Knox Press, 1990), 452.

Exegetical Perspective

demonstrated by their performance of "offerings in righteousness" (Mal. 3:3). Righteousness (*tsedaqah*) is an essential quality of the covenant made with Moses and the people at Sinai (see Exod. 19:1–6). This covenant, the ideal of Torah living, is held up by the majority of the prophets. Thus, to these idealized times of the past, Malachi calls this Second-Temple people to return (Mal. 3:4).

Read thusly, the message of these verses is basically a conservative one, as it calls for a return to the idealized past to avoid the threat of judgment. The "good old times" are invoked and promised as a possibility, if only the people and the priesthood change their current ways: this is what a simplistic reading would suggest.

To arrive at a more differentiated interpretation of the present-past-future continuum in Malachi and other prophetic books of the Second Temple period, one needs to consider the sociohistorical context of the Judeans under the Persian Empire.[2] A mixed multitude of those who returned from the exile in Babylon, those who never left the land, and those who since had moved there and intermarried, these fifth-century-BCE Judeans are living together uncomfortably with competing messages as to what faithful living entails now (see, for example, Isa. 56:1–8; Ezra 9:1–2, 10–15; Neh. 5:1–5). Which of the rival leaders clamoring for power are they to follow? The Levitical purists? The Isaianic reconciliationists? The radical apocalypticists?

Malachi does not exactly take sides. Instead, he offers another possible direction, namely, to go back to the principles of the covenant so as to be rewarded (see Mal. 3:16–4:6). While sympathizing with the Levitical purists, the prophet upholds Moses as a model of righteousness and thus faithful living (Mal. 4:4). If those principles of the past are to be lived out in the present and future, then fundamental change may be possible. Even the possibility of the return of the prophet Elijah is promised. Though its details remain enigmatic, the result is a vision of intergenerational reconciliation (Mal. 4:5–6).

Analogies and allusions abound between the people addressed by Malachi and contemporary congregations in the United States. Competing voices proclaim the "right" direction; rival leaders clamor for power. What would constitute faithful covenant living during this season of Advent?

ANGELA BAUER-LEVESQUE

Homiletical Perspective

God's promise, spoken through Malachi, is finally fulfilled, what will look different in our church? our world? our lives? A word of warning about this approach: this text is not an occasion to attack enemies or to point out all the things that some imagined "they" are doing wrong. Rather, *we* are the ones who are going to be refined. *We* are the ones in need of refining.

Look inside. Look inside yourself. Look inside your congregation. Look inside your church. What will God's refining look like? Perhaps the faces in our pews will reflect the rainbow of pigmentation in God's world more than they do. Perhaps there will be fewer luxury cars in the church parking lot and more beds for the homeless. What will our worship and our stewardship look like if "the offering of Judah and Jerusalem [and Chicago and Dallas and Tuscaloosa and Juneau and First Presbyterian and St. Martin's Lutheran] will be pleasing to the LORD" (v. 4)? These would be worthwhile questions to ponder.

In closing a sermon prepared with either of these approaches, it would be very helpful to emphasize that the promise of this restoration and refining is sure. It will happen, and it will happen under God's control and in God's time. The refining is not waiting for us to feel good about it. God's promise is sure, and it is good news. We will be re-formed in God's image, and it will be good. No matter how we feel about it now. No matter what we may be afraid of now. When we are refined and purified as God promises, it will be good.

SETH MOLAND-KOVASH

---

2. Pierre Briant, *From Cyrus to Alexander: A History of the Persian Empire* (Winona Lake, IN: Eisenbrauns, 1998).

Luke 1:68-79

68"Blessed be the Lord God of Israel,
  for he has looked favorably on his people and redeemed them.
69He has raised up a mighty savior for us
  in the house of his servant David,
70as he spoke through the mouth of his holy prophets from of old,
71 that we would be saved from our enemies and from the hand of all
    who hate us.
72Thus he has shown the mercy promised to our ancestors,
  and has remembered his holy covenant,
73the oath that he swore to our ancestor Abraham,
  to grant us 74that we, being rescued from the hands of our enemies,

Theological Perspective

Zechariah's canticle sits among six offerings of praise in the infancy narratives of Luke 1–2 (1:42–45, 1:46–55, 2:13–14, 2:29–32, 2:38). Unlike the other five, which focus directly on the birth of Jesus, Zechariah's canticle honors John's birth as a sign of what is done and what is to come. Presented as two distinct movements—praise (vv. 68–75) and prediction (vv. 76–79)—the song is both general and specific in celebrating fulfilled promises to the nation and in celebrating the meaning of an individual life. In this way, Luke's text paves the way for Advent reflections, both individual and communal.

Called the Benedictus, Zechariah's song is based on a hymn of "the poor of the Lord." Since Zechariah and Elizabeth were among the Jewish upper class (he was a priest and she was descended from Aaron), his use of a song of the poor signals the reversals of fortune interpreters traditionally identify as central to the book of Luke. Zechariah's celebration of salvation for the nation also captures the historic debate about whether Jesus was to be understood as a political or spiritual messiah. On one hand, references to a "mighty savior . . . in the house of his servant David" (v. 69) who rescues the people "from the hands of our enemies" (v. 74) and who promises "peace" (v. 79), in a text written shortly after the Roman-Jewish war, suggests

Pastoral Perspective

The ministry of the church is a complex and combustible concoction of fear and joy. Indeed, if I were to chart the heartbeat of the church, it would spike from fear and anxiety to joy and gratitude, with little resting in between. For example, if you want to see a spiking line in the church I serve, just ask about money. You see furrowed brows as storm clouds begin to gather, and you can almost feel the collective energy taking a precipitous drop. By contrast, ask about our Community Club tutorial program and you will get a big smile, and you can feel the group energy soar like an eagle.

The characters in the Gospel of Luke can also be described as vacillating between joy and fear. Let's sketch, for example, the story of Zechariah and Elizabeth. Luke tells us that Elizabeth is barren and getting on in years (for Luke, a definitive line down). Then the angel Gabriel appears to Zechariah to announce that Elizabeth will bear a son named John, who will be the forerunner of the coming savior of Israel (line up). At this news, Zechariah is terrified with disbelief, and so the angel renders him mute (line down). Then Elizabeth conceives and bears a son (line up). When it comes to naming the child, everybody questions Elizabeth's naming him John (line down). Then Zechariah confirms this name for his son, his mouth is freed, and he is able to speak

might serve him without fear, [75]in holiness and righteousness
before him all our days.
[76]And you, child, will be called the prophet of the Most High;
for you will go before the Lord to prepare his ways,
[77]to give knowledge of salvation to his people
by the forgiveness of their sins.
[78]By the tender mercy of our God,
the dawn from on high will break upon us,
[79]to give light to those who sit in darkness and in the shadow of death,
to guide our feet into the way of peace."

Exegetical Perspective

Our passage, called the Benedictus, after the first word of its Latin translation, has been beloved by the church for two millennia. Zechariah's prophetic song separates neatly into two parts. In verses 68–75, he praises the God of Israel for fulfilling God's covenant to God's people; in verses 76–79, Zechariah gives his son a broad job description. Set into worship on this Second Sunday in Advent, our passage introduces the faithful words of Zechariah, whose journey of faith we follow throughout chapter 1.

Narrational prose brackets the song. Verse 67 carries on the discussion about John, a miracle baby and child of promise, by describing the upcoming speaker as "his father Zechariah." This is important, for throughout the prophecy the speaker, Zechariah, remains secondary to both his message and his baby son. Verses 67–79 are distinctly Trinitarian: The God of Israel is praised (v. 68) and someone called "the dayspring" is coming from heaven (v. 78 KJV). Verse 67 has Zechariah "filled with the Holy Spirit" and verse 80, also in narration, sums up the child John's early life and hints at Zechariah's strong mentoring influence, for the child "became strong in spirit."

The miraculous dominates. John's birth is miraculous because his parents are past child-siring/bearing years (v. 18). Zechariah's prophecy is miraculous because he suddenly speaks; nine

Homiletical Perspective

Advent continues; our ruminations go deeper. We wait, watch, wonder if we will ever know peace. Will we find peace in our own souls? Will there be peace on earth? Peace is the traditional theme for the Second Sunday of Advent—not just peace as the absence of violence, but peace that passes understanding, peace that heals and makes whole, peace that allows the wolf to live with the lamb and the leopard with the kid, peace that allows a little child to lead the people and bring them back into full communion with God, peace that ensures there will be no more hurting or destruction on God's holy mountain because the whole earth will be full of the knowledge of God (Isa. 11:6–9).

The Benedictus, Zechariah's great hymn of prophecy, praise, and blessing clearly moves us toward that unfathomable, whole, creation-healing shalom of God. Here we find ourselves waiting and watching for something that we deeply desire, wondering if it will ever come. We may long for peace but we know we live in a world in which there is much too little of it, both personally and politically.

In preaching on this text, it may be useful to give Zechariah's hymn some literary context. Like Mary later in this chapter, Zechariah is surprised by a visit from the angel Gabriel. Like Mary, he questions the announcement of a miraculous pregnancy, that he

Luke 1:68-79

Theological Perspective

political/physical redemption. On the other hand, salvation "by the forgiveness of . . . sins" (v. 77) commonly is considered a spiritual reference. Some interpreters, such as Stephanie Buchanon Crowder and Alfred Plummer, overcome the tension of the two positions by affirming the importance of both dimensions. Crowder says that "Luke uses faith to speak to the contextual reality of believing readers and imperialistic leaders" to address "the holistic well-being of those who have such faith."[1] Plummer says the text refers to "political redemption" that is "accompanied by and based upon a moral and spiritual reformation."[2]

Among the first words he utters after at least nine months of silence, Zechariah's song, like Advent, celebrates the new era to be brought by the incarnation. As a privileged male leader from the ruling classes, Zechariah's character is in tension with an important reversal theme in the infancy narratives that focus predominantly on women and in the book that presents outsiders (such as women, the poor, and foreigners) as favored by God. In content, however, the Benedictus is consistent with celebration of divine work that characterizes other songs in the infancy narratives.

In this first movement of the song, Zechariah praises God for the favor indicated by the new era, since the coming incarnation means that prophecies "from of old," promises "to our ancestors," and the "holy covenant" with Abraham all are fulfilled. By making these announcements, Zechariah takes on the role of prophet, even as he points to fulfillment of prophecy. His relatively privileged status as a priest who understands his nation as being favored by God, but who nonetheless identifies with the oppressed circumstance of Jewish people whose homeland is occupied, captures the complexity of the situation of human beings, understood by some Christian theologians as being both friends and foes of God.

The reference to fulfillment of promises to ancestors (v. 72) brings this complexity into historic view, since by its story ancient Israel is implicated in the global legacy of conquest. The meaning of this fulfillment is framed as having both historical and contemporary dimensions. As the full fruition of promises anticipated by Jewish ancestors as far back as Abraham, the fulfillment relates to the entire Jewish history up to Zechariah's time; yet

Pastoral Perspective

(line up), but the people are terrified (line down). On and on, the lines spike up and down throughout the rest of the Gospel—from John's proclamation of judgment (line down) to Jesus' baptism (line up) to the temptation scene (line down) to the call of the first disciples (line up) to the conflict with religious authorities (line down). So Zechariah's song seems a bit disingenuous to me, when, as he is praising God for the coming Savior, he describes the ministry of those who will follow the Savior, suggesting that we will "serve [God] without fear."

I have never served in a ministry that was completely without fear. Fear of failure or rejection, or something like this, seems to be a constant companion in ministry. To be sure, there is lots of joy that can be added to this mix, but I am also under the impression that fear is an accompaniment of any serious ministry. For while in Luke, Jesus, an angel, or a messenger is always telling us to not to fear, Jesus also tells disciples that if they want to follow him they must "take up their cross daily" (9:23) and that their ministry will be as sheep among wolves (10:3), which are not exactly comforting descriptions of the service of God! After all, the life of ministry is about confronting the principalities and powers that rule the world, and the prospect of doing so is understandably fearful.

I am reminded that the late psychiatrist Dr. Murray Bowen had a theory that there are times in any society when anxiety peaks. At such times, terrorism, fundamentalism, and toxicity infect all of society.[1] This sounds like the United States since 9/11, doesn't it? And it is not likely to improve. In election years, political speech becomes more polarizing, and rhetoric within the church is often no different. Anyone who has attended a church judicatory meeting knows how fever pitched the debates can be, as conservatives stereotype liberals for their perceived laxity in morals and general disregard for the Bible, and liberals portray their conservative counterparts as puritanical and legalistic prigs. Will we ever get beyond the anxieties that produce these stereotypes? In such a toxic environment, how is it possible to raise our heads above collective, self-perpetuating fear?

A story about British philosopher Geoff Midgley might be instructive. By his own admission, Midgley tended to look on the gloomy side of life. In the early 1980s, one day as he was having tea with his

---

1. Stephanie Buchanon Crowder, "The Gospel of Luke," in *True to Our Native Land: An African American New Testament Commentary*, ed. Brian K. Blount et al. (Minneapolis: Fortress Press, 2007), 158.
2. Alfred Plummer, *A Critical and Exegetical Commentary on the Gospel according to S. Luke*, 5th ed. (New York: T. & T. Clark, 2000), 40.

1. See Peter Steinke, *How Your Church Family Works: Understanding Congregations as Emotional Systems* (New York: The Alban Institute, 1993), foreword.

months earlier, the angel Gabriel decreed a punishment of silence (v. 20) and maybe deafness (v. 62) because of Zechariah's unbelief. The text groups the naming and circumcision of John and Zechariah's prophecy (v. 59–79), giving the impression they happened together. But this may not necessarily be so.

Zechariah's name means "God remembered." And God's remembrances dominate verses 68–75. Zechariah includes himself in the prophecy because of the pronoun "us" and possessive adjective "our." Zechariah prophesies that God has remembered God's holy covenant, the oath God swore to Abraham our father. God has remembered to show mercy and to rescue God's covenant people from the hand of their enemies. God has redeemed God's people. God remembers God's covenant promises.

God's character figures prominently in the song. God is strong; God has raised up a horn of salvation, a symbol of strength, for us. God saves us from those who hate us. God has shown mercy to our ancestors and now to us. God gives us the security to do what we want to do most of all: serve God with awe, and serve God the way God wants to be served, in righteousness and holiness. A keynote of God's character is God's tender mercy.

God has sent holy prophets throughout the ages, and the small son whom Zechariah now addresses (vv. 76–79) is the latest in that line. John will be called a prophet of the Most High. His job is to go before the Lord to prepare the way for him. John will do this by giving God's people the knowledge of salvation via the forgiveness of their sins (v. 77). Later, John calls people to repentance (Luke 3:3), and Jesus confirms he is a great prophet (Luke 7:26–28).

John's birth and calling come because of the tender mercies of our God (Luke 1:78). One of God's tender mercies is sending someone called the Rising Sun, the Dayspring, to us (Mal. 4:2). Zechariah's prophecy also outlines the job description of this Rising Sun, this Dayspring. The Dayspring will shine on those living in darkness and shadowed by death. It turns out that we, those to whom Zechariah speaks and those who hear his prophetic word, are those living in darkness and shadowed by death. The Dayspring will guide our feet into the path of peace.

Zechariah's prophecy exudes joy. This is amazing, because Luke introduces Zechariah as something of an old grump. Zechariah's response to the angel visitor is skeptical: "How can I be sure?" (Luke 1:18). He doesn't believe God's representative that this restorative miracle could happen to Elizabeth and

and his wife in their old age will have a child. As ancient Sarah laughed at such news, Zechariah challenges the angel's proclamation. Unlike Mary, he is punished for his incredulous response to the angel's announcement. Perhaps a man of his years and stature, a priest of the most high God, ought to be better prepared for such visitations than a peasant girl. Perhaps the elderly priest is, and ought to be, held to higher standards of accountability than a teenager still finding her way in the world. Perhaps there is a standard here by which the more seasoned and mature are expected to set examples, to lead the way for the young. Tom Wright says that "Often it's the old people, the ones who cherish old memories and imaginations, who keep alive the rumor of hope. . . . Zechariah comes across in this passage, especially in the prophetic poem, as someone who has pondered the agony and the hope for many years, and who now finds the two bubbling out of him as he looks in awe and delight at his baby son."[1]

Because Zechariah is mute and deaf, a preacher might develop some sort of interior monologue in which Zechariah meditates on his fate and gathers the thoughts that culminate in this hymn of ecstasy and blessing. Surely Zechariah's season of being mute and deaf leaves him with time to wait, watch, and wonder. His physical state forces him in on himself to consider the entire course of his life—his faithful service as a priest, his faithful love for Elizabeth, his faithful belief that God would redeem God's people. He has time to consider the long arc of his life and how it has been disrupted by the sudden appearance of the holy at a time and in a manner he was not expecting.

Finally, Zechariah is faced with the hubbub surrounding the naming of the baby. The people of the village see that something out of the ordinary has happened to him, but they do not understand what he is going through. In the midst of the naming crisis he finds his voice. In response to people wondering, "What then will this child become?" the old priest breaks out in his ecstatic song of prophecy and blessing.

Who will this baby be? He will be called John, "God's gift" or "God is gracious." He will be integral to fulfillment of the ancient prophecy of how God will redeem God's people. He will prepare the way for the coming Messiah. In Luke's account of Zechariah's song, quotations from Israel's prophets

---

1. Tom Wright, *Luke for Everyone* (London: SPCK; Louisville, KY: Westminster John Knox Press, 2004), 18.

Luke 1:68-79

Theological Perspective

composition of the book in the shadow of the recent Roman-Jewish war (66–70 CE) and during ongoing occupation by Rome gives "being rescued from the hands of our enemies" (v. 74) immediate relevance.

The second movement relates specifically to the life of John the Baptist, whose birth is the immediate source of the song. Unlike the first part of the canticle, which offers praise by articulating what God is fulfilling, the second part of the canticle offers new promises by making predictions about John's life. Here Zechariah continues in the role of prophet as he foretells John's future. In the moment of the prophecy, Christians will see Zechariah as providing continuity between prophecy of the First and Second Testaments, since his words about John, his son, occur within the same song that memorializes fulfillment of Jewish prophecy. As a seer foretelling John's future, Zechariah steps outside his parental role and addresses the infant objectively as "you, child." He identifies John as one who makes way for the work of the incarnation by delivering knowledge about salvation and forgiveness. Offered because of God's "tender mercy," the forgiveness coming through the incarnation will make it possible to see differently. New sight, resulting from the dawn breaking in and giving light, insinuates possible paradigm shifts and the reversals identified with Luke's Gospel. Perhaps those identified as enemies earlier in the song may become friends. In fact, Luke's Gospel and Acts feature many such reconciliations—the conversions of Zacchaeus and Paul and the openness to Gentiles being typical.

Among other possibilities suggested by the new light and inbreaking dawn, the potential to overcome enmity is particularly implied in interpreters' suggestion that "to give light" refers not only to new knowledge for Israel, but also to Gentile inclusion. The idea that both need light presents an element of Luke's reversals, since by implication there is a leveling of everyone as "in darkness." Christians will see the paradigm shift suggested here as a reflection of the newness annually anticipated in Advent. However, it is distinct from the ordinary "annual anticipation" when the shift is seen as a call for personal, social, and political *reversals* in our own time.

ROSETTA E. ROSS

Pastoral Perspective

landlady, they were talking about the dismal stories in the newspaper that day—stories about the cold war and the potential of nuclear holocaust. Suddenly he blurted out, "The world is too horrible! If we had a button we could press that would finally blow the whole thing up, which of us would be able to help pressing it?" "Oh I wouldn't," she said. "I'm terrified of electric things." This, he reported, cheered him up considerably.[2] A little humor can reframe and give perspective to fear. In Luke 10, Jesus does something similar as he sends his disciples out on a mission with little more than the word "peace." He tells them, if people accept this word, so be it; but if not, kick the dust off your feet. This is what you might call a lean or focused view of ministry that doesn't get distracted with successes and failures, threatening circumstances, or finances. What Jesus describes is a ministry without fear that is focused on what we are called to be and do; it doesn't get preoccupied with troublesome issues or people.

Peter Steinke, who is a church consultant, tells the story about working with a church that had been going through months of discontent. Steinke began by asking twenty leaders to redefine their problems without focusing on a person or issue as presented in the original problem. As they did so, they began to focus on their vision for their church and how each was accountable for that vision.[3]

And so we are back to Zechariah's hope to "serve God without fear." He undoubtedly had in mind oppression-free practice of Judaism. I find these stories instructive as I picture how to serve God without fear in a toxic society such as ours. By the grace of God, we can follow Jesus empowered with the gospel and the words he gave to the disciples, "Peace be with you."

ROGER J. GENCH

---

2. Mary Midgley, *The Owl of Minerva* (London: Routledge, 2005), 202.
3. Steinke, *How Your Church Family Works*, 52–55.

Exegetical Perspective

himself. The angel, now introducing himself as Gabriel, takes umbrage and pulls rank. Gabriel reminds Zechariah that he, Gabriel, stands in the presence of God. As such, he has the authority to rebuke. And he does! Gabriel decrees Zechariah's speechlessness until his prophetic words come to pass. Perhaps Zechariah was too talkative, too enamored of his own opinions. Throughout decades of waiting for a child, perhaps these opinions had talked him into his present unbelief.

Now alone with his thoughts, unable to communicate except in signs and writing (1:22, 62–63), Zechariah's nine-month "time out" led to profound changes in personality and faith. Maybe he read the scrolls, for his prophecy relies heavily on earlier words from Genesis, Psalms, Ezekiel, and Samuel. Zechariah, in his incubation of silence, meditated on an upcoming great move of God. Domestically, he probably listened to his wife! When he next appears in the text (vv. 67–79), Zechariah, transformed, fairly bubbles with joy! Like an explosion after much pressure, joy bursts forth, cascading good words on all. Zechariah literally sings! This new, energized Zechariah, ready for fatherhood, tenderly talks to his baby boy.

Although Zechariah's is quite possibly the most endearing, heartwarming prophecy over a child in the biblical text, what makes the prophecy so compelling is that Zechariah is not primarily concerned about himself or about his miraculous son. Instead, Zechariah's prophecy exalts God, points to the dominant work of the Dayspring, and foretells God's tender mercies on upcoming generations of God's covenant people. Zechariah conveys a sense of wonder that he is part of it. He—with all his arrogance and unbelief—basks now in the love, forgiveness, mercy of God.

God in the silence of centuries has done preparatory work for Israel. God in the silence of nine months has done preparatory work in Zechariah. God saved Zechariah from his own unbelief. God can save Israel from enemies. Zechariah's prophecy looks forward. God moved on Zechariah and Elizabeth's behalf and linked their personal miracle of a son to wider miracles for Israel. Zechariah doesn't understand it. He doesn't have to. He rejoices and lets God manage the details. Zechariah will spend his remaining days a happy "praiser" mentoring this miraculous child.

ROBIN GALLAHER BRANCH

Homiletical Perspective

are interwoven with Zechariah's own words of commissioning and blessing for his infant son. John will be the bridge between the law and its fulfillment, the prophet who will proclaim the Messiah's presence, the voice who will call the whole creation to repentance in response to the promise of salvation.

This ancient hymn is set in two parts. The first deals with social redemption, salvation of the people; the second addresses more personal redemption, salvation of the soul. Repentance that leads to forgiveness is to be John's message, repentance and redemption that are both personal and corporate. The preacher may raise questions about the need for repentance in many ways and in all sorts of contemporary contexts. This is an opportunity to invite people to look deeply into their own hearts to see what changes may be needed, to understand where they must turn around and head in a different direction in their own lives. There are also many opportunities to ask where repentance and redemption are needed in the social and political realities of the world in which we live. What might Zechariah predict that his son John would preach to us in this Advent?

If, in the end, peace is the theme for the day, it is the preacher's challenge to make peace from Zechariah's ecstasy. Zechariah's hymn makes clear that true peace—in our hearts and in our world—will come only when we are right with God, when we have laid aside our own ambitions and passions, or at least turned them over to God. The condition of souls and the condition of creation is troubled by self-centeredness, self-absorption, and failure to understand what is available in true communion with God, what God has offered us in the ancient covenant and offers us still in the coming of Jesus, the Christ. Though we may live in between times, when we do not yet fully walk in the way of peace, Zechariah promises that his little boy, John, will prepare us to bridge those times as we live toward God's reign in hope.

RANDLE R. MIXON

Philippians 1:3-11

³I thank my God every time I remember you, ⁴constantly praying with joy in every one of my prayers for all of you, ⁵because of your sharing in the gospel from the first day until now. ⁶I am confident of this, that the one who began a good work among you will bring it to completion by the day of Jesus Christ. ⁷It is right for me to think this way about all of you, because you hold me in your heart, for all of you share in God's grace with me, both in my imprisonment and in the defense and confirmation of the gospel. ⁸For God is my witness, how I long for all of you with the compassion of Christ Jesus. ⁹And this is my prayer, that your love may overflow more and more with knowledge and full insight ¹⁰to help you to determine what is best, so that in the day of Christ you may be pure and blameless, ¹¹having produced the harvest of righteousness that comes through Jesus Christ for the glory and praise of God.

Theological Perspective

The passage that opens the apostle Paul's letter to the church at Philippi is striking in its emotion and intimacy. It suggests a deep, and potentially enduring, relationship. The key theological themes are remembering, joy, and fellowship. Paul's recollection elicits thanksgiving, his joy is rooted in shared tribulation, and the longing for fellowship can only be fulfilled in Christ.

Collective Remembering. The early-twentieth-century French sociologist Maurice Halbwachs addressed the question of the social character of human memory. Halbwachs believed memory could function only within a collective context. Within this social context groups develop the memories that shape the reality in which they live. The memory to which the apostle Paul refers in this passage is of that order. His remembering is not mere reminiscing. It is the foundation of the reality that this Christian community celebrates—a memory centered in the person and work of Christ. The community of faith is a community of memory because the remembrance of Christ becomes real only in a social context. This is why the memory of his time with his readers elicits thanksgiving.

Friedrich Nietzsche is credited with developing the notion of memory as a social bond. He argues that "will to remember" is the basis for human social

Pastoral Perspective

As in last week's reading from 1 Thessalonians, in this Sunday's Epistle lection the apostle Paul prays that the faithful will be blameless before God. Paul raises the issue of blamelessness halfway through his letter to the church at Thessalonica. To the Philippians, he leads with it. By the tenth verse he is praying that they may be "pure and blameless" in the day of Christ.

To be "pure and blameless" is a status to which many likely aspire, but its reference in the text can present pastoral problems. Given the pervasiveness of discussions about blame, however, blamelessness is better addressed than ignored. The question is for what purpose are the hearers of the word to be pure and blameless—to look better or to live better? According to Paul it is the latter of course, to the end that a "harvest of righteousness" is produced—but will raising the issue of blame achieve such a harvest?

Who is confident, as Paul seems to be, that in the day of Christ, "pure and blameless" is how they will be found? Who has ever done anything that they knew, with hindsight at least, was just plain wrong? Who has been involved in a situation that turned out badly and, if honest about it, knew that the outcome was their responsibility, perhaps even their fault? Has anyone done anything for which they are to blame?

Exegetical Perspective

On this Second Sunday of Advent, as Malachi shouts from the mountaintop his prophecy that God is a refining fire, Paul whispers from prison his prayer that God will help Philippian Christians to become pure and blameless. But his depiction of these two virtues is hardly about avoidance of impurity. Rather, Paul begins in his prayer to paint a picture of active love itself, the starting point toward purity and blamelessness and the catalyst for unified community. These prayed hopes are not confined to antiquity, of course. Paul would desire them for us too, and so they reverberate through the two intervening millennia and whisper into our own twenty-first-century lives and churches.

Paul and the Philippians. In this brief opening interlude of thanksgiving, Paul previews his letter's main themes: his own joy and his hope for theirs (1:4 and 4:4); his gratitude for their "sharing in the gospel" through financial support (1:5 and 4:15); their dearness to Paul (1:8 and 4:19); his hope that their "love may overflow" (1:9 and 2:1–11); and their ability to discern what is truly valuable (1:10 and 3:2; 4:2). It is no accident that Paul uses his thanksgiving period as a table of contents. First, it is his custom. Each of his letters except Galatians features this kind of a paragraph, in which the author reestablishes his

Homiletical Perspective

A few years back a pastor wrote a letter in which he said:

> During Advent the lectionary suggests what I call "John the Baptist/end of the world" texts. The stories surrounding the birth of Jesus are not addressed until Christmas. I think this is a huge mistake. If the community is known by the stories it tells, then the church following the common lectionary stands in some danger of losing the stories surrounding the birth of Jesus. The ominous result might be that our children will grow up knowing more about the Grinch than they will know about baby Jesus. Therefore, during Advent I toss the lectionary out the window and preach the birth narratives, beginning with Elizabeth and Zechariah in Luke's gospel.[1]

The pastor has a point. The lectionary gives us birth narratives during Christmastide (like the resurrection stories we have during Eastertide). It expects us to *begin* celebrating Christmas on Christmas Day. That may make good liturgical sense, but unfortunately the culture has declared that on December 26, Christmas is over (with the exception of those few brave souls who celebrate Boxing Day instead of Gift Return Day).

---

1. My colleague in ministry shall remain nameless here for obvious reasons.

Philippians 1:3-11

Theological Perspective

relations. Society would crumble if we could not depend on one another to remember tomorrow what we promised yesterday. Nietzsche, in his typically pessimistic way, sees this memory as something that the heroic individual grasps by his own power. He argues that religion misuses memory as a place where human pain can be warehoused. This is why he states that "only something that continues to hurt remains in the memory." For the apostle Paul the memory of his time with his readers not only contains hurt, but brings forth joy. That joy, unseen by Nietzsche, is not dependent on the heroic will of the individual Christian, but is something rooted in shared tribulation. In this way, it is the memory of Christ as seen in them that creates the unbreakable bond between Paul and his readers.

The twentieth-century political theologian Johann Baptist Metz is credited with developing the notion of a dangerous memory. He describes these memories as ones "in which earlier experiences break through to the center-point of our lives and reveal new and dangerous insights for our present. They illuminate for a few moments and with a harsh, steady light the questionable nature of things we have apparently come to terms with, and show up the banality of our supposed 'realism.' They break through the canon of all that is taken as self-evident, and unmask as deception the certainty of those 'whose hour is always there' (John 7:6). They seem to subvert our structures of plausibility. Such memories are like dangerous and incalculable visitants from the past."[1]

The kind of memory to which Paul refers is dangerous to the extent that it continues to break in on the present of the Christian community. It is dangerous because the memory of Jesus renews itself in the life of the community. But not only does the memory of Jesus break in from the past; it is a forward memory that draws the community into a future that is already transforming the present. This is what Paul is referring to in the recurrent phrase "the day of Jesus Christ," which seems to point to both the memory of the love they share and the hope for its fulfillment. This "day of Jesus Christ" both grounds and sustains the relationship between Paul and his readers.

A Letter of Friendship. Gordon D. Fee and others have found helpful analogies to Paul's letter in the "friendship letter" genre of the Greco-Roman

Pastoral Perspective

If they have, is it possible for them to be pure and blameless in the day of Christ, whenever that may be? Might it be that in his enthusiasm Paul has gone overboard in his praise for the Philippians? Does this praise run the danger of producing the opposite of what such praise intends? If it is true that "no one is good but God alone" (Mark 10:18), and "since all have sinned and fall short of the glory of God" (Rom. 3:23), from whence comes Paul's confidence with regard to the Philippians' blamelessness in the day of Christ? Research suggests that being praised for a positive quality may encourage lying if praiseworthy behavior is not maintained,[1] and the reality of human sinfulness virtually guarantees that praiseworthy blamelessness will not be sustained.

Being pure and blameless is an admirable goal. The world would be a better place if there were a larger store of blameless behavior. But raising the specter of blame may not produce the desired end of fewer blameworthy acts, because of the dynamics of the blame game. Even mentioning the issue of blame may pull us into the blame game's orbit. The difficulty in dealing with blame is at least as old as the story of the garden of Eden. God asks the man if he ate the fruit of the forbidden tree. The man admits doing so but blames the woman for his behavior. She in turn blames the serpent (Gen. 3:11–13).

Where does the blame game get us? When confronted with their blameworthy behavior, the man and the woman in the garden did not accept responsibility. They were unwilling to be held accountable. Likewise, if to be a good Christian is to be blameless, but despite our best intentions we are to blame at least on occasion and for some things, we may try to deflect or deny blame when confronted with our guilt. The desire for blamelessness can produce falsehood rather than righteousness. In writing to the Romans, Paul seems to have reached this conclusion. To the Romans Paul admits "I do not do the good I want, but the evil I do not want is what I do" (Rom. 7:19). If this is so, can Paul or any of us be pure and blameless on the day of Christ? In Romans, Paul rejects the works righteousness that might be read into this passage to the Philippians.

How do you react if you fear being blamed? Some have overactive consciences and succumb and accept blame when they are not to blame. Beaten down by messages of their unworthiness, they take the blame for things for which they are not responsible.

---

1. Johann Baptist Metz, "The Future in the Memory of Suffering," *Consilium* 36 (1917): 15.

1. Claudia M. Mueller and Carol S. Dweck, "Praise for Intelligence Can Undermine Children's Motivation and Performance," *Journal of Personality and Social Psychology* 75, no. 1 (1998): 41.

relationship with his audience and reveals the matters that he will address in the letter. Second, the apostle did not invent the technique. We learn from the papyri and inscriptions that this practice was common in more-than-personal-but-less-than-formal letters in antiquity.[1]

The length of this thanksgiving—it is Paul's longest—seems to reflect an especial intimacy with and enthusiastic love for the Philippian church. This impression receives strong support from the striking use of the Greek term *pas* ("all") three times in a nine-word stretch: "I thank God *whenever* I think of you . . . praying for *all (pase)* of you *always (pantote)* in *all (pase)* my prayers" (v. 3). Paul backs up that overflowing prose with the specific language of love in verse 8, where he tells the Philippians that he cares constantly for them and cherishes them with the "bowels" of Christ (*splanchna*).

The Purifying Power of Agapaic Love. As pastoral prayers often do, Paul's turns eventually toward exhortation. In verses 9–11, Paul reveals the content of his all-the-time-for-all-of-them prayers, and it looks like a call to growth. He wants the Philippians' *agapē* to increase. And that increase should take a recognizable form in its intended outcome (*eis* used to signal purpose) of knowledge and insight. Once more, this new love-soaked cognition is not the end point in itself, but will reach its intended outcome (*eis* again to signal purpose) when the Philippians can discern what is very best. Then that sense of "true value" finds its ultimate fulfillment in a "pure" and "blameless" Philippian people. To summarize, Paul asks God for more love that produces more knowledge that produces a clearer sense of what is important that ultimately purifies these Christians. The end is purity. Love practiced in community sets off the chain of events that leads to it.

Paul's prayer for an increase in the community's love sets the table for the rest of the letter. *Agapē*, the first named hope of the prayer, appears verbally in 2:2 and is the overarching theme of 1:12–2:11. Paul surrounds an exhortation to other-oriented community (2:1–4) with the "visual aids" of his own example (1:12–26) and the example of Christ Jesus (2:6–11). Just as the imprisoned Paul looks not to his own interests but to the advance of the gospel (1:12–18) and the well-being of the Philippians' faith (1:21–26); and just as the flesh-assuming and cross-

Why is our lectionary shaped the way it is? Early on, the expectation of the Messiah was a paschal event, but then it changed to an Advent theme, and the focus shifted from the coming of the Messiah to the *second coming* of the Messiah. This made sense in the early church that had an active eschatology (sleep in shifts!). The return of Jesus was palpable; Christians could feel it. How many Christians today wake up every morning and think, "This could be the day that Jesus comes back"? My grandmother was a member of the Pentecostal Holiness Church, and that is the way she believed! She would run out in the face of an oncoming storm and look up into the clouds, just to check and see. How many of your people feel that way today and want to hear those kinds of sermons. Some? Yes. Many? No.

So we have a call to make. There are two possibilities if one chooses not to "throw the lectionary out the window": (1) take the texts as they are, or (2) take the two major Advent themes for the first two Sundays (the coming reign of God and the exhortation to preparedness) and then move to the birth narratives.

Whichever choice is made can still engender useful and imaginative sermons grounded in the lectionary texts, even from those letters of Paul that almost never get preached during Advent. To that end, I suggest considering at least one of the Pauline texts provided for this Advent, especially if such themes as waiting, hope, expectation, God's future story and ours, are rising in the congregation.

Today's text from Philippians 1:3–11 is similar to the Epistle text from last week, 1 Thessalonians 3:9–13. Paul thanked God persistently for the churches in Thessalonica (night and day) and Philippi (constantly), longed to see them both, and prayed that both of them would be "blameless" when Christ returned.

There are several differences, however, in the two little texts. And at least two of them strike me as appropriate for the Advent pulpit. In verse 6 Paul writes, "I am confident of this, that the one who began a good work among you will bring it to completion by the day of Jesus Christ." The day of Christ, Fred Craddock writes, "is a Christianized version of the Day of the Lord in the Old Testament and refers to the Parousia, the coming of Christ."[2] It appears that Paul was affirming that God would bring the work of the little Philippian church to

---

1. Paul Schubert, *Form and Function of the Pauline Thanksgivings* (Berlin: A. Töpelmann, 1939), 10–39 and 142ff.

2. Fred Craddock, *Philippians*, Interpretation Series (Atlanta: John Knox Press, 1985), 20–21.

Philippians 1:3-11

Theological Perspective

world.[2] Aristotle's first-order friendship was based on virtue. These friendships carried such commitment and social significance, that to have friends was automatically to have enemies. Paul's care for his readers is also a watchfulness regarding the enemy. Paul refers obliquely to shared enemies when he says that "all of you share in God's grace . . . both in my imprisonment and in the defense and confirmation of the gospel." Paul's letter here is a quintessential example of a friendship letter of the highest order. Paul says, "I hold you in my heart" (v. 7, note), and remembers their "sharing in the gospel from the first day until now" (v. 5). Clearly, this letter is one written to friends and carries little or none of the patron/protégé tenor of some of his other letters.

If there is a theology emerging in this "letter of friendship," it is a theology of friendship. The emerging literature on the theological and philosophical meaning of friendship may be enriched by looking again at this text. Glenn Morrison, in his article "Pastoral Care and Counselling: Towards a Post-Metaphysical Theology of Friendship," draws upon the thought of Emmanuel Levinas and illustrates the link between hope and friendship. Morrison outlines "a theology of friendship that finds its roots more in an eschatological future world (Isa. 64:4; 1 Cor. 2:9) rather than economics, politics, or utopia. . . . The poor and the suffering are not 'objects' of knowledge and nor are they 'objects' of mission. Before all thematisation, everyone has a face beyond the being of self-interest. It is particularly in friendship that the true and beautiful faces come to mind/consciousness." Morrison concludes that friendship is a "grave responsibility" and that "accordingly, if we want to be like the disciples, called to a life of superindividuation (expiation), then we have to allow our compassionate lives to be deepened by friendship."[3] In an age of superficial relationships and impersonal communication, the friendship that is spoken of in this letter suggests depth and duration. When Paul talks about longing for you "in the bowels of Jesus Christ" (v. 8 KJV; "with the compassion of Christ Jesus" NRSV), it is clear that this friendship has a profundity that surpasses that of even the most passionate genteel aristocrats. This letter communicates the essence of both faith and friendship.

JAMES H. EVANS JR.

Pastoral Perspective

Others have underdeveloped scruples and refuse to take responsibility for anything, shamelessly shifting the blame to others, even when their culpability is undeniable. In either case, raising the issue of blame can be counterproductive.

The issues of blame can loom large especially in a season of preparation such as Advent. As we prepare heart and mind, home and church for the inbreaking of incarnation, as we ready ourselves for the good news of great joy that is Christmas, the pitfalls of the blame game are prominent. With pressure to produce a picture-perfect holiday, some will fall prey to the temptation to look for someone to blame if things don't turn out as well as expected. With the plethora of competing needs and wants that are fueled by consumer notions of what makes a good holiday, is it possible to meet the great expectations that abound? Amid assumptions of holiday cheer, is it possible to resist blaming self or others if relationships sour and happiness is not achieved?

In order to address the difficult dimensions of blamelessness, the preacher may preach against the text. Another option is to look for a way to understand Paul's prayer for our blamelessness that can help rather than hinder. The key to this approach may be found in the opening words of the prayer in verses 9 and 10: "And this is my prayer, that your love may overflow more and more with knowledge and full insight to help you determine what is best." To set blamelessness in the context of overflowing love and increasing insight, instead of judgment, sheds new light on blame. Seen from the perspective of love, blame can be associated with responsibility rather than affiliated with condemnation. From the vantage point of love, assessing blame can teach us how to step up and do better next time, rather than leaving us mired in guilt or ensconced in defensiveness and denial. The love we await in Advent is such a love—a love that will overflow and leave us, if not fully blameless, at least closer to it than we otherwise would be.

PHILIP E. CAMPBELL

2. Gordon D. Fee, *Paul's Letter to the Philippians*, New International Commentary on the New Testament (Grand Rapids: Eerdmans, 1995), 3.
3. Glenn Morrison, "Pastoral Care and Counselling: Towards a Post-Metaphysical Theology of Friendship"; dlibrary.acu.edu.au/research/theology/ejournal/aejt_9/morrison.htm.

Exegetical Perspective

bearing Christ considered not his own comfort but humanity's need (2:6–8)—so the Philippians should think of others as more important than themselves (2:3) and look not to their own interests but to the interests of others (2:4). Paul's concern about this stems from a threat of fracture in the community under some sort of pressure from outside the community (1:28). Later, the two church leaders Euodia and Syntyche are similarly summoned to think the same things (*ta auta phronein* in 2:2 and 4:2) in the Lord. The interconnectedness of love and group unity is implied throughout the letter.

Lest we imagine that the function of Paul's prayer in 1:9–11 is entirely hortatory, it is important to recall Paul's famous confidence in God's activity among the Philippians: "I am confident of this, that the one who began a good work among you will bring it to completion by the day of Jesus Christ" (1:6). By way of reiteration, Paul follows up the examples and exhortations of 1:12–2:11 by stating his strong confidence that God will accomplish them: "It is God who is at work in you, enabling you both to will and to work for God's good pleasure" (2:13). It is because Paul knows an active God that he can utter this prayer for divine enabling so confidently. Another reason for Paul's confidence is the Philippians' track record with him—the very active love for which he thanks God in 1:3 and thanks them in 4:10–20. By their generous material support for Paul's ministry, they have shown themselves altogether capable of considering Paul's interests over their own. It seems he wants them to apply that skill to the way they treat one another in Christian community. God has already accomplished their deference toward him; Paul prays for and awaits their deference to one another.

Twenty-first-century Western culture loves love, but holds an arm's-length disdain toward purity and blamelessness. We speak of Puritans with a superior sneer, and anyone who imagines that there could be no blame or blemish on a character is counted to be living in a bygone world. But in his opening words to these dear brothers and sisters, Paul envisions a deferential divine love that ultimately purifies those who embody it. In this Advent season of preparation, preachers may be able to rehabilitate Christian purification by removing it from its captivity to caricatures and placing it squarely in the middle of active love lived out in Christian community.

ALLEN HILTON

Homiletical Perspective

completion before Jesus returned, which Paul expected soon. If that is the case, then Paul was wrong. The day of Christ did not come and has not come in the shape he expected, and the work of the church—whether in Philippi or in Laramie, Wyoming—has not come to completion. Furthermore, none of us can claim to have completed all the good work assigned to us by God. My grandfather did not finish the house he was building. My teacher did not finish the book he was writing. My friend did not finish seeing her child through school. An old preacher once showed me a line he liked from a European writer. I do not remember the writer, but I remember the line: "All [people] fail, do they not, at what they want to do most."

But wait! I do not believe Paul was saying that each of us and every church will finish the good work God gave us in this lifetime, however short or long that life is. Many years ago a young couple asked me to do a memorial service for their stillborn child. The one thing I remember saying in that service was my conviction that "all life comes to completion in God." I still believe that. As Reinhold Niebuhr put it, "Nothing that is worth doing can be achieved in our lifetime; therefore we must be saved by hope."[3] Yes.

This passage may help our friend who wants to move the birth narratives forward. Advent puts our wait for the day of Christ into clearer perspective. Our wait is not for the arrival of one who may come tomorrow or ten thousand years from now. In Galatians 2:20 Paul said, "It is no longer I who live, but it is Christ who lives in me." This season reminds us of the "nowness" of the day of Christ, when the Parousia comes to us and is willing to stay. Prayer, love, knowledge, and insight, Paul says, will help us best to be prepared for his presence and for understanding that all life and all work will come to completion in God. Jesus is showing us how and doing so now. Pay attention.

JOSEPH R. JETER

3. Reinhold Niebuhr, *The Irony of American History* (New York: Charles Scribner's Sons, 1962), 63.

Luke 3:1-6

[1]In the fifteenth year of the reign of Emperor Tiberius, when Pontius Pilate was governor of Judea, and Herod was ruler of Galilee, and his brother Philip ruler of the region of Ituraea and Trachonitis, and Lysanias ruler of Abilene, [2]during the high priesthood of Annas and Caiaphas, the word of God came to John son of Zechariah in the wilderness. [3]He went into all the region around the Jordan, proclaiming a baptism of repentance for the forgiveness of sins, [4]as it is written in the book of the words of the prophet Isaiah,

"The voice of one crying out in the wilderness:
 'Prepare the way of the Lord,
  make his paths straight.
[5]Every valley shall be filled,
  and every mountain and hill shall be made low,
 and the crooked shall be made straight,
  and the rough ways made smooth;
[6]and all flesh shall see the salvation of God.'"

Theological Perspective

While it is unfortunate—both theologically and exegetically—that the lectionary divides in two the Luke 3:1–18 narrative, which really is one story, it is also fascinating to appreciate the dynamic in this pericope that, I believe, stands at the heart of the biblical message. In God's salvific work, there is a mysterious interplay of divine and human, or ordinary and extraordinary, or regular and miraculous. On the one hand, the advent of the son of Mary and Joseph of Nazareth was a function of long historical development culminating in the socio-political situation recorded in detail in the first verses of this passage; on the other hand, the "word of the Lord" concerning the advent of the Word made flesh (John 1:14) came miraculously to a lonely preacher in the wasteland without any human mediator.

This is the culmination of the narrative of the whole salvation history as presented in both covenants of the Bible. Christian faith—differently from, say, all the strands of Hinduism(s)—is firmly rooted in real history, not only in "salvation" history, but in "general" history with all its twists and turns. At the same time, the coming of the word of the Lord is in no way conditioned or limited by the preparation of historical events. Think of Moses with his proclamation of the exodus, or Jeremiah and his announcement of the return from exile, or

Pastoral Perspective

In his own commentary, John Calvin wrote that talk in verse 3 of this passage about John the Baptizer "proclaiming a baptism of repentance" should be taken as both a beginning theology of baptism and a caution to pastors to speak clearly when performing and explaining the sacraments. On the theology side, Calvin hears an affirmation of the centrality of repentance and forgiveness in baptism. On the public speaking side, he advocates no "murmuring of magic undertones by some exorcist but the effect of a clear and distinct voice proclaimed for the building up of faith."[1] All this from "proclaimed"! Yet the rhetorical side of Calvin's dual reading should not be dismissed too soon, for there might be pastoral insights in generalizing the idea of doing what's necessary to get the message across. Removing barriers to communication might be as much a pastoral imperative in our day as any.

The warrant for John's ministry, from Isaiah 40, reinforces this imperative in its own way. The voice in the wilderness cries out for the way of God to be prepared with relentless urgency. This urgency can be heard as a call to rhetorical sensitivity among those who proclaim the word of faith. Here is

1. John Calvin, *Commentary on a Harmony of the Evangelists, Matthew, Mark, and Luke*, trans. A. W. Morrison (Grand Rapids: Eerdmans, 1972), 1:116.

Exegetical Perspective

This week's reading depicts the beginning of the ministry of John "the Baptist." The reading, short as it may be, fills the important role of introducing a new prophet. First, in echoes of the OT prophets, Luke sets John's ministry in the political context of the time (cf. Isa. 1:1; Jer. 1:1–3; Ezek. 1:1–3; Hos. 1:1; Amos 1:1; Mic. 1:1; Zeph. 1:1; Hag. 1:1; Zech. 1:1). This historical setting deserves more than passing attention. First, it serves as a reminder that God's promises come to fulfillment within the context of physical history. Both John and Jesus, unlike mythical heroes from Greek mythology, for example, existed in historical time and space and functioned within a specific cultural situation. Additionally, Luke makes very clear how convoluted and tightly wound this situation was: he includes a large number of Roman rulers scattered throughout Judea and the realm in his list, several of whom will make appearances elsewhere in Luke–Acts, as well as two Jewish leaders listed under the singular term of "high priest." In this way, Luke signals the tension between the Roman realm and the Jewish religion, a tension compounded by the ambiguity within the religious leadership itself.

Navigating Roman rule in Judea was complex. Religiously, the Romans encouraged emperor worship and even introduced images of the emperors

Homiletical Perspective

Advent is a season of preparation. At home people are cleaning, getting out their Christmas decorations, purchasing a tree, baking, hosting and attending parties, and simply getting ready for Christmas. But into our Advent "busy-ness" each year enters John the Baptist. He interrupts our schedules and demands that preparations of a different kind be made. John demands that we get ready for Jesus. Before we can bask in Christmas joy and the birth of a special baby, John forces us to examine ourselves and our world. In the style of the Old Testament prophets before him, John challenges Advent people with a message of personal and corporate self-examination. Advent, John reminds us, is a time to prepare to welcome Jesus and not simply our invited Christmas houseguests.

When I was a teenager, I used to tease my mother about some of her most particular preparations for company. She would get down on her hands and knees and comb the fringe of the oriental carpets in our living and dining rooms so that there were no knots and the entire fringe was perfectly lined up. It looked beautiful when she was finished—so neat and orderly. I tried to point out that one kick or shuffle of our guests' feet and the beautifully arranged fringe would all be in disarray again, but she would hear nothing of my analysis. She wanted everything,

Luke 3:1-6

Theological Perspective

any other Old Testament prophet: there is a mysterious, intriguing interface of "historical" and "suprahistorical." This is a dynamic that belongs to the heart of a Christian view of history and salvation and should not be too cheaply eased by well-meaning homilists.

What makes Luke's narration of the first Advent so intriguing is the pedantic attention to historical details. The first verse of the pericope lists no less than seven historical political figures. Why? To anchor the story of salvation history in the concrete, tangible history of the world. Tiberius Caesar, Pontius Pilate, Herod, Philip, and others; what do they have to do with the gospel, the good news? Nothing, in their own estimation—they would not have been enthused to find their names in an obscure tract of a marginal religious movement of the time. Yet they have everything to do with it—in the estimation of this story's narrator. Later Christian theology picked up Luke's philosophy of history by including the name of Pontius Pilate in the creed. Oddly enough, the church pronounces his name in every liturgical gathering when the people of God remember and recall the great salvific events of the Triune God.

The one whom the Eastern Orthodox tradition regards as the last prophet of the Old Covenant enters abruptly onto the stage shared by the leading world rulers as if he were the culmination of the historical process and international politics. The Baptist comes from nowhere, and in the middle of nowhere he receives the Word of the Lord. Unlike the other Synoptics, Luke gives almost as careful attention to the annunciation of John as to the advent of the Savior, including the parallel narration of their birth and naming. Yet at the same time the evangelist is careful to place the prophet from the desert into a proper perspective: he is—as Irenaeus aptly puts it—the "little boy . . . who guided Samson by the hand" (see Judg. 16:26) and "who showed to the people the faith in Christ."[1]

The message of the last of the Old Testament prophets—and the first in the New Covenant—was but a continuation of the proclamation of his predecessors, namely, that of repentance, call for radical change, *metanoia*.

The invitation to repent, however, was not a legalistic stipulation but, rather, a door to forgiveness. In his remarks on this passage, Calvin

1. Irenaeus, *Exegetical Fragments* 27 (http://www.newadvent.org/fathers/0134.htm; accessed November 24, 2007).

Pastoral Perspective

dramatic imagery for making connection, for finding available means to communicate so that God's desire for creation might be known: straightened paths, valleys and mountains made into plains, rocky ways made even (Isa. 40:4–6).

A hundred years ago there were precious few paved roads. Now they are the landscape. Clear-cutting makes the way straight, and asphalt smoothes it. Bridges raise valleys and tunnels level mountains. We are now sped from here to there in ways that both illuminate and obscure the power of this passage. The imagery would be brought back to life by time spent in lands where roads are still rocky and sometimes impassable, where nature is less easily overcome and travel takes more planning than simply keying in one's destination on a navigation screen. When I must discover my way from here to there through wit, endurance, force of will, good fortune, and the grace of those who might help, I may better understand how Luke imagines the scouting mission that is Christian preaching. There are challenging and circuitous paths on which to venture, high mountains to climb, and many valleys in which to tumble on the way between what must be said of God and how that can be heard. The work of speech in the church is arduous and complex, even as it is passionate and single minded. And the work requires different approaches for different terrains.

The imagery of leveling and straightening need not be taken as counsel to sameness or uniformity, as if the operative characteristic of flattening is the resulting plain. The imagery is best taken at a step removed, so that the prophet's call is to the *action* of making, opening, and clearing the way for God, rather than to some fixed image of the *result* of that work.

What stands between, as impediments to preaching or noise to hearing? Paul Riceour wrote about the "pre-homiletic" work of the preacher, the work we must do, not simply to prepare a sermon, but to prepare a congregation to hear. This work is *global*, as interpretive work is done throughout the church to understand the gospel, but it is also profoundly *local*—in a time, in a place, with and among a particular group of people, against specific cultural pressures, and in favor of a particular relationship between speakers and hearers. Each preacher will develop her or his own understandings of impediments and how to respond to them, but a handful of themes might guide the way.

The classic question of *character* comes to mind, for each preacher must determine with others what

into the holy and iconoclastic city of Jerusalem. Politically, Herod the Great had been brutal to the people with his taxes, and his sons continued such a policy. The people of Israel were ripe for change, longing for God once again to deliver God's people and set them free from the yoke of oppression.

It was in this historical setting that God spoke again. When Luke announces, "the word of God came to John son of Zechariah," he is proclaiming the triumphal return of the presence of God among the people of God. Luke reiterates that John is the "son of Zechariah" (1:5–25) because he follows the formula for the call of an inspired prophet as seen in the OT. The setting also is important, the wilderness (*erēmos*) being a key place of activity in Luke, whether of testing (4:1, perhaps 15:4) or of prayer, withdrawal, and miracles (4:42; 5:16; 8:29; 9:12). The wilderness locale for John while he waited to begin his ministry (1:80), as well as his ascetic lifestyle, has even led some to speculate that John either trained with the Essenes in Qumran or was familiar with them.

Verse 3 gives us a brief summary of John's ministry upon receiving the word from the Lord. He appears to have been an itinerant preacher who confined his work to the region around the Jordan, never crossing the hills to Jerusalem or leaving the wilderness region entirely. Herod Antipas built up the city of Tiberius on the Sea of Galilee, into and out of which the Jordan River flows, so he would have been in good position to hear the condemnation John spoke regarding him and Herodias his wife (vv. 19–20; Matt. 14:1–12), a message that led to John's imprisonment and death. Interestingly, though, after setting John in this political setting, Luke concerns himself very little with John's political interactions, focusing instead on the "baptism of repentance for the forgiveness of sins."

What John means by "repentance" in this context will be explained further in next week's reading, in verses 7–18. But here we may note that John's baptism is not identical to that of the baptism commanded upon the resurrection of Christ. While both baptisms signify a commitment to a new life and repentance from the old, this baptism is one of preparation for the impending judgment, an acceptance that repentance alone—not status, blood, or ritual—can bring about forgiveness when the judgment arrives. In Luke's setting, then, John's baptism is the preparation for the ministry, life, and death of Jesus, because those who accept John's call show themselves humble before God and willing to submit to God's word, ready to acknowledge the

down to the fringe on the carpet, to be perfect when we were preparing for guests. She attended to every detail.

The advent of guests prompts the host not only to straighten up, but also to fix things around the house—a broken doorknob, a loose towel rack, the burned-out lightbulb, the leaky guest toilet. Preparing for company often causes the hosts to look at their home, to examine their surroundings with a whole new perspective. Suddenly the countertops are too messy, the broken chair inadequate, the silverware too tarnished. Preparing for guests demands self-examination as much as it involves a "to do" list.

John the Baptist does not seem like a character who would have likely understood all that is involved in welcoming company to our homes. He spent most of his time in the wilderness eating locusts and wild honey, after all—hardly the place for a bed-and-breakfast. But if John wasn't thoughtfully straightening rug fringes, he did understand how a people ought to welcome their God. His bold preaching in the wilderness called people to preparation. His challenging words called people to self-examination, along with a "to do" list, if they were going to be ready to receive the one coming after him. John's prophetic message called people to get ready to receive Jesus.

The Advent preacher, quoting John the Baptist, will challenge people to a different kind of preparation, one that calls them to examine their lives, their values, and their priorities. If worshipers are rightly to prepare to receive the Prince of Peace at Christmas, they must be willing to go through the detailed preparation process just as they do when planning for company at home. Outside the church, people are drinking eggnog with their neighbors, singing along with Bing Crosby in the elevator, and hanging the popcorn garland on their Christmas trees. But, in worship, the people of God hear the challenging words of John the Baptist, calling for a different kind of preparation. John the Baptist and his message of repentance cannot be avoided. He appears in the Advent lectionary readings each year, causing the preacher, and thus the parishioners, to listen and to respond to his challenging words. John confronts us, commands our attention, and demands our responses.

John's challenge is to repent and prepare. True repentance (*metanoia* in the Greek) means literally, to change one's mind, turn around, reorient oneself. John calls all people to turn to God and from sin, to

Luke 3:1-6

Theological Perspective

took pains to convince his readers that they find the gospel rather than the law in the Baptist's message: "For John does not say, 'Repent ye, and in this way *the kingdom of heaven* will afterwards be *at hand;*' but first brings forward the grace of God, and then exhorts men to *repent*. Hence it is evident, that the foundation of repentance is the mercy of God, by which he restores the lost."[2] The North African church father Tertullian saw the same gospel truth: that call for "repentance should . . . prepare the home of the heart, by making it clean, for the Holy Spirit, who was about to supervene."[3] Etymologically the word translated "forgiveness" comes from a Greek word meaning "to let go." Only God has the authority and power to let go of our sins; the humble and obedient response to the call to repentance is yes to God's reaching out to us to deliver us from evil.

The advent of the one who lets go of our sins is placed in this pericope in the widest possible salvation-history framework: with reference to the prophecy from the beginning of Second Isaiah (40:3–5), a key messianic and eschatological promise according to which all flesh shall see the salvation of God. In keeping with the apocalyptic expectation that underlies the texture of the Gospels, the imagery of mountains being flattened and valleys raised, crooked roads made straight and rough ways smooth, the Advent Sunday message is linked with the final advent of eschatological salvation, which includes not only the chosen nation but also the nations. At the day of Pentecost to which our text also points, the Spirit was poured out on "all flesh" as an anticipation of the final salvation. A key theological theme in Luke is the inclusion of all in God's salvific invitation and reaching out: both men and women, poor and rich, Gentiles and Jews. This Advent Sunday is a great place for us to be reminded of that.

VELI-MATTI KÄRKKÄINEN

Pastoral Perspective

are the particular habits of pastoral and personal life that accomplish her credibility to name sin with compassion, to proclaim God's forgiving Spirit, and to invite others to respond to that Spirit. The character question may also be raised about the congregation. What practices of communal life are fitting to make a mere group into a people, an audience into a listening congregation ready to hear? How is a specific congregation's identity shaped through study, counsel, critical reflection on the world, sacrifice for the sake of mission, mutual care and forbearance, encouragement, celebration, prayer, and more?

What of *circumstance*? Here is a biblical mandate to pay attention to material things—comfort of worship space, effectiveness of amplification, accessibility for the disabled, and more. What of poverty, violence, distraction, and other cultural realities inside and outside the sanctuary that rise as if a jagged climb between a freeing word and folk's ability to hear it? How might strength and wisdom to address such challenges be found?

What styles of *perceiving and thinking*, whether concrete or abstract, random or sequential, affect how a message is shaped and how it is heard?[2] How can we craft messages that fit ways in which hearers grasp ideas? We must be open to a variety of speaking styles, both as speakers and hearers, and take the time necessary to learn about them.

What *spiritual and theological formation* is required to keep people in the conversation long enough to hear the Spirit speak? And how do bringers of Christ restore in hearers abused by modern media the ability to receive rightly ways of communicating characteristic of biblical witness: narrative, symbolism, rhythm, irony, mystery, and metaphor? In a culture in which messages are consumed instantly and tomorrow forgotten, where battling sound bites of crafted deception parade as discourse, and where distraction abounds, the prehomiletic work of recreating a rhetorical environment in Christian worship and Christian witness worthy of the nonviolent, liberating, Christ-glorifying word we carry might be the most urgent pastoral task we have. Preparing the way. Making paths straight.

WESLEY D. AVRAM

---

2. John Calvin, *Commentary on a Harmony of the Evangelists* [1558], vol. 1, on Matthew 3:1–6/Mark 1:1–6/Luke 3:1–6 (http://www.ccel.org/ccel/calvin/calcom31.ix.xxvii.html; accessed November 24, 2007).
3. Tertullian, *Considering Repentance* 2, in *Ante-Nicene Fathers*, 10 vols. (Grand Rapids: Eerdmans, 1989), 3:658.

2. Distinctions between perceiving and ordering the world here are based on the work of Anthony Gregoric.

Exegetical Perspective

Messiah of the Lord. The first step in preparing for the coming of the Lord is repentance from sins, a message that reverberates from the Hebrew prophets and is highly relevant to the Advent season.

John prepared for his ministry and proclaimed his message in the wilderness, so Luke can see John as the fulfillment of Isaiah's prophecy of a voice proclaiming in the wilderness (*erēmos* again) to prepare the way for the Lord. Isaiah 40:3–5 was originally a word to the exiles in Babylon and so brought comfort to the people of Israel, that their time of oppression would end with God's rescue—that God had not forgotten them and would not neglect them. By using this text from Isaiah, Luke skillfully plays upon the messianic hopes of the Israelites; hearing these words, they would understand John was the voice that was to prepare them to receive the promised redemption. Thus John's message really is "good news" (v. 18), for his message of repentance *is* the one that prepares the way for the Lord, while those who accept and act upon it show themselves ready for the Lord to enact his comfort. Luke uses Isaiah's words to show the continuity between the ministries of John and of Jesus: John's coming was not only predicted, but his message was the one that truly began the good news. Although Luke contains John's entire ministry separate from and prior to that of Jesus, despite the overlap of their ministries and the fact that John baptized Jesus (Matt. 3:13–17, a detail Luke omits from his account of the baptism in Luke 3:21–22), Luke presents one seamless message proclaimed by the two, first prepared for by John and then embodied by Jesus.

As our congregations enter worship on this Second Sunday of Advent, what current realities of state and church, of sin and repentance, will Luke's words summon? There are many to choose from. They span the pages of our newspapers and diaries. Whatever they may be, Luke's lection delivers a timeless word: to accept John's message of repentance is to be ready for Messiah.

MARIAM J. KAMELL

Homiletical Perspective

seek God's forgiveness, and to prepare the way of the Lord. Later he will give very specific and practical examples of what this rightly oriented life will entail (3:10–14), but this week we live in the poetic world of the prophet Isaiah, who called all people to prepare for the Lord by making crooked paths straight, lifting up valleys, and making rough places plain. The punch and promise of the poetry is saved for last: "all flesh shall see the salvation of God."

Prepare the way of the Lord! If that is the central message of our passage, there is meaning in God's choice of John, the wilderness-dweller, as messenger. In Luke, the word of God comes neither to the Emperor nor to the governors, and not even to the high priests. It comes to simple John, son of Zechariah, whom Luke introduces in the first chapter of his Good News. John the Baptist is to us a great prophet who prepared the way for Jesus, but compared with the political and religious leaders of his day, he was just an ordinary guy—and yet, God chose John, and not the luminaries of his time, to be the messenger. God sent the message to John, not in Rome, not in Jerusalem, but out in the wilderness. Not the seat of political or religious power, but the wilderness, the often scary and confusing place where God had spoken to God's people in the past and through which God had led God's people to a new and promised life. God's choice of John and where God spoke to John are indications of what God expects from us. Our repentance, our turning around, will likely involve us looking at the structures and the systems and the people of the world around us in new and different ways.

"Prepare the way this Advent," the prophet John cries out. John makes us uncomfortable. Maybe this is the Advent preacher's job as well—to make us uncomfortable enough truly to repent and prepare for the coming of Jesus.

KATHY BEACH-VERHEY

THIRD SUNDAY OF ADVENT

Zephaniah 3:14-20

14Sing aloud, O daughter Zion;
   shout, O Israel!
  Rejoice and exult with all your heart,
     O daughter Jerusalem!
15The LORD has taken away the judgments against you,
   he has turned away your enemies.
  The king of Israel, the LORD, is in your midst;
   you shall fear disaster no more.
16On that day it shall be said to Jerusalem:
  Do not fear, O Zion;
   do not let your hands grow weak.
17The LORD, your God, is in your midst,
   a warrior who gives victory;
  he will rejoice over you with gladness,
   he will renew you in his love;

Theological Perspective

As Christians travel ever further in the journey of anticipation that is Advent, the prophets continue to yield important insights into the meaning of the season, and the character and fulfillment of God's promises. This week's lection from the prophet Zephaniah carries within it the communal memory of suffering and divine judgment, yet anticipates fulfillment of God's promises.[1] Prominent theological themes in this text include (1) God's exaltation of the suffering and the outcast and (2) incarnation.

God's Exaltation of the Suffering and the Outcast.
Zephaniah is acutely aware of the corruption and injustice perpetrated by Judah's leaders. Right up to the admonition to "wait" in 3:8, Zephaniah details the spiritual and political oppression perpetrated by the leaders in Judah, and God's impending punishment: destruction. As a result of the social injustice, the oppressed are fearful and ashamed, while the powerful are haughty and corrupt and reject divine correction. While the prophet recounts all the ways in which God will deal with the

1. Although it is commonly agreed that this text was written during the continued Assyrian domination in Jerusalem, the prophet invites his hearers to gather for praise in anticipation of coming restoration. See Marvin A. Sweeney, *Zephaniah: A Commentary*, Hermeneia (Minneapolis: Fortress Press, 2003), 193–208.

Pastoral Perspective

"Thank God we can't know the future, or we'd never get out of bed." Playwright Tracey Letts scripts an unhappy adult daughter to pass along the family pessimism to her own daughter. *August: Osage County* is a Pulitzer Prize– and Tony Award–winning play about a family convened on the occasion of the father's funeral. Some families rise to the occasion of good behavior during a crisis. This one sinks even deeper in dysfunction. The alcoholic father has committed suicide; the pill-addicted widow-mother is mean and manipulative. One of the daughters who seems happy and healthy is revealed to be in love with her cousin, who is revealed to be her half brother; another is trying to hide a marital separation, and another is about to marry a pedophile. The granddaughter is stoned and promiscuous. They all smoke something and drink too much and swear excessively. All of that is the context of the disturbing and riveting line: "Thank God we can't know the future, or we'd never get out of bed." The playwright reflects a pervasive, corrosive milieu of fear and grim resignation in our time. In his time, the prophet Zephaniah rehearsed a similar drama of human sin, involving "violence and fraud" (1:9), arrogance, and immorality that produced disaster, reproach, and shame. But, thank God, Zephaniah knows something of God's future.

he will exult over you with loud singing
18 as on a day of festival.
I will remove disaster from you,
so that you will not bear reproach for it.
19 I will deal with all your oppressors
at that time.
And I will save the lame
and gather the outcast,
and I will change their shame into praise
and renown in all the earth.
20 At that time I will bring you home,
at the time when I gather you;
for I will make you renowned and praised
among all the peoples of the earth,
when I restore your fortunes
before your eyes, says the LORD.

Exegetical Perspective

The short biblical book of Zephaniah locates itself in the seventh century BCE during the reign of King Josiah of Judah (640–609 BCE), who elsewhere in the Bible, namely, in the books of Kings and Chronicles, is characterized as the last great king, whose only equal was the great King David. Zephaniah, however, witnesses another reality in the streets of Jerusalem. Lamenting idolatry, corruption, and injustice, the prophetic message found in the book of Zephaniah is constructed in a way that sets the stage for the Josianic reform of 621 BCE, a major movement to reintroduce the statutes and ordinances of the Sinai covenant (see the Deuteronomic Code in Deut. 12–26). The identity of the prophet remains unclear, even though the superscription of the book traces his roots back four generations (Zeph. 1:1), which is unusual for biblical prophets.[1] The fact that his father's name is Cushi has made some scholars wonder about a possible Ethiopian heritage of this prophet. The matter is complicated by royal Israelite heritage invoked in King Hezekiah. In any case, the need for legitimization of Zephaniah the prophet appears strong, be it for the color of his skin in a place of power or for the content of his message.

1. See for example, Mária Eszenyei Széles, *Wrath and Mercy: A Commentary on the Books of Habakkuk and Zephaniah*, trans. George A. F. Knight (Grand Rapids: Eerdmans, 1987).

Homiletical Perspective

A first reading of this passage inspires thoughts of a word of hope in the mist of despair, a word of God's sure and strong promise to lift up those who are bowed down. It would be easy (and perhaps beneficial) to preach an end to fear and the rejoicing of those who are saved and protected by the Lord.

But how do we hear this word authentically in our context? How do we hear words of promise spoken to a people in exile in our own situation? Words of promise and restoration were spoken through Zephaniah to people who knew national devastation, who knew isolation from community and home. Privileged people in twenty-first-century North America hear these same words from a perspective of ease and comfort. We may and do experience the fears that war arouses, personal fears and anxieties, but it cannot be denied that our own experience is very different from that of Zephaniah's original hearers. It would be too easy to apply Zephaniah's words directly to our dis-eases and our dis-comforts.

So where can we enter this text? Where can we see ourselves in it? How can we hear this promise as authentic good news? Perhaps the first step is to recognize and to help people to understand a bit about the challenge in hearing this text. Perhaps we need to talk just a bit about our situation and about

Zephaniah 3:14-20

Theological Perspective

oppressors, he reserves a special word for those who have suffered at their unjust hands: "I will deal with all your oppressors at that time. And I will save the lame and gather the outcast, and I will change their shame into praise and renown in all the earth" (3:19). In reading this text during Advent, we anticipate the Gospel reading for the fourth week, in which Mary sings praises unto God, who lifts up the lowly and brings down the powerful (Luke 1:46–55). The same themes are echoed, also, in Revelation 21:4: "mourning and crying and pain will be no more." In these two texts, as in the lectionary text for today, the relationship between the season of Advent and the advent of the kingdom of God start to become clear. God's promises have about them a preference for protecting and lifting up the lowly, the suffering, and the oppressed. We find an unfolding of God's promises in many places throughout the biblical narratives: in the prophetic word, in the coming of Jesus, and in God's alternative future, the kingdom of God. Jürgen Moltmann defined this as the essence of theological hope: "biblical thought always understands hope as the expectation of a good future which rests on God's promise."[2] Of course, readers should not move too quickly to associate Zephaniah's words with either the birth of Jesus or an eschatological future. At the same time, however, as the Christian celebration of the birth of Jesus nears, readers are challenged to remember the character of God's continuing and living promise to protect and exalt the lowly. This is the context in which the prophetic word, the coming of the Messiah, and the shape of the kingdom of God derive their meaning. It also is the context in which the character of God is revealed.

It is important to note, however, that Zephaniah's praise of the humble ought not be interpreted solely as a universal valorization of self-effacing humility. Rather, the prophetic word affirms that God's purposes are to make right systems of injustice, to heal the shame that results from oppression. In the exaltation of the humble and lowly, Zephaniah finds both a divine rejection of the abuses of power and a divine promise to protect the weak and the outcast.

Incarnation. Twice in this text (vv. 15, 17) the prophet affirms God's presence with the people, affirming that God is and will continue to be in their midst. God's presence does two things in these

2. Jürgen Moltmann, "Hope," in *The Westminster Dictionary of Christian Theology*, ed. Alan Richardson and John Stephen Bowden (Philadelphia: Westminster Press, 1983), 271.

Pastoral Perspective

In these weeks we hear from Malachi, Jeremiah, Zephaniah, Isaiah, and Micah. The prophet is as much the voice of Advent as is the evangelist. Why? Prophets say what no one wants to hear, what no one wants to believe. Prophets point in directions no one wants to look. They hear God when everybody else has concluded God is silent. They see God where nobody else would guess that God is present. They feel God. Prophets feel God's compassion for us, God's anger with us, God's joy in us. They dream God's dreams and utter wake-up calls; they hope God's hopes and announce a new future; they will God's will and live it against all odds. Prophets sing God's song and sometimes interrupt the program with a change of tune.

Zephaniah's song calls people to lament and repent. Jerusalem is idolatrous and complacent; the nations are corrupt. God is indignant. Today's text needs to be heard in its context in order to capture the abrupt shift in the joyful imperative, "Sing aloud. . . . Rejoice and exult!" God's promised salvation interrupts a tirade of judgment with a song of joy. The "day of darkness and gloom" (1:15) is supplanted by a day of gladness.

Zephaniah, thank God, knows the future and wants us to get up and rejoice! The future will be different from the present and even different from the future that had been foreseen. There will be no disaster, no reproach, no shame, no fear. Why do we listen to the prophets during Advent? Because centuries before the birth of Jesus Christ they were messengers of essential good news: "Do not fear. . . . The LORD, your God, is in your midst." The prophet teaches the evangelist a basic phrase in the language of God, and again the prophetic word is a pastoral word, spoken into the heart of human experience.

"Do not fear" is not a plea, but a declaration. Luke speaks it to instill confidence in unsuspecting recipients of God's news: "Do not be afraid, Zechariah," "Do not be afraid, Mary." Later in the story we will hear, "Do not be afraid . . . I am bringing you good news of great joy." Another Gospel proclaims at its end, "Do not be afraid. . . . He is not here, for he has been raised" (Matt. 28:5–6).

Zephaniah and Luke join voices in a persistent, insistent biblical refrain. "Do not fear" is repeated over and over again because human beings are afraid of many things. Read between the lines that follow in verses 16–20, and we read our own souls: We fear that God is not in our midst and that the enemies of good and God are winning. We fear that our hands are weak and powerless, atrophied by lack of useful

Exegetical Perspective

The book of Zephaniah consists predominantly of judgment oracles (eight out of nine in the book) invoking the day of the Lord (*yom YHWH*) (Zeph. 1:2–3:8), a special day when all will be judged and found in breach of the covenant. Indeed, the prophet Zephaniah announces cosmic destruction (1:2–3; 3:8), which includes particular attention to the people of Judah and Jerusalem, singling out the priesthood as particularly sinful and idolatrous (1:4). The language, reminiscent of the book of Isaiah (see Isa. 1:21–31; 2:5–22; 10:1–4; 28:1–13; etc.), has led some scholars to suggest that Zephaniah was a student of Isaiah of Jerusalem. Others have ascribed the Isaianic echoes to a postexilic editor. The fact that the prophet denounces Israel's sin as pride and puts his hope in a faithful remnant also fits well into an Isaianic tradition. The short book ends in a ninth oracle, an oracle of salvation for this very remnant, and those eschatological verses make up the lectionary reading for the Third Sunday of Advent in Year C.

Zephaniah 3:14–20 opens with an exhortation to daughter Zion and to Israel to sing. Addressed with female appellations, the people are to rejoice wholeheartedly (v. 14). The subsequent hymn belongs to the song tradition of women in the Hebrew Bible.[2] It especially echoes women's songs in times of crisis and celebration in other prophetic books (see, for example, Jer. 9:17–22; 31:2–6). The promises picture God having reversed judgment and reclaimed the throne (v. 15). As in the time before the institution of the monarchy, in these eschatological times there is no need for a human king. Indeed, accepting God as king reverts to the arrangements of the Sinai covenant (see Exod. 19:1–6), the kind of relationship between God and people that the Josianic reform will favor. As a consequence, Jerusalem is admonished to fear no longer, because God will not only bring victory over the enemy but also join in rejoicing and song (vv. 16–17). Indeed, God will join together with the people in singing this hymn of praise.

Part of this promise is what the NRSV renders "he will renew you in his love"; the NIV reads "he will quiet you with his love"; and the Tanakh translation says, "He will soothe with His love" (v. 17b). While the NRSV gets its translation from the wording in the Septuagint, the other two translations mentioned try to render the corrupted Masoretic text with a possible emendation. Both

2. Carol L. Meyers, "Of Drums and Damsels: Women's Performance in Ancient Israel," *Biblical Archeologist* 54 (1991): 16–27.

Homiletical Perspective

the situation of Israel in Zephaniah's time, so that we are all on the same page about the historical and cultural distance we face as we hear this text and attempt to understand what it might mean for us.

It might be helpful to begin a treatment of this text with a brief (re)telling of some of the historical and cultural context of the prophet. Whether written before or after the conquest of Judah by Babylon, this text was written in the context of that event or its threat. This text was first heard as a part of a divine judgment against Jerusalem. Earlier portions of Zephaniah speak out forcefully against the people of Jerusalem, promising retribution for their lack of faith. In this text itself, Zephaniah looks beyond the punishment to the restoration. This cycle of punishment and restoration is key to God's relationship with God's people, from the beginning of Genesis down to the present day. God will always restore. There is good news for any day and for any age.

The people to whom Zephaniah spoke this word were experiencing profound challenges. Their nation was embarrassed on the international scene: they were a pawn in the movements of the great world powers Babylon, Assyria, and others. Foreign armies were a constant threat and sometime reality. Lack of food and water, the basic necessities of life, accompanied this instability.

It is into this reality that Zephaniah speaks of restoration and an end to shame. Zephaniah promises not only an end to shame: Zephaniah promises that Israel will be praised throughout all the earth. What a radical promise this was to the fearful lot who first heard it!

After recognizing the profound differences between our own situation and that of Zephaniah's Israel, two interrelated approaches lend themselves to a hearing of this text as authentic good news for our time. We could first approach it from the context of our own challenges and fears and shames. If God can restore the fortunes to a nation bowed down before the powers of the world and dragged away into slavery, then God can also banish our fears and our challenges.

In a related way, we also may want to proclaim the universality of this promise. God's promised messianic kingdom and restoration of fortunes are not just for us and for our challenges. They are for the whole world. In God's messianic kingdom, oppressors will be dealt with (v. 19), because there will be no oppressed and no oppressors. In God's messianic kingdom, all the lame and the outcast will be restored. There will no "in groups" and "out

Zephaniah 3:14-20

Theological Perspective

verses: it protects and it rejoices. The people will live without fear, trusting that God saves them from disaster and enemy attack. God's presence does more than remove threats, however. God's presence among the people is animating, in that God rejoices with them, renews them, and exults over them. God frees and strengthens the people by being present among them, such that their hands should not "grow weak." John Calvin interpreted the prophet's words in this way: "And it is what we also know by experience, that when fear prevails in our hearts we are as it were lifeless, so that we cannot raise even a finger to do anything: but when hope animates us, there is a vigor in the whole body, so that alacrity appears everywhere."[3] God's living among the people releases them from fear and shame, invigorating them to work for the good.

God's promises to those who suffer are not effected from a divine distance, but by God's very presence among the people. God comes to humanity in flesh, most assuredly. The Advent season walks us forward toward that birth the angels sang. But Zephaniah assures us that God also comes to humanity in the community of faith. God's presence heals, enlivens, and challenges humanity to lean into God's promises for an alternative future. As the United Presbyterian Church affirmed in the Confession of 1967, "Already God's reign is present as a ferment in the world, stirring hope in (women and men)." In dwelling among the people, God nourishes and makes real the promised future of peace and joy that theological hope imagines. This is a strong and hopeful message that will hearten the faithful on this Third Sunday of Advent.

JENNIFER RYAN AYRES

Pastoral Perspective

work and helpful use, exercised in holding on but needing both physical and spiritual therapy to reach out. We fear insignificance, doubting that we matter in the course of events and dreading that we will be crushed by them. We fear political defeat and natural disaster. We fear shame and reproach, that our faults and foibles will be discovered and render us less than the person we had fooled ourselves and others into thinking we were. We are afraid that we won't have enough, won't be enough. We even fear that God may keep God's promises, and interrupt the safety of our fears and the familiarity of our enemies with something new. Zephaniah's pastoral word to the people of God acknowledges our fear and dispels it with a promise of a transforming joy and not a threat of judgment.

This text illumines the liturgical practice of lighting a rose-colored candle on the Advent wreath on the Third Sunday of Advent. Congregations that continue the liturgical color of purple for this season, rather than blue, have a visual symbol for an interjection of joy. Purple candles recall a time when Advent paralleled Lent as a season of penitence and was marked by practices of prayer and fasting. But on the Third Sunday a rose candle was lighted to symbolize joy, and the penitential fast was lifted. The Third Sunday of Advent is traditionally called Gaudete Sunday, from the Latin imperative, "Rejoice!" The name sounds the note of the epistle for this day, in which Paul enjoins the Philippians, "Rejoice in the Lord always; again I will say, Rejoice. . . . The Lord is near" (Phil. 4:4–5). In year A, the church hears the prophesy of Isaiah and the promise of the desert rejoicing and blossoming as the rose at the Messiah's coming (Isa. 35:1–2).

We are not a people who welcome interruptions. Zephaniah reminds us that through prophetic interruptions God offers us glimpses of a hopeful future that goes beyond getting us up in the morning. It frees us from fear and moves us to rejoice.

DEBORAH A. BLOCK

3. John Calvin, *Commentaries on the Twelve Minor Prophets*, ed. and trans. John Owen (Grand Rapids: Eerdmans, 1950), 4:303.

concepts—the earlier one of the promise of God's love calming the people and the later one of God renewing God's covenant love—can hold meaning in an interpretation of this eschatological ecstasy. God's presence among the people will make all the difference at every level.

Such divine presence will bring universal liberation from oppression, illness, and social ostracism, Zephaniah proclaims (vv. 18–19). Indeed, the vision of a utopian society is invoked to motivate the audience to change the status quo. And as if such a vision was not enough, a homecoming with fame and fortune awaits at the finale (v. 20).

The lectionary reading for the Third Sunday in Advent harvests the climax of the book of Zephaniah, while the book as a whole feasts on juxtapositions. There is Jerusalem the unfaithful and corrupt placed alongside Jerusalem the city of universal rejoicing and justice; there is the contrast between idolatrous and purified—a city of violence versus a dove (that is, a city of peace). Within the book of Zephaniah, without the context of judgment and impending destruction, the concluding promises do not make sense.

What does that mean for the Advent lectionary? What happens when the lectionary passage is heard without its context? Or put theologically, what meaning does promise have without preceding judgment? Frankly, it remains shallow, like Pollyanna. Notably, throughout the Bible, promise does not come separated from judgment and suffering. Biblical writers have not offered comfort to the comfortable. Rather, eschatological passages succeed instances of death, destruction, and despair. Those who are oppressed now will be rejoicing in justice.

Thus, while certainly all congregations need occasions for celebration, the crucial connection between judgment and promise in this Advent text needs to be made clear. A lectionary that leaves out the former by not naming the dominant realities of death, exploitation, and despair, and a sermon that does not name contemporary instances thereof, deprive their hearers of the depth of the biblical message.

ANGELA BAUER-LEVESQUE

groups," there will be no favored nations and unfavored nations. There will be no scattered nations and refugees, for all of God's people will be brought home and gathered (v. 20).

This kind of proclamation takes seriously the privileged position from which we North Americans hear this text. We largely do not experience extreme deprivation or shame, but because we love the world, we listen to that pain in the peoples of other nations and other classes. Then, informed and compassionate, we can pray in solidarity with our sisters and brothers around the world who do experience the world in ways much more like the experience of Zephaniah's hearers. We pray for an end to all disasters and conflicts, and we trust in God's promise for restoration.

As we pray in solidarity with our sisters and brothers around the world, we recognize that God's promise is also for us. At the end of the day, once we have recognized the differences between our own fears and the fears originally addressed by Zephaniah, we can say that God will banish our fears as well. God will ultimately bring an end to our pain and our suffering, whatever nature that pain and suffering take.

It is not inauthentic to claim the promise of restoration for ourselves as well. God brings good news to all people through the promise of Messiah and the final kingship of the Lord (v. 15). The good news is for the privileged of this world, as well as for those bowed down in this world. The good news is a promise of restoration to right relationships. When God promises that we will be praised throughout the world, the promise is based on who we are as God's children, and not on our own might or strength. When we are in right relationship with one another and with God, then we will be renowned and praised in all the earth (v. 20).

SETH MOLAND-KOVASH

Isaiah 12:2-6

²Surely God is my salvation;
   I will trust, and will not be afraid,
  for the Lord God is my strength and my might;
   he has become my salvation.

³With joy you will draw water from the wells of salvation. ⁴And you will say in that day:

  Give thanks to the Lord,
   call on his name;
  make known his deeds among the nations;
   proclaim that his name is exalted.
⁵Sing praises to the Lord, for he has done gloriously;
   let this be known in all the earth.
⁶Shout aloud and sing for joy, O royal Zion,
   for great in your midst is the Holy One of Israel.

Theological Perspective

Perhaps the most significant signature of the Advent season is its celebratory air. Gleaming lights and other decorations, pageants by children and adults, baking, giving, and well-wishing all reflect the anticipation of the season. Advent also is a time of singing. Advent songs celebrate the season and express joy and thanks in expectation of what God will do. This text, a song that celebrates divine strength by offering praise, giving thanks, and proclaiming divine deeds, likewise anticipates what is to come.

The hymn that comprises Isaiah 12 concludes the first division of the book and is situated in the largest portion of what now generally is identified as First Isaiah. However, unlike its surrounding material, this chapter is late. Thematic resemblance to Isaiah 40 and following suggest that it was likely composed in the 500s BCE, amid the exile to Babylon, not during the prophetic work of First Isaiah (between 734 and 701 BCE) with which other portions of the first division are identified. Interpreters believe the hymn was added here by an editor to complete the narrative sequence preceding it. As chapter 11 predicts return, the praise hymn of chapter 12 appropriately anticipates celebration of that return. Interpreters call the text a celebration for the second exodus, since the return predicted resembles movement of the people out of captivity

Pastoral Perspective

As a child, I used to have endless fun playing Monopoly—the board game in which one aims to amass wealth by buying property and extracting rent from fellow players who, because of an unfortunate roll of the dice, land on the squares that you own. Dad used to give my brother and me twice the amount of money the rules allowed. I presume the assumption was that he was smarter than we were, but this meant that if my brother or I landed on a prized square like Park Place or Boardwalk, we had more money to buy up the property, to buy a hotel or two, and to charge exorbitant fees from the other less fortunate players. From this game I learned two contradictory realities about life that are always held in tension and that continue to puzzle me to this day. The first is that life is lived on a competitive, but unequal, playing field in which winning and losing is based somewhat on merit but also significantly on the social benefits of being born of a certain class, race, gender, and with a certain amount of intelligence, and physical prowess. The second lesson I learned is that God is somewhat like my dad, an uncommonly generous giver of very good gifts, the benefits of which I often exploit and misunderstand. While I grew up wishing I had been born into privilege, in my church I was taught that I was good enough, and that God loved me even when I

Exegetical Perspective

Isaiah 12, a prophetic song in six verses, bursts with joy and promises God's presence. This triumphant song with its messianic implications exuberantly closes a section of eleven chapters about Judah and Jerusalem. Its joyful message fits well the traditional theme of the Third Sunday of Advent.

Little is known about Isaiah, the son of Amoz, but he clearly knows the international scene of his day. His work opens by describing visions he saw concerning Judah and Jerusalem during the reigns of Uzziah, Jotham, Ahaz, and Hezekiah, kings of Judah (Isa. 1:1). These kings reigned 792–686 BCE.

While chapter 12 provides a joyful interlude, chapters 13–23 speak of God's upcoming judgment on Babylon, Philistia, Moab, Damascus, Cush, Egypt, Edom, Arabia, Jerusalem, and Tyre. The structure of Isaiah 12:1–6, a prophecy about God's glorious work and the upcoming reign of God's king, is simple. The song breaks neatly into two sections, verses 1–3 and 4–6. The second person singular in verse 1a changes to the second person plural in verse 4a. Both sections begin with the phrase, "In that day you will say."

Verse 1, not part of the lectionary reading, nonetheless merits attention. An unnamed person accepted chastisement, experienced God's anger, and now enjoys God's reconciliation. John Calvin points out the inherent biblical truths of verse 1. The faithful ascribe

Homiletical Perspective

Another Sunday in Advent, and we are invited to seek out, in our waiting, watching, wondering, the joy that might be present in the depths of our midwinter ruminations, even amid experiences of exile and threats of destruction. Joy is commonly the theme for the Third Sunday of Advent. Clearly there is joy in this beautiful passage that ends the first section of Isaiah, joy now known, as well as joy anticipated, for the ways in which God redeems and restores God's people.

The rhythm of the first chapters of Isaiah fluctuates between dire predictions of destruction and profound promises of salvation. To begin with, we are confronted with a "sinful nation, people laden with iniquity, offspring who do evil, children who deal corruptly, who have forsaken the LORD" (Isa. 1:4). There are sections that treat the Assyrian threat to Israel and Judah. There are harsh words about the people's iniquity, their failure to keep covenant, their straying after idols and abandonment of the one true God in favor of the latest fashion.

At the same time, the first part of Isaiah contains magnificent words that proclaim God will yet provide salvation for God's wayward and recalcitrant people. The great culmination of these promises comes in chapter 11, in which the prophet tells of the "shoot" that "shall come out from the stump of

Isaiah 12:2-6

Theological Perspective

in Egypt. Verse 12:2 is a near verbatim restatement of Exodus 15:2, which is a part of the song of celebration of Moses and the people after crossing the Red Sea. Since there are two movements in the chapter, some interpreters identify the text as two songs divided by a change from singular to plural at the end of 12:3. The entire text may be understood as a doxology since, like other doxologies, it "is an act of confident hope that things in time to come . . . will be happily resolved."[1]

Both units of the passage move joyfully beyond the textual present time of exile in anticipation of a victorious homecoming day celebration. The lection opens with a verse stating the expectation of salvation through God's work. Because of the surety of this salvation that will come through divine power, the singer looks forward to "trust" and not "fear." Christians observing Advent will readily identify with celebration of the coming salvation indicated in 12:2 and 3, in spite of textual references to political and physical salvation of the people of Israel from being conquered and dispersed. The national salvation in the text is distinct from the spiritual salvation many Christians anticipate during Advent, even though there are traditions within Christianity that point to the material as well as the spiritual meaning of salvation. Still, many streams within the Christian tradition advocate defining salvation as exclusively religious.

There may be "new" news for some Advent listeners who for the first time hear in this text words about physical remedy to challenges they face. The first unit of the hymn ends with a reference to a festivity that includes drawing water. Interpreters say this may refer to an actual ritual that celebrates "wells" or "springs" of help God provides, or which celebrates, as do Jeremiah 2:13 and 17:13, God as a "fountain of living water." Alongside joyous singing and other festivities hailing the event of deliverance, the water celebration may be seen rhetorically as very similar to Christmas pageants during Advent. Both function to commemorate the event being celebrated. Both are rituals and thereby are abstracted from the actual event commemorated. Both depend on repetition for effect. An important function of rituals, especially intensified through repetition, is to help shape and strengthen group identity by memorializing commonly held beliefs about who a community is. The editors' intent in

Pastoral Perspective

squandered the gifts I had been given. I also learned in church that the world of grace and salvation is always in tension with the world of meritocracy and privilege.

The clash between these two worlds is reflected in this lesson from Isaiah. Isaiah 12 looks forward to the day when God's anger over the people's turning away from the Torah is turned into a word of comfort. Walter Brueggemann points out that the use of "comfort" in verse 1 of chapter 12 looks forward to the use of this same word in Isaiah 40, which announces the homecoming of the people of God who are in exile.[1] Thus Isaiah 12 not only anticipates a day when Jerusalem will be destroyed and the people taken into exile; it also anticipates homecoming. Homecoming must certainly be included among the many "deeds" of God referred to in the text.

Salvation as homecoming is noteworthy because it is a gift. In Isaiah's view, the people have done nothing to deserve the gift. In other words, the gift is not based on merit. Moreover, the people certainly did not deserve the gift on account of the privilege of being in covenant relation to God, because they had abused the privilege. The nature of this gift is highlighted by the use of an image of water being drawn from a well of salvation. In his commentary on Isaiah, John Calvin said this of the image: "Everything necessary for supporting life flows to us from the undeserved goodness of God. . . . [Isaiah] appropriately compares the mercy of God to a fountain, which satisfies those who are thirsty and dry."[2]

Yet I must admit that I find the language of gift incommensurate with the Monopoly model of the world in which we live—a world where meritocracy will get you only so far and where privilege is often abused. In this world, the language of gift carries the connotation of either exploitation or something we don't deserve. I have a friend who calls terms like grace, gift, and salvation the "language of Zion," by which he means the strange language of the church that is in tension with the language of the world.

In her book *Economy of Grace* Kathryn Tanner reframes the traditional language of the church using the modern economic language of competition. In the world of games and economics, competition is based on a win-lose model; for someone to win, someone has to lose. When playing a game, winning and losing can be fun. But in economics, where possessions and the privileges thereof are often

---

1. Walter Brueggemann, *Isaiah 1–39* (Louisville, KY: Westminster John Knox Press, 1998), 109.

1. Walter Brueggemann, *Isaiah 1–39*, Westminster Bible Companion (Louisville, KY: Westminster John Knox Press, 1998), 109.
2. Quoted in Brueggemann, 110.

mercy to God and expect God's mercy; they know that God's chastisement will not prevent God's compassion; they anticipate individual attention of joy and comfort; they do not despair; and they know that God's anger is brief.[1] While God does not need praise, both the person of verse 1 and the people of verse 4 need to praise God. Why? Because praise profits both.

Verse 2 describes the coming of the Messiah, when full salvation occurs. It begins with an emphasis: "*Hinneh*! Behold! God is my salvation!" The result of this statement? "I will trust and not be afraid!" Isaiah's song exudes confidence. Salvation is God's gift; this knowledge is a solid foundation for confidence. It banishes distress and uneasiness. A believer evidences cheerfulness upon being reconciled to God and strength because God is his or her strength. God is a believer's song. God's kindness upon a believer encourages perseverance in thankfulness.

Joy springs from God's favor (v. 3). As joy progresses, it becomes the sacrifice of praise (see Hos. 14:2; Ps. 50:23; Heb. 13:15). An individual's confidence comes from the assurance that eventually God—and therefore the godly individual and godly community in tandem—will be victorious. The God who faithfully began the salvific process carries it through to completion for the individual and community. Salvation and God's other graces form a constant running fountain from which a believer draws. The springs or wells of salvation produce life-giving water. Deep, constant, pure water—a lovely poetic metaphor—is essential for life. God's grace is not a onetime thing; the broad concept of salvation/ deliverance occurs repeatedly throughout a believer's and a community's life. God's salvation is as faithful as a deep, underground spring.

The springs of salvation poetically represent God's power, love, and care.[2] God opened and closed the subterranean springs for the flood (Gen. 7:11; 8:2). Springs bubble and rivers dry up at the divine command (Pss. 74:15; 104:10; 114:8). A bride's love for her groom resembles a garden spring (Song 4:15). Joel 3:18 speaks of a fountain flowing from the Lord's house. God's undeserved goodness never ceases. It calms, refreshes, cleanses, restores, provides life, covers, and satisfies. It does all this thoroughly and abundantly. Later, Isaiah encourages all who are thirsty—whether believers or not—to come and drink; no money is necessary (55:1).

Jesse," the promised Messiah. Chapter 11 also contains the wonderful description of the peaceable kingdom over which the Messiah will reign.

With these words of possibility proclaimed, we see that indeed Israel may yet be restored and the people redeemed. They may yet avoid the experience of exile, or, failing that, return rejoicing to the home from which they have been dragged into exile. There will be no more struggle to sing God's songs in strange lands (Ps. 137). In the words of the old hymn, "There would I find a settled rest, while others go and come; no more a stranger, or a guest, but like a child at home."[1] Such is the promise of redemption proclaimed to the people as they face wearying days of exile. With such a promise ringing in their ears, what is left but to sing a song of joy?

Biblical scholar William Herzog says that "Isaiah 12 celebrates with exultant joy the coming of God's salvation to a land that had dwelt in the deep darkness of God's judgment."[2] Do we know now anything of being wayward and recalcitrant? Where do we dwell in darkness and live with the threat of destruction? What does it mean to live in fear? We who live these early years of the twenty-first century know something of that in a world in which whole cultures of fear have been built around the threats (real and perceived) of terror, terror from both the privileged and from the dispossessed. We clutch national identities, sustaining a perceived need for enemies, which in turn serves to justify the economics of military industrial complexes. Hospitality disappears, and strangers and foreigners are seen as a threat and not welcomed. Everyone in his or her own way dwells in the shadow of death. Will God's great light shine once more? How can we find our way through the morass to singing songs of joy in the night?

Many will be preaching to those who know only too well about exile, about oppression, about destruction. They will know firsthand what it is like to live in fear of economic collapse, of neighborhood violence, of undocumented status. Others will know these threats only spiritually. Can one experience exile in the upper middle class? Shaping this text will differ for hearers from different social location. It will be a challenge for those in privileged positions to help their congregations understand the deep, raw joy of those who celebrate what little they have and

---

1. John Calvin, *Commentary on the Book of the Prophet Isaiah*, vol. 1, trans. William Pringle (Grand Rapids: Baker Book House, 1981, reprint), 387–88.
2. Bryan E. Beyer, "ma'yan, spring," in *New International Dictionary of Old Testament Theology and Exegesis*, Willem A. VanGemeren, gen. ed. (Grand Rapids: Zondervan, 1997), 2:1018–19.

1. Isaac Watts, "My Shepherd Will Supply My Need," *The Worshipbook* (Philadelphia: Westminster Press, 1970), \#477.
2. William R. Herzog II, *New Proclamation, Year C, 2006–2007, Advent through Holy Week* (Minneapolis: Fortress Press, 2006), 26.

Isaiah 12:2-6

Theological Perspective

anticipating songs of celebration after the return likely includes this identity-forming function. Christian Advent celebrations serve the same function and, in fact, are at least partially appreciated and enjoyed because of their familiarity and repetition of meaningful elements. An important and necessary distinction between the two celebrations is the relationship of the Jewish water ritual to the national identity and the disconnection of Advent and other Christian celebrations from national identity.

In the passage at hand, the ritualizing occurs not only in the song of celebration, but also in the construction of this text through use of devices like the formulaic expression "and you will say in that day" (v. 4, also in v. 1) to indicate distinct movements in the song and to remind readers of the text's relationship to events to come. What follows is the admonition to appropriately acclaim the divine work that is anticipated: to give thanks by calling God's name, to proclaim divine deeds, to honor God's name, to sing praises, and to shout for joy. These all are required "for" the "gloriously" "great" deeds God will do.

Reading this text through the lens of the New Testament, Advent readers and listeners may find especially noteworthy the charge to praise the divine work of salvation "among the nations" and "in all the earth," beyond the people of Israel (vv. 4, 5). Those celebrating Advent also may see the incarnation prefigured in the charge to rejoice at the presence of "God with" (in the midst of, v. 6) the people of Israel. Ironically, these two interpretations, which many Christians will understand as pointing to the inclusion of Gentiles and which some will understand as a supersession of Judaism by Christianity, occur in relation to a text that identifies the election of Israel ("O royal Zion," "the Holy One of Israel," v. 6). An important challenge to those celebrating Advent is to overcome the potential tendency to glorify one's own group at the expense of other groups and to remember the promise of Advent as providing welcome to everyone. For some, this welcome to all and respect for religious traditions of others will present a conflict that is difficult to overcome.

ROSETTA E. ROSS

Pastoral Perspective

exploited, winning and losing can be devastating. By marked contrast, in the noncompetitive economy of grace, the goods that are given by God are given in an indiscriminate and recklessly extravagant manner, and seemingly without God's suffering loss.[3] Moreover, in the economy of grace, even when we fail to give in return, God keeps giving (just as every time we played Monopoly, my dad keep would giving us more money than the game allowed, even though we exploited the privilege).

Indeed, when God gave of Godself in Christ, we humans even exploited the gift of incarnation. Even though we use the language of suffering for the crucifixion of Christ, the resurrection is a witness to the fact that for God, to give is to gain, because the Christ event empowers us to see the win-win world of the gift-giving God who frees us from the win-lose world based in meritocracy that never satisfies, or in privilege that is always abused. Isaiah 11 looks forward to this win-win world of the gift-giving God in its idyllic vision of the future, when "the wolf shall live with the lamb, the leopard shall lie down with the kid, the calf and the lion and the fatling together, and a little child shall lead them" (Isa. 11:6).

Perhaps the language of Zion—the language of grace, gift, and salvation—is not so strange after all. For what is so strange about a world of winners? Where the environment is not exploited in order to make a profit? Where people don't work for their poverty? And where the phrase "homeless person" is an oxymoron? Let us draw deeply from such "wells of salvation" and look forward to the day when homecoming will be a reality for all of God's people.

ROGER J. GENCH

---

3. Kathryn Tanner, *Economy of Grace* (Minneapolis: Fortress Press, 2005), 25–26, 64–65.

Exegetical Perspective

In the second section, 12:4–6, the prophet commands others to make known God's deeds among their neighbors, the nations mentioned starting in chapter 13. Calling upon God represents worship's essence. God's salvation made known to the Israelites is too glorious to be kept solely in that community. Infectious joy needs to spread throughout the whole earth.

What began with an individual's excitement now becomes a community's excitement. What started as an individual's charge to praise now expands to a community's responsibility to give thanks, make known God's deeds, and exalt God's name among the nations. God bestows amazing honor: God condescends to use the believing community in extolling and spreading the glory of God's own name.

Joy about God escalates in volume. Sing, believing community! God has done glorious things! Singing accelerates to shouting, even the high-pitched shouting that is the specialty of women in the prophet's community.[3] Evidently God not only likes but also commands noisy worship! The desire of a godly community is that God's goodness become known to all humankind so that all may call upon God and all may join in a cacophony of singing, shouting, praising, thanking, and worshiping God. God's people face a fun and fulfilling future exalting God's great name. God's king will reign. What started as an individual's joy eventually will be experienced by everybody.

Notice God's provision in Isaiah 12: forgiveness, comfort, salvation, strength, a song, joy, springs of salvation, a job to make known his deeds and proclaim God's name, and finally God's presence. Isaiah 12 resembles the Song of Moses, Exodus 15:2; Psalm 118:14; and the Song of the Lamb, Revelation 15:3–4. God's saving power in the Messiah (Isa. 53:1ff.) eclipses the joy of salvation during the exodus. The Holy One of Israel (12:6) is unique, separate, transcendent, present, and distinct—but not aloof.

Isaiah 12—a song of praise, shout of thanksgiving, exclamation of joy—responds to God's goodness glimpsed in the present and assured of for the future. Both individual and community must sing, because God not only is great but also will dwell in the midst of his beloved, believing community.

ROBIN GALLAHER BRANCH

Homiletical Perspective

who relish with passion the promises of redemption. It will be a challenge to help the already comfortable understand what the promise of comfort might mean to the dispossessed and struggling.

For the preacher in less affluent circumstances the challenge might be to help congregants have hope and rejoice in the promise of what is to come, but is not yet. Or it might be a challenge to speak truth to power, to become agents of their own transformation in the name of Jesus, the Christ, and through the empowerment of the Holy Spirit. For all of us, there is a challenge to bridge the gap between haves and have nots, to bring about some sort of jubilee in which goods and services, resources and hope are distributed more equally. Then we might find ourselves living together on that holy mountain, in peace and harmony, singing together in deep and abiding joy.

Walter Brueggemann tells us that Isaiah 12 is a pair of psalmic interpolations in which "the doxology is an act of confident hope that things in time to come (we don't know when) will be happily resolved." It is "an act of buoyant and determined hope that refuses to give in to debilitating present circumstance. . . . The doxology is to be one of thanks, of glad acknowledgement of Yahweh's goodness and generosity." There is unrestrained corporate joy in deliverance of the people. Brueggemann again says, "Israel restored is called to give thanks, to call upon the name, make known, praise, shout, sing for joy. Israel cannot now restrain itself, for the unexpected, undeserved, inexplicable has happened. It is the sort of thing about which one cannot keep quiet. The *news* must be shared."[3]

So we too on this Third Sunday of Advent are called to sing for joy, to celebrate the ways in which God has delivered us, is delivering us, and will deliver us, until there is true peace, shalom, wholeness on earth and goodwill throughout the entire creation. "With joy you will draw water from the wells of salvation. . . . Shout aloud and sing for joy." For, in the words of another old hymn, "Since love is Lord of heav'n and earth, how can I keep from singing?"

RANDLE R. MIXON

---

3. John D. W. Watts, *Isaiah 1–33*, Word Bible Commentary 24 (Waco, TX: Word Books, 1985), 184.

3. Walter Brueggemann, *Isaiah 1–39*, Westminster Bible Companion (Louisville, KY: Westminster John Knox Press, 1998), 109–10.

Philippians 4:4-7

[4]Rejoice in the Lord always; again I will say, Rejoice. [5]Let your gentleness be known to everyone. The Lord is near. [6]Do not worry about anything, but in everything by prayer and supplication with thanksgiving let your requests be made known to God. [7]And the peace of God, which surpasses all understanding, will guard your hearts and your minds in Christ Jesus.

Theological Perspective

The apostle Paul here writes to a community to whom he has become attached. His affection for them is obvious throughout the letter. This affection makes Paul's customary defense of his apostolic authority unnecessary. Karl Barth notes that "we have to think here of extraordinary trust between author and readers, which rendered that designation of himself superfluous."[1] In 4:4–7 Paul powerfully exhorts his trusted Philippian friends to rejoice. This rejoicing comes in the face of trials and tribulations. Yet this command to rejoice, or to live joyfully, grounds this pericope theologically. The central theology of this passage is a theology of joy. The meaning of this joy or rejoicing cannot be separated from the tone and tenor of the letter as a whole. The intimacy or friendship that Paul shares with his readers is the immediate context of their common joy "in the Lord."

This joy Paul commends is not something that one can pursue. This is one of the differences between this joy and what is referred to as happiness in contemporary social discourse. It is not accidental that one of the foundational texts of American social and political life affirms that one has the right to

Pastoral Perspective

Late in her life, my grandmother started attending a church different from the one in which she had been raised and that she had attended for most of her years. When I asked her about her new church home, she said she liked it there because of the positive message she received. For the first time in her life, she felt God's loving presence. "God wants me to be happy," she said. "I never knew that before. I thought church was about keeping me from doing what I was not supposed to do. And I never felt like I was good enough." Late in life my grandmother heard a word of God's grace and experienced a joy she had never known before. She began to heed Paul's instruction to the church in Philippi: "Rejoice in the Lord, always; again I will say, Rejoice."

My grandmother's awareness of the joyful nature of Christian life is consistent with the tone of the Third Sunday of Advent, known traditionally as Gaudete (Latin for "Rejoice") Sunday, when the disciplines of Advent preparation are relaxed, celebratory rose replaces penitential purple as the liturgical color, and the foretaste of Christmas joy is proclaimed. The joyful posture of the day is seen in Paul's invitation to "rejoice in the Lord always." The mood of this day is captured by the children's round that puts Paul's words to music.[1] The Third

---

1. Karl Barth, *Epistle to the Philippians* (Louisville, KY: Westminster John Knox Press, 2002), 10.

1. "Rejoice in the Lord Always," in Pamela Conn Beall and Susan Hagen Nipp, *Wee Sing Bible Songs* (Los Angeles: Price Stern Sloan, 1986), 62.

Exegetical Perspective

On this Third Sunday of Advent, as many churches light the pink candle symbolizing joy, the lectionary offers one of the most encouraging passages in all of Paul's epistles. "Rejoice in the Lord always!" "Do not worry about any thing." Experience the "peace that passes understanding." These dear words mostly float through our consciousness detached from their gritty real-life setting of danger at the Philippians' door, doctrinal dogs nipping at their faithful feet, and strife between two of their leaders—not to mention prison chains wrapped 'round the one who wrote them. Noticing the sometimes-dark context from and into which these bright words are spoken will help preachers reach people in their pews who think they're supposed to be smiling peacefully as Christmas approaches but aren't sure why or how.

The Philippians are dear to Paul. The genre of the epistle is a "friendship letter." The Philippians have been generous in supporting his ministry (4:10, 14–16). But not everything is rosy for them. Paul sees fault lines. The specific descriptions of the Philippians' challenges lie in three different sections of the letter. The first mentions "opponents" (*antikeimenoi*, 1:28) who have caused them suffering (*paschein*, 1:29). Whether this threat is physical or social, Paul is concerned that the church might divide in the face of it (1:27b).

Homiletical Perspective

For many congregations the Third Sunday in Advent is reserved for the choir's Christmas cantata, which means the preacher is limited to a brief meditation, if that.

This text may be the perfect word for such a message. It's a familiar text for most people. And there are important messages in each of the four verses, in addition to the overall theme of rejoicing.

Verse 4. That *chairete* can mean both *rejoice* and *farewell* is interesting. Craddock suggests that the sense of verse 4 favors *rejoice* and Morna Hooker says that *farewell* makes no sense.[1] I cannot but feel that the word may be pulling the Philippians toward a future with Christ but without Paul instead of rejoicing over what had already been accomplished. Does this also apply to us?

Verse 5a. "Let your *gentleness* (or *generosity* or *Christlikeness* or *magnanimity* or *consideration of others*) be known to everyone." This is not, I believe, an invitation to toot your own horn like the hypocrites in Matthew 6:5, who stand and pray in the synagogues and on the street corners so they may be

---

1. Fred Craddock, *Philippians*, Interpretation Series (Atlanta: John Knox, 1985), 20–21; Morna Hooker, "Philippians," in *The New Interpreter's Bible*, vol. 11 (Nashville: Abingdon Press, 2005), 540.

Philippians 4:4-7

Theological Perspective

"the pursuit of happiness." There is within the statement itself a clue to the difference between joy and happiness. Happiness is something that is pursued, and happiness is tied up in the pursuit. But joy is something else altogether. It is a "joy" that the English essayist C. S. Lewis described as the best translation he could make of the German idea of *Sehnsucht*, or longing. Lewis was overtaken by this joy.

Barbara A. Holmes also addresses this notion of joy as it manifests itself in the African American church. She notes that "a common presumption is that black church worship practices are subsumed in liturgical enthusiasm and joyful expressions of adoration and praise."[2] She argues, however, that at the heart of the understanding of joy in the African American worship experience is not unrestrained frivolity, but a deep longing. This longing, more often than not, challenges and even defies expression; that is, this joy is experienced as an "unspeakable joy." This understanding is reflected in Paul's exhortation to the Philippians to "rejoice." Out of this understanding of joy, three auxiliary theological themes come into view.

Joy Brings Patience. Paul writes, "Let all men know your forbearance" (v. 5, RSV). This joy to which Paul refers brings patience. This patience must be distinguished from resignation or inactivity. It is, to quote the German theologian Dorothee Soelle, a "revolutionary patience."[3] The phrase is borrowed from a South African poet, Breyten Breytenbach. "It is not enough to rail against the descending darkness of barbarity. . . . One can refuse to play the game. A holding action can be fought. Alternatives must be kept alive. While learning the slow art of revolutionary patience." Like the joy from which it springs, this patience has the character of longing. It is a waiting that is filled with wanting. And like the joy from which it springs, it must be allowed or even compelled to expression in the public square. The patience is a Christian virtue because it requires trust in God.

Prayer as the Answer to Anxiety. "In nothing be anxious; but in everything by prayer and supplication with thanksgiving let your requests be made known unto God" (NKJV). Paul's advice to his readers to counter the anxiety of their lives with

Pastoral Perspective

Sunday in Advent is a day not to be troubled. It is a day to bask in the assurance of God's peace that passes understanding.

Yet the experience of joyful peace is not always easily found amid the great anxieties and expectations that the season can engender. My grandmother's straightforward need to hear a joyful word near the end of her life is a different circumstance from the one in which others may find themselves amid Advent. In fact, for some there is not a more anxious time in all the year. Some parishioners will be laboring under mounting pressure to have everything "just right" for the holidays as Christmas draws ever closer. For others, the world intrudes in even more jarring ways. In verse 4 Paul imagines faithful prayer as the solution to its opposite. But despite "prayer and supplication . . . made known to God," pain and heartache can overwhelm. Sorrow and tragedy cannot necessarily be held at bay, even on days reserved for rejoicing. Amid the cacophony of the world's vagaries and demands, "the peace of God, which surpasses all understanding," can prove elusive despite Paul's assurance that it "will guard your hearts and your minds in Christ Jesus" (v. 7).

During Advent attention is needed to the distinction between the material happiness that the commercial world promises and the abiding joy of Christian faith that cannot be bought at the mall but can sustain us, come what may. After all, Paul issues this exhortation to rejoice from the cell of a dark Roman prison (Phil. 1:13). Joy that emerges from a deep connection with our spiritual source is a far cry from the fleeting rush achieved through the acquisition of the season's latest toy. The depth of acculturation to consumer values, however, makes this message challenging to preach in ways that are not trite and simplistic.

This challenge is compounded by the varying economic circumstances represented in our congregations. To preach against materialism to those without basic necessities can be insensitive and offensive (Jas. 2:15,16). But avoiding the problematic nature of materialism may leave others untouched by the gospel's claims on their lives. Many in a rich country like the United States find themselves in a predicament not unlike the rich young ruler who approached Jesus because he knew something was missing in his life. Jesus, diagnosing the ruler's spiritual ailment as his attachment to his wealth, told the man to sell his holdings and give to the poor. The man went away sad, unwilling to part with his

---

2. Barbara A. Holmes, *Joy Unspeakable: Contemplative Practices of the Black Church* (Minneapolis: Augsburg Fortress Press, 2004), 6.
3. See Dorothee Soelle, *Revolutionary Patience*, trans. Rita Kimber and Robert Kimber (Eugene, OR: Wipf & Stock Publishers, 2003).

Exegetical Perspective

The community may also be hearing alternative teachers whom Paul unflatteringly calls "dogs" and characterizes as "the false circumcision" (3:2). While we can't know whether this is an on-the-ground threat or a possible eventuality, the language of Paul's autobiography (3:4–11) echoes his concern in the letters to the Galatians and Romans, namely, that a law- and circumcision-based Christianity will confuse the Philippians into imagining that they can accomplish righteousness through their deeds (3:9).

The third struggle in Philippi is a conflict between two female leaders of the congregation named Euodia and Syntyche (4:2). We ought to notice on the way the presence of female leaders who were coworkers with Paul, which, contrary to widespread perception in our time, was his customary practice (see Rom. 16). These two women are at odds, though, and the interpersonal issue is also a congregational one. To demonstrate this, Paul exhorts Euodia and Syntyche in the same language he earlier used to call the larger group to unity: "think the same thing" (*to auto phronein* in 2:2 and 4:2).

When Paul's famous "Rejoice in the Lord always!" arrives in an ancient Macedonian living room, then, it is not a tranquil and untroubled company who hear the scroll read out. The Philippians are troubled by external threats and internal strife. They are glad to have a note from Paul, but in the face of all this struggle they may wonder if their rejoicing might need to wait for happier times. "Rejoice . . . always? Really? Do you know what my day was like?" But it turns out that Paul does know. It is no accident that the apostle displays his own hardships so prominently at the beginning of the letter. He offers himself as an example to the suffering Philippians. Imprisoned and beset by ill-intentioned rivals (1:12–18), Paul tells them his response: "I rejoice." His simple ground for this joy also recurs in our passage: Christ. In his case, he celebrates the fact that Christ's good news is going forth. Similarly, in verse 4 the reason for their rejoicing is not pleasant circumstances but the steady good that is "in the Lord." "Rejoice in the Lord," says Paul, "because prosperity and happy times and the other potential reasons for rejoicing can't be counted on to continue 'always.'"

A similar dynamic appears in 4:6–7. When Paul calls the Philippians to prayer instead of anxiety, they might answer back that he doesn't know how utterly valid their reasons for being anxious are—but his personal situation lies in the background refuting such a claim. Because of the practice of prayer, even Paul's chains, with all the uncertainties of life that

Homiletical Perspective

seen by others. It is, rather, closer to the well-known statement by Sri Lankan ecumenist D. T. Niles: "Evangelism is one beggar telling another beggar where to find bread."[2] Some years ago I went with a group to the Rio Grande Valley of Texas. Hundreds of refugees from Honduras and El Salvador were being detained by the Immigration and Naturalization Service prior to deportation and the risk of their deaths in home countries. Pastor Feliberto Pereira, himself a refugee from Cuba, was known to all the detainees as one who would try to help them. When we arrived, I was stunned and just stepped back to watch as the people flocked to Feliberto, to greet him, to touch him, to thank him, to plead with him. It reminded me then of a scene in a movie about Jesus. It reminds me now of the sort of obvious gentleness Paul pictures.

Verse 5b. "The Lord is near." What an affirmation that is! When we think of the Parousia, the *second* coming, it is easy to distance that from our daily experience—except for those folk who watch the skies when a storm is approaching, as my grandmother used to do, hoping to see Jesus coming on a cloud (Acts 1:9–11), I suspect most people think of the expected return of Jesus Christ as a precious residue of days long gone by, if they think of it at all.

But if "the Lord is *near*," that is different. Yes, Paul never gave up his eschatological understanding of the Parousia. But, says Craddock, "it may also be taken in the sense of the present experience of the church."[3] Was Jesus present in an African man at a gypsum market in West Africa, in a hobo outside a Toddle House café in Texas, in the beloved Alberta Lunger when she walked into a room? It seemed that way to me.

Verse 6. This is a simple statement of something hard to do: "*Do not worry about anything, but in everything by prayer and supplication with thanksgiving let your requests be made known to God.*" It is interesting that Paul, who lauds prayer as the pathway to faith and joy and peace, who encloses his prayers for the churches in his letters, also says in Romans 8:26: "We do not know how to pray as we ought," clearly including himself among the deficient. The just-mentioned Alberta Lunger told a group her life had been crumbling and she could think of nothing else to do other than pray. We asked

2. D. T. Niles, cited in *The New York Times*, May 11, 1986, section 6, p. 38. Some versions of Niles's statement use "Christianity" instead of "Evangelism."
3. Craddock, *Philippians*, 21.

Philippians 4:4-7

Theological Perspective

prayer is no simple catchphrase designed to simply mask the terror, contingency, and uncertainty of their daily existence. It is a call to take those anxieties to God in prayer and allow God to refashion them. This prayer is not just the presentation of a wish list to God. This prayer is enriched, tempered, and qualified by "supplication and thanksgiving." Supplication suggests that the one who prays comes before God with supreme humility. This humility does not grow out of any doubt about the power of God to accomplish God's will, but the contrary. In the face of an omnipotent God, one can only be humble. Thanksgiving suggests that the one who prays comes before God with supreme gratitude. This gratitude does not grow out of any confidence in one's own worthiness, but the contrary. One can be truly grateful only to the extent that one acknowledges one's unworthiness before God. The humility implied by supplication and the confidence implied by thanksgiving are both necessary to the kind of prayer that will allow Paul's readers to "be careful for nothing" (v. 6 KJV).

Joy Brings Peace. The kind of joy and prayer to which Paul refers brings peace. This peace is not equivalent to the satisfaction of basic human needs, as important as these are. The satisfaction of basic human needs is a human striving and is within the will of God. However, the will of God is that we experience more than this satisfaction. Our joy cannot be complete without peace. This peace is found only, as the prophet Isaiah notes, in those whose minds are stayed on God (Isa. 26:3). Not only is this peace rooted in God; it is also a positive peace—not simply the absence of conflict or strife, but the active pursuit of a right relationship with God. But perhaps most important to this understanding of peace is Paul's wonderful notion that this is a peace "which passes all understanding." One could point to the idea that this Christian sort of peace is nonrational, suprarational, or perhaps even, irrational. However, the context of this phrase suggests that the focus is not on the relationship between Christian peace and secular notions of peace, even the *Pax Romana*. Rather, the phrase suggests that it is a peace that finds its ultimate fulfillment both within and somewhere beyond the realm of human reason. It is a peace that may pass our understanding but, in God's realm, is blessedly within our reach.

JAMES H. EVANS JR.

Pastoral Perspective

things, because of the grip they had upon him (Luke 18:18–23). For the dispossessed, gospel joy is liberation. For the privileged, it is relinquishment.

Although it starts from differing sides of experience, the spiritual dilemma that materialism poses for the dispossessed and the privileged may be similar. In their presence or their absence, neither material riches nor the yearning after them can deliver the happiness alleged. Both being "rich in things" and desiring to be rich in things can leave one "poor in soul," if happiness is seen as an end in itself rather than a byproduct of faithful living. In a sermon in which he adopted the persona of the apostle Paul, Martin Luther King Jr. addressed the problem of pursuing happiness rather than living the gospel: "The end of life is not to be happy. The end of life is not to achieve pleasure and avoid pain. The end of life is to do the will of God, come what may."[2]

The key to rejoicing without focusing on the individual pursuit of happiness as an end in itself may be found in verse 5: "Let your gentleness be known to everyone." Other translations for "gentleness" are "magnanimity" (NEB) and "consideration for others" (REB), and these alternatives speak to the communal and compassionate vocation of Christian communities.[3] An excerpt from a Communion liturgy captures the vision of the Christ's table where all are welcomed and mutual concern is manifest in the words "sharing by all will mean scarcity for none." By offering who we are and what we have, we can practice "consideration for others" and "rejoice in the Lord always." The Third Sunday of Advent is a good time to remember that both my grandmother and Martin Luther King were right. God wants us to be happy, but happiness is not the purpose of life; doing God's will is. As the joy candle is lit, give thanks for your gladness. Remember also all who are in sorrow, and care for them. Gospel joy is always shared joy.

PHILIP E. CAMPBELL

---

2. Martin Luther King Jr., *Strength to Love* (Philadelphia: Fortress Press, 1981), 144.
3. Morna D. Hooker, "Philippians," in *The New Interpreter's Bible*, vol. 11 (Nashville: Abingdon Press, 2005), 540.

they represent, do not undermine the "peace of God, which passes understanding" and "guards [his] heart and mind in Christ Jesus." When Paul invites the Philippians to such peace through prayer, he does so with the credibility of someone who has ample reason to be anxious but chooses prayer and peace.

Between the two exhortations to rejoice and to pray lies a less familiar one. Paul calls his friends to a gentleness (possibly "moderation") that they should display openly to the world (4:5). This outward-looking orientation "to all people" is Paul's remedy for these embattled Christians, both spiritually and communally. If Paul has faced his chains by celebrating the gospel's advance (1:14, 18) and by thinking of the Philippians' well-being over his own (1:24); and if Christ Jesus considered humanity's need more important than his divine status (2:6–8); then the Philippians ought to respond to their own strife and struggle by preferring the other in community (2:3) and keeping their collective eye on the waiting world outside (4:6). All this they should do because "the Lord is at hand"—both temporally in a forward-looking expectation and presently in a spiritual nearness. In the words of J.-F. Collange, "the solution to the problems of the Philippian church is not to be found in some kind of introspection but in a desire to turn outwards towards others."[1]

The text's beautiful last sentence—a direction of the mind to true and honorable and just and pure and lovely and gracious and excellent and praise-worthy things—offers the Philippians an alternative to endlessly orbiting around their suffering.

And so our weary Advent worshipers, not quite sure their life warrants rejoicing, have their encouraging answer: Fear not! For the joy we celebrate today is anchored, not in bright circumstances but in the Christ-aided direction of our minds toward joy, toward others, toward God in prayer, and toward God's best things. That is a joy that can withstand even the dark travails of Advent!

ALLEN HILTON

her how long it took her to get through. "Twenty years," she said. She taught many of us how to pray, encouraging us never to give up. I suspect it also took Paul a good long while to learn how to pray and to encourage the first-century and the twenty-first-century churches to do the same. He never gave up. Thanks be to God.

Verse 7. "And the peace of God, which passes all understanding, will guard your hearts and your minds in Christ Jesus." We often hear this text at funerals, and appropriately so. Deaths, especially tragic deaths, can leave us with our ability to understand the will of God completely shattered. All of us who have pastored have heard the crying "Why?"

We live in such an unbelievably violent time that we long for the presence of the Prince of Peace. We sing Advent hymns like "Christians all, your Lord is coming, hope for peace is now at hand," and then on Christmas Eve, we lift our candles in lullaby to the one who "sleeps in heavenly peace." Probably none of us think that this may have been the last peace that Jesus would know in this world, apart from that which came to him in prayer.

I was driving down the street one day with an old pastor friend and peace advocate in the car, and I am sure we were talking about great things. Suddenly he said, "Slow down, there's a school zone." He went on to say, "I still work on big issues and always will, but I'm paying more attention these days to little things, like casual meetings and driving in traffic, because I've come to realize that the peace I get there is the only peace I'm going to get in this world."

Why can we not live in peace? Are we destined to know only that peace "which passes all understanding"? Possibly. That peace is of God and it is good. It comes to us when we need it most and, with no other options, yield ourselves to God. The only way we will ever "understand" peace is one small act of peace at a time and welcoming the One who comes to us, the One who understands.

JOSEPH R. JETER

---

1. J.-F. Collange, *The Epistle of Saint Paul to the Philippians*, trans. A.W. Heathcote (London: Epworth, 1979), 144.

Luke 3:7-18

⁷John said to the crowds that came out to be baptized by him, "You brood of vipers! Who warned you to flee from the wrath to come? ⁸Bear fruits worthy of repentance. Do not begin to say to yourselves, 'We have Abraham as our ancestor'; for I tell you, God is able from these stones to raise up children to Abraham. ⁹Even now the ax is lying at the root of the trees; every tree therefore that does not bear good fruit is cut down and thrown into the fire."

¹⁰And the crowds asked him, "What then should we do?" ¹¹In reply he said to them, "Whoever has two coats must share with anyone who has none; and whoever has food must do likewise." ¹²Even tax collectors came to be baptized, and they asked him, "Teacher, what should we do?" ¹³He said to them, "Collect no more than the amount prescribed for you." ¹⁴Soldiers also asked him, "And

Theological Perspective

The passage for the Third Sunday of Advent confronts the preacher with some very cumbersome and complex tasks of interpretation for today's congregation. What do we make of the "brood of vipers" sayings? Or what possibly could the preacher say of the meaning of the "stones" out of which "God can raise up children to Abraham," or the "ax . . . at the root of the trees," or "unquenchable fire"? And to make the task even more challenging, how are we to speak of baptism in the Spirit (as if water baptism weren't a complicated enough topic in itself)?

Perhaps the best way to begin to theologize about this passage is to start from where things seem to be obvious and unambiguous, namely, from the Baptist's call for repentance in terms of practical ethical exhortations. The preacher from the desert addressed the crowd, tax collectors, and soldiers, with an uncompromising demand for fairness and justice. Generosity and unselfishness were the proper "fruit" of repentance. This is nothing less than a mental and spiritual U-turn, true *metanoia*. For the Baptist, repentance had less to do with how fervently one prays or how faithfully one attends the worship service; instead, it had everything to do with how one handled riches, executed public service, and exercised stewardship.

Pastoral Perspective

Luke describes John the Baptist's rhetorical method as *exhortation* (*parakalōn*, v. 18). This is to explain the mix of irony, hyperbole, criticism, warning, self-effacement, direction, and anticipation that appear in this story. This rhetoric feels as untamed as the wilderness prophet who speaks it. It wakes us up, directs us to repentance, and shows us the impossibility of this life so that we know our need for Jesus. A pastoral reading might begin from an exploration of John's rhetoric, of *parakalōn*.

Normally taken as finger-pointing direction to good behavior, the richer historic meaning of *parakalōn* is easily lost on modern hearers. For these urgent calls carry a fuller ethical intent than simple commands. They summon a way of being, an integrity of action, memory, and identity, that is not only compelling, but can even be comforting and reassuring. One exhorts others to act out of what they already know and affirm, out of the deepest values of the tradition and people that they claim, and that the exhorter claims with them. Exhortation binds exhorter to exhorted, and them together to values they share, in a way that simple command-and-response does not. As exhortation, proclamation of the gospel is a far richer rhetorical act than simply winning an

we, what should we do?" He said to them, "Do not extort money from anyone by threats or false accusation, and be satisfied with your wages."

¹⁵As the people were filled with expectation, and all were questioning in their hearts concerning John, whether he might be the Messiah, ¹⁶John answered all of them by saying, "I baptize you with water; but one who is more powerful than I is coming; I am not worthy to untie the thong of his sandals. He will baptize you with the Holy Spirit and fire. ¹⁷His winnowing fork is in his hand, to clear his threshing floor and to gather the wheat into his granary; but the chaff he will burn with unquenchable fire."

¹⁸So, with many other exhortations, he proclaimed the good news to the people.

Exegetical Perspective

Luke finally gives a sample of John's preaching. He has already declared John's role in preparing the people to avoid judgment; so to illustrate this he turns to John's message. This man, who prepared people for Christ's coming, still teaches preachers and congregations how to prepare for the Lord's coming.

The first part of the message is the pronouncement of verses 7–9. John denounces his hearers as a "brood of vipers," a term Matthew interprets as directed against the Sadducees and Pharisees (Matt. 3:7). Luke generalizes the saying to the "crowds," highlighting that this call to repentance is for everyone, not merely the leaders. The question that follows might be sarcastic, but since the people flock to hear John, it might also be a warning. God's wrath is coming, so John seeks to discern whether people will heed his warning. He follows his question with a practical exhortation to "bear fruit." In light of the coming day of judgment, God expects his people to behave, not merely believe. John does not immediately define this fruit, but goes on to attack one other comfort the people might hold to themselves, namely, proper bloodline.

Throughout their history, the people of Israel knew themselves to be the people of God as defined

Homiletical Perspective

No one wants to be chastised by John the Baptist this close to Christmas. No preacher wants to read this text when preparing for his third Advent sermon. No parishioner wants to be challenged by John's words as she sits in the pew enveloped in thoughts of final Christmas preparations and purchases. Again this Third Sunday of Advent, however, the lectionary delivers us to John and his challenging words from the wilderness.

There is no getting to Bethlehem and the sweet baby in the manger without first hearing the rough prophet in the wilderness call us to repentance. This seems the obvious and first point to take from this Luke 3 text. Trying to avoid or sugarcoat John's words is just not possible. Faithful and fruitful arrival at the manger will be possible only after the careful self-examination and recommitment called for by John. The Advent preacher may as well own up to this before moving forward with the text. Just as it could not have been easy for John to call the very crowds who were following him a "brood of vipers," so too it is not easy for the twenty-first-century Advent preacher to call the comfortably assembled, pre-Christmas worshipers to reprioritize and return to lives focused on the love of God and the love and care of neighbor.

Luke 3:7-18

Theological Perspective

This much is clear from the text without doubt. At the same time this may be the toughest part of the text. No wonder Advent preachers start busily looking for the "spiritual" meat in the text, something "deeper," something more upbuilding! It may be because, as the North African father Tertullian once noticed when commenting on this text: "Repentance [is] more competent to heathens than to Christians."[1] It seems as if this message is not for encouragement or consolation! Or is it? Is it not good news, *euangelion*, the gospel, to hear that a proper way to prepare for the Advent of the Humble Servant is to let the divine ax cut off our greed, self-indulgence, egoism, hypocrisy, and the like and throw them into the unquenchable fire of God's judgment?

The good news, the gospel, however, does not stop here—nor does it properly start here. In preparing the homily on this passage, the preacher who wants to tune into the Baptist's wavelength—and I dare to say, into the wavelength of the New Testament gospel—needs to wear simultaneously two hats, that of an *eschatologist* and that of an *ethicist*. The latter hat has already been placed on the pastor's head, so let us try the first one.

Everything about this text is eschatologically pregnant. It is about the *advent*, coming, appearance, arrival of something new, something unexpected. The text is filled with such language, familiar from the Old Testament apocalyptic literature: "coming wrath," "ax," "winnowing fork," "threshing floor," "unquenchable fire." The text is about the beginning of the end!

According to all the prophets, repentance is necessary for the entrance of the kingdom. Yes, any ethical U-turn is a desired end goal in itself in that it helps improve the personal, communal, social, and political conditions of this world—yet its "end" is yet to come. The Advent Sunday is but the beginning of God's unending eschatological advent. That's why church fathers such as Irenaeus spoke of two advents of the Savior, the first when Christ came as "a man subject to stripes" and the second when he comes "burning the chaff with unquenchable fire."[2] The Baptist's call for repentance lives in the dynamic of the eschatological tension. Then, and only then, bearing the fruit of repentance is of lasting value; the fruit of repentance becomes the "first fruit" of the harvest to come.

Pastoral Perspective

argument, convincing others to change their ways, or informing.[1]

Consider the irony and hyperbole with which John addresses those who had come out into the wilderness to be baptized. He is "proclaiming a baptism of repentance for the forgiveness of sins" (v. 3). The apocalyptic context is obvious, as John proclaims imminent judgment in expectation of imminent salvation in the coming Messiah. Irony enters, however, as John seems unsatisfied with success. John suspects the motives of those who have come out to ask for the very baptism he is "proclaiming." He calls them a brood of snakes. "Who warned you to flee from the wrath to come?" he asks (v. 7). Ironically, it may have been John himself.

This is not an evangelistic approach to try at home. For these are not mere bystanders. They are people who have come to him—folks who are likely to join, and even to pledge during the next stewardship campaign. They are the joiners. While John's name-calling tactic might not be the best choice today, a preacher may nevertheless be called to challenge even these joiners to deeper levels of self-reflection and repentance than they have walked in the door prepared to perform.

Matthew's version sets John in conflict with the Pharisees, who used status, learning, and accomplishment as ways of weakening John's exhortations: "Do not begin to say to yourselves, 'We have Abraham as our ancestor'; for I tell you, God is able from these stones to raise up children to Abraham" (v. 8). Yet the presence of soldiers in Luke suggests that the conflict is also between Jews and Gentiles more broadly, implying that Jews were claiming pride of place by virtue of Abraham. There is a certain satisfaction in seeing an oppressed people taking a place of privilege against soldiers of their oppressors. Yet John shouts that before God, the repentance of each is as important as the other. This is a call to take stock of the ways we hide behind tradition, national or ecclesial identity, wealth, ethnicity, or position. We are all liable to God's judgment, as the ax is at the tree. We are all called to bear fruit as part of our repentance.

John calls the good works that make hearers worthy of their baptism "fruit" borne from the tree of their lives. It is not enough lazily to claim oneself the fruit of Abraham (or of the Roman army). It is not enough to presume that because one is a child of the

---

1. Tertullian, *On Modesty* 10, in *Ante-Nicene Fathers*, 10 vols. (Grand Rapids: Eerdmans, 1988), 4:84.
2. Irenaeus, *Against the Heresies* 4.333.1, in *Ante-Nicene Fathers*, 10 vols. (Grand Rapids: Eerdmans, 1988), 1:506.

1. See Wesley D. Avram, "Exhortation," in Thomas O. Sloane, ed., *Encyclopedia of Rhetoric* (New York: Oxford University Press, 2001), 279–83.

Exegetical Perspective

by being descendants of Abraham through Jacob. John now removes this security from them. His grammar forbids them to even *begin* to comfort themselves with their history. Instead, he forces each hearer to a personal decision, not one resting on a communal heritage. His next statement reveals the power of God, for God need not depend upon human heritage for a people; instead, the God who made humans from dust can craft a *faithful* people even from the rocks. The key here is faithfulness (i.e., "fruit"): Abraham was characterized by his faith, so to be a true child of Abraham, one must also exhibit such faithfulness. For failure, the threat of judgment looms ever closer, graphically depicted as an ax at the roots of a tree (parallel to Jesus' parable in Luke 13:6–9). John's syntax points to the imminence of this judgment: the people of Israel are not promised more time; instead, they are warned that judgment is ready. After 2,000 years we may read this warning with apathy, but the warning is as potent today as it was then. We do not know when the ax of judgment may fall, so true believers must always seek to live faithfully.

The next verses, 10–14, form a triple pattern. Three groups, the crowd, the tax collectors, and the soldiers, ask John what they must do. Each group receives a practical answer: care for the needy and practice truth and justice. John says not a word about ritual, about the temple, about sacrifice. Whether or not Luke's John knows the final sacrifice that will be entailed in the Messiah's ministry (see John 1:29), it is clear that his message concerns social justice more than religious ceremony. We should note, however, that he commands each group slightly differently, according to their roles and possessions. He admonishes the crowds to share their wealth, whether food or clothing, with those less fortunate. They are not commanded to distribute everything they have and thus become the needy and the naked, but to share from their excess, however minimalistically defined. He commands the tax collectors to be fair and honest in their work in a field known for its corruption and greed. The soldiers, a surprising group of participants, are warned about the greed that their position enabled them to act upon. Contentment is never an easy lesson, particularly when we have the means to attain what we wish, but it is a crucial fruit of repentance, for it reveals a steadfast trust in God and God's work and will.

Ultimately, because of the dynamism of John's preaching, his audience begins to hope that he is not merely the one sent to prepare, but the coming one

Homiletical Perspective

Two themes stand out as possible directions for a sermon on this text.

First, one could focus on the question asked of John three different times in this short passage. First crowds, then tax collectors, and finally soldiers ask John, "What should we do?" John's advice to all of them is very practical and pointed. His answers reflect his knowledge of the vocations and values of those who ask the question, and his answers all involve acts of mercy and justice. In response to the question, "what should we do?" John is clearly saying, share, keep no more than you need, be fair, treat others with care, and be honest. Twenty-first-century Christians are asking the same question of their preachers, of their church, of their faith. Advent, a season of preparation and self-examination, is a perfect time to address this question head-on in a sermon. As Christians prepare for Christmas, maybe more than any other time of the year they are outwardly focused. Churches and charities receive more donations in December than any other month of the year (in part because of the tax benefit, I know, but also because of Christmas-season generosity). The people gathered in the pews on the Third Sunday of Advent are eager to bear fruit. This text offers the preacher the opportunity to share practical and personal examples of how the faithful might act toward others in ways that reflect the faith we have in our saving Lord, whom we anxiously await during Advent. John's responses had to have been tough to follow. He instructed the crowds, the tax collectors, and the soldiers to make unselfish choices, to live within their means, and to do what is just. This instruction from John certainly would translate well in most mainline churches today. Advent worshipers could leave with a clearer sense of how they are called to live with answers to "what should we do?"

Second, one could engage Advent worshipers in a sermon that focuses on the meaning of baptism and offers an opportunity for the reaffirmation of baptism in worship. One does not ordinarily think of baptism or reaffirmation of baptism as important elements in Advent worship. However, this rich text begs the connection. What better way to help worshipers truly prepare their hearts and lives to receive the Christ child than to have them reaffirm their baptismal vows and remember the life to which they each were called when they passed through the baptismal waters?

In the denomination in which I serve, the liturgy for reaffirmation of baptism, just as in the liturgy of

Luke 3:7-18

Theological Perspective

Eschatology, as much as any other theological topic, has been mishandled in Christian preaching. The Advent passage at hand is a critical reminder to the preacher of the need to avoid two easy and often-tried mistaken strategies. (1) Eschatological urgency aside, as is the case in much of bourgeois *Kulturprotestantismus* (Protestantism adapted to the needs of modern culture), the Baptist's call for repentance is easily reduced to a "world-improvement" program, a.k.a. classical liberalism, which thinks of Jesus mostly or even only as an ethical teacher. (2)Eschatology divorced from its this-worldly and ethical rootedness, as is the case in much of fundamentalistic *Left Behind* mentality, writes off the ethical demand with a spiritualization strategy that leads to an escapist "safe exit" strategy from this world.

The Advent passage reminds us of the strange figure of the Baptist, who took the advent of the Messiah so dead seriously that nothing less than complete *metanoia* with an ethical U-turn was required. At the same time, the Advent passage presents to us the desert preacher who tied the advent of the Messiah to the eschatological advent of God. To that context belongs the promise of the baptism with the Spirit and fire. It is going to be an eschatological Spirit baptism. Whatever else the Spirit baptism may mean, in this passage it is a judging and cleansing act. Fire, of course, speaks here—as in much of the rest of the Bible—of judgment and purification; as Karl Barth succinctly put it, "Baptism with the Spirit is concretely the divine cleansing and reorientation of men."[3]

Because of the way this paragraph ends, some interpreters may be tempted (!) to engage the theological debate about various interpretations of Spirit baptism—from Barth's equation of it with the whole process of salvation, to the Pentecostals' understanding of Spirit baptism as subsequent to new birth in terms of empowerment, to some Catholic charismatics' effort to hold on to both. Pentecost Sunday, with its reference to the beginnings of the church and pouring out of the Spirit, would provide preachers an opportunity for that discussion. This passage, for Advent, however, in my opinion, is not a viable place to engage that topic, since it easily leads the homilist away from the main concern discussed above: the ethical/eschatological or eschatological/ethical dynamic of the Advent theme.

VELI-MATTI KÄRKKÄINEN

Pastoral Perspective

church, a "good citizen," or a person of status, one is secure before God. Don't confuse sitting on the limb with being either the tree or its fruit. For the tree might not be so strong or fruitful as one thinks. Shifting the metaphor, it might be more a snake than a tree. Recall that John does not call his hearers vipers; he calls them a brood of vipers. The "brood" (*gennēmata*) are the children, produce, even *fruit*.

The use of "brood" links the name calling to the question about who warned them to flee the wrath to come. Surely the snakes from whom they had come could not have. On whom, then, must they depend for the exhortation they need? Is the accusation here against his hearers, or against their *ancestry*, their *authority*, or, by extension, their *tradition*?

Whose message is strong enough to lead us to the repentance to which we are called? Not the church's, for it is too much a snake pit. Not our own insight, for we are as needy as anyone in the crowd—hoarding coats and food when others are in need (v. 11). We are as the tax collectors—dependent upon unjust structures for our livelihood. We are as the occupying army—caught in a culture of exploitation and violence.

The exhortation: be a *tree*, by bearing fruit of integrity by sharing (v. 11), by caring for persons in your charge (v. 13), by acting with equity and justice (v. 14). Yet also be *fruit*, part of a fertile tree. Bind yourself to the only proclamation that can truly lead you to the repentance to which baptism calls you. It is not in the wake-up call, or the mission statement, or the preaching alone that we will be brought to the fruitful garden where the snake can no longer tempt us and the ax cannot threaten. It is in the One who does more than water the tree. It is in the One who is the life of the tree itself, its metaphorical fire. It is in the One who is coming.

This is pastoral exhortation, calling our hearers back to what they have claimed in their baptism, and uniting the church in a call to integrity, self-reflection, mutual confession, and openness to the One who puts in us our Advent hope.

WESLEY D. AVRAM

---

3. Karl Barth, *Church Dogmatics*, IV/4, ed. G. W. Bromiley and T. F. Torrance (Edinburgh: T. & T. Clark, 1936–1981), 30.

himself. It is quite probable that John is asked this on more than one occasion. Messianic hopes were prevalent at the time, so a charismatic preacher who teaches repentance and judgment and does not fear to speak against the powers of the day (cf. v. 19) would raise people's hopes. Instead, John, in verse 16 confirms his position as preparer, contrasting his ministry with that of "the one who will come." John's baptism of water is a symbol for repentance, but the coming one's baptism will be a baptism of power. Previously, the Holy Spirit settled on individuals to empower them for ministry (cf. Saul or David), but soon those who see and accept the true Messiah will be baptized in it and empowered for life accordingly.

John follows this promise, however, with another warning, again drawn from agriculture. He depicts the Messiah holding a winnowing fork, prepared to sort the wheat, those who have truly repented and have borne the proper fruit, from the chaff, those who failed to heed the warnings of John and so continue their own selfish lifestyles. "Burning," of course, indicates punishment, a fate contrasted with the positive image of being "gathered" into the barn. It is interesting to note the two opposing uses of "fire" in verses 16 and 17. First, "fire" (*pyr*) indicates one of the baptisms of the coming Messiah, standing apposite the "Holy Spirit" as an image. In verse 17, however, this fire (*pyr*) brings about the destruction of those who failed to repent and obey.

Ultimately, Luke summarizes John's message as good news (*euangelizō*), thereby including it within the good news of Jesus' life, death, and resurrection. Indeed, John's is not a separate message from that which Christ preached. Before one can receive the Spirit, before one can understand that Christ is Messiah, one must repent from self-sufficiency. Repentance is defined as humble obedience, the natural result of meeting with God and accepting the truth of the gospel. Consistently throughout Scripture, God called his people to repent, a call still resonating. John, as prophet to Jesus, teaches that repentance entails a life characterized by honesty and concern for those in need.

MARIAM J. KAMELL

adult baptism and profession of faith, includes questions in which believers are asked to renounce sin and evil and to turn to God in Christ. Additionally, believers are asked if they will promise to live as faithful disciples of Jesus Christ.[1] This is exactly what John commands those who followed him into the desert. Repent! Turn around and return to God! And when they ask what their lives should look like when they have followed his commands, he tells them to live generously and justly.

A colleague always addresses the infant after he has baptized her, saying, "Little child, you belong to God; you always have and you always will, and now the mark of Christ is upon you." It is the meaning of this mark that John called his followers to embrace. John wanted to ensure that those who had followed him into the wilderness were aware of the serious life-altering consequences of being baptized. John cautioned folks truly to understand the demands placed upon them once they had been marked. And he cautioned the crowds about the one who was still to come, Jesus the Messiah, whose baptizing and call would be "changing you from the inside out" (v. 16 *The Message*). This is what the church of Jesus Christ believes about baptism today. We are cleansed, renewed, and changed forever. We believe we are sent from the font to serve.

The preacher might ask fellow worshipers, "Can anyone tell, by observing our lives, that we bear the mark of Christ and are living as his faithful disciples?" We must, according to John, live the faith we claim to possess. Authentic Christian living always has that challenge. "It's your *life* that must change, not your skin. . . . What counts is your life" (vv. 8–9 *The Message*). While this may not be the challenge worshipers have come to hear in Advent worship, it is what John the Baptist offers.

This text of challenge and instruction is rich in opportunity for the preacher weary of another Advent Sunday with John the Baptist.

KATHY BEACH-VERHEY

---

1. Theology and Worship Ministry Unit, "Reaffirmation of the Baptismal Covenant for a Congregation," in *Book of Common Worship* (Louisville, KY: Westminster John Knox Press, 1993), 466.

Micah 5:2-5a

²But you, O Bethlehem of Ephrathah,
   who are one of the little clans of Judah,
from you shall come forth for me
   one who is to rule in Israel,
whose origin is from of old,
   from ancient days.
³Therefore he shall give them up until the time
   when she who is in labor has brought forth;
then the rest of his kindred shall return
   to the people of Israel.
⁴And he shall stand and feed his flock in the strength of the LORD,
   in the majesty of the name of the LORD his God.
And they shall live secure, for now he shall be great
   to the ends of the earth;
⁵and he shall be the one of peace.

Theological Perspective

As we approach Christmas on this Fourth Sunday of Advent, we hear from the eighth-century prophet Micah, who, make no mistake, is not happy. In his day, there was not "peace on earth, goodwill to all." No, the world was not as it should be—not as God intended it to be. He speaks for many of the children of Israel in the southern kingdom of Judah, made anxious and insecure by the external threat of invasion by the Assyrians and the internal threat of the loss of home and hearth at the hands of their own leaders in Jerusalem. Here Micah asserts that God does not accept this state of affairs and will send a leader to set things right. However, this leader will come from a surprising place and rule in an astonishing way.

Historians tell us that many in Judah suffered displacement and economic hardship after the fall of the northern kingdom in 722. To keep Assyria at bay, rulers of Judah paid tribute for several generations and evidently passed those expenses on to the poor. In addition, refugees flooded into Jerusalem and elsewhere in the southern kingdom from the north and from territories Sennacherib, the Assyrian king, sliced off from Judah and gave to the Philistines. In a time when resources were not plentiful, the increased population and need for more food

Pastoral Perspective

Among the most beloved of Old Testament texts, these extraordinary verses in Micah speak hope to despair with a clarity and power that is nothing less than thrilling. Micah concedes that the situation is grim: the nation is in extreme distress, Jerusalem is under siege, and the king has suffered humiliation. The people see no hope. But Micah sees hope. He sees beyond the current circumstance to what God is promising to do. Our God is a God of promises, and Micah is God's messenger. Despite the evidence of despair and defeat that is everywhere present, the messenger gives speech to the future God has guaranteed.

And, oh, what a future! It includes a ruler like no other, return from exile, food, and peace. The best is summed up in this marvelous phrase: "and they shall live secure" (v. 4b). Security. This is the thrilling substance of our Advent hope. In this manifestly insecure world, marred by terror, war, poverty, accident, tsunami, and the ordinary but nonetheless anguishing events of old age, illness, and death, our God promises a security that the world cannot give.

North Americans have this in common with ancient Israelites: a sense of insecurity pervades our lives. Like the ancients we typically look toward perceived seats of power for rescue, hoping that our

Exegetical Perspective

Micah 5:2–5a is a messianic poem that combines the royal imagery of a strong Davidic ruler with the picture of a peaceful shepherd of a restored community. The Hebrew of this passage is quite difficult and obscure in both its vocabulary and syntax. Its fragmentary or overly terse economy of words causes English translations to differ widely from one another. While the lectionary's timing expresses the ancient Christian reading of the text as an anticipation of Jesus, it will help preachers to know the social location of its first audience.

The book of Micah is attributed to a prophet from Moresheth who prophesied during the reigns of the Judean kings Jotham, Ahaz, and Hezekiah (ca. 740 to at least 727 and perhaps as late as 698 BCE). During this time the Near East was dominated by the Neo-Assyrian Empire, which conquered and deported much of the northern kingdom of Israel in the decades prior to its final defeat in 722. Micah (or his editors) also likely witnessed the utter devastation of the southern kingdom of Judah in 701 by the Assyrian king Sennacherib, who claims to have taken "forty-six strong cities" and countless smaller towns from Hezekiah's embattled nation and to have besieged Jerusalem. Micah's first three chapters are mainly oracles of doom and

Homiletical Perspective

When Micah took up his pen to write this book in 735 BCE, David had been dead almost three centuries. But his reign would survive throughout all of Israel's history, down to the present moment, as the messianic model. David would come again, and his second coming would extend even the empire he established long ago. Micah was weary with the spirit of idolatry that permeated the eighth century BCE. The injustice of the nation's judges and the corruption of its priests had set a yearning in the hearts of the decent believers to anticipate the coming of the Messiah, a new David. As the first David had hailed from Bethlehem, so would the final glorious messiah-king, David.

But war was at hand, and the prophet reminded them of the horrors of battle and siege that were surely on the way. "Marshal your troops, O city of troops" (Mic. 5:1 NIV). Such is the common cry of international politics. It always has been, it always will be. The only hope of blessing the nations is for the nations to see that Micah 5:1 has never been a solution to the long-term cycles of war and peace. Toynbee's march of civilizations—twenty-eight of them now—sees the beginning of every civilization rising in the triumph of war, and dissolving in the horror of siege.

Micah 5:2-5a

Theological Perspective

encouraged landowners to lower wages and expand their properties.[1]

The trickle-down effects of these conditions were, according to Micah, deadly. The "heads of Jacob and rulers of the house of Israel" coveted and seized fields, oppressed small farmers and pushed them off their land, took bribes, and generally declared "war against those who put nothing into their mouths" (2:1–9; 3:2–11).

For this kind of treatment, YHWH did not choose the people of Israel and give them the land of Canaan. God's promise to Abraham of a land, protection, and blessing came with the stipulations, through Moses, that the people and their leaders would not covet, steal, deceive, and murder. Though the rulers, priests, and prophets in his day believed that the Lord was with them and that "no harm shall come upon us," Micah countered, "Because of you Zion shall be plowed as a field; Jerusalem shall become a heap of ruins" (3:12).

Micah also announces that a new and different kind of ruler is on the way. The new leader is to come not from Jerusalem, the city of David the king, but from Bethlehem, the small, rural village where David the peasant was born (5:2). This ruler will come from humble origins, as had David. There will be then a reversal. The poor outside Jerusalem will have a champion. During the time of Hannah and Elkanah, parents of Samuel, "there was no king in Israel; all the people did what was right in their own eyes" (Judg. 21:25). In her prayer Hannah looked forward to a just king, because YHWH "raises up the poor from the dust; he lifts the needy from the ash heap" (1 Sam. 2:8). YHWH led her son, Samuel, to two peasants— Saul and David—to do just that. And they did—until the temptations of power overtook them.

Micah is convinced that, once again, YHWH will act on behalf of those who are unjustly subjugated, exploited, and demoralized—even if it the perpetrators are the royal successors of David. He believed, with Dr. King, that "the arc of the moral universe is long but it bends toward justice."[2]

However, the nature of the future ruler differs from the kind of warrior king Saul and then David became; this ruler will be "one of peace" (5:5a). Through this one, YHWH "shall judge between

1. Delbert R. Hillers, *Micah: A Commentary on the Book of the Prophet Micah* (Philadelphia: Fortress Press, 1984), 2–8.
2. Martin Luther King Jr., "Where Do We Go from Here?" Eleventh Anniversary Convention of the Southern Christian Leadership Conference in Atlanta on August 16, 1967, from Philip S. Foner, *The Voice of Black America* (New York: Simon & Schuster, 1972); also available online at http://www.stanford.edu/group/King/publications/speeches/Where_do_we_go_from_here.html.

Pastoral Perspective

leaders will see to our needs and to the needs of the most vulnerable among us. Or we look toward established professionals (doctors, lawyers, bankers, public engineers, clergy) to protect us from what threatens and makes us feel vulnerable.

Yet, while we are looking toward prime ministers and presidents, satraps and senators, Micah is jumping up and down, waving his arms, desperately trying to point us in an entirely different direction. He is pointing to a small, out-of-the-way place: a town called Bethlehem. He is pointing to a leader who stands "in the strength of the LORD" (v. 4), rather than in the strength of weapons or power or wealth or territory. Here is a difference that makes a difference.

It takes one's breath away, this promise. In these few verses, tucked away in a slim prophetic book, Micah captures the ache with which we live each day and the hope that is in us for a future that only God can deliver. Life is precarious, and so too are the so-called securities we purchase with our dollars and in which we place so much trust: insurance policies, savings accounts, credit cards, physicians, and elected officials. Like us, they are here today but gone tomorrow.

Christians understand God's provision of true security in the One whose birth the church is soon to celebrate. Christ is our security. He is bread for our hunger, drink for our thirst, and life for our death.

It is fitting on this Sunday that the pastor imitate the prophet Micah by pointing to stories in which hope and help have come from unexpected quarters and unlikely people. For instance, today's Gospel reading from Luke describes a meeting between Mary and Elizabeth, two cousins with no pretensions to greatness. Mary visits Elizabeth in an unnamed city "in the hill country." Yet a babe leaps, the Holy Spirit turns up, and Elizabeth, sensing the wonder of what is occurring, cannot hide her astonishment that God's blessing and presence would deign to visit her humble abode.

The pastor may then point to other stories in which rescue and hope have arrived in unlikely ways. These can be small stories (the neighbor who brought relief to an ill elder) or larger (the community activist who started the soup kitchen) or even larger (the Brazilian rubber tapper who took on corporate giants[1]). The point is that Micah inspires

1. Chico Mendes was a Brazilian rubber tapper and labor leader. In 1988 he was slain by a group of powerful ranchers for what the *New York Times* called "defending the forest."

condemnation appropriate to this period. Later tradition (Jer. 26:18–19) reports that Micah prophesied the destruction of Jerusalem, as recorded in 3:12: "Zion shall be plowed as a field, Jerusalem shall become a heap of ruins." Since Jerusalem did not fall until 586 BCE, an eighth-century prophecy would seem premature. Chapters 4–5 are oracles of a hopeful future, which includes the promise (4:10) that God will rescue Zion after exile in Babylon rather than Assyria. Apart from some conservative scholars, most critical scholars accordingly argue that this pericope, part of the longer unit of 4:1–5:9, is exilic or postexilic in date.

This prophetic oracle begins with God's direct address to Bethlehem (5:2). The reference to the Judean clan of Ephrathah explicitly links the coming ruler to the ancestral house of King David, who was "the son of an Ephrathite of Bethlehem in Judah, named Jesse" (1 Sam. 17:12; see Ruth 1:2 and 4:11). Some translations identify Bethlehem as "the least of the clans" rather than "one of the little clans of Judah," just as David was the youngest or "least" (NRSV "youngest") of the eight sons of Jesse (1 Sam. 16:11). The favorable prophecy of "one who is to rule (môšel) in Israel" (v. 2b) on God's behalf provides a sharp contrast to the previous verse's humiliating image of the ruler (šôpet) of Israel being struck on the cheek with a rod (5:1b). The one who "shall come forth" (yṣ') (v. 2b) is identified by the same verb that describes the appearance of a Davidic messiah in Isaiah 11:1: "A shoot shall come out (wĕyāṣā') from the stump of Jesse." The related Hebrew word translated "whose origin" (môṣā'ōtāyw) (v. 2c) does not appear elsewhere in the Bible (cf. Ps. 19:6), but it refers to the dynasty founded by David. The phrases "of old" and "from ancient days" also describe the ancient lineage of the great eleventh-century king of Israel. Yet, for all of its royal and Davidic imagery, the text seems purposefully to avoid the title of "king" (melek) in describing the Israelite leader (cf. Mic. 4:7).

The beginning of verse 3 is odd, but the Hebrew text implies that God will deliver up Israel to persecution until "she who is in labor has brought forth" (yôledâ yaladâ) the anticipated new ruler. The woman in labor (yôledâ) also appears in Micah 4:9–10 as daughter Zion, who writhes in agony and is exiled to Babylon, where she will be rescued and redeemed by God. Verse 3 states that "the rest of his kindred shall return to the people of Israel" after her delivery. As an eighth-century oracle, this text could prophesy the return of the deported northern and southern tribes of Israel after the Assyrian invasions

Micah's promise, though he saw only the mystical outline of things to come, was that, in the closing years of what we would later call the pre-Christian era, a very small town would call the grand centers of empire to a new idea. Instead of another boring, bloody generalissimo, there would arise a shepherd king: "And he shall stand and feed his flock in the strength of the LORD" (5:4). Judah's harvest center, Bethlehem ("house of bread"), a small village, would place a shepherd king in the very center of history's long line of tyrants and despots. But God would be clear with this prediction. It would not be just any old Bethlehem—this Bethlehem would be the one located in the smaller region of Ephrathah.

The best prophecy always gets specific with its zip codes. The address of the Messiah is certain. Out of the myriad villages (and most villages of ancient Israel were thought to have about a thousand inhabitants), here was the specific place that offered the world a new way of establishing the peace. The point is that this specific Bethlehem in Ephrathah was the place where the international shepherd king would rise.

It is hard for us to imagine impressive historical heroes as coming from very small towns. We are all a bit guilty of the Nathanael syndrome. When Philip told Nathanael that he had found the Messiah, Nathanael replied, "Can anything good come out of Nazareth?" (John 1:46). Philip certainly was smug. "Now Philip was from Bethsaida, the city of Andrew and Peter" (John 1:44). You would think that, being from a nowhere place, Philip could see the glory of nowhere places. There is wonderful mystery in God's supply of heroes. Strategic babies may be born just about anywhere. Bethlehem is proof of that. Every baby is a potential king. Jesus is proof of that. Bethlehem was a one-camel town, "one of the thousands," but it was over these simple fields that Ruth the Moabite gleaned for heads of broken grain. Here in Nowheresville, Judah, David tended sheep and wrote poetry. And here it was that shepherds were startled that even they could get in the history books if the time was just right and it happened to be their turn to do the midnight shift with the sheep. Bethlehem within the space of half an hour would know more angels than Rome saw in a thousand years of its existence. Why all this angelic folderol?

Micah reminds us that God is just doing God's constant biblical task of saving the world. God did it with one small nation called Israel and one small town named Bethlehem. But the metaphor

Micah 5:2-5a

Theological Perspective

many peoples, and shall arbitrate between strong nations far away; they shall beat their swords into plowshares, and their spears into pruning hooks; nation shall not lift up sword against nation, neither shall they learn war any more" (4:3). This ruler will resolve the conflicts between and among the nations diplomatically, through arbitration. There will be no need for swords or spears, because there will be no need for war. The residents in those nations, including the beleaguered peasants of rural Judah, "shall sit under their own vines . . . and no one shall make them afraid" (4:4). This one will usher in an era of international and domestic harmony, and the flock of Israel will be fed "in the strength of the LORD" (5:4).

No, according to Micah, this ruler will bring peace not with a sword, which might suggest that the ruler brings peace with arbitration, diplomacy, and service. He will feed his flock in the strength of the Lord. It is, evidently, a strength of a different sort than many in his day imagined. It is a strength that shows itself in service. It is a notion of power or strength that corresponds to that of Jesus. When he was asked by his disciples to allow them to sit at his right hand—the place of power or strength—Jesus responded, "Among the Gentiles those whom they recognize as their rulers lord it over them, and their great ones are tyrants over them. But it is not so among you; but whoever wishes to become great among you must be your servant" (Mark 10:42–43).

Micah's people saw so much greed and deception in high places. Could they believe with him that "the arc of the moral universe bends toward justice"? Could they believe that "the one of peace," whose only weapon is gentleness, would win for them security and safety, when they experienced so much violence around them? Could they believe that someone from little, out-of-the-way Bethlehem would be "great to the ends of the earth"? Can we?

STEPHEN B. BOYD

Pastoral Perspective

us to look for God's activity in people and places that are off the map, in the Bethlehems and the stables of our world and lives. We are invited to follow the prophet's gaze and so turn our full attention to God. It is the pastor's joy and responsibility to be ever vigilant as to where God is acting and to keep an ear cocked for those through whom God is speaking. More often than not, God is in the nooks and crannies, the alleys and kitchens. Advent's call then is a call to eyes, ears, and hearts that are trained to expect the unexpected and to listen for the least likely voices.

In addition, the pastor may wish to assign for this Sunday the Christmas carol "O Little Town of Bethlehem." The carol's story begins with a simple visit to Bethlehem but has grown to stretch around the world. On Christmas Eve in 1865, a young Episcopal priest named Phillips Brooks approached Bethlehem on horseback and then worshiped in its ancient Basilica of the Nativity. The simplicity and beauty of the service made a lasting impression on him. Three years later, while he was serving as the rector of Holy Trinity Church in Philadelphia, the Sunday school children asked Brooks to write a new Christmas song. The memory of his Christmas Eve in Bethlehem came rushing back, and he penned the words in a single evening. On Christmas morning in 1868 the little children of Holy Trinity first sang a song that has become one of the best loved of all the carols.

It took years for the carol to wend its way into the hearts of Christians around the world. As it did so, the priest who crafted its words grew to become one of the great preachers of the nineteenth century. Large of stature at six foot four, Phillips Brooks grew to be even larger in his theological and moral reach.

The pastor might consider inviting a child to read these stirring words of assurance from Micah. Or why not invite a children's choir to sing the carol? Hope often comes to us softly. The sound of children's voices is a reminder to us of the Child to whom the ancient texts point: the One who brought everlasting light to our dark streets; the One who alone is our security.

NANCY S. TAYLOR

Exegetical Perspective

(745–701 BCE), when a new messianic king of peace would appear (Isa. 9:2–7 and 11:1–5). Historically, no such return of refugees occurred. As a sixth-century oracle, this passage would seemingly predict the restoration of the Davidic dynasty after the return of Judeans from Babylon, beginning in 538 BCE (cf. Amos 9:11; Hos. 3:5). Since the Davidic monarchy was not restored at that time, this text has been applied by later Jews and Christians to an expected time of troubles preceding the messianic age. In the NT, Matthew 2:6 very roughly paraphrases Micah 5:2–4 to explain the birth of Jesus in Bethlehem as a fulfillment of this prophecy (cf. John 7:42).

The description of the messiah's reign in verse 4 is difficult in the Hebrew. The phrase "And he shall stand and feed his flock" translates just two Hebrew words: "And-he-will-stand and-he-will-shepherd" (*w'md wr'h*). The phrase "feed his flock" does not appear in the Hebrew. The shepherd is a common metaphor for kingship throughout ancient Near Eastern royal literature, and the metaphor is more fully developed in Ezekiel 34:1–24. The gentler image of God as a protective shepherd is effectively evoked in Psalm 23, as well as in Isaiah 40:11: "He will feed his flock like a shepherd; he will gather the lambs in his arms, and carry them in his bosom, and gently lead the mother sheep." Although the common royal and divine imagery of a shepherd is appropriate to the messianic context, it also evokes David's actual boyhood role in Jesse's house (1 Sam. 17:34; 2 Sam. 7:8).

The second half of verse 4 is rather opaque. The NJPS translation—"And they will dwell [secure]"—conveys the fragmentary quality of the line. Indeed, some scholars amend the text from "they will dwell" (*wyšbw*) to "they will return" (*wyšwbw*). Combined with the following verb, "he shall be great," the phrase suggests the safety of the reunited people and the greatness of their king, but the uneven Hebrew poetry is far from clear. The passage concludes (5a) with a royal or messianic title, "the one of peace" (*zh šlwm*). This title is similar to the Prince of Peace (*sr šlwm*), attributed to the ideal Davidic king by another eighth-century Judean prophet, Isaiah (9:6), in the lectionary reading for Christmas Eve.

NEAL WALLS

Homiletical Perspective

suggested in Micah 5:3 is that if God was the Father of the dream, Israel, at least at Christmas, should be celebrated as the Mother. It is hard for us to stretch our mind around this idea, for Mary forever remains the blessed mother of Christ. Almost every time the Bible speaks of Mary it refers to her as blessed—but equally blessed was the nation. It is odd how nations tend to take on the names of relatives. With Germany it was the Fatherland. With the United States it is Uncle Sam. Those who live in the land of the great bear call their nation Mother Russia. In this passage, Israel the son becomes mother Israel. It is she, not the virgin mother of our Lord, who endures the birth pangs that precede the incarnation. This more national metaphor seems to see how Israel, the people of God, has always been the promised parent. When Israel's travail of birth is over, the kingdom will be born. Then all of the world's people—every tribe and nation—will come back to join the messianic family. The world will be one.

Then will end the ruthless game tyrants have always played. The game is this: if I kill all my enemies, the only ones left on earth will be my friends. The real name of this game is genocide. When Hitler tried to rid himself of the Jews, this was his rationale. When the American frontiersmen tried to rid themselves of the Cheyenne, this was their motive. When the terrible enemies of the Masai wanted to stamp them out, this was the rationale. When the Shiites thought to eliminate the Sunni in Iraq, this was their rationale. But when at last the shepherd prince issues from the birth canal of mother Israel, "He will stand and shepherd his flock in the strength of the LORD, in the majesty of the name of the LORD his God. And they will live securely, for then his greatness will reach to the ends of the earth. And he will be their peace" (vv. 4–5a, NIV).

CALVIN MILLER

Psalm 80:1-7

¹Give ear, O Shepherd of Israel,
  you who lead Joseph like a flock!
 You who are enthroned upon the cherubim, shine forth
² before Ephraim and Benjamin and Manasseh.
  Stir up your might,
    and come to save us!

³Restore us, O God;
  let your face shine, that we may be saved.

⁴O Lᴏʀᴅ God of hosts,
  how long will you be angry with your people's prayers?
⁵You have fed them with the bread of tears,
  and given them tears to drink in full measure.
⁶You make us the scorn of our neighbors;
  our enemies laugh among themselves.

⁷Restore us, O God of hosts;
  let your face shine, that we may be saved.

Theological Perspective

The psalmist cries out on behalf of a hurt and beleaguered Israel, a nation both captive and divided. "Give ear, O Shepherd of Israel. . . . Stir up your might, and come to save us!" The plea begins with an insistent demand that God listen, be attentive, and really hear this community's cry for deliverance. The desperate tone indicates that God has stretched Israel's patience beyond its limits. Waiting is at an end, hope is exhausted, and God must act now. The unsparing full-throatedness of this communal lament expresses both the darkness of the present reality and the character of Israel's relationship with God—a relationship of trusting intimacy unfettered by convention. Lament is also protest. It is an honest bewailing of an intolerable situation, an exposure of culpability, and a demand for restoration.

The first two verses invoke a God whom Israel has known in the past as shepherd, and acknowledges in the present as enthroned in majesty. Israel's experience of God gives rise to expectations for the future—only the future is now, it is immanent. Familiarity with God's love and power, combined with impatience, causes Israel to place blame for the current calamity at the divine doorstep. Israel personalizes and takes ownership of the age-old theodicy question; however, instead of

Pastoral Perspective

Advent is the broccoli of the Christian banquet, what you have to get through before digging in to the sweet treats of Christmas. We know it is good for us, but we would skip it if we could. Pastors try to hold back the yuletide, scolding our flocks for requesting Christmas carols out of season and preaching texts from Jeremiah or Malachi. But by the Fourth Sunday of Advent, even our liturgically disciplined eyes are focused on the dessert cart, which is why the plaintive cries of Psalm 80 are rarely heard from the pulpit. *Restore us, O God of hosts!* Yet if we look around our congregations, we see many people in need of restoration and healing. For these fragile souls, Psalm 80 offers the bread of life, speaking of a steadfast faith in God in the midst of sorrow and tragedy.

Psalm 80 is a song of communal lament. While scholars cannot pinpoint the exact time and place in which the text was composed, we can surmise the general circumstances. The people are deep in mourning, feeding on the "bread of tears" (v. 5). Their neighbors have abandoned them, their enemies mock them, and, worst of all, their God seems to be ignoring them. In this bleak and hopeless moment, the psalmist cries out to God, pleading for divine intervention.

What is striking about this psalm is the complete trust in God that is implicit in the text. From the

Exegetical Perspective

This psalm seems woefully out of place at the end of the Advent season. Intruding upon the blissful anticipation of Christmas, the psalm slaps the reader with an anguished complaint to God and desperate call to divine action. The first seven verses (eight in the Hebrew) consist of an opening petition (vv. 1–3), a direct complaint to God (vv. 4–7), and a concluding petition (v. 7) that is nearly identical with verse 3. The psalm continues with a more graphic complaint (vv. 8–13) and concludes with a petition (vv. 14–19). The refrain ("Restore us, O God [of hosts]; let your face shine, that we may be saved") repeated in verses 3, 7, and 19 gives the psalm its unity. The psalm thus is structured by the prayerful rhythm of petition and complaint, with petition bracketing the psalm as a whole. It leaves little room for praise (see only vv. 1b–2). The superscription of the psalm provides the title "covenant" (*'edût*), better translated as "testimony." Psalm 80 is a "testimony" of protest and petition.

Historically, the psalm seems to have its origin in the northern kingdom rather than in Jerusalem or somewhere else in Judah. In verse 2, certain northern tribes are listed, including Benjamin, originally a northern tribe but later incorporated into the southern kingdom as a buffer against northern aggression. The psalm holds a favorable attitude toward the northern kingdom, much in contrast to,

Homiletical Perspective

This close to Christmas, with Mary's visit to Elizabeth playing on the main screen, few listeners will hear the strains of the psalm coming through the walls from the small theatre next door. Yet, read from the Christian perspective on this particular Sunday, the psalm contains the prayers of the people that are answered in Mary's pregnancy. Along with the prophecy from Micah, the psalm is our reminder that this pregnancy is not God's pastoral answer to one person's prayer for a child, but God's eschatological answer to a whole people's prayer for a savior. In the readings from the Hebrew Bible, then, preachers may find valuable antidotes to the domestication of the Advent season.

As the church prepares to celebrate God's presence in Mary's child, Psalm 80 mourns God's absence from the life of the nation. God is not listening (v. 1a). God has withdrawn from the people to go sit upon the cherubim (v. 1b). There is no mighty activity coming from God's direction (v. 2b), no sign of God's shining face (v. 3). Although the people fill their prayers with imperatives ("give ear," "shine forth," "stir up your might"), God does not respond.

The psalmist interprets this silent treatment as a manifestation of God's wrath, although God has sent no message to that effect. God is angry with the people's prayers, the psalmist guesses. Given the

Psalm 80:1-7

Theological Perspective

philosophizing, the psalmist pleads and protests. Israel points to God's anger as the source of their suffering; God has given them tears for their bread and their drink and made them the laughingstock of their neighbors as well as their enemies. There is no argument here, but rather a statement of fact. Whether God is directly afflicting Israel is not the point. Whether Israel's own folly and sinfulness justify God's anger is not the point. At the moment, Israel is experiencing the misery of life without God, an unsustainable life in which every other relationship is out of joint. The driving focus is not really on God's culpability, but rather on Israel's need for God's return. This lament is a manifesto of faith in what God can do, and in fact must do. Whatever the current calamity, all will be well, all will be restored, if God will deign once again to let God's face shine upon Israel. In the darkness of suffering, Israel has no illusions about where true power lies, where salvation lies, but simply wants to prevail upon this divine power to put things right once again.

The language of restoration, however, the language of "putting things right," is based on the standard of the past. In the past, God has been a faithful shepherd and caring guide. The psalmist wants that secure, golden past back again. God the shepherd led Israel out of Egypt, formed Israel into a people united and uniquely God's own. Now division, destruction, and darkness afflict this people. In the midst of disorientation, Israel has only the comforting memory of God's past deeds by which to orient itself, seeking the salvation it has known before. "Restore us, O God of hosts; let your face shine, that we may be saved" (v. 7). But when God's face shines, when God comes to save, it is always a new moment, a moment of reorientation to a new future. And reorientation can be destabilizing.[1]

The Christian community prays this psalm on the liturgical cusp of dawn, facing the coming of this longed-for light, this desired radiance, this Christmas. Four weeks of preparation—or a lifetime of longing—and here we are again, on the aching edge of brilliance, though still in darkness. What will it mean when the light bursts over that edge? In many ways, it will depend upon how we own and interpret our darkness, individually and as a people. We too are hurt and beleaguered, a nation both captive and

---

1. Walter Brueggemann, drawing on Ricoeur, analyzes the function of the Psalms as expressive of life patterns of disorientation and reorientation. "Alongside language that describes what is, there is a language that evokes what is not" (Walter Brueggemann, *The Psalms and the Life of Faith*, ed. Patrick D. Miller [Minneapolis: Fortress Press, 1995], 28).

Pastoral Perspective

start, the author acknowledges the sovereignty and *agency* of God. The shepherd of Israel, who sits upon the throne, has the power to bless and to curse. Yes, the Lord has brought a great calamity upon the people, but there is no word of reproach or demand for restitution. There is no hint of "how could you do this to us after all we have meant to one another?" Instead, the psalmist accepts the tragic situation in order to preserve the possibility that God will yet show mercy and save the people. In other words, if you believe that God has the power to save you, then you must also trust in the Lord when things go wrong.

Of course the psalmist does not mince words when it comes to recounting the dire circumstances in which the people find themselves, nor is there any mistaking who has caused these things: "*You* have fed them with the bread of tears." "*You* make us the scorn of our neighbors." As a pastor, I am struck by the honesty. So often our prayers and sermons are sanitized until no one—not even the Almighty— could possibly take offense. Yet to preach Psalm 80 requires an unflinching account of what is wrong, how we feel about it, on whom we blame it, and what we want God to do. Unfortunately, most of us hesitate to make such bold requests for fear of being disappointed or appearing arrogant.

During a summer of clinical pastoral education, I visited a woman who had received a terminal diagnosis. As we held hands, I cautiously picked my way through a prayer, asking for peace, for strength, for healing of body and soul—nothing controversial or unattainable. When I had safely concluded my prayer, the woman squeezed my hands and added, "Almighty God, I want you to take this cancer away from me. I know you have the power, and I want you to do it. I want to be healed and I want to go home. Amen." When she finished, she looked into my worried face and said, "Don't be shy with God. If I don't ask for what I want, how can I hope to get it?" *Restore us, O God of hosts!*

Another striking aspect of Psalm 80 is the source of salvation. Three times the psalmist repeats the refrain: "Restore us, O God (of hosts); let your face shine, that we may be saved." The shining face of God is reminiscent of Moses's return from Mount Sinai and the transfiguration of Jesus. It is symbolic of being in the actual presence of God. This is the salvation the people desire: once again to be in the presence of the Holy.

Yet as much as they might desire this, the people cannot achieve it of their own accord. The chasm

for example, Psalm 78 and much of 1 and 2 Kings, where Judah is the exclusive recipient of God's favor. The verses of this psalm that follow the lection indicate a national catastrophe in the north. As a "vine" lovingly cultivated by God, Israel flourished and spread throughout the divinely gifted land of Canaan until its walls were breached and a "boar from the forest" ravaged it (v. 13). Cast metaphorically, the catastrophe refers to the fall of the northern kingdom in 722 BCE, brought about by the imperial power of the day, Assyria.

The prayer of Psalm 80 is the community's desperate cry for God's salvation in the aftermath of invasion and exile. But the remnant does not blame the Assyrian invaders for the disaster. Rather, the blame is placed squarely upon God, who has force-fed them with the "bread of tears," and disproportionately so: not just double but triple for anything deserved (v. 5). The enemies of Israel do what they do because God has allowed them, indeed provoked them (v. 6). The community charges God with willful neglect, with angrily refusing to attend to their prayers. The verb in verse 4 literally means "exude smoke": God *fumes* against the people's prayer.

Psalm 80 has nothing much to do with waiting serenely for God's advent. Quite the contrary, it has all to do with hastening God's appearance or epiphany. The prayer functions as a wake-up call to God: "Rouse your might and come to our salvation!" is the community's alarm-cry (v. 2b, my trans.). The anguish of the community's desperation is matched only by the exultation God is given in the prayer.

Perhaps more apropos of Advent is the psalm's elevated language about God. Shepherd, king, and light signify God's saving presence. As in Psalm 23:1, the image of the shepherd is also the image of king. Like David, the shepherd boy anointed by God to shepherd a people, God serves as king over a people by leading "Joseph like a flock" (v. 1; see also Pss. 95:7; 100:3b). The psalm recalls God's leading of the people out of Egyptian bondage and settling them in a new land, in green pastures. But this is no ordinary shepherd. This shepherd king is "enthroned upon the cherubim" (v. 1b), upon the outstretched wings of fearsome winged creatures (definitely not the chubby cherubs of Western art!) that grace the Holy of Holies in the temple.

Most prominent in the psalm is the association of God with light. Three times in the refrain, God is implored to let the divine countenance "shine" (vv. 3, 7, 19). The opening petition, in addition, commands God to "shine forth" (v. 1b; see also Deut. 33:2).

syntax of verse 4, we do not know whether God finds the content of those prayers offensive or God is simply too furious with the people to hear a single word they say. Either way, this psalm is worse than a soliloquy. Instead, it is the one-sided pleading of a desperate subject whose mouth is pressed against a shut door, speaking to an offended sovereign who will not speak back.

Everything is God's fault in these verses. The people are eating and drinking tears because that is all God has given them. God has made them the scorn of their neighbors. Because of God, they must endure the muffled laughs of their enemies, which are apparently more shameful to them than outright guffaws. All of this is the fault of the Shepherd of Israel, for withdrawing from the flock.

On one hand, this sounds like the whining, blaming language of people who refuse to take responsibility for their own actions. *Who* has made them the scorn of their neighbors? *Whose* behavior has given their enemies reason to laugh? Heard another way, however, the same language gives voice to the people's utter dependence on the God of hosts. Whether they behave well or badly, whether they eat lamb chops or the bread of tears, they know that the whole of their lives comes to them from God. Without the shining presence of the God of hosts, all they have to look forward to is dying in the dark.

The Christian preacher who chooses to make reference to these verses has several ways in. In the first place, there are bound to be more than a few in the congregation who dread the coming holidays. For them, the bright lights of the season only accentuate their own darkness, just as the church's focus on God's coming presence only deepens their sense of God's absence. The preacher who can allow the psalmist to speak to and for these people (instead of treating both them and the psalmist like depressives who are about to be cured by the gospel) may help lighten the holiday blues. Sometimes being saved does not require us to be cured. All we need to be saved is to hear the truth about our lives spoken out loud in the community of the faithful.

Preachers who wish to follow the psalmist's lead more closely will acknowledge the ways in which the whole nation has its face pressed against God's door, beseeching God with the same ancient imperatives: give ear, shine forth, stir up your might. Even when we disagree about what that might look like on the national or global scene, it is difficult to disagree that the world needs help. As the church unfurls her seasonal banners of peace and love, we are given the

Psalm 80:1-7

Theological Perspective

divided. We are captive not only to personal sin, but to a national lifestyle built on resources extracted from others, principally the world's poor and the earth upon which the poor depend more viscerally than the affluent. As a church, we are divided in our response to our nation's exercise of power in the world, and we are held captive by the patterns of war and death-dealing in which we cannot help but be complicit.

I write as an early-twenty-first-century American, but as we read the lament of a powerless nation from our position of national power, we can ironically own the psalmist's lament: we are increasingly a laughingstock to our neighbors and scorned by our enemies. We are entrenched in a darkness expressed in increasing acts of violence in our local communities, especially among our youth. We are entrenched in a darkness marked by the misery of God's absence, and we have an existential need to own this darkness and our disorientation and dislocation within it. Like the psalmist, the beginning of our salvation lies in our capacity to cry out full throated and unsparingly to God, who alone can save us. Like Israel, we must acknowledge the depth of our need, the extent of our vulnerability, and our utter dependence upon God. Like Israel, our temptation is to cry out for restoration, for the salvation we knew before. However, just as this darkness is marked by contours and portents unlike any previous darkness, this salvation will be marked by contours and portents unlike any previous salvation.

As God's people today, we stand in darkness, trembling on the cusp of dawn waiting to be saved. What is the radiance, the light, we so desire? What will it mean when the Christ light bursts upon us? When that light comes, what new future will be revealed? And what will it mean to reorient our lives, our church, our nation, our world—according to the contours of this new moment of salvation?

KATHLEEN MCMANUS

Pastoral Perspective

between God and humanity cannot be bridged from our side. "Restore us, O God" is a cry for God to act. In our modern, do-it-yourself society, such an admission of powerlessness is a radical statement of faith and poses a challenge to our inflated sense of autonomy and agency. It also provides a bridge to the coming birth of Christ, who Christians believe to be the ultimate divine act of restoration. Consider John's enigmatic account of the incarnation: "What has come into being in him was life, and the life was the light of all people. The light shines in the darkness, and the darkness did not overcome it" (John 1:3b–5). *Restore us, O God of hosts; let your face shine, that we may be saved.*

Psalm 80 speaks to those people who find themselves bereft of the Christmas spirit, people lacking the spiritual, physical, or financial resources to join in the party. For those who have lost a loved one or just a job, for those who have become disabled or depressed, for those who wonder if war will ever end—Psalm 80 speaks a word of patience, faithfulness, and hope. It takes suffering seriously and asks God to respond. This is good news, though only in the long term. As in real life, there is no quick fix here, no sudden change in circumstances. The psalmist's community has long suffered and may continue to suffer. But the psalmist does not lose faith, nor should we. Instead, the author honestly expresses great sorrow and greater faith— faith that God will one day gather us in and we will be saved.

Perhaps this is not a word that will delight the palate of people already anticipating the decadent celebration of Christmas. Yet for those whose sorrow knows no season, Psalm 80 offers a nourishing meal of hope.

SHAWNTHEA MONROE

Exegetical Perspective

God's shining presence is associated with Zion, the cradle of God's abode and "the perfection of beauty" (Ps. 50:2). To "shine forth" is to execute judgment against the proud (Ps. 94:1–2). The language of God's shining face recalls the venerable benediction in Numbers 6, given to Aaron and his sons to be delivered to the congregation: "The LORD bless you and keep you; the LORD make his face to shine upon you, and be gracious to you; the LORD lift up his countenance upon you, and give you peace" (vv. 24–26). Indeed, the popularity of the benediction is confirmed by the discovery of two seventh-century-BCE silver amulets in a burial cave near Jerusalem (Ketef Hinnom) that contain abbreviated versions of the blessing in Numbers 6. The blessing of God's shining face was literally worn on the body.

The shining face of God connotes the blessing of shalom. In Psalm 80 it conveys salvation and restoration, the outcomes of Gods epiphany or "manifestation." Actually, "emanation" would be a more appropriate term. The "shining" denotes an effulgent blast of light that brings not terror but restoration, salvation in the place of destruction. Salvation emanates from divine care expressed by God's smiling, resplendent countenance, as it were. Such salvation is restorative; it marks the re-creation of a community decimated by violence and deprivation.

No wonder the community does more than simply wait for God's restoring presence; it urgently prays, cajoles, proclaims, implores, and anticipates, as if every spoken word in prayer could hasten God's return so that the people can return (v. 18). Such is the salutary outcome of epiphany, of the shining star that leads wise men and kings, as well as shepherds and sheep, all "like a flock," to the King.

WILLIAM P. BROWN

Homiletical Perspective

annual opportunity either to wrap ourselves in them so that we cannot see beyond our own party decorations or to let them slap us in the face as the wind of God tries to bring both them and us to life.

Those who choose to include the whole psalm in worship will find another intriguing possibility at verse 14, where the psalmist pleads with God to "turn again." In Hebrew, this amounts to a plea for God's own repentance. While Psalm 80 contains no call to penitence, no acceptance of blame for what has befallen Israel, here we have the subtle recognition that human repentance can only go so far. If the people live, it is not because of anything they have done or failed to do. In the end, it is only God's repentance that can save life.

In the context of the Christmas season that is now fully on the horizon, this opens the possibility of treating Psalm 80 as a prayer that is answered in the Christ event. Christian interpreters have exercised this option for centuries, with mixed results. Preachers who choose it this year will exercise caution on a number of counts.

As always, when they preach from the Hebrew Bible, Christian interpreters will note that this sacred text is shared by two distinct religious traditions that do not read it the same way. Preachers will also model for their listeners how to turn toward the light of Christ without leaving Israel in the dark. Finally, they will support their congregations to give thanks for the whole long history in which the one Shepherd of the sheep has cared for the flock—from Genesis to now, through absence and presence, with tears and laughter, in darkness and in light—without ever failing to answer the prayers of the people, though always in God's own good time.

BARBARA BROWN TAYLOR

Hebrews 10:5-10

⁵Consequently, when Christ came into the world, he said,
  "Sacrifices and offerings you have not desired,
    but a body you have prepared for me;
⁶ in burnt offerings and sin offerings
      you have taken no pleasure.
⁷ Then I said, 'See, God, I have come to do your will, O God'
      (in the scroll of the book it is written of me)."

⁸When he said above, "You have neither desired nor taken pleasure in sacrifices and offerings and burnt offerings and sin offerings" (these are offered according to the law), ⁹then he added, "See, I have come to do your will." He abolishes the first in order to establish the second. ¹⁰And it is by God's will that we have been sanctified through the offering of the body of Jesus Christ once for all.

Theological Perspective

What a curious text to be considering on the final Sunday before the birth of Jesus! For those who are willing to travel back to the days of Mary and Joseph, the effort will yield great insights.

The world of the espoused parents-to-be was one marked by guilt and shame. Unlike the people of the secular twenty-first century, the ancient children of Israel were schooled in the laws of God. They had been taught to keep God's law with scrupulous care, living lives of moral purity, ethical integrity, and religious reverence. Nobody kept those standards perfectly. Given the absolute otherness of God, all were deemed unworthy to stand in the presence of the Holy One. Accordingly, when the writer of Proverbs spoke eloquently of the fear of God being the beginning of wisdom, it was to promote not a mere reverence or awe, but an overwhelming, terrifying fear.

What hope might a sinner possess? How could one approach the throne of the Sovereign? Along with the teachings of law came teachings about an elaborate sacrificial system, introduced in the book of Exodus and expounded at length in Leviticus. Such a system called for the presentation of animals—goats, bulls, birds, and especially sheep— to be given as sacrificial offerings to the Sovereign. In most cases, the animal would be killed, suggesting

Pastoral Perspective

When I was in seminary, Will Willimon was my professor for worship and sacraments. Sometimes the lectionary will skip over selected verses, and those were the ones that Dr. Willimon would often pull out to preach. They did not skip over any verses in this pericope in Hebrews, but I wish they had backed up and included verse 4: "For it is impossible for the blood of bulls and goats to take away sins."

It is impossible for us to rid ourselves of sin. If we could do that, we would not need Jesus. If we could fix ourselves, we would not need a Savior. The hope that the church holds out for the world on this Fourth Sunday of Advent is that God has done something for us that we cannot do for ourselves. Jesus came on a mission to retrieve us.

How many ineffective ways have we all tried to take away our own sins? We have used all the classic defense mechanisms of denial, rationalization, and projection. We have tried pietism and even secularism. The culture around us has become somewhat numb to sin.

In Karl Menninger's book *Whatever Became of Sin?* he writes,

> It is surely nothing new that men [*sic*] want to get away from acknowledging their sins or even thinking about them. Is this not the religious history of mankind? [*sic*] Perhaps we are only more glib

Exegetical Perspective

The central portion of Hebrews consists of a lengthy exposition of the significance of the death of Christ, which culminates in today's reading, a quotation from Psalm 40 and an exegetical comment. So on this blessed last Sunday before Christian congregations around the world celebrate the Son's birth, we visit his death. In order to understand the function of the passage, it is necessary to keep in mind the previous exposition.

The reflection on the death of the great high priest begins at 8:1–6 with an evocation of the "heavenly tabernacle," which, according to Exodus 25:39–40, served as a model for the earthly tabernacle. With the dichotomy between the heavenly and the earthly in place, the exposition proceeds (Heb. 8:7–13) with a lengthy citation of Jeremiah 31:31–34, a prophecy in which God promises to make a "new covenant" with Israel, with its laws written on human hearts, not on tablets of stone. What follows shows how that prophecy was fulfilled in the death of Jesus, understood to be the ultimate Day of Atonement sacrifice. The argument first focuses (9:1–10) on the "old" Day of Atonement ritual that took place in the earthly tabernacle, a ritual that could not "perfect" (v. 9) the conscience of the believer. In contrast stands the self-sacrifice of Christ, consummated in the heavenly tabernacle

Homiletical Perspective

In the Fourth Sunday of Advent, as we turn the corner toward Bethlehem, our Epistle brings us the extraordinarily direct voice of the Christ saying, "Here I am!" The voice lays aside the entire sacrifice system of the Hebrew Scriptures in favor of the One who does God's will by giving his own body. This bold passage is completely reliant upon the immediately preceding verses; when Christ speaks in verses 5–7, we hear that he comes to do what the law could not accomplish. The law only approximates a relief from sin. Actually even this language of relief from sin is problematic. Verses 1–4 make it clear that the law could never accomplish it. Evidence rests in the yearly renewal sought in repeated sacrifices. The need to repeat them evidences their ineffectiveness to purge sin. Christ comes to do what no sacrifices of our efforts could accomplish. Advent creates in us an eager anticipation (celebration) of Christ's sacrifice in our behalf.

Verses 5–7 recapitulate a passage from Psalm 40 (vv. 6–8). The language has been changed in several places, which reorient our hearing to the contrast of Christ's "sacrifice" over and against those of the Levitical traditions (see 9:11–14). These changes between Psalm 40 and Hebrews 10 themselves offer preachers four points to consider in shaping the sermon. Debates over whether some of these changes are the results of scribal errors or authorial

Hebrews 10:5-10

Theological Perspective

that the human person offering it was now relieved both of one's guilt and of the death penalty that had been hanging over one's head. This elaborate system of propitiation for sin defined a paradigm by which the ancient children of Israel measured their lives.

Amid such a sin-stung community Jesus was born to Mary and Joseph. The writer of our passage introduces Jesus as one who stood in critique of the Levitical system, agreeing with the sacrifices' repeated reminders of the sin-and-guilt problem, but challenging their efficacy in resolving that problem. The fact that those sacrifices would need to be offered repeatedly—especially the ultimate sacrifices offered on the annual Day of Atonement—served as an obvious admission of their inadequacy. "If they work so well, why do you have to keep repeating them?" the writer was inquiring. No, a better sacrifice was needed.

Into Israel's story breaks the Savior who offers his body as a once-for-all sacrifice for sins. Only a human, a perfectly obedient human, entirely free from sin, could be offered in place of our fallen humanity and thereby absorb the guilt, shame, and punishment deserved by us all.

Whenever we encounter texts that speak of old covenant vs. new covenant, law vs. grace, or as in verses 9, "the first" and "the second," we must face the challenge of displacement theology, in which the new covenant teaching of Jesus and the apostles is portrayed as a replacement for an inferior, old covenant of Abraham, Israel, and Moses. In this case, the supposedly inferior "old" practice being displaced is that of animal sacrifices for the purpose of reconciling sinful humans to the holy God. Was anti-Semitism so prevalent among the early Christians that they felt free to dismiss the teachings of their Hebrew counterparts as well as the ancient roots of their faith practices? Shall today's church promote such anti-Jewish thinking and behavior?

The difference outlined between the old and the new here finds comparable critique in the Hebrew life of Israelis in the time of Jesus. The blood sacrifice system introduced in Exodus and expounded in Leviticus had been revived when Herod's temple was built. Though that temple hardly compared to the great temple of Solomon, the practice of offering sacrifices was proceeding at full steam in Jesus' day. However, in the three centuries prior to Jesus' birth, the Diaspora of Jews after the exile generated the synagogue system, along with the growing influence of the rabbis. Separated as they were from Jerusalem and its temple, they could

Pastoral Perspective

nowadays and equipped with more euphemisms. We can speak of error and transgression and infraction and mistakes without the naïve exposure that goes with serious use of that old-fashioned pietistic word "sin." But although it has disappeared from serious use in our workaday vocabularies, perhaps it has not gone from the back of our minds.[1]

If we have no sin, then we are not in need of a Savior. If we have no need of Savior, then we have no need to be grateful to God for our salvation. If we lack gratitude to God for salvation, then there is no need to live one's life as a steward of all that God has given to us. We stand alone. We are self-made. Christmas can be nothing more than the celebration of a winter solstice.

The Fourth Sunday of Advent is an excellent time to talk about sin and our need of a Savior. The writer to the Hebrews does not shy away from it. Jesus is on a mission to retrieve us: "And it is by God's will that we have been sanctified through the offering of the body of Jesus Christ once for all" (v. 10).

Someone told me about taking a mission trip and seeing a large wall with a variety of paint colors on it. They asked one of the locals about the wall, to which they replied, "Oh that? When Americans come over, they have to have something to do. If we do not have anything for them to do, we just get them to paint on that wall." That is a true story!

Jesus did not come to paint on a meaningless wall. He came to reconcile humanity to God (2 Cor. 5:18–19). He came to deal with separation issues. He came to mend what was broken, to rebuild what had been destroyed, to bury the hatchet, to recover what was lost, and to make peace between God and us. Jesus was very clear about his mission. He was not just painting on a nebulous wall. He was removing the wall that exists between God and us.

Some people think we can save ourselves by other means. If we just educated everyone, then the human race could be saved. What we call sin is simply ignorance. Knowledge will lead us home. That sounds right until you consider the fact that many highly educated people have done some incredibly immoral things. Can education alone really save us?

Some people think science can save us. Discover that cure, and all will be well. But for all the good that science does, it also has given us the capacity for

---

1. Karl Menninger, *Whatever Became of Sin?* (New York: Hawthorn Books, 1973), 24.

Exegetical Perspective

(9:11–14), a unique offering of the heavenly high priest made through "the eternal Spirit" (v. 14). The significance of this paradigmatic sacrifice consists in its function as a covenant-inaugurating event (9:15–21). The argument here seems artificial and based on wordplay equating "covenant" and "testament," notions expressed by the same Greek word (*diathēkē*). Yet the playful expression garbs a serious point: the death of Christ is an atoning event precisely because it establishes a social reality in relationship with God, the kind of covenant promised by Jeremiah.

The next stage of the argument (9:23–28) returns to the image of a heavenly locale in which Christ's sacrifice was consummated. The phraseology (e.g., "heavenly things themselves" v. 23) recalls technical Platonic language used of the ideal realm and the emphasis on the uniqueness of Christ's sacrifice (v. 26) also evokes the unitary realm of the ideal. The passage thus reinforces the strong dichotomy between heavenly and earthly realms with which the whole exposition had begun, and it seems to highlight a mythical understanding of Christ's priestly death. This step in the argument, however, simply sets the stage for the concluding passage, which "demythologizes" the imagery used thus far and indicates the way in which the new, interior covenant is in fact established.

The final stage of the exposition (10:1–10) begins with the metaphor of a shadow cast by something real, an image evocative of Plato's myth of the cave in *The Republic*, which would cohere with the reading of the previously dominant heavenly-earthly dichotomy in idealist terms. Yet our homilist now undercuts that expected development of the antithesis. What casts the shadow is not an abstract, heavenly ideal, but "the good things to come" (v. 1). The ultimate source of the "shadow" that is cast backwards in time proves to be a specific human body (v. 10). The homilist thus uses a well-worn trope (bodies cast shadows) to make a serious point. The idealist implications of his argument thus far do not disappear but are applied in a striking new way. The ideal "heavenly" reality on which the ancient tabernacle was modeled turns out to be the very fleshly body of the one who offers himself to God. His action in doing so establishes a precedent and a model for all those who would live lives of fidelity to God. In doing so, they fulfill the prophecy of Jeremiah.

To drive home this point, and thus stitch together the complex themes of his exposition, the homilist

Homiletical Perspective

redactions between ancient translations do not detract from the principal effort to illustrate that God prepared the way for Christ and, as Christ speaks, Jesus seeks to do God's will. Anticipation in Advent builds upon Christ's desire to offer will and body in sacrifice for humanity.

Preachers will have to wrestle over how to understand the atonement in the Christology of this letter. The language and imagery of sacrifice in this passage and surrounding material draw directly upon the idea of blood atonement as sin offering. Preachers are not spared from deciphering to what extent this metaphoric language and imagery is to be concretized in our atonement theology. How are we to preach that "without the shedding of blood there is no forgiveness of sins" (9:22)? Is Christ's sacrifice a blood offering to appease the wrath of God over human sin? Is atonement grounded in the willing and obedient servanthood of Christ, who moves sacrificially in service to God's love and will for humanity, in God's own effort to reconcile us, thereby purging humanity from the essence and ultimate destruction of sin? Verses 8–10 may help the preacher in answering the questions raised by the changes made from Psalm 40. God takes no pleasure in sin offerings. The author interprets atonement at the center of Christology. And we intensely ponder, "What is the advent of Christ?"

Christ is the sacrifice. Once and for all, this sacrifice overcomes the limitations of humanity to approach God and to be purged from sin. It is God's will that sacrifice no longer would be required. God's will and Christ's willing servanthood, even unto the sacrifice of blood and body, sanctify us (v. 10). In the birth of Christ, God enters humanity; and in our behalf Christ creates a new access to God.[1]

It is difficult to preach on the notion of sacrifice. Christ knows sacrifice is to be his life. But there is something disturbing about sacrifice as the will of God for appeasement or ransom. Questions still persist. In the reconciliation of humanity, how do we reconcile the love of God, the very character of God, with blood offering? Cannot sacrifice be a way of life that seeks life? Cannot the blood offering be a willing servanthood that seeks life and relationship in the face of death, even death wrought by sin? Clearly, we should not seek to escape the language and imagery of atonement in passages such as this. The power for preaching the atonement still lies in God's willingness and even plan to overcome God's

---

1. William G. Johnsson, *Hebrews* (Atlanta: John Knox Press, 1980), 68–73.

Hebrews 10:5-10

Theological Perspective

present blood sacrifices only by taking long, arduous pilgrimages to the city of David. Instead, they offered prayers, songs, and offerings in synagogue worship services. The rabbis leading such worship lifted up not bloody sacrifices but teachings of the Scriptures to the people they were shepherding. The teaching office of the rabbis serving thousands of synagogues eventually eclipsed the sacerdotal office of priests serving the one temple. Ultimately the Roman destruction of Jerusalem and her temple in 70 CE brought to an end the whole priestly sacrificial system, and the rabbis in synagogues generally interpreted the transition from a sacrificial cultus system to a teaching and pastoral system as God-inspired.

Soon they were looking upon the sacrificial system as an antiquated, primitive version of their religion, and the synagogue system as a modern improvement upon the former. It maintained the most important elements—the law of Moses as the great gift of God to the world—while dispensing with the lesser elements of bloody sacrifices. And they could hearken to such passages as Psalm 40:4–6, written centuries before, to affirm the priority of obedience over sacrifice.

Accordingly, the writer to the Hebrews was following a pattern of critique that was being voiced by the great rabbis of the first century of the Christian era. One major improvement lauded by the rabbis in those days entailed the formation of character. The law was given, they taught, not simply to point to sin but also to effect a shaping of character—purity, integrity, honesty, reverence—that ought to mark the lifestyles of the people of God. In this light, our writer also quotes Psalm 40:6–8 but takes the liberty of placing those words on the lips of Jesus. The sacrifice God seeks, indeed has sought for centuries from the children of Israel, is not that of burnt offerings but that of a life lived according to the will of God. "See, I have come to do your will," he says (v. 7).

Accordingly the work of Jesus is one that is intended to shape the character of the people who would follow Jesus. As the passage further expounds—echoing the teaching of Hebrews 8:8–13, in fulfillment of Jeremiah 31—God is inscribing God's laws into the hearts and minds of God's people, so that they shall live as the psalmist aspired to do.

JACK HABERER

Pastoral Perspective

nuclear war. With all of our scientific advancements over the past fifty years, we have not made a dent in immorality. Science does not address greed, pride, lust, envy, slothfulness, or any of the other deadly sins.

Some people have even argued that piety can save us. Purify your mind and body, and you will be saved. But pious sin manifests itself in boardrooms, in legislature, even in the White House. And the worst thing about pietism is its twin sister, self-righteousness. Jesus had an easier time talking with someone who knew she was a sinner than with someone who believed he was without sin.

We need to be retrieved. We need to be forgiven. We need to be restored. We need for somebody to come and get us because we are lost. We need to be reconciled with God. The blood of bulls and goats does not work.

Somebody is sitting there on this Fourth Sunday of Advent in desperate need of salvation. Someone is sitting there, even in church, lost. Somebody is covered up with guilt and shame. Somebody is hiding from all of it while the person next to them is weeping; "We are out of bull's blood and we have killed all the goats. Tell me about this Jesus and what he can do for all of us."

Thank God Jesus wasn't confused. Thank God he would not settle for less. Thank God that Jesus knew how severe the nature of our sin is, how dangerous and deadly it is, and that he responded accordingly. Thank God he didn't get sidetracked with thinking that he could save the world by other means. Thank God "that we have been sanctified through the offering of the body of Jesus Christ once for all" (v. 10).

STEVEN P. EASON

Exegetical Perspective

uses Psalm 40:6–8 (LXX 40:7–9), understood to be something said by Christ as he "enters the world" (v. 5). This is the second time that Hebrews echoes the voice of Christ. As in the earlier case (2:12–13), Christ speaks with the words of Scripture, primarily the words of the Psalms. The text cited is not the original Hebrew, but the Greek translation, which in verse 6 rendered "you have given me an open ear" with "a body you have prepared for me." The Greek rendering is essential to the point that will be made with the text.

The original psalm, attributed to David, celebrated God's saving mercy and described the situation of the psalmist, who "waited patiently for the Lord" (Ps. 40:1), who had experienced deliverance from the "desolate pit" (v. 2), and who prayed for the continuance of God's "steadfast love and . . . faithfulness" (v. 11). As he described his own situation, the psalmist invoked a contrast frequently found in the prophets between the external religiosity of cultic sacrifice and the devotion of a faithful heart (vv. 6–8). These are the verses chosen for citation as words of Jesus.

Perhaps the most obscure part of the citation is the psalmist's reference to being inscribed in the "scroll of the book." Both the Hebrew original and the Greek translation are difficult, but the Greek phrase literally means "in the heading of the scroll." Our homilist probably understands this to mean, to use a modern equivalent, that the "title page" of sacred Scripture has on it the name of the Son and high priest. Scripture in its totality points to the Son's faithful commitment expressed in these verses.

The commentary (vv. 9–10) intensifies the contrast expressed in the words of the psalm. The willingness to "do your will" is a principle that abrogates the system of sacrificial offerings. Here the polemical strain of Hebrews, denigrating the whole sacrificial system of the temple, comes to the fore. What replaces that system is the "will" first expressed by the speaker of the psalm, now understood to be the incarnate Son, and eventually lived out by those who would follow in his footsteps. Through faithful commitment to the will of God, shared by the Son and all the children of God, comes sanctification (v. 10) and ultimately the "perfection" that consists of access to God (v. 14).

HAROLD W. ATTRIDGE

Homiletical Perspective

own disdain for sin within humanity with God's own life in humanity.

The character of God is known not only in God's disdain for human sin—sin that seeks self-fulfillment with the subjugation of relationship with God. God's character is known in God's unmerited grace and faithfulness to God's own love for humanity. Preaching the advent of Christ names the sacrifice of Christ within God's love for humanity. God does not permit God's own disdain or wrath to define God's character or nature. Even in cutting the Sinai covenant, God declares that though human sin may bear historical effects, it will not govern God's being or ultimately delimit God's relationship with humanity. Even in giving the law on a second set of tablets, God is determined to extend grace beyond justice, because God is "merciful and gracious, slow to anger, and abounding in steadfast love and faithfulness" (Exod. 34:6). These are the words of God in a self-descriptive proclamation. God's love forever seeks to overwhelm God's own wrath. The incarnation is God's mercy, grace, steadfast love, and faithfulness. The sacrifice of Christ is God's refusal to move ultimately in disdain for humanity, but rather to move in behalf of humanity. The advent of atonement is something other than the satisfaction of divine justice. God extends divine grace beyond even divine justice in this new covenant through Christ.

Our Advent sermons ironically point forward to what has been already accomplished once and for all. Again in this new covenant, God declares that forgiveness is the determined will of God. Christ is the agent. The Epistle reading for this Fourth Advent Sunday declares we are sanctified by Christ's sacrifice (v. 10), but anticipates the divine proclamation of verse 18: "Where there is forgiveness . . . , there is no longer any offering for sin." The birth of Christ anticipates God's own agency in behalf of humanity and our salvation.

DALE P. ANDREWS

Luke 1:39-45 (46-55)

[39]In those days Mary set out and went with haste to a Judean town in the hill country, [40]where she entered the house of Zechariah and greeted Elizabeth. [41]When Elizabeth heard Mary's greeting, the child leaped in her womb. And Elizabeth was filled with the Holy Spirit [42]and exclaimed with a loud cry, "Blessed are you among women, and blessed is the fruit of your womb. [43]And why has this happened to me, that the mother of my Lord comes to me? [44]For as soon as I heard the sound of your greeting, the child in my womb leaped for joy. [45]And blessed is she who believed that there would be a fulfillment of what was spoken to her by the Lord."

[46] And Mary said,
 "My soul magnifies the Lord,
[47] and my spirit rejoices in God my Savior,
[48]for he has looked with favor on the lowliness of his servant.
 Surely, from now on all generations will call me blessed;

Theological Perspective

This passage is commonly known as the visitation; it includes the meeting of Mary with her relative Elizabeth (vv. 39–45), and the song Luke records as Mary's response to Elizabeth's blessing (vv. 46–55). The two passages are best read and preached on together, for Luke clearly intended to link the births of John the Baptist and Jesus.

Mary Visits Elizabeth (vv. 39–45). Mary's motivation for visiting Elizabeth presents a practical theological problem for interpreters seeking to highlight her as an example of faith. Did she need confirmation and encouragement to continue believing God? Or should the word of Gabriel have been enough for her? Her response to Gabriel in verse 38 seems unequivocal, but we moderns find it easy to imagine that she might have had second thoughts and doubts afterwards. Calvin concedes as much and commends Mary for seeking confirmation: "There is nothing we should reckon odd in her seeking to confirm her faith by going to see the miracle which the angel had effectively brought to her notice. The faithful may be satisfied with the unadorned Word of God, and yet neglect none of his works which they realize provide support for their faith. Mary was above all right to seize upon the help afforded her, if she did

Pastoral Perspective

Waiting is not a skill that comes naturally, and so the impulse to ignore Advent is a strong one. By the Fourth Sunday of Advent it is almost irresistible. Many congregations open the floodgates, break out the Christmas carols, and rename it "Christmas Sunday." This text from Luke offers both warrant and road map for resisting this temptation. (Warning: pastoral courage must be supplied separately.)

By making the Magnificat portion (1:46–55) of the text optional, the lectionary pushes us toward the intimate narrative about the meeting of Mary and Elizabeth. The scale of this story hardly seems grand enough for one of the most well-attended Sundays of the church year. But it may be just what we need. Many people come to worship on this day battered by the gauntlet we politely call "the holidays." The stress of balancing work and home expands beyond the normally dangerous levels of contemporary life, as families aim for an anachronistic holiday ideal. Those who grieve or doubt or question find little platform or patience for their concerns. Many families feel envious of others whose Christmas card pictures look more prosperous, or more harmonious, or just plain more beautiful. Emotions are raw, and cultural nostalgia crowds out gospel truth as

⁴⁹for the Mighty One has done great things for me,
  and holy is his name.
⁵⁰His mercy is for those who fear him
  from generation to generation.
⁵¹He has shown strength with his arm;
  he has scattered the proud in the thoughts of their hearts.
⁵²He has brought down the powerful from their thrones,
  and lifted up the lowly;
⁵³he has filled the hungry with good things,
  and sent the rich away empty.
⁵⁴He has helped his servant Israel,
  in remembrance of his mercy,
⁵⁵according to the promise he made to our ancestors,
  to Abraham and to his descendants forever."

Exegetical Perspective

In the encounter of Mary and Elizabeth, Elizabeth becomes the first human witness to the good news the angel brought Mary in the annunciation (1:26–38). Both women are pregnant with significance, for between them they bear the messenger and the message. Through narrative, speech, and song of praise the characters in this lection prophetically proclaim the gospel: God is working salvation for us in Jesus. The meeting between these two women is about the confirmation of hope, the fulfillment of a promise. The rest of the Gospel makes explicit the means and nature of that fulfillment through Jesus' teachings, parables, healings, death, and resurrection.

The optional second part of the lection (vv. 46–55) is a song in praise of God, the Magnificat. The song itself contains no reference to a birth, so Luke may have adapted it from a different source than that of the birth narrative into which it is sandwiched.[1] At any rate, the context supplies the connection: Mary extols God as savior, now fulfilling in the Christ event what was promised through the prophets. The full passage (vv. 39–55), which joins the birth narrative of Jesus to the one of John,

Homiletical Perspective

This text cries out to be preached in all of its wildness and absurdity. The story calls for preachers who can enter into and express the joy, amazement, foolishness, and danger enacted in the encounter between Mary and Elizabeth. Here we preachers encounter God's embarrassing and threatening "challenge to good order."[1] Here we come face to face with the upside-down world inaugurated by the incarnation of Jesus. The text is best interpreted not by serious academic commentaries or pious religiosity, but by the folk traditions and street theater of the Feast of Fools and Carnival, in which the social hierarchies of the day are lampooned and subverted, and the lowly are raised to places of honor (Harris, *Carnival*, 140). The church prepares this week for Jesus' birth, not through serious theological reflection, but through subversive laughter, singing, and astonishment.

The scene is absurd. The coming of the Messiah who will redeem Israel is anticipated and proclaimed, not by archangels or high priests or emperors or even ordained preachers. Rather, two

---

1. François Bovon, *Luke I: A Commentary on the Gospel of Luke 1:1–9:50* (Minneapolis: Fortress Press, 2002), 56.

1. Max Harris, *Carnival and Other Christian Festivals: Folk Theology and Folk Performance* (Austin: University of Texas Press, 2003), 25. My approach to this text relies on Harris's work; see esp. pp. 9, 25–26, 45, 140–41, 153–54, 170, 222–24.

Theological Perspective

not wish to reject what the Lord had deliberately put before her."[1]

While Mary did receive confirmation and encouragement from Elizabeth, Luke may have made a different point, namely, that Mary went to *offer* confirmation and encouragement, rather than to *receive* them. Gabriel's announcement brought Elizabeth's situation to mind, and it "connected the dots," as they say, and she concluded that Elizabeth needed to know what God was doing. In one of his homilies on the Gospels, Bede observed: "[Mary] went so that she could offer her congratulations concerning the gift which she had learned her fellow servant had received. This was not in order to prove the word of the angel by the attestation of a woman. Rather it was so that as an attentive young virgin she might commit herself to ministry to a woman of advanced age."[2]

Another key theological theme highlighted in this passage is the work of the Holy Spirit. Mary's presence turned out to be significant confirmation for Elizabeth. As Mary approached, Elizabeth's child "leaped in her womb," and she was filled with the Spirit and offered a blessing upon Mary and her unborn son. Elizabeth's blessing acknowledges the special role that Mary has as the mother of the Savior: "Blessed are you among women" (v. 42) and "blessed is she who has believed that what the Lord has said to her will be accomplished" (v. 45 NIV). Elizabeth's knowledge of Mary's condition is revealed by the Holy Spirit, so that subsequent blessing is prompted by the Spirit. Here as elsewhere in Luke and Acts, the Holy Spirit imparts God's Word and prepares people to hear and receive it.

Mary's Song (vv. 46–55). Like an aria in an opera or a duet in a musical, the Magnificat stops the action of the Gospel in order to celebrate the greatness and covenant faithfulness of God. God is sovereign in the world and displays God's greatness by displacing the proud and the powerful, sending the rich away empty handed (vv. 51–53).

God is great, but equally important—and harder to believe for many in our day—God is good. God's demonstration of power is not merely a show of force, but is intended to remind Israel that they belong to God and can count on their God to help

Pastoral Perspective

people look backward, rather than God-ward, for inspiration. "A mere trifle consoles us," as the French savant Pascal put it, "for a mere trifle distresses us."[1]

To our lonely and fragmented souls, Luke bequeaths a wonderful pre-Christmas gift: a small story about a genuine connection between two pregnant women of different generations. In this text we see God at work in a deeply personal way that also just happens to change the world! The work of the Holy Spirit is made manifest as the baby in Elizabeth's womb (John) responds to Mary's greeting. As well-timed baby kicks often do, this one opens up the recipient to a new awareness and understanding of unfolding events. (Does the kick during a job interview mean take the position or run away fast?) A brave pastor might ask parents in the congregation to share their baby-kick stories during the sermon. Mary's greeting of Elizabeth starts a cycle of *recognition followed by response* that could further echo spontaneously through the congregation. The scriptural world can absorb the present reality.

Though Zechariah, the officially sanctioned priest, is silent during this episode, it is the unassuming "preacher's wife," Elizabeth, who functions as a de facto prophet. Prompted by the Holy Spirit, she articulates for Mary an outline of the special role the younger kinswoman has been called to play. Elizabeth's prophetic witness also encourages and strengthens Mary. Recognizing her own vocation in Elizabeth's description, she is empowered to share the bold words of the Magnificat. Once again, response follows recognition. What began as a simple visit to the home of a sidelined priest in the "hill country" issues forth in a pronouncement of global political and economic import.

A sermonic shift of focus to the Magnificat could highlight the world-changing aspects of the impending birth. But a faithful reading might also, for this one day at least, stay closer to the personal dimensions. God gives Mary and Elizabeth two things they each lacked: community and connection. God removes their isolation and helps them to understand themselves more fully as part of something larger than their individual destinies. Together they are known more fully, and begin to see more clearly (cf. 1 Cor. 13:12), than they do as individuals. This is truly an Advent message—of hope and understanding that starts out slowly and quietly. We anticipate its growth and full

---

1. John Calvin, *A Harmony of the Gospels Matthew, Mark and Luke,* ed. D. W. Torrance and T. F. Torrance, trans. A. W. Morrison (Grand Rapids: Eerdmans, 1972), 31.

2. Bede, *Homilies on the Gospels* 1.4, quoted in Arthur A. Just Jr., ed., *Luke,* Ancient Christian Commentary on Scripture: New Testament 3 (Downers Grove: InterVarsity Press, 2003), 21.

1. Blaise Pascal, *Pensées,* trans. W. F. Trotter (New York: Random House, 1941), 48.

prophetically proclaims the promise of a birth and is thus well suited to the last Sunday in Advent, the last, long breath before the birth of Christmas.

The reading is part of Luke's extended and interlaced birth narratives of John the Baptist and Jesus (1:5–2:52), which precede the respective public appearance of both men, in the same order. Biblical birth narratives—for example, of Jacob, Moses, Samson, and Samuel—tend to accompany concrete instances of historical salvation, hence the pertinence to Luke's main theme: the arrival of the messianic savior (1:32), who is "holy . . . a son of God" (1:35, my trans.). Jesus and John the Baptist, whose birth is unmentioned in the other Gospels, are intimately related—Luke makes them relatives—because both are the working of "the Lord . . . God, my savior" (vv. 46–47) and the fulfillment of what "God spoke to our ancestors" (v. 55).

The lectionary reading begins (v. 39) with Mary setting out to visit her "relative" Elizabeth in a Judean hill town, around eighty miles distant[2] from her home in Nazareth of Galilee (v. 26). She enters the house of Zechariah and greets Elizabeth in one of the most famous "recognition scenes" of all time, extraordinary because the recognition is utterly intrauterine! The spiritual commotion of fetal John—his own first prophecy—turns Elizabeth into a prophet: she is "filled with the Holy Spirit" (v. 41) and utters a prophetic blessing: Mary is "blessed . . . among women" even as the "fruit of [her] womb" is "blessed" (v. 42). To the usual blessing of progeny—a familiar biblical motif: Elizabeth, like so many significant OT mothers, was barren (v. 7)—is added the supreme blessing of becoming "the mother of my Lord" (v. 43), the bearer of the "beloved son" of God (3:22).

When they meet, Elizabeth learns what Mary already knows. Thus informed, Elizabeth makes the important connection between Mary's blessing and Mary's believing (v. 45) what God spoke to her through the angel; an implicit contrast is with Zechariah's doubtful response (1:18–20). "Happy are you" (v. 45), Elizabeth exclaims, although the reader shortly learns through Simeon's song that Mary's soul will necessarily taste also sorrow over her son (2:35). As God is the ultimate source of fertility and birth (see Gen. 20:18, 30:2; 1 Sam. 1), the womb is a profound symbol of potential for the new and surprising, the unexpected and joyous: "the child in my womb leaped for joy" (v. 44). This motif of joy

marginalized, pregnant women—one young, poor, and unwed, the other far beyond the age to conceive—meet in the hill country of Judea to celebrate (and possibly commiserate about) their miraculous pregnancies. A baby leaps in the womb. Blessings are shared. Astonishment is expressed. Songs are sung. By two pregnant women. The story is not only odd and joyful; it is fleshy, embodied, earthy, appropriate as a forerunner to the incarnation, which derives from the Latin root *carn-* ("flesh"), which is also the root of the word "carnival." In the women's actions, the world is indeed turned upside down. Hierarchies are subverted. The mighty are brought down. Two marginalized, pregnant women carry the future and proclaim the Messiah.

Mary's song, her Magnificat, gives voice to this subversive incarnation that she and Elizabeth embody. Indeed, the fact that Mary sings the Magnificat is itself odd and subversive. This young, unwed, pregnant woman—a thoroughly marginal person in her culture—proclaims one of the most important prophetic words in Scripture. The image is extraordinary, even comical: young, pregnant Mary gives voice to a song for the ages, a song that invites us beyond our realistic expectations and our numb imaginations. She herself seems amazed at what has happened, as her opening words indicate: "My soul magnifies the Lord, and my spirit rejoices in God my Savior, for he has looked with favor on the lowliness of his servant" (vv. 47–48a). And the rest of her song announces the larger implications of the upside-down world God has inaugurated: "He has scattered the proud in the thoughts of their hearts. He has brought down the powerful from their thrones, and lifted up the lowly; he has filled the hungry with good things, and sent the rich away empty" (vv. 51b–53). Mary proclaims the promised, topsy-turvy future of God as an already-accomplished fact—possibly because that future can already be glimpsed in God's choice of Mary as the bearer of the Messiah. The song proclaims the reality and promise that the singer embodies. Indeed, the song ironically foresees the end of the very social structures that ground Mary's own worth in her ability to bear a son.

Mary's song inspired the Feast of Fools, a name variously given to all or part of the Christmas revels that were celebrated for centuries throughout the church. The Feast of Fools, in fact, became a literal acting out of the Magnificat, an odd witness to the God "whose inclination is to topple human power

2. "The feasibility of such a journey . . . taking perhaps four days, by a woman alone is not germane to this type of story" (C. F. Evans, *Saint Luke*, TPI New Testament Commentaries [London: SCM Press, 1990], 169).

Luke 1:39-45 (46-55)

Theological Perspective

them. God's power and greatness display God's goodness. As A. W. Tozer observed nearly fifty years ago, "The greatness of God rouses fear within us, but His goodness encourages us not to be afraid of Him. To fear and not be afraid—that is the paradox of faith."[3] Mary's fear of God is unafraid, and in her song we hear of both sides of God's goodness in action, the grace *and* the mercy of God. Mary bears witness to the grace—the unmerited favor—of God, who has done great things for her and looks with favor upon the lowly and fills the hungry with good things. God's mercy (Heb. *hesed*; Gk. *eleos*) is found in forgiveness and long-suffering patience with the weakness and corruption of humanity.

We also discover here that humility is the proper attitude of God's people in response to God's goodness. Calvin observed: "If we contrast Mary's poor estate with high estate we may see that Mary, in emptying herself, elevates God alone. This is no paean of false humility, but the plain and sincere statement of a conviction that she had graven on her heart" (Calvin, *Harmony*, 35). God has claimed us as his eternal possession, and we rejoice in God's goodness.

The Magnificat rounds off this celebration of God's goodness by recalling God's covenant faithfulness to Israel (v. 55). The covenant of God with God's people is the golden thread that binds together the Old Testament and the New Testament, the old Israel and the new Israel: "I will walk among you, and will be your God, and you shall be my people" (Lev. 26:12). Calvin noted: "Understand this, God spoke in this way to the Fathers of old, that the grace offered to them might come down to later generations also, for then by faith, an adoption was made of all nations, that they too might be spiritual sons of Abraham, who were not by nature" (Calvin, *Harmony*, 40–41). The best hope of the Christian in every age finds its voice in Mary's song, and it has rested securely on this: God is good, and God keeps promises.

ROBERT REDMAN

Pastoral Perspective

manifestation, but we do not yet experience it. For many in the typical congregation, this Sunday may be their only opportunity to hear a genuine message of Advent, as distinct from Christmas.

The development of hope within community takes time. How many Marys and Elizabeths (or Zechariahs and Josephs) might there be sitting in the pews, awaiting an opportunity to connect more deeply with the people around them? How many long to connect their small story with the larger stories of God? How might our churches encourage the cycle of recognition and response that widens the reach of the Holy Spirit? Much can be learned from sitting quietly with our brothers and sisters as the world pushes us relentlessly toward a louder, larger, and ever more expensive December 25. In our postmodern context, the texts of Advent are deeply countercultural. Churches of the Christendom era enjoyed an easy familiarity with the wider culture: town Christmas trees, carols sung in school concerts, Christmas cards sent by politicians to their donors. Now the big, flashy events are largely focused around the twin idols of celebrity and consumerism. For good and for ill, the church has been marginalized. The preacher of this Sunday's good news can welcome the faithful into this marginality, because marginal people, like expectant mothers in the ancient Near East, have time to listen and wait. Those who are alienated by their culture might just be visited by the Holy Spirit.

It is hard to know what brings people to church on the Fourth Sunday of Advent. Perhaps they are there every Sunday, or maybe today is somehow special? Perhaps they were asked to light the Advent candles or sing in the pageant or bake cookies for coffee hour? They may not be on open display, but doubts and hurts are close to the surface for many. Congregants need to sit for a while with a people— and a God—who will accept them as they are, not as they feel they are expected to be. Experiencing true acceptance in worship, they may find themselves asking Elizabeth's question: "And why has this happened to me?" (1:43). This very human-sized story prepares us for the grand, history-changing birth that is yet to come. The congregations that linger here will be strengthened, prepared, and deepened for their Christmas celebration.

MICHAEL S. BENNETT

3. A. W. Tozer, *The Knowledge of the Holy* (San Francisco: Harper, 1961), 84.

culminates in the angelic announcement of Jesus' birth (2:10–14).

Mary's song is the first of three in Luke's introductory section. There follow the Benedictus ("Blessed be the Lord God of Israel") of John's father, Zechariah (1:68–79), and then the Nunc Dimittis ("You are now dismissing") of Simeon (2:29–35). The effect of this interweaving of narrative and prophetic praise songs is a stately, almost worshipful stage setting for Jesus' public activity in Luke, which picks up after the appearance of John the Baptist in the wilderness. The Magnificat relates Mary's present joy and overflowing praise (vv. 46–47) as a response to what God has done, both for her personally in granting her the admiration of all future generations and for God's more encompassing salvation (vv. 50–55). The central affirmations of the Magnificat are God's capacity to act, God's holiness, and God's mercy (vv. 49–51). God's history with Israel functions thus as a guarantee and a proof of the efficacy of the revelation in Christ.

There is a strong socioeconomic tone of the acts of God praised in the Magnificat (esp. vv. 51–53). This kind of imagery recalls the hymnic language of the OT, particularly other songs of praise sung by individuals,[3] often women (e.g., the Song of Miriam, Exod. 15:21, and the Song of Deborah, Judg. 5). Such emotional language and triumphal imagery, however, is not a Jewish or Christian counterpart of the triumphalist imperial propaganda of Virgil's *Aeneid*. It is not the voice of the powerful of the earth speaking here, but the voices of the marginalized and relatively powerless early Christian movement. Picture Nicaraguan peasants or the marginalized people of Sudan. But Luke's motif of God's reversal of fortunes (vv. 51–53) is not intended to raise violent resistance or to drive the wealthy and powerful to despair; these verses must rather be read in light of the examples later in this Gospel—say, of the rich ruler (18:18–30) or Zacchaeus (19:1–10)—where the well-off are exhorted to deal with their wealth in a way that brings them into a positive relation with the poor in order to partake in the same promised salvation.

STEPHEN A. COOPER

structures and to raise the downtrodden to a position of honor and feasting" (Harris, *Carnival*, 140). Preachers of this text, rather than treating it with deadly seriousness, can learn from the spirit of the Feast of Fools, which subverted the pretensions and hierarchy of both the church and the society:

> Throughout medieval and early modern Europe, Christmas was a time for festive reversals of status. As early as the ninth century, a mock patriarch was elected in Constantinople, burlesquing the Eucharist and riding through the city streets on an ass. And as late as Innocents' Day (28 December) 1685, in the Franciscan church of Antibes, lay brothers and servants "put on the vestments inside out, held the books upside down, . . . wore spectacles with rounds of orange peel instead of glasses, . . . blew the ashes from the censers on each other's face and hands, and instead of the proper liturgy chanted confused and inarticulate gibberish."
>
> Cross-dressing, masking as animals, wafting foul-smelling incense, and electing burlesque bishops, popes, and patriarchs mocked conventional human pretensions. So did the introduction of an ass into the church, in commemoration of the holy family's flight into Egypt, and the braying of the priest, choir, and congregation during mass.[2]

When churches get too serious, this Magnificat can become sourly prophetic and angry. But for preachers, this Sunday is an occasion for bold, daring speech, like Mary's, which proclaims the upside-down world inaugurated by Jesus' incarnation. It is a Sunday to declare the politically, socially, and ecclesially subversive character of Jesus' arrival, which will be joyful good news to folks like Mary, but may be threatening to those in power. This Sunday, finally, offers preachers the opportunity to "play the fool." It is a day to prepare for the incarnation by lampooning the "powers that be" (including the powers in the church) with the topsy-turvy news of the gospel, which is first celebrated by two pregnant women laughing and singing, and which enters the world through a young, unwed mother and a child laid in a manger because there was no room in the inn.

CHARLES L. CAMPBELL

---

3. Bovon, *Luke I*, 55.

2. This quotation, in Harris, *Carnival*, 140, is from E. K. Chambers, *The Medieval Stage* (London: Oxford University Press, 1903), 1:317–18.

Isaiah 9:2-7

²The people who walked in darkness
   have seen a great light;
  those who lived in a land of deep darkness—
   on them light has shined.
³You have multiplied the nation,
   you have increased its joy;
  they rejoice before you
   as with joy at the harvest,
   as people exult when dividing plunder.
⁴For the yoke of their burden,
   and the bar across their shoulders,
   the rod of their oppressor,
   you have broken as on the day of Midian.

Theological Perspective

"It's always darkest before the dawn."

Isaiah writes at a time when things were about as bad they could get for those in the kingdom of Judah. They had been betrayed from without and within. Their northern, sister kingdom of Israel had plotted with Syria to invade them. However, this potential calamity had been averted by yet another—the invasion of Israel by Assyria and the fall of Samaria. Large areas of the promised land in the north had been "brought into contempt"—annexed—by Tiglath-pileser III (9:1). Now, Assyria, led by an arrogant, boasting king, threatened Judah with a similar fate (10:12). King Ahaz of Judah, though warned against idolatry by Isaiah, subjected Judah to the violent Assyrian king.

It was as understandable as it was tempting for the people of Judah, including her kings, to seek an alliance with one of her neighboring kingdoms—Assyria, Syria, Babylon, or Moab—in order to assure her safety and security, her peace. It only made good geopolitical sense. One must fight fire with fire; one must meet power with power.

But Isaiah rejected that turn, that strategy. Why?

In *The City of God*, St. Augustine defines peace as "the calm that comes from order." For him, that order is founded on the equilibrium of, or balance between and among, all the parts of the body, the body and

Pastoral Perspective

Into the darkness of national chaos and despair, Isaiah's words shine a light that illuminates the shape and form of the central claim of his good news: rescue is coming. To those who sit in darkness, or fear, or failure, or want: rescue is coming!

Imagine the moment after a battle when the terrifying noises of screaming planes, whining missiles, and grenade blasts suddenly, unbelievably come to an end. The smoke clears, the dust settles, the sun reappears, and you touch your own body and find that you are whole; you made it through.

Such is the feel and import of these verses from Isaiah. The prophet carries us from darkness to light, from despair to hope, from terror to comfort in a matter of seconds.

For Christians this news of rescue comes in the shape and form of a child. This is the single reason the church is gathered on Christmas Eve: "a child has been born for us, a son given to us." This verse is located in the center of tonight's reading and is the pivot around which the passage revolves. Indeed, it is the pivot around which revolves the whole Christian enterprise.

The pastor will therefore want to center the sermon on the child to whom the church is gathered to pay homage. Just as grandparents, aunts and uncles, cousins, neighbors, friends and coworkers

⁵For all the boots of the tramping warriors
and all the garments rolled in blood
shall be burned as fuel for the fire.
⁶For a child has been born for us,
a son given to us;
authority rests upon his shoulders;
and he is named
Wonderful Counselor, Mighty God,
Everlasting Father, Prince of Peace.
⁷His authority shall grow continually,
and there shall be endless peace
for the throne of David and his kingdom.
He will establish and uphold it
with justice and with righteousness
from this time onward and forevermore.
The zeal of the LORD of hosts will do this.

Exegetical Perspective

The hopeful proclamation of the reversal of fortunes, light amid darkness, and a child's birth makes this beautiful passage a most appropriate text for the celebration of Christmas Eve. Rejoicing replaces lament, and victims become victors in the prophet's hymn of thanksgiving. This appropriateness for Christmas makes it striking that, aside from Matthew 4:15–16, which paraphrases Isaiah 9:1–2 to explain Jesus' residence in Capernaum at the beginning of his public ministry, the Gospels do not connect the Isaiah text to Jesus' nativity or messianic identity (cf. Luke 1:79). Indeed, nowhere does the NT quote or allude to the famous messianic titles (vv. 6–7) of this prophetic song. The preacher does holy work who helps a congregation imagine how this promise of a Hebrew royal birth to end Assyrian hegemony anticipates the birth of the nonroyal teaching wonder worker we celebrate on this sacred evening.

Historical Context. The book of Isaiah is attributed to Isaiah son of Amoz, who prophesied in Jerusalem during the latter half of the eighth century BCE and witnessed the rise of Neo-Assyrian imperialism. Under the aggressive policies of its king, Tiglath-pileser III (ca. 745–727 BCE), Assyria eventually conquers or annexes much of Syria and its neighbors, including the kingdom of Israel with its

Homiletical Perspective

Christmas is a time for the widening of the kingdom. God is not ever to be labeled or libeled as a tribal God with a small sectarian geography. The problem with making friends with all the world at once is that the world we make friends with tends to teach us their values and philosophies. Syncretism is the marriage of opposing ideas and values by welding uncommon beliefs and symbols into a new kind of fabric that holds some of the values of each of the faith systems, but generally weakens the strongest ideas of both.

When opposing cultures come together and live together, they often bring into being new ways of seeing the world. When Oeastre and Jesus came together in the newly missionized areas of England and northwest Europe, Jesus brought in communion and Oeastre brought in her fertility symbols of rabbits and baby chickens perhaps. When Christians lived with the Romans for a while, the desired holiday of his birth became associated with the Latin Saturnalia. And then there's Christmas! Into this odd syncretism of elves and apostles, reindeers and shepherds, snowmen and magi, Jesus and Santa spin in a common blender and generally speaking, the non-Christian elements come to the froth at the top of the spin. The dominant interpreter of this spin is what the majority of the people emphasize or believe. Does the emperor have on new clothes? Nearly everybody thinks so. And the few who do not,

Isaiah 9:2-7

Theological Perspective

the soul, humanity and God, and the people constituting the political community.[1] It is a comprehensive and compelling notion. To be at peace means that every aspect of our own person and every relationship we have with others, from those closest to us to those across the globe, exist in a tranquil harmony. In such a world, no one is threatened by violence, exploitation, or abuse; no one has reason to fear. For Augustine the political realm experienced peace "by means of an ordered harmony of authority and obedience." He believed in a great chain of being where some ruled and others obeyed. Living in the period after Constantine, when the Christian church was supported and protected by the power of empire, Augustine assumed that that authority involved the power of the emperor's sword.

Back during the period of the cold war, when there was enmity between the West and East, the United States employed a strategy of peace by means of the doctrine of mutually assured destruction (MAD). The idea was that if the United States and the Soviet Union had sufficient nuclear weapons to destroy each other, if one or the other fired first, they would be assured of annihilation by the other. Therefore, neither would dare use nuclear weapons in a first strike. In a sermon Dr. Richard Groves made the following observation. "This is like saying that two people are holding a gun to each other's head. Now, there are a lot of ways to characterize that situation, but 'peace' is not the first one that comes to mind."[2]

Isaiah would agree. In his mind, peace could not be won by the forced submission of some to others, even others as powerful as Tiglath-pileser III or the kings of Syria, Babylon, or Moab. For him, the harmony that assured security and peace could not be produced by force, imposed from above by those at the top of the social hierarchy—no matter how powerful they appeared to be. Rather, he announced that "a child has been born for us, a son given to us. . . . His authority shall grow continually, and there shall be endless peace" (9:6a, 7a). On this one rested authority and the titles "Wonderful Counselor, Mighty God, Everlasting Father, Prince of Peace" (9:6b). Peace rests on the foundation of wisdom, strength, steadfastness, and a nonviolent intent. Isaiah looked to the One whose "fire is in Zion" (31:9). From this fire, Isaiah believed the "light has shined" (9:2). He counseled Judah to hold out

---

1. In Augustine, *The City of God*, trans. Gerald G. Walsh et al. (Garden City, NY: Image Books, 1958), Book 19, chap. 13, 456.
2. Preached at the Wake Forest Baptist Church, Winston-Salem, NC, 1988.

Pastoral Perspective

gather to lay eyes upon a newborn infant, so we sinners draw near on Christmas Eve to lay eyes upon this child. Every child is a gift from God and, therefore, an intimation and reflection of the gift of *this* child who is our light, our rescue, and our good news. Tonight let the church be stable and manger, swaddling the child in our embrace and in the embrace of our aching human hearts. After all, it is for him that our painters have painted, our musicians composed, our architects designed, our martyrs died, our healers healed, our activists agitated, and our preachers preached. We have come from far and wide to gaze upon this gift from God. It is for him and to him that our carols ring out on Christmas Eve.

Taking a cue from Isaiah, the pastor might labor attentively over the sermon: whittling, trimming, and snipping at it until it contains as few sentences as possible. After all, Isaiah describes his context, points to the child, and pronounces the future in six concise, yet stunningly wrought verses. The pastor may wish to ponder what few beautiful words might be employed to carry this exquisite message. As an act of pastoral care, surprise and delight your uneasy holiday congregation with a combination of beauty and brevity. Look with compassion upon the strangers, the doubters, and the sheepish footdraggers who were pressed into attendance this evening by circumstances beyond their control. Surely on this night of all nights we can trust the carols and candles, the readings and music, the liturgy and the season itself to have their way with the ecclesiastically wayward.

The pastor may wish to begin his or her reflections where Isaiah begins: by naming whatever darkness is palpably experienced by members of the congregation, by the nation, and by the nations of the world. What is the substance of the darkness in which the pastor and the congregation are gripped? What constitutes the yoke, burden, bar, and rod? What do these feel like and look like? How do these define and limit our lives as individuals and as a nation? Just as Isaiah spoke into the truth of the lives of his compatriots with utter honesty, so must the church today speak from and to the truth as experienced by those in our pews—yet not only by those in our pews, but also by those in Africa, Asia, the Middle East, and Latin America. For this child who has been born for us, has been born for *all of us*.

The soldiers' boots to which Isaiah refers bespeak an aggressive human posture, a way of relating to the world with violence and dominance that, in turn,

capital at Samaria. In opposition to the looming Assyrian presence, King Rezin of Damascus and King Pekah of Samaria form a coalition to resist the encroaching empire. They invite King Ahaz of Jerusalem to join them in imitation of successful confederacies against Assyrian aggression in the previous century. When Ahaz refuses to join their coalition, they besiege Jerusalem in order to replace him with a more malleable king, referred to as the "son of Tabeel" (Isa. 7:6). Such a puppet king is a threat not only to Ahaz, but to the entire Davidic dynasty. This conflict, called the Syro-Ephraimite War (734 BCE), is described in Isaiah 7:1–2 (cf. 2 Kgs. 16:5–9).

According to Isaiah 7:14, the prophet assures Ahaz of God's support with the sign of Immanuel. Rather than waiting on God's deliverance from the armies of Pekah and Rezin, however, Ahaz willingly submits to Tiglath-pileser III and sends him a large payment. The Assyrians then destroy Damascus (732 BCE) and annex large portions of Israel. The Assyrian deportation of Galilean populations (2 Kgs. 15:29) provides the dire context of Isaiah 9:1 and its gloomy "darkness." In this historical context, Isaiah's poem reflects a vision of renewed independence and the assurance of an unbroken line of succession for the Davidic dynasty in the aftermath of the Syro-Ephraimite War. The text may thus have been composed as a hymn in celebration of the birth of a Davidic crown prince, a coronation hymn for Hezekiah's royal inauguration, or some less specific event. Whatever the ancient social context, the text is a beautiful proclamation of a hopeful future and its vision of a just and righteous leader is timeless in its appeal.

Exegetical Remarks. Following the "gloom," "anguish," and "contempt" of 9:1, our passage begins with the powerful symbol of light shining in the darkness (v. 2). The imagery of darkness and light is common in the book of Isaiah (e.g., 2:5; 42:6; 49:6; 60:1), and later biblical writers further develop this symbolism. "Deep darkness" renders the Hebrew word *lmwt*, read as "shadow of death" in older translations of Psalm 23:4 (also Matt. 4:16 and Luke 1:79). In Hebrew poetry "the land of deep darkness" also denotes the land of the dead (Ps. 107:10–14; Job 10:21–22). In an eighth-century context, darkness symbolizes the Assyrian conquest, while light symbolizes freedom from foreign oppression.

Verse 3 addresses God directly for the first of three times (vv. 3–4) to commend what God has accomplished. The first phrase makes little sense in

cast down their eyes and remember what it was like before the majority opinion emerged. Alas, over time the herd urge had set a new standard, and all the dissenters must agree that the group's perception is the only one that really matters. Those who clearly see that the emperor had no clothes must agree that he has new clothes. They must either shut up or look odd in a culture that has settled the matter in their own minds. Fortunately for us, Matthew and Luke's account of the origin of Christmas still survives and demands that the honest believer steer around the wreckage of North Pole mythology and fix Christian geography squarely in Bethlehem of Judea.

In the closing verses of Isaiah 8, the prophet is begging Israel not to be contaminated with the spirit of secularity that owns the nations around them. The world grows dark when it feeds on group opinion.

> Now if people say to you, "Consult the ghosts and the familiar spirits that chirp and mutter; should not a people consult their gods, the dead on behalf of the living, for teaching and for instruction?" surely, those who speak like this will have no dawn! They will pass through the land, greatly distressed and hungry; when they are hungry, they will be enraged and will curse their king and their gods. They will turn their faces upward, or they will look to the earth, but will see only distress and darkness, the gloom of anguish; and they will be thrust into thick darkness. (Isa. 8:19–22)

Perhaps Jude emphasizes the constant war of the people of light, to contend for the light, lest the light become darkness and they see no more. It is fearful and never-ending work to keep the mind straight in a world that wants to bargain for truth by asking what it would hurt if we make Jesus and Astarte consorts, for instance. Jude began his letter with a spirit of reluctance, "Beloved, while eagerly preparing to write to you about the salvation we share, I find it necessary to write and appeal to you to contend for the faith that was once for all entrusted to the saints" (Jude 3).

Isaiah in his own mind had watched his nation come down to a time when the light was growing dim. It wasn't as if some enemy was stealing the light. It was the good people who were to blame. It is the masses who opt for darkness. They choose it because in some sense they find that darkness requires very little maintenance, while light requires a constant struggle. But there is no glory in darkness; a people dedicated to it are finally lost beyond redemption. Amos saw that when the darkness had completely saturated a culture, it would terminally bypass redemption.

Isaiah 9:2-7

Theological Perspective

for the real thing—an authentic and lasting peace brought by the One who would establish the "throne of David and his kingdom" with "justice and righteousness" (9:7).

But why and how could they wait? In the midst of darkness, in the midst of injustice and unrighteousness, why should a people hold out for peace founded on justice? How can they? They can, because, though they "walked in darkness," Isaiah says they "have seen a great light" (9:2). Had they seen it? Or had Isaiah seen it?

Exegetes point to a bit of ambiguity here in the use of the past tense. Has this Prince of Peace already appeared? If so, why is this one not known? Or did Isaiah himself see it, as he experienced his own vision and call in the temple (6:1ff.)? In this "great light," did he see creation as God intended it to be, ordered by wisdom, strength, steadfastness, and peace? Is that a vision that can guide us today?[3]

There are many of us who also live in darkness. In the United States during the first decade of the twenty-first century, there are those who argue that we too are surrounded by enemies at every turn; they are all around us, ready to destroy us, our cherished institutions, and our way of life. In the face of the fear, even terror, it is tempting to put our trust in the powerful—those who, seeking their own interests, promise to protect us. In this, our own darkness, Isaiah poses the questions: Will we make room for the Prince of Peace, who orders the world with justice and righteousness? Will we prepare to follow him in peacemaking?

STEPHEN B. BOYD

Pastoral Perspective

beget more of the same. The image of boots leads inexorably to Isaiah's next image, of soldiers' blood-soaked garments. Isaiah then contrasts these images with that of the mantle of authority that rests so lightly upon the shoulders of the one to whom the prophet points. Clothes do not merely "make the man." They can affect the way we feel and act; they can signal aggressiveness or gentleness.

Years ago, while serving as a chaplain in a juvenile detention center, I heard a seventeen-year-old confess that he acted particularly badly when he was wearing his big, heavy hunting boots. He loved those boots, he said. He loved wearing them. They made him feel like a man. Yet, when he wore them, he turned into a bully. The boots tapped into a part of him that was ugly, aggressive, cruel, and domineering. He confided to us that when he was not wearing them he felt and acted more gently. From the day this young man arrived at this self-understanding and named it aloud to his peers, he began to change.

How does the Christian exchange tramping boots for "feet shod with the preparation of the gospel of peace" (Eph. 6:15 KJV)? How do we dress for and witness to the one whom Isaiah names as the Prince of Peace? How do we proclaim with our lips and embody in our lives that which we read in our Bibles and sing in our carols: peace on the earth, goodwill to all? How do we practice gentleness in the presence of this gentle gift from God? A child has been born for us and a son given to us—for and to *all of us*—and nothing will ever again be the same.

NANCY S. TAYLOR

---

3. Brevard Childs, *Isaiah* (Louisville, KY: Westminster John Knox Press, 2001), 70–80.

Exegetical Perspective

Hebrew, but the NRSV translation—"You have multiplied the nation"—provides a nice poetic parallel with "you have increased its joy." The people respond to God's actions by rejoicing as at harvest and dividing plunder.

Following the "light" and rejoicing of the previous two verses, verses 4–5 offer dark images of oppression, war, and bloodshed. The prophet claims that God has already broken the yoke of Assyrian oppression "as on the day of Midian," a reference to Gideon's defeat of Midian in Judges 7. The poetic parallelism of the "yoke," "bar," and "rod" of Assyria's oppression is also found in Isaiah 10:24–27. Verse 5's description of burning "all" the blood-soaked boots and garments of slain enemy soldiers is reminiscent of Ezekiel's eschatological vision of war's end in 39:9–10. Although such militaristic language of defeated enemies is unsettling, contemporary readers should appreciate the ancient writers' sense of relief and joy in freedom from warfare.

Like verses 4 and 5, verse 6 begins with the Hebrew word *kî* ("for, because") to introduce the third reason for the people's rejoicing: "For a child has been born for us." The poet speaks for the entire community to celebrate the birth of a royal heir. Scholars frequently compare the royal titles in verse 7 to ancient Egyptian throne names, and many commentators understand verse 6a as part of an enthronement ritual utilizing divine adoption language (cf. Pss. 2:7; 110:1). As royal or messianic titles, these names are not attributes of their human recipient. That is, the infant in this poem is not Mighty God and the Everlasting Father; he is named in honor of the heavenly Father. The culmination of the list in the fourth name, "Prince of Peace," answers the poem's militaristic context by offering a vision of a peaceful future.

Verse 7 describes the reign of the royal child with the hyperbolic language common to royal psalms (e.g., Ps. 89:19–37). The first phrase may originally have been a fifth throne name, but the text is not clear. Authority, peace, justice, and righteousness are explicitly linked to the throne and kingdom of David. Isaiah 11:1–5 similarly describes the righteous rule of the Davidic heir, while Psalm 72 details the royal duties of justice and integrity. The poem concludes with a final prophetic declaration: "The zeal of the LORD of hosts" will accomplish this wondrous future.

NEAL WALLS

Homiletical Perspective

The time is surely coming, says the Lord GOD,
    when I will send a famine on the land;
not a famine of bread, or a thirst for water,
    but of hearing the words of the LORD.
They shall wander from sea to sea,
    and from north to east;
they shall run to and fro, seeking the word of the LORD;
    but they will not find it.

In that day the beautiful young women
    and the young men
shall faint for thirst. . . .
    they shall fall, and never rise again.
                    (Amos 8:11–13; 14b)

To Isaiah's mind, the darkness that resulted from not safeguarding or treasuring the light, was about to disappear.

The people who walked in darkness
    have seen a great light;
those who lived in a land of deep darkness—
    on them light has shined.
                    (Isa. 9:2)

With this light, this holy pure light, will come a new reign of joy. This light will come from a God who has offered them a utopian day—light that denounces all the old symbols of battle for a universal peace.

For all the boots of the tramping warriors
    and all the garments rolled in blood
    shall be burned as fuel for the fire.
                    (Isa. 9:5)

Who will be the source of this universal light?

For a child has been born for us,
    a son given to us;
authority rests upon his shoulders;
    and he is named
Wonderful Counselor, Mighty God,
    Everlasting Father, Prince of peace.
His authority shall grow continually,
    and there shall be endless peace
for the throne of David and his kingdom.
    He will establish and uphold it
with justice and with righteousness,
    from this time onward and forevermore.
The zeal of the LORD of hosts will do this.
                    (Isa. 9:6–7)

Isaiah didn't know his name, but we do, and he comes to this darkened present world to remind us that darkness is not forever; light is. And when we have sifted out the odd syncretisms of this holy night, we will find exactly what the magi did. Only the light leads. Only the light is eternal.

CALVIN MILLER

Psalm 96

¹O sing to the Lord a new song;
  sing to the Lord, all the earth.
²Sing to the Lord, bless his name;
  tell of his salvation from day to day.
³Declare his glory among the nations,
  his marvelous works among all the peoples.
⁴For great is the Lord, and greatly to be praised;
  he is to be revered above all gods.
⁵For all the gods of the peoples are idols,
  but the Lord made the heavens.
⁶Honor and majesty are before him;
  strength and beauty are in his sanctuary.

⁷Ascribe to the Lord, O families of the peoples,
  ascribe to the Lord glory and strength.

Theological Perspective

On this eve of Christmas, many churches will reenact the beloved ritual of processing to the crèche and placing the baby Jesus in his manger. In some cases, the presider will perform this act; in others, this honor will be given to one of the youngest members of the assembly. Perhaps this latter choice is most fitting for the enthronement of the humble Christ child. In contrast, our psalm majestically announces the enthronement of a king who reigns in splendor—YHWH, the divine king who reigns over all other gods and principalities. This enthronement has its impetus in Israel's experience of salvation in its own history, and its confident expectation of God's future coming in a reign of justice, peace, and abundant life in a fulfillment that will embrace all the nations.

This psalm of praise is proclaimed against the backdrop of Israel's memory of suffering. Through enslavement, oppression, war, and famine, through uncertainty and doubt in God's promise, through experiences of humiliation and vulnerability, through the instability of life seemingly devoid of God's presence, God's faithfulness has prevailed, God's power has come to save, and Israel knows its reality as once again firm, secure, and stable.

The language of the psalmist is praise and exaltation, the exhortation to "sing a new song." Not only Israel but all living things are called into a chorus

Pastoral Perspective

Described as an enthronement psalm, Psalm 96 is really an invitation for all the world to rise up and praise the Lord. What could be more appropriate on the night we celebrate the birth of Jesus, our true sovereign? "O sing to the Lord a new song; sing to the Lord, all the earth!" Yet what appears at first to be a simple song of praise allows for multiple pastoral interpretations—especially in uncertain times.

The great challenge of Christmas Eve is to craft a sermon that feeds the faithful but also ministers to the needs of the skeptical (or for other reasons) unchurched. Honesty is the key. As I prepared my Christmas Eve sermon one year, I overheard a young woman trashing Christmas. This self-described pagan was explaining to a friend how the early church co-opted the winter solstice. "Even the colors of red and green originated with the druids. The whole Christmas thing is such a fraud!"

Of course, it's true. Early Christians did "borrow" from many preexisting traditions. Back in the third century Emperor Aurelius established the winter solstice as the birthday of the invincible sun. Then in 336 CE, the early church, backed up with Roman authority, determined that December 25 would be celebrated as the birth of Jesus, the true invincible son. Indeed, many of our Advent and Christmas traditions are reinterpreted pagan

⁸Ascribe to the LORD the glory due his name;
  bring an offering, and come into his courts.
⁹Worship the LORD in holy splendor;
  tremble before him, all the earth.

¹⁰Say among the nations, "The LORD is king!
  The world is firmly established; it shall never be moved.
  He will judge the peoples with equity."
¹¹Let the heavens be glad, and let the earth rejoice;
  let the sea roar, and all that fills it;
¹² let the field exult, and everything in it.
  Then shall all the trees of the forest sing for joy
¹³ before the LORD; for he is coming,
  for he is coming to judge the earth.
  He will judge the world with righteousness,
  and the peoples with his truth.

Exegetical Perspective

Psalm 96 bursts upon the tranquil manger scene of Christmas Eve with a tidal wave of praise inundating all of creation with the message of God's sovereign rule. Psalm 96 is one in a series of enthronement psalms that includes Psalms 93 and 95–100, each celebrating the Lord's kingship over the nations and all the earth. The lection, for example, builds on the theme of God's sovereignty expressed in Psalm 95 (see 95:3 and 96:4–5).

The psalm is divisible into four sections: praise with proclamation (vv. 1–6), praise with tribute (vv. 7–10), creation's praise (vv. 11–12), and, by way of conclusion, the fundamental reason for praise (v. 13). The final verse is key to the entire psalm: all praise serves to herald God's coming "to judge the world with righteousness and . . . faithfulness" (my trans.).

The psalm opens with a ringing command to sing "a new song" addressed to "all the earth" (see also 40:3; 98:1; 144:9; 149:1). The old, tired song of lament is a thing of the past; a new situation gives birth to a new song, a song of praise (cf. Isa. 43:18–19). As Psalm 96 makes clear, fundamental to such praise is proclamation, the substance of praise. And the substance of proclamation is the Lord's greatness and awe (v. 4). God's glory puts everything else to shame, including the gods, idle idols that they are. The Psalms sometimes speak of the gods

Homiletical Perspective

While Psalm 96 stands little chance of serving as a preacher's central text on Christmas Eve, it may still provide the preacher with a shape for the sermon. This enthronement psalm sings a new song to the God above all gods, calling all who hear it to proclaim God's salvation and declare God's glory. Neither the salvation nor the glory is theoretical. God's "marvelous deeds" are concrete in Israel's memory. Those who sing this new song do so with the old song of Exodus 15 ringing in their ears. If the psalm can actually be sung this evening—with flourishes from several tambourines—then those who share Israel's memory may find themselves with Moses and Miriam on the far side of the Red Sea, dancing with joy at their deliverance.

The psalm evokes creation as well, reminding those who sing this song that they do so in a chorus that includes the heavens and the earth, the sea and all that fills it, the field and everything in it, and the trees of the forest, as well as all the families of the peoples. The safety this psalm proclaims ("salvation," v. 2) is inclusive of every created thing. The stability of the world is a done deal ("it shall never be moved," v. 10). The justice announced here ("equity," v. 10) leaves out no one and nothing. The divine sovereign in this psalm is no local god, both identified with and exclusively focused on the fortunes of one particular

Psalm 96

Theological Perspective

of praise to God. The new song is a response to YHWH's brand-new deeds, deeds transforming reality and bringing to birth a new order—not only among humankind but throughout creation. This "new order" is the establishment of all things in right relationship— what the psalmist calls righteousness (v. 13). The stable ordering of lives and all life, the firm foundation of the world, rests on the rule of God. However, the efficacy of God's rule, it seems, depends upon Israel's acknowledgment of the one true God and the rejection of all idols. It depends upon Israel's free entry into relationship with this God, a relationship of honesty and trust, and above all, a relationship that gives God God's due. "Giving God God's due" entails reverencing the order of creation and humbly acknowledging the existence and participation of all other nations.

Israel experiences salvation as having come from God, and always coming from God. There is no other source of this salvation, a salvation that is nevertheless ongoing: God's reign is already established and yet is always being established on the earth, even as faith is proclaimed in the future fulfillment of that reign.

In the Christian community, we look back tonight to the birth of Jesus as the decisive fulfillment of that always-coming reign of God, and yet we still look forward to the fullness of that reign when Christ will come in glory. What can it mean for *this* Christian community to announce the once-and-future coming of Christ? What can it mean to proclaim Christ as ruler of the nations? In doing so, what idols of our age must we actively reject?

The idols of our age are legion, and they are insidious; they are the idols of empire, which permeate even the structures of our churches. As a people, we are held captive by the belief that our security lies in our military might, material wealth, and the forces of globalization. Globalization has multiple meanings, both positive and negative; in essence, however, it is a consciousness that is enveloping the world. In this sense, Mary Grey characterizes globalization as analogous to spirituality, because it is a force that engages the whole person—mind, body, and heart. Thus globalization is a spiritual crisis, and capitalism is a new religion in its idolatry of money. "It has hijacked our imaginations and our desires." Furthermore, Grey asserts, "capitalism aims to subordinate every other interest and is deliberate, systemic, hierarchical and patriarchal."[1]

---

1. Mary C. Grey, *Sacred Longings: The Ecological Spirit and Global Culture* (Minneapolis: Fortress Press, 2004), 16.

Pastoral Perspective

customs, originally designed to appease the pagan gods.

But the pagan gods are not the God of Abraham. As Psalm 96 declares: "For great is the LORD, and greatly to be praised; he is to be revered above all gods. For all the gods of the peoples are idols, but the LORD made the heavens." The message is clear: we worship God, not so that God will be great; we worship God because God *is* great. The creator does not depend upon the creature for his glory, just as Christmas does not depend upon the originality of its traditions in order to be holy. For people who struggle with the meaning of Christmas, Psalm 96 provides a pastor with an opportunity to explore the differences between the idols we create for ourselves and the one Creator God.

Read from a different angle, Psalm 96 opens up a conversation about the environment and our role as the crowning glory of creation. After establishing that the Lord is great, and calling all people to extol God's holy name, the psalmist moves on, focusing on the righteousness of God. The last three verses culminate with these words: "Let the heavens be glad, and let the earth rejoice; let the sea roar, and all that fills it; let the field exult, and everything in it. Then shall all the trees of the forest sing for joy before the LORD; for he is coming, for he is coming to judge the earth. He will judge the world with righteousness, and the peoples with his truth" (vv. 11–13).

What causes the earth to rejoice? Not only that God is king, but that the Lord is coming to judge the *earth,* not just the people. That's what makes the trees shout for joy. The good news declared in Psalm 96 is that God, who has made heaven and earth and all creatures that inhabit the earth, will render justice to all of creation. In other words, the dolphins and the redwoods will have their day in court. Such a suggestion should give us pause, perched as we are on the eve of our annual Christmas binge. What does justice look like for the rest of creation? Are we "doing right" by the environment? If we take seriously the psalmist's claim that God is the author of all creation, we must also take seriously our effect on that same creation. This message will matter to both faithful and skeptic.

Yet the most important pastoral message found in Psalm 96 is the message of God's unchanging presence in the world and in our lives. Some years ago, a woman came to visit her pastor in great distress. Her parents had recently sold the family home and moved to a retirement community in the Southwest. Although it had been a decade since she

revering the Lord and, in the same breath, of them being mere artifacts fashioned by human hands (see 97:7; 115:3–8; 135:15–18). Psalm 82 fills the narrative gap by recounting God's judgment against the gods, sentencing them to death for their failure to implement justice in the world. Only the Lord can lay claim to creation and to justice (v. 5). Idols are created; God creates. The distinction for the psalmist is categorically absolute. As for human beings, they ambiguously hold the middle ground; they are both creators and created. Nevertheless, the attributes of majesty and strength belong to God alone. Poetically objectified, they serve as the vanguard for God's entrance into the sanctuary (v. 6).

The centerpiece of the psalm (vv. 7–10) opens with a command to "ascribe to the LORD" (literally "give"), similar to the opening verses of Psalm 29, which addresses not a human congregation of worshipers but an assembly of divine beings. The peoples in Psalm 96 are commanded to "give" to the Lord "glory," "power," and the "glory of his name" (vv. 7–8a). How is that so, particularly if God already possesses glory and greatness (vv. 3–4)? What more does God need? To "give" God the glory is, yes, to acknowledge God's glory, to recognize God's supreme honor. But the language is more suggestive: God is actually edified by such acknowledgment. In the Psalms, praise is meant to "exalt," "make great," "lift up," "glorify," "magnify" God. Such language suggests a transference of power from the one giving praise, the worshiper, to God, the recipient of such praise and the object of worship. In short, hymnic praise strengthens God in some measure. At the very least, it helps establish God's renown in the world, or as Jewish theologian Abraham Heschel puts it: "For to worship is to expand the presence of God in the world. God is transcendent, but our worship makes Him immanent."[1]

Authentic praise, thus, is no empty exercise; praise carries the weighty function of giving to God what is due God. Psalm 96 conjoins giving glory to God with offering gifts to God, that is, tribute (v. 8). As the first section affirms, powerful praise—praise that yields power to God—is naturally declarative. Built into the act of praise is the proclamation of God's sovereignty over the nations, summarized in the cry "The LORD is king" or perhaps better translated, "The LORD reigns!" (v. 10a). This terse acclamation is found elsewhere, primarily in the enthronement psalms (93:1; 97:1;

faith or nation. The Lord of this psalm is the Lord of all. Before this throne, there can be no more warring among the nations about whose truth or rightness shall reign on earth. There is only one judge of the world's rightness, only one arbiter of the peoples' truth, and this one holds no passport from any nation on earth.

A Christmas Eve sermon that follows the shape of this psalm will focus on the continuity of God's care from the beginning of creation to the present moment. The birth of the Christ is consistent with this care. At his coming, the congregation is invited to welcome their newborn king by singing a new song based on the songs that have long saved the lives of God's people. This child is descended from the house of David. Abraham and Sarah's blood runs in his veins. He is named for Joshua. The covenant is as much his cradle as the feed trough in which he lies.

A sermon that follows the pattern of the psalm will announce the good news and give concrete evidence of it. In English translation, more than half of the verbs in this psalm are imperatives: sing, bless, proclaim, declare, ascribe, worship, say. Six more verbs are in the future tense: the world will never be moved (v. 10); God is coming to judge the peoples with equity (v. 10); when that happens, all the trees of the forest shall sing for joy (v. 12). That leaves at least seven verbs in the present tense: great is the Lord and greatly to be praised (v. 4); strength and beauty are in God's sanctuary (v. 6); all the gods of the peoples are idols (v. 5); the world is firmly established (v. 10). Like the Lord's Prayer, this psalm mixes verb tenses. The God who acted in ages past and who will one day act again is also acting right now.

Perhaps because the psalm ends in the future tense—or is it because the case for divine activity in the present is so hard to make?—the proclamation of salvation tends to be treated eschatologically. The good news of God's reign is projected into the future, as if that were the only place where it might be believable. Granted, the world is in rough shape, and in many places the church is no better. Proclaiming hope in the future is always a safer bet for the preacher than bidding trust in the present. Yet if the divine help and justice announced on this holy night remain theoretical, then there is reason to wonder why anyone present should care.

The courageous preacher will not surrender the evening's news to those who report it on television. While the media paralyze viewers with story upon story of war, natural disaster, genocide, and domestic violence, there are other stories to be told. The

1. Abraham Joshua Heschel, *Moral Grandeur and Spiritual Audacity: Essays,* ed. Susannah Heschel (New York: Farrar, Straus & Giroux, 1996), 110.

Psalm 96

Theological Perspective

We are hardly aware of all the ways we are caught in this pervasive, systemic web. Willing or not, we are subject to the widespread conviction that our nation has a divine right to order the affairs of other nations through economic pressure or military might; we are complicit in an operational ethic that establishes a Western notion of "quality of life" as the arbiter of who lives and who dies; we multiply our creature comforts at the expense of the very cosmos our psalmist calls into praise. We are captive to the idols of patriarchy and white supremacy: the ingrained, often unconscious belief that the male is the perfect human, and the white male is the perfect exemplar. Where and how do our churches and faith communities continue to worship at the altars of these idols? We cannot celebrate the historical birth of Christ without taking an inventory of the present obstacles to Christ's birth in our own age.

The coming of Christ in our day depends upon our willingness to allow the grace of God's reign to dissolve our devotion to the idols of our age. We are able to "sing a new song" only because God goes before us, supplying us with this grace. We are able to sing a new song only to the extent that we are willing to receive this grace and allow it to transform our lives. Glitter and bright lights have been spread throughout the land this holiday season. It is Christmas on the surface But the authenticity of this Christmas for the church rests upon our willingness to do what it takes to give birth to Christ in all the arenas of our lives—today. That may require the humility of a child willing, once again, to lay the baby Jesus in his simple manger and worship him as he is. This is the enthronement God chooses.

KATHLEEN MCMANUS

Pastoral Perspective

had lived with her mom and dad, the final sale of the house had thrown her into deep depression. She explained it this way, "No matter how many times I've moved over the years or how many mistakes I've made, I always knew I could go home. That house has been the one constant in my life and now it's gone."

We live in a rapidly changing world marked by exponential growth in technology and economic globalization. As populations have become more mobile, the bonds of community have weakened. In my congregation, nearly a quarter of the parishioners are transient, staying no more than four or five years before they are relocated by an employer. When asked why they are joining my church, the majority of new members respond, "Because I feel welcome here." Everyone is searching for home, longing for that elusive sense of stability and safety.

To people who live in an ever-changing world in uncertain times, the good news of Psalm 96 is that God's presence is unchanged and eternal. Come what may, the Lord of hosts offers strength in times of trouble and comfort in times of sorrow. In the midst of desperation, God brings hope; in the face of oppression, God promises justice. And because this mighty One is also the Creator, "the world is firmly established; it shall never be moved" (v. 10). I am reminded of the last line of Isaac Watts's hymn "My Shepherd Will Supply My Need": "There would I find a settled rest, While others go and come; No more a stranger, or a guest, But like a child at home." Looking out upon a sea of new faces on Christmas Eve, there is no better word: Welcome home!

SHAWNTHEA MONROE

Exegetical Perspective

99:1), and it acknowledges the auspicious moment of God's ascendancy to rulership, a moment considered everlasting. Such is the paradox of the eternal now: celebrated for the moment, acknowledged for eternity. That moment is fulfilled in the verbal utterance of God's supremacy, but it is the utterance that also declares God's everlasting reign (see Ps. 10:16). The claim of God's sovereignty makes a comparable claim about creation: the world is firmly established as much as God's kingship remains unassailably secure. The earth "trembles" before the *mysterium tremendum* of God's presence, but it shall not be shaken (vv. 9b–10). To claim God's sovereignty is to claim creation's perdurability, and to claim creation's perdurability is to claim God's justice among the peoples (v. 10).

As for creation, the final stanza (vv. 11–12) exhorts praise from the nonhuman realm, from the celestial heavens to verdant trees. Especially noteworthy is the sea, whose roar is more likely to be threatening than edifying. Usually the sea's "roaring" requires divinely induced silencing (65:7; 93:3–4). But here the sea's roar is left unsuppressed as a vehicle of praise. Chaos is transformed. To borrow from Psalm 42:7, "deep calling to deep" is filled with liturgical mystery. Not only does the sea give praise; also "its fullness," that is, all life that dwells therein, even the great sea monsters (see Gen. 1:21; Ps. 104:25–26). Nature itself, the psalmist implies, has a liturgical voice, and in Psalm 96 that voice is the voice of irresistible joy.

The final verse marks the occasion of nature's praise. Praise heralds God's coming, and God's coming is purposeful. The NRSV translation has God coming "to judge," like a judge holding a hearing. But no specific crimes are listed in the psalm. God's coming is for a much broader cause, namely, the cause of justice, of justice informed by "equity," "righteousness," and "faithfulness" (vv. 10, 13). Fairness and compassion characterize God's justice. God's justice is justice infused with salvation that only the sovereign of all creation can implement, and it is justice met with praise and joy. Joy to the world!

WILLIAM P. BROWN

Homiletical Perspective

preacher who wishes to galvanize the paralyzed will spend time hunting for true stories of inbreaking salvation, justice, and stability right here on earth. Where are people looking out for other people, even at risk of their own safety? Where are just verdicts being rendered? Where are small groups of people creating islands of peace and plenty amidst high seas of war and scarcity? Where are saving things happening that have no earthly explanation, except that somehow or another the universe seems predisposed to love life more than death?

If the evidence for these divine realities is slim and easily assailed, then that should not discourage the preacher from citing them. Just as small and vulnerable is the Christ child whose reign is proclaimed this evening. If evidence can be found nowhere else, then pray to God it may be found in the listening congregation.

Depending on the character and witness of that congregation, the preacher may also follow the psalmist's lead in another way, announcing that God's salvation is not limited to any one people or nation or religion. This God's ear listens throughout the earth, seeking new songs wherever they may be found. National gods are idols. Any people who claim a privileged place for themselves in God's politics have not yet fully responded to the good news that God is one. On Christmas Eve, when the temptation may be greatest for those present to claim special status in God's eyes, both the psalm and the Gospel announce that in the birth of this holy child, God delivers "good news of great joy for all the people" (Luke 2:10).

BARBARA BROWN TAYLOR

Titus 2:11-14

¹¹For the grace of God has appeared, bringing salvation to all, ¹²training us to renounce impiety and worldly passions, and in the present age to live lives that are self-controlled, upright, and godly, ¹³while we wait for the blessed hope and the manifestation of the glory of our great God and Savior, Jesus Christ. ¹⁴He it is who gave himself for us that he might redeem us from all iniquity and purify for himself a people of his own who are zealous for good deeds.

Theological Perspective

Many a pastor will preach to many a stranger on Christmas Eve. Can anything be said that will reach folks whose faith, if it ever existed, has waned until this is the only worship service they will attend this year? Can a preacher's words reach a person who has made this annual pilgrimage to worship only under the compulsion of a spouse, parents, in-law, or friend?

The one message that can cut through the fog of disinterest and/or defiance is the essential gospel of Jesus Christ. This brief passage from Titus summarizes that gospel almost as succinctly as John 3:16, and does so with the unenlightened in mind. Titus was serving a congregation on the island of Crete, whose inhabitants the author characterizes in terms that are less than flattering. "It was one of them, their very own prophet, who said, 'Cretans are always liars, vicious brutes, lazy gluttons'" (1:12).

Certainly that is an overstatement, an insulting caricature. In a time when we have been sensitized to avoid using such stereotypes, it would be tacky to use such pejorative expressions in our preaching. However, the writer's approach can serve as a reminder to a preacher that on this day, of all days, she or he must speak to the minds and hearts of folks who do not share our theological jargon, our ecclesiastical code words, or even our culture and

Pastoral Perspective

Can you get away with preaching from Titus on Christmas Eve? I may be wrong but I can hear some of the good church folk saying, "Come on, preacher, do not mess with the Christmas story. Just tell us about the shepherds and the baby Jesus wrapped in swaddling clothes lying in a manger."

That is a sweet story, if you leave out Herod killing all of the children in and around Bethlehem who were less than two years old. Then there are all those discrepancies between Matthew's and Luke's versions. Most folks do not care about all of that; they just want to hear the story, as they know it, told again. Every year it is a challenge for the preacher to connect all of that to the real world in which we live. Titus may help you do that.

Titus is in Crete. He is trying to establish a church in the midst of a culture that is apparently somewhat of a mess. Sound familiar? The American church gathered on Christmas Eve is in the midst of an increasingly secular culture. Paul writes this brief letter of encouragement to Titus but does not underestimate the magnitude of the challenge to make Christians out of Cretans. He quotes one of their own prophets who said, "Cretans are always liars, vicious brutes, lazy gluttons" (1:12). Paul agreed. "That testimony is true" (1:13a).

Exegetical Perspective

In the imagined scenario of the letter, Paul[1] addresses his follower Titus, who has been left behind in Crete to lead the Christian community there as a kind of regional overseer. Paul gives Titus admonitions about the qualities of leaders also found in the other Pastoral Epistles (1 and 2 Timothy). Thus Titus, like the men whom he is to appoint as local leaders, is to be "blameless, married only once," with decent children (1:6). Leaders must "not be arrogant or quick-tempered or addicted to wine or violent or greedy for gain" (1:7), but instead should be "hospitable, a lover of goodness, prudent, upright, devout, and self-controlled" (1:8). Such respectable leaders should be able to enforce right doctrine (2:1) and practice. What constitutes correct doctrine is not specified, but appropriate behavior is treated in some detail. People above all should behave in ways appropriate for their station in life. Women should manage household affairs and be submissive toward their husbands (2:3–5). Young men should behave well and respect public opinion (2:6–8). Slaves should submit to their masters (2:9–10). All should be subject to those in authority (3:1–2). This line of exhortation,

Homiletical Perspective

Grace is the dynamic feature of this passage. The role of grace in the NRSV translation indicates a significant theological transition from the understanding of grace made known in covenantal relationship and the grace made known in Christ, at once and for all the world.[1] Titus lifts up the universal understanding of grace—an approach that may be necessitated by the Gentile identity of the addressee and the intended communal context. In Christ, grace is made directly available.

The theological notion of grace in teaching piety through such cultural phenomena as household codes is significant and most likely problematic to preachers. Quite frankly, preaching from Titus can be a troubling task. Preachers risk theological and hermeneutical conflicts if we attempt to isolate our treatment of verses 11–14 from the context of the household codes and the questions that emerge from the multiple forms of submission urged in verses 1–10. This letter calls upon older women to mentor younger women into submission to their husbands. It also urges slaves to be submissive to their masters with complete fidelity. In each instance, this counsel

---

1. The Epistle to Titus attributed to Paul is probably the work of a disciple standing in the tradition of the great apostle who has adapted his teaching to the new circumstances of the church toward the end of the first century CE.

1. Alan Smithson, "Grace and the Character of God," *The Expository Times* 115, no. 3 (2003): 75.

Titus 2:11-14

Theological Perspective

values. The whole letter to Titus presents the apostolic faith in terms that almost anybody can grasp, and we do well to follow that example in leading worship on such a day as this.

The opening of verse 11 presents our message in crystallized terms: "The grace of God has appeared." Grace by definition is invisible. It is a concept, an idea, like goodness, friendliness, hope, patience. In life we experience and observe such ideas and concepts only in bits and pieces. For example, when a person extends a hand to shake yours, you glimpse friendliness. When a person acts unruffled and unperturbed after you have made the person wait, you catch a vision of patience. But the idea does not in itself "appear." However, that all changed in the incarnation. When Jesus was born in Bethlehem's manger, he embodied the character and communication of God, now enfleshed for all to see.

Accordingly, this passage parallels the incarnational message of John 1, where the apostle says, "In the beginning was the Word, and the Word was with God, and the Word was God. . . . And the Word became flesh and lived among us, and we have seen his glory, the glory as of a father's only son, full of grace and truth" (John 1:1, 14). The Word—*logos*—of God became embodied, enfleshed in the person of Jesus, so that the glorious, truthful, grace-filled character and content of that Word was now observable.

The appearance of the Savior had an immediate goal in mind: to make for God a people of God. From the call of Abram (Gen. 12:1–3) to the commissioning of Moses (Exod. 6:7), from the promises of Ezekiel (37:23, 27, et al.) to the warnings of Hosea (1:8–10), from the exhortations of Paul (2 Cor. 6:16) to the proclamations of Peter (1 Pet. 2:10) and even the revelations to John (Rev. 21:3), the mission of God to form a people of and for God drives the biblical story. Jesus "gave himself for us that he might redeem," says verse 14, "for himself a people of his own."

This people will be identifiable by their character. While the means of salvation for them is grace, the freely given mercy of God, the outworking of that grace transforms a person toward the image of Jesus, who himself "renounce[d] impiety and worldly passions" (v. 12) and lived a life that was "self-controlled, upright, and godly . . . zealous for good deeds" (vv. 12, 14). He gave himself—in birth and death—to "redeem us from all iniquity and purify for himself" this people for God (v. 14).

A comparable parallel to this text is found in Ephesians: "For by grace you have been saved

Pastoral Perspective

Can you imagine the search committee at Crete advertising for a new pastor?

SOLO PASTOR wanted by small congregation in Crete. Our people are known to be liars, vicious brutes, and lazy gluttons. Their minds and consciences are corrupted. They profess to know God, but they deny him by their actions. They are detestable, disobedient, and unfit for any good work. A great challenge for the right person. Low pay and few rewards. No manse.

The challenge for the church in our modern American culture is not too unlike that of the challenge before Titus in Crete. How do you make a Christian out of a Cretan? Can Cretans really celebrate the birth of Christ on Christmas Eve?

There will probably be a lot of Cretans in the church on Christmas Eve. Some will be regulars, others will be once-a-year people. It is a wonderful opportunity to present the gospel to all of them. They need to hear more than just an old story of something that happened a long time ago. How does the gospel slam into our modern culture? How is this Jesus born again and again and again into this stable, with all of the Herods, wise people, and shepherds? If Christmas Eve says anything (other than a Cretan winter solstice holiday), it lays claim to God showing up in a place like Crete. In spite of our lack of self-control, our disobedience, our passions and pleasures, our malice and envy, our controversies, divisions, and basically worthless lifestyle, God comes to Crete! God has come to us in Christ!

The preacher might consider pulling some fresh evidence from the newspaper that would easily convict us as a latter-day Crete. I would look for the absurd. It would not be so much to evoke guilt among the good people who have gathered for a Christmas Eve service as to remind them of what they already know is true. They live in an increasingly secular society where being a Christian has rapidly become a minority commitment. They get Crete. By identifying with them the preacher can join them in listening for a word of hope for the church in Crete. Does God even know we are here? Do we have the power to make this work? Is this Christian thing just wishful thinking, or can you really make a Christian out of a Cretan? Will God do that?

Crete becomes a metaphor. It represents the world to which Jesus came. It represents our world. It represents us. It is that place of resistance to being obedient and faithful to God. It is a place run by

Exegetical Perspective

familiar from other Christian writings of the late first century, promotes a form of Christian life in harmony with the generally accepted values of its social environment. The yearning for respectability is certainly understandable, although the absence of a prophetic critique of conventional assumptions is regrettable.

Within this general appeal to reaffirm societal values stands the passage read today, an affirmation of fundamental claims of the gospel understood as a warrant for the exhortations dominating the text. The gospel proclaimed in these verses, however, has a power that transcends the use to which it is put in the context of this epistle and moves among us on the great festival occasion of Christmas Eve.

The fundamental affirmation is that "the grace of God has appeared, bringing salvation to all." The formula preserves Paul's emphasis on the centrality of God's gracious action in Christ, providing a relationship with God unmerited by those to whom it was offered. Indeed God's action in Christ offered "salvation" to "all" irrespective of their identity as Jews or Greeks, slaves or free, male or female (Gal. 3:28). The epistle does not indicate any knowledge of the Christmas story as told in Matthew or Luke, but it does have a lively sense of the significance of the grace of God incarnate in Christ.

The implications of the "appearance" of grace are, as often in the Pastoral Epistles, ethical. Grace is a phenomenon that does not simply work at a spiritual level unconnected to lived reality. Like the philosophical schools of antiquity, it trains its recipients in specific ways, first, to avoid "impiety and worldly passions" (v. 12). Other ethical instructions of the period specify with more precision what vices are to be avoided, such as Paul's "works of the flesh" (Gal. 5:19–21), and the vice lists of Colossians (Col. 3:5–9) and Ephesians (Eph. 5:3–5). Here a summary reference to the ways of the world suffices.

In contrast, but expressed with similar brevity, are the virtues to be pursued. These correspond closely to the qualities of ideal leaders sketched in the first chapter. Like a good philosopher, one must be "self-controlled" and like any good citizen of the empire, one must be "upright and godly" (v. 12).

Two considerations warrant this attention to rather conventional moral norms, both of which distinguish the Christian community from its environment. The first is the eschatological horizon within which the community lives. "We wait," says the author, "for the blessed hope and the

Homiletical Perspective

is couched in such terms as being a "credit," or a faithful witness, to our God of the gospel. How is our "submission" a faithful witness? We should be careful in answering this question. Likely no age has escaped the manipulation of submission into forms of oppression. Misogyny and slavery are wretchedly mutating examples throughout the ages and well into our own time. Some are tempted to dismiss these problems as an eisegetical intrusion of contemporary cultural hermeneutics. This charge is weak, even if potentially helpful. While we may risk drawing the correlation uncritically, we may not be exposing the correlation strongly enough, nonetheless.

Preaching "submission" as a demonstration of the saving grace of Christ misses the theological mark of the text. While different church traditions will vary in their theology of Scripture itself, all of our church traditions wrestle with biblical traditions that are difficult to substantiate. In fact, we have living traditions today that perpetuate oppression based in such texts as Titus 2. Still, preachers will discover that verses 11–14 can liberate our sermons this Christmas Eve. Grace is our trainer. As some have put it, grace is in the business of educating us into piety that seeks to give witness to the grace of God in Christ.[2] This letter attempts to teach us the powerful witness of a virtuous or moral life—even if parts of that moral life are understood in dangerously submissive terms. Grace drives us into life that gives witness to the gift of Christ. The transformation by means of grace does not seek a false holiness in self-righteousness or for its own sake. Instead grace seeks life that does no harm to self or any relationship with another; and more than this, it seeks to live into reconciled life with God and one another.

Another feature of this grace is that the call to virtuous living seeks to build community even in the cautions underscoring "worldly passions" (v. 12). The very idea that an epistle would delineate household relationships should focus our attention upon the various relationships in our lives. To what degree then does grace operate in our relationships? The call to live upright and godly lives (v. 12) gives witness to the power of grace to transform us. An overwhelming proclamation emerges from this text. The grace of forgiveness and salvation is not a passive enterprise that somehow simply offers eternal promises. Forgiveness and salvation have

---

2. Klaus Bockmuehl, "'. . . to live soberly, righteously, and godly in the present age.' A Meditation on Titus 2:12," *Crux* 21, no. 4 (December 1985): 3–4.

Titus 2:11-14

Theological Perspective

through faith, and this is not your own doing; it is the gift of God—not the result of works, so that no one may boast. For we are what he has made us, created in Christ Jesus for good works, which God prepared beforehand to be our way of life" (2:8–10).

Of course, many unchurched individuals perceive the message of Christianity to be little more than a constricting moralism. What is missed by them, and often misrepresented by preachers, is the fact that Jesus and the apostles saw the transformation of one's character as a liberation from enslavement to fleshly and worldly passions. A full-orbed proclamation of the gospel, one that does not shy away from the message of character formation, will lift up the freedom available to those being empowered by the Holy Spirit to show forth the positive character qualities of the Savior.

This summary word to Titus operates within two eschatological bookends. Already noted above is the incarnation being celebrated on Christmas morning. The other bookend held in view in the season of Advent is Jesus' anticipated second coming. Advent is, by definition, the season of waiting, a time existentially to engage the waiting of the people Israel, as modeled by such figures as Mary and Joseph, Simeon and Anna (Luke 2:25–38). And it is a season for all of today's believers to remember that we do not simply revel in the present gifts of grace but also anticipate something more. We "wait for the blessed hope and the manifestation of the glory of our great God and Savior, Jesus Christ" (v. 13).

In this Bethlehem-born Christ, God makes grace visible by taking away our sin, forming us as a new people, and offering us a glorious and endless future. A Christmas Eve sermon based on these words of Titus may well touch the heart and mind and open the eyes of the unchurched who have been drawn to worship not just by persuasive cajoling but also, we trust, by the Spirit of God.

JACK HABERER

Pastoral Perspective

humans. It is the other kingdom, but it is not a place outside of God's grace and covenant.

Jesus shows up on the doorstep of poverty and gross immorality. That is Crete. He shows up on the doorstop of leprosy and even death. We know about those. He shows up at the tables of self-righteous people, and he comes to those who are bound in chains and cast out into the cemeteries because nobody knows what to do with them. More Crete. Jesus touches people whom other people will not touch. He pulls people out of the ditch and gives them sight. He yanks them up off the mat and lets them walk. He forgives sins that have stained so deep that no human effort can cleanse them from the soul.

If Christmas Eve says anything, it says that God comes to Crete! Those are precisely the kind of people for whom Jesus was sent. Was that not what the angels were sent to proclaim?

> "Look out! Get ready! You are not going to believe this! The God of all that is has decided to come to earth to bring salvation for all!"

Paul said it this way: "He [God] it is who gave himself for us that he might redeem us from all iniquity and purify for himself a people of his own who are zealous for good deeds" (v. 14).

You may be having Communion at your Christmas Eve service. The Titus text goes well with the bread and the wine. We might come to this Table as Cretans, but by God's grace we leave as somebody else. We leave as Christians, people who reflect the nature and character of Christ. God's kingdom is another culture. You don't have to leave Crete to get it. You just have to leave everything in Crete that is keeping you from receiving it.

The Table is a sign of God's consistent and unrelenting love for people like us. At this Table we are reminded that

> the grace of God has appeared, bringing salvation to all.

Even to Cretans! Thanks be to God.

STEVEN P. EASON

Exegetical Perspective

manifestation of the glory" (v. 13). This disciple shares Paul's hope, although not with the same degree of fervor that could speak of the "groaning of creation" anticipating its final deliverance (Rom. 8:22). The focus of hope is the second coming of Christ, identified as our "great God and Savior" (v. 13). Although it is just possible to construe the phrase to refer to God and the Savior as two discrete persons, the more natural construal of the Greek attributes the title of "God" to Christ. Such language conforms to the practice of Christians, well attested by the end of the first century (e.g., John 1:1; 20:28; Heb. 1:8), of identifying Christ as "God," however that identity was understood.

The second warrant for adopting the recommended lifestyle is christological. Verse 14 encapsulates an understanding of the significance of the death of Christ that has implications for the behavior of his followers. His death was an act of "redemption," buying people back from their slavery to "iniquity," as at 1 Corinthians 6:20. That death was also, as in the Epistle to the Hebrews, a priestly act that effected "purification." Purity here is understood not simply as a ritual requirement, but above all as a moral quality. Those who have been purified constitute a new people (cf. 1 Pet. 2:9) "zealous for good deeds" (v. 14). The emphasis on good works, though phrased more baldly than would be Paul's custom, is consistent with the Pauline understanding that the implications of "justification by faith" will be a life of love in action (e.g., Gal. 5:14; Rom. 13:8–10), bearing the "fruits of the spirit" (Gal. 5:22–26).

The concluding admonition focuses on Titus, understood to be a rather young man, a "child in the faith" (1:4). He is encouraged to preach the message outlined for him "with authority" (2:15), a reference not so much to the office that he holds but to the conviction that comes to expression in his procla-mation. Although some of the recommendations made to Titus may seem very time-conditioned, the fundamental shape of the gospel that motivates them remains consistent with Paul's teaching and makes the admonition to proclaim that message "with authority" as relevant today as in the first century.

HAROLD W. ATTRIDGE

Homiletical Perspective

agency themselves, and in this world. As we have learned from the Hebrews text in the Fourth Sunday of Advent, Christ is God's agent of grace. But that grace has agency as well. In concert with the work of salvation wrought by Christ, the Holy Spirit sustains the power of grace to renew us continuously. The work of the Holy Spirit enables us to live into our inheritance (Titus 3:3–7). Titus reminds us that we are empowered by grace and even called to respond to grace to work in concert with God.[3]

An important homiletic interplay with this text involves how we contend with our frustrations in living into the moral and spiritual calling. People who wish to live faithfully wrestle endlessly with their impiety. Maybe we do not wrestle enough. We flirt with temptations that subtly feed our passions, irrespective to some degree of the destruction we wield upon relationships and the well-being of others. In tragic events or gross offense it may be easier for us to exercise self-restraint, as the text urges; although our ability to inflict destruction, even self-destruction, is bewildering. But what of our "household" relationships? Our overlapping households are comprised of the dominant circles of relationships—home, church, work, neighborhood—that constitute our spheres of community. Grace is indeed our trainer! Redemption to life eternal and the call to moral life defined in nurturing relationships are driven by grace. The gift preachers may offer to congregants is to take the time to nurture discipleship in the grace of moral living. A call to submission may not serve well the enduring message of this teaching passage. Grace calls us into a humility that seeks to honor the grace of God to forgive and restore us. Grace calls us into a humility that seeks to honor the multiple relationships throughout our overlapping households or spheres of community. The training power of grace may be its capacity to illumine the image of God in another. We pray for God to give us God's own love for the other when we recognize that our love is in dire need of grace. If we preachers are careful with our encoding, we might risk preaching that responds to the grace we receive and teaches disciples to live faithfully through the worship community and well into our divergent households.

DALE P. ANDREWS

3. Lewis R. Donelson, *Colossians, Ephesians, First and Second Timothy, and Titus* (Louisville, KY: Westminster John Knox Press, 1996), 174–77.

Luke 2:1-14 (15-20)

¹In those days a decree went out from Emperor Augustus that all the world should be registered. ²This was the first registration and was taken while Quirinius was governor of Syria. ³All went to their own towns to be registered. ⁴Joseph also went from the town of Nazareth in Galilee to Judea, to the city of David called Bethlehem, because he was descended from the house and family of David. ⁵He went to be registered with Mary, to whom he was engaged and who was expecting a child. ⁶While they were there, the time came for her to deliver her child. ⁷And she gave birth to her firstborn son and wrapped him in bands of cloth, and laid him in a manger, because there was no place for them in the inn.

⁸In that region there were shepherds living in the fields, keeping watch over their flock by night. ⁹Then an angel of the Lord stood before them, and the glory of the Lord shone around them, and they were terrified. ¹⁰But the angel said to them, "Do not be afraid; for see—I am bringing you good news of great joy for all the people: ¹¹to you is born this day in the city of David a Savior, who is the Messiah, the Lord. ¹²This will be a sign for you: you will find a child

Theological Perspective

In the wonderful play *The Greatest Christmas Pageant Ever*, a family of poor kids—aptly named Herdman—hijack a children's Christmas pageant, taking all the choice roles by intimidation and force. As the performance degenerates into chaos, the youngest Herdman, who plays the angel announcing Messiah's birth to the shepherds, yells out over the din, "Hey! Unto you a child is born!" Thankfully, the great good news of Jesus' birth, the event of the incarnation, can still cut through the noise of our distracted culture and our own restless souls.

At least three incarnational themes have roots in this passage: its historical location, its spiritual location, and its social location.

1. The manger of Bethlehem indicates the *historical location* of the incarnation. The names of Caesar and Quirinius reveal Luke's historical consciousness. God entered human history as a baby boy born to Mary in Bethlehem. "For in him all the fullness of God was pleased to dwell" (Col. 1:19). Philosophers and religious thinkers over the years have stumbled over the "scandal of particularity," God locating himself in human history as Jesus. Modern humanity seems to expect that if God reveals himself at all (a big "if"), then God is revealed in universal truths and principles, and not particularly in space and time in history. The older

Pastoral Perspective

In a decree that seems emblematic of the propensity of governments to overreach, the Roman emperor declares that "all the world" should be registered. And like a state governor whose name appears on the interstate sign posting local speed limits and seat-belt laws, Quirinius gets free campaign publicity as well. Though the NRSV's "registered" is undoubtedly a better translation of the Greek than the KJV's "taxed," one suspects the older rendering gets more directly to the heart of the matter. Whatever governments count and catalog, they soon enough will tap as a source of revenue. And the convenience of citizens will not be a top priority as the collection policies and procedures are implemented.

Many in the congregation on Christmas Eve will arrive weary from travel or will be receiving guests who have made long journeys. The aftertaste of airport security checkpoints (and the ticket taxes that pay for them) and parking regulations (keep that car moving!) should help hearers to find sympathy for Mary and Joseph as they are herded along to Bethlehem at a very inconvenient time in their lives. We can imagine a modern Mary prying her shoes from her pregnancy-swollen feet to accommodate the X-ray operator. Joseph reluctantly discards the baby oil and Mary's favorite hand lotion he had thoughtfully packed for the trip. No liquids

wrapped in bands of cloth and lying in a manger." [13]And suddenly there was with the angel a multitude of the heavenly host, praising God and saying,

[14]"Glory to God in the highest heaven,
    and on earth peace among those whom he favors!"

[15]When the angels had left them and gone into heaven, the shepherds said to one another, "Let us go now to Bethlehem and see this thing that has taken place, which the Lord has made known to us." [16]So they went with haste and found Mary and Joseph, and the child lying in the manger. [17]When they saw this, they made known what had been told them about this child; [18]and all who heard it were amazed at what the shepherds told them. [19]But Mary treasured all these words and pondered them in her heart. [20]The shepherds returned, glorifying and praising God for all they had heard and seen, as it had been told them.

Exegetical Perspective

This reading provides the Christmas tableau of baby Jesus in the manger and of shepherds watching their flocks by night, who receive the heavenly Christmas proclamation: "there is born to you today a savior in the city of David, Christ the Lord" (v. 11, my trans.). This passage is the culmination of the preceding narratives about the births of Jesus and John. It concludes with the shepherds spreading the news, "proclaiming all they had seen or heard" (v. 20) and so, with Mary (v. 19), becoming links in a series of human witnesses transmitting the heavenly witness of the angelic host (for its extension, see Acts 1:8). Heaven and earth pause for a moment in awe, with audible wonder, joy, and praise at what God has wrought.

Luke opens this part of his extended introductory section by dating the events, like a Greek and Roman historian, by the reigning emperor and local Roman ruler: Jesus was born amid a general census under Augustus Caesar (v. 1) and during the office of the imperial legate in Syria, Quirinius (v. 2). But the calendar math does not work well. The general phrase "in these days" of verse 1 seems to refer back to "the days of King Herod of Judah" (1:5), who died in 4 BCE. This is difficult to reconcile with the dates for the office holding of Publius Sulpicius Quirinius, appointed governor of Syria in 6 CE and charged to

Homiletical Perspective

Christmas Eve is a challenging occasion for preachers. The service of worship is not a time for lengthy sermons or wordy theological analyses from the pulpit. Rather, it is an occasion for sharing the story, singing hymns and carols, and pondering the mystery. On this occasion, less from the pulpit may in fact be more. The goal is not to explain the odd arrival of the Messiah, who is born to a poor, unwed mother and laid in a manger because there is no room in the inn. Rather, the goal is to help the story come alive in all of its radicalness and to draw people into the newness suggested by Luke's birth narrative.

Luke proclaims the odd, astonishing arrival of a new world, a new time. The story can be told in ways that help the congregation glimpse the implications of this newness. The story begins, "In those days . . ." It begins in the old time, chronological time, time shaped by the "powers that be." The emperor reigns. Time is denoted by who is in power: "Quirinius was governor of Syria" (v. 2). Here is the story time in which many people live even today: the time of the census and taxes and authoritative orders and pronouncements; time shaped by business as usual, by the world's accepted power structures; history defined by those in positions of authority. Indeed, the way people "tell time" is a significant theological

Luke 2:1-14 (15-20)

Theological Perspective

philosophers expressed it this way: the finite is not capable of the infinite (*finitus non capax infiniti*). As Lessing put it, "the accidental truths of history can never become the proof of necessary truths of reason."[1] On this view, one "marginal Jew" living in the first century CE in a backwater province of the Roman Empire could not possibly be the full and complete revelation of God.

The manger of Bethlehem is God's counterargument: this decisive act of revelation and reconciliation was not an announcement of universal principles or truths; instead it was a baby. The manger shouts back that God is capable of dwelling among his people. The first baby steps of the infant Jesus were the fulfillment of the age-old covenant promise: "And I will walk among you, and will be your God, and you shall be my people" (Lev. 26:12).

2. The celebration of the angels indicates the *spiritual location* of the incarnation. The Bethlehem manger is the divinely appointed intersection of heavenly and earthly realms that brings peace on earth and fosters goodwill among mortals. The angels bear witness to this when they declare peace on earth, an end to the estrangement between God and humanity. Gregory the Great noted: "Because the King of heaven has taken unto himself the flesh of our earth, the angels from their heavenly height no longer look down on our infirmity. Now they are at peace with us, putting away the remembrance of the ancient discord."[2]

In Luke's account, angels bear witness to the event of the incarnation. As God enters space and time, so the hosts of the heavenly realm break into the earthly realm to announce the incarnation. Interestingly, the angels participate only indirectly in the event by foretelling its coming (Luke 1) or announcing its happening (Luke 2). Given the widespread interest in angels in popular culture, Christians need to be reminded that angels point only to Christ and his ongoing ministry of revelation and reconciliation, and not to themselves.

3. The announcement to the shepherds indicates the *social location* of the incarnation. One might expect the Son of God to be born in more dignified surroundings and celebrated by more upscale admirers. In the first of many "great reversals," God bypasses the proud and the powerful (Luke 1:51–52)

---

1. G. E. Lessing, *On the Proof of Spirit and Power*, quoted in Alistair McGrath, ed., *The Christian Theology Reader* (3rd ed., Oxford: Blackwell, 2007), 296.
2. Gregory the Great, *Homilies on the Gospels* 8.2, quoted in Arthur A. Just Jr., ed., *Luke*, Ancient Christian Commentary on Scripture: New Testament 3 (Downers Grove, IL: InterVarsity, 2003), 42.

Pastoral Perspective

beyond this point. No exceptions. Times like this efficiently shatter our myths that we control our own destiny or really have power as individuals.

The truly rich can purchase some distance from such experiences: first-class tickets with shorter lines (or even private jets!) and a comfortable hotel duvet and bubble bath at the end of the day. For Mary and Joseph there is, famously, "no place for them in the inn." When we think of the holy family as uniquely deprived, however, we may be making a false assumption that distances them from our own experience. Nowhere does the text tell us they could not afford better lodgings. They may simply be the victims of a travel economy overtaxed by the emperor's sudden urge to count his subjects. We do not have to be homeless to find an imaginative place of entry into this story. Nor do we need to take the distant posture of those who only help the homeless. If we have ever spent a night in an airport because the cancelled flights overwhelmed the local hotels, then we can understand.

In parallel to Mary and Joseph's travel saga, Luke tells the story of the shepherds. Here we have people who are truly in a different category. While "all the world" is rushing around to comply with Augustus and Quirinius, the shepherds are "living in the fields, keeping watch over their flocks by night." Like migrant workers or the newly homeless family who live in their car, they move from place to place largely unnoticed by the bureaucracies. They are, quite literally, not worth counting. Ironically, their life looks peaceful in comparison to Mary's and Joseph's. If the extended lection is read, we learn that they are summoned to Bethlehem not by a legal decree, but rather decide to "go now . . . and see this thing that has taken place." Maybe they arrive on foot, or perhaps they roll into town unnoticed at the unsecured bus station down across the tracks. No X-ray lines. No government functionaries. No lists. No inns are even considered. They arrive without incident, and they return "glorifying God" instead of muttering under their breath about the indignities of their journey.

Most of the church people who hear sermons delivered by people who read books like this will have a much easier time relating to Mary and Joseph's journey to Christmas Eve than they will to the journey of the shepherds. Instead of romanticizing the "poverty" of Mary and Joseph, this text invites us to see them as people much like us— trying to make their way in the world, squeezed by rising taxes and family demands, weary from a

Exegetical Perspective

conduct a census in Syria and Palestine. Also, despite smaller censuses under Augustus, nothing suggests he ever ordered a universal census (as Luke in 2:1 states). Finally, enrollments in censuses and registrations of property were done in the place of residence, not the place of birth.[1]

Whatever the extent of Luke's familiarity with these political events, one narrative function for the sentence is to bring Jesus' parents out of their home-town, Nazareth in Galilee (v. 4), and into Bethlehem of Judah. Although Luke does not refer to the specific prophecy (Mic. 5:2) that Matthew employs to anchor the birth of the Messiah in Bethlehem (Matt. 2:6), he does present Jesus, the son of Joseph who is "from the house and hometown of David" (v. 4; 1 Sam 16:1), as having the requisite messianic ancestry. A second narrative function may be to imply an oppressive political setting, in which self-involved rulers can move subjects around their map like pawns on a chessboard (see 2 Sam. 24 and Ps. 87:6).

Both the means of dating and the travel itinerary serve to frame the spectacle Luke creates of wonder and joy fitting the occasion of the savior's birth. The manger, the vulnerability of the setting of the birth, and the resourcelessness of his parents to secure better lodgings (2:7) all mirror the vulnerabilities of sub-jugated peoples like Jews (3:12–14) and marginalized groups like early Christians (21:12–19) to local and imperial rulers. Yet the humble setting puts no damper on the joyous event. The Christmas joy of the birth story and the "joy" of the resurrection news at the end of the gospel (24:41, 52) frame the largely somber tone of the Gospel and the dolorous passion narrative.

Luke presents Jesus' birth as the birth also of a message, the good news of the gospel. The implications of what is being revealed—what is inside the wrapping—are indicated in Jesus' first sermon in a Nazareth synagogue and made fully manifest at the Gospel's conclusion (4:14–21; 24:46–49), but are here expressed summarily by the angel announcing to the shepherds "news of great joy for all the people: to you is born this day . . . a Savior" (v. 11). That Jesus is specified as Mary's "firstborn son" (v. 7) serves not only to sustain the earlier statement of her virginity (1:27) but also to highlight the status of the firstborn son as partic-ularly beloved to women, who in the patriarchal culture were under pressure to produce male offspring (see Gen. 30:1–4).

1. See a full discussion in C. F. Evans, *Saint Luke*, TPI New Testament Commentaries (London: SCM Press, 1990), 190–97.

Homiletical Perspective

act, as Luke recognizes. So the story begins in the old time—the old age: "In those days . . ." Even the words sound tired and hopeless.

But something happens, and the story ends on "this day" (v. 11). A new time has entered the world—a new age. "This day" is not merely a temporal notation, but an eschatological affirmation; it is *kairos* time, not *chronos* time. It is time shaped by the character and quality of the new event that has happened and changed the world—the birth of the Messiah. This new time is characterized not by the drudgery of business as usual or the threat of imperial power, but by the inbreaking of the heavenly realm, the song of angels, and the "good news of great joy for all the people" (v. 10). From the viewpoint of the emperor—the "powers that be"—it may even be a treasonous time. For "this day" has a political dimension; this new time is a direct challenge to the imperial world of "in those days." There is a new Savior, a title formerly reserved for the emperor. There is a new Messiah, the royal, anointed one who will liberate Israel from Roman occupation. And there is a new Lord, who will inaugurate a new reign (v. 11). Indeed, this new reign is signaled by its announcement to lowly shepherds, rather than to those in the halls of power. A story that begins with a threatening decree of Emperor Augustus ends with the joyful, treasonous proclamation and praise of shepherds. Something odd and extraordinary has happened indeed!

Contemporary preachers may want to attend specifically to one dimension of this new time that has entered the world. With the Messiah's birth comes a time characterized not by fear, but by the freedom and joy of the announcement "Do not be afraid," which is repeatedly proclaimed by the angels (v. 10; see also 1:13, 1:30). "Those days" are governed by fear. The political powers, in both Jesus' day and our own, play on fear to get their way—whether it be the fear of the emperor, the fear of terrorists, the fear of the "other" (the immigrant), or the fear of death. But with "this day" comes a new possibility. The first words spoken after Jesus' birth are "Do not be afraid; for see—I am bringing you good news of great joy for all the people" (v. 10). Contemporary preachers may seek to tell the story in such a way as to move believers from the fear that grips so many lives to the joyful "fear not" of the angels' proclamation. Such a message would be remarkable good news on Christmas Eve.

As astonishing as this change from "those days" to "this day" is, however, the way in which the new time

Luke 2:1-14 (15-20)

Theological Perspective

in favor of a stable surrounded by livestock and visited by lowly shepherds—"not . . . enfolded in Tyrian purple, but . . . wrapped with rough pieces of cloth . . . not . . . in an ornate golden bed, but in a manger." Bede quotes from 2 Corinthians, "Though he was rich, yet for our sake he became poor, so that by his poverty we might become rich."[3]

While it is clear that Christ came to be Savior for all persons, rich and poor alike, it is also equally clear that God chose to dwell among the least and the lost. Shepherds had little status and did menial work for low pay. Yet God has "lifted up the lowly" (Luke 1:52) by making humble shepherds the first to visit him. Thus the Savior spent his first hours surrounded by the lost ones whom he came to seek and save (Luke 19:10). Jesus' later practices underscored the earthiness of the incarnation as he chose to be with the poor, the marginalized, and the outcast.

This social location of the incarnation continues to challenge our notions of who is blessed by God: "on earth peace among those he favors" (v. 14). The favor of God—the grace of God—comes not to those who think they've earned it by birth or education or success in the world. The grace of God sneaks into our world under the radar of our religious expectations, in the person of Jesus. The "good news" the angels proclaimed turns out to be better than we thought or dared to dream, for it offers the promise of peace with God and the favor of God through him who is the Savior on the basis of his love and covenant faithfulness. In welcoming the announcement of Jesus' birth, we too can treasure and ponder in our hearts what Mary treasured and pondered in hers.

In the words of Phillips Brooks, "O holy Child of Bethlehem, descend to us we pray / Cast out our sin and enter in, be born in us today. / We hear the Christmas angels the great glad tidings tell. / O come to us, abide with us, Our Lord Emmanuel."

ROBERT REDMAN

Pastoral Perspective

variety of struggles, and badly in need of someone to understand their identity as individuals who are precious in God's sight. And that "someone" is born right in the midst of their harried rush toward antiquity's equivalent of the April 15 tax-filing deadline.

Truly Jesus is born *to* us and *for* us. By locating the birth story at the registration under Quirinius, Luke is placing it firmly in the realm of "everyday Joes" (and everyday Marys)—of the people who come to our churches not just for Christmas Eve, but also for baptisms, weddings, and funerals—who are trying to understand ordinary lives in light of the extraordinary news of the gospel. These people need a savior, and God has provided one.

Though we are the ones who are properly positioned to receive the newborn king, we are not the ones who really understand him or are called upon to announce his arrival. That belongs to the shepherds, to those who have fallen off, or never entered, the economic hamster wheel that so engrosses the rest of us. In a later encounter with powerful authorities, the adult Christ declares, "give to the emperor the things that are the emperor's, and to God the things that are God's" (Luke 20:25). Because the shepherds have nothing of interest to the emperor, they are free to glorify and praise God fully and without reservation.

Though modes and technology have changed dramatically since Luke's day, the twin travel narratives of this passage are remarkably accessible to postmodern pilgrims who make their way to hear them again on Christmas Eve. Weary like Mary and Joseph, we are longing to learn structures of meaning that reach beyond our daily concerns for survival and compliance with life's many demands and decrees. Unfamiliar teachers, until now marginalized and ignored like the shepherds, will show us the way. But because Jesus himself *is* the way, we are welcomed not as strangers but as expected guests.

MICHAEL S. BENNETT

---

3. Bede, *Exposition of the Gospel of Luke* 1, quoted in Just, *Luke*, 38–39.

Exegetical Perspective

The details of the narrative focus the reader's attention on a moment in time and space. The "great joy" (v. 10) of the proclamation of the savior's birth greets this opening of heaven to earth, a motif communicated through a double and intensified vision, first of "the glory of the Lord" (v. 9) and then of "a multitude of the heavenly host" (v. 13). This latter vision is of angelic worship and praise of God in the words that epitomize the Christmas message: "Glory to God in the highest heaven and on earth peace among those of God's favor!" (v. 14). God inclines to people drawn by the weight of the divine love: peace—fulfillment, not a mere absence of strife—is love's gift.

This meeting of heaven and earth, as Luke conceives it, does not presuppose any infusion of a divine substance into an earthly vehicle—such as some interpretations of the Johannine prologue might suggest—but the fulfillment of a divine intention for human salvation, much as was the baby born as a sign in Isaiah 7:13–16 (v. 17 is not part of the original oracle). Luke's understanding of the virgin birth of the Messiah does not suppose any theory of incarnation, but works with a "chosen one" Christology (see the speeches in Acts, e.g., 2:22, 36; 5:31).

The optional segment (vv. 15–20) narrates the shepherds' going to Bethlehem, seeing the scene, relating the angelic message, and at their departure witnessing to "all they had seen and heard just as it was told to them" (v. 20). These verses are dominated by terms of hearing, seeing, speaking—or being told—and other forms of declaring. This fits the basic sense of the lection as about revelation and witness, about a movement from heaven to earth and the spread of that movement on earth. That horizontal movement for Luke extends "to the ends of the earth" (Acts 1:8), but the night on which it begins, when time stops in that very specific humble stable, a new thing of God is born.

STEPHEN A. COOPER

Homiletical Perspective

arrives is even more surprising. The turning point in the story occurs in one extremely understated verse: "And she gave birth to her firstborn son and wrapped him in bands of cloth, and laid him in a manger, because there was no room for them in the inn" (v. 7). Before this verse, the story is "in those days." After this verse, "this day" has arrived. Yet the event of the birth itself is shared with few details and little fanfare.

The words of the Christmas carol "O Little Town of Bethlehem" come to mind: "How silently, how silently, the wondrous gift is given!"[1] Those words have often sounded rather sentimental and idealized to me, as if Mary gave no cries during childbirth, Jesus was not a squalling newborn baby, and there was no commotion around the manger. Surely there was plenty of noise surrounding Jesus' birth, though such details are obviously not important to Luke. But maybe that's not the kind of "silence" the hymn has in mind. "In those days," Jesus' actual birth really does not make much "noise." It is simply the unexceptional birth of another child to poor parents in a small, crowded backwater town in the empire. No one in any position of power would have noticed. There would have been no royal birth announcements. In this sense the birth was indeed a "quiet" one, as the understated words of Luke's story suggest.

But that is the wild and holy mystery of Christmas Eve, and preachers do well not to add too many details or try to explain it away. This "quiet" birth is the pivotal moment in the story, in our story. For afterward, the shepherds are startled, and an angel proclaims, "To you is born *this day* in the city of David a Savior, who is the Messiah, the Lord."

CHARLES L. CAMPBELL

1. Phillips Brooks, 1868.

Isaiah 52:7-10

⁷How beautiful upon the mountains
　　are the feet of the messenger who announces peace,
　who brings good news,
　　who announces salvation,
　　who says to Zion, "Your God reigns."
⁸Listen! Your sentinels lift up their voices,
　　together they sing for joy;
　for in plain sight they see
　　the return of the LORD to Zion.
⁹Break forth together into singing,
　　you ruins of Jerusalem;
　for the LORD has comforted his people,
　　he has redeemed Jerusalem.
¹⁰The LORD has bared his holy arm
　　before the eyes of all the nations;
　and all the ends of the earth shall see
　　the salvation of our God.

Theological Perspective

Today, we celebrate the incarnation—the coming of God in the flesh at a particular time in history and to a particular geographical place in the Middle East. In this Old Testament lesson, Second Isaiah, speaking from exile, offers a profound vision that rivets our attention to the wondrous nature of God and salvation. Among the affirmations he offers are (1) God cares deeply about *this* world—so deeply, in fact, that God intends not to rescue us from it, but to redeem this world through us; (2) where we are matters; that is, if God wants to redeem *that* place (Zion/Jerusalem), God wants to redeem *this* place.

How beautiful, indeed, are the feet of the messenger who brings to a people exiled in a strange land the good news that the Lord will return to Zion/Jerusalem; but then, this is simply the way God is. As Isaiah surveys the history of God's dealing with the Hebrew people, he sees continuity in God's character and a pattern of liberation that has been repeated in the past and will be repeated again. God's people went down to Egypt, where they were aliens and oppressed. More recently, the Assyrians oppressed them. But God brought them out of Egypt—redeemed them—and delivered them from the hand of the Assyrians. God will also deliver them from the oppression of the Babylonians, restore them to Jerusalem, and establish peace (52:3–7).

Pastoral Perspective

A movie director would surely begin where Isaiah begins: by concentrating on the feet. Feet, running along a mountain path. Accustomed to such terrain they are practiced, swift, and deft. They are also dirty, dusty, calloused, perhaps even bleeding. What makes them beautiful is the message we hear when the focus widens to the runner's mouth: good tidings, peace, and the news that God reigns! The message itself, shouted aloud and borne aloft on the mountain air, arrives before the messenger.

The camera then moves to the sentries stationed upon the wall who have heard the message. The sentries are singing! And why wouldn't they be? After all we are told that they see the return of God "eye to eye." Moses spoke to God "face to face" (Exod. 33:11, Num. 12:8). Now the sentries see God eye to eye. The intimacy and immediacy of this act of divine self-revealing is disarming. The guards let down their guard and break into song.

The image of the ancient sentries, eye to eye with God and singing from their lookouts, forces the question: What does God look like? What does the return of God look like? What does God's reign feel like? For Christians that question is answered on Christmas morning. God looks like an infant. His name is Emmanuel. Here is God's latest revealing:

Exegetical Perspective

This exuberant piece of Hebrew poetry celebrates the good news of God's triumphant return to the ruins of Jerusalem as its comforter, redeemer, and savior. Scholars attribute this passage to the so-called Second Isaiah, an anonymous but virtuoso poet, prophet, and theologian who was active during the Babylonian captivity of Judah (ca. 586–538 BCE). This prophet apparently composed most or all of chapters 40–55 of the canonical book of Isaiah as a means to exhort and persuade his audience in exile to prepare for God's "new thing," the return of the Jewish community to Zion (e.g., 43:19). While Jeremiah instructs the deported Judeans of an earlier generation to settle in Babylon (29:1–9), Second Isaiah delivers the good news of exile's end with "second exodus" imagery. The important theological concepts of God's "redemption" (v. 9) and "salvation" (vv. 7, 10) are typical of Second Isaiah's hopeful message of restoration after catastrophe.

Immediately prior to Isaiah 52:7–10 is a prose section (vv. 3–6) that briefly rehearses the difficult history of Israel, from Egyptian bondage to Assyrian oppression. Our text exults in the power and determination of the Lord to act anew in overturning empires and liberating the exiled community from Babylonian captivity. All the nations of the earth will witness the vindication of God's ways. The verses

Homiletical Perspective

It is Christmas and time to celebrate the great gift. For the great gift is always liberty in some form. If there had been a Fourth of July or a Bastille Day among the Hebrew people, it would have risen from this passage. And when our Christmas is about the greatest gift, we receive it through this passage. We are prone to go to the romantic accounts of the origin of Christmas. Mary would be in blue, Joseph in soft beige, looking over a naked child whose arms are open wide to embrace the world. After such a romantic script beginning, we would smile warmly and agree that we have fulfilled our obligations and kept Christ in Christmas, and hurry off to our eggnog and opening of gifts. We might even remark that God gave his greatest gift to us on Christmas and agree with the apostle, "Thanks be to God for his indescribable gift!" (2 Cor. 9:15).

The Christmas passages from the Old Testament do not give up the romance of the coming of Christ, but they do center their high poetry on liberty. This liberty—to all who have lived in chains and slavery—is the real gift. The passage that introduces this Christmas text tells of Israel's two imprisonments. "For thus says the Lord GOD: 'Long ago, my people went down into Egypt to reside there as aliens; *then* the Assyrian, too, has oppressed them without cause'" (v. 4, italics my addition). In all this

Isaiah 52:7-10

Theological Perspective

In discerning the work of God in these past, paradigmatic events and then looking forward to similar events, Isaiah engages what Justo González refers to as a typological hermeneutic. That is, Isaiah looks at historical events as "types" or "figures," important in their own right, but pointing beyond themselves toward a future event/s. González differentiates this method of interpretation from an allegorical approach that sees concrete, historical events as mere shadows of more important, spiritual truths, and from literalist readings that freeze historical events in an unrepeatable past.[1] The theological foundation for a typological interpretation of the Scriptures includes several convictions. First, God created the world, and human beings are meant to flourish in it, not above it. Second, God's purposes for the earth and for humanity have been, are being, and will be realized on earth as they are in heaven.

In his last sermon at the Bishop Mason Temple in Memphis, on the eve of his assassination, Dr. King made poignant use of the same interpretive key. Commenting on the threats of violence he had received, Dr. King acknowledged, "We've got some difficult days ahead." However, he affirmed that God "allowed me to go up to the mountain. And I've looked over. And I've seen the promised land. I may not get there with you. But I want you to know tonight, that we, as a people will get to the promised land. I'm not worried about anything. I'm not fearing any man. Mine eyes have seen the glory of the coming of the Lord."[2] Like Isaiah, Dr. King discerned in the exodus story a historical trajectory of God's work in the world that moved through time into the present. He perceived an unmistakable momentum that carried him, those who had suffered the atrocities and indignities of slavery and segregation, those who marched and protested, those gathered in Memphis that night, and those who would come after them. He sensed that he, like Moses, might not see a new America, but that his people would see and experience vindication and a place where they would flourish.

If this world matters to God, so too does every place in it. One of the promises God made to Abraham was that the Hebrew people would have a place of their own—a place where they and their progeny could flourish. Isaiah believed that God intended to keep that promise: "for the Lord has

1. Justo González, *Christian Thought Revisited* (Maryknoll, NY: Orbis Books, 1999), 56–57.
2. James Washington, ed., *A Testament of Hope* (San Francisco: Harper & Row, 1986), 286.

Pastoral Perspective

human and humble, a testimony to the yearning of our God to bridge the distance between us.

That bright truth does not end the conversation. Even with the gift of Jesus, we do not always experience God as reigning. Too often it feels as if God is nowhere to be found. On Christmas morning we are reminded that God rarely chooses to exercise God's sovereignty in the ways we expect or desire . . . or, for that matter, even notice. It is, therefore, a good morning for the church to wrestle with what it means to worship a God who appears in our midst as a child, poor and lowly and without weapons, crown, or wealth. In what ways do we honor our God's style of reigning? How do we imitate it, practice it, and teach it?

The camera proceeds to pan the crumbled walls and the vacant homes of those who were carried into exile. The lens rolls over Jerusalem's dilapidated structures and looted shops, as even these are invited to join the singing. It is a magical image, but one that evokes the symbiotic relationship between human community and the architecture of beloved and familiar places . . . places where babies were born, couples married, children raised, and grandparents buried. These are places that, brick by brick, had been built by the sweat of self, neighbors, and sons. In Isaiah's image, the city itself sings out a song of welcome to God and to Israel.

What does locale (home, meeting house, geography, city or town, village or countryside, school or cemetery) mean to your congregation? How do these participate in forming the human community that is at the heart of the divine invitation? On Christmas morning our homes and sanctuaries are festooned with greenery, candles, trees, lights, and other decorations so that they too may participate with us and share in the celebration of this day. The gift of this child through whom and in whom we see God eye to eye is cause for a party day, a feast day. One and all—sentient and inanimate—take up the festivities. The pastor may wish to contemplate how to capture and express in the liturgy and sermon the exultant joy of Isaiah's proclamation.

One possibility is to recall that Christmas Day is a day for singing, a day for carols. As the church will undergo a long fast from carols until this time next year, it is well to gorge on them now while they are plentiful. Martin Luther, who loved Christmas, claimed that "music is a fair and glorious gift of God." Music, he said, "makes people kinder, gentler, more staid and reasonable. The devil flees before the sound of music almost as much as before the Word

following our passage (vv. 11–12) similarly exhort the Jews to exit Babylon in safety, carrying the temple vessels, accompanied by the presence of the Lord in a new exodus.

Compared to prophetic oracles that instruct Zion herself to proclaim the Lord's return (e.g., Isa. 40:9), this lectionary passage offers a more dramatic and rhetorically nuanced perspective on God's return to Jerusalem. As a poem rather than a prophetic oracle, Isaiah 52:7–10 uses an unidentified narrator to provide the point of view, beginning with a third-person description of the approaching herald (v. 7) and the reaction of the city sentinels to the appearance of the Lord (v. 8). Verse 9 includes a second-person address to Jerusalem before describing the salvific activity of God. The passage culminates in verse 10 with the inclusive first-person-plural reference to "our God." While readers essentially overhear the good news that the speaker declares in verses 8–9, they are drawn in to the poem's exultant conclusion as participants in God's triumph.

This exilic poem offers no exegetical difficulties. The language is clear, and poetic forms are elegantly constructed. Verse 7 sets the stage by introducing the herald who approaches the ruined city of Zion with the exclamation, "How beautiful upon the mountains are the feet of the messenger" or herald. With finely wrought poetic parallelism, the herald "announces peace," "heralds good news," and "announces salvation" to Jerusalem (my trans.). The Hebrew word for "peace" (šalôm) also denotes wholeness or welfare, which is good news indeed to the devastated land. The word "salvation" (yešû'â) is central to the message of Second Isaiah, who uses forms of the verbal root more than fifty times in his sixteen chapters. The actual content of the herald's message is delivered or summarized with the royal proclamation, "Your God reigns!" While Zion has been abandoned and desolate, she has not been forgotten by the Lord her God in the theology of Second Isaiah (see 49:14–26). The image references a herald announcing the procession of a triumphant sovereign, who is approaching a city within his realm.

Verse 8 moves from third-person description to a second-person address (beginning with the interjection qôl, translated "Listen!" in the NRSV): "Listen! Your sentinels lift up their voices." The outpouring of human emotion provides this passage with its rhetorical power, as "together they sing for joy" (yḥdw yrnnw). The narrator does not actually describe the Lord's appearance but lets the reader experience the event from the perspective of

journey into servitude and back, no money was exchanged. The purchase was arranged without the transference of a shekel, "For thus says the LORD: You were sold for nothing, and you shall be redeemed without money" (v. 3).

For all of Israel's history, she has wrangled with her imprisonment—exiled twice in the Old Testament, and fleeing into dispersion after the New. From Masada to her post-Auschwitz years, she knew no settled boundaries. Even now her enemies are many and will, if their boasts hold, "wipe her off the map." Naturally she is tired. It is hard work to be in chains and dream incessantly of freedom. Weary with her incessant bondage, she has ever dreamed of living in the land God once gave to Abraham. Her poverty of spirit and her indigence have called her to bend her ear to God's promise:

> Ho, everyone who thirsts,
>   come to the waters;
> and you that have no money,
>   come, buy and eat!
> Come, buy wine and milk
>   without money and without price.
>   (Isa. 55:1)

Perhaps there is only one real gift at Christmas. It is liberty. In *A Christmas Carol* we allow Dickens to play some Halloween themes against Christmas. Maybe we are not destined to understand Christmas aright until we play some Fourth of July themes against the incarnation. Coming out of Assyria, (or Persia, who kept Israel in chains after Assyria was vanquished), the poet cried,

> Speak tenderly to Jerusalem,
>   and cry to her
> that she has served her term,
>   that her penalty is paid,
> that she has received from the LORD's hand
>   double for all her sins.
>   (Isa. 40:2)

Then the prophet goes on to beg a highway in the desert, where the hills are leveled and the valleys lifted up, so that his poor bedraggled slaves will have a smooth course from the lands of whips and iron to the land of milk and honey.

It is Christmas born long ago, before there was anything cyber and anything technical. The news was brought by caravan and travel gossip. Unless, of course, it was really important news—then it was brought by a runner, an athlete whose marathon commitment to good news drove him across the arduous mountains, where his whole frame ached

Isaiah 52:7-10

Theological Perspective

comforted his people, he has redeemed Jerusalem" (v. 9b). Now the ruins will sing for joy. And this glad-making hope isn't confined. Isaiah even widens the reach of God to all broken-down places, everywhere—including the Babylon in which his people find themselves. In the expansive vision of the prophet, that locus of God's concern, the splendid salvation that comes from God, now extends even to "all the ends of the earth" (v. 10).

The one whose birth we celebrate today also believed that. George Tinker, a member of the Osage Nation and a theologian, observes that, for Native Americans and other indigenous peoples, space, not time, is of prime importance. He sees in Jesus, particularly in the Markan narrative, a similar sensibility. The Gospel begins with an affirmation derived partly from Second Isaiah, "I am sending my messenger ahead of you, who will prepare your way" (Mark 1:2). Then Jesus came into Galilee proclaiming the good news, saying, "The time is fulfilled, and the kingdom of God has come near" (Mark 1:15). Tinker notes that the kingdom has, then, a decidedly spatial dimension—its extension is identified as "the Way" and it has come near.[3] Indeed, it has; starting in and throughout Galilee, Jesus went "proclaiming the message in their synagogues and casting out demons" (Mark 1:39). Before his death, Jesus told his disciples that, after he "was raised up," he would go before them to Galilee (Mark. 14:28). At the tomb, his followers were told that, if they were to see him, they had to meet him in Galilee (Mark 16:7–8), where they would take up again the work of extending God's kingdom. According to the Lukan narrative, the kingdom would then be extended from "Jerusalem, in all Judea and Samaria, and to the ends of the earth" (Acts 1:8).

As we contemplate today the coming of Jesus, where do we expect to meet him? Will he be in Bethlehem? Will he be in Jerusalem? Will he be in Galilee? Will he be in Memphis? Or will he be around the corner and up the street?

STEPHEN B. BOYD

Pastoral Perspective

of God."[1] Providing opportunity for the congregation to sing well and joyfully, to sing loudly, confidently, and with abandon, to break forth into singing with the ancient sentinels and the waste places of Jerusalem, will no doubt require some planning. It is not the natural proclivity of all congregations to sing with abandon, heads up and voices raised. The pastor who prepares carefully and enables the congregation to sing out will find that it has been well worth the effort.

Singing our carols as if we mean them is one way to express the profound implications of Isaiah's message: that the Lord has comforted his people. How can you help your congregation feel this, believe it, and live into it? Nietzsche is said to have complained that the trouble with Christians is that they don't look redeemed. Christmas Day is a day we had better look and act redeemed. The pastor will want to model this by looking and acting both redeemed and comforted in a way that is convincing to the congregation!

The passage began with a camera trained on the feet of a messenger. It moved to the watchmen, swept over Jerusalem, and rested for a moment on a people comforted. For the final scene the camera pulls back until the viewer can take in all the nations, indeed, all the ends of the earth. This is no parochial God who reigns over a tribal community. This is John of Patmos's God of gods, King of kings, and Lord of lords (Rev. 19:16). This is the one God to whom the whole earth belongs. Isaiah announces that it is this God and none other who has returned and whose reign is now inaugurated.

NANCY S. TAYLOR

---

3. George E. Tinker, *Spirit and Resistance: Political Theology and American Liberation Theology* (Minneapolis: Fortress Press, 2004), 95–98.

1. From the foreword to the *Wittenberg Gesangbuch* (1524), Martin Luther's hymnbook.

Exegetical Perspective

Jerusalem's sentinels: "for in plain sight they see the return of the LORD to Zion." The reader, like the "ruins of Jerusalem," must accept the testimony of the witnesses to these events. As men whose duty is to stand guard and watch for dangerous advances against the city, sentinels provide an appropriate metaphor for prophets, who are also the first to perceive a new thing. In this case, however, the sentinels (and prophet) do not see approaching danger. What they witness causes them to burst forth in song, because what they see is "the return of the LORD to Zion," advancing like a king in royal procession to his own city. Second Isaiah shares the good news of the Lord's return to redeem Jerusalem, perhaps in response to Ezekiel's visions (chaps. 8–11) of God's presence abandoning the defiled city to its destruction in 586 BCE.

Just as the narrator in verse 8 describes the sentinels' joyful outcry, the poet in verse 9 commands the "ruins of Jerusalem" to "break forth together into singing." The image of war-torn ruins bursting into joyful song because God has comforted its refugees is poignant and effective. Although the NJPS translates the verbs of this verse in the future tense, the NRSV states that God has already "comforted" (*niham*) the people and redeemed (*ga'al*) the devastated city. God's actions of comforting and redeeming God's people are typical of Second Isaiah, which opens (40:1) with the divine imperative to "Comfort, O comfort my people." Note also the common parallelism that poetically identifies Jerusalem with God's people in both 40:1 and 52:9.

In verse 10, the "LORD has bared his holy arm" as a demonstration of power before all the nations of the world (cf. Ps. 98:1). Although the verb used here is not common, the metaphorical "arm" (*zerôa'*) of YHWH is a traditional reference to God's ability to deliver Israel, used especially of the exodus events (e.g., Deut. 11:2). Second Isaiah effectively applies this metaphor elsewhere, such as in 40:10 and 51:5, 9. Comfort is found in the strength of the Lord, who will once again act in the sight of "all the nations" even unto the "ends of the earth," to deliver Israel from a foreign land and domination. This beautiful passage appropriately concludes (in Hebrew as well as English) with the exultant news of "the salvation of our God." In this lection, contemporary Christian congregations join ancient Hebrew exiles in a song of hope.

NEAL WALLS

Homiletical Perspective

from the effort of bringing the good news. His feet were crusted with calluses and torn by the rocks and thorns of his course.

But they were not ugly feet. They were beautiful. He brought good news! He published peace. Joy swelled around his shout, "Your God reigns" (Isa. 52:7). The voice of the lone runner passes to the village criers, "The LORD has comforted his people. . . . The LORD has bared his holy arm . . . and all the ends of the earth shall see the salvation of our God" (Isa. 52:9–10).

I have a friend who was imprisoned for two years in Castro's Cuba at the beginning of that regime. He was a missionary in the same prison with other missionaries. He had a single Bible that he tore into many sections and then secretly circulated among all the missionaries who suffered imprisonment with him. His wife was not imprisoned with him but elected to stay in Cuba and took an apartment near the prison where her husband was being held. She knew where his cell was, and there was—miracle of miracles—a window in that cell. She would take their very young son and walk him past the prison every day. And on every day that she could, she would stop the baby carriage and take the child from the carriage and play with the baby in clear view of her husband's cell. She knew he was watching, and it was her delight to remind him of the steadfastness of God in the dark times. The mother and child were free, of course, and in the passing of years, her husband too was set free.

There was great rejoicing among all of us who had prayed for this particular prisoner to be set free. Then the great news came. Like the words of a mountain courier, the good news came running to us on beautiful feet. Still, it was hard for me not to play his liberation against a courageous mother, bouncing a little boy on her knee. There is only one gift, and when the couriers come to announce our liberty, eggnog and reindeer lose their significance. We are free. The couriers and watchmen have told us the center message of every Christmas, and it is this:

"Your God reigns." (Isa. 52:7)

CALVIN MILLER

Psalm 98

¹O sing to the LORD a new song,
for he has done marvelous things.
His right hand and his holy arm
have gotten him victory.
²The LORD has made known his victory;
he has revealed his vindication in the sight of the nations.
³He has remembered his steadfast love and faithfulness
to the house of Israel.
All the ends of the earth have seen
the victory of our God.

⁴Make a joyful noise to the LORD, all the earth;
break forth into joyous song and sing praises.

Theological Perspective

All the ends of the earth have seen salvation, the victory of our God; God is vindicated in the sight of all the nations. So proclaims the psalmist who seems to be conducting a universal, symphonic hymn of praise: "O sing to the LORD a new song. . . . Make a joyful noise to the LORD, all the earth. . . . Sing praises . . . with the lyre, . . . with trumpets and the sound of the horn. . . . Let the sea roar, and all that fills it. . . . Let the floods clap their hands; let the hills sing together for joy at the presence of the LORD, for God is coming to judge the earth." Indeed, on this Christmas Day we celebrate God's decisive coming in the humble birth of Jesus. Yet this psalm announces a coming of cosmic proportions— proportions that echo the Gospel of John, which today proclaims that the Word through whom all things came to be now has become flesh.

The incarnation we celebrate today finds its full meaning in the paschal mystery from which the church itself is born. Antecedent to the Christ event, the psalmist projects this event's eschatological fulfillment from the vantage point of the "now" of ancient Israel, a "now" transformed by YHWH's eternal faithfulness. Israel has experienced God as a God of life, even in the midst of death. Despite suffering and failure, Israel has been upheld by God's

Pastoral Perspective

Like Psalm 96, Psalm 98 is an enthronement song. There is no proposition argued, no plea for divine intervention, no words of thanksgiving or cries of remorse. Instead, Psalm 98 is simply an exuberant expression of praise to God, who "has done marvelous things!" Though perfectly appropriate as a call to worship or prayer of invocation, it is harder to imagine the psalm as the basis for a Christmas Day sermon—that is, until you listen more closely to the psalmist's tone and tune.

Reading the text from a Christian perspective, the questions of Advent have all disappeared. There is no "O Come, O Come, Emmanuel" or "Watchmen, Tell Us of the Night." No, Psalm 98 is worded in the imperative, as if to say, "Hey, you! Sing!" Furthermore, the song to be sung is unfamiliar, not one of the old chestnuts we know by heart. God has pulled off a remarkable feat, beyond our wildest dreams or deepest hopes: the Lord has come in the flesh. In fulfillment of the promises made to the house of Israel, God's steadfast love and faithfulness have now taken human form. The world as we once knew it has changed in composition; God reigns. Such an astonishing turn of events requires its own new composition, for none of the old tunes will do. *"O sing to the LORD a new song!"*

⁵Sing praises to the LORD with the lyre,
  with the lyre and the sound of melody.
⁶With trumpets and the sound of the horn
  make a joyful noise before the King, the LORD.

⁷Let the sea roar, and all that fills it;
  the world and those who live in it.
⁸Let the floods clap their hands;
  let the hills sing together for joy
⁹at the presence of the LORD, for he is coming
  to judge the earth.
  He will judge the world with righteousness,
  and the peoples with equity.

Exegetical Perspective

Assigned for Christmas Day, Psalm 98 is a natural continuation of the psalm lection for Christmas Eve, Psalm 96. Both share the language of praise and proclamation. If Psalm 98 distinguishes itself in any way from its cousin, it is by its musical flair. Praise is mandated with musical accompaniment (vv. 5–6). Content-wise, both psalms sing out the same message of salvation given for the sake of the world. It is indeed a message worth repeating, especially on a day of new birth!

Psalm 98 divides itself into two sections (vv. 1–3 and 4–9), each opening with a command to praise. The first section articulates the content of that praise. The lengthier second section specifies the manner of praise and who (or what) is included within the circle of singers. As with Psalm 96, today's lection concludes with the overall reason for praise, namely, the Lord's coming "to judge the earth" (v. 9).

The psalm opens with the mandate to sing a "new song." For a new day, only a new song is appropriate (see also Pss. 40:3; 96:1; 144:9; 149:1). What would constitute an "old song" in the ears of the psalmist? Perhaps the song of lament that constitutes most of the Psalter. One recalls God's command in Isaiah: "Do not remember the former things, or consider the things of old. I am about to do a new thing; now

Homiletical Perspective

God reigns. God is compassionate and just. The God who enacted creation, covenant, exodus, and return from exile is still acting and will never cease from acting to save what God loves. God's people have ample cause for praise.

This is the condensed version of the good news in today's psalm, which Christians have sung from earliest times as a song about Jesus. Even if the psalm never surfaces in the sermon for Christmas Day, those who sing "Joy to the World" proclaim its gospel by heart. The Lord is come. Let earth receive her king. Let us our songs employ—and not just us, but all creation—sounding the joy of welcoming our Savior. Here, at last, is a sovereign who rules the world with truth and grace instead of guile and force, who will make the nations prove righteousness and love instead of dominance and might. As the new king is seated on his throne, the psalmist orders all creation to join in singing a new song, for this Lord has done marvelous things.

Jesus is not named in the hymn, any more than he is mentioned in the psalm, yet Christians recognize in him the continuity of God's saving work. To say or sing Psalm 98 on Christmas Day is to identify Jesus with God. To call him Savior is to make the connection between his incarnate purposes

Psalm 98

Theological Perspective

saving power. Amid all the vicissitudes of history, God has made salvation known, albeit in fragmentary ways. The psalmist seizes upon these fragments and identifies them with the God of the promise; he expands them to fill the earth and the cosmos, envisioning the whole creation bathed in this promise, come to fulfillment in its final utterance.

We who honor that final utterance in Christ still await the completion the psalmist celebrates. Like Israel, we seize upon the fragments of salvation we have known; we ground ourselves in the triumphs of love, healing, and justice wherever they are immanent in our relationships, our communities, and our world. Here we recognize God's incarnation and the down payment on the eschatological fulfillment of the promise. Such glimpses of grace and fragmentary experiences of salvation, however fleeting, reflect the resurrection from which we live. To proclaim the birth of Christ is also to proclaim his death and resurrection, the victory that God has already won. It is to proclaim that this victory of salvation already belongs to us who live in Christ. But wait—if this victory pertains only to those who "live in Christ," what are we to make of the psalmist's universal sweep? How are we to understand the cosmic significance of his vision? And how are we to imagine this already-possessed, yet still-awaited salvation?

If God's salvation extends to the ends of the earth, then it transcends the human limitations of our faith constructs and the boundaries of our particular churches. It transcends our impoverished notions of what it can mean "to live in Christ." The psalmist exults in a vision of salvation that transcends Israel, encompassing all the nations and indeed the forces of nature itself. Can we who proclaim the coming of Christ do less? We may be baptized and very much formed by our particular Christian traditions. Yet, when we proclaim Christ, we profess faith in a transformed humanity, a new heaven and a new earth. We profess faith in a new creation brought about by God's power beyond all human designs. That power is at work in history; that new creation begins with hope for a people experiencing *threatened humanum,* hope rooted in the fullness of the *humanum* encountered in Christ.

Edward Schillebeeckx uses the term *humanum* to signify the full flourishing that God desires for humanity.[1] We can begin to imagine salvation over

---

1. See, for example, Edward Schillebeeckx, "Questions on Christian Salvation," in *The Language of Faith, Essays on Jesus, Theology, and the Church* (Maryknoll, NY: Orbis, 1995), 110.

Pastoral Perspective

The psalm is in the imperative because God's work has been accomplished. Note the past tense in verses 1–3: "has done . . . have gotten . . . has made known . . . has revealed." Nothing is left unfinished, things will simply unfold. What God has accomplished is the ultimate victory (NRSV) that is salvation (NIV). There is great comfort in this proclamation, especially for those who worry about God's mercy and salvation. What excites the psalmist is not the potential for victory or the possibility of salvation, but rather the fact of it. When Christian ears hear these words, especially on this bright Christmas morning, our hearts move to the manger. It is done. The birth of Jesus is the spark that brings true light to the world, a light—as John's Gospel reminds us—that no darkness can overcome. God's steadfast love and faithfulness has brought about this good news.

Listen more closely and you will notice how unusually orchestrated this new song is. It is a loud text, ringing with the cries of human voices and the clang of instruments as well as the roar and clatter of the natural world. This might strike the listener as discordant, letting all these sounds take up the same tune, but theologically, the music is stunning.[1]

First comes the lyre, David's harp traditionally used to accompany singing. An agile and melodious instrument, the lyre was meant to entertain royalty. Next, we hear the trumpets, official instruments used by priests in sacred celebrations. With only a four- or five-note range, the trumpets were used to call people to worship and now call all creation to praise God. Then comes the horn, with its two-note blast, most often used to signal armies across great expanses. On this day, the instruments of war now herald God's salvation. All people and all instruments are joined in celebration, but beneath those more familiar sounds, there is an even greater noise.

Recall that in Scripture, in both the Old and New Testament, the sea is a mysterious and dangerous force. Formless and void, it is the chaos out of which God called all creation into being. It holds both fish for eating and the great leviathan, the feared creature of the deep. Yet, in response to God's marvelous work, even the sea joins in the chorus, roaring with praise. The flood waters, which extinguished all life in the time of Noah, clap in celebration as the mountains, where previously God had come closest to earth, ring with songs of praise. Some in our

---

1. Information about the musical instruments can be found in *The HarperCollins Bible Dictionary,* ed. Paul J. Achtemeier (San Francisco: HarperCollins, 1996), 717–20.

it springs forth, do you not perceive it? I will make a way in the wilderness and rivers in the desert" (Isa. 43:18–19). For this writer of the exile, the "things of old" recall the punishment of exile and its attendant despair, which he draws into parallel with the earlier "exile" of God's people in Egypt (see Isa. 43:16–17). The "new thing" is the inbreaking newness of God's saving work, specifically the release of the exiles and the community's restoration in Palestine. Whatever the poetic liturgist of Psalm 98 considers "old" and no longer relevant, it is swept away by the exuberant proclamation of salvation that pulses through every verse.

The "new song" is about God's new and "wonderful things" (my trans.), the things of salvation wrought by God's "holy arm" and "right hand" (v. 1). Such anthropomorphic references are not to be dismissed as primitive references to the Deity. No, they vividly connote potency and directness on the part of God. Other than this psalm, only Isaiah refers to God's "holy arm," by which Israel's salvation is displayed to the nations (Isa. 52:10). The psalmist, too, may have God's deliverance of the exiles in mind. Nevertheless, the wonders wrought by God are inclusive. Such salvation, the psalm and Isaiah concur, is eminently public, and internationally so. "Before the eyes of the nations" and witnessed by "all the ends of the earth" is God's righteousness revealed (vv. 2, 3b). And yet such salvation is evidenced specifically with God's elect, Israel. It is in Israel's behalf that God has "remembered his *hesed*" (v. 3a). *Hesed* designates God's freely initiated commitment to caregiving, a divine quality to which the psalmists repeatedly appeal as a matter of expectation grounded in historical precedent. It is by God's *hesed* that Israel is delivered and that God is recognized as the saving God for all generations. God's action in behalf of Israel is witnessed even cosmically, as the psalm will demonstrate at the end.

The second section of the psalm opens like the first, with a command to worship, this time accompanied by musical instruments. Lyre, trumpet, and shophar (or ram's horn) all join in to support the congregation's praise of God. Psalm 150 yields an even fuller picture: lute, pipe, drums, and cymbals are also included, not to mention dance, all creating a kinetic symphony of praise. But what remains primary for Psalm 98 (up until vv. 7–8 at least) is the human voice of praise. The congregation is to "sing," "shout," and "rejoice," and the words are the words supplied by the psalm. But what about the non-human participants mentioned: sea (and marine

and the eternal purposes of God. Both Father and Son operate with steadfast love and faithfulness (v. 3). Both will come to judge the world with righteousness, and the peoples with equity (v. 9).

Repeating this psalm on Christmas Day, Christians place the birth of Jesus in line with the rest of God's mighty acts. These "marvelous things" include making the world, choosing Israel, giving Torah, parting the Red Sea, speaking through the prophets, ending the exile in Babylon, and sending a Jewish child to embody the divine Word. In all of these events and more, God has acted to save God's people. Faith is not a matter of believing what can never be proved but of remembering what God has already done. The only faith required is to trust this same God to go on acting to save the world from chaos until the whole earth rests at peace in God's presence.

Preachers who do not make use of the psalm's content may still make use of its form, composing a sermon in three movements that move from past to future tense.

The first movement (vv. 1–3) includes vivid examples of marvelous things God has done in the past. While scriptural things certainly belong on the list, so do things from the life of the world. This may require the preacher to make bold claims about God's sovereignty, but such claims would not have sounded strange to the first singers of this psalm. The Lord they praised was not the Lord of their own faith or nation only but the Lord of the whole world. Preachers aware of the ways in which such language has been used against those of other faiths may take time in this movement to describe the difference between religious triumphalism and divine salvation. God's agenda is righteousness and equity, unhindered by the self-interest of any one religion.

The second movement (vv. 4–6) bids the congregation to make a joyful noise to the Lord—if not with lyre, trumpets, and horn, then with any musical instruments close to hand. Having been led to recall the manifold reasons for praising God, the faithful are now called to deliver. Make noise, the psalmist commands. Break into song, sing praises, make a joyful noise before the king. Preachers will note that these verbs are not invitational but imperative. Praise is not optional today. Subjects who remain silent at the enthronement of their new king are out of line. No one who hears what God has done in Bethlehem is allowed to remain mute. Following the psalmist's lead, preachers used to cajoling their congregations from the pulpit may decide to experiment with more forceful language on

Psalm 98

Theological Perspective

against the suffering reality of the *threatened humanum* everywhere and always present in our world. In protest and resistance to all that damages human beings and the earth, in active engagement in creating the conditions under which justice and love might flourish, we begin to articulate in word and deed the meaning of salvation.[2] While we of necessity speak of salvation over against negative experiences of suffering, we do so on the basis of those concrete positive experiences of salvation that ground our hope, and to which we humanly cling. We begin to act toward the salvation already given in Christ.

The psalmist, on the other hand, boldly attempts positively to evoke the fullness of salvation that we dare not define. His lavish and exuberant imagery necessarily crosses all rational borders in a grand effort to render what cannot humanly be rendered. The incongruity of floods clapping their hands and hills singing is commensurate with the incongruity of the human imagination vis-à-vis the eschatological fullness of salvation, and this is the point. The psalmist knows it is beyond him adequately to express the universal sweep of God's salvation. He settles for depicting the wild rejoicing of the earth and all creation in response to the marvels of God. This earth, this creation, is abundantly alive. In the twenty-first century, this image of abundant life critically contrasts with what we know of our earth's devastation. The fullness of salvation extends to the flourishing of the earth and all it contains, for its own sake and for the sake of the most vulnerable of its human inhabitants.

God "is coming to judge the earth," to "judge the world with righteousness, and the peoples with equity." This righteousness, this equity, inheres in the harmony of interdependence and right relationship that signifies what it could possibly mean "to live in Christ." To live in Christ is to live according to the Word through whom all things were created, the Word that has taken flesh in history. It is, inversely, to encounter that Word in all that is created, the earth as well as the human other, and there to reverence Christ with humility and grace. Thus will all the ends of the earth see the salvation of our God.

KATHLEEN MCMANUS

Pastoral Perspective

Christmas congregations will be consoled to hear that their darkest chaos might even find a way into the divine symphony.

Everything that makes a sound, beautiful or barbarous, takes up the new song, creating a strange but holy harmony throughout the world. Yet, if you listen, you may discover this is not only the new song sung in response to God's salvation; this is the sound of salvation itself.

Some years back, as part of our Homecoming Sunday, we organized a congregational band to accompany the first hymn of the new church year. The invitation was extended to anyone who played, or longed to play, an instrument. Talent and experience were optional; only desire was required. People of all ages and abilities signed up, and the orchestration included, among other things, one banjo and two accordions. On Sunday morning, I wandered into the sanctuary just as rehearsal was ending. Karen, who plays first-chair horn in the symphony, was sitting next to Carolyn, an awkward sixth-grader who had only recently taken up the instrument. With some trepidation, I asked Karen how it was going. "I love it! Carolyn is sitting there and hasn't hit one right note, but she's beaming with pride! This is the church at its best!"

Jesus came to save us—not because we deserved it, but because we needed it. He came for all, not just for those with talent and experience. The salvation of God is for all people as well as all creation, and this present victory comes with a promise of a final triumphant return. Such good news fills our hearts with songs of thanks and praise.

And what a wonderful contrast this noisy psalm is to the reverent and well-mannered music of Advent and Christmas Eve. Having come to the manger singing "Silent Night" by the hush of candlelight, what could be more fitting than to greet the new day and let loose with the wild song of God's salvation! The text invites us to sing Isaac Watts's big, bold adaptation of the psalm, "Joy to the World," and give it everything we've got . . . even an accordion!

SHAWNTHEA MONROE

2. Schillebeeckx, *God the Future of Man* (New York: Sheed & Ward, 1968), 154–56.

Exegetical Perspective

life), earth, torrents, and mountains? (Psalm 96 also includes trees and fields [v. 12].) Their praise is not speech as we know it. The psalmist broadens the horizon of discourse to accommodate the respective speech patterns, as it were, of nonhuman, indeed allegedly "inanimate," creatures: the seas "thunder" and the "torrents clap their hands." Such is the sound of nature at praise. They together "rejoice aloud" to be heard (v. 8b), if only we have ears to hear. At least God and the psalmist do. Nonhuman nature, the psalmist testifies, has its own language of praise, and it comes naturally. Natural, then, is the traditional picture of the manger scene surrounded not only by Joseph and Mary, the shepherds, and the magi, but also by beasts of burden. The lowing of the cow, the braying of the donkey and camel: each gives its appropriate praise to the newborn king. And just as the sea's thunderous roar is transformed into praise, so can also the threatening hiss of the serpent.

But, one may ask, has nature's voice of praise been stifled? One does not have to look far in our world, filled as it is with pollution and other scourges, whereby the fullness of the sea is no longer so very full and the bright sky is darkened. The psalm concludes with an announcement of God's coming in judgment (v. 9). What kind of judgment is envisioned? As in Psalm 96:13, divine judgment is not restricted to courtroom drama and legal decisions. No, God's judgment is justice for the sake of the world, the justice that is required to reopen voices stifled by human hubris and greed, in order to let the full symphony of God's good creation play loud in a surround sound of praise.

WILLIAM P. BROWN

Homiletical Perspective

Christmas Day. Some may halt their sermons for one verse of a well-known hymn (or a brief medley with instrumental accompaniment). Others may seed the pews ahead of time with tambourines, thumb harps, party horns, and kazoos, choosing an opportune moment during the sermon to command the congregation to pick these noisemakers up and make a joyful racket.

The third movement (vv. 7–9) reminds those present that they celebrate in concert with all creation. The preacher may simply evoke the sounds of this concert—the roaring of waves, the singing of humpback whales, the splashing of waterfalls, the chirping of hills full of birds—or find some way to pipe the actual music over the speaker system, making sure that a baby's cry is included somewhere in the mix. Either way, the point is to help those present on Christmas Day situate themselves in the cosmic context of God's salvation. The God who comes to judge the world will be the one who made it and who inhabited it in the flesh. God's "victory" (the NRSV v. 1–2 translation of "salvation") means to include everyone and everything.

Depending on the preacher and the congregation, there is room in today's sermon for the proclamation that Jesus is part of something bigger that God is doing. The birth of this Savior may be decisive, but it is neither the only nor the last such event in the royal history of God. The form that divine salvation assumed in Bethlehem may have been different from the form it took in the wilderness of Sinai, but it came from the same source. Jesus is no anomaly. His birth demonstrates both the constancy and ingenuity of God's purpose. The God who acted in him is still acting and will never cease from acting to save what God loves.

On Christmas Day, God's people use all available verb tenses. We are not stuck looking backwards, into the past tense of God's being with us. We celebrate Christ's reign in our lives now, even as we anticipate the future, when the Lord of love and faithfulness will give the whole world fresh cause for praise.

BARBARA BROWN TAYLOR

Hebrews 1:1-4 (5-12)

¹Long ago God spoke to our ancestors in many and various ways by the prophets, ²but in these last days he has spoken to us by a Son, whom he appointed heir of all things, through whom he also created the worlds. ³He is the reflection of God's glory and the exact imprint of God's very being, and he sustains all things by his powerful word. When he had made purification for sins, he sat down at the right hand of the Majesty on high, ⁴having become as much superior to angels as the name he has inherited is more excellent than theirs.

⁵ For to which of the angels did God ever say,
"You are my Son;
today I have begotten you"?
Or again,
"I will be his Father,
and he will be my Son"?
⁶And again, when he brings the firstborn into the world, he says,
"Let all God's angels worship him."

Theological Perspective

Who would ever preach a Christmas Day sermon on a text not found in the opening chapters of Matthew or Luke? The writer of Hebrews might. While we cannot determine the authorship of this letter (Apollos? Priscilla? We don't know), we do know that this writer wanted the readers to understand the amazing story of the incarnate Son of God. The Letter to the Hebrews lauds the exalted child of Bethlehem. While the early Christians probably did not throw parties to celebrate Jesus' birthday—the celebration of Christmas came a couple centuries later—this correspondence elevated for those believers the wondrous story of God-in-Christ entering and elevating the world.

The prologue (vv. 1–4) reflects themes that would be later used in the writing of the introduction to the Gospel of John. That writer felt no need to retell the story of the virgin, her espoused fiancé, their awkward journey, the birth of the child, or the visits of shepherds and magi—stories that were well known. John speaks of the incarnation in metaphysical-metaphorical terms: the enfleshment of the eternal Word of God, the appearance of light overcoming darkness, the rejection of that light by some and the birthing as God's children of those who accepted him, the revelation of glory and truth. The introduction of the Fourth Gospel runs deep,

Pastoral Perspective

This passage begins with the words, "*Long ago . . .*" (1:1a). The writer starts by remembering. Let us look back to see what God has done, so that we can lay claim to what God is continuing to do.

What a powerful way to get at the pastoral perspective of a Christmas story! The writer of Hebrews starts out remembering. Christmas morning is a great day to remember. We remember Mary, Joseph, and the innkeeper. We remember the story of the shepherds and the wise men coming to visit the Christ child. We remember what the angels sang, what gifts were given, and we even remember what the stars were doing that night. It is a good thing to remember what God has done "*long ago.*"

But the writer to the Hebrews makes a shift: "*In these last days (God) has spoken to us by a Son*" (1:2a).

How has God been speaking to us? Where do we lay claim to that story? The danger of Christmas is leaving it in the "*long ago.*" The danger is in leaving it back there, where it is safe, not intrusive, doesn't ask anything of us, makes no changes. It is easier for us to forget how controversial this old Christmas story is.

We have preached on everything from the three gifts of the wise men to the straw in the manger. We have analyzed it up one side and down the other. This makes it difficult for the preacher to say anything new, because it has been beaten to death

⁷Of the angels he says,
  "He makes his angels winds,
    and his servants flames of fire."
⁸But of the Son he says,
  "Your throne, O God, is forever and ever,
    and the righteous scepter is the scepter of your kingdom.
⁹You have loved righteousness and hated wickedness;
    therefore God, your God, has anointed you
      with the oil of gladness beyond your companions."
¹⁰And,
  "In the beginning, Lord, you founded the earth,
    and the heavens are the work of your hands;
¹¹ they will perish, but you remain;
    they will all wear out like clothing;
¹² like a cloak you will roll them up,
    and like clothing they will be changed.
  But you are the same,
    and your years will never end."

Exegetical Perspective

The first four verses of the Epistle to the Hebrews summarize the whole of this rich "word of exhortation" (13:22). Echoing classical rhetoric, they display elaborate verbal devices, with dramatic alliteration (several word-initial *p* sounds) and assonance (repetition of long vowels, especially *o*). The verses are arranged chiastically, framing the reference to Christ's atoning death. Their theology highlights the significance of the "great high priest," the Son whose exaltation at God's right hand assures his faithful followers. The exordium also anticipates many of the homily's major themes. By doing all of this in such beautiful incarnational language, the homily offers the Christmas-Day preacher an entryway into the deep mystery of the holy birth.

Verses 1–2, highlighting God's speech, a key theme of the discourse, also introduce an antithesis between the "prophets," through whom God spoke to the ancestors, and the Son, who speaks at the end of days. A similar antithesis governs chapters 8–10, where Jeremiah's promise of a "new covenant" introduces a contrast with the old cultic order.

The reference to Christ as Son is one of the two focal points of the Christology of Hebrews. A catena of scriptural quotations following this exordium emphasizes the exalted status of the Son, set higher than any angel. Chapter 2 will emphasize the

Homiletical Perspective

The task of preaching on this day can be at once one of the easiest and yet more daunting responsibilities for any preacher. Preacher and congregation are drawn to the gospel story because the birth narrative ushers us into a celebration of God's gift of grace to humanity in Christ. But Year C of the lectionary pushes us to deal with the christological themes underscoring Jesus' divine standing in creation and redemptive history. This introduction to the letter does not proffer the typical initial greetings to a congregation. Instead, it is a tightly woven prologue to the theological treatment of Christ's identity between God and humanity.

The tight weave of the passage may tempt the preacher into a sermon composition replicating the rhetorical strategies, parallelisms, and numerous features illustrating Christ's identity. These include artistic alliterations and metered speech in the original language, variations of syntax, and parallelisms in chiastic structures, meaning, and sounds of clauses, all along with approximately seven identifiable features outlining the letter's Christology.[1] A preacher would do well to remember that the letter has thirteen chapters to work with these themes and traits. The

1. William L. Lane, *Hebrews 1–8*, in Word Biblical Commentary, vol. 47, ed. David A. Hubbard and Glen W. Barker (Nashville: Thomas Nelson Publishers, 1991), 5–19.

Hebrews 1:1-4 (5-12)

Theological Perspective

and so does the introduction to the Letter to the Hebrews.

The writer begins by setting the story in context. Like Matthew or Luke telling of the Savior's family lineage, or like John telling of Jesus' eternal preincarnate existence, this account begins with his oracular roots. Can we imagine that Jesus speaks the word and will of God? Well, the writer reminds the readers of others who have so spoken before.

In the past, says the writer, God was speaking. Note that that reflection, written as a participle, suggests an ongoing task of communicating. However, that ongoing task operated intermittently. The opening phrase of the letter translates, literally, "In various ways and various times . . ." God was speaking in drips and drabs. The people Israel do buy the idea that the Sovereign of the universe breaks into human history to reveal the eternal purposes and plans, and they are used to hearing those words piecemeal.

God has spoken again, but in a different way, a final way. God has spoken—aorist tense, suggesting finality and completion—to us. The word of God recently spoken is the complete message, the final word, the total revelation. Understandably so. God has spoken through God's own Son.

Note that this introduction prepares the way for the whole letter to follow, which will refer many times to the words of God given throughout Israel's history, especially Israel's cultus. The letter will affirm the validity of those words while declaring that they were always hinting and pointing ahead, as types and symbols, in anticipation of the final revelation and fulfillment—which has now been accomplished in Jesus Christ.

The writer next launches into a set of metaphors in order to paint a picture of the Christ whom he is lauding. Consider "the radiance of God's glory" (v. 3 NIV). Just about every movie about Jesus casts in that role a star who exudes a beatific gaze. His face radiates beauty, reverence, winsomeness, and kindness. But is that what is intended by "the radiance of God's glory"? Written by a scholar of the ancient biblical texts, one who sees Jesus through high-priestly eyes, perhaps the writer is reintroducing the readers to a vision of glory regularly expressed in the context of Israel's God-encounters. Those most glorious moments occurred when the presence of God broke into their world, manifest by what became known as the "glory," the appearance of fire and other phenomena, dubbed in the intertestamental period the "Shekinah glory." Consider the burning bush, the

Pastoral Perspective

over the years. Even so, the congregation is very happy for us just to tell the story again. It is heartwarming, even if it is not completely accurate.

Christmas morning may be an excellent time to be creative in remembering. On several occasions I have invited people into my sermons. Rather than having me tell their story, I have them do it. Right in the middle of the sermon I simply say to the congregation, "I want you to hear this story from Mary Jones. She just returned from Congo with incredible experiences that bring light to what Jesus is saying to us this morning." At that point Mary steps into the lectern and briefly tells her story. It has been well rehearsed. I go over it with the speaker. I have invited as many as three people into a sermon to bring something to light.

If the writer of Hebrews is looking back to see God's activity in order to lay claim to that activity in the present and the future, it could be a powerful experience to invite one to three people into the sermon on Christmas morning to look back into the more current past and ask, "Where has God been speaking to us?"

I realize the dangers of this, but I think the risk is worth it. Knowing some of your people's stories and experiences, you can choose people who bring a balance and a variety to the sermon. There may be someone in your congregation who has experienced God's grace in a new and fresh way after the loss of a loved one. You may have a soldier who has returned from war who has a similar story of the birth of Christ in the most unlikely place. You might invite a youth who has had a significant experience on a mission trip or a college student who has done a summer mission project. If you have any members going to seminary from your church, this could be a good time for them to tell how this Christ has been incarnate in their lives. You could have someone who has been battling a deadly disease and yet has come in touch with this Christ who is born in the midst of pain and suffering. I would use a variety of ages and a variety of experiences.

I want to hear how God is speaking to us now if I am in a marriage that is deeply in trouble. I want to hear about it when my son or daughter is living in the prodigal's pigpen. I want to hear it when I just got laid off from the only job I have ever known at the textile plant that is now moving offshore. I want to hear it just after the doctor leaves the room having told me that it is cancer. I want to hear it when I watch the news tonight and see thirty-nine more soldiers and citizens killed by a car bomb in the

solidarity of the incarnate Son with his "brothers and sisters" (NRSV v. 10, "children") of flesh and blood. The combination of heavenly status and full humanity is the way God speaks a definitive word.

The next clause (v. 3) uses poetic language, similar to Wisdom of Solomon 7:25–26, to speak about the Son's significance. The first image, "reflection (NRSV, or "radiance" NIV) of God's glory," anticipates language used by Christian theologians to describe the ways in which Son and Father relate as a unity with two distinct identities. The second image, "imprint of God's very being," uses a different metaphor, but with a similar thrust. The "imprint" or "stamp" bears the exact likeness of what is imaged. The term for God's "very being" (*hypostasis*) will have a long history in Christian theology, with a sometimes confusing range of meaning. The term reappears at 3:14 and 11:1, in each case with etymological plays. Here the philosophical connotations predominate. The Son is the visible impression of the very "reality" of God. The next usage will evoke the ethical demand to "stand fast" for one's belief (the NRSV 3:14 translation "first confidence" misses the crucial etymological play). The final usage (11:1) will combine the two senses, suggesting that the hope that makes the ideal real consists in taking a stand for one's faith.

The next clause (v. 4) suggests the Son's role in creation, both at the initial moment of divine creativity and in the ongoing divine sustenance of the created order. The affirmation again evokes the figure of Wisdom, present with God at the creation (Prov. 8:22–31), who "pervades and penetrates all things" (Wis. 7:24). Similar affirmations about the cosmic role of Christ are found in other early Christian hymnic confessions (1 Cor. 8:6; John 1:1–3) influenced by the Wisdom tradition.

The exordium's central affirmation focuses on distinctive themes of Hebrews. "When he had made purification for sins" (v. 3) hints at the interpretation of the death of Christ as a sacrificial act, the key insight developed in chapters 8–10. The later chapters will specify that Christ's sacrificial death is the reality to which the Yom Kippur ritual pointed as a shadowy sketch.

Having completed his priestly act, Christ "sat down" at the side of the "Majesty on high," a circumlocution for God. The reference to Christ's session evokes a key text, Psalm 110:1, that recurs throughout the homily (1:13; 8:1; 10:12). Early Christians frequently used this psalm to express their belief that after his crucifixion Christ was exalted to

irony of course is that this letter is better described as a sermon. It is a sermon because of its commitment to exhortation and the exaltation of Christ. Today one's sermon will likely need to focus upon one or two of the text's features. Perhaps the continuity of today's Epistle reading with a couple of texts from the Hebrew Scriptures or with the companion Gospel reading for this lectionary year will prove helpful in selecting one's theme.

A prominent correlation occurs between verse 2 and the Gospel of John 1:3–4. An important distinction given to Jesus is that he is heir to God, already being the one through whom the world was created (cf. Col. 1:16 also). Previous revelation has been through the ancestors and prophets of the faith. This distinction is not a triumphant rejection of such historical revelation. The authority here issues from oneness with God from the very beginning of creation as heir apparent (John 1:1–3). Celebrating the birth of Christ begins with the Son's connection to creation already. That connection is empowered by the Son's oneness with God in creation. What may become distinctive in the preaching event then is how this revelation takes shape. Care should be given not to reject God's self-revelation in history, as with the ancestors and prophets. In fact, Christ is a historical revelation as well. Yet the christological theme here is that the very one in whom God reveals Godself from the beginning of creation is the one through whom God ultimately reveals Godself even in the humility of the incarnation. The sermon can proceed from this revelation in two essential veins: one may proceed to celebrate the birth of Christ as one who is known through his connection with creation; or one may develop how Christ's life within creation reveals the character of God and faithfulness to humanity. Of course, these options are simply facets of the essential theme of Christ's transcendence over, and yet powerful work through, creation.

Another correlation upon which many scholars build further the theme of inheritance draws from Psalm 2:7–8: "You are my son; today I have begotten you. Ask of me, and I will make the nations your heritage, and the ends of the earth your possession." Psalm 2 is a royal psalm reflecting on the Davidic reign. The significance for our passage from the Letter to the Hebrews is in the language of inheritance and sovereignty. This correlation is substantiated further by another allusion to the Psalms. Verse 3 seats Christ "at the right hand of the Majesty on high." The placement of Christ at God's

Hebrews 1:1-4 (5-12)

Theological Perspective

pillar of fire and smoke that led the people out of slavery and through the wilderness, and the glory presence that indwelt the Holy of Holies in the traveling tabernacle and later in Jerusalem's temple.

This image appears also spoken in the Fourth Gospel when it says, "And the Word became flesh and lived [literally, "tabernacled"] among us, and we have seen his glory, the glory as of a father's only son, full of grace and truth" (1:14).

The writer of this letter is stating, in concert also with Colossians 1:19, that in Jesus all the fullness of God dwells. Indeed, in Jesus, God's presence was evident in vivid terms: he radiated God's Shekinah glory.

Then again, Jesus manifested even more than that representation of God's glory. He was the very essence of God. The fiery presence of old suggested that God is a purifying and powerful deity. But so many other divine character traits were not revealed in that manifestation. Jesus, as God in the flesh, embodied the fullness of God, manifesting the full character of the one whose holiness is compassionate, whose judgment is forgiving, whose power is redeeming, whose knowledge is comprehensible, and whose sovereignty is self-emptying (per Phil. 2).

Jesus' ultimate demonstration of God's essence showed forth when in his death, resurrection, and exaltation he accomplished the purification of sins. Again, this cultus scholar is introducing a theme that will repeat itself frequently in this letter: Jesus is the high priest who offered himself as the final sacrifice for the forgiveness of sins.

For these reasons, Jesus is greater than the angels. What? The writer launches into a string of biblical quotes to argue that Jesus is superior to these heavenly beings. Is that not already obvious? As a matter of fact, while angelic creatures play a small role in the Hebrew Scriptures, they were the object of great fascination and veneration in the milieu of Jesus and the earliest church. This fascination became cardinal doctrine for the Qumran community, which looked for two messiahs, one kingly and the other priestly, both of whom would serve the archangel Michael. The prominent role of the angels in the birth narratives of Matthew and Luke both validates Jesus' identity and puts them in the subordinate role of witnesses.

Put this all together, and the message of Christmas rings forth.

JACK HABERER

Pastoral Perspective

dusty, chaotic streets of Baghdad. I want to hear it as I stand at the grave looking at a box that contains my mother or father, my spouse, or my child.

That is not all. If the marriage is hopping, I want the still-speaking God to move us both into deeper wholeness and discipleship through it. If the kids are well, I want God to guide my support. I just got promoted at work: I want to know how to do justice with my new power. Doc says no cancer. What will God do with my new lease on life? Whether amid darkness or light, I really want to believe that this God of *long ago* is speaking to us now—right now.

It is a shame that not all of our churches have Christmas morning worship services. We have the most powerful message on earth to proclaim on that morning. That is not the day for the church to be closed. Christmas morning is about salvation (Heb. 5:9b.) It is a gift that comes to the world when we need it most, but it is a gift that the world apparently has a difficult time receiving. God waits for this gift to be opened, to be received, to be cherished, and to be responded to in faith. We, as God's people, are called to live as those who have received this gift in hopes that others might receive it as well. We live with the hope that the entire world might be saved through this Christ who was born on Christmas Day. This God of *long ago* continues to speak to us today. That is good news on Christmas morning! That is good news on any morning!

STEVEN P. EASON

Exegetical Perspective

heaven in triumphant vindication (Eph. 1:20; 1 Pet. 3:22). Our author will creatively use verse 4 of the same psalm, in which a royal figure is addressed as a "priest according to the order of Melchizedek," to ground the claim that Christ is a special high priest, whose death is a special kind of sacrifice. Christ's being seated at the right hand of God plays an important role in the psalm. In that position, Christ has achieved a heavenly glory to be shared with all his brothers and sisters (Heb. 2:10). There too, on a throne of grace (4:16), he is in a position to intercede for the faithful.

The exordium closes with an a fortiori argument (i.e., "to the stronger" or "how much more . . . !"), typical of Hebrews. The note that Christ has inherited a name (v. 4) introduces another important theme, inheritance. Woven through the homily (6:17; 11:8), the theme will culminate in the notion that by his death, Christ has left a will/testament that provides his followers an inheritance (9:15–17). The "name" that Christ has "inherited" is not made explicit, although the citation of Psalm 2:7 in verse 5 suggests that it is "Son," the designation used for Christ from the beginning of the exordium.

The superiority of his name parallels Christ's superiority to the angels, who are but servants (1:14). The following collection of biblical verses (vv. 5–13) explores the theme of Christ's superiority to the angels. The texts may have originally celebrated Christ's heavenly enthronement, although they now seem to have been reinterpreted in terms of the prologue's incarnational theology.

The catena begins with citations of Psalm 2:7 and 2 Samuel 7:14, which speak of the "begetting" of the Son. Verse 6 cites Deuteronomy 32:43 in Greek, part of the Song of Moses, to evoke the angelic hymnody accompanying the introduction of the Son into the world. Verses 7–8 contrast the ways in which the Psalms speak of angels and the Son. Psalm 104:4, read very literally, suggests that "angels" are made fleeting elements of fire and wind. Psalm 45:6–7, cited in verses 8–9, by contrast addresses the Son as "God" and affirms the eternal character of his throne. Psalm 102:25–27, cited in verses 10–12, affirms the eternality of the one who laid the earth's foundations, here understood to be the Son, as verse 3 suggests. The collection of citations ends as did the prologue, with a reference to the Son's eschatological enthronement, alluded to in Psalm 110:1. On this holy morning, flesh and eternity join.

HAROLD W. ATTRIDGE

Homiletical Perspective

right hand for eternity, which recurs in verse 13, unmistakably echoes Psalm 110. The reign of Christ is established from creation, but in verse 3 we see it reflected as God's "glory" and in God's "very being." While the sustaining power of Christ named in verse 3 is reminiscent of Wisdom literature as well, Jesus lives into his reign by fulfilling his saving mission. This is a consistent theme throughout the letter. Ironically, the evidence of Jesus' sovereignty or oneness with God lies in the humility and faithfulness of enduring suffering for the sake of humanity.[2]

Preachers may find quite useful here the juxtaposition of Christ's reign over creation with God and Jesus' faithful humility in birth and suffering. The juxtaposition suggests ways in which we may discover the power or glory of God in the most unlikely of places. Given that this day celebrates the birth of Christ, this juxtaposition is almost built into the event. A newborn is our most vulnerable creature and yet precious gem in humanity. A newborn is protected by moral law and therefore all sorts of legal statutes. In the weakest state of life, we find the majesty of God. In the newborn's dependency, we discover the sanctity of life. The juxtaposition becomes a source of revelation. Jesus is the agent of God's self-revelation in both his incarnation and his mission.

The revelation does not begin or cease with Jesus' death and resurrection. Christ is exalted above creation, above heavenly creatures, as one with God. His exaltation is part of the revelation. This prologue is careful to demonstrate that the exaltation of Christ extends from and exceeds the promises of earlier revelation. While the Letter to the Hebrews builds upon this prologue to highlight the supremacy of Christ over the angels, the prophets and priests of covenantal tradition, and the faith of the ancestors, preachers will find that the exhortation and exaltation of Christ builds upon the humility of Jesus in the incarnation and suffering servanthood for the sake of creation. In his most vulnerable commitments, Christ's divinity is imaged in the glory of God and secured in the reign of God.

DALE P. ANDREWS

2. Thomas G. Smothers, "A Superior Model: Hebrews 1:1–4:13," *Review and Expositor* 82, no. 3 (Summer 1985): 333–35.

John 1:1-14

[1]In the beginning was the Word, and the Word was with God, and the Word was God. [2]He was in the beginning with God. [3]All things came into being through him, and without him not one thing came into being. What has come into being [4]in him was life, and the life was the light of all people. [5]The light shines in the darkness, and the darkness did not overcome it.

[6]There was a man sent from God, whose name was John. [7]He came as a witness to testify to the light, so that all might believe through him. [8]He himself was not the light, but he came to testify to the light. [9]The true light, which enlightens everyone, was coming into the world.

[10]He was in the world, and the world came into being through him; yet the world did not know him. [11]He came to what was his own, and his own people did not accept him. [12]But to all who received him, who believed in his name, he gave power to become children of God, [13]who were born, not of blood or of the will of the flesh or of the will of man, but of God.

[14]And the Word became flesh and lived among us, and we have seen his glory, the glory as of a father's only son, full of grace and truth.

Theological Perspective

John begins his Gospel with a poetic theological meditation on the Word, the *logos*, which sets the stage for the narrative as John intends the reader to understand it. The prologue is thus like the overture to a musical or an opera that offers bits of the melodies or motifs to be more fully developed later. In the prologue John offers a theological framework for understanding the person of Jesus in his relationship to God and to us.[1]

The key theological themes of the prologue include the identity of Jesus as the incarnate Word of God, and the reality of revelation and reconciliation mediated by the Word.

The Identity of Jesus and the Reality of Incarnation. The prologue identifies Jesus as the incarnate Word of God (v. 14). The term Word, or *logos*, is a rich and nuanced word, meaning mind or rationality, but also speech or communication. As John deploys it, the *logos* of God is both substantial and dynamic. As mind or rationality, *logos* conveys the content of God's thinking; as speech, it conveys action and realization. In Jesus, God speaks God's mind.

Almost from the beginning, debate arose on how to interpret the prologue. Did John mean to identify

1. Earl F. Palmer, *The Intimate Gospel: Studies in John* (Waco, TX: Word, 1978), 15.

Pastoral Perspective

For many Protestant Christians, the opportunity to worship on Christmas Day is limited to those few years when Christmas falls on a Sunday. The wisdom of ceding a holy day to (rampant) consumerism and (over) eating aside, it is certainly the case that the common practice of not worshiping on Christmas Day leads to a compressed, if not truncated, Christmas celebration. In Roman Catholic and other more traditional liturgical churches, the Christmas experience *begins* rather than *concludes* on Christmas Eve.

Reclaiming Christmas Day also entails recasting Christmas Eve. In the expanded two-day celebration, Christmas Eve is focused on expectation and anticipation at its peak. Mary and Joseph arrive at the place of nativity and, like any expectant father and mother, find themselves embroiled in the hustle and bustle that immediately precedes birth. As nurses or midwives attend, the anticipation of mother and father mounts until . . . finally . . . that moment of delivery! The night both peaks and concludes with "Joy to the World." Christmas Day, on the other hand, is for settling in. As with a typical birth experience, the crowds are mostly dispersed. Mother and father have time to spend alone with the newborn child. Exhausted and overwhelmed by the previous night's events, words are used sparely. Punctuated perhaps by naps, snacks, and short visits,

Exegetical Perspective

To what can we compare the opening of the Gospel of John? To none of the other Gospels' openings, but only to the first words of Genesis. John's Gospel is about the one in whom there was "life" (v. 4) and about the new family of God for those "who believe in his name" (v. 12). The events of the Gospel are recent history, but the evangelist conceives them as bound up with the beginning of all things, namely, the realities the first verse presents: God and God's Word. The idea of Christ as the incarnate Word (*logos*) of God is unique to John. It arose out of the particular history of this community, and the term *logos,* Word, is used with this special meaning only in the opening.

Scholars identify John's opening as a prologue. It is characterized by a liturgical quality and extends to verse 18, as is evident from the literary device called an *inclusio* (or "closing in"), employed by ancient authors to mark the boundaries of a passage by repetition of the same word or idea. The statement in verse 1 that the "Word was with God" (the preposition "with" generally means motion toward, but can also indicate proximity) is echoed and unpacked by verse 18's description of the "only begotten Son" as "in the bosom of the Father" (KJV). Verses 15–18 form the prologue's final section and bring the story down to the present of those

Homiletical Perspective

The lectionary's move from Christmas Eve to Christmas Day is stunning. On Christmas Eve worshipers go home having pondered the human arrival of the Messiah, who was born to a poor, unwed mother and laid in a manger because there was no room in the inn. These same worshipers return on Christmas Day (actually the first day of the twelve-day Christmas *season*) to hear the proclamation that this child is the Word become flesh, the Word who "was with God" and "was God," and who participated in the creation of "all things" (vv. 1–3). The child born in Bethlehem is the preexistent divine Word, one with God, who brings into being light and life.

The poetic opening words of John's Gospel move the church theologically from "birth" to "incarnation." The canvas on which the Gospel paints the person and work of Jesus now becomes very large indeed. It encompasses "the beginning" and includes identity with God and the work of creation. The church now encounters not simply the unique and extraordinary birth of Jesus, but the coming of the one who, in the words of the Nicene Creed, is "God from God, Light from Light, true God from true God." This very one has become flesh and lived among us—literally "tabernacled" among us, as the glory of God "tabernacled" with the people of Israel.

John 1:1-14

Theological Perspective

Jesus with the Word and with God in a metaphorical sense or in a realistic sense? Those who took the latter approach used the term *homoousios* to describe the relationship between Jesus the Logos and God. Some may think of the word today as a contentious and esoteric technical term, but in fact, *homoousios* was a fairly common Greek word that meant "made of the same stuff." On the other side, the theological "conservatives" of the day, the Arians and the moderate semi-Arians, read the prologue as mythical and poetic, and balked at the realistic use of *homoousios* as an open door to polytheism. Jesus is undeniably a lot like God, they argued, a true window to the divine; but it is going too far to say that he was actually God. This view has resurfaced periodically in the history of the church, particularly since the Enlightenment.

In opposition to the Arians, Athanasius and others encouraged a realist reading of the prologue. They took John to mean that the incarnation is a real event in space and time within the cosmos God created. For these fathers, the prologue is more than metaphorical; it is a realistic witness to an actual event, namely, the appearance of God in and through the man Jesus. They went on to point out that if Jesus is not in fact the Word of God, then his life and teaching is merely a human word, devoid of any meaningful revelation and impotent for salvation.

The difference between these perspectives ought not to be taken lightly or dismissed quickly, because it reveals divergent assumptions about the nature of God and the nature of the universe. At root in the modernist application of the Arian and semi-Arian perspective is an assumption of an impersonal and silent God and an autonomous and closed universe, a world in which divine interaction is not possible except in indirect modes. On this view, the prologue can make sense only metaphorically, since a real incarnation is inconceivable. The alternative views God as a dynamic and personal being, capable of self-communication, and the universe as contingent creation, open by divine design to the activity of God. In this view, the prologue works as a realistic witness to an actual event, namely, the appearance of God in and through the man Jesus.

The Incarnate Word as the Mediator of Revelation and Reconciliation. In the prologue, John introduces the twin themes of light and life, which feature prominently in the rest of the Gospel. They are not a poetic piling on of images, but rather carefully

Pastoral Perspective

it is a day for the quiet realization that life will never again be the same. The question of the moment is "What Child Is This?"[1]

The prologue to the Gospel of John is legendary for the exegetical, theological, and homiletical challenges it presents. Few other passages of the Bible have been subjected to as much prolonged and varied scrutiny as this one. Fortunately, the pastoral question for Christmas Day is narrower and, though potentially aided by the vast history of interpretation, does not require it: How does this passage help us to "settle in" to life with the newborn savior who will change our lives forever?

When compared to the very concrete narratives of the preceding days in the lectionary (Luke 1:39–55 and Luke 2:1–20), the poetic language of John 1:1–14 seems almost to float untethered from daily life. Pregnant women, kicking babies, a decreeing emperor, weary travelers, a swaddled baby, visiting shepherds—John's version offers no such enticing details and characterizations as it begins the gospel story. Instead we have the language of mystery: "In the beginning was the Word, and the Word was with God, and the Word was God." Our desire to be entertained is thwarted. But our need to be grounded is met, paradoxically, in this vision of a savior who refuses to be pinned down to overly precise human expectations.

In avoiding the temptation to wish poetry away, we are rewarded with a text that can be our quiet companion on this day of watching and listening for the signs of life's new meaning. The prologue is what literary critic Frank Kermode aptly called a "threshold poem," concerned with "how that which *was* crossed over into *becoming*."[2] Its nuanced words, while frustrating to the prosaic mind, offer a fountain of resources for probing the liminality of Christmas Day. Before the birth we were not alone. We knew God and worshiped God. But now our knowing is different, and our worship can never again be the same. We are crossing a threshold.

Over against Luke's "cast of thousands," John's prologue contains only three "characters" (if we can even properly call them that). Two of them, God and the Word, overlap in a complex and (humanly) difficult way. The third, John the Baptist, seems oddly and abruptly inserted into the poem's flow. Verses 6–9 remind us that Jesus has a prehistory. Like every

---

1. I am indebted to my colleague and friend the Rev. Don Bailey-François for his reflections on the rhythm of these days.
2. "John," in *The Literary Guide to the Bible*, ed. Robert Alter and Frank Kermode (Cambridge, MA: Harvard University Press, 1987), 445.

who have experienced "grace and truth" through Jesus (v. 17).

The conclusion of John's Gospel cites an unnamed disciple—alluded to throughout as "the one whom Jesus loved" (e.g., 13:23; 21:20)—as the authority for the writing of the Gospel (21:24). This "beloved disciple" may have been a previous adherent of John the Baptist (1:35–40), perhaps from a prominent Jerusalem family (18:15–16). Under his influence, the "community of the beloved disciple"[1] developed the characteristic high Christology of the Gospel. These "Johannine" Christians probably experienced rejection from the local synagogue (9:22; 12:42) late in the first century for calling Jesus God and thus offending Jewish monotheistic sensibilities (10:33).

John clearly did not share this fear. Although the earliest biblical use of the notion of the "word of God" involved the communication of a "word" to and through a prophet (e.g., 1 Sam. 3:21; Amos 3:1), the "word" of God developed into a quasi-separate reality (e.g., Isa. 55:11). In the Hellenistic and Roman period, this idea features in some Jewish works, for example, in the apocryphal Wisdom of Solomon: "your all-powerful word leaped from heaven" (18:15). A similar development happened with God's wisdom, whose feminine gender in Hebrew led to an image of Lady Wisdom as God's assistant in creation (Prov. 8). Just as in the prologue all things are created through the Word (1:3, 10), Wisdom was called "the fashioner of all things" and "a breath of the power of God" (Wis. 7:22, 25). The mid-first-century Alexandrian Jew Philo (who was deeply influenced by Plato) made wide usage of the "word" (logos) of God as the medium of God's self-communication, going so far as to use the term "God" to refer to "God's most ancient word."[2]

Whatever parallels may obtain between John and the concepts of Greek philosophy and Hellenized Jewish thought, the prologue emphasizes the mission of the incarnate word to humanity (vv. 9, 14, 18) and the response to the proclamation of Jesus (vv. 7, 11–14). The Word is not simply a medium of God's revelation considered as knowledge about God; for what the Word reveals, it transmits: God's love for humanity (3:16).

The opening verse's echo of Genesis draws attention to the idea that the Word belonged to God before the creation of the world. The first verse

1. See Raymond E. Brown, *The Community of the Beloved Disciple* (New York: Paulist Press, 1979).
2. David T. Runia, *Philo in Early Christian Literature: A Survey* (Minneapolis: Fortress Press, 1993), 83. The quotation from Philo is from *Somn.* 1.229.

As John suggests, poetry, rather than explanation or analysis, may be the best way for preachers to bear witness to this remarkable news that can never be captured in human words.

The prologue of John is so dense and rich that it may overwhelm the preacher, particularly on Christmas Day, which, like Christmas Eve, is not a time for many words or theological arguments. There is no way the preacher can cover everything in the text; he or she will inevitably have to focus the sermon. Yet the entire text needs to be heard in its poetic density and complexity. With this challenging situation in mind, the first task of the preacher is simply to read this text well. The proclamation of the Word—the same Word that was in the beginning and was God!—begins with the reading of the text. Preachers should thoroughly prepare for this reading, considering the thoughts and emotions to be conveyed, and practicing the best ways to faithfully interpret and "perform" the text for the assembled congregation. In addition, hymns or anthems may be chosen that also give rich poetic voice to the text. In these ways, the fullness of John's poetry may be heard by the congregation in deep and powerful ways.

The sermon itself, like the text, should paint on a big canvas. This text calls for some large and stunning claims. The preacher seeks to draw the congregation into the grand sweep of the Incarnate One's work. One approach might involve a focus on creation. From the beginning the Word's work is creative and creating. Just as God *speaks* creation into being in Genesis 1, so in John 1 "All things came into being through [the Word], and without [the Word] not one thing came into being" (v. 3). The Word, which becomes flesh and lives among us, is the very creative power of God. And the Word's creative work seeks the light of salvation and fullness of life for all people (v. 4).

As the Word made flesh, Jesus embodies and enacts the creative work of God. Indeed, the sweep of Jesus' work may be proclaimed as the inauguration of the *new creation*. John's Gospel suggests this approach. Just as John's prologue links Jesus with the creation story in Genesis 1, so John's resurrection account links Jesus with the creation story in Genesis 2. In John 20:11–18, one finds a man (Jesus) and a woman (Mary) in a garden (Mary supposes Jesus to be the gardener), an allusion to Adam and Eve in Eden. Just as God through the Word began the original creation on the first day of the week, so God through the risen Word inaugurates the new creation on the same day of the week.

John 1:1-14

Theological Perspective

chosen to communicate the reality of divine revelation and reconciliation that is mediated to humanity through the incarnate Word, who is equally the mediator of creation (v. 3). At the heart of John's understanding of Jesus is the conviction that in him we behold the fullness of both divine revelation and reconciliation. Athanasius wrote: "He was made man that we might be made god [*theo-poietheomen*]. He manifested himself by a body that we might receive a conception of the unseen Father. He endured the hubris of humanity that we might inherit incorruptibility."[2]

As the life (*zōē*) of people, Christ is the source and sustenance of all life. But John means more than just physical existence; the Word made flesh mediates new life that is the result of reconciliation with God. God overcomes sin and death by embracing and defeating them in Jesus, who became flesh of our flesh and bone of our bone. Jesus' encounters with lepers illustrate this point dramatically. Humanity did not drain life from Jesus; rather, he injected dying humanity with life. The Word is also the light (*phōs*) that enlightens life. This reality of revelation through the incarnation of God in Jesus Christ was particularly important to Luther and Calvin. Jesus is not merely a human word among many words; he is uniquely the Word of God by virtue of the incarnation.

Reconciliation and revelation are thus not two separate realities, but two sides of the same coin. The healing power of Christ renews and restores our minds, enabling us to embrace the truth of God in Jesus Christ. As Karl Barth observed, "This is the beginning of all beginnings in Christian thinking and speaking, the presupposition of all presuppositions with which the Christian community approaches the world. When we say Jesus Christ, this is not a possibility which is somewhere ahead of us, but an actuality which is already behind us. With this name in our hearts and on our lips, we are not laboriously toiling uphill, but merrily coming down."[3] Therein lies the deep joy of Christmas.

ROBERT REDMAN

Pastoral Perspective

child who is born, he is part of a family legacy. John's presence in the poem ties Jesus to ancient Israel and to the prophetic tradition. This savior of the world is also a human being with a particular identity that may embarrass us in some circles. He isn't timeless, or universal, or generically spiritual. He was born at a specific time, to a specific people, who practiced a specific religion. He is also tied to a tradition that places fidelity to God's truth above the niceties of diplomacy. He is likely to cause some trouble.

The verses before and after John's appearance in the poem literally foreshadow the trouble that is to come. This birth brings light to the world, but that light will be made more visible by the surrounding darkness. Light is defined by the shadows that surround it. Every parent knows that a newborn infant will both face, and cause, difficulties as he or she grows up. The poem's realism, while not detailed in prediction, is absolute in conviction. Darkness exists. It is real and terrifying. But the light of life will persist and prevail. One ancient commentator captures the drama superbly: the life that is light "is chased by the darkness, but is not overtaken by it."[3]

So, while Christmas Day is a day replete with worry and foreboding, it is ultimately a day of hope. Verse 14 makes the promise explicit. The Word has encamped among us, we have seen glory, a glory full of grace and truth. We receive that promise only in faith. John refuses to pin down our hopes to anything more specific than the One who was, and is becoming, the Word. Like parents of a newborn, we are startled that we would be released back into the world with such vagaries. Should we not have to pass a test? Could a nurse come to live with us and show us what to do? Is there a list of rules to keep us all safe? No, there is just the Child—his life and presence—and the promise of "grace upon grace" (John 1:17) that unfolds in the chapters ahead.

MICHAEL S. BENNETT

---

2. Athanasius, *On the Incarnation* 54:3, quoted in Joel C. Elowsky, ed., *John 1–10*, Ancient Christian Commentary on Scripture: New Testament 4a (Downers Grove, IL: InterVarsity Press, 2006), 43.
3. Karl Barth, *Church Dogmatics*, IV/2 (Edinburgh: T.&T. Clark, 1963), 46.

3. Gregory of Nazianzus, *Oration 39*, in *The Nicene and Post-Nicene Fathers, Second Series*, vol. 7, ed. Philip Schaff and Henry Wace (Peabody, MA: Hendrickson Publishers, 1994), 685.

Exegetical Perspective

formally consists of three clauses, each disclosing something about the Word: its When, How, and What. The reality of the Word is distinct from God, which the Greek of verse 1 makes clear through the use of the definite article in the second clause: "and the Word was closely oriented to the God" (my trans.). The first two clauses lay out the rationale of the third, so the reader understands how this "Word" can be called "God" (without a definite article). The Word's status, role, and work are related in the rest (vv. 2–5) of the first section.

The second section (vv. 6–9) zooms in from the cosmic frame to a single man "sent from God" (v. 6). John the Baptist, who came "to witness about the light" (v. 7), is for the evangelist foundational to the history of the Word, as his witness marked the revelation of the "true light, which enlightens everyone" (v. 9). The image of the Word as light—a metaphor for knowledge in biblical and other traditions—that "shines in the darkness" (v. 5) stands in contrast to the "darkness" that recalls the "darkness" before creation (Gen. 1:2), again relating creation and salvation.

The prologue's third section sharpens the focus on the Word's salvific appearance on earth (vv. 10–13). The Word's presence in the world met a twofold response, but those who "received him" become a new people, "children of God" (v. 12), who belong now to God in a special relation described in familial terms. All this follows from the author's incarnational theology: "the Word became flesh and lived among us" (v. 14). "Lived" could be more literally translated as "pitched his tent" or "tabernacled,"[3] recalling the intimacy of God's dwelling amid the Israelites through the wilderness route out of Egypt.

The exegesis yields a mesh of three interwoven stories: of creation, salvation, and the birth of the church. The prologue relates these themes inextricably to the evangelical proclamation: God's love for humankind and God's will to save result in a new community demarcated not by its fleshly descent or inclination but on a new mode of interrelatedness among those "begotten by God" (v. 13, my trans.).

STEPHEN A. COOPER

Homiletical Perspective

The Gospel of John frames Jesus' person and work by allusions to the creation stories. The Gospel thus invites preachers to proclaim the new creation that has come into the world in the Word made flesh, and encourages preachers to share "glimpses" of this inbreaking new creation they have witnessed in the church and the world. Moreover, because "all things" have been created through the Word, preachers may boldly affirm that nothing and no one is outside the creative, life-giving purposes of the Word. Although the conflict between the Word and the world (the *kosmos* in rebellion against God) continues (vv. 5, 10–11), the creation is not autonomous; it has no existence apart from the Word, and it can thus be redeemed. To borrow Paul's words, nothing can separate us from the love of God in Christ Jesus (Rom. 8:38–39).

John's prologue not only provides the content for preaching on Christmas Day. It also suggests the character of Christmas preaching (and possibly all preaching). Such preaching will take the form of testimony, like the preaching of John the Baptist (vv. 7–8) and the preaching of the early church (v. 14). Preachers are given no "proof" regarding the Word made flesh, who has embodied the very glory of God among us (v. 14). Rather, preachers can only share the living Word we have *seen* and *believed* (v. 14)—in the text, in the world, in the church, and in our lives.[1] Preachers stand in the pulpit with no other "foundation" than this Word, on which we boldly bet our lives. But this Word "was with God" and "was God"; this Word created "all things." This Word became flesh and lived among us, full of glory and grace and truth. So faithful witness is enough. Through the preacher's testimony, the creative Word will empower others to see and believe and live.

CHARLES L. CAMPBELL

---

3. Andrew T. Lincoln, *The Gospel according to Saint John* (London: Continuum, 2005), 104.

1. For a helpful book on the testimonial character of preaching, see Anna Carter Florence, *Preaching as Testimony* (Louisville, KY: Westminster John Knox Press, 2007).

1 Samuel 2:18-20, 26

18Samuel was ministering before the LORD, a boy wearing a linen ephod. 19His mother used to make for him a little robe and take it to him each year, when she went up with her husband to offer the yearly sacrifice. 20Then Eli would bless Elkanah and his wife, and say, "May the LORD repay you with children by this woman for the gift that she made to the LORD"; and then they would return to their home. . . .

26Now the boy Samuel continued to grow both in stature and in favor with the LORD and with the people.

Theological Perspective

In this text we encounter the young Samuel growing in "stature and favor." He was a gift from God to his barren mother, Hannah, and she returned him to God as a gift. Samuel was dedicated as a Nazirite, committed to the service of God from infancy. We find him now a young man, serving as a priest in the house of the LORD. He wears the linen ephod, a garment that marks his identity as a priest. But he also wears another garment, a robe made by his mother. She brings him a new one each year when she comes on annual pilgrimage with her husband to make sacrifice. Eli, the old priest, blesses Samuel's parents and prays that God will repay them with many children, for they have given Samuel to God.

Young Samuel will grow into a great prophet who will oversee Israel's transition from a tribal confederacy to a unified nation. In this text we meet him as a young man surrounded by the trappings of the priesthood, the grandeur of religious ceremony, and the solemnity of ritual service. In this context, he is a witness to both great faithfulness (in Eli, who listens for a word from God, even though God was strangely silent "in those days") and petty corruption (in Eli's scoundrel sons, who help themselves to the sacrificial meat and the bodies of the women serving at the temple).

This story raises two theological themes related to identity. First, notice that the story is remarkably

Pastoral Perspective

The four verses of this brief lectionary text prompt reflection on at least four affirmations that touch the lives of parishioners in every pew.

Our Children Are Not Our Own; They Belong to God. A radio news story reported that many summer camps have established online photo galleries to keep anxious parents informed about their child's daily activities. Parents can—and do—check the photo galleries daily and complain when pictures are not updated regularly. One parent, upon viewing the photos, noticed a scratch on a child's arm and promptly telephoned the camp to find out what had happened.[1]

Such overanxious parenting, also known as "helicopter parenting," is not limited to early childhood, but extends to high school, college, and even into the work world. "From Vanguard Group and St. Paul Travelers to General Electric and Boeing, managers are getting phone calls from parents asking them to hire their 20-something kids. . . . Parents are calling hiring managers to protest pay packages and trying to negotiate."[2] Clinging tightly

1. Diane Orson, "Summer Camp Makes Room for E-Contact," *All Things Considered*, National Public Radio, August 6, 2007.
2. Sue Shellenbarger, "Helicopter Parents Now Hover at the Office," *The Wall Street Journal* Executive Career Site, www.careerjournal.com , accessed July 26, 2007.

Exegetical Perspective

The birth of a first child, like the beginning of a new year, is cause for celebration. Every instinct is to focus on fulfilled hopes and unencumbered possibilities. Today's reading from Samuel's birth narrative accents three reasons why the faith community celebrates the promise of new beginnings.

— The child Hannah prayed for (1:9–11), the boy she promised to dedicate to God's service if God granted her prayer (1:27–28), is now "*ministering* before the Lord" (2:18; cf. 2:11). The verbal form "ministering," coupled with the report that Samuel wears a "linen ephod," an apronlike garment that is a priestly vestment (cf. 2:28), indicates that Samuel is "engaged in the service of the LORD as an attendant" (2:18 NJPS).

— Both Samuel's ministering and his parents' joy (cf. 2:1–10) are nested within a blessing (2:20). This is the first occurrence of the word "bless" in 1 Samuel, and it signals at the outset that a life conceived in the hope of parents who faithfully wait on God's promises will be nurtured by God's abiding care.

— As Samuel grows up physically, he grows more and more into the will and purposes of God. The description of Samuel's maturation in verse 26 is pregnant with both affirmation and promise, as the Gospel lesson from Luke 2:41–52 makes clear

Homiletical Perspective

This passage can present a radical challenge to parents who, after bringing their children to church at Christmas, may be considering joining the church "for the sake of the kids." It can also be a year-end testimony to the power of God to raise up new things, even as old things are dying away.

Participating in the life of a congregation is often considered part of a well-rounded upbringing. That was not the reason Hannah brought her child to Shiloh. In gratitude for the gift of a son, Hannah gave God—her son! The very thing Hannah asked for was what she gave back to God. Hanna's dedication of her son to the service of God serves as an example of how a relationship with God casts everything else in a new light. Overwhelming gratitude like hers—which comes from knowing that God notices and responds to us—is what allows martyrs to give their lives joyfully, missionaries to leave home and family for distant lands, and ordinary Christians to make extraordinary sacrifices for the gospel.

In essence, what Hannah did was much like what parents do when they present a child for baptism or dedication. At that moment they turn their child back over to God. It should be made clear that Hannah's gift of her son was not a cold act of ideological frenzy such as we might associate with some disturbing sect. Hannah still loved her son and

1 Samuel 2:18-20, 26

Theological Perspective

forthright about its assessment of the degree to which we are relatively free and relatively constrained in the choices we make about our lives. Samuel's growth in favor is contrasted with the path of destruction chosen by Eli's sons (2:12–17). Samuel freely chooses to serve God; Eli's sons freely choose to corrupt themselves. No one forces them, yet neither Samuel nor Eli's sons choose with absolute freedom. Samuel has been dedicated to the service of God and favored by God from birth. Eli's sons have also been dedicated from birth, but they will not listen to their father's dire warnings because "it was the will of the LORD to kill them" (2:25b).

Jonathan Edwards reflected on the nature of human freedom and its relationship to God's sovereignty. "The will always is," he taught, "as the greatest apparent good is."[1] We freely pursue and willingly choose what seems good to us. Human beings, he concluded, are free to do what we want. But we do not choose our wants; we do not determine our desires. We may act on our desires, but we do not choose what our desires will be. We are both free and constrained.

In contemporary society, we are often reluctant to confront constraints on our freedom, hesitant to acknowledge the degree to which our identities are shaped by forces beyond our control. Yet this reluctance may lead us to overestimate our freedom. Especially in contexts of affluence, refusal to acknowledge how we have been shaped by our contexts may lead us to believe that we have earned our privileged lives and, consequently, that those who live on the margins have also, somehow, received what they deserve.

We may even come to believe that we may somehow merit the favor of God. The central insight of the Protestant Reformation, that God redeems humanity without regard for merit,[2] flies in the face of our reluctance to confront our own limitations. God claims us, not because we are worthy, but because we cannot be. (This leaves unresolved some troubling questions about those whom God appears not to claim. Including the passages about Eli's sons omitted from the lectionary may prompt conversation about the mystery of God's judgment and the scope of divine mercy.) Affirming that God has freely chosen us means that the central fact of our

1. Jonathan Edwards, *Freedom of the Will*, ed. Paul Ramsey (New Haven, CT: Yale University Press, 1957), 142.
2. See, for example, Martin Luther, "Preface to the Epistle of St. Paul to the Romans," in *Martin Luther: Selections from His Writings*, ed. John Dillenberger (New York: Anchor Books, 1962).

Pastoral Perspective

to children, many parents make their sons and daughters the center and focus of their lives.

In contrast, here are Hannah and Elkanah. They cherish their son. No one can dispute that. They have waited long and prayed fervently for his arrival. But as much as they love Samuel, their lives are shaped not by their devotion to him, but by their devotion to God. They worship, praise, sacrifice for, give thanks to, submit to, and serve not Samuel, but God. They recognize that God has different plans for Samuel from what they might have envisioned, but they surrender their plans and submit to God's. They do what they can to help Samuel fulfill God's purposes for his life, "making a little robe and taking it to him each year."

Hannah and Elkanah model the kind of parenting Christians promise to undertake when we stand at the baptismal font with our little ones. When our children are baptized, we rejoice that "they are marked as God's own forever." This may mean that God will have different plans for our children from those we might choose: the daughter may be sent to China to teach English, the son may be called away from a law degree into the ministry. Surrendering our children to God's keeping and will is easier said at the font than done day to day.

But do it we must. Our job as Christians is to center our lives not on our children, but on God. Our job as parents is to help our children remember whose they are and to support them in their becoming the men and women God intends. To do that, we remember that our children are not our own: they belong to God. Hannah and Elkanah can help us do that.

God Is Already Preparing the Future. Eli's sons are scoundrels. The Bible says so. Despite the faithfulness of their father Eli, these sons have "no regard for the LORD" (2:12). Surely this is a point for a preacher to ponder, bearing in mind the untold number of faithful congregants who must share Eli's heartbreak at his adult children's rejection of the God he has worshiped and served.

Eli's sons are corrupt. They have failed to do the Lord's will and work. But God does not let their faithlessness thwart the divine purposes. Even before God's judgment has been passed on the sons, God is already preparing a solution to the ruptures their sin has caused. God chooses Samuel.

In the same way, God will not let the sins of Israel thwart God's great purposes. Long before the people could see, God prepared the antidote to their sin, the

Exegetical Perspective

(cf. Luke 2:52 and 1 Sam. 2:26). When Luke uses the Samuel narratives to exegete the birth of Jesus, he invites us to remember and celebrate the promise that growing into the "stature" of God means to be filled with the "wisdom" and "grace" (Luke 2:40 NIV) that commend not only God's applause but also the respect of "people" who yearn for possibilities that surpass the exigent limitations of life.

New beginnings, however, mark points of departure, not arrival. They are but first steps toward a destination that clarifies—and becomes more complex—as the journey unfolds. The lectionary reading is therefore an important entry into the celebration that today's liturgy invites, but these verses alone do not provide the full context for understanding and appropriating the promise of new beginnings. The following mitigating circumstances, according to the larger narrative (1 Sam. 1–6), should be factored into today's celebration.

1. As Samuel was ministering before the Lord in Shiloh (1:24), others there were learning what it meant to be a priest. Both before (2:12–17) and after (2:22–26) the selected reading for today, the narrative focuses on the sinful behavior of Eli's sons, Hophni and Phinehas, the presumptive heirs to his priestly office. They are described as "scoundrels" (v. 12; literally "worthless sons") who take offerings dedicated to God for their own use (cf. Lev. 7:30–36; Num. 18:17–18) and "lay with the women who served at the entrance to the tent of meeting" (v. 22; cf. Num. 25:6–15). The specific acts referenced here are not altogether clear, but the narrative leaves no doubt that the sons' behavior shows contempt not only for their father but also for God. The judgment oracle that announces their death (2:27–36) pivots on a central truth (v. 30) that may be lost if one focuses only on the hope and joy that attends Samuel's beginnings: "Those who would serve God place themselves under God's grace and God's judgment, not just under God's grace."[1]

2. As Samuel continues to grow in stature (2:26) and as the word of God continues to be revealed to him in Shiloh (3:19–21; see especially the narrative in 3:1–18), the Philistines "muster for war against Israel" in Aphek, a city about twenty miles to the east, in the Sharon valley (4:1). The backdrop is the conflict with the Philistines, especially as depicted in Judges (most famously in the Samson stories, Judg.

1. B. Birch, "The First and Second Books of Samuel: Introduction, Commentary, and Reflections," in *New Interpreter's Bible*, vol. 2 (Nashville: Abingdon, 1998), 989.

Homiletical Perspective

cared for him deeply. Her love was evident in the gift that she took him on her regular visits to Shiloh. She always brought him a little robe. It was nothing extravagant, but one can imagine the love she poured into each stitch as she made the robe, thinking of her son and whispering prayers of gratitude to God for the gift of his life. One hopes that the presents we give our loved ones are as loaded with care and gratitude.

A sermon on this text will also have to address the fact that God gave Hannah other children in response to her dedication of Samuel to God's service. One might infer from this story that we can strike bargains with God. The preacher needs to make clear that Hannah dedicated Samuel with no expectation that she would receive other children in return. She presented her son to God out of sheer gratitude. The gift of more children to her and Elkanah was an example of God's free and expansive generosity.

The homiletical point here is that we can expect God to do great and wonderful things and can trust God's goodness always to surprise us, but we cannot manipulate God. When parents present their children in baptism or dedication, it is done with no strings attached. They cannot predict what God will do with their children or how their own lives will be affected, but they know that what follows will be in character with God's gracious and merciful nature.

This text challenges the church to examine its ministry critically, making sure that it does not contribute to any misperception that it exists merely to provide nice programs to enrich the lives of children. It is tempting for a congregation to buy into a consumerist mentality that promises numerical growth by appealing to parents' desires to give their children the very best. A congregation faithful to the gospel will be honest with parents about the radical nature of involving their children in the life of the church. A church that is doing a faithful ministry of Christian nurture is preparing children to take up the cross. We need to be sure that is really what parents want their children to do.

As the year draws to a close, many Christians are reflecting on the past. For some, the passing year has marked the end of a relationship or the death of someone they love. For others, a job has ended or a season of life has closed. Some congregations will mark the end of an era with the departure of a pastor or the shutting down of a once-thriving ministry. Maybe the community or the nation is

1 Samuel 2:18-20, 26

Theological Perspective

identities—that we belong to God—is beyond our control, beyond our choosing. We simply follow the desires of our hearts toward the God who made our hearts and their desires for God's own self. No wonder our hearts are restless until they find their rest in God.[3]

A second theological theme related to identity emerges from this good news that we belong to God, not because we have chosen God, but because God has chosen us. This time the theme is baptismal. Hannah and Elkanah acknowledged that Samuel belonged to God. This fact superseded but did not obliterate his family identity. His parents dedicated him to the service of God but visited every year. Samuel is literally clothed in his dual identity, wearing the garment of the priest and the robe of his mother. We can imagine Hannah thinking about and praying for her son as she makes him a new robe each year. We can almost see how delighted she and Elkanah would be to find Samuel well and growing in stature and favor. Eli too acknowledges that his sons belong to God and trusts the judgments of God to be both merciful and just. Yet his sons are also his own, and so he tries to warn them of the consequences of their evil.

There is a remarkable moment in the sacrament of infant baptism when parents hand their child over to the pastor. By this act we remember that through baptism the child's identity is no longer determined primarily by his or her family of origin but by membership in the church. Through baptism, the child participates in the death and resurrection of Christ and is welcomed into a new identity as a member of the Christian church. Parents, in other words, acknowledge that their child belongs first and foremost to God and that this identity supersedes family identity. But rather than obliterate family identity, baptism reinterprets it. Now parents are understood to be stewards of a life that belongs to God.

KENDRA G. HOTZ

Pastoral Perspective

coming of Christ. As James Newsome writes, "The judgment of God never takes place in isolation, but it is always limited and shaped by [God's] continuing love. . . . God's act of redemption from judgment is often underway before the act of judgment itself begins."[3]

We too are scoundrels. We rebel against God. There is much in us and in the world that is corrupt—but God will not let our sin thwart God's great purposes. God is already preparing our future, and the future of the whole creation.

We Grow in Favor with the Lord through Life in a Worshiping Community. We do not come fully formed into the Christian life. The life of faith begins at our baptism, but if we are to mature as faithful Christians, having the relationship and the ministry God intends for us, then we must grow beyond our baptism, "grow in stature and in favor with the Lord" (v. 26). Even Jesus did not come "fully formed" into his ministry: he too had to "increase in wisdom and in divine and human favor" (Luke 2:52).

Sadly, studies indicate that many Christian adults have a sixth-grade-level understanding of the faith. Apparently many people simply stop growing in their faith when they reach adolescence.

Samuel matured into his faith and ministry by being part of a living, worshiping congregation. He had a guide and mentor in Eli, he worshiped regularly in the temple, and he was surrounded by the company of God's people. Would that every boy and girl—and every man and woman—were so richly blessed!

Our Children Have a Place in the Worship of God. Samuel "was ministering before the LORD." He wore a linen ephod, a liturgical garment, which indicates that he had an official and particular role to play in the worship of the Lord. Could this image of Samuel's ministering before the Lord foster some reflection on the place of children in our worship? In some traditions, children light candles. Are there other ways in which children can join in leading worship, such as reading Scripture or writing prayers? Today's text from 1 Samuel suggests that the answer to all of these questions is yes.

KAREN PIDCOCK-LESTER

---

3. This is a paraphrase of Augustine's famous prayer in *Confessions*, trans. R. S. Pine-Coffin (New York: Penguin Books, 1961), 21.

3. James D. Newsome Jr., *I Samuel/II Samuel*, Knox Preaching Guides, ed. John Hayes (Atlanta: John Knox Press, 1982), 23.

Exegetical Perspective

13–16), that occurred throughout the early period of Israel's settlement in Canaan. First Samuel 4–6, usually referred to as the "ark narrative," reports the outcome of one such engagement: The Philistines rout the Israelite army; the Israelites, confident that God will turn defeat into victory, counter by bringing the ark from Shiloh (4:3–4). The Philistines capture the ark (4:10–12); back in Shiloh, a new son is birthed into Eli's house, his name, Ichabod, interpreted to mean "the glory has departed from Israel" (4:19–22), bears witness to the collapse of Israel's hopes. This narrative goes on to report the eventual return of the ark to Israel (1 Sam. 5–6), but at no point does it connect the resolution of this crisis to Samuel. It is the "hand of God" that is heavy on the Philistines (5:6, 7, 9, 11). It is the power of God, this narrative asserts, over, beyond, and when necessary *against* all human claims to power, that governs Israel's destiny.

At the end of Samuel's birth narrative, we are told that the "word of the LORD" came to him in Shiloh (3:21) and that the "word of Samuel came to all Israel" (4:1a). With this promise of Samuel's beginnings as an essential mediator of God's word to Israel, he disappears from the scene, and the focus shifts from the internal problems he confronts in Shiloh to the external threats Israel confronts with the Philistines. Samuel will reemerge in chapter 7 and will play a major role in the ensuing story of Israel's journey toward the new leadership that will emerge with the installation of Saul, then David, as king (1 Sam. 8–15). Hovering over this unfolding story, however, is a word from the people in Beth-shemesh. Having received the ark back into their presence, they now prepare for a new beginning, in truth, a resumption of a beginning, by asking, "Who can stand in attendance on the LORD, this holy God?" (6:20 NJPS). It is this question that must guide those who will dedicate themselves anew to grow "both in stature and in favor with the LORD and with the people."

SAMUEL E. BALENTINE

Homiletical Perspective

reeling from some loss or tragedy. The astute preacher will know.

The story of young Samuel takes place as an era in Israel's life is drawing to a close. Sadly, it is an ignominious end. The story of the promising young Samuel is embedded in the story of the end of the house of Eli. The downfall is brought on by the corruption of Eli's sons Hophni and Phinehas as well as Eli's passive complicity in their sin. Even as Israel's worship is being degraded and the seeds of a humiliating defeat are sprouting, the boy who will usher in Israel's most glorious era is growing "both in stature and in favor with the LORD and with the people" (v. 26).

God remains true to the promises made to Israel, even as the priests at Shiloh degrade Israel's worship. This same God remains faithful as the old year gives way to the new. We can be sure that even as the old dies away, God is already preparing things for God's people that are fresh and new.

A sermon may point to such signs of redemption, but the preacher must take care not to be too confident in identifying signs of God's work in the midst of loss. Often those things that offer hope turn out to be no more than polished relics of the old order. It is unlikely that the Israelites who grieved the debacle that was taking place at Shiloh looked on the boy Samuel as a ray of hope. What a sermon *can* affirm is that God is engaged in redemptive work. God does not abandon God's people forever. As we look back over God's dealings with Israel and the church, we see that God has remained faithful. We have every reason to believe that God will still be faithful into the new year.

STEPHENS G. LYTCH

Psalm 148

¹Praise the LORD!
 Praise the LORD from the heavens;
  praise him in the heights!
²Praise him, all his angels;
  praise him, all his host!

³Praise him, sun and moon;
  praise him, all you shining stars!
⁴Praise him, you highest heavens,
  and you waters above the heavens!

⁵Let them praise the name of the LORD,
  for he commanded and they were created.
⁶He established them forever and ever;
  he fixed their bounds, which cannot be passed.

⁷Praise the LORD from the earth,
  you sea monsters and all deeps,

Theological Perspective

The central theological claims of Psalm 148 are both cosmological and anthropological. The cosmological claim is that all creation is summoned to the common task of giving praise to the God who is its initial source of—and its final resource for—being. The first six verses focus on the outer reaches of the cosmos, the heavens, the heights, those upper reaches of the universe with their animate and inanimate denizens (angels, sun, moon, and shining stars). Almost as if the psalmist has not stretched far enough into those upper reaches, the psalm appeals again to the "highest heavens" and to the "waters above the heavens." In Hebrew cosmology this amounts to an exhaustive reference to all that is "out there."

The reason that praise of God is demanded of the highest and outermost reaches of creation is because these have been uttered into being by God's own command and they have been founded and bounded by God's own act. As vast as all that is "out there" may be, God is vaster yet. Small wonder that Anselm came in prayerful appreciation to understand God as that than which nothing greater can be conceived. Thus, when this soaring majesty of the universe confronts the yet more soaring majesty of its source, praise is the only fitting response.

Verses 7 through 13 bring this cosmology down to earth, as it were. The roll call turns from heaven to

Pastoral Perspective

The weeks leading up to Christmas Day are a blur of frenetic activity. There seems to be an endless round of parties we must attend. There are frequent and exhausting trips to buy presents for our loved ones. Special meals are prepared. We clean our homes with extra care and decorate them with all of our Christmas finery.

Since this Sunday falls between December 26 and January 1, all of the hectic busy-ness that has defined our lives before Christmas will be behind us. In many churches, the attendance on this Sunday is considerably smaller than the crowds who flocked to the church for Christmas Eve worship. How, then, should we approach this particular Sunday as God's people? How should we respond to the divine imperative, God's call, to worship?

As a community of faith, we have the opportunity to step back from the frenzy of the holiday season and reflect upon our lives. When we hear the psalmist today, we hear the call to give praise to God. Beginning with the opening word of the psalm, "Hallelujah," which is translated "Praise the LORD," the community of the faithful—including both the created order and all of humanity—is enjoined to be part of the universal worship given to God.

In a way that brings the creation accounts of Genesis 1–2 to mind, the psalmist specifically

⁸fire and hail, snow and frost,
stormy wind fulfilling his command!

⁹Mountains and all hills,
fruit trees and all cedars!
¹⁰Wild animals and all cattle,
creeping things and flying birds!

¹¹Kings of the earth and all peoples,
princes and all rulers of the earth!
¹²Young men and women alike,
old and young together!

¹³Let them praise the name of the L<small>ORD</small>,
for his name alone is exalted;
his glory is above earth and heaven.
¹⁴He has raised up a horn for his people,
praise for all his faithful,
for the people of Israel who are close to him.
Praise the L<small>ORD</small>!

Exegetical Perspective

Psalm 148 appears to be a routine song of praise composed of the typical elements: invitation to praise (vv. 1–5a; 7–13a), accompanied by reasons for praise introduced with "for" (vv. 5b–6; 13b–14). But Psalm 148 is anything but ordinary. The first indication of its extraordinariness is the expanded length of the invitation to praise, matched by an expansiveness of content. While most songs of praise push toward inclusivity (see Pss. 96:1; 97:1; 99:1; 100:1; 117:1), Psalm 148 is the ultimate in this regard, inviting praise from the highest "heavens" (v. 1) to the depths of "the earth" (v. 7), including representative "residents" of these realms. Psalm 150:6, the final verse in Psalms, is often cited as exemplary of the universal reach of the Psalter's invitation to praise. It is a good example, but its sweeping invitation to "everything that breathes" is surpassed by Psalm 148, which invites praise from everything that exists! Breath is not required for praise. Even the inanimate "residents" of the two realms participate in this outpouring of praise.

Scholars sometimes cite Psalm 148 and similar texts (see Pss. 96:11–12; 98:7–8) as evidence that ancient folk believed everything was "alive." This is possible, but it is more likely that we are dealing here with literary personification. In any case, Psalm 148 is testimony to God's involvement with the entire

Homiletical Perspective

Just as beginning writers are taught to "Show, don't tell," beginning preachers are taught not to tell congregations what to do. We will be more effective, we are taught, if we open up the text in such a way that the congregation is moved to faith and action. It is a challenge, then, to preach a psalm that uses the imperative "praise" ten times in fourteen verses. It goes against our education by telling the listener exactly what to do: praise the Lord.

The psalm moves briskly through the created order, exhorting each element to praise. It begins with the celestial realm: the angels, the heavenly court, the sun, moon, and stars. The earthly world follows: from the chaos of the sea and its monsters to the wildness of weather, the good gifts of fruit trees for eating and cedar for building, the creatures around us in their variety and beauty. Finally, humanity is called to praise, in an uncommonly inclusive list that includes women and children alongside kings and princes. The psalm is reminiscent of the children's book *Goodnight Moon*, in which the child falling asleep says goodnight to everything in sight. Here the psalmist does the same, cataloging all of creation and drawing everything in it together for a rally of remembrance and praise of the creator's holy name.

As imperatives go, this is not a hard sell. Who among the faithful would say it is inappropriate to

Psalm 148

Theological Perspective

earth and again all the elements of earthly locale, fanciful and routine, are summoned to praise. Here the unruly, natural forces of the world (sea monsters, deeps, fire, hail, snow, frost, and stormy wind) are also bounded by the God whose command they fulfill in being what they are. Moreover, the landscape itself is captured in the summons (mountains and hills), along with the flora that it nurtures (fruit trees and cedars). Finally, the (presumed) sentient creation is included as animals, domesticated and otherwise, human and nonhuman, are all summoned to the chorus of praise.

Just as the nonhuman animals are comprehensively named (wild animals, cattle, creeping and flying creatures), so the full range of humankind is embraced in the call, both the privileged and the ordinary (kings, princes, rulers, young and old, men and women). Together with those "outer reaches" of the cosmos, these "inner reaches" are embraced as the universal combined choir that acknowledges the glory of that One above earth and heaven, than which nothing greater can be thought, and the origin and destiny of all creatures, great and small.

Thus the overarching cosmological claim of Psalm 148 is that the proper purpose of all that exists, known and unknown, seen and unseen, is to give adoration and praise to God. As Patrick Miller has observed, this language of praise is "the speech that is truly primal and universal. All existence is capable of praising God and does so. In such speaking, God is identified."[1] For his part, Walter Brueggemann has noted that in this way creation itself is witness to the reality of God as Creator, adding that in polemical theological discourse this has sometimes been designated (and discounted) as "natural theology."[2] Yet that is precisely the cosmological claim of Psalm 148—all nature acknowledges *theos* in its chorus of praise.

But what of the anthropological claim of this text? Karl Barth has suggested that this psalm impresses a deep humility on humankind. "As we must say of [human beings] that [they are] what [they are] only in gratitude towards God, we shall have to say the same of all other creatures."[3] So the first element of the psalm's anthropology is not what distinguishes humanity from the rest of creation, but

1. Patrick D. Miller, *Interpreting the Psalms* (Philadelphia: Fortress Press, 1986), 73.
2. Walter Brueggemann, *Theology of the Old Testament: Testimony, Dispute, Advocacy* (Minneapolis: Fortress Press, 1997), 157.
3. Karl Barth, *Church Dogmatics*, III/2 (Edinburgh: T. & T. Clark, 1960), 172.

Pastoral Perspective

summons several celestial entities—from angels to the sun and moon to the waters above the heavens—to worship God. The reason given for the praise of the natural world is simple: God created all of them, and they all function according to God's purposes. In fact, their faithfulness to fulfill their function becomes a way for them to give praise to God.

We know that every Sunday, indeed every day, should be acknowledged as an opportunity for God's people to give praise to God. This Sunday, though, provides a unique perspective from which to do so. Poised at the ending of one year and just before the beginning of another, this day can serve as a sanctuary from the busy-ness of life to allow us to consider our relationship with God and the blessings inherent in it. This Sunday after Christmas can be seen as a "hinge" time as we, the followers of Christ, look back to the blessings of the previous year and especially that blessing represented by Christmas Day—the birth of the Messiah, the Savior of the world. From our position during these in-between days at the end of the year, we are also able to look ahead to the possibilities and promises of the coming new year as we continue in faithfulness with God.

The church should take at least three lessons from this section. First, humanity is linked to the created order in both the worship of God and in the hope of the final consummation, when God's salvation is made complete. As Paul wrote, the created order waits for its final transformation to its original and intended glory that will come when the children of God are themselves finally transformed and made whole through God's redemption (Rom. 8:18–25). Our worship should reflect this eschatological hope.

Second, as humanity is linked with the created order in this way—as partners in worship and salvation—humanity should be more mindful of its responsibility for the created order as God's stewards of it. This awareness is expressed across a broad spectrum of Christian thought. In 2001, in a general audience address, Pope John Paul II cautioned humanity to remember our responsibility to care for the natural world as a trust for future generations. The Mennonite Church in Canada emphasizes the duty of humanity to care for the land and all that lives on it. Many evangelical Christians recognize the need for human beings to live lightly on the earth.

Third, we can give praise to God by fulfilling our functions in life, whatever they may be. The understanding of divine call varies from faith community to faith community, with some groups recognizing only a "call to ministry" as a valid call of

Exegetical Perspective

creation, a comprehensive relatedness that is reinforced by the ninefold repetition of "all" (vv. 2, 3, 9, 10, 11, 14). Not surprisingly, the reasons for praise mention God's creative activity (vv. 5b–6) and suggest God's sovereign claim over "earth and heaven" (v. 13b; "exalted" and "glory" are elsewhere associated with royal sovereignty). Plus, many of the "residents" of the two realms of heaven and earth recall elements of creation in Genesis 1.

As in Genesis 1, Psalm 148's movement is from the heavenly realm toward the mention of humanity. Unlike Genesis 1 and Psalm 8, however, there is no mention of "dominion" (Gen. 1:26; Ps. 8:6). To be sure, there is power language present ("kings," "princes," "rulers"), but these normally powerful people are no more important than anyone else. As Konrad Schaefer concludes, "All are equal in God's sight."[1] This conclusion applies not only to the human community but also in some sense to the larger community constituted by all the "residents" of the earthly realm (vv. 7–10)—from "sea monsters" to "fruit trees" to "flying birds." At this point, Psalm 148 is reminiscent not only of Genesis 1 but also of Genesis 9:8–17, where parties to the first biblical covenant include "every living creature" (Gen. 9:10, 12, 15, 16) and "the earth" itself (v. 13), as well as humans and God. Again, in concert with Genesis 1 and 9, Psalm 148 is testimony to God's relationship with the entire created order. In short, God loves the whole world.

If anyone or anything is singled out for special attention, it is "the people of Israel" (v. 14). How does one interpret the apparent tension between the universality of verses 1–13 and the particularity of verse 14? A historically oriented, ideological approach might suggest that Psalm 148, located near the end of the Psalter, arose in the Persian or Greek periods and that it tells the people of Israel what they needed or wanted to hear—that this tiny, oppressed people, struggling for survival amid the world's great empires, is being attended to by no less a being than the God of all creation. The phrase "raised up a horn" suggests being endowed with strength (see Pss. 75:10; 89:17; 92:10; 112:9). Given this interpretive direction, the ambiguous phrase "praise for all his faithful" could be taken as a description of Israel's favored status.

A more theological approach, however, is suggested by the shape of the canon. God's covenant with humankind, the creatures, and the earth itself

1. Konrad Schaefer, *Psalms*, Berit Olam: Studies in Hebrew Narrative and Poetry (Collegeville, MN: The Liturgical Press, 2001), 343.

Homiletical Perspective

praise God? To a preacher, the psalm offers the opportunity to make a simple offering of praise. This is an invitation we often need to hear. After all, it is a constant temptation in church work to see only the challenges: the entrenched leadership or the members who yearn for the former pastor's return. The psalm calls us back to the good news that God is good and worthy of praise and that our first job as believers is to offer that praise.

In this spirit, the preacher might speak with the psalmist's joy to the celebration of transitions: the beginning of a new ministry or the completion of an old one; pledge drives or evangelism campaigns; baptisms, weddings, and, in some contexts, funerals. Framing these transitions in a context of praise can shift a congregation's attention from anxiety to joyful opportunity.

The text's imperative to praise is also a challenge. The uncomfortable truth is that we do not praise God very often. We may not even know what it would look like to do so. Praise abounds in our culture, but it is cheap praise: praise for an athlete that lasts only through the news cycle; praise for employees that is intended only to improve morale and increase the bottom line. True praise is hard to come by, and the praise of God is virtually absent outside Sunday morning.

Even when we do praise God, is it with the wild abandon of the psalmist? Do we get so caught up in the glory of God that we call on all creation to join us in praise? Or do we praise meekly, with dusty hymns half-sung on Sunday morning?

The preacher might ask: What keeps us from praising like the psalmist? What must we look past to see the glory of God that moves us to praise? What must we remove from our ears before we hear the songs of angels, winds, and sea monsters? Are there preoccupations that call our minds away? Are there temptations that cut short what little praise we offer? Where are the impediments to our praise? Are they in our work? Are they in our families? Are they perhaps even in our churches?

The text also challenges us with its close focus on creation as an instrument of praise. By naming the many elements of creation, it calls us to an awe of what God has made, of those things that praise God simply by being. The earth—specifically its weather and its flying, swimming, crawling, and walking creatures—is called to praise the Lord. As human activity continues to bring about global climate change and extinction, have we hindered creation's ability to praise God?

Psalm 148

Theological Perspective

what unites humanity to all the rest. As the repeated refrain of the psalm makes clear, that unity is found in the wonder of praise to God.

Yet the theological anthropology of Psalm 148 has a dialectical dimension. Notwithstanding the unity of humanity with the rest of creation in the chorus of praise, humanity has a special vocation within this shared, common vocation. Barth argues that if the rest of creation also praises the Lord, "it is not they who in Psalm 148 call upon [humans] to do so, but [humans] who [call] upon them to render this act of worship" (Barth, *Church Dogmatics*, III/3 173). He concludes that the difference is a difference of *responsibility* for gratitude toward God that differentiates the special vocation of humankind. One can make a similar point by calling attention to the way in which verse 14 acknowledges that because Israel is near to God, it knows and can speak the exalted name.

Thus, beyond the unity with all creation, what if any anthropological distinctiveness is there for humanity in general and the people of God in particular? Barth's allusion to *responsibility* is most suggestive. Just because humanity can voice the praise native to all creation, humankind has a unique responsibility. But there is more to this responsibility than Barth names. The responsibility is not just to call upon the rest of creation for praise, but to attend to the well-being of the rest of creation so that it survives to give praise.

Put baldly, the theological anthropology of Psalm 148 is finally a theological ethic that requires the human family to take care of creation as a *status confessionis*, as a fundamental accompaniment of its core belief that humanity's chief end is to glorify God and enjoy God forever. Knowing that this chief end is shared with all creation means that we have a fundamental responsibility to support and nurture the highest beings of heaven and the lowest creatures of earth (from mountain tops to snail darters), so that their voices continue unabated in the universal, combined choir.

D. CAMERON MURCHISON

Pastoral Perspective

God. Many others, however, see utilizing one's talents and skills in both volunteer opportunities and daily work as a way of fulfilling God's call in our lives. Thus, skilled teachers and doctors and lawyers can worship God with their lives as they exercise their abilities in the world.

The human race is able to vocalize praise for the rest of creation. Humanity, then, has a responsibility to serve as the surrogates of praise for all the other inhabitants of the cosmos. The splendor of God, the very holiness of God's nature, ought to make us want to give such worship. Indeed, within the psalm there is the suggestion that, at the very least, the faithful are to praise God because God "has raised up a horn for his people" (v. 14), that is, God has bestowed dignity upon them.[1]

As the minister incorporates this passage in worship, she should take care to remember those for whom the holiday times are not particularly joyful. There will be those who go through the holidays alone, those who may have received frightening medical diagnoses, and those who have recently lost jobs. For these members of our communities of faith, the psalmist's call to praise may sound hollow. Here, a key would be to focus the call to give praise because of the attributes of God—God's steadfast love and faithfulness, God's loving grace to be with us, and God's strength to sustain us—and not for the particular circumstances a person may face.

Since Christmas is past, it would be easy to think that the occasion for joy is past. Yet, as God's community of the faithful, we can join with the universe and rejoice as we give praise to God on this Sunday, as we should do every day.

W. MICHAEL CHITTUM

---

1. James L. Mays, *Psalms*, Interpretation Series (Louisville, KY: John Knox Press, 1994), 445.

Exegetical Perspective

in Genesis 9 precedes the covenant with Abraham, Sarah, and their descendants. The blessing of and promise to Abraham include a commission—that in or through Abraham and his descendants, "all the families of the earth shall be blessed" (Gen. 12:3). Here particularity is in the service of universality. A similar conclusion could apply to Psalm 148. Israel is strengthened by God to effect a blessing not only for "all the families of the earth," but also for all the creatures and features of creation! According to this interpretive direction, Israel's "praise" is not so much a special status but rather a special responsibility or mission. God's people, then and now, praise God by enabling the rest of creation to be what God has called it to be.

As Terence Fretheim concludes, Psalm 148 "contains an implicit call to human beings to relate to the natural orders in such a way that nature's praise might show forth with greater clarity."[2] The ecological implications are profound; praise, for instance, would involve the preservation of species that are disappearing at an alarming rate. Not only is the integrity of creation, and perhaps the future of the earth as we know it, at stake; but so also is God's desire to be in relationship with, and thus praised by, the whole creation. As Fretheim puts it, "God is enthroned not simply on the praises of Israel [see Ps. 22:3]; God is enthroned on the praises of his creatures."[3]

The missional emphasis, along with the issue of relating particularity and universality, is evident also in the immediate context, Psalms 146–50. The "faithful" (Ps. 148:14) are featured in Psalm 149:1, 5, 9; their mission is "justice" (NRSV "judgment," v. 9). Despite the violent-sounding language (cf. Ps. 2:8–9), "justice" is what the sovereign God wills (see Pss. 96:13; 97:2; 98:9; 99:4; 146:7) and the mission God has entrusted to the earthly king (see the exegetical perspective on Ps. 72:1–7, pp. 201–5). The final form of the Psalter seems to suggest that the mission of the former monarchy is now entrusted to all God's "faithful." The particular relationship between God and Israel is featured in Psalms 147 and 149, but in the center of this particularity stands Psalm 148 and its extraordinarily expansive invitation to praise. God will properly be praised only by a universal, indeed cosmic, congregation!

J. CLINTON MCCANN JR.

Homiletical Perspective

For a framework, the preacher might adopt the psalmist's rhetorical use of lists. As the text lists the elements of creation and exhorts them one by one to acts of praise, the preacher could catalog impediments to praise, challenging the listener to remove them.

Another approach might be to mirror the psalm's rhetorical movement, which can be read in at least two ways. The first is a cosmological movement from the outside in, and from the strongest to the weakest (or, in the case of women, those who seem to be weakest). In descending order, this list includes heaven, angels, and the waters of heaven; the waters of earth, the wind, and land; plants and animals; and finally rulers, young and old, along with women and children. In a sermon of celebration or exhortation, the preacher could follow the same pattern by listing the groups within a congregation—perhaps from the long-term members to the newcomers, or from the leaders to those who hide in the back pew—calling them to common praise or mission.

The psalm's rhetorical movement can also be described emotionally: it starts high, goes low, and comes back up. Calling the heavens to praise God is a joy and no challenge at all. But when the focus shifts to creation, it becomes a list of fearful things: sea monsters, the deep, fire, hail, and wind; forces of destruction called to praise God. To those whose homes have been leveled in a hurricane, it is an enormous challenge to imagine the wind praising God. Then the movement swings back up, to the rulers and peoples united in praise. The preacher could use a list of similar shape to challenge a congregation. It is easy to say that God is praised through a congregation's outreach ministry, Sunday school, or annual bazaar. But what about the conflicts and topics that cannot be broached? Can the community face those challenges in a way that praises God? Can it face them in a way that moves their common life back up into united praise?

DREW BUNTING

2. Terence Fretheim, "Nature's Praise of God in the Psalms," *Ex Auditu* 3 (1987): 29.
3. Ibid.

Colossians 3:12-17

¹²As God's chosen ones, holy and beloved, clothe yourselves with compassion, kindness, humility, meekness, and patience. ¹³Bear with one another and, if anyone has a complaint against another, forgive each other; just as the Lord has forgiven you, so you also must forgive. ¹⁴Above all, clothe yourselves with love, which binds everything together in perfect harmony. ¹⁵And let the peace of Christ rule in your hearts, to which indeed you were called in the one body. And be thankful. ¹⁶Let the word of Christ dwell in you richly; teach and admonish one another in all wisdom; and with gratitude in your hearts sing psalms, hymns, and spiritual songs to God. ¹⁷And whatever you do, in word or deed, do everything in the name of the Lord Jesus, giving thanks to God the Father through him.

Theological Perspective

This is one of the classic New Testament passages that speak, in effect, of "sanctification," that is, of the new life that the Holy Spirit works in us. This sanctification is a work of God *in* us; it flows *from* the purely divine work of "justification"—the act whereby Christ's righteousness is imputed to us, a work of grace alone, in which our actions have no part. Yet if justification is uniquely the work of God, sanctification is a work of God that also involves us. We participate in it. But how? What is our role? How does God's action relate to ours in this matter of new life? These are questions that the Pauline letters can help us with, though what we find here is less of an outright explanation than a set of metaphors or images for the relationship between the Spirit and our lives.

In the present passage, the leading metaphor for that new or sanctified life is a metaphor of clothing: we lay aside one coat, as it were, and put on (*enduō*) another. The one we discard is our "old self," with its "anger, wrath, malice, slander, and abusive language" (v. 8), and what we "put on" (RSV) is our "new nature" (vv. 9–10; cf. Eph. 4:24), with its "compassion, kindness, humility, meekness, and patience" (v. 12). This is a way of talking about a change in our condition, but that change is not imagined as something happening "inside" us, as an

Pastoral Perspective

Mohandas Gandhi is popularly known as one who confronted empires. Yet those who knew him, or have studied him, acknowledge that he often spoke of a more complex struggle against tyranny. The conflict is not only with the British, he would say, but also within our own communities and "with myself." The Pauline vision generally, and the specific pastoral advice in this text, is rooted in just such a multidimensional understanding of reconciliation. There is a seamlessness to the task that communities of faith are forever separating into parts and assigning graded priority.

Empires do dominate, then as now. But such domination has its claws in us, too. This is why the struggle is not merely against "flesh and blood"— the particular personalities or ideologies that guide the beastly ravaging of governing regimes—but also against what Paul spoke of as "principalities and powers"—the *spirit* of those regimes, whose cunning capacity transcends political structures. We who claim allegiance to God's reign are standing in the need of prayer.

While it is true that this epistle to the church at Colossae is a deeply felt entreaty, it would be a mistake to read these admonitions as a first-century call to civility (something like, "y'all play nice"). The Colossian correspondent is not saying, "You can catch more flies with honey than with vinegar."

Exegetical Perspective

The birth of Jesus inaugurates a movement on the part of God to make new the very nature of faithful human beings. Colossians 3:12–17 is the backend, yet the very goal, of what it means to be "raised with Christ" (3:1–2). This goal is sketched in the previous verses: "[You] have put on the new nature, which is being renewed in knowledge after the image of its creator" (v. 10; RSV). The corporate goal of redeemed humanity—manifested in the church—is a unity that erases ethnic, cultural, and social distinctions (v. 11).

The structure of our passage is built on the shift from the "old/previous" existence to the "new/transformed" existence now available through Christ's death and resurrection (Col. 2:11–15; 3:1). Paul sets up this structure in Colossians 3:2 with the injunction to "set your minds on things that are above, not on things that are on earth." This idea is then extended to the metaphor of "putting off" and "putting on" clothing (esp. 3:9–10). The baptismal act of conversion and transformation is often symbolized in early Christianity with the removal of old clothing and the reclothing of the baptismal candidate in a new garment (the NRSV favors the language of "clothing oneself" over "put on" at 3:10, 12, 14). Removed clothing is to be destroyed (v. 5; "put to death") or permanently set aside (v. 8; "get

Homiletical Perspective

Note the context for our passage. The theme of stripping off the old self and putting on the new begins with Colossians 3:5. The contrast between what is old and what is new, what is dead and what is alive, what is on earth and what is above, begins with Colossians 3:1. It seems likely that when the apostle refers to taking off old clothing and putting on the new, he is not only metaphorical. He reflects the early Christian practice of baptism, where the candidate strips off the old clothes before entering the baptismal waters, emerges, and is clothed anew. Colossians 3:11 reminds us of Galatians 3:28, another use of the baptismal story to confirm and shape the unity of all believers in Christ. Colossians says, "In that renewal there is no longer Greek and Jew, circumcised and uncircumcised, barbarian, Scythian, slave and free; but Christ is all and in all."

Colossians 3:12–17 then presents a vivid portrait of what it looks like to live as one clothed entirely in Christ—what it means to be part of the community where "Christ is all and in all." A sermon on this text could provide the opportunity to remind the congregation of the implications of their own baptism.

There are at least three main moves in the text itself. The preacher could either lead the congregation through these moves in order or could focus on one as the theme for the sermon.

Colossians 3:12-17

Theological Perspective

act of our own wills; rather, the change is in the values and behaviors we choose to (as it were) enclose or envelop us. Paul likes this clothing metaphor, using the same verb elsewhere to talk about other changes in our condition—what happens in the resurrection of the dead (when the body "puts on imperishability," 1 Cor. 15:53ff.) or in the life to come (when we "put on" a "heavenly dwelling," 2 Cor. 5:3 [RSV]).

A theme related to the metaphor of clothing here is the imitation of Christ. It becomes explicit only once, in verse 13, where the Colossians are told to forgive each other "just as the Lord has forgiven you." Commentators typically note here that in the Pauline literature, "Lord" always refers to Christ, and therefore apparently it is Christ's forgiveness that we are to mirror in our relations with each other. This, together with subsequent references to Christ in verses 15–17, makes it reasonable to go back to verse 12 and read the list of characteristics there—our new clothes—as characteristics of Christ as well. In that case, the metaphor of putting on clothing may be even itself a way of talking of imitation: we wear Christ as our clothing, taking him as our model. In turn, the train of thought here is not far from Paul's powerful exhortation to the Philippians to take on the "mind" of Christ (Phil. 2:5).

Through verse 14, the clothing metaphor is at work. But then in verse 15 the metaphorical language changes. Suddenly Paul is speaking not of what we "put on" around us—an *outside* metaphor, as it were—but rather what is *inside* of us, namely, the "peace of Christ," which is to "rule in your hearts" (v. 15), and the "word of Christ," which is to "dwell in you richly" (v. 16). This peace in turn expresses itself outwardly again through what we teach others and through the singing of "psalms, hymns, and spiritual songs." This is a marked shift in imagery, and it brings a problem with it: namely, that this interiorized language is not as suited as the clothing metaphor to answer the question of how the new life comes about. What do we do, in other words, to bring the peace and presence of Christ into ourselves? One answer, obviously, is that this is the Spirit's work and not finally our own. True enough. Yet the text is clearly exhorting the reader, and so some action must be envisioned. But what action?

Perhaps the metaphorical shift is itself the key; perhaps the idea is that the outside change becomes precisely the condition, or invitation, for the inside change. In other words, I put on my coat, and then I warm up inside: two events, but really only the

Pastoral Perspective

This tutorial is more than tactical instruction for an orderly march into the mission. Rather, the mission itself entails a disciplined pattern of redemptive life together.[1] There is more than functional purpose for being clothed with compassion, kindness, humility, meekness, and patience. Bearing with one another, forgiving each other, binding us to each other—such work is not for the faint of heart. This is not conflict-avoidance advice. Forget putting on a happy face and accentuating the positive. This is about what to do when bare-knuckled emotional brawls break out.

Our common experience is that the most blistering disputes are among intimates, with people we know well. Rarely are anger and the impulse to vengeance as ravenous as when they arise between those who spend a lot of time together, who share memory and coherent purpose. Maybe it is precisely because of our proximity that our familial disagreements get so prickly.

Years ago and late one night, while packing for an early-morning trip, my spouse and I got into a disagreement that escalated beyond a difference of opinion. Somehow it got personal. (The definition of "conflict" is difference plus tension.) Too tired to carry on, we simply ditched the conversation and cut the lights. Our quarrel was still rumbling in my gut the next morning as I sat in the airport lounge waiting for a predawn flight. I finally worked up the resolve to put a quarter in the pay phone, dial our home number, and mumble a brief "I'm sorry about last night."

"Me, too," came the blessed response. We did not attempt in that moment to resolve the difference—I do not even remember what it was about. What I remember is this: that simple exchange drained the poison from the moment, and that the initiative took more resolve than any of my trips into conflict zones as a professional peacemaker.

We live in a culture that faintly praises kindness, humility, meekness, and patience, but these qualities are neither honed by nor honored among perceived history makers. Such qualities are upheld as a kind of etiquette for the personal sphere but ignored (even scoffed at) by real-life decision makers. Being "tough on crime" and "strong on national defense" are coveted reputations among electoral candidates; and such perceptions typically translate well in all leadership circles, even in the church.

Among the most promising directions in Christian discipleship training is that of "conflict

---

1. Dietrich Bonhoeffer's *Life Together* is the modern classic on this subject.

Exegetical Perspective

rid of all such things"). Moralists (e.g., Cicero, Seneca, Epictetus), before and after the time of Paul, shaped individual and community instructions in terms of avoiding vices and pursuing virtues. The clothing metaphor in Colossians 3 is shaped by this moralist stance of listing vices to be avoided ("Put to death earthly things") and virtues to be pursued ("clothe yourselves with compassion, kindness . . .").

Paul believes that his audience has undergone a fundamental change—the beginning of a transformation. Yet how each individual and the community as a whole clothe their person(s) is a matter of intentionality and focus ("set your minds"). Paul, rejecting the false teachers' insistence that forms of philosophy and strict regulations are necessary to counter vice, writes that they are therefore a missed step on the road to redemption and salvation (2:16–23). Paul, like typical moralists of the time, calls upon the commonsense nature of his audience to recognize and avoid vices (3:8; anger, wrath) and to give constant mental assent to virtuous characteristics (3:12; compassion, kindness). Paul also counsels the practice of early Christian community worship. Notably absent in the argument is the role of the Holy Spirit in the process of virtuous transformation. The Holy Spirit's role might be inferred from the ideas of "raised with Christ" (3:1) or "new nature" (3:10 RSV) or "being renewed . . . after the image of its creator" (3:10 RSV). One may well wish to supplement this aspect of 3:12–17 with the discussions of the Holy Spirit's role in Galatians 5–6 and Romans 6–8.

In Colossians 3:12–17, virtuous contemplation and practices center around three aspects: love, peace, and thankfulness. The virtue list begins with the exhortation "clothe yourselves" and is specifically addressed to "God's chosen ones, holy and beloved." Generally, rhetorical emphasis in a list lands on the first and last items. In this case, the list begins with compassion—a deep inward feeling of care toward another. While compassion is not developed as a thematic element prior to this use, this word stands nicely as the necessary position from which the following virtues are practiced. In the flow of the argument, kindness, lowliness, meekness, patience, and forbearance/forgiveness promote stable community formation and prepare the ground for the household rules for husbands, wives, children, slaves, and masters that follow (3:18–4:1). The emphasis on forbearance/forgiveness is obvious from the length of treatment, the emphasis throughout the letter on forgiveness as the gracious action of God/Jesus (1:20; 2:13–15), and its connection,

Homiletical Perspective

The first motif, found in verses 12–15a, is a description of how to dress for church. The apostle is not concerned as we so often are with whether blue jeans have any place in the sanctuary. The apostle is concerned with the way we dress our souls. The virtues that the epistle commends are entirely social. Right dress is not a matter of individual piety; it is a matter of how we relate to one another in Christ (since of course Christ is all in all).

The passage reminds us of 1 Corinthians 13, another description of how believers think and act toward one another. Compassion, kindness, humility, meekness, and patience are all relational virtues—they mark how we think and behave toward one another in the community.

The apostle shows the practical value of such virtues: they provide the framework and the motivation for settling disputes among believers. The reminder that we should forgive as we are forgiven echoes the Lord's Prayer—perhaps quite deliberately. This reminder can also send the preacher back to the Gospel parable of the unforgiving servant (Matt. 18:23–35).

In these verses there are three great realities that make possible the well-dressed congregation. The first reality is the call of God, sine qua non. The second is the reality of Christian love, which here, perhaps even more explicitly than in 1 Corinthians, is evident primarily in the harmony of the whole congregation. The third is the reality of Christ's peace—Christ's shalom. Colossians picks up the familiar Pauline symbol of the church as the body and here makes clear what binds the members together: the peace that can only be the gift of God.

The last sentence of Colossians 3:15 provides a kind of transition to the next theme—the theme of right worship: "And be thankful." Thankfulness is both the gift of God to the church in Jesus Christ and the response that the church brings to God. The Greek term for "thankful" in this sentence is *eucharistoi*. We have no evidence that the apostle already thought of the central act of Christian worship as eucharist, but the call to thankfulness does move beautifully into the next theme of the passage: the shape of Christian worship.

In Protestant churches, at least, we are great at proclaiming the word of Christ (or "of God" or "of the Lord"; see the notes for v. 16 in the NRSV) as a central part of Christian worship. What we often undervalue is the generative power of the word. We are more apt to pray that the word of Christ beat on our congregation loudly than that it dwell in them

Colossians 3:12-17

Theological Perspective

former event is an action on my part. Here monastic spirituality may offer an analogy to the movement and meaning of this passage. As the historian Jean Leclercq has explained, historically, Christian monasticism has developed a distinctive understanding of how we learn, and, accordingly, of how we change.[1] The monk's or nun's whole life itself becomes the means of that change, itself the expression of what he or she knows. The texts of the Bible, for example, are not to be treated as objects to be understood, containers of ideas to be questioned or debated; rather, they are to be taken into oneself through the whole shape of daily life. That is, as a regular part of the rhythm of monastic living, one reads the texts and incorporates them into prayer and worship, so constantly that the Bible's words and ideas become one's own. In that sense the texts and their ideas stand no longer as objects outside the self but are rather woven within it, elements of one's own thinking and speaking. They shape the person's life. The "inside" transformation that then can occur is potentially very deep. Yet the action called for is but an "outside" action, a "putting on" of—in this case, a form of life as prescribed by a monastic rule—or, for those of us outside the monastery, by such a text as this one from Colossians. The Spirit, in any case—the same Spirit that finds expression in song (v. 16; cf. 1 Cor. 14:15 and Eph. 5:18–19)—operates *with* that action of ours, to work the deeper changes of sanctification.

JOHN W. COAKLEY

Pastoral Perspective

transformation" theory and practice.[2] Among the key insights are these:

1. Conflict is given in our personal and public lives. The issue is what we do *when*, not *if*, it erupts.
2. Fear is the quality that makes conflict so explosive. Scripture has a lot to say about the struggle between faithfulness and fearfulness.
3. You do not have to be a saint or a rocket scientist to develop the skills to handle conflict. Everyone can learn to analyze the dynamics of conflict and develop habits of redemptive response.
4. The traditional responses to conflict are fight or flight; but there is a third option, which Jesus taught and Paul reinforced (most eloquently in his letter to the Roman church).
5. Conflict is an opportunity to deepen relationships. Think of your nearest, dearest relationships. Chances are good that you have endured turbulence together.
6. Practicing nonviolence within the family of faith may be the best training ground for the work of reconciliation in the larger world. Dealing with conflict is part of our spiritual formation, and not simply a nuisance to be managed or resolved with the least amount of energy and time.

Practicing nonviolence is, in fact, another way of talking about forbearance and forgiveness, notions that frame this set of pastoral recommendations. Reconciliation is not the suppression of conflict any more than peace is the absence of violence. Ditching the conversation and cutting the lights is actually a form of apostasy—a denial of the holy, beloved calling that has gripped us.

The practice of forgiveness is neither simple nor easy. It certainly does not mean "forgive and forget"—at least, not in the way that sentiment is commonly used as a cover for subservience in the face of injustice. Our ability to forgive others is reflective of our lived experience of being forgiven by God. This is our distinctive insight.

As with any insight, however, an imperative is implied—and a discipline, which involves tutoring and training. Practice leads to habits; "muscle memory" is formed so that the word of Christ comes not just to visit but to dwell (v. 16). And inch by inch, step by step, our words and deeds become consonant with that name.

That is worth singing about.

KENNETH L. SEHESTED

---

1. Jean Leclercq, *The Love of Learning and the Desire for God* (New York: Fordham University Press, 1961).

2. See Carolyn Schrock-Shenk and Lawrence Ressler, eds., *Making Peace with Conflict: Practical Skills for Conflict Transformation* (Scottdale, PA, and Waterloo, ON: Herald Press, 1999).

therefore, as a key element in the "new nature . . . being renewed in knowledge after the image of its creator" (3:10 RSV).

In the moralist tradition, all the virtues working together produce *the virtue*, which for Paul is *love* (contrast, for instance, the stoic chief virtue of *self-control*). The supreme emphasis on "love" (3:14) is indicated by the modifier, "above all," by the repetition of "clothe yourselves," and by putting it in final position as a transition to Paul's next subject, harmony/peace. Paul's emphasis on "love" as chief virtue is often indicated by its first-place listing (see Gal. 5:22: "The fruit of the Spirit is love, joy, peace, patience . . . ").

Development of virtues in the context of care for others ("love") produces "perfect harmony" (v. 14). This is the "peace of Christ," not only a deep-felt presence ("rule in your hearts") but also the result of Christ's cosmic peacemaking efforts that battle with and overcome all ruling authorities and powers (chaps. 1 and 2; esp. 2:9). The ruling Christ is the "head" of the whole body, leading it to maturity in growth (2:19) and uniting all (Jews and Gentiles; slave and free; those who turn away from false teaching; those who forgive—1:26–27; 2:18–19; 3:11, 13) into *one body*.

The proper response for virtuous formation, strong community cohesion, and the revelation of God's working through Christ for peace and rule is *thankfulness* (note the repetition of this theme in vv. 15b–17). Emphasis on the "word of Christ" and "teaching and admonishing" indicates ongoing *reproclamation* of the saving work of God in Christ and the benefits accounting to all believers ("in all wisdom"). This is accomplished in *worship*, with its variety of expressions (v. 16) and its goal of gratitude and praise to God. This is a deep-felt response of believers that must be given expression with others in word and song. Vibrant churches know the need for thankfulness within and its natural expression outward. Proper teaching and preaching cultivates, strengthens, and reminds congregants that gratitude to God is the very air we breathe. Verse 17 indicates that proper moral reasoning about human relationships within the household of faith (3:18—4:1) must start in the context of thankfulness: "*whatever* you do, *in word or deed*, do everything in the name of the Lord Jesus, *giving thanks*."

ROLLIN A. RAMSARAN

richly. We might think about Scripture reading and preaching as sowing seed. The seed that falls on the soil of a loving and thankful congregation will bear its own fruit in worship. God's own wisdom grows among the people. Now, wonderfully, the word of Christ is not the product that one Christian, the preacher, provides for passive clients, the congregation. The word flourishes and bears fruit among the people. It is there in the communal teaching, admonishing, and perhaps especially in the communal singing. How would it be if after an especially powerful hymn the worship leader declared: "The word of the Lord" and the congregation replied: "Thanks be to God"? That would be Colossian worship. (If you want to tie this text to the Gospel lesson for this week, notice that in Luke Jesus brings and becomes the wisdom of God, come to the place where the people worship. In the story he lives out the injunction: "Teach and admonish one another in all wisdom.")

The final theme is the "whatever you do" theme. Even though the apostle has just been talking about Christian worship, he does not mean that only what we do in worship is to be done in the name of the Lord Jesus. In Decatur, Georgia, there is a church that might have been named with Colossians in mind: The Thankful Baptist Church. Colossians claims that, as with Thankful Baptist Church, when we dress up for each day's work, we dress ourselves in Christ, with thanksgiving. In a religious marketplace that pushes happy Christianity, Colossians speaks a word for thankful Christianity. Thankfulness is harder to come by than happiness, but immeasurably better to count on. Thankfulness is captured and modeled in e. e. cummings's fine poem "i thank You God for most this amazing day" (the poet's deliberate use of the small "i" for the self and the capital "You God" is a major key to thankfulness).[1] Thankfulness is the classic attitude of faithful prayer: "You have given me so much, O God—I ask but one thing more, a grateful heart."

DAVID L. BARTLETT

---

1. e. e. cummings, *Poems: 1923–1954* (New York: Harcourt, Brace & World, 1968), 464.

Luke 2:41-52

⁴¹Now every year his parents went to Jerusalem for the festival of the Passover. ⁴²And when he was twelve years old, they went up as usual for the festival. ⁴³When the festival was ended and they started to return, the boy Jesus stayed behind in Jerusalem, but his parents did not know it. ⁴⁴Assuming that he was in the group of travelers, they went a day's journey. Then they started to look for him among their relatives and friends. ⁴⁵When they did not find him, they returned to Jerusalem to search for him. ⁴⁶After three days they found him in the temple, sitting among the teachers, listening to them and asking them questions. ⁴⁷And all who heard him were amazed at his understanding and his answers. ⁴⁸When his parents saw him they were astonished; and his mother said to him, "Child, why have you treated us like this? Look, your father and I have been searching for you in great anxiety." ⁴⁹He said to them, "Why were you searching for me? Did you not know that I must be in my Father's house?" ⁵⁰But they did not understand what he said to them. ⁵¹Then he went down with them and came to Nazareth, and was obedient to them. His mother treasured all these things in her heart.

⁵²And Jesus increased in wisdom and in years, and in divine and human favor.

Theological Perspective

Traditionally, this Sunday is known as the Feast of the Holy Family, and one purpose of it was to portray the family unit of Jesus, Mary, and Joseph as the model for all Christian families. However, this reading from Luke presents a less than idyllic, if realistic, depiction of family life with teenage children: we meet the young Jesus acting impetuously, seemingly oblivious of the impact his actions have on others. Despite the fact that he eventually caves in to his parents' demands, it is clear that a decisive break has occurred. Jesus is separating himself from his earthly parents and is dedicating himself to the service of his heavenly "Father" (2:48–49). Although his parents have been told that Jesus will be the savior and Messiah, these revelations come as a surprise, even a shock. Here Jesus "looks like something less than the son one dreams of."[1]

Another thread in this passage concerns Jesus' innate sense of the divine wisdom that exceeds that of normal human beings like his parents. Many commentators have focused on Jesus' comprehension of the law (v. 47), his pronouncement that he would naturally be found in his "Father's house" (v. 49), and his growth in "wisdom" (v. 52), as these affirm him as

1. Sharon H. Ringe, *Luke* (Louisville, KY: Westminster John Knox Press, 1995), 47.

Pastoral Perspective

The late Dr. Albert Ellis devised a controversial psychological program—rational emotive behavior therapy—that challenged the therapeutic models of more traditional and much-longer-term analysis. His method was action based, his theories punctuated by exclamation points. Ellis was definitively "anti-whining," and over five decades advanced increasingly accepted short-term, direct-approach techniques that morphed into popularized versions like television's Dr. Phil, whose motto, "Get real!" has captured the current cultural moment.

All who now read the story of young Jesus in the temple are susceptible to interpreting it through this ubiquitous cultural lens; numerous clergy have adopted Dr. Phil–type approaches to addressing Christian life, especially family life. After all, family matters are hot topics for sitcoms, talk shows, counseling gurus, and politicians of every stripe. The church can hardly ignore such rampant overexposure of family dynamics and their variously described, massaged, and processed psychological detritus. Throw in family antics of the Christmas season for flavor, and the cultural family stew is complete.

Everyone has stories to tell from their early days, especially from those tender transitional years when childhood gives way to more adult preoccupations and behaviors. And what parent cannot recall a

Exegetical Perspective

This story of the second visit of the young Jesus to the temple (see Luke 2:22–39) serves as a transition between Luke's infancy narratives and his account of the ministry of the mature Jesus, which begins with chapter 3. It also marks the transition between what others say about Jesus (Gabriel, Simeon, the angels at Jesus' birth) and his own words, which begin in this passage (v. 49). Jesus' trip to Jerusalem at the time of Passover anticipates his final journey to Jerusalem during the same festival. Jesus' engagement with "the teachers," which in this context can only mean teachers of the law, anticipates his later engagement with scribes and Pharisees about the law. In fact, such discussions of the Jewish law characterize the ministry of Jesus from beginning (4:1–13) to end (24:25–27), as they do his ministry as a whole (e.g., 7:26–27; 10:25–28; 20:17–18, 37–38, 41–44).

The teachers' amazement at the young Jesus' words (2:47) foreshadows the people's amazement at the mature Jesus' wisdom (4:32; 20:26). The word "amazed" is also used to describe people's reaction to many of Jesus' miracles. A similar word is used to describe the reaction of Jesus' parents to this scene in the temple (2:48), indicating that even those closest to him had difficulty coming to terms with him. Finally, Luke's account of Jesus prior to his public

Homiletical Perspective

Whether the creators of the lectionary meant to or not, they have set up a scene similar to the one sketched in Luke's Gospel. On this First Sunday after Christmas, the temple is no longer crowded. The annual festival has ended. The visitors have packed their donkeys and headed home, trailing ribbons and wrapping paper behind them. In their wake, the peace in the temple is palpable. There are plenty of seats for those whose devotion is year-round, and plenty of time to talk together about things that matter.

Among them is the boy Jesus, whose relationship with his parents undergoes considerable strain in today's story. His motive for staying in the temple after they have headed home is unclear. Maybe he loses track of time, like any boy caught up in something he loves. Maybe he has had enough of childish things and wishes to mark his maturation with an exclamation point. Maybe he does not think he is lost.

Whatever his motive, he does not waste any courtesy on his mother when she finds him in the temple talking with the teachers. "Why were you searching for me?" he says, making her distress *her* problem. "Did you not know that I must be in my Father's house?" No, she did not know that, any more than Joseph did. Jesus' parents do not understand what he is talking about, Luke says, which is our clue

Luke 2:41-52

Theological Perspective

one who unusually reflects, even basks in, the divine wisdom. Early Christian interpreters argued that these passages proved that Jesus is truly the Son of God. "Just as everything else about him was extraordinary," Origen argued, "so his boyhood was extraordinary as well, that it might be filled with the wisdom of God." Jesus' questions in the temple did not reveal ignorance but that he had already perfected the Socratic method. The discovery of Jesus in the temple gives practical instruction concerning holiness: "For it is there that the Son of God is found. If you ever seek the Son of God, look first in the temple; hasten thither. There you will find Christ, the Word and Wisdom—that is, the Son of God." Some contemporary commentators argue that the paschal mystery is also foreshadowed, and with it the way such holiness is achieved: Jesus is lost and discovered "after three days" (v. 46), which refers to his coming resurrection.[2]

Yet another thread concerns not Jesus' divinity, but his humanity. Although Luke's infancy narratives reinforce Jesus' status as a Messiah in the Davidic line, they also make clear that Jesus was raised within a particularly observant family that followed the customs and traditions of the Judaism of his day (vv. 41–42). Jesus' observance and obedience also provide teaching on the incarnation. "In a word," John Calvin argued, "if we do not choose to deny that Christ was made real man, we ought not to be ashamed to acknowledge that he voluntarily took upon him everything that is inseparable from human nature." Even in these moments Jesus "performed the office of Mediator," and this casts light on the surprising ways that God's wisdom is revealed in the context of ordinary life. For John Wesley, this passage also provides practical teaching regarding progress in holiness—Jesus, though perfect, continues to grow in perfection, and thus "it plainly follows" that even "pure" Christians "have room to increase in holiness" and "in the love of God."[3]

Each interpretive thread portrays the incarnation, but in a way that offers contrasting views of what the incarnation means in human life. For centuries, theologians tried to understand the incarnation in terms of determining the precise relation between the human and divine in Jesus, often treating the two natures as mutually exclusive. Given the different threads in this passage, these efforts are not

---

2. Origen, "Homily 19," in *Homilies on Luke*, trans. Joseph T. Lienhard, SJ (Washington: Catholic University Press, 1996), 82.

3. John Calvin, *Commentary or a Harmony of the Evangelists Matthew, Mark and Luke*, trans. W. Pringle (Grand Rapids: Eerdmans, 1949), 167; John Wesley, *Explanatory Notes upon the New Testament* (London: Epworth Press, 1929), 211.

Pastoral Perspective

moment or two when a child has somehow disappeared from sight and care? Indeed, this writer well remembers a moment during a Christmas vacation when his son vanished in a crowd at an amusement park; sheer panic aroused a frantic search. Great, rushing relief, frustration—even a dissipating anger—accompanied our reunion.

Parental matters, teenage issues, family life, family trips, coming-of-age stories, and being single in family-style congregations provide pastoral touchstones for the perceptive religious practitioner when addressing this unique story from Jesus' childhood. Still, from a strict interpretive point of view, they are mostly beside the point. The text does not lend itself to psychological analysis, even if congregants are naturally predisposed to provide it. The interpreter needs a sensitive touch when honoring both their lived experience—especially within the Christmas season—and the christological emphasis within the story. How to create a dance between these elements might provide one approach to the pastoral task.

This is first and last a story about Jesus and his human development and growing awareness. Within the arching biblical narrative, it provides his first personal report about his unique relationship with God. Nevertheless, consideration of the family context here does provide a window into the elemental human characteristics of Jesus' life as well as our own. He has a mother and father who care for him; they are part of a larger community that honors religious tradition (they travel to Jerusalem for Passover among friends and relatives); he honors these relationships; he matures and grows; he listens, learns, and teaches; time passes from one stage to the next. In all this, his humanity is described and affirmed. These details inspire poignant pastoral connection for the worshiping community.

Yet no congregant is truly like Jesus, and his uniqueness seems the seminal aspect of this story. Just as Luke's birth narrative revealed Jesus' special position, this story provides a transitional marker emphasizing his growing self-knowledge of his need to be "in his Father's house" (v. 49). Later, when visiting Jerusalem at the end of his life, Luke reports that Jesus returns to the temple to drive out those who were selling things, saying, "My house shall be a house of prayer; but you have made it a den of robbers" (Luke 19:46). His Father's house is his house too and demands his attention. Where is our attention?

As time progresses and Jesus continues to move into his human maturing, he invites all others to consider "his house, their house." Eventually the

---

ministry begins (1:8) and ends (2:41) in the temple, as in fact does the Gospel as a whole (24:53).

This story is only loosely connected to the material that precedes it. There are fewer Semitisms (Hebrew-influenced expressions) here than in the previous stories; the narrative shows no awareness of the virginal conception of Jesus; and Mary and Joseph are both identified as Jesus' parents, with Mary referring to Joseph as "your father" (v. 48). For these reasons, some scholars have posited a special source for this narrative, which Luke ties into the prior narrative with bracketing comments about Jesus' maturation (2:40, 52). The language is straightforward except for the phrase in verse 49, variously translated as "in my Father's house" (NRSV) or "about my Father's business" (KJV). In context, the former is more likely, since Jesus' parents search for him and find him in the temple, to which Jesus then refers. The fact that Jesus' parents find him "after three days" probably does not covertly refer to the resurrection, since Luke's term for that period of time is uniformly "on the third day." Why Jesus stayed behind is not stated or implied, and it is useless to speculate on the possible reason(s). It is not clear from Jewish sources whether a boy of twelve was obligated to go to Jerusalem to celebrate the Passover. In this instance, Jesus probably simply accompanied his parents, although neither children nor women were obligated to make the pilgrimage.

This is the only story in the canonical New Testament that refers to Jesus as a youth. That lack prompted later tradition to create stories of the young Jesus, many of which are collected in the apocryphal *Infancy Gospel of Thomas* (not to be confused with the more widely publicized *Gospel of Thomas*). Stories there range over an eight-year period, with Jesus from five to twelve years of age. They portray Jesus mostly as miracle worker (at five he makes birds out of mud, claps his hands, and makes them fly away; later, when he helps his father in the carpenter shop, he stretches a board too short for its intended use), often with malevolent results (he causes a boy who jostles him in the marketplace to die, strikes blind those who subsequently complain, and raises a boy who fell from a roof to his death so he can testify that Jesus did not push him off, as some had claimed). The noncanonical Gospel ends with a quotation of Luke 2:41–52 conflated with Luke 1:42, along with some additions. With his knowledge, Jesus silences the teachers in the temple who question him; the teachers subsequently tell Mary they have never seen nor heard such "excellence and wisdom."

that Luke's motive in telling this story may be more important than anyone else's.

In this singular story Luke includes at least three themes that will remain central for him throughout his Gospel: (1) the importance of the temple in Jesus' life, (2) the boundaries of Jesus' family, and (3) Jesus' authority as a teacher of God's word. Each theme suggests sermon possibilities for this particular Sunday after Christmas.

The Importance of the Temple in Jesus' Life. In Luke's Gospel, Jesus is carried into the temple before he can even walk. His parents are both observant Jews who do all that Torah requires of them. Having circumcised their son on the eighth day of his life, they carry him to the temple a little less than a month later to present him to the Lord (vv. 22–24). There Simeon and Anna both recognize him as destiny's child, seeing something in him that amazes even his mother and father.

In today's story Jesus returns to the temple for one of the three annual pilgrim festivals described in Torah. As before, the temple turns out to be the place where others see something in him that his parents do not. Later he will come back again and again as an adult, drawing both followers and critics with his teachings. For Luke, the temple really is Jesus' home—his "Father's house"—where he finds his purpose and the people who can spot it in him.

On this Sunday after Christmas preachers might find parallels in the local church, where those who are not our kin sometimes see things in us that our kin cannot. What young person will not welcome the good news that parents do not know everything? Parents may also profit from the reminder that there are other adults in the community of faith to look after their children when those children seem lost to their own families. Finally, there may be Simeons or Annas sitting there just waiting for permission to say what they see when they look at the children of this congregation.

The Boundaries of Jesus' Family. The first theme leads naturally to the second. Jesus' parents do not miss him for three days, because they are not traveling as a nuclear family. They are traveling with a caravan of extended family and friends. When they return to the temple, they find Jesus happily relating to an even-further-extended circle made up of those who teach Torah in "his Father's" house. Later in Luke's Gospel, Jesus will widen the boundaries of this circle beyond the house of Israel, offering the

Luke 2:41-52

Theological Perspective

without cause, but they can miss the incarnation's deeper teaching, which is that the divine completes, but does not obliterate, human nature in all its fullness and complexity.

In the context of this passage, the incarnation teaches that God can be found even in difficult familial circumstances. It teaches that God's wisdom is available to the young as well as to the old, which means that we must make room for God to surprise us with unexpected revelations given by unusual messengers. It teaches us that though God's wisdom and holiness remind us of our limitations, it is precisely within these limitations that wisdom is often revealed. The incarnation represents the moment in which this wisdom enters the human sphere in all its contradictions, so that nothing is left without transformation and transfiguration.

To be certain, this passage takes place within a larger narrative surrounding Jesus' establishment of the kingdom of God, and we should avoid any interpretation that would limit this narrative in any way. Jesus' decision to do the business of his "Father" and his grasp of wisdom foreshadow not only the entire scope of his earthly ministry, but more specifically the moment where he stands in the synagogue in Nazareth and proclaims, "The Spirit of the Lord is upon me" (4:18). Even so, we should not limit the ways in which this passage reflects the mystery of the incarnation as it is worked out in the life of this particular family. Like the moment in the Gospel of John where we read that Jesus wept (11:35), to lose this encounter in its surrounding narrative would bring its own impoverishment.

That the incarnation took this shape in the life of the holy family gives hope for families of all kinds and conditions on this day. The model of living that the holy family offers is not, as is sometimes depicted in romantic paintings and portraits, that of a family perfectly ordered and without division or differences. Rather, it is of a family that lives into messy moments with the confidence that God in Christ Jesus has entered and redeems them from within.

WILLIAM J. DANAHER JR.

Pastoral Perspective

gospeler/theologian John will report a fully mature Jesus saying this to his friends: "In my Father's house there are many dwelling places. If it were not so, would I have told you that I go to prepare a place for you? And if I go and prepare a place for you, I will come again and will take you to myself, so that where I am, there you may be also" (John 14:2–3). Again, where is our attention?

In the critical incident when Jesus was twelve years old, his understanding concerning his relationship to his Father's house seems age-appropriate and, yes, also astonishing and perplexing, if not a little irritating as Mary and Joseph experience him—a very human parental response (Luke 2:48). And we observe that Jesus provokes astonished perplexity and occasional irritation for all those who are captured by his precocious and holy charisma. From time to time it is helpful to remind today's seekers and followers that Jesus' potentially irksome provocations can catalyze their spiritual maturity. As in most healthy families, children will rise up to become their parents' teachers, often to the parents' chagrin.

Throughout this story a sense of agitated imperative prevails. Jesus is missing; filled with anxiety, his parents must return to find him. When they discover Jesus in the temple, he asks them directly about this: "Why were you searching for me? Did you not know that I must be in my Father's house?" (v. 49). They must look for him, and he must be within his Father's house. This tells us something about the nature of Jesus' identity, as well as that of his parents. They each do what they must. For the time being, there is seeming conflict in these differing necessities, which could be understood from the vantage point of a naturally occurring evolution in the parent/child relationship. However, in this case the tension has a more fundamental root that pertains to Jesus' radical identity. This leads to interesting considerations about the varieties of "musts" that drive our behaviors, how they confirm our identities, and how they merge with the one essential "must" that pertains to our relationship with the youth of Nazareth.

Despite his unique position, Jesus was obedient to his parents as Mary "treasured all these things in her heart" (v. 51). This is a fitting conclusion for this vignette, but also a potentially useful beginning for the person in the pew who has brought a fair amount of cultural and personal luggage into the room.

STEPHEN BAUMAN

Exegetical Perspective

It was not unusual in ancient times to tell stories of renowned people who at the age of twelve or so gave an indication of their coming stature. Such stories are told of the Buddha in India, Osiris in Egypt, Cyrus the Great in Persia, and Augustus in Rome. It is therefore not surprising that one such story does appear in our Gospels; what is perhaps remarkable is the restraint with which this story is told.

Finally, the narrative's Jewish roots are very evident. The setting at the time of the Passover, the location of the central elements of the story in the temple, and Jesus' obedience to his parents all make these roots manifest. Not immediately apparent are the links between stories of the young Jesus and accounts of the young Samuel. For instance, the Magnificat of Mary in Luke 1:46–55 contains clear echoes of the hymn of Samuel's mother, Hannah, in 1 Samuel 2:1–10. The custom of Mary and Joseph going to Jerusalem to celebrate the Passover is reflected in the similar custom of Samuel's parents (1 Sam. 1:3, 21; 2:19). The twofold reference to Jesus' maturing (Luke 2:40, 52) is reflected in a similar twofold reference to the young Samuel (1 Sam. 2:21, 26). Thus, from the beginning the story of Jesus in Luke is closely bound up with the story of Israel. In his own way, Luke makes this connection as evident as Matthew does (the latter by repeating the phrase "this occurred in order to fulfill what was said").

The Jesus who appears in this narrative thus recalls the roots of Christianity in the history of Israel. The story shows Jesus to be fully human in his maturation in wisdom and in stature, anticipating his total dedication to the mission with which his Father has entrusted him. This temple story also portrays the resulting necessities under which Jesus fulfills that mission, from this early announcement of the necessity of being in his Father's house to the subsequent necessities of his ministry: preaching the kingdom of God (4:43), casting out demons and performing cures (13:32–33), and finally suffering many things, being killed, and being raised from the dead (9:22; 17:25; 22:37; 24:7, 26).

PAUL J. ACHTEMEIER

Homiletical Perspective

good news of God's embrace to all within the sound of his voice.

As becomes clear in today's story, the enlarging of family boundaries does not come without stretch marks. Jesus speaks as sharply to his mother here as he does in John's Gospel (2:4). In Mark's Gospel, he does not speak to her at all but only *about* her (3:33). Later in Luke's Gospel, Jesus erases any doubt about what such behavior means: "Whoever comes to me and does not hate father and mother . . . cannot be my disciple" (14:26). What happened to "Honor your father and your mother"?

Jacob Neusner takes up that question in his book *A Rabbi Talks with Jesus*.[1] While preachers will want to do their own reading, Neusner makes the point that in the Israel of Jesus' time, Torah was understood to take precedence over genealogy, so that "the master of Torah gains a new lineage."[2] While this Jewish understanding never became license to abandon the family, it did underscore the seriousness of Torah study.

On this First Sunday after Christmas, preachers might explore what the serious study of God's word does to one's sense of family. What happens to a person when she decides to stop accepting what her family tells her and to start studying with other teachers instead? Is conflict inevitable, or is it possible to honor one's family of origin as well as one's ever-expanding family of faith?

Jesus' Authority as a Teacher of God's Word. While Luke stays concerned throughout his Gospel with Jesus' inclusion of all the nations in the redeeming work of God, he never erases Jesus' Jewishness. Here at the beginning of Jesus' adulthood we see him in a self-devised confirmation class, exchanging questions with teachers in the temple. When he preaches his first sermon (4:18–19), he will make good use of his Jewish education.

On this First Sunday of Christmas, preachers might attend to the ways in which Jesus grows sturdily *from* his religious roots, not *in spite of* them. This boy who was filled with wisdom as a child (v. 40) will increase in wisdom as he grows (v. 52). He is Sophia's child as well as Mary's, whose first awareness of his parentage comes to him in his Father's house.

BARBARA BROWN TAYLOR

1. Jacob Neusner, *A Rabbi Talks with Jesus* (New York: Doubleday, 1993), 37–57.
2. Ibid., 48.

Sirach 24:1-12

¹Wisdom praises herself,
    and tells of her glory in the midst of her people.
²In the assembly of the Most High she opens her mouth,
    and in the presence of his hosts she tells of her glory:
³"I came forth from the mouth of the Most High,
    and covered the earth like a mist.
⁴I dwelt in the highest heavens,
    and my throne was in a pillar of cloud.
⁵Alone I compassed the vault of heaven
    and traversed the depths of the abyss.
⁶Over waves of the sea, over all the earth,
    and over every people and nation I have held sway.
⁷Among all these I sought a resting place;
    in whose territory should I abide?

Theological Perspective

Wisdom's praise of herself in Sirach raises at least two significant theological issues for the Sundays following Christmas, when the church focuses its celebration on the incarnation. The first theme concerns the doctrine of revelation. God-with-us in Christ points to the broader question of *how* God is with us and how God is made known *to* us. Theologians have traditionally spoken of God's self-revelation in two ways: (1) general revelation, referring to the ways God is made known to us through the natural world and is accessible to our reason; and (2) special revelation, referring to the ways in which God is made known to us through God's self-revelation in the history of Israel and especially in the life, death, and resurrection of Christ.

In Sirach, Wisdom is present and active in creation as both Word and Spirit. "I came forth from the mouth of the Most High, and covered the earth like a mist" (v. 3). The word of God calling creation into being and the spirit of God covering all the earth are presented in Sirach in personal form as Wisdom. Although Wisdom refers to God as her "Creator" (v. 8), she is also affiliated with language that the Bible usually reserves for the creator. In Job, it is God who travels across the vault of the heavens and searches out the depths of the sea, but here that journey is Wisdom's. In Exodus, it is God who is

Pastoral Perspective

"Pastor, can we talk?" The request comes from all kinds of people: the thirty-something engineer considering his dream job offer, which would require moving his family across a continent; the mother of three adolescent children who discovers her husband snorting cocaine in the bathroom; the executive vice president who is uneasy about business practices at her company; the sixty-year-old son whose widowed mother has had three driving violations in just as many months; the conscientious citizen who will cast a vote in the next national election; the members of the property committee weighing budget matters. They all wrestle with decisions and seek counsel.

Though these earnest believers face widely different dilemmas, at their core the dilemmas pose the same question: "What does God want me to do?" Most of the faithful really do want to do what God wants, but they need wisdom to do it. What issues does this reading from Wisdom literature raise? What insights does it offer?

What Is Wisdom? Wisdom is not information or knowledge or experience, though certainly these three can contribute to the gaining of wisdom. Wisdom is that which leads to a good life, that is, a life that both pleases God and gives us pleasure.

⁸"Then the Creator of all things gave me a command,
   and my Creator chose the place for my tent.
He said, 'Make your dwelling in Jacob,
   and in Israel receive your inheritance.'
⁹Before the ages, in the beginning, he created me,
   and for all the ages I shall not cease to be.
¹⁰In the holy tent I ministered before him,
   and so I was established in Zion.
¹¹Thus in the beloved city he gave me a resting place,
   and in Jerusalem was my domain.
¹²I took root in an honored people,
   in the portion of the Lord, his heritage."

Exegetical Perspective

New Testament writers often tied their teaching about the mysteries of God revealed in Christ to the Old Testament's wisdom tradition, principally identified with the books of Proverbs, Job, and Ecclesiastes. This wisdom tradition continues in Sirach (in some English Bibles, The Wisdom of Ben Sira), written in Jerusalem in the second century BCE, against the sociopolitical backdrop of Hellenism's challenge to Judaism. The Vulgate's Latin title, Ecclesiasticus (see REB, NAB, NJB), literally, "church book," reflects the book's extensive use in early Christian catechesis.

To counter the seductive appeal of regnant Greek thought, which prized the pursuit of wisdom through human inquiry, Sirach seeks to convince a Jewish audience that its own intellectual heritage, preserved in the Torah, prophets, and the "other books of our ancestors," is a sufficient guide for those who are "lovers of wisdom" (foreword, NAB). The central argument is set forth in the opening poem in praise of Wisdom, personified here, as elsewhere in the sapiential tradition, as a woman: "All wisdom is from the Lord. . . . It is he who created her; . . . he poured her out upon all his works; . . . he lavished her upon those who love him" (1:1a, 9a, 9c, 10b; cf. Prov. 1:20–33; 8:22–36; 9:1–6; Wis. 7–9). Other poems on Wisdom's role in creation

Homiletical Perspective

"What are your New Year's resolutions?"

That is a question we are likely to hear from members of the congregation in the days following Christmas. What are you going to do differently in the coming year? What changes are you going to make so that the way you actually live is more like the way you want to live?

Everyone wants to negotiate life well, and most of us, when we are honest, know we could do that better. A few years ago *The New York Time Book Review* started a separate bestseller list for "Advice, How-to and Miscellaneous" books, since titles in those categories were crowding out the traditional fiction and nonfiction lists. Knowledge about how to live right was and is in demand.

Some of the world's oldest literature consists of compendia of advice on how to do well and prosper, how to live properly and gain esteem. In the religion of ancient Israel that advice for sound living was found in the Wisdom literature. Wisdom is personified as one who was with God at the creation and who covers the whole earth. She offers human beings sound guidance for negotiating life. What makes her counsel so authoritative is the fact that it emanates from the very source of life. When we heed the counsel of Wisdom, we live as God intends us to live and save ourselves from the folly of a life gone astray.

Sirach 24:1-12

Theological Perspective

present with the people in the pillar of cloud, but in Sirach, the pillar of cloud is Wisdom's throne. Clearly, then, Sirach closely identifies Wisdom with God's own self.

Although Sirach did not envision such a concept, Christians in the act of worship may be forgiven for transferring this language into Trinitarian form. God-with-us is present with us and made known to us in creation. This is the heart of what is meant by general revelation, and God's choice of creation as a context for self-revelation is deeply entwined with the affirmation that creation is good.

In Sirach, Wisdom rules over all the nations. "Over every people and nation," she affirms, "I have held sway" (v. 6b). But she has found in Israel, especially, "a resting place" (v. 7). For Thomas Aquinas, it would be perfectly natural for Wisdom, who is made known in nature, to forge a special relationship with Israel. According to Aquinas, general revelation is corrected, complemented, and made complete in special revelation. God's self-revelation in nature may be misunderstood by sinful humanity, and so its essential truths are repeated and clarified in God's great acts in the history of Israel and the life of Christ. As we receive special revelation, our erroneous and idolatrous interpretations of general revelation are corrected. Finally, special revelation offers humanity truths that cannot be contained by the natural, and so, without overwhelming or negating nature, grace completes and perfects it.[1] John Calvin described this relationship between general and special revelation by using the metaphor of a book and eyeglasses. Although God has clearly written in the book of nature truths for all to behold, our sin has distorted our vision, so that we now require the corrective lenses of Scripture if we are to read that book rightly.[2]

Reading from the edifying, if not canonical, books of the Apocrypha helps us to understand how Jewish thought about the nature of God and God's relationship to the world evolved during the intertestamental, or Second Temple, period. Understanding how Greek philosophical concepts entered the Hebrew world, giving Jews new language and categories for expressing their faith, allows us to understand the world in which Jesus lived and worked. It also reveals to us the fundamental continuity between the Old and New Testaments.

Pastoral Perspective

Wisdom is the way to the life for which we are created.

Believers want to find that way. They know that the ways of the world are often at odds with the ways of God, so they try to look at their situation not from a human point of view but from God's perspective. "Common sense suits itself to the ways of the world; wisdom tries to conform to the ways of heaven."[1]

Is it not preposterous for mortals to attempt to discern the ways of heaven? Sirach says, "No. Wisdom is available on earth. Wisdom has been established in Zion . . . in Jerusalem is Wisdom's domain. . . . Wisdom has taken root in an honored people" (vv. 10, 11, 12). The Creator established Wisdom in creation, then revealed it in Torah and brought it to life in Christ. Now it is possible for God's people to gain wisdom.

"With all wisdom and insight God has made known to us the mystery of his will," says Ephesians in the Epistle lection for this Sunday (1:8). Wise human beings can actually come to think like God, or at least to understand life as God sees it. We might be inclined to dismiss this claim as presumptuous, were it not for Paul's words in Philippians, "Let the same mind be in you that was in Christ Jesus" (2:5).

How Do We "Get" Wisdom? Since divine wisdom is available to human beings, parishioners may well ask this question. We do not *get* wisdom, Sirach tells us; wisdom is *given*. It is not something we can acquire or attain by effort or intelligence, but something we receive as a gift. It is a spiritual gift graciously conferred by the Spirit of the most wise God. "For the LORD gives wisdom; from his mouth come knowledge and understanding" (Prov. 2:6).

How do we receive the gift? Not from the pastor! We receive the gift from the Holy Spirit through prayer, through contemplation of the Word, through holding fast to God's commandments, through pursuing a life of discipleship. If believers want to think with the mind of Christ, they are invited, or rather, instructed, intentionally to seek it. What parishioners need from the pastor is not the answer to their dilemmas, but spiritual direction as they go to the well of wisdom, the Spirit of the living God.

What If We Do Not "Get" It? What if the seeking parishioner does not gain certainty, despite fervent efforts to discern God's wisdom? What if her life of

---

1. Thomas Aquinas, *Summa Theologica*, Blackfriars edition, vol. 3, trans. Herbert McCabe (London: Eyre & Spottiswoode, 1964), 1a.13, 5–6.
2. John Calvin, *The Institutes of the Christian Religion*, trans. Ford Lewis Battles (Philadelphia: Westminster Press, 1960), 1.6.1.

1. Joseph Joubert, "Pensees," in *Living Pulpit*, July/September 2000, 33.

are located at critical sections of the book (6:18–37; 14:20–15:10; 42:15–43:33). Of these, none is more critical than the hymn in 24:1–22, which constitutes the center of the book, both structurally and thematically.

The introduction (vv. 1–2) is a third-person description of Wisdom praising herself in "the assembly of the Most High." The reference to the assembly draws upon Canaanite descriptions of the council of gods over which El, the creator god, presides. The Old Testament utilizes the image of the divine council in several places (Isa. 6; Ps. 82; Job 1–2) to refer to the heavenly beings who attend God. Woman Wisdom, Sirach says, enjoys a place of honor in this assembly. On the one hand, Wisdom's heavenly location confirms that she dwells with God. On the other, the brief but important reference to "her people" hints that what she has to say, adumbrated in the verses that follow, is not for God's ears alone.

In the first stanza (vv. 3–7), Wisdom associates herself with God's cosmic act of creation. As an intimate of the God who spoke the cosmos into being (Gen. 1:1–2:4a), Wisdom comes from the "mouth" of God, and like the primordial waters she "covers the earth like a mist" (v.3; cf. Gen. 1:2; 2:6). Extending her reach to the "vault of *heaven*," "the depths of the *abyss*," and "all the *earth*" (vv. 5–6a), Wisdom encompasses the three spheres of the unformed mass from which God brought forth the wonders of an ordered world (cf. Gen. 1:1–2). Overseeing the entirety of what God has created, Wisdom describes herself as a "in pillar of cloud" (v. 4), a surrogate of the God whose guiding presence promised the Israelites safe passage through the wilderness (Exod. 13:21–22). The last verse in this stanza (v. 7) introduces the central question of the poem: where, among all the places in the cosmos over which it holds sway, will Wisdom find a resting place?

The second stanza (vv. 8–12) provides the answer to this question. At God's command, Wisdom sets up her tent in Jacob; she receives her inheritance in Israel. More specifically, she pitches her tent in Zion, in the "beloved city" of Jerusalem, and from there she "ministers" (*leitourgeō*, "provides divine service") unto God (vv. 9–10). The language draws upon the imagery of both the tent of meeting/tabernacle, which provided the visible symbol of the presence of God as Israel journeyed the wilderness, and the temple in Jerusalem, in which, according to Sirach, Wisdom now administers the priestly rituals that keep God and world connected in worship. This

One of the challenges of preaching Wisdom from the Bible is providing some context for the lists of sayings that make up most of the literature. Merely reminding people of the many things Proverbs, Ecclesiastes, and Sirach say they should do soon overwhelms even the most devout persons. Today's passage tells us two important characteristics of Wisdom that inform the way we should live: (1) She is found in community, and (2) she occupies herself with serving God. When our resolutions are grounded in community and service to God, they have a fighting chance of surviving until June.

Even though Wisdom is everywhere, from the highest vault of heaven to the deepest abyss of the earth, she desires a place to settle down, a place to rest and call her home. Those whose work takes them to many far-flung places may sympathize with her. There can be a certain satisfaction that comes with knowing how to live in many places. Going from place to place can broaden our understanding of the world and give keen insights. Nevertheless, most travelers come to appreciate a place to call home, a place to settle, to nurture long-term relationships and to be accessible to those who matter most.

In a culture that encourages us to construct our identities by choosing who we want to be, Wisdom reminds us that, like her, we are created to live in relationship with others. The raging popularity of virtual online communities such as chat rooms, blogs, and personal information pages is testimony to how we cannot live in isolation. We need to be connected to others.

A sermon on this text can invite those who hear it into a specific kind of community whose purpose is not to enhance the life experience of its members but to serve God. Wisdom dwells in a specific community, Israel. God chose that community to be a blessing to all the nations, and Wisdom finds her home there ministering before God (v. 10). The sermon can also challenge the church to be a community that is shaped by Wisdom, a community that exists not to provide for the needs of its members but to serve and glorify God.

In this season when we celebrate the incarnation, specificity is an important theme. Sirach tells us that Wisdom dwells in a specific place, Zion, and is engaged in a specific activity, ministering to God. A sermon preached during Christmas cannot help but recall that the Wisdom of the ages has come to us in a specific person. Reading this passage, the words of John's prologue come to mind, "The Word became

Sirach 24:1-12

Theological Perspective

God's self-revelation to the Hebrew people was reinterpreted and deployed theologically in ever-new historical and cultural contexts by the Hebrew people themselves in the postexilic world. Sirach shows clear signs of having been influenced at least indirectly by Stoic philosophy, with its confidence that the *logos* provided the rational structure for the cosmos that allowed the human mind to comprehend it.

The easy identification of Word and Wisdom in Sirach's hellenized Jewish world contributed to the early Christian identification of Christ with both Word and Wisdom, providing an important second theme for theological reflection. The personification of Wisdom as a woman in Sirach, as in Proverbs, opens space for theological reflection on the nature of our language for God. All human language about God must of necessity be metaphorical. Our words can only gesture toward divine reality. When we speak theologically, we are speaking of what we cannot finally know. The Pseudo-Dionysius explained that all finite theological language falls short of its infinite object. Whatever we say of God will always be partly false, that anonymous sixth-century author reminds us, because it will always be tied to some aspect of the creation that the creator utterly transcends. For this reason, the Pseudo-Dionysius preferred halting language that pointed to its own incapacity to contain the Divine.[3]

We can become so tied to certain metaphors—God as shepherd, God as Father, God as king—that we fail to recognize their limitations. We can begin to confuse our metaphors for God's reality, transforming our words into idols. God is no longer understood to be *like* a Father but *is* Father. When these metaphors are predominantly masculine in character, the idolatry damages our ability to value women as equal recipients of God's gifts and to love men as the creatures they are. One of the surest ways to break our idolatry and expand our vision of God is to deploy the full range of biblical metaphors and images for God, including its feminine imagery. This passage from Sirach can provide an opportunity to reflect on the nature of our language about God and to begin an exploration of the wide variety of canonical feminine images for God.

KENDRA G. HOTZ

Pastoral Perspective

faith is marked by doubt and questions? She is not alone. And she is not necessarily unfaithful. In fact, she may be closer to wisdom than she thinks. "The fear of the LORD is the beginning of wisdom" (Ps. 111:10). When we are aware that our human understanding is limited, we manifest a different fruit of the Spirit, humility. And there can be no wisdom without humility. "Knowledge is proud that he has learned so much; Wisdom is humble that he knows no more."[2]

Abraham Lincoln, trying to discern God's wisdom as he led the country through the darkest days of the Civil War, urged the people to do the right as God gave them to see the right. Sometimes, even though we have done our best to seek divine rather than human wisdom, we nevertheless must act without the assurance of clarity and certainty. In those times, we understand what prompted Thomas Merton to pray, "My Lord God, . . . the fact that I think I am following your will does not mean that I am actually doing so. But I believe that the desire to please you does in fact please you, and I hope that I have that desire in all that I am doing. And I know that if I do this, you will lead me by the right road."[3]

On the Other Hand, If You Think You Have "Got" It, Think Again. In talking about discerning the mind of God, perhaps there is never a place for certainty. Certainty can lead to arrogance, if we forget that human knowledge is limited and inevitably skewed by sin. How much damage is done by human beings who claim to know the mind of God?! Though Sirach tells us that wisdom has taken up residence among us, the language of the text—soaring, full of mystery, awed by the vastness and majesty of God—forbids us to whittle God's wisdom down to our size. We can never be glib about knowing the will of the creator of the universe.

KAREN PIDCOCK-LESTER

---

3. This is a theme throughout the writings of the Pseudo-Dionysius, but see esp. "The Divine Names," in *The Complete Works*, trans. Colm Luibheid (New York: Paulist Press, 1987).

2. William Cowper, "The Task," quoted in *Living Pulpit*, July/September 2000, 32.

3. Thomas Merton, *Choosing to Love the World: On Contemplation*, ed. Jonathan Montaldo (Boulder, CO: Sounds True, Inc., 2008), 99.

Exegetical Perspective

affirmation of Wisdom's accessibility is striking, because it moves beyond conventional sapiential thinking. Job 28, for example, describes wisdom as essentially beyond human grasp; God "knows its [wisdom's] place" (Job 28:23), but "mortals do not, . . . it is not found in the land of the living" (Job 28:13). A comparison with *1 Enoch* 42:1–2 (first century CE), which concedes that Wisdom sought a place on earth to reside but returned to heaven in frustration, is still more instructive. Sirach's claim that Wisdom finds a home in Jerusalem does not go as far as today's reading from the Gospel of John, but it is an important signpost pointing in this direction. John's term for the "Word that became flesh and *lived* [*skēnoō*] among us" (1:14) comes from the same root as the word for Wisdom's "tent" (*skēnē*; Sir. 24:8) in Zion.

The reading ends by affirming that Wisdom resides with an "honored people" (v. 12). Coupled with the words "her people" in verse 1 and the multiple mentions of Israel in verses 7–11, the text affirms that God has chosen to dwell with a special people, the Jews, in ways that distinguish them from all others. A full exegesis of this idea invites careful reflection on the wider framework that informs the Bible's election theology. That God favors some people over others is an important biblical truth that lies at the core of both Judaism and Christianity. It is also, sadly, a truth vulnerable to misunderstanding by both Jews and Christians, who throughout history have often yielded to the temptation to claim that they alone have access to the full truth of what God has revealed. For the worship that today's text invites, we should read beyond verse 12, for the remainder of this hymn is an important reminder that what takes "root" in a chosen people should send out its branches far and wide (vv. 13–17); its fruits should summon *all God's children* (see the note on v. 18 in NRSV) to a banquet of delights that is inexhaustible (vv. 19–22).[1]

SAMUEL E. BALENTINE

Homiletical Perspective

flesh and lived among us" (John 1:14). As Wisdom dwelled in Jerusalem, the eternal glory of God came to dwell in human flesh. In him we know the One who created the heavens and the earth, the One who is the source of Wisdom. He draws us to himself and transforms us into new people whose sins are forgiven and whose hearts are attuned to the Wisdom of the ages. In Christ we become what God has made us, "created in Christ Jesus for good works" (Eph. 2:10). In him we attain right living not by working hard at keeping our resolutions but by being transformed into new creatures who belong to the community of faith that is dedicated to serving God.

A sermon on this text could begin by inviting the congregation to consider different places they might look for help in living the right way. The preacher who knows her or his congregation will have some idea where those places are. The preacher could go on to point out that life at its best is not lived willy-nilly but in accord with a certain quality that enriches our experience of life and gives us equilibrium when times are tough. The Bible identifies that quality as Wisdom. The preacher might then go on to say how Wisdom springs from God and is the foundation of a life lived as God created it to be. One characteristic of God is that God comes to us in particular ways. Just as Wisdom rested in Israel, God's incarnation comes to us in Jesus. In Jesus we find Wisdom. The Holy Spirit guides us in the ways of Wisdom. So perhaps the wisest resolution this New Year would be, "I'm going to grow in my relationship with Jesus."

STEPHENS G. LYTCH

---

1. For further reading, see J. Kaminsky, *Yet I Loved Jacob: Reclaiming the Biblical Concept of Election* (Nashville: Abingdon, 2007).

Wisdom of Solomon 10:15-21

[15]A holy people and blameless race
  wisdom delivered from a nation of oppressors.
[16]She entered the soul of a servant of the Lord,
  and withstood dread kings with wonders and signs.
[17]She gave to holy people the reward of their labors;
  she guided them along a marvelous way,
  and became a shelter to them by day,
  and a starry flame through the night.
[18]She brought them over the Red Sea,
  and led them through deep waters;
[19]but she drowned their enemies,
  and cast them up from the depth of the sea.
[20]Therefore the righteous plundered the ungodly;
  they sang hymns, O Lord, to your holy name,
  and praised with one accord your defending hand;
[21]for wisdom opened the mouths of those who were mute,
  and made the tongues of infants speak clearly.

Theological Perspective

Unfamiliar to most Protestant preachers because of its designation by their branch of the Christian church as part of the Apocrypha, the Wisdom of Solomon offers an important theological contribution to all branches of Christianity. That contribution is its resolute attempt to use the language and concepts of a new (for first-century-CE Judaism) cultural milieu to give life to the Hebrew tradition in an alien setting. "This effort at using Greek philosophy and rhetoric in the service of biblical religion makes the author to some extent also a pioneer in enculturation, or adapting the religious message to different thought patterns and modes of expression."[1] If further encouragement is needed, it is worth noting that as they reflected upon the person of Jesus and the doctrine of the Trinity, such Christian thinkers as Ignatius, Origen, and Augustine made use of the Wisdom of Solomon, albeit in a variety of ways.[2]

Given the endeavor of Wisdom of Solomon to express a distinctive faith in an unfamiliar cultural and conceptual context, it furnishes a kind of theological model for preaching. If nothing else,

---

1. Daniel J. Harrington, SJ, *Invitation to the Apocrypha* (Grand Rapids: Eerdmans, 1999), 57.
2. David A. deSilva, *Introducing the Apocrypha* (Grand Rapids: Baker Academic, 2002), 152.

Pastoral Perspective

Earlier in this book, the writer describes wisdom as "radiant and unfading" (6:12) and states that "the beginning of wisdom is the most sincere desire for instruction" (6:17). Wisdom has long been prized as a defining goal for what it means to be truly human. The problem comes as we try to define precisely what wisdom is.

Often we call someone wise based on the amount of knowledge she has. We believe that the person who knows more facts, somewhat like a trivia champion, has greater wisdom than others do. But that is not always the case. A person can know many things without being able to apply these facts to a particular situation and thus ends up making a foolish decision.

I was reminded of this in a recent conversation with a young friend who was facing a tough decision and came to talk to me about it. As we reviewed the pros and cons of different courses of action, my friend stated, "I like to talk to other people to get a different perspective on my situation. I especially like to talk to someone who I think has more wisdom than me, rather than someone my own age. I have a lot more wisdom than most people my age." This prompted me to ask, "What do you think wisdom is?" My friend replied, "I believe that wisdom is the profound interpretation of knowledge and experience."

Exegetical Perspective

Written in Greek by a Jewish sage, probably in the late first century BCE in Alexandria, Wisdom of Solomon is an extraordinary example of the importance and necessity of interpreting Scripture anew for new times and places. The author clearly knew and respected Judaism's emerging canon—the Torah, Prophets, and Writings (including Proverbs, Job, and Ecclesiastes, earlier works in the wisdom tradition)—but he reread and reinterpreted these texts in conversation with Greek philosophy and Hellenistic culture. His setting and his audience, consisting most likely of Hellenistic Jews like himself as well as non-Jews schooled in Greek philosophy and Hellenistic culture, demanded nothing less.

What the author drew most prominently from Hellenistic thinking was a new anthropology that, unlike the anthropology of the Hebrew Bible, made a distinction between body and soul. To be sure, the translation "soul" shows up frequently in the NRSV, but it generally translates a Hebrew word that more accurately means "self" or "whole being," without a distinction between a material body and an imma-terial soul. This newfound distinction clearly provided new interpretive options. For instance, the existence of an immaterial, eternal soul meant that Sheol no longer has to be understood as the realm of the dead to which all are destined. Rather, immortality

Homiletical Perspective

It is a good idea for preachers to focus more on their given texts than on the events of the liturgical year, lest we end up preaching the calendar and not the Word. But this text invites us to a seasonal reading for two reasons. First, the reality is that congregations are almost certainly focused on Jesus during the season of Christmas. Preaching this text in isolation asks a congregation with Jesus on their minds to change their focus and risks losing their attention altogether. Second, this text welcomes a Christian/Christmas interpretation, not only because it recounts a part of the salvation story that culminates in the incarnation, but also because the text is already imposing its own ideas onto preexistent texts.

The fourteen verses leading up to this passage tell the story of salvation history from creation to the exodus, but the author modifies the story to fit an understanding of divine Wisdom. The author argues that it is Wisdom who acts on Israel's behalf, as opposed to the Lord, in Exodus. The author tweaks the details, calling the Israelites a "blameless race" (despite their repeated disbelief in the wilderness), referring to the Egyptians' being cast up "from the depth of the sea" (a later tradition not described in Exod. 15:30)[1] and specifying that the mute and

1. David Winston, *The Wisdom of Solomon* (New York: Doubleday, 1979), 221.

Wisdom of Solomon 10:15-21

Theological Perspective

effective preaching seeks to utter the theology of the religious tradition in categories and experiences that make sense to particular hearers in particular times and places. Attention to this preacher's theological method is thus salutary for all preachers.

The assigned text is part of a major turning point in the structure of the book as a whole, opening the third (and final) portion of the book by turning from an account of the nature of wisdom to wisdom's role in Israel's early history (Adam to Moses). One of the most fascinating characteristics of the entire tenth chapter is the writer's ability to summarize the biblical narrative of Israel's origins while only rarely identifying by name either figures or events. The opening verse of this passage, along with each successive verse, illustrates this perfectly: "A holy people and blameless race wisdom delivered from a nation of oppressors" (v. 15). Those who know the narrative will recognize the reference to the people of Israel delivered from Egyptian slavery. And the same is true as the passage continues, recounting wisdom's embodied role in Moses, her guidance on a "marvelous way," sheltering them by day and as a "starry flame through the night" (v. 17). Only when the decisive moment of rescue is rehearsed is there a familiar place reference—the Red Sea.

This fascinating retelling of the story without much reference to conventional narrative markers serves several purposes. Harrington is probably right in describing it as a rhetorical device that "presumes that readers can identify the figures and may promote their active involvement."[3] Even a contemporary reader is likely to have a somewhat unusual experience of reading and mentally being challenged to make the connection to the unspoken names and places of the biblical narrative that are summarized here. One has to supply what is not said in order to grasp what is said. But in addition to this rhetorical and pedagogical purpose, there is also a theological purpose at work. The burden of the retelling is to reunderstand the mode of God's saving presence and action in the history of Israel.

And the ringing reiteration throughout the passage is that God embodies Godself as wisdom in accomplishing these mighty works of rescue and redemption. Wisdom is the agent who "delivered" Israel, who "withstood dread kings," who "guided" and "sheltered," who "led through deep waters," who "drowned their enemies," who "opened the mouths" of those thus delivered in resounding praise of this

3. Harrington, *Invitation*, 67.

Pastoral Perspective

That discussion seems to illuminate the passage from the Wisdom of Solomon. The writer extols Wisdom as the essential piece in God's work in the lives of God's people. True wisdom provides the proper (and often profound) interpretation of life's events.

In the previous verses of this chapter, the writer gives a number of examples of how Wisdom has been involved in the history of the people of Israel. Beginning with the first-formed man (Adam) and continuing through a righteous man who was sold (Joseph), the writer shows how Wisdom has protected, delivered, and comforted the righteous ones of Israel.

In the passage for this Sunday, the writer begins by reminding the readers that Wisdom delivered a holy people from its oppressors. This obvious reference to the exodus event must have evoked many responses from the original readers of this text. They would have remembered the hardships faced by those ancient ancestors. The exodus text stressed the ruthlessness of the Egyptians in dealing with the Israelites, the cruelty of the taskmasters, and the harsh reality that the Pharaoh ordered midwives to kill all newborn Hebrew boys at delivery. Readers and hearers would have identified with the feelings of despair experienced by the enslaved people as they watched Moses negotiate their release from bondage. Despair turned to hope as the Israelites finally began the trek out of Egypt only to turn to despair again as—facing the sea ahead of them—they watched the Egyptian chariots approaching. Then came the moment of ultimate triumph as the people of Israel passed through the waters safely and the sea swallowed the pursuing Egyptians. In all of this, the writer of today's text asserts, Wisdom played an active role and was in fact responsible for delivering the people from their hopeless situation.

Readers and hearers of the Wisdom of Solomon likely faced their own hopeless situations. This book was probably written during a time when many Jews were tempted to embrace the paganism of their conquerors. After all, they must have believed, it is hopeless for us to think that we will be able to survive or thrive in such an atmosphere by practicing our faith. They may have even doubted the presence and power of God in the face of such overwhelming evidence of the power of the pagans. This word, then, becomes a word of hope in a hopeless situation to the Jewish people: remember what God has done; seek the Wisdom of God; remain faithful and you too shall be rescued.

becomes an option, and immortality is a major theme of Wisdom of Solomon (see 1:15; 3:4; 5:15; 6:17–20). Then too, when God's justice need not be worked out solely in a this-worldly realm, there are new options for approaching big issues like theodicy and eschatology, both of which figure prominently in the book (see 3:10–5:23).

While drawing deeply from Hellenistic philosophy, the author was faithful to his Jewish inheritance. For instance, the opening chapter features a word/concept critically important in the Torah, Prophets, and Writings—"righteousness" (1:1, 15; the two occurrences form an inclusio for chap. 1). This word/concept is important throughout Wisdom of Solomon, including chapter 10, which is usually viewed as a conclusion to the book's first major section (1:1–11:1). Chapter 10 maintains the focus on wisdom that characterizes this first section but also provides a transition to the second major section of the book (11:2–19:22). It offers a review of the Torah story— from Adam (10:1–2) to Cain (10:3) to Babel/Abraham (10:5) to Lot (10:6–8) to Jacob (10:9–12) to Joseph (10:13–14) to Moses and the exodus (10:15–11:1)— that lays the groundwork for the detailed exposition of the exodus plagues in 11:2–19:22.

In the cases of Noah, Abraham, Lot, Jacob, and Joseph, each character is described as a "righteous man" (10:4, 5, 6, 10, 13). Israel too is characterized as "righteous" (10:20). The author's point is that the righteous are "preserved" (v. 5), "rescued" (v. 6), "guided" (vv. 10, 17), "prospered" (v. 10), "protected" (v. 12; see v. 1), and "delivered" (vv. 13, 15), while the "unrighteous" (v. 3), "ungodly" (vv. 6, 20), and "oppressors" (vv. 11, 15) are punished. If they persist in their wickedness, they perish. Given the movement of chapter 10, as well as the content of the second major section of the book, the climactic and paradigmatic example of how God prospers the righteous and punishes the unrighteous is the exodus. Despite a tendency in this direction perhaps, God's pursuit of righteousness does not amount to a rigid retributional scheme, since the author also allows for the effective operation of God's "grace and mercy" (3:9; 4:15).

The author's use of the Torah clearly privileges the story aspect of the Torah rather than the stipulation aspect. It is likely that traditional Jewish rituals were viewed with suspicion by the author's intended audience, including many Hellenistic Jews in Alexandria; so the author ignores the Torah's legal material in favor of a review of the Torah's plotline from Adam to Moses. Faithful to the Torah itself, this review has the effect of holding together creation and redemption.

infants are part of the praise of "the Israelites" described in Exodus 15:1. If the author of Wisdom can expand on Exodus in this way, it seems perfectly reasonable for a Christian preacher to expand on Wisdom. The compilers of the lectionary seem to have had such interpretation in mind.

1. The text has three foci: Wisdom as nurturer, Wisdom as agent of justice, and Wisdom as enabler of praise. The author describes Wisdom as nurturer, guide, deliverer, rewarder, and leader. This language evokes a divine protection and love that is steadfast and trustworthy, with us not just in times of crisis but on a daily basis. God guides us, not only in the wilderness but on the way to work. God nurtures us, not only with bread from heaven but with daily bread. Yet, like the Israelites who demanded miracle after miracle, we sometimes lose sight of the good things God has done for us and need to be reminded of them. Indeed, the Christmas season itself is a reminder, a time when we remember the greatest thing God has done for us in Christ.

2. Wisdom is also the agent of God's justice in this passage. It is Wisdom who enters the soul of Moses and brings the plagues on Egypt, Wisdom who pours the Red Sea back into place and drowns Pharaoh's army, and Wisdom who casts their bodies out from the waters for the Israelites to see. This is a fearful justice. We quail to be reminded that God is active in the world, and not always to our benefit. We are challenged by this fact to look honestly at our selves and our way of life. Are we doing God's will? Do the food we eat, the cars we drive, and the clothing we wear accord with God's commandment to do justice and walk humbly? What might it look like for God's Wisdom to act with justice in our lives? This text calls our attention beyond the Christmas season, past the first awed moments of the incarnation and even beyond the resurrection to Christ's return and the new Jerusalem. Before creation is perfect, it will be perfected. In the face of God's justice, what within us will be perfected? By the Second Sunday after Christmas we have opened the gifts, taken the wrapping paper to the curb, and popped the New Year's cork. We may have an acute sense of our culture's excesses and be ready to hear a word about justice.

3. Lastly, Wisdom is the enabler of praise. When the people see the Egyptians killed, they sing to the Lord "with one accord." These words are significant because of their resonance with other sacred texts in which heavenly beings sing "with one accord,"[2] as the

2. Ibid., 222.

Wisdom of Solomon 10:15-21

Theological Perspective

"defending hand" of the Lord. Only here, at the end of the passage, is "the Lord" named, with wisdom being the preferred way of speaking of God from the start. While the extent to which this divine wisdom is identified directly with God may be unclear, ideas drawn from Hellenistic philosophy clearly are being used to express God's agency. Thus wisdom is employed in a genuinely metaphysical sense (not merely poetically, as appears to be the case in Proverbs), describing God's agent in creation and the continuing, redemptive interaction of God with the "holy and blameless people."

But the theological elephant in the room of this text is doubtless the gendered representation of wisdom. The pronoun must be "she," because wisdom is feminine. While it may be easier to ignore the significance of a gendered wisdom when wisdom is represented primarily in pithy epigrams, there is no escape when wisdom is the active agent of God's redemptive work. The only theological point one can take from the association is that at the very least God encompasses the feminine as well as the masculine. If this is woman Wisdom, she is not meek, mild, or subservient. It is precisely *she* who did all those things we may typically associate with God's mighty work: delivering, inspiring, withstanding, guiding, sheltering, and leading.

There is a natural approach of Christian theology to such a text as this one from the Wisdom of Solomon that makes ready and understandable correlations to a theology of the Spirit. It works well enough to substitute "spirit" for "wisdom" at every point in the text. Such a change is virtually seamless and maintains a powerful sense of the active agency of the Divine reaching into every historical moment of the salvation story, from the events of liberation, through the days of preparation/preservation, to the culminating celebration on the far banks of the Red Sea. But if Christians want to make that translation, we should consider keeping the pronoun "she" as we make it. To do so will give us the opportunity of hearing in full profundity the claim of this text that God's power—specifically, redemptive and saving power—embraces the feminine as much as the masculine.

D. CAMERON MURCHISON

Pastoral Perspective

This is a needed word for our congregations as well. People of faith face a number of "isms" (such as materialism, capitalism, and political activism) that would lay claim to their sole devotion. Many become enamored with these powerful rivals to the claims of God. It may be easy for some to succumb to the siren calls of these competing ideologies, even believing that somehow these other forces are doing the work of the kingdom of God. Wisdom, though, calls to the faithful, reminding us all of the miraculous deliverance effected by God, and seeks to have us remain faithful to God alone.

It is not only abstract external forces that can affect the faithful. People of faith also face seemingly hopeless personal situations that can lead to despair. I remember an elderly couple on vacation in Florida, thinking everything was going right in their world, when the husband died from a massive heart attack. I picture a young mother tenderly rocking her one-year-old baby on the pediatric oncology floor of the hospital and trying to comfort him, having lost two previous children to cancer before they reached two years old. I think of a faithful couple who had just received word that their adult son had been found dead with a self-inflicted gun wound. I recall a loving family gathered around a hospital bed in the ICU, watching their loved one struggle to take his final breaths. Each of these scenarios could lead to a sense of insurmountable hopelessness and despair. Wisdom stands ready to invite such as these to sing hymns to God's holy name and to praise God for God's defending hand by reminding them of God's previous works of deliverance.

On this oft-missed Sunday of the Christian year, it is well for us to hear the words of hope that come from the Wisdom of God. As Wisdom provides the profound interpretation of life, God's people can remember and live in faith.

W. MICHAEL CHITTUM

Exegetical Perspective

While the exodus may be the climactic and paradigmatic example of God's intent to set things right, God's larger purpose is to set the whole world right. The strategy of addressing the work to "you rulers of the earth" (1:1) is in keeping with this universal purpose, and the grounding of redemption in God's creative work also furthers the author's purpose of appealing to Hellenistic persons, both Jewish and non-Jewish, who had become accustomed to thinking in terms of the universals of Greek philosophy. As almost always in Scripture, the author wrestles with the tension between particularity and universality (see exegetical perspective on Psalm 148, pp. 153–57).

Drawing upon the tradition of personifying Wisdom as a woman (see Prov. 1:20–33; 8:1–36; Sir. 24), the author proclaims that Wisdom's activity is responsible for what might be called a righteousness history that unifies the Torah and God's work in general, consistently vindicating righteous persons and demonstrating the immortality of righteousness (see 1:15–16). In this regard, Wisdom of Solomon goes well beyond the portrayal in Proverbs and Sirach of Wisdom as an agent of creation (Prov. 8:22–31; Sir. 24:3–7) and also well beyond Sirach's claim that Wisdom "was established in Zion" (24:10). Here, Wisdom's work in shaping a righteousness history is indistinguishable from what the Torah describes as God's work (see also the divinelike characteristics of Wisdom in 7:22–23). This is clearly evident in 10:17–19, in which major episodes in the exodus story are Wisdom's doing, including the deliverance of Israel at the Red Sea and the defeat of Pharoah's armies (vv. 18–19; see Exod. 14:13–31). Verse 20 alludes to the Song of the Sea (Exod. 15:1–21); verse 21a may be a poetic description of Moses's transformation from not being able to speak (Exod. 4:10–17) to leading the people in song (Exod. 15:1); and verse 21b is probably an allusion to Psalm 8:2.

Precisely how the author conceived of the relationship between Wisdom and God is not clear. Michael Kolarcik's conclusion is helpful: "The author has gone as far as possible in the personification of God's wisdom without creating a separate entity as an intermediate being between human beings and God."[1] In any case, Wisdom here is doing very incarnational sorts of things, even though the concept of incarnation will not be introduced until a few years later in the prologue of the Gospel of John, the Gospel lesson for the day.

J. CLINTON MCCANN JR.

---

1. Michael Kolarcik, "The Book of Wisdom," in *New Interpreter's Bible*, vol. 5 (Nashville: Abingdon, 1997), 448.

Homiletical Perspective

angels sing before the shepherds at Jesus' birth (Luke 2:14). The Israelites' song is an emulation of the heavenly chorus, if not a participation in it. Although Wisdom does not prompt the song, it enables the people to sing it in unity by giving voice to the mute and infants. The text challenges us to ask whether we are united in our praise of God. In congregations or denominations that are divided, are we able to sing to God as one in thanksgiving for our salvation? What would God's Wisdom have to do before we could sing that way? How would we be changed?

The singing of the mute and infants can also prompt more specific questions about our congregations. Are there members of our communities who are excluded? This question is particularly relevant to communities that include people with special needs. The blind, the developmentally delayed, those who cannot walk: does our worship make room for their praises? How might Wisdom move in our congregations to open their mouths? How will they teach us new ways to praise God?

The inclusion of all people in praise also echoes themes from Jesus' own life: the healing of the deaf mute (Mark 7:32–37), the participation of children (Luke 18:16; Matt. 19:14), and the prayer for the disciples' unity (John 17:20–21). In the Christmas season, it is noteworthy that Wisdom's salvation story is made complete by the participation of infants.

Throughout the text, we are reminded that God's Wisdom is active in the world. As nurturer and agent of justice, Wisdom acts in the world outside us on our behalf. When it opens our mouths to praise, Wisdom acts in the world by entering our souls as it entered Moses's soul. It is good to remember God's presence and activity at any time, especially when we celebrate God's perfect presence in the incarnation.

DREW BUNTING

Ephesians 1:3-14

³Blessed be the God and Father of our Lord Jesus Christ, who has blessed us in Christ with every spiritual blessing in the heavenly places, ⁴just as he chose us in Christ before the foundation of the world to be holy and blameless before him in love. ⁵He destined us for adoption as his children through Jesus Christ, according to the good pleasure of his will, ⁶to the praise of his glorious grace that he freely bestowed on us in the Beloved. ⁷In him we have redemption through his blood, the forgiveness of our trespasses, according to the riches of his grace ⁸that he lavished on us. With all wisdom and insight ⁹he has made known to us the mystery of his will, according to his good pleasure that he set forth in Christ, ¹⁰as a plan for the fullness of time, to gather up all things in him, things in heaven and things on earth. ¹¹In Christ we have also obtained an inheritance, having been destined according to the purpose of him who accomplishes all things according to his counsel and will, ¹²so that we, who were the first to set our hope on Christ, might live for the praise of his glory. ¹³In him you also, when you had heard the word of truth, the gospel of your salvation, and had believed in him, were marked with the seal of the promised Holy Spirit; ¹⁴this is the pledge of our inheritance toward redemption as God's own people, to the praise of his glory.

Theological Perspective

The purpose of the Letter to the Ephesians is to instruct a specifically Gentile audience what it means to be Christian. These opening verses state that meaning very grandly. Through the medium of Jesus Christ, the author tells his readers, they were chosen as children of God since before the creation itself, as a part of God's very plan eventually to "gather up all things in him." So the passage places their Christian identity, and by extension our own, in context of the whole history of God's working. Two fruitful concepts that have roots in this passage are *election* and *recapitulation*.

The idea of *election*—that is, God's choosing of persons—has been intensely discussed, especially in the West since Augustine. This passage has been key. Comparison with another key passage, Romans 9, will help to highlight what this one contributes to the discussion. In the Romans passage, an anguished Paul had considered the apparent rejection of the gospel by his fellow Jews in light of the question of election. In the process he asserted, as a principle, the mysteriousness of God's workings: God "has mercy on whomever he chooses, and he hardens the heart of whomever he chooses" (v. 18). Here in Ephesians, the writer similarly has in mind the idea of election as a matter of God's freely chosen purpose and echoes the Romans passage, which he surely knew. The

Pastoral Perspective

The following exchange is fictitious—although quite plausible—imagining the voices and perspectives of three particular friends.

Aaron, the traditionalist: Attention to the opening lines of this letter from Paul to the church at Ephesus is among the most-needed antidotes to the nihilism and moral confusion so evident in the world generally, and in our culture specifically—from the inaugural line about blessing "the God and Father of our Lord Jesus Christ" (v. 3), to the admonition to holiness (v. 4), to the emphasis on Christ's salvific blood atonement (v. 7) and the confirming presence of the Holy Spirit (v. 13). In Christ, and Christ alone, do we find our salvation. By grace, and grace alone, are we redeemed. This stuff will preach!

Bob, the modernist: Aaron, I do sometimes think you exist to get under my skin! All the comments you just made have the effect on me of someone raking fingernails across a chalkboard. First of all, Paul almost certainly did not write this letter (though neither he nor his pseudonymous friends ever escaped their chauvinism). And your obsession with *Father* language is beyond me. Don't you realize this impoverishes the prayer life of more than half the human family and reifies patterns of gender discrimination? Furthermore, focusing on Jesus'

Exegetical Perspective

The movement away from Christmas in the church calendar is the movement from a surprise reordering of the world in Christ's coming to the very fullness of God's restoration and redemption. The Letter to the Ephesians emphasizes the surety of God's plan—both in its recounting of the whole plan of God *now revealed* and in its explanation of the believer's place within that plan. The structure of the letter as a whole is the movement from the most general to the more specific: the cosmic structure of the world under Christ's rule (chaps. 1–2), the church as holy place/temple within that world (chaps. 3–5), the ordered household within the church (chaps. 5–6), and the individual believer within the household, portrayed as one arrayed for battle with virtuous armor (chap. 6).[1]

Our text opens with a Jewish blessing formula: "Blessed be the God and Father of our Lord Jesus Christ" (1:3). This is a slight variation from the Pauline letter standard that has the opening salutations followed with a thanksgiving/prayer (cf. 2 Cor. 1:3–7). The Scriptures of Israel indicate that the story of the people of God is construed as a journey with God in covenantal agreement. Blessings were a

1. J. Paul Sampley, "Ephesians," in *The Deutero-Pauline Letters: Ephesians, Colossians, 2 Thessalonians, 1–2 Timothy, Titus,* ed. Gerhard Krodel (Minneapolis: Fortress, 1993), 20–23.

Homiletical Perspective

How do you preach on a long benediction?

The exegetes remind us that Ephesians 1:3–14 is one long sentence, one subordinate clause piled upon another, as if the apostle has learned his rhetorical style from William Faulkner, or vice versa. We can try to use the text to make theological points, or we can illustrate the text with appropriate narratives; but the text itself sings rather than discusses, praises rather than tells. The letter that follows is full of theology and of narrative too. There is the theology of the church's unity—Gentiles gathered into the family where Jews had belonged from the beginning. There is the theology of the church's ministry—all the diverse gifts working together to build the church toward maturity. There is an implicit story of who Jesus is, image piled upon image: he is our peace; he is the church's head and lover. There is the hortatory reminder of what it means to be Christ's people—struggling against rulers and authorities and cosmic powers.

But here, at the beginning, is a benediction. The whole letter is driven from God to God in a cycle of gratitude and grace.

What about a sermon that simply noted the passage's movements and strophes, driving toward the repeated refrain: Praise God!

There is a strophe praising God for election (vv. 3–6). Election gets a bad press from us because we

Ephesians 1:3-14

Theological Perspective

Ephesians writer changes the context of that idea and in the process gives it a different focus, for the Romans passage presents the idea of the inexplicability of God's choices as the fruit of Paul's intense reflection on biblical accounts of the acts of God, such as the stories of God's preference of Jacob over Esau, the hardening of Pharoah's heart, and various sayings of the prophets. The author of Ephesians elevates the idea to a general principle, or rather to an event (so to speak) outside of time as we know it: "before the foundation of the world." He no longer focuses, as Paul had done, on the deep irony of the history of salvation. Rather, he wants to impress on his Gentile readers the certainty of their own election as God's "children through Jesus Christ" (v. 5). This choosing, which predated the creation itself, is therefore not conditional on anything that has *happened* in that creation but is rather "destined" (v. 5), as a function of the will (vv. 5, 9, 11) and grace (vv. 6, 7) of the creator.

This strong assertion of *God's* agency in salvation, coupled with the mention of predestination, raises the crucial issue that theologians have debated concerning election, namely, the proper way to speak of *human* agency, of "works," in relation to God's choosing. For Calvin, the fact of God's own "good pleasure" (v. 5) alone as the "efficient cause" of our salvation, implies specifically that the Lord "expressly sets aside all merit," "does not look at what we are, and is not reconciled to us by any personal worth."[1] The Ephesians author's repeated references to "grace," the recurrence of the Greek word *charis* and its derivatives, make this text a great expression of the doctrine of salvation as absolutely free, rather than in any sense conditional. The author of Ephesians also says, however, that God made the choice "*in order* for us to be holy and blameless," which clearly implies the importance of human action, and attempts to make sense of God's otherwise mysterious action. Whether holiness is only a matter of human response to the unilateral action of God (e.g., Luther, Calvin), whether it implies synergy or cooperation between humans and God (e.g., Chrysostom), or whether predestination must be understood only as God's foreknowledge of the holiness of those who are chosen (e.g., Wesley,[2] over against Luther and Calvin), becomes a matter of many debates. This passage opens the way to those

1. John Calvin, *The Epistles . . . to the Galatians, Ephesians, Philippians and Colossians* (Grand Rapids: Eerdmans, 1965), 127.
2. John Wesley, *Sermons*, ed. Albert C. Outler (Nashville: Abingdon Press, 1985), 2:402.

Pastoral Perspective

blood sacrifice turns the Ground of our Being into a child abuser, just as identifying God's grace solely as a response to human weakness reduces the I-Thou relationship into a pattern of codependency. And this *inheritance* language, coupled with the claim that we alone are "God's own people," fosters the kind of hubris that has undermined the church's therapeutic and civil-reconstructive purposes throughout much of our history.

Charles, the postmodernist: Would somebody hand me a shovel, so I can dig my way out of this compost pile of a conversation? Both you guys are locked into the rationalist assumptions of this passage. Don't you understand the deterministic function of such "cosmic" constructs ("before the foundation of the world," "gather up all things")? I mean, the twentieth century—ushering in the "age of optimism" about human potential to make history turn out right—was the bloodiest in recorded history, and virtually all its campaigns of butchery were undertaken on calculated, "scientific" grounds. Think of Stalin's gulags, the Nazis' extermination camps, the U.S. atomic bombings of Hiroshima and Nagasaki. Furthermore, can't you see that assertions about *truth* mask the competition between self-appointed superpowers? Putting a "religious" face on this power struggle makes the irony that much more cruel. Your God, all gods, are killing us—and the planet itself! If we have any survival options left, all such metanarratives must be deconstructed.

§§§

Pity the pastor whose flock has gathered from each of these pastures!

But wait. The geo-cultural backdrop to the Pauline corpus is not unlike the ideological clash summarized above. Remember that this original Christian missionary movement took place both (1) among Jewish communities formed in Hellenistic culture outside Judea and its priestly-temple ethos *and* (2) among Gentile communities to whom Paul and his fellow missionaries were vigorously and radically extending fellowship at YHWH's table. The cultural chaos, then as now, included profound questions of legitimate authority, the applicability of inherited holiness codes and behavioral norms, and the breakdown of religiously sanctioned social hierarchies. One of the most pressing motives for composing and circulating these epistles was to answer questions such as these: How can a harmony, rather than a cacophony, be created from this choir loft of distinctive voices? Is there a center to this swirling whirlwind? What is the particular shape of our set-apartness, and

Exegetical Perspective

significant part of the covenantal formula between a people and its god in the Near Eastern context. Blessing the god was the means by which a recounting of the divine gifts and benefits on behalf of the people was enacted. Israel adopted covenantal ideas as a means to praise God and reinforce its expression of loyalty through faith and obedience: exclusive worship of the one God, covenant stipulations for community life, relationship to God through ritual forgiveness, mercy, and deliverance. Paul's blessing now asserts that the covenant faithfulness of God *to all people* is grounded in the events surrounding Jesus Christ.

Many are the gifts of our God. Paul's recounting of God's activity and benefits on behalf of the people of God centers on the sense of plan and purpose. Note the expansive semantic field in 1:3–14: "chose us . . . before the foundation of the world"; "destined us"; "good pleasure of his will"; "mystery of his will"; "his good pleasure"; "a plan for the fullness of time"; "destined according to the purpose of him"; "his counsel and will." God has always had and continues to bring about a plan and purpose to benefit God's people. The prominent use of the past tense (aorist indicative) indicates the destiny of God's people as an accomplished fact. The gifts and benefits of God are relational, personal, and close in presence. Believers are chosen to be holy and blameless (lit. "without blemish"). This description parallels the language for sacrificial animals and cultic priests of Israel. Believers, like selected animals and priests, have the quality to be in the presence of God. Holiness is a gift of God obtained through Christ's death ("blood") so that believers might be granted freedom from harm's power ("redemption") and forgiveness of their errors ("trespasses"). God's plan has at its core a lavish outpouring of grace and love for human creation such that we might obtain a filial/family relationship with God as children (v. 5, Gk. "sons").

We are made for praise and worship of the creator God. It is both destiny and gift, the very order of things. We come to understand ourselves and our place in God's plan and purpose through the very knowledge of it. God has not withheld this from believers—God openly reveals wisdom and things that previously have been hidden (such as the *inclusiveness* of God's plan, evident in the joining of Jews and Gentiles, see Eph. 3:1–6). Our destiny is "marked by the seal of the promised Holy Spirit" (v. 13) such that we have a "pledge of our inheritance" (v. 14)—we will be God's people. This passage reminds us of God's goodness and faithfulness, motivating our hearts to return

Homiletical Perspective

are eager to protect our "free will." The earliest Christians, including the author of this epistle, were not concerned with debating the philosophical tension between determinism and free will. They knew two things. God is sovereign of all. We receive God's sovereign goodness through faith. Descriptively, both those things were true.

The doctrine of election is finally not so much a doctrine as a doxology anyway. What do we know about God? That through Jesus Christ, God gives grace and mercy. What do we know about ourselves? That through Jesus Christ, we have received grace far beyond any achieving or deserving. What is the only possible response to this affirmation? Gratitude and thanks. "Blessed be the God and Father of our Lord Jesus Christ."

One strophe praises God for redemption (vv. 7–8a). This might be where we want to focus our sermon on the Second Sunday of Christmas. Again, this is not so much an argument about redemption as a lyrical affirmation of redemption. It is a song about Christ's blood—not in the maudlin detail of so many nineteenth-century Christian hymns, but in the strong affirmation that it is only through Christ's loss that we gain God. It is a song about forgiveness. It is a song about generosity. God is not only generous; God is extravagant. In some churches we have tried to make John Newton's familiar hymn less offensive: "Amazing Grace, how sweet the sound that saved a wretch like me" becomes "Amazing Grace, how sweet the sound that gave new life to me." Grace that gives new life is pretty good grace; but only those of us who know what it is to be wretches (not every day, not all the time) have a clue about amazing grace. Because we know God's redemption, we can preach and pray: "Blessed be the God and Father of our Lord Jesus Christ."

A strophe praises God for eschatological fulfillment (vv. 8b–10). To be sure, Ephesians believes that the faithful already participate in God's promise "with every spiritual blessing in the heavenly places" (v. 3), but along with other early Christian writers, the apostle holds that the completion of God's mysterious and blessed plan will happen only in the "fullness of time." The author does not describe the details of that completion—neither the temperature of hell nor the furniture of heaven. Rather with typical *theo*logical emphasis, the author reminds us that God will gather up all things into Godself. The claim reminds us of 1 Corinthians 15:28, "When all things are subjected to [God], then the Son himself will also be

Ephesians 1:3-14

Theological Perspective

debates, and though it surely has not *resolved* them, preachers do well to think these matters through from the perspectives of both their own and others' traditions. There is much richness here.

The notion of *recapitulation*, in contrast to that of election, concerns the ends rather than the origins of God's actions. The writer declares that one of the gifts that the chosen ones possess is the knowledge of the divine plan to "gather up all things"—or as the Vulgate translates it, "recapitulates all things" (*anacephalaiōsthai*, v. 10)—in Christ. The phrase suggests a glimpse of what God intends to occur in the creation in the "fullness of time" (v. 10)—that is, in that end time that is already being anticipated in the present. The Christian writer who has perhaps made the most of that glimpse given here is the second-century church father Irenaeus of Lyons. In the context of arguing for the goodness and singleness of God and for the continuity of the old and new covenants (over and against the so-called gnostics' contention that the Father of Jesus Christ is not the same as the God of the patriarchs and prophets), Irenaeus developed his understanding of the "recapitulation." What Christ did on earth, Irenaeus argues, was precisely to undergo, stage by stage, the whole experience of human beings—thus "recapitulating" it in himself—specifically in order to bring the human together with the Divine in a restored relationship. Thus, as Irenaeus paraphrases verse 10, Christ "summed up in himself all things which are in heaven and which are on earth," *re*establishing the longed-for harmony between the two rather than rescuing us, as though from some alien environment.[3] In fact, for Irenaeus, the idea of summing up or recapitulation as it appears in this passage becomes nothing less than a term for the incarnation itself, in the sense of a reconciliation of the creation to the Creator, just as the author of Ephesians would have it.

JOHN W. COAKLEY

Pastoral Perspective

how is Jesus' lordship different from that of Caesar? This last question is fruitful and has pastorally relevant implications for the contemporary church.

More than ever, we are realizing the truth in the aphorism "what you see depends on where you stand." Scholars increasingly help us locate the historical contours of Scripture, allowing us to view the text in three-dimensional ways. The canon's imperial backdrop—especially that of the Roman Empire for the Newer Testament—allows us to uncover assumptions and histories we hardly recognized before.

When in 31 BCE Octavian (who took the name of "Augustus," meaning "revered") defeated Anthony for control of Rome, he was acclaimed as "Savior" who had brought "peace" to the whole world. One inscription spoke of Caesar as the gift of "Providence," "equal to the Beginning of all things" who "put an end to war and set all things in order." He "gave to the whole world a new aura" and, beginning with his birth, marked "the beginning of good news *(euangelion)*" and thus was "god-manifest," with citizens to celebrate his reign in "assemblies" *(ekklēsiai).*[1]

This is the landscape of *Pax Romana,* the empire that secured *peace, fruitful security, and an expanding global economy.* Is it any wonder that the early Christian community chose the phrase *Pax Christi* as the counterclaim?

This prologue testifies that a new order is unfolding, despite the chains that shackled the apostle even in his writing; that the very foundations of creation are inscribed with our names; that our mistakes do not make us a mistake in God's eyes, for indeed we have been adopted out of the penurious life of the conquered and into the inheritance of the Beloved's. Ground is being laid here with details to follow: that the disordered life of "fleshliness" results in creating "children of wrath" (2:3), whereas "grace and peace" characterize Christ's *ekklēsia;* that the "dividing wall of hostility" (2:14) is destined for collapse, resulting in the welcome of all, whether "far off" or "near" (2:17), turning "strangers and aliens" into "citizens" (2:19) in the empire of God, whose Lord himself abolishes all lording and whose "economy of undeserved grace has primacy over the economy of moral deserts."[2]

KENNETH L. SEHESTED

---

3. Irenaeus of Lyons, *Against Heresies* 5.20, in *Ante-Nicene Fathers*, vol. 1 (Grand Rapids: Eerdmans, 1981), 548.

1. Richard A. Horsley, *Jesus and Empire: The Kingdom of God and the New World Disorder* (Minneapolis: Fortress Press, 2003), 23–24.
2. Miroslav Volf, *Exclusion and Embrace: A Theological Exploration of Identity, Otherness and Reconciliation* (Nashville: Abingdon Press, 1996), 85.

Second Sunday after Christmas Day

gratitude, praise, loyalty, and obedience for the cosmic plan of God in Christ.

One final element in this text needs exploration—the role of Christ. In addition to Christ's important position as redemptive agent as described above (1:7), his key role in Ephesians is as reigning heavenly Lord. As usual, the Pauline thanksgiving (here, the "blessing") introduces key elements that are further developed throughout the letter. Christ has been vindicated from death to assume a reigning role in heaven—and believers, in some way, are raised to reign with him (Eph. 2:4–7). These ideas are found in embryo in verse 3 ("who has blessed us in Christ with every spiritual blessing in the *heavenly places*") and in verse 6 with the use of the unique title of "*Beloved*" for Christ.

The early Christian reflection on the Psalter of Israel provided a means of expressing Christ's redemptive and ruling role. The most quoted psalm in the NT, Psalm 110, stands behind the idea of Christ's position in the "heavenly places." "The LORD says to my Lord, 'Sit at my right hand until I make your enemies your footstool'" (Ps. 110:1). Paul elaborates this idea most fully at the end of chapter 1 (vv. 20–23; "seated him at his right hand in the heavenly places"). The early Christian idea of the "beloved" in the context of sonship crystallized in the portrayal of Jesus' baptism in the Gospels (Mark 1:11: "You are my Son, the Beloved"). Ephesians 1:3–6 employs the image of the *sonship of believers* as adoption through the "Beloved" Christ (cf. 1 Cor. 15:12–28). The Gospel portrait of Jesus' sonship in baptism is based on the kingly adoption of a son as found in Psalm 2:7: "[The LORD] said to me, 'You are my son; today I have begotten you.'" These two royal psalms, Psalm 110 and Psalm 2, form the basis of Jesus' role as kingly redeemer, now ruling over all powers and bringing about the full destiny of the faithful.

To preach this text—and to preach—is to give *assurance* of (1) God's goodness, (2) God's faithful plan for the people of God, and (3) the continual resolve of God to reorder the cosmos with righteousness and peace through the kingly rule of Christ.

ROLLIN A. RAMSARAN

subjected to the one who put all things in subjection under him, so that God may be all in all." (Lots of Christian preaching appropriately focuses on the future of the individual Christian. Ephesians focuses on the future of God.) Because God's plan is unfailing and unlimited, "Blessed be the God and Father of our Lord Jesus Christ." Praise God.

So Ephesians gives us one strophe on election, one on redemption, and one on eschatological fulfillment—three stanzas on what God is doing in Jesus Christ. Then in the fourth strophe the author turns to the believers, the church, us. What does life look like in the light of election, redemption, and final hope? First, believers are incorporated into Christ's own life through adoption. Second, believers live for the praise of Christ's glory. Ephesians enjoins what it displays: faithful life is the life of praise. Third, believers live by the word of truth, believing in the Gospel. Fourth, believers are marked by the Holy Spirit. The author does not here go into detail on how the Holy Spirit marks its own, but Ephesians 4 will spell out what Ephesians 1 only suggests. "And do not grieve the Holy Spirit of God, with which you were marked with a seal for the day of redemption. Put away from you all bitterness and wrath and anger and wrangling and slander, together with malice, and be kind to one another, tenderhearted, forgiving one another" (4:30–32). Because God in Christ has called and shaped the church, because we are adopted into God's own family, "blessed be the God and Father of our Lord Jesus Christ."

It is not easy to preach poetry. Most of us are amateur poets at best, and the strongest poetry (like Eph. 1) is so packed with image and allusion that we tend to overload our sermons and our congregations both. Yet, if we see in this passage a hymn that moves us through the story of salvation—from election, to redemption, to final hope—and then turns back to us, we may find sufficient blessing, not just to preach about doxology, but to preach the thing itself.

DAVID L. BARTLETT

John 1:(1-9) 10-18

¹In the beginning was the Word, and the Word was with God, and the Word was God. ²He was in the beginning with God. ³All things came into being through him, and without him not one thing came into being. What has come into being ⁴in him was life, and the life was the light of all people. ⁵The light shines in the darkness, and the darkness did not overcome it.

⁶There was a man sent from God, whose name was John. ⁷He came as a witness to testify to the light, so that all might believe through him. ⁸He himself was not the light, but he came to testify to the light. ⁹The true light, which enlightens everyone, was coming into the world.

¹⁰He was in the world, and the world came into being through him; yet the world did not know him. ¹¹He came to what was his own, and his own people

Theological Perspective

Biblical commentators have long considered this passage—known as the prologue to John's Gospel—a polysemic masterpiece. Some have viewed it as poetry that draws from gnostic and Hellenistic imagery in order to capture the interest of Gentile and Greek readers. Jesus' title as "the Word" (v. 1) is reminiscent of gnostic figures, and the dichotomies between light and darkness (v. 5), as well as those born of God and flesh (v. 13), suggest, John Chrysostom believed, that the prologue explores terrain that "the disciples of Plato and Pythagoras enquired into"—but even if the languages of these belief systems bear a family resemblance to each other, it is clear that the prologue views Jesus as unique. Instead of reinforcing these dichotomies, Jesus resolves them: "all things came into being through him, and without him not one thing came into being" (v. 3). Jesus even resolves larger dichotomies implicit in the prologue—between eternity and time, between heaven and earth, between the beginning of all things and the things that have a beginning. In other words, Jesus is God's infinite reconciliation entering into time and space. Therefore the dichotomies in the prologue are not epistemological or metaphysical, as in these other belief systems. The determination to stand in the

Pastoral Perspective

This wondrous passage provides a profound theological argument for the entire Gospel of John and introduces most of its principle themes. Initially, it may not seem naturally to lend itself to specifically pastoral considerations, yet the context of the Christmas season illuminates significant linkages to the faith and experience of those who gather for worship and study. Indeed, this passage speaks to the very heart of the Christmas message by answering this question: "Who is the child of Bethlehem, and why should we care about his birth?"

Worshipers during the season of Christmas include many who have only peripheral identification with Christianity and with Jesus in particular. Those who have been actively engaged with the tradition nevertheless bring their own idiosyncratic versions of the generic question above. In the very last days of December and first days of January, most worshipers who gather at services are emotionally spent by festivities—or lack thereof—and may have lingering ambivalence about relatives, overindulgences, or vestigial loneliness. The passing holiday leaves a variety of emotions in its wake that may obscure the profound meanings to be gleaned in the Christmas stories. Much is made of the cultural accretions that have built up over the years,

did not accept him. [12]But to all who received him, who believed in his name, he gave power to become children of God, [13]who were born, not of blood or of the will of the flesh or of the will of man, but of God.

[14]And the Word became flesh and lived among us, and we have seen his glory, the glory as of a father's only son, full of grace and truth. [15](John testified to him and cried out, "This was he of whom I said, 'He who comes after me ranks ahead of me because he was before me.' ") [16]From his fullness we have all received, grace upon grace. [17]The law indeed was given through Moses; grace and truth came through Jesus Christ. [18]No one has ever seen God. It is God the only Son, who is close to the Father's heart, who has made him known.

Exegetical Perspective

In words probably intended to recall the opening phrase of Genesis, where "in the beginning" God's Word was active as the agent of creation, our author succinctly states the basic conditions of the creation of the world. In light of the key phrase in 1:14 ("the Word became flesh and lived among us"), the author casts this opening statement in four stanzas (vv. 1–5, 6–8, 9–13, 14–18) that alternate between divine and historical perspectives, moving progressively to the climactic passage on the incarnation.

The prologue begins with what at first appear to be some abstract speculations on the nature of the Word (Logos), a concept that points both to a word and to the logic that informs the structure of the world, making it intelligible to humans and thus able to be described by words. Although this concept was a key to Stoic thinking, and to the writings of Philo, who sought to combine the Hebrew Scriptures with such philosophy, it quickly becomes apparent that the author is pointing to history (v. 5) rather than to timeless speculation.

The import of this first segment is to make clear that this Logos is divine but does not exhaust within itself the totality of divinity. The grammar of verse 1 makes clear that when one says "God," one has said all one can say about "Logos," but the reverse is not

Homiletical Perspective

John's prologue can be difficult to read out loud, and it is no easier to preach—especially for a congregation coming down from the rich narratives of previous weeks. Shepherds, angels, and even teachers in the temple are all easier to imagine than John's light, glory, grace, and truth. As lovely as those words are, they are largely abstract concepts that the preacher, like John, will need to bring to earth.

This is the second appearance of John's prologue in three weeks, the other being on Christmas Day. The verses shift here, allowing the preacher to consider verses 14–18. In these additional verses John compares the revelations of God through Moses (the law giver) and Jesus Christ (the grace and truth giver). Preachers will note here there is no denigration of the first in favor of the second. Both revelations have come from God, and both have shaped the people of God. This is not a text for proclaiming the superiority of one faith over another.

It is instead a text for focusing on the person of Jesus, in whom the God "no one has ever seen" is made known. Since the First Testament says that both Moses and Job saw God, preachers might spend some time thinking about how those earlier sightings compare to this one. In Jesus, John says, the Word becomes flesh. The intangible light, glory,

John 1:(1-9) 10-18

Theological Perspective

light and to be a child of God is a moral decision to accept Jesus' reconciliation.[1]

Commentators have also considered the prologue a summary statement of the second person of the Trinity and of the incarnation's role in redemption. For Augustine, God's begetting of the Word (v. 1) is analogous to the way words form in human minds: "Thou canst have a word in thy heart, as it were a design born in thy mind, so that thy mind brings forth the design; and the design is, so to speak, the offspring of thy mind, the child of thy heart." Therefore, as the moment in which the "Word became flesh and lived among us" (1:14), the incarnation is the revelation of the triune mind of God, the contemplation of which enables the renewal of human minds: "View what was made by the Word, and then thou wilt understand what is the nature of the world." For Calvin, the first verse of the prologue, "In the beginning," speaks of a beginning prior to the creation of the heavens and the earth described in Genesis. In this way, "the evangelist asserts the eternal divinity of Christ, telling us that he is the eternal God," who is "placed above the world and all creatures and before all ages." God's agency regarding the created order is therefore continuous with the new creation of humanity through the grace of regeneration. For Calvin, the incarnation represents the "new office" of "Mediator" that the "Son of God" occupies so that fallen humanity can partake of the light and life originally given in creation.[2]

Finally, more recent commentators view the prologue as an overture or an outline of John's ensuing Gospel. The words "light" (3:19–21), "life" (6:35–45), "glory" (16:33–17:10), and "truth" (17:33–38) will recur later, and therefore the prologue introduces these governing motifs in order to provide structure to the ensuing narrative. As motifs, these words are not exhaustively defined in the prologue, but become clearer as the story unfolds. In addition, some find in the prologue summaries of Jesus' earthly ministry as it is related later. The references to John the Baptist (1:6–8, 15) anticipate later appearances (1:19–34; 3:22–30), and the central description of Jesus coming to "his own"

1. John Chrysostom, "The Works of St. Chrysostom," in *Nicene and Post-Nicene Fathers*, vol. 14, ed. P. Schaff (Grand Rapids: Eerdmans, 1956), 5. For more on the gnostic or Hellenic imagery in the prologue, see Claus Westermann, *The Gospel of John in the Light of the Old Testament*, trans. S. S. Schatzmann (Peabody, MA: Hendrickson, 1998), 2–3.
2. Augustine, *Lectures or Tractates on the Gospel according to St. John*, in *Nicene and Post-Nicene Fathers*, vol. 7, ed. Philip Schaff (Grand Rapids: Eerdmans, 1956), 10. John Calvin, *John*, ed. Alister McGrath and J. I. Packer (Wheaton, IL: Crossway Books, 1994), 13, 15, 18.

Pastoral Perspective

swamping the humble origins of the observance. Dead trees need to be hauled out to the street, bills need to be paid, life resumes, and a natural yet unspoken question lingers: What was that all about, anyway?

Responding to this query, John thunders with resounding eloquence, "In the beginning was the Word, and the Word was with God, and the Word was God. . . . What has come into being in him was life, and the life was the light of all people. . . . the Word became flesh and lived among us. . . . grace and truth came through Jesus Christ" (John 1:1, 3b–4, 14, 17b). John stipulates nothing less than this: God poured God's own self into human form. This eternal Word was God's proactive agent in the creation of all things—even life itself—and in a paradoxical condescension took form as a baby of the most humble origins. This astonishing proclamation overwhelms the limits of human imagination. More questions leak out: How could such a thing be possible? What does this mean for me?

Questions lurk just below the surface for everyone who encounters this story with any seriousness. One pastoral tack might be actually to provoke these queries in listeners. For instance, consider the "darkness" that did not overcome the light of the eternal Word. That darkness takes many forms, and any given Christmas season provides an ample supply of examples: wars, human devastation, greed, torture, oppressions of every variety, and also the darkness that comes with existential ennui, depression, confusion, helplessness, and hopelessness. All this darkness is unable to overcome the light of the eternal Word, the very life force that continually animates the entire created order, even every individual within the range of the proclamation.

This is a wonderfully hopeful message, nearly too good to be true and nearly impossible to believe: all this "light" in one human—Jesus. The juxtaposition between light and dark prompts consideration of a decisive choice: Do we wish to live in this light's bright illumination or remain in collusion with the power of darkness? The hope rooted within the power of creation itself comes with acknowledgment of the true identity of Jesus Christ. To accept him is to gain the "power to become children of God" (v. 12), which is a matter not of bloodlines but of God's gracious action. To see Jesus in this manner is to see Jesus' Father as well. Seeing Jesus is the closest humanity will ever come to actually seeing God. This is John's claim.

If this is true, the pastoral outcomes spill forward in a wondrous cascade. If Jesus is truly God, then God

true: there is more to God than just the Logos. Since the NT does not contain a developed doctrine of the Trinity, such language makes eventual reflections on the Trinity inevitable. In addition to being the agent of all of creation (v. 3), the Logos is also identified with the terms "life" and "light," both central concepts in the Fourth Gospel. In this Gospel, "life" does not refer to the quality of animated beings so much as to the life God gives only through the Logos, namely, eternal life. In verse 4, such life is identified with "light," providing again the clue to the significance of light in this Gospel. Where light is spoken of, eternal life is also present. Thus when Jesus brings light to those in darkness—when he brings sight to the blind, for example—he is also bestowing eternal life. The fact that Jesus repeatedly talks of bringing light and eternal life (5:24; 8:12; 10:28; 12:46; 17:2) indicates that when John speaks here of Logos, he already has in mind the incarnate Jesus. This is confirmed in verse 5, where the light characteristic of the Logos appears in the darkness of fallen creation. Finally, unable to be defeated by that darkness, the light is a clear reference to the incarnation and, indeed, to Jesus' resurrection from the dead. Thus the very structure of creation underlies Jesus' incarnation, cross, and resurrection.

The next segment (vv. 6–8) turns from the eternal prologue to the appearance of Jesus and to the historical prologue: John the Baptist. The immediate context of this insertion—Jesus as the light—may imply that some had seen that light in John. If that is the case, it is countered by the specific statement in verse 8: John is not that light. Nevertheless John, as a witness sent by God, is central to the appearance of Jesus. John witnesses to who he really is so that those who hear John and see Jesus may have faith in Jesus.

The third segment (vv. 9–13) resumes the thought of verse 5, with the added note that Jesus is the true light, thus rendering all lesser lights unnecessary for understanding Jesus, and therefore God. Jesus is the primary revelation of God in this Gospel, and as the Logos, the divine Word, underlies all other revelations of God. For John, revelation is basically Christ-centered, perhaps most clearly indicated later in 14:6—Jesus is the way, the truth, the life, the only one who can give access to the Father. Verse 10 points to the whole tragedy of Jesus' rejection by the world in whose creation he had been instrumental, indicating that the author has had the career of Jesus in mind from the beginning of his description of that creation. The tragedy is heightened in verse 11—he came home, and his own

grace, and truth of God are embodied in him. God puts skin on those divine attributes so that followers who want to know how they sound and act have someone to show them.

Jesus is not God in verses 10–18 of this text. Jesus is God's Son, who is "close to the Father's heart." Preachers unafraid of body parts may choose the translation indicated in the NRSV footnote: there Jesus is "close to the Father's bosom," an image that evokes the maternal as well as the paternal body of God. While no one has seen God, Jesus apparently knows where to lay his head. Like the beloved disciple who will later lay his head on Jesus' bosom, this Son knows how to listen to the heartbeat of his Father.

While John's prologue is printed on the page as prose, it reads more like poetry. While some preachers may decide to explain the poetry—diagramming John's long sentences and taking them apart—others may decide to answer poetry with poetry—choosing language as rhythmic, mysterious, and bold as John's language to extend his theme. Like John, preachers may stick with Jesus as their subject, reaching further into John's story of his life for instances of the ways in which he made God's light, glory, grace, and truth concrete. On the Sunday before Epiphany, this makes particular sense.

Preachers may also stay true to John's Gospel by focusing on the ways that the coming of the Word made flesh has enabled those who follow him to embody God's word as well. To "all who received him," John says, "who believed in his name, he gave power to become children of God" (v. 12). In other words, Jesus is not alone in this word-made-flesh business. He has brothers and sisters able to do the works that he does and more (14:12), since he has returned to the bosom of the Father.

Almost everyone has a word that he or she has a gift for bringing to life. For one person the word is "compassion." For another it is "justice." For someone else the word is "generosity." For another it is "patience." Until someone acts upon these words, they remain abstract concepts—very good ideas that few people have ever seen. The moment someone acts on them, the words become flesh. They live among us, so we can see their glory.

Congregations embody words as well. Plenty of congregations think they have to embody all the words in the gospel, but they do not. They have to put flesh on only one or two of them. Some congregations do a great job of making "hospitality" real. Others have a flair for "prayer." Every now and then you find a congregation that brings the word

John 1:(1-9) 10-18

Theological Perspective

who "did not accept him" (1:11) anticipates Jesus' ministry in Galilee and Jerusalem (4:1–12:50) as well as his death and resurrection (18:1–20:29). But if this is so, it is clear that the Gospel of John only partially fulfills the promises described in the prologue. Most of the concluding lines of the prologue describe the faithful community's share in the incarnation, in which Jesus' followers become "children of God" (1:12), participate in his glory and truth (1:14), and receive from him grace upon grace (1:16). These events, however, are not fully revealed in the Gospel of John itself.[3]

Taken together, these interpretations in the commentarial tradition justify the practice of reading the prologue during Christmas. As the first interpretation makes clear, the prologue describes not only the way things came to be through Jesus Christ, but the way all things are reconciled through the incarnation. As the second makes clear, the incarnation not only establishes that Jesus is the source of this reconciliation, but invites us to participate in it through the renewal of our minds. Fidelity to the incarnation, then, involves seeing ourselves and our world with the "mind" that is "in Christ Jesus" (Phil. 2:5). Finally, as the third makes clear, the incarnation calls us to participate in Christ's own work of reconciliation. Just as we do not know the true meaning of "light," "life," "glory," and "truth" until we see these words within the narrative of Jesus' life, death, and resurrection, so too must these words be related to our own lives of faithful following. Are we willing to stand with the light of Christ as it continues to shine in the darkness? Are we willing to be children of God in response to God's willingness to be born a child for us? These are questions the prologue asks each time it is read.

WILLIAM J. DANAHER JR.

Pastoral Perspective

is not separate from fleshly existence, but profoundly and intimately present. Our material existence matters. It matters in an absolute sense by virtue of God's blessing it, but it also matters to God relationally. If Jesus is truly God, then God came to share in human experience, human suffering, human agony of every kind—even the most gruesome of human deaths. God is not far away. God is as close as our next breath and bears the pain we bear as well as celebrates the joy in which we exult. This very message is the truth that captured and transformed the heart of this writer as a kind of pastoral intervention.

The theology of John is perfectly matched to our felt and experienced human condition—actually, more than matched. If we are bearing an unbearable loss, God is present in our suffering. If our nation is embroiled in international conflict, God is embedded with us in the human predicament. There is no darkness, even unto death, in which God is not intimately acquainted and engaged, present and powerful, loving and true. Jesus is our gracious companion, friend, savior, life, light, lover—words fail. Yet the Word is the source of life itself, and Jesus is our touchstone and more, our key to understanding and living the truth of his wisdom as John captured it in the fifteenth chapter of his Gospel: "No one has greater love than this, to lay down one's life for one's friends" (15:13). This is the same Word who was with God at creation, the same who was said to be the "light of all people." This paradoxical mystery of power and self-emptying, exaltation and humiliation, captured in the first verses of John lies at the heart of the essential Christian proclamation. This proclamation directly addresses the situation of those who are within earshot of the message.

This situation pertains to human vulnerability. Nothing is more vulnerable and dependent than a newborn: "The Word became flesh and lived among us." When connected to specific and tangible examples of human, vulnerable (fleshly) existence, this statement packs a pastoral wallop.

STEPHEN BAUMAN

---

3. For one example of this interpretive tradition, see Rudolph Bultmann, *The Gospel of John: A Commentary*, trans. G. R. Beasley-Murray, B. W. N. Hoare, and J. K. Riches (Philadelphia: Westminster Press, 1971), 13–83.

people rejected him. Yet it is not unmitigated tragedy. Some did in fact receive him, and to them he gave power to become children of God. Verse 13 makes it clear that one becomes God's child only through faith in Jesus, not by being born into a specific people. In John, as in the whole NT, the people of God now includes both Jews and Gentiles. It is made up of all who accept Jesus for who he is, not of those born into a particular ethnic group.

The climax of the prologue is stated in verse 14: the eternal, divine, creative Word became a person of flesh and blood in Jesus. In this Jesus, God's own glory is visible. As Jesus will later explain, "The one who has seen me has seen the Father" (14:9). Thus Jesus not only speaks the Word of God; he is the Word of God. Jesus not only speaks the truth; he is the truth. Jesus not only does the work of God; he is God. For that reason he is the source of boundless grace (v. 16). Jesus is the source of grace and truth, as Moses was the source of the law (v. 17), the implication being that in Jesus a new order has arrived—based on accepting God's grace in Jesus, not on being a member of the group that received the law. Interestingly enough, no contrastive "but" connects the two clauses about law and about grace and truth. They are simply two declarations about God's dealing with creation.

That is the God who is made known in Jesus (v. 18). God remains beyond the realm of human perception. For our Gospel, knowledge of God can only be mediated, not received directly. And the one who mediates that knowledge is Jesus, who, as the beginning of the prologue makes clear, was with God prior to all creation and remains with God in all eternity.

PAUL J. ACHTEMEIER

"prophetic" to life, while there is another one around the block that puts skin on the word "service." Congregations like these know that when you preach the gospel, it is not always necessary to use words. By the grace of God, you may also volunteer your own flesh for bringing the words to life.

Of course congregations can also bring some deadly words to life, the same way individuals can. "Judgment" can be a real killer. So can "busy" and "self-absorbed." Since it is sometimes hard to tell whether you are embodying the words you mean to embody or letting some other, more malignant, words leak through, asking other people to guess your words can be a great help. When a visitor leaves a church service on a Sunday morning, what are the first three words that come to her mind? A preacher might ask the members of a congregation what they hope those words might be (as well as what they fear those words might be). It is never too late to bring one of God's life-giving words to life.

Preachers who decide to explain John's poetry will highlight his literary genius. He has essentially rewritten the opening verses of Genesis in his prologue, placing the Word with God from the beginning. Like Sophia (see Prov. 8:22–31), the Word was God's companion in creation. Unlike her, the Word was not God's creation but the true light of God (v. 9). Much later in the story, when the soldiers come to arrest Jesus in the garden, they will bring lanterns and torches as well as weapons with them (18:3). John alone includes this ironic detail, underscoring the blindness of those who bring lights to arrest the Light of the world.

With the season of Epiphany dawning this coming week, preachers who follow any of these leads will make sure that "Light" is capitalized, in the minds of the congregation if not in the text—for the coming of the Light is what John announces, in the person of Jesus Christ.

BARBARA BROWN TAYLOR

Isaiah 60:1-6

> [1]Arise, shine; for your light has come,
>   and the glory of the LORD has risen upon you.
> [2]For darkness shall cover the earth,
>   and thick darkness the peoples;
>   but the LORD will arise upon you,
>   and his glory will appear over you.
> [3]Nations shall come to your light,
>   and kings to the brightness of your dawn.
>
> [4]Lift up your eyes and look around;
>   they all gather together, they come to you;

Theological Perspective

H. Richard Niebuhr likens revelation to a moment when we are reading a "difficult book, seeking to follow a complicated argument, [and] we come across a luminous sentence from which we can go forward and backward and so attain some under-standing of the whole."[1] The same might be said for an epiphany. There comes some moment when an important truth suddenly becomes clear, and we can reinterpret our past and rethink our way forward in light of it. At Epiphany—one of the most important and neglected holidays of the Christian year—we come to one of those moments when an event, the first revelation of Christ to the Gentiles, grabs hold of us and changes everything. Now the past makes sudden sense; now the future calls for a new direction. Epiphany points us to God's universal love and universal sovereignty.

In light of Christ's revelation to the Gentiles—in this case, the wise men from the East who come following a star and find a child—a theme of central importance in the Hebrew Bible suddenly crystallizes for us, so that we understand God's self-revelation in the history of Israel differently and lean into God's coming reign with renewed hope. Our passage from

1. H. Richard Niebuhr, *The Meaning of Revelation* (New York: Macmillan Publishing Co., 1941), 68.

Pastoral Perspective

In crisp, staccato syllables, the prophet challenges the people of Israel to move out of the darkness and march into the brilliance of God's new day. The prophet's syllables reverberate across the centuries to the people of the new Israel, as the church has long thought of itself. They challenge us to move out of the waiting of Advent darkness and the mystery of Christmas dawning, and march into the brilliance of Epiphany's bright day. The imperative and emphatic tones of this text pose several pastoral issues for the preacher and congregations.

The Darkness Is Real and Pervasive. "Darkness shall cover the earth, and thick darkness the peoples" (v. 2). Thick darkness is not new to the people whom Isaiah addresses in his day or our own. Isaiah's contemporaries dwelt in the thick darkness of Babylonian exile. Today parishioners and preacher dwell in the twenty-first century's version of exilic darkness. The preacher does not need a laundry list of current horrors to set forth what it means to dwell in thick darkness; she can all too easily compile her congregation's own list from daily headlines and weekly pastoral visits. But it is worth the preacher's time to reflect on the fact that Isaiah voices what God knows—the grim realities of life in this sinful world and just how thick the darkness can get.

your sons shall come from far away,
    and your daughters shall be carried on their nurses' arms.
5Then you shall see and be radiant;
    your heart shall thrill and rejoice,
because the abundance of the sea shall be brought to you,
    the wealth of the nations shall come to you.
6A multitude of camels shall cover you,
    the young camels of Midian and Ephah;
all those from Sheba shall come.
They shall bring gold and frankincense,
    and shall proclaim the praise of the LORD.

Exegetical Perspective

"How lonely sits the city that was once full of people! How like a widow she has become, she that was great among the nations!" (Lam. 1:1) With these words a poet describes Jerusalem's despair during the days of Babylonian exile (586–538 BCE). Like a person ravaged beyond repair, the city sobs, its stomach churns, its heart turns over, even its gates and roads mourn, for its inhabitants have been stripped of the life they once knew. Jerusalem stretches out her hands, she calls for help, but as the deadening refrain that runs throughout Lamentations 1 makes clear, "there is no one to comfort her" (1:17; cf. vv. 2, 9, 16, 21).

These grief-wracked words—"no one to comfort her"—convey the only future Jerusalem can see, until the anonymous prophet who speaks in Isaiah 40–55 dares to imagine a new beginning. In the heavenly council, God issues a directive, "Comfort, comfort my people. . . . Speak tenderly to Jerusalem" (40:1–2). The prophet, responding to God's directive, speaks the words he is given, and a message of hope begins to take shape, promise by promise (e.g., 49:13; 51:13; 59:20). The prophet punctuates the promises with repeating imperatives directing Jerusalem to prepare to celebrate what God is about to do: "Rouse yourself, rouse yourself! Stand up, O Jerusalem" (51:17); "Awake, awake! . . . Put on your beautiful garments, O Jerusalem. . . . Shake yourself

Homiletical Perspective

A sermon faithful to this text will begin in the imperative mood. The operative words to the congregation are "Arise, shine. . . . Lift up your eyes and look around." The preacher's goal is to get the people to notice God's rising glory and join in the throng that is streaming toward it.

One place to start is by reminding the congregation what is going on in worship. When we gather to sing praise, hear the good news of the gospel, and bring our offerings in worship, we are recapitulating the drama that Isaiah describes. Sometimes our worship seems far removed from the majesty and drama in this text. Anyone who has ever sat through a worship committee meeting that has dragged on while those present try to untangle ushering procedures and assign responsibility for washing the communion ware may have a hard time seeing the connection. The preacher's task is to keep reminding the people that what we do in worship has cosmic significance.

When we gather to worship, we are in the company of people from all nations of all ages. That is not readily apparent to the casual observer who looks out over most congregations in North America. Churches are still some of the least diverse institutions in terms of race and socioeconomic standing. Isaiah opens the window to something

Isaiah 60:1-6

Theological Perspective

Isaiah jumps off the page in light of Christ's luminous sentence. To understand the content of this epiphany, we must begin with the exiles from Judah as they wait in Babylon for the word that will send them home. In the middle of the sixth century before Christ, things seem as dark as they have ever been, with little left to sustain the hopes of the Judeans. They are exiled from their land; the temple has been destroyed; and the dynasty of David has come to disastrous end. In the midst of a people without land, temple, or leader, Isaiah describes the deep joy that they felt at the promise from King Cyrus of Persia that they could return to their land: the nations that have dominated Judah will ultimately come to kneel before it; the exiles will return to the land; lost sons and daughters will be gathered together again. Isaiah even describes how the sea to the west will pour its abundance into the land and the desert to the east with the wealth of camel caravans bringing gold and frankincense will pour wealth into Zion. The poverty and shame of exile will be overcome when all the wealth of the world pours into Zion and the city of exiles becomes a light to the nations. Isaiah bids the people, "Arise, shine; for your light has come."

But this light that has come to Israel is not for Israel alone. "Nations shall come to your light, and kings to the brightness of your dawn." Throughout the Old Testament, God has used foreigners, outsiders, women, the least expected and sometimes most unsavory characters to fulfill God's will. Although the people and the authors often missed this crucial truth, God has always been the universal sovereign over all humanity and, from the beginning, intended to bless all the families of the earth through the covenant with Abraham.

This first theological theme—the recognition of God's universal sovereignty—points to a second important theme for reflection, especially when the passage from Isaiah is paired with the passage from Matthew: the Christian appropriation and reinterpretation of the Old Testament. When the Gospel of Matthew describes the wise men coming from the East, the writer draws on the rich imagery of Isaiah to do it. The exiles likely imagined Israel's oppressors bowing down before the restored nation, paying tribute as vassal states, but Christian tradition has redeployed the imagery of Isaiah for christo-logical purposes. The exegetically careful preacher will be attentive to and respectful of the original context and meaning of the passage. The Isaiah of the exilic community could never have imagined the

Pastoral Perspective

The Darkness Is Thick, but It Is Not Total. "*Your light has come*" (v. 1). Even now, there is light shining in the darkness. It is as though the world were a blackened stage. No house lights are on, no footlights, no stage lights. The actors cannot see where they are going; they grope their way through their scenes. Then from above the stage, beyond the catwalk, a single spotlight cuts into the darkness with a cone of brightness, casting a circle on the floor. The light shines on some of the people who stumble blindly in darkness.

Why have these people, and not others, been elected to enjoy the privilege of standing in the cone of light? Why has the Lord risen upon *them*, the Lord's glory appeared to *them*? The one who shines the spotlight does not say, but it is clear from Isaiah's previous chapters that it is not because they are better "actors" than the rest of the cast. They are merely chosen.

It is grace that has shined this light. Grace has chosen the ones who find themselves dwelling in the brightness of the circle. It is not their light that shines, but the light of the Lord, and it falls on whom it will. Preacher and parishioners would do well to ponder what it means to be chosen and how life is different under the light of God's grace.

Grace Has Its Privileges. "*Then you shall see and be radiant; your heart shall thrill and rejoice*" (v. 5). Those on whom light is shining can see things others cannot yet see: the abundance, wealth, color, and exuberance of life in the new realm. They see the future rectification of the world's fortunes, when injustices are put right and God's proper order is restored. Those who have been forced to pay tribute to foreign powers will in turn be paid with "the abundance of the sea and the wealth of nations," with gold, frankincense, and caravans of camels. The mighty will be put down from their thrones and the lowly lifted up (Luke 1:52).

Isaiah proclaims that the people on whom light has shined will be able to see what grace is doing if they "lift up [their] eyes and look around" (v. 4). If they do, they will be radiant. Their hearts will thrill and rejoice, for they will be able to live with a vision of the new realm, and in the confidence that this realm is already coming to pass.

The preacher and parishioners might lift up their eyes and look around, considering together the question, Where do we see the abundance and wealth of God's realm breaking into the present darkness? And seeing, they can live in the hope and thrill of it all.

Epiphany of the Lord

from the dust, rise up, O captive Jerusalem" (52:1, 2). The call to prepare for God's arrival reaches a crescendo in Isaiah 60–62, the immediate literary context for today's reading, which likely comes from the same prophet, or one of his disciples, working in the early postexilic period.

The opening section (vv. 1–3) begins with feminine imperatives—"Arise, shine"—as the prophet continues (e.g., 51:17–23; 54:1–17) to address Zion as a woman in distress. The days of waiting for the "glory of the Lord" to be revealed (40:5) are over. The days when darkness covered the earth and left people groping like the blind for a way forward (59:9–10) have ended. The light of God has come, and that light, the shimmering radiance of "*his* [the Lord's] glory" (v. 2), the prophet now twice declares to Zion, is "*your* light" (vv. 1, 3). The possessive pronoun "your" signals God's extraordinary gift to Jerusalem, a gift rendered palpable in the gathering of children who will assuage a mother's grief (v. 4) and in the wealth of offering brought from afar by other nations (vv. 6–13). But this gift is not Jerusalem's to hoard. It is a gift of light that shines its promise "to the nations" (cf. 42:6; 49:6), and thus, as verse 3 indicates, all those who see it, "nations" and "kings" beyond Israel, will come to its brightness. The lectionary does not include verses 19–22 in the reading, but interpreters will want to include them in their reflection, for they extend the promise of the "everlasting light" that shines in Jerusalem in eschatological directions (cf. the imagery of the "new Jerusalem" in Rev. 21:22).

The second section (vv. 4–7; v. 7 should be included) also begins with feminine imperatives: "Lift up your eyes and look around." The summons reiterates God's earlier response to Zion in 49:18. As a mother whose children were dead or dying, Zion lamented that God had forsaken her (49:14). Now, once again, the prophet summons Zion to lift her head and see what God is doing. Sons and daughters are coming from far away (60:4), their arrival a first sign that those forcibly removed from their mother are on their way home. Along with them comes "the wealth of nations," gold and spices from desert traders in Midian, Ephah, and Sheba, flocks and rams from Kedar and Nebaioth. Such abundance surely enriches Jerusalem, but here again a close reading of verses 6–7 is instructive. These gifts proclaim "the praise of the Lord," not the splendor of Jerusalem. They glorify God's house, not Zion's.

The reference to the "nations" coming to Zion's light (v. 3), their offerings in hand (vv. 4–7), merits further comment. Such language, especially when

more that is going on: God is gathering the multitudes. The local gathering that hears the sermon on this text may seem like a stunted version of the sacred throng in Isaiah, but the worshiping congregation is a representation of something beyond itself. It is the resident manifestation of God's expansive realm. No congregation can ever be a complete reflection of the variety of all the people God means to gather together. Even the magi of Matthew 2 (who are brought to mind by v. 6) are pale incarnations of Isaiah's vision. The best those wise men could do was to represent the nations bringing their treasures to the Lord. Yet even they are apt reminders of the larger drama described in Isaiah. When we gather to worship, we are part of that spectacle. An Epiphany sermon on this text will be aware of that context.

The sermon can also challenge the congregation to live into the promise that people of all nations will one day gather together to worship the Lord, even as they gather in their separate places on any given Lord's Day. Sometimes the very things people love most about their churches are the things that keep them from fulfilling the mission of being a light to the world that beckons others to Christ. Many churches that take pride in saying, "We are a friendly church," really mean they are friendly to each other. Isaiah's vision reminds us that the healing and solace we find in the community of faith are not the ultimate reason the church exists. God restores us to wholeness within the community of faith so that we can take our place in the procession and make room for others to join us.

A sermon that shows the church its place in Isaiah's vision needs to address both the satisfaction and the despair it is likely to elicit in its hearers. There is satisfaction in knowing that you are part of something much greater than yourself. It is uplifting to know that you belong to the multitude that includes the magi, saints, martyrs, and faithful people of all generations. There is also disappointment in realizing how far your particular community of faith is from embodying that cosmic reality. This is the point where specific examples can help the congregation envision what it looks like to be that sacred throng in its particular context. Depending on the circumstance, the preacher can point out ways Isaiah's vision is being realized in the church's life and suggest ways the church can live further into that vision. Some churches form genuine partnerships with local faith communities that have a different racial ethnic or socioeconomic

Isaiah 60:1-6

Theological Perspective

use to which Christians put these verses. Does that mean that using the Old Testament in this way is invalid, exegetically careless, or disrespectful of the pre-Christian past?

Niebuhr's proposal about the nature of revelation is especially useful for addressing this question. If the incarnation is the luminous sentence, "the event in our history which brings rationality and wholeness into the confused joys and sorrows of personal existence and allows us to discern order in the brawl of communal histories,"[2] then it is entirely legitimate to reimagine meanings for texts far beyond what they might originally have borne. This does not excuse us from carefully investigating and respectfully presenting texts in their original contexts; but neither does it prohibit us from making new use of them. Christ, the luminous sentence, sheds new light on the past. The thoughtful preacher can fully affirm that Isaiah means what Isaiah might never have meant, that the nations come to the light of Israel to bow down before an entirely different kind of king.

Epiphany reveals that even in his infancy Jesus Christ is for all humanity, not only for the chosen few. He is for the outsiders; he comes to draw people together: wise men from the East, Syrians from the north, Egyptians from the south, Romans from the west. The truth that grasps us in the moment of epiphany, the moment when Christ is revealed to the Gentiles, is that Jesus Christ is the very love of God incarnate, and that love cannot be confined to ethnic or national identity; it cannot be restricted by gender or claimed only by the powerful and privileged. Jesus Christ, as the new king of Israel, is in fact, Jesus Christ the sovereign ruler over all the earth. In him, at last, God's promise that Israel will be a light to the nations is fulfilled. The expansive scope of God's love in Jesus Christ means that all are invited, all are included. God's sovereign grace reaches out and calls in every last one of God's beloved children who will come from every compass point to worship God, to kneel before Christ, and to dine at the heavenly banquet.

KENDRA G. HOTZ

Pastoral Perspective

Grace Also Has Its Responsibilities. *"Arise! Shine!"* (v. 1). This is not an invitation. It is a command. The light has not come merely to rescue a chosen few from darkness. The light has come so that others will be drawn out of the darkness into the circle of light. "Nations shall come to your light, and kings to the brightness of your dawn" (v. 3). Grace elects not for privilege but for service.

Those who are privileged to stand in the light have a responsibility not just to receive the light, but also to respond to it. "Arise! Shine!" cries Isaiah, "*You* have the light . . . now *show* it! Get into that darkness and start shining."

How? How do the people reflect the light? That is the preacher and congregation's task to discern. They must find their own way to arise, to shine, to stand up in the darkness, and to declare, in word and deed, what grace has granted them to see.

KAREN PIDCOCK-LESTER

---

2. Ibid., 80.

Exegetical Perspective

coupled with verses 8–16, may be pressed into a thin interpretation that equates the "glory of *the* LORD" that shines in Jerusalem with Jerusalem's right to lord *its* glory over all others. Thus, the imagery of "foreigners" laboring on Israel's behalf (v. 10), of nations who refuse to serve Israel perishing (v. 12), of the children of those who once oppressed Israel now bowing at its feet in submission (v. 14), may be shoehorned into an ideology of political sovereignty that claims power over others at the expense of obedience to God. The burden of the exegete is not to skip over these texts, and others like them in Isaiah (e.g., 40:17; 43:3–4; 45:23–25; 49:23, 26), but to weigh them carefully against the witness of other texts that extend the horizon for understanding. Thus, for example, the imagery of God's intention to "bring forth justice to the nations" (42:1), of God's salvation extending to "the ends of the earth" (45:22; 49:6), of God's "covenant of peace" (54:10) extending its promise to "nations that do not know" Israel's God (55:5) and to "foreigners" who do but fear they will not be included in God's purposes (56:3–4, 6) serves as an important counterweight to any presumptive claim to know the full truth about God's love and mercy.

The epiphany we remember and celebrate this day is framed by an important reminder. *Before* the summons to "arise" and "shine" is spoken, there is a prefacing word: God comes as Redeemer to those "who turn from transgression" (59:20). *After* the "Redeemed of the LORD" (62:12) have seen the light and committed themselves to walk in its path, there is another word from God: "I held out my hands . . . to a rebellious people, who walk in a way that is not good" (65:2). Such are the expectations that attend the promises from God we celebrate. Such is God's grief when our celebration makes no difference in the way we live.

SAMUEL E. BALENTINE

Homiletical Perspective

composition. Some, often working through their denominations, form partnerships with churches in other nations.

These partnerships are not based on one group giving and the other receiving. Rather, both groups work hard to find ways they can give to each other. Some churches identify ways that public policies or economic trends and housing patterns isolate groups of people from one another, contributing to the social segregation that is reflected in so many congregations. They then find ways they can address the forces that isolate them from those who are different. One task of a sermon on this text will be to help the congregation discern how Isaiah's vision shapes its life together.

The conclusion of Flannery O'Connor's short story "Revelation" can help the preacher envision his or her congregation as part of Isaiah's throng. The protagonist, Mrs. Turpin, is a woman who prides herself on her proper and upright life. She is constantly annoyed by those around her whom she perceives to have fewer social graces, less integrity, and little common sense. One evening at sunset, as she is watering down the hog pen on her farm, a light falls on her eye and she sees a "bridge extending upward from the earth."

> Upon it were whole companies of white-trash, clean for the first time in their lives, and bands of black [people] in white robes, and battalions of freaks and lunatics shouting and clapping and leaping like frogs. And bringing up the end of the procession was a tribe of people whom she recognized at once as those who, like herself and [her husband] had always had a little of everything and the God-given wit to use it right. . . . She could see by their shocked and altered faces that even their virtues were being burned away.[1]

A sermon on Isaiah 60 helps the church hear the voices shouting hallelujah and see the parade of souls streaming toward heaven. Then it guides the particular gathering of believers to find its place in the procession.

STEPHENS G. LYTCH

---

1. Flannery O'Connor, "Revelation," in *Complete Stories* (New York: Farrar, Straus & Giroux, 1986), 508–9.

Psalm 72:1-7, 10-14

¹Give the king your justice, O God,
   and your righteousness to a king's son.
²May he judge your people with righteousness,
   and your poor with justice.
³May the mountains yield prosperity for the people,
   and the hills, in righteousness.
⁴May he defend the cause of the poor of the people,
   give deliverance to the needy,
   and crush the oppressor.

⁵May he live while the sun endures,
   and as long as the moon, throughout all generations.
⁶May he be like rain that falls on the mown grass,
   like showers that water the earth.
⁷In his days may righteousness flourish
   and peace abound, until the moon is no more.

. . . .

Theological Perspective

Core theological convictions about the exercise of power, divine and human, are at the heart of Psalm 72. Recognized as belonging to the royal psalms that were used in the rituals of inauguration, it describes the character and the scope of the power that belongs to God and is expected to be embodied in the rule of God's anointed one. Put in classical theological language, God's sovereignty is mirrored in the king's sovereignty. The passage is in the form of a prayer, a series of intercessions to God, which implies that the mirroring of divine sovereignty in human sovereignty is not a foregone conclusion. It is, as James Mays acknowledges, "not about any particular king; rather, it is concerned with the office and vocation of kingship."[1]

The challenge for Israel's kings was not simply the exercise of power. It was instead the challenge of the character of the power that is wielded. Verses 1–4 underscore this character by emphasizing judging the people righteously and the poor justly, defending the poor, delivering the needy, and crushing the oppressor. And the impact of such rule is described in verses 6–7 as like rain falling on mown grass, like refreshing showers watering the earth. This arresting

Pastoral Perspective

The Scripture passages for Epiphany Sunday are filled with references to kings. On this Sunday when the church celebrates the divine revelation of the Messiah, the prophet Isaiah writes of the kings who shall come to the brightness of the divine dawn. The text of Matthew's Gospel is even more explicit; there, we read of King Herod the Great, the three wise men from the East (who are not identified in the Gospel as kings but have been made so in our imaginations), and the infant king Jesus, born in Bethlehem.

Thus Psalm 72, frequently identified as an enthronement psalm, fits into the readings for today. In most translations, this psalm has a superscription identifying it as a psalm of Solomon, but the text itself is general enough that it could have been used for any of the kings of Israel. As James Mays writes, "It is not about any particular king; rather, it is concerned with the office and vocation of kingship."[1] Can there be any important applications from it for churches that exist outside of kingdoms?

In poetic fashion the psalmist enumerates the qualities of a good king, asserting righteousness and justice as the watchwords of a royal administration. These qualities provide the bedrock on which the

1. James Luther Mays, *Psalms*, Interpretation Series (Louisville, KY: John Knox Press, 1994), 236.

1. James L. Mays, *Psalms*, Interpretation Series (Louisville, KY: John Knox Press, 1994), 236.

¹⁰May the kings of Tarshish and of the isles
    render him tribute,
  may the kings of Sheba and Seba
    bring gifts.
¹¹May all kings fall down before him,
    all nations give him service.

¹²For he delivers the needy when they call,
    the poor and those who have no helper.
¹³He has pity on the weak and the needy,
    and saves the lives of the needy.
¹⁴From oppression and violence he redeems their life;
    and precious is their blood in his sight.

Exegetical Perspective

Psalm 72 is traditionally categorized as a royal psalm, and it is likely that it originated and functioned as a prayer for the Judean king, perhaps upon the occasion of his coronation. In this regard, it is a companion to Psalm 2, which probably also functioned as part of a coronation liturgy. What is absolutely certain, however, is that both Psalms 2 and 72 (and the other royal psalms—Pss. 18, 20, 21, 45, 89, 110, 132, 144) outlived the institution of monarchy. Furthermore, in the cases of Psalms 2, 72, and 89, these royal psalms occupy strategic positions in the final form of the Psalter. Along with Psalm 1, Psalm 2 serves to introduce the Psalter; Psalm 72 concludes Book II; and Psalm 89 concludes Book III.

Since Psalm 89 laments the rejection of the monarchy (see vv. 38–51), it serves as fitting preparation for Book IV, which features prominently the assertion of God's reign (see Pss. 93, 95–99). The effect of the Psalter's final form is to deflect attention away from the monarchy as such and to invite attention to the centrality of God's reign and God's sovereign purposes for the world. To be sure, royal psalms continue to appear in Books IV and V; but the final one in particular, Psalm 144, suggests that the promises and responsibilities formerly attached to the monarchy have been transferred to the whole people of God (see exegetical perspective on Psalm 148, pp. 153–57). The

Homiletical Perspective

The first hurdle to leap in preaching this text is convincing the congregation of its relevance. It is, after all, a text that was probably used in the coronation of kings.[1] In a democratic society where church and state are kept distinct, a prayer for a king who rules by divine providence seems out of place—and there is no way to hide the fact that this is exactly what the psalm is about. But within it there is also a word for us about leadership and what it means to be righteous and just.

The text raises questions about leadership, specifically about godly leadership and the responsibilities of those in authority. The fact that we have authority does not automatically make us worthy of it. We rely on God to help us use it wisely. The psalm begins "Give the king your justice, O God, and your righteousness." The text asks that the king will exercise his authority with justice, righteousness, and a passionate concern for the poor and helpless. But the source of those virtues is clear: they are given to the king by God.

In fact, the extent of the king's authority depends on how he embodies those God-given virtues. The psalmist tells us that foreign kings will pay him tribute "*for* he delivers the needy when they call"

1. Mitchell Dahood, *Psalms 51–100* (New York: Doubleday, 1968), 222.

Psalm 72:1-7, 10-14

Theological Perspective

rendition of power and sovereignty not merely as authoritative rule but as authoritative rule that delivers the needy (vv. 12–14) differentiates power in God's hands sharply from power in human hands. The sovereignty for which this psalm prayer intercedes "is the creation of God's kingdom, a human community not left on its own or potentially victim to whatever strong forces seek to control and dominate others, but rather truly shepherded and secured by God's rule through the human ruler."[2]

Of course even cursory knowledge of the history of Israel's kings reveals that this ideal for the mirroring of God's justice in the dominion of those kings did not regularly come to fruition. The association of this psalm with Solomon, who did choose to pray for wisdom to judge his people with justice (1 Kgs. 3:3–14), seems appropriate to that extent, but the recorded failures of Solomon's vocation as king show even him as a flawed example of the model. Yet there are different ways to ponder this gap between God's redemptive exercise of power and humanity's too frequent debasing of dominion. Psalm 72, if taken with ultimate seriousness, is regarded by James Mays as a "prescription for failure," creating a tension that led to prophets who looked forward toward "one who is to come" (Mays, *Psalms*, 238). This line of reflection has led in Christian appropriation of the psalm to read it as a prayer for the coming of the Messiah.

Another way to ponder the gap between the divine and human exercise of power is to construe Psalm 72 as so much "liturgical, ideological cant" that serves to benefit the elites who celebrate the liturgy but ignore the embodiment it demands. Walter Brueggemann has acknowledged that this reservation about the functioning of the psalm is in order, but also argues that the psalm continues as a constraint against human acquiescence to the gap. Instead the gap has to be confessed again and again, not just by elites but by the whole community as it listens afresh to the psalm. "The visionary insistence of kingship is that faithful kingship mediates Yahweh's sovereignty precisely in the performance of the transformation of public power in the interest of communal well-being." Elsewhere Brueggemann adds that "the psalm is not only an ideal of what the just king must do, but also a public critique of the unjust king who fails to merit the condition and therefore cannot sustain peace and prosperity."[3]

2. Patrick D. Miller, *Interpreting the Psalms* (Philadelphia: Fortress Press, 1986), 91.
3. Walter Brueggemann, *Theology of the Old Testament: Testimony, Dispute, Advocacy* (Minneapolis: Fortress Press, 1997), 612; and *Solomon: Israel's Ironic Icon of Human Achievement* (Columbia: University of South Carolina Press, 2005), 218.

Pastoral Perspective

reign is built. Most specifically, the king is to be concerned about the needs of those who are marginalized in society and have no other advocate. As this good king governs, the society will be one in which peace abounds and the needy experience the saving justice that God desires for them.

The expression of hope in this psalm for a divinely inspired reign exhibiting good leadership is not a hypothetical exercise. The people knew what bad leadership could mean. In 1 Samuel 8:11–18, the prophet Samuel warned the people about the unjust acts that kings might commit. His list included the confiscation of the best land, the taking of slaves and livestock, and the elimination of the people's freedom.

Two passages from Jeremiah on justice are particularly fitting for the church to hear. In Jeremiah 22:3, the prophet is instructed to deliver a warning to the king of Judah that he should act with justice and do no wrong to the alien, the orphan, and the widow. In Jeremiah 23:5, a companion piece, God indicates that God will raise up a king who will achieve the justice and righteousness necessary for God's kingdom. It is this last verse that has important implications for the church in understanding Psalm 72.

Even though the superscription for Psalm 72 refers to Solomon and we believe it was used in Israel as an enthronement piece for the line of ancient kings, there has been a tradition within the church to see this psalm as a prophetic reference to Jesus the Christ. Certainly the church should remember Jesus' proclamations concerning justice and righteousness, taking note of his actions revealing God's justice. In his inaugural sermon in the Gospel of Luke (4:16–19), Jesus identified his mission as bringing good news to the poor and providing release to the captives. In the Sermon on the Mount in Matthew's Gospel, Jesus pronounced blessings on those who had a hunger for righteousness (5:6). As the faithful church, we can remember how, throughout all of the Gospels, Jesus interacted with women (such as the Samaritan woman in John 4 and the woman with a bleeding disorder in Matthew 9), lepers (whom Jesus healed), and the outcast, like the tax collector Zacchaeus (Luke 19). According to the Gospels, Jesus met all of their needs and provided complete healing.

This can lead to some disquieting questions for faithful Christians. For example, we can ask ourselves: How often have I been less concerned with justice for the poor and the outcast than with my own economic advantages? How often have I turned

Exegetical Perspective

royal psalms, including Psalm 72, thus function in the final form of the Psalter as testimony to God's desire to implement concretely the divine will on earth.

What is God's will? Psalm 72 answers this question directly, featuring a triad of words that are among the most important in the Bible: "justice" (vv. 1, 2, 3; NRSV "defend the cause of" in v. 3 would better be translated "establish justice for"), "righteousness" (vv. 1, 2, 3, 7), and *shalom* (v. 3 NRSV "prosperity;" v. 7 NRSV "peace"). The repetition of these three words in verses 1–7 is intentional and important. It is already clear in verses 1–7 that the establishment of justice, righteousness, and peace is inseparable from the empowerment of the "poor" (vv. 2, 4) and "needy" (v. 4). These two keywords recur in verses 12–14, making clear that justice and righteousness are not to be merely abstract ideals or empty slogans. Rather, justice and righteousness involve the creation and implementation of what we would call today an equitable economic system (maybe even "welfare reform"!), in which the most vulnerable members of society are especially valued and protected (v. 14).

Indeed, utilizing language that is often used of God's activity, the king is to be nothing short of the savior (v. 13; see v. 4, in which NRSV translates the same verb as "give deliverance") and redeemer (v. 14) of the poor and needy and their children (see NIV, which more accurately translates v. 4 as "save the children of the needy"). In Israelite law, the responsibility of redemption in the earthly realm fell to family members; see, for instance, Ruth 4:1, where NRSV uses "next-of-kin" to translate the word it usually renders as "redeemer." In essence, the king is to value, protect, and provide for the most vulnerable members of society, treating them as members of his own family. Everyone is to be treated like royalty!

Not coincidentally, God is described elsewhere as willing and doing exactly what the king is entrusted with in Psalm 72. This is especially the case in Book IV of the Psalter, which, as suggested above, seems to respond to Psalm 89 by featuring the proclamation of God's reign. In Psalm 98:9, for instance, God is "coming to establish justice (on) earth. He will establish justice (in) the world with righteousness" (my trans.; see also Pss. 96:13; 97:2, 6; 99:4). A comparison of Psalm 72 and Psalms 96–99 makes it clear that the monarchy was entrusted with doing on earth what the heavenly king wills (see the Lord's Prayer, "thy will be done, on earth as it is in heaven"): justice and righteousness.

Homiletical Perspective

(v. 12). The implied claim is that God not only pays attention to how we use our authority, but ensures that our authority expands to the degree that we exhibit godly virtues.

God pays attention to how we use authority—but that is not a threat; it is an invitation to participate in God's economy. The king of Israel is God's agent, and his job is to make God's virtues a fact of daily life. This idea calls to mind Paul's description of Christians as ambassadors of Christ (2 Cor. 5:20).

The preacher might ask, how well do we live up to the psalmist's standard of authority? Do we understand it as a gift from God or as a reward we attain for ourselves? Is the listening community on fire for godly virtues? How does it use its cultural authority as the church?

We might also view it from the perspective of the Israelites. Do we expect mercy, justice, and righteousness from our leaders? Do we pray for them to receive these gifts? These questions pose a particular challenge to Americans. Do we believe our nation's massive power and authority derive from our righteousness?

Those in authority tend to view mercy, righteousness, and justice as very good ideas—edifying abstractions—without asking whether they are actually implementing them. This text, however, challenges us to embody those virtues by putting them in very concrete terms. The king will act by giving deliverance to the needy. Deliverance is more than temporary relief. It is a fundamental change, a reordering of conditions for those in need. The king will "crush the oppressor" (v. 4), not talk about how they should stop oppressing. He will "[save] the lives of the needy" (v. 13), not tell them to pull themselves up by their bootstraps. The psalm is a call to action.

The most striking example is the final verse of this reading: "from oppression and violence he redeems their life, and precious is their blood in his sight." In ancient Israel, to redeem a person was to assume the role of family member. It was to seek vengeance if he or she were murdered, or for a man to marry his brother's widow. The king is called to view all those in need as his family and to act accordingly. To redeem a people is to be in a relationship of extraordinary intimacy with them.

Our congregations have authority in our culture; like the king, churches are often perceived as recipients of godly virtues. Do we, like the king, have an intimate relationship with those in need? Do we recognize them as our sisters and brothers? Do we

Psalm 72:1-7, 10-14

Theological Perspective

As preachers approach Psalm 72 on Epiphany, both of these ways of assessing the gap, between God's sovereign justice for communal well-being and humanity's fractured mirroring of such power, have a place. In the Epiphany of the Lord we surely are called to celebrate the reality that the embodiment of sovereign power has been incarnated in Jesus, bringing a light that can never be extinguished by even the grossest human failures. Against them all stands the appearing of this heir of David who has come and who the faithful believe will come again. Especially on Epiphany their voices can join the prayer of Psalm 72 as a petition for the consummation of the reign of God that has come near in Jesus.

Just because of this confidence, the second line of reflection on the distance between God's sovereignty and all earthly attempts (earnest or halfhearted) to practice God's rule can be taken up again. This approach claims the psalm as public critique of the human exercise of power and seeks to reorder it in the light thereof. Translating from the governance of kingship to democratic society, we may speak of the theological and ethical responsibilities of governments and public policies they and their citizenry establish for communal well-being—especially for the needs of the poor. One simple illustration may be noted: in the economic domain we may call attention to the way in which conventional economic lending practices turn biblical tradition on its head and end by burdening most those who have the least in the way of economic resources.

Epiphany, as the day that brings to culmination the celebration of the one in whom the perfect reign and power of God has been realized, invites both responses. Together, they allow us to avoid the pretension that we can perfectly reflect the community creating justice that characterizes God's purpose, as well as to eschew a self-indulgent refusal to attempt to bend public power toward genuine communal well-being.

D. CAMERON MURCHISON

Pastoral Perspective

a blind eye to unjust situations in my community? How often have I participated in actions that demeaned others? Could I do more to ensure that justice will roll down like water?

This suggests at least two courses of action for the contemporary church. First, followers of Jesus need to be actively engaged to ensure that justice and righteousness are priorities for the civic leadership in their towns. Those in civil government who undertake to lead all of the community should model their decisions on the standards set in this psalm.

Second, since the church is now the embodiment of the presence of God on earth, and since we are to emulate Jesus' life and example in the world, people of faith should be the first people in the community in whom the call to justice and righteousness should take root. The people of the church should seek ways in which they can show forth the love of God to all people by working for justice and righteousness. Obviously, this might be made manifest in different ways in the many different communities where our churches stand. Perhaps a church could raise a voice for affordable housing or volunteer to winter-proof the home of an elderly person. Perhaps it could engage in food drives throughout the year, not just at Thanksgiving or Christmas. A church service could be devoted to recognizing agencies in the community who work for justice and righteousness, providing an opportunity for the members of the church to volunteer for these agencies.

Brian Wren, a contemporary hymn writer, wrote a hymn based on Psalm 72 entitled "With Humble Justice Clad and Crowned," which could be used in the worship service on this Sunday. The hymn emphasizes the understanding that the complete fulfillment of God's righteousness and justice was seen in the life and ministry of Jesus the Christ. As the glory of God is revealed to us and through us, we too will be the ones to ensure that God's righteousness will reign.

W. MICHAEL CHITTUM

Exegetical Perspective

When Psalm 82 is added to the picture, it is even clearer that for the Psalms, the fundamental criterion for true divinity is the establishment of justice and righteousness (see Ps. 82:2–4). Indeed, as Psalm 82:5 suggests, the failure to establish justice and righteousness will mean that "all the foundations of the earth are shaken"—that is, the world falls apart! The agricultural and cosmic imagery in Psalm 72—mountains, hills, sun, moon, rain, grass, grain—serves the same function. Only in the presence of justice and righteousness, for which the king is responsible as God's earthly agent, will the world operate as God intends, yielding universal *shalom* (vv. 3, 7; see also v. 17, which echoes the promise to Abraham and Sarah and their descendants in Gen. 12:3, as well as their mission to effect a blessing for "all the families of the earth").

Of course, this pattern of promise and responsibility highlights one of the major aspects of the history of the monarchy—namely, its failure. Very seldom did the kings actually serve as agents of God's justice, righteousness, and peace, thus evoking the criticism of the prophets and their pleas for justice and righteousness (see Isa. 1:17, 21; 5:1–7; 32:14–20; Jer. 22:15–16; Amos 5:15, 24; Mic. 6:8; Zech. 7:8–10). Even Solomon, whose name is attached to Psalm 72, is remembered not only for his wisdom and international influence, but also for his oppressive policies that led to the dissolution of the united monarchy. Eventually the monarchy disappeared, but the royal psalms did not. In particular, Psalm 72 remains an enduring witness to the content of God's will and to God's commitment to implement justice and righteousness on earth. Within the Psalter, as suggested above, there is evidence that this mission, once entrusted to the monarchy, became the calling of the whole people of God.

For the Christian church, Psalm 72 is a reminder that the titles accorded to Jesus by the early church were drawn primarily from Israel's royal tradition, especially "Christ" (Heb. *messiah* = "anointed one" = Gk. *christos*). The author of the Gospel of Matthew probably had Psalm 72:10–11 in mind when he composed 2:1–12. Such an interpretive move should not be understood as a prediction of Jesus' messiahship (although the author of Matthew may have understood it this way). Rather, to read Psalm 72 in the light of Jesus is to affirm the Christian conviction that Jesus truly understood, enacted, and embodied the will of God in a ministry aimed at setting things right, especially for the poor, weak, and needy, and that Jesus called and calls his followers to do the same.

J. CLINTON MCCANN JR.

Homiletical Perspective

see them on Sunday morning, or only at the soup kitchen?

The text refuses to let us keep the pain of the poor and needy at arm's length. Instead, it grounds any authority we have in our willingness to embrace their pain. When politicians tell us they feel our pain, we write it off as a cheap attempt at empathy, designed to win our vote. But the psalmist calls the king literally to feel the pain of his people, to assume it as his own and redeem them.

The image of a king who truly feels his people's pain and redeems them is a familiar one to Christians. By assigning this text to the feast of the Epiphany, the lectionary invites us to read it in the light of the incarnation. Its language of reversal ("deliverance to the needy . . . crush the oppressor") echoes the Magnificat. The image of rulers falling down before the king calls to mind the elders of Revelation 4:10 and the Christ hymn of Philippians 2:10. The language of deliverance, redemption, and salvation calls to mind the crucifixion and resurrection.

Reading the text in the light of Christ's Epiphany turns its challenge on us. The psalmist speaks of a different king, one who rules over his people. But Christians share in their Lord's reign. We are Christ's body, and so each of us is called to the same standard of righteousness, justice, and mercy as the king in this psalm.

This is a political text. It was originally used as a coronation prayer for a worldly ruler. But more importantly, it is political because it expects something of the people. It challenges our approach to social justice and our response to government policies. It challenges our daily lives, where its message of deep intimacy with those in need may be more difficult to hear.

In fact, the text may challenge us more than it challenged Israel. In the monarchic period of Israel, the psalm challenged only the king. In a democracy, it challenges every citizen. In the body of Christ, it challenges every member.

DREW BUNTING

Ephesians 3:1-12

¹This is the reason that I Paul am a prisoner for Christ Jesus for the sake of you Gentiles—²for surely you have already heard of the commission of God's grace that was given me for you, ³and how the mystery was made known to me by revelation, as I wrote above in a few words, ⁴a reading of which will enable you to perceive my understanding of the mystery of Christ. ⁵In former generations this mystery was not made known to humankind, as it has now been revealed to his holy apostles and prophets by the Spirit: ⁶that is, the Gentiles have become fellow heirs, members of the same body, and sharers in the promise in Christ Jesus through the gospel.

⁷Of this gospel I have become a servant according to the gift of God's grace that was given me by the working of his power. ⁸Although I am the very least of all the saints, this grace was given to me to bring to the Gentiles the news of the boundless riches of Christ, ⁹and to make everyone see what is the plan of the mystery hidden for ages in God who created all things; ¹⁰so that through the church the wisdom of God in its rich variety might now be made known to the rulers and authorities in the heavenly places. ¹¹This was in accordance with the eternal purpose that he has carried out in Christ Jesus our Lord, ¹²in whom we have access to God in boldness and confidence through faith in him.

Theological Perspective

The passage is about Paul's apostleship as well as about the cosmic significance of the gospel and the nature and task of the church. These are all themes found elsewhere in the Pauline writings; but here we are no longer watching the emergence of Pauline ideas as they take shape in the heady context of the Corinthians' or the Galatians' early encounters with the gospel. Instead, the author is beginning to create "doctrine." He is thinking about the enduring significance of Pauline ideas for posterity. We may miss the emotional immediacy of the earlier letters. But we *are* posterity, after all, and the question of enduring significance, embedded here in the text itself, is also our question.

As for Paul, the author of Ephesians reminds his second-generation Gentile readers that it was ultimately from Paul that they had received the gospel and that he himself had received it by a personal revelation (v. 3). Paul had indeed written to the Galatians that "I did not receive [the gospel] from a human source, nor was I taught it, but I received it through a revelation of Jesus Christ" (Gal. 1:12). But there Paul was asserting his teaching over against the teachings of others. The implied question was, why should you believe me rather than them? The answer was because he spoke directly from God, from a revelation. Here in Ephesians, by contrast, competing

Pastoral Perspective

Although the apostle does not use *epiphany* ("manifestation") in this text, he likely had something similar on his mind. Something new has happened in Jesus. Better yet, the Word—God's "eternal purpose" (v. 11)—can now be "seen" (v. 9) in ways previously unimagined. This "mystery" is *news* even to the heavenly hosts (v. 10). There is something of a Copernican revolution underway. The entire universe of God's providence has been revised: not only in the context of a Roman imperial venue (the apostle is again writing from jail), but also in the redemptive story centered in Israel's promise.

In the church's history, Epiphany has three traditions. One is to commemorate Jesus' baptism. Another is to signify his birth. The third is to recall the arrival of the magi of "We Three Kings" fame, so often enacted in annual congregational Christmas pageants by children in bathrobes. In each case, the context inaugurates a confrontation between the Incarnate One and those who presently define reality.

As a baptismal occasion, this manifestation inspired Jesus' first sermon in the temple at Nazareth, eventually enraging the faithful to the point that they attempted to launch him over a cliff (Luke 4:29).

As a birth announcement, this manifestation so infuriated Rome's Herodian rule that infant boys in the region around Bethlehem were exterminated. The

Exegetical Perspective

This passage centers on the apostle Paul, the ostensible writer of the letter (Eph. 1:1). The historical questions of authorship (authenticity or pseudonymity) will be left to one side here. As canonical Scripture, we seek to understand how this text functions with the rest of Ephesians to encourage faith in the life of the church. Nothing in 3:1–12 contradicts the autobiographical information given to us in other passages from the so-called indisputable letters of Paul (see Gal. 1:11–2:14; Phil. 3:4–6; 2 Cor. 11:21–30). Paul is described as a prisoner, without any location indicated. References to Paul as a prisoner are common in his letters (2 Cor. 6:5, 11:23; Phil. 1:13–14; Col. 4:3, 18; Phlm. 1, 9) and in Acts (16:23; chaps. 21–28).

The rhetorical form of this text is that of autobiographical narrative. Recent work on Pauline autobiography gives us some helpful guidance on identification and interpretation.[1] Autobiographical narrative was rhetorical in nature: historical descriptions were subject to effective arrangement and promotion of thematic elements of exhortation—not simply an attempt to do comprehensive cataloging of events in a person's life. Autobiographical

1. George Lyons, *Pauline Autobiography: Toward a New Understanding*, SBL Dissertation Series 73 (Atlanta: Scholars Press, 1985), 17–73, 223–27.

Homiletical Perspective

In many of our congregations and denominations, we spend a fair amount of time puzzling about what God intends to do with the Jewish people. The crude way to put the question is, "Will the Jews be saved?" The more sophisticated way is to ask, "What is the role of God's covenant with the Jewish people in this time of God's covenant in Jesus Christ?"

The question for the writer of Ephesians and for most of the first generation of Christians was very different: "Will the Gentiles be saved?" Or "What is the role of God's covenant in Jesus Christ *given the fact that God's covenant with the Jews is irrevocable?*"

From time to time, every preacher would do well to talk honestly and clearly with the congregation about the relationship between Christians and Jews in God's providence. For congregations steeped in the language of the Gospels of Matthew and John, it may sometimes seem that God has finished with the synagogue and encamped exclusively in the church.

That is probably too simple a reading of those Gospels, and it is directly contradictory to what we find in Ephesians or in Romans 9–11. In light of Ephesians, one could preach a helpful sermon on the fact that God has called Israel and that God does not renege on that calling. For Ephesians the mystery, the surprise hidden from the beginning of time, is that Gentiles are welcome into God's family too.

Ephesians 3:1-12

Theological Perspective

teachers are not the issue. The point is rather to explain to readers the meaning of teaching they have already accepted. The implied question is not about the *authority* of Paul's teaching but rather about its *significance*. To say that he had it from revelation becomes now a way of saying how momentous it is. Momentous indeed, it is in fact a "mystery" that concerns God's very "plan" (v. 9), now revealed for the first time (v. 5)—and they, the Gentiles, are essential to that plan, "sharers in the promise" (v. 6).

Presented this way, the theme of the *newness* of the gospel looms large. What has been made known to us was "in former generations . . . not made known to humankind" (v. 5). This is an important point for preaching. It resonates with Jesus' claim to have revealed "things hidden from the foundation of the world" (Matt. 13:35)—and, fundamentally, with believers' essential experience of the gospel as "making all things new" (Rev. 21:5).

But the declaration of newness here also implies a problem. For what about the Old Testament? Is the author ignoring it? Already in the fourth century, John Chrysostom asked in this context whether the truth of the gospel was indeed not "made known" before the time of the apostles. For "how can Christ say . . . that Moses and the prophets wrote 'these things about me'?"[1] Was the truth of the gospel then so new? There is an obvious answer, which in fact Chrysostom (and after him many other interpreters) supplied: namely, that the gospel was always known, but not in its "completeness." Thus John Calvin would later write that the prophets had indeed prophesied that "at the advent of the Messiah, the grace of God would be proclaimed throughout the whole world," but they had "left the time and manner undetermined." It is in this sense that the Ephesians author can speak of newness.[2]

This is all well and good, but one wonders if the answer quite does justice to the passage at hand. Of course Calvin and Chrysostom have it right that the truth of gospel is present throughout the Scriptures. Yet in fact this is not a truth that the Letter to the Ephesians acknowledges by itself. The Ephesians author, presenting the gospel as something new, tends to ignore the relation of the church to Israel (past or present), which it in effect replaces. In this sense, Ephesians stands in some tension with the undisputed letters of Paul and indeed with much of

---

1. Quoted in *Ancient Christian Commentary on Scripture: New Testament*, vol. 8, ed. Mark J. Edwards (Downers Grove, IL: InterVarsity, 1999), 147.
2. John Calvin, *The Epistles . . . to the Galatians, Ephesians, Philippians and Colossians* (Grand Rapids: Eerdmans, 1965), 160.

Pastoral Perspective

threat prompted Mary and Joseph to flee with baby Jesus to Egyptian political sanctuary (Matt. 2:13–16).

As an announcement of international import, the manifestation implicated visiting dignitaries ("from the East") in a web of political intrigue, forcing them to take back roads out of town and out of reach of despotic revenge.

Common to each variant is the insistence that this manifestation of God's intent will disrupt the world as presently defined. Those for whom this "world" is "home"—all who profit from current arrangements, from orthodoxies of every sort—will take offense at this swaddling-wrapped revolt. Something new is being built; a new cornerstone (Eph. 2:20) is being laid. That is the good part. The bad part is that existing structures may be razed to make room.

To understand the goodness of this news, one of our first pastoral tasks is to ask, For whom is this news *bad*?

The primary scandal on which the apostle focused within the early Jesus movement involved something akin to racial/ethnic discrimination. There were some among the Jews who had inverted the Hebrew people's "election" by God for redemptive purpose into the assumption of being God's elite. For them, the world was divided between Jews and non-Jews (as today we divide the population between white and nonwhite). The Gentiles—goyim—were the *others*. Much like what happened at the 1787 U.S. Constitutional Convention, where it was agreed that each African American slave would count as three-fifths of a person, the Gentiles came up short in the alleged divine apportionment scheme.

No wonder, then, the shock over the apostle's insistence that the *others* were no longer strangers and aliens but now fellow heirs, members of the same body, sharers in the promise. For some, the apostle's "dividing wall" of "hostility" (2:14) was actually a retaining wall, a provision of sanctuary, a needed safeguard, and essential security "fence."

The religious overlords of the day were not happy, even within significant parts of the Jesus movement. Their world was being deconstructed. The apostle was assaulting sacred demarcations, breaching holy boundaries, challenging the "historical understanding" of the faith; and, by implication, threatening the very character of God. It was a lot to swallow—probably even for some Gentile Christians who, in their new-convert enthusiasm, wanted to be completely immersed in the inherited protocol of righteous standing.

This new thing God is doing, the apostle emphasized, was not absolutely new. It was embedded

information will (1) build the ethos (character) of the writer as one to imitate because of his or her consistency in words and deeds, (2) reinforce a key theme(s) already introduced in the letter, and (3) exhort hearers without giving the impression of self-boasting.

Chapter 3 of Ephesians (our text, Eph. 3:1–12, and the prayer that follows in 3:14–21) is clearly delineated in the flow of the letter. The final verses of chapter 2 indicate the growth and joining together found in the *household of God*—the holy temple/dwelling place of God. Chapter 4 picks up this image of the household of God and begins to elucidate it as the building up and knitting together of the *body of Christ*. Tucked in between is our chapter 3, introduced by Paul, the *prisoner*. After chapter 3 solidifies Paul's role in and devotion to the divinely ordained movement of the gospel, Paul begins to exhort his readers by first repeating his designation as *prisoner* once more in 4:1.

Ephesians 3:1–12, then, functions as an important digression, and it contains autobiographical remarks that build Paul's character as a teacher about community growth. These remarks are sparse: Paul as prisoner; his call to and stewardship of the gospel; his status as "the very least of all the saints" (cf. 1 Cor. 15:9). The purpose of our passage is to review and reiterate a certain theme that, as Paul puts it, "I wrote [about] above in a few words" (3:3). This important theme, this "mystery" revealed to Paul by revelation, this fruition of God's divine plan hidden previously to humankind, is now evident: "the Gentiles have become fellow heirs, members of the same body, and sharers in the promise of Christ Jesus through the gospel" (3:6). These "few words," of course, are contained in the rather lengthy passage of 2:11–19. Hence, the autobiographical narrative is repeating and reinforcing a previous theme as expected. Paul knows this gospel, proclaims it to Gentiles, and lives in such a way as to bring full harmony between Jews and Gentiles as destined by God's plan. This is *worthy of imitation on the part of believers*—and Paul, as a teacher, is worthy to be listened to with regard to community instruction (4:1ff).

Following his drawing out of the mystery of God's plan—the inclusion of the Gentiles and Jews into God's people by the work of the creator God in Christ Jesus—Paul gives result and purpose to this new twist: "so that through the church the wisdom of God in its rich variation might now be made known to the rulers and authorities in the heavenly places" (3:10). This verse sets the stage for the

Another possible motif for the preacher is to suggest the ways in which God continues to reach out surprisingly to people we might have thought beyond the pale of God's mercy. The Jewish Christians of the time of Ephesians were apparently surprised to discover that God had invited the Gentiles to God's mercy too. What divine invitations have we failed to notice, or even opposed?

Another way to preach the text would be to play it over against the Epiphany Gospel text, the visit of the magi. In that story, the Gentiles come from afar to seek Jesus. In Ephesians, it is God in Christ who has set out to seek the Gentiles. The Ephesians text is not about wise men who figure out the astrological signs that lead to Bethlehem. The text is about God's hidden wisdom now revealed to all of humankind in Jesus Christ (see v. 11). And while in Matthew's Gospel the Gentile magi bring riches to Christ, in Ephesians the apostle brings the "boundless riches of Christ" to the Gentiles.

The preacher will also notice that the word "mystery" (*mysterion*) appears three times in the Greek version of our text, in verses 3, 4, 9. (The NRSV rightly uses "mystery" again in v. 5 as the implied subject of the verb.) A sermon might pick up on the fact that whereas in contemporary parlance a mystery is a puzzle to be solved, for Ephesians a mystery is a treasure to be revealed. Mysteries are hidden because God has the power to hide and to reveal. (Words for "reveal," "revelation," or "make known" occur in vv. 3, 5, 9, 10.)

In the early Latin translation of the New Testament, the Greek word *mysterion* is translated *sacramentum*. Not only is Ephesians' understanding of mystery somewhat different from our contemporary understanding, but Ephesians' understanding of "sacrament" is somewhat different from the understanding of the later church. For Ephesians, the one true sacrament is Jesus Christ, intended by God from before the ages to be the full revelation of God's astonishing grace. The secondary sacrament is the mysterious and magnificent fact that all humankind—Gentiles as well as Jews—now have access to God.

Another possible theme for preaching is the strong stress on God's eternal, and sometimes hidden, purposes. There is no hint in Ephesians of the claim that Jesus was God's great Plan B. There is no suggestion that it was only when God's original strategy for the redemption of the world went bust that God determined to send Jesus as a last resort. Jesus is the first resort of the mystery of God, God's

Ephesians 3:1-12

Theological Perspective

the rest of the New Testament. But we should at least listen to it in its own right, before adding the rest of the truth from other scriptural sources.

Finally, the passage makes reference to the "rulers and authorities," to which "through the church the wisdom of God in its rich variety might now be made known" (v. 10). We know now that these "rulers and authorities" or "powers," which appear often in the Pauline writings, are not to be understood simply as supernatural beings. Rather, they signify the very forces at work in human life or, as Walter Wink has put it, "all the tangible manifestations which power takes," including prevailing cultural practices and ideas, social and political systems, and institutions.[3] They are not in themselves evil, but are part of God's good creation. Yet as a function of sin in the world they tend to be demonic, claiming our allegiance in place of God, and thus must be "disarmed" and defeated (Col. 2:15).

What is unique about the present passage is that only here is the *church* explicitly pictured as confronting these powers and principalities. In Ephesians, the church indeed appears more explicitly as a theme—as something to be considered in its own right—than anywhere else in the New Testament. Whereas in the undisputed letters, Paul tends to think about the nature of the church only when addressing particular situations (e.g., 1 Cor. 12), here in Ephesians the church is something coherent and universal. For instance, the author describes it as a metaphorical building with foundation and cornerstone (2:19–22; cf. 4:11–16) or personifies it as Christ's bride (5:21–23). So too here, the author is thinking in large terms: as something new and vital in the history of the world, the church brings the gospel to bear on all the workings of society.

JOHN W. COAKLEY

Pastoral Perspective

from the beginning of God's "eternal purpose," now becoming manifest—brought to the light, revealed—in Christ Jesus. Maybe the apostle, steeped in Torah training, was stumbling onto the obscured implication of the promise made by God to Abram: that Sarai was not forgotten, was "known" by God, and that together they would be a blessing to many nations.

Novelist Flannery O'Connor is credited with this startling paraphrase of the well-known line from John's Gospel: "You shall know the truth, and the truth will make you odd." Immersion in the "mystery" of Christ is surely an odd-making adventure. But there is another factor at work as well, which might be captured in a similar reworking of John's line: "You shall know the truth, and the truth will set you free. But first it will make you miserable."

The misery factor in spiritual formation is an implication of the new cornerstone being laid, of the dividing wall crumbling, of the "new creation" (2 Cor. 5:17) emerging. This dislocating, deconstructing experience does not mean God is a sadist and likes to see us squirm. It is simply the detoxifying process that accompanies the recovery from addiction to "the way things are."

For pastoral leaders charged with guiding congregations into this new creation—bringing down hostile walls both within and without—one comprehensive way to imagine the task is by asking, What are the borders that need to be crossed, the boundaries that need to be broached, the walls that need to fall? What are the "human traditions" (Col. 2:8) that are confusing and confounding the believing community's confessional practice? Given our habits of trusting only what we can see with our eyes, how can we strategically locate ourselves in compassionate proximity with those who are battered, bruised, and broken by the world's reigning *disorder?* Where, and how, can we intentionally place ourselves in ways that allow our blinders to be loosened, expanded, and eventually removed?

Good teachers know the truth in this aphorism about learning: I hear, and I forget. I see, and I remember. I do, and I understand. How do we develop in our congregations a thirst for being *doers* of the Word and not hearers only (Jas. 1:22)? What does it take to help our folk make the transition from being *convinced* to being *convicted?* How can we recommend the "ministry of reconciliation" so that it is embraced as a *spiritual discipline*—a way of exposing ourselves to the grace of God through Christ Jesus—rather than merely an occasional effort to do kind things in the world?

KENNETH L. SEHESTED

---

3. Walter Wink, *Naming the Powers: The Language of Power in the New Testament* (Philadelphia: Fortress Press, 1984), 5.

remainder of the letter in two very important ways. First, Paul continues the theme of the "church" (the gathered people of God in a particular location) as the means by which God's plan is coming to fruition in the present. "Rich variation" represents the discussion of giftedness and leadership through the Spirit, discussed in Ephesians 4:1–16: "maintain the unity of the Spirit," "each of us given grace according to the measure of Christ's gift," "the gifts he gave were that some would be apostles, some prophets, some evangelists, some pastors and teachers . . . ," "as each part is working properly, promotes the body's growth in building itself up in love." Second, Ephesians 3:10 indicates that the work of the church *in doing good* contests with the powers and authorities in the heavenly places—the church living rightly makes extension of the risen Christ's rule (Eph. 1:8b–14). Thus in Ephesians 4:17–5:20 Paul exhorts the church, "Live as children of light—for the fruit of the light is found in all that is good and right and true" (5:8b–9), "take no part in the unfruitful works of darkness, but instead expose them" (5:11).

Paul's autobiographical remarks are carefully constructed with respect to the issue of self-boasting. He makes no dramatic claims, disparages no one else, and downplays his own self-importance ("a prisoner," "wrote . . . in a few words," "I am the very least of all the saints"). The key element here is attribution of all credit to the "god" and the leaving aside of any self-claim. This is abundantly evident with the use of passive verbs ("God's grace that was given me" [3:2]; "the mystery was made known to me" [3:3]; "I have become a servant according to . . . God's grace" [3:7]), the theme of the divine plan in Ephesians, and the use of prayer (both v. 13 [left out of the lectionary reading] and 3:14–21).

Preaching and teaching this passage begins with a recognition that the *presence* of the living Lord continues through the faithful living and witness of Christ's church. It is modeled through Christian leaders who prioritize the healing, changing, exposing power of the gospel. This gospel seeks unity in a fallen world and strives to overcome the distinctions in race, class, gender, and other inequalities that hinder the reign of God's generous, overflowing, and infectious love.

ROLLIN A. RAMSARAN

intention from the beginning, God's secret from before creation for the redemption of creation.

Notice too how here, as in the rest of Ephesians, there is a very high sense of the significance and power of the church. This wisdom of God (which is greater than the wisdom of the magi and immeasurably greater than the wisdom of Herod and his minions) has been given to the church—and the church is not called just to share this mystery "in house," not just to mumble churchy things like some secret code among the initiate. The church is to declare this wisdom to the "rulers and authorities in the heavenly places" (v. 10). For the writer of Ephesians there was a close link between earthly and heavenly power. Earthly authorities manifested rules and dominions of more than earthly origin. The church does not sit idly by or silently accede while the powers and principalities do their work. We speak truth to power and the "rich variety" of God's wisdom against the deadly uniformity of this or that official line.

A final theme in our text is that of "access." It might be homiletically fruitful to play with the way "access" is used in our common language today. For example, when a computer shows "Access denied," we search for the password that will let us in. To get access to our money, we use the ATM card and the PIN. For Ephesians, Christ is a little like that, but also so much more. The verbal root of the Greek noun has to do with ushering someone into the presence of another, sometimes into the presence of a ruler. The Greek texts seem to suggest that Jesus Christ is the one who ushers us into the presence of God. Jesus Christ is the host, the guide, the door, the maitre d' at the great feast of God's mercy, where the table is prepared for Jews and Gentiles alike. Here is a most astonishing feast for a most astonishing group of guests.

DAVID L. BARTLETT

Matthew 2:1-12

¹In the time of King Herod, after Jesus was born in Bethlehem of Judea, wise men from the East came to Jerusalem, ²asking, "Where is the child who has been born king of the Jews? For we observed his star at its rising, and have come to pay him homage." ³When King Herod heard this, he was frightened, and all Jerusalem with him; ⁴and calling together all the chief priests and scribes of the people, he inquired of them where the Messiah was to be born. ⁵They told him, "In Bethlehem of Judea; for so it has been written by the prophet:

⁶'And you, Bethlehem, in the land of Judah,
   are by no means least among the rulers of Judah;
for from you shall come a ruler
   who is to shepherd my people Israel.' "

Theological Perspective

One tradition holds that Epiphany celebrates the sharing of the gospel with the Gentiles, who are represented by the magi mentioned in this passage. In order to emphasize the universality of Christ's saving mission, early commentators imaginatively reconstructed the physical characteristics of the magi to represent different races and unpacked the symbolism of the gifts brought to the Christ child. In a treatise attributed to the Venerable Bede (672–735), the magi are first named: "Melchior" was described as "an old man with white hair and a long beard," "Gaspar" as "young and beardless and ruddy complexioned," and "Balthasar" as "black-skinned and heavily bearded." The gifts of the magi (2:11) are also interpreted: gold represented an appropriate gift due a "king," frankincense symbolized "an oblation worthy of divinity," and myrrh "testified to the Son of Man who was to die."[1]

Although such constructions are now recognized as historically invalid, they resonate with one message of this passage. The magi are an anticipation of the Gentile Christians of the early Christian community. They know Jesus only from what has been revealed in nature, and thus their grasp of this revelation is not

1. Raymond Brown, *The Birth of the Messiah* (New York: Doubleday, 1993), 199.

Pastoral Perspective

From Matthew's point of view, the three magi were authentic spiritual seekers. Even though their methodology was stargazing, they discovered a remarkable truth that transcended their immediate context and led them into alien territory. In a surprising location far from home, they found what they had been searching for in the birth of a child to a young peasant woman.

We live in a time of great spiritual agitation; our culture is rife with seekers of every sort, who attempt to make their way to the most fulfilling destination as they respond to deep interior longing. Many follow or dabble in myriad spiritual approaches, including ancient esoteric traditions like astrology and psychic phenomenon, as well as amalgams of Eastern practices and Western science. Every variety of religious expression is as available as a click of a mouse or a meeting with one's next-door neighbor.

The church has often condemned or ridiculed these alternative spiritual means and their practitioners, yet in this famous story of the wise men's trek to Bethlehem, Matthew takes a different measure of the integrity of their purpose. Indeed, even Jewish scholars are summoned to confirm the potential in the magi's quest. From Matthew's perspective these foreign exotics are better informed about the nature of this child than most inhabitants

⁷Then Herod secretly called for the wise men and learned from them the exact time when the star had appeared. ⁸Then he sent them to Bethlehem, saying, "Go and search diligently for the child; and when you have found him, bring me word so that I may also go and pay him homage." ⁹When they had heard the king, they set out; and there, ahead of them, went the star that they had seen at its rising, until it stopped over the place where the child was. ¹⁰When they saw that the star had stopped, they were overwhelmed with joy. ¹¹On entering the house, they saw the child with Mary his mother; and they knelt down and paid him homage. Then, opening their treasure chests, they offered him gifts of gold, frankincense, and myrrh. ¹²And having been warned in a dream not to return to Herod, they left for their own country by another road.

Exegetical Perspective

Contrary to popular perception, Matthew does not speak of three magi, nor does he refer to them as kings. The number three was apparently deduced from the number of gifts, although one early tradition put the number at twelve. The image of kings was perhaps deduced from Psalm 72:10–11 and/or Isaiah 60:3. Rather than picturing them as three royal riders outlined against the desert sky, it would perhaps be more accurate to think of a larger caravan including magi, servants, supplies, and the like, who have apparently been traveling for weeks if not months. We are not told how long an interval had passed between the time the magi sighted the star and their arrival in Jerusalem, but Herod's subsequent order to kill all children two years old and younger (v. 16) indicates an extended period of time. They were therefore not with Jesus at the same time as the shepherds, of whom Matthew knows nothing.

The word "magi," from which the English "magic" is derived, is used pejoratively in the remainder of the NT (e.g., Acts 8:9–24; 13:6–11) but here refers not so much to magicians as to astrologers who studied the heavens for portents of significant events. Although many early church fathers assumed they came from Arabia and early Christian art portrayed them in Persian dress, the most likely point of origin for the magi was Babylon, the seat of

Homiletical Perspective

Today's text from Matthew offers a rare opportunity to rescue the magi from their fixed places in the annual Christmas pageant and restore them to their biblical roles as key witnesses to both the threat and promise of the Christ child.

If preachers mixed the Gospels the same way such pageants do, they might do more than put wise men and shepherds on the same stage. In true Matthean fashion, they might announce that a prophecy has been fulfilled in today's text—the prophecy that Simeon delivered in Luke's Gospel when he first set eyes on the infant Jesus in the temple: "This child is destined for the falling and the rising of many in Israel, and to be a sign that will be opposed so that the inner thoughts of many will be revealed—and a sword will pierce your own soul too" (Luke 2:34b–35).

The arrival of the wise men in Jerusalem signals the fulfillment of Simeon's prophecy. When King Herod hears why they have come, his deadly, duplicitous thoughts are revealed: a new king of the Jews will not only threaten his own position and that of his heirs; the very rumors may bring Rome crashing down on him like a fist. Herod knows how to deal with messianic movements and tax revolts. In short order—beyond the bounds of today's text—he orders the slaughter of every baby boy in the town of

Matthew 2:1-12

Theological Perspective

as strong as what has been revealed to the Jews in the Scriptures concerning the Messiah. Nonetheless, Matthew contrasts the magi, who sincerely wish to pay homage to the "king of the Jews" (2:2, 11), and Herod, who claims to be "king of the Jews" and seeks to destroy rather than worship the true king. The real issue therefore is not what birthright one has, but what kind of disciple one seeks to become in light of the revelation of Christ, however faint that revelation might be. The magi, then, are model believers, and the Gospel of Matthew ends in a way that recalls this beginning: with the disciples paying "homage" to the risen Lord (28:17) and receiving the command to "make disciples of all nations" (28:19).

The imaginative constructions of the magi's gifts by early commentators also resonate with another implicit message in the passage regarding generosity. The magi's visitation and gifts are a response to the greater gift of the Christ child himself. As an expression of God's infinite generosity, in which God actually gives God's self, there is no way to enter the economy established by the Christ child as equals or to offer anything in return that can match the gift that has been given. Rather, the gifts of the magi are symbolic, even sacramental, offerings signaling that disciples of Jesus are called to participate in this infinite generosity by giving themselves to God and others freely. This theme of generosity also recurs in Matthew's Gospel and is particularly evident in the parable of the laborers in the vineyard (20:1–16) and the judgment of the "Gentiles" or "nations" (25:31–46).

Alongside the tradition celebrating the sharing of the gospel with the Gentiles, another tradition holds that Epiphany celebrates the "revelation" or "manifestation" of Christ following the literal meaning of the Greek, *epiphaneia*. Here the magi's observation and following of the "star" (2:2, 7, 9) serves as physical marker of a new outpouring of heavenly light. As with the visitation of the magi, early commentators also engaged in imaginative reconstructions of the manifestation of the star and the revelatory light it sheds. On Epiphany, Leo the Great (400–461) wrote, "A star with new brilliance appeared to three wise men in the East" that "was brighter and more beautiful than others" attracting the "eyes and hearts of those looking on." The determination of the magi to "follow the lead of this heavenly light" expressed a willingness to be "led by the splendor of grace to knowledge of the truth." In this way, "they adore the Word in flesh, wisdom in infancy, strength in weakness, and the Lord of majesty in the reality of a man." Similarly, so should

Pastoral Perspective

of Jerusalem. At the end of their journey, of course, these wise men from the East discover a truth that transcends all others—their seeking is both honored and rewarded.

In the Sermon on the Mount, Matthew reports Jesus saying this: "Ask, and it will be given you; search, and you will find; knock, and the door will be opened for you" (Matt. 7:7). Jesus was addressing himself to a crowded hillside of people, no doubt representing every sort of background. There was no litmus test for their seeking. Jesus himself was eventually excluded from the accredited list of rabbis and teachers, ultimately led to the cross as a condemned outsider. Those who would follow him broke with established norms. The seeking that he advocated was a radical departure from status-quo thinking.

This suggests an important corollary for today: any seeker, whether by chance or authentic pursuit, can find his or her way to the manger. Certainly the church would not exist but for the determination or simple faith of seekers who stumbled into the hay surrounding Jesus' birthing trough. On any given Sunday—or other day of Christian worship—those gathered will include a number of persons who could be classified as seekers rather than, say, as fully committed or truly knowledgeable. Yet among the various amateur spiritualists who attend may be some who are better able to kneel at the manger than those who have worshiped for a lifetime. Not every committed Christian in name has a taste for actually kneeling in the dust and muck of a barn in a backwater town with astonished recognition that this is where God prefers to make an entrance.

The musty sentimentality with which this story has been swathed for cradle Christians obscures the radical implications in God's condescension to humanity. Everyone has been invited to God's natal party, even those who have been traveling radically different paths on their search for their true home. Those who have visited the manger many times as a matter of rote habit could be invited to rediscover the promise held in honest seeking, for surely even the most well-schooled Christian needs regular reminding that no one is above another, that no one has a corner on the complete truth, and that even the baptized travel a path with many distractions, some leading to disastrous ends with pious-sounding names. Given the ingrained repetition of this story for many churchgoers, it is worth reminding the congregation that this child savior will one day say things like, "The last will be first, and the first will be last" (Matt. 20:16).

Exegetical Perspective

ancient astronomical studies. That magi traveled west to visit important kings is attested by ancient writers (Pliny, *Natural History* 30.1, 16; Dio Cassius 63.1–7; Suetonius, *Life of Nero* 13), who report their visit to Nero in 66 CE.

The fact that the magi explain to Herod the astral event that brought them to Jerusalem implies that they were among the few experts who made it their business to follow such events. There is no indication that Herod was aware of any startling astral occurrence such as a nova, comet, or meteor. Both the grammar of the phrase and Herod's inquiry about the time of the star's appearance (v. 7) indicate that the magi's report in verse 2 is to be read as their seeing the star "at its rising" rather than the less accurate rendering "in the East."

Herod's response to the arrival of the magi is to assemble the Sanhedrin (v. 4) and ask them about the appearance of such a "king of the Jews," whom he interprets as God's anointed one, that is, the Christ. Their response is a citation from Micah 5:1, 3, reflecting some of the language of 2 Samuel 5:2 (although the citation is not drawn directly from the Hebrew texts nor the Greek translation of them). While the typical Matthean citation formula ("this happened to fulfill what the Lord had spoken by the prophet") is absent here, it is clear that the author understands this to be one more instance of the career of Jesus fulfilling OT prophecies.

Herod's disturbance at the news the magi bring (v. 3) and his desire that they report to him what they discover (vv. 7–8) clearly anticipate his reaction reported in Matthew 2:16–18 and accurately reflect Herod's murderous response to any threat to his rule.

The report of the magi's exaggerated joy when they saw the star on their arrival in Bethlehem (four different words are used to describe it in v. 10) implies they had not seen the star since they set out for Jerusalem, and did not see it again until they arrived in Bethlehem. There, the second sighting confirmed the accuracy of Herod's experts' advice to them. The text does not state that the magi saw the star going before them (v. 9), only that they rejoiced when they saw it on their arrival in Bethlehem (v. 10).

The gifts offered (v. 11) are probably not intended to be symbolic or to provide the means of defraying the costs of the trip, but are simply the sorts of gifts brought on important occasions (cf. Isa. 60:6; Song 3:6). After receiving information in a dream—a persistent theme in Matthew's infancy narratives (1:20; 2:12, 13, 19)—the magi disobey Herod's request that they inform him of the results of their

Homiletical Perspective

Bethlehem. As Matthew's new pharaoh, he prompts the holy family's flight to Egypt, providing Matthew with several new parallels between the life stories of Moses and Jesus.

For a close look at the often-ignored sociopolitical dimensions of this story, preachers might consult *The First Christmas: What the Gospels Really Teach about Jesus' Birth* by Marcus Borg and John Dominic Crossan.[1] These two Jesus scholars have spent most of their academic lives getting to know the first-century context of the Gospels as well as the Gospels themselves. When they put the two together, they strike sparks that may intrigue preachers and congregations alike.

The feast of the Epiphany is one of the seven principal feast days on the Christian calendar. It is also a fixed day—the twelfth day after Christmas—so that it migrates through the days of the week. While the lections for this day are not customarily transferred to the nearest Sunday, preachers may still decide to do that in order to give this major feast its due.

In many parts of the world, Epiphany is a bigger holiday than Christmas, with rituals of gift giving tied to treasure-bearing wise men instead of a jolly fat man in a red suit. In some places, children leave shoes filled with hay outside their homes. The hay is for the camels of the wise men, who leave gifts for the children in the shoes as thanks before resuming their journey to Bethlehem. Preachers in search of such rich details need do no more than type "Epiphany" into a search engine on their computers (hint: start with "Epiphany in Ethiopia"). Telling such stories is one way to link local Christians to their brothers and sisters around the world. It is also a way to note—and perhaps critique—the effects of our own culture on the practice of our religion.

Preachers wishing to deliver a more theological sermon may take one step back from the story in order to discern Matthew's purpose in telling the story. In many ways this story would seem more at home in Luke's Gospel, where the inclusion of the Gentiles in the redeeming work of God is a central theme. In Matthew's far more Jewish Gospel, the story both fulfills the prophecy of Micah 5:2 in the text and points toward a feature of some messianic expectations of the time, namely, that when Messiah comes, he will hold open the doors of the kingdom for all of God's righteous ones, Jew and Gentile alike. The magi are the first Gentiles to recognize the

1. Marcus J. Borg and John Dominic Crossan, *The First Christmas: What the Gospels Really Teach about Jesus' Birth* (New York: HarperOne, 2007).

Matthew 2:1-12

Theological Perspective

we raise our "hearts" to the "shining beauty of eternal light," revere the "mysteries devoted to human salvation," and put our "energy" into all that has been done on our behalf.[2]

As with the other commentarial tradition, it is unlikely that the magi possessed anything like the incarnational Christology of the Christ child Leo described. However, even if this reading is historically invalid, there is a nascent Christology found in this passage. The light of revelation suggested in this passage does not differ in kind from what God has shed previously in the acts and messianic promises recorded in the Scriptures, as is evident from the allusions in Matthew's nativity story to Moses's birth (Exod. 2:1–10), Balaam's blessing of Israel (Num. 22–24), and Micah's prophecy (Mic. 5:2). But it is clear that the light of God shines most definitively through Jesus Christ, and subsequent events in the Gospel of Matthew repeat the dynamic movement of the magi's acceptance and Herod's rejection of this new revelation: Jesus' proclamation of "the good news of the kingdom" (4:23), his acceptance by his disciples as the "Son of God" (14:33), and his rejection by "the chief priests and elders of the people" (27:1).

Finally, in the Gospel of Matthew discipleship is often likened to a kind of shining, which recalls the light from the star that shined on the Christ child. Jesus tells his disciples, "You are the light of the world. . . . let your light shine before others, so that they may see your good works and give glory to your Father in heaven" (5:14, 16). That disciples are called to shine is important to remember in the season of Epiphany, for now that Christ has ascended and the Spirit has been given, we are the ones through whom this light shines forth.

WILLIAM J. DANAHER JR.

Pastoral Perspective

Epiphany offers the religious practitioner an opportunity to reflect on holy humility and to find pastoral means to prick the conscience of the "saved" to discover the wonderful gifts in those who yearn for connection with the living God but may not know the same name for God. God's compelling hospitality constantly regenerates the family of faith. Preaching and teaching that honors Augustine's famous claim that, "Our hearts are restless till they find their rest in Thee, . . . O Lord,"[1] will exude a passionate spiritual modesty that reflects the universal human quest for reunion with our creator, the author of our lives, and the lover of our souls. In this we are all alike.

The pastoral situation concerns this spiritual hunger. This is the longing that can be identified in the famous story of the magi. Like other reversal stories in the Gospels, this one challenges the assumptions of the first and satisfies the thirst of the last. Churches that characterize such hospitality reflect the radiance of the Christ child and serve as a beacon for all who are restless for their true home. In this way, the star of Bethlehem is replicated a thousandfold over churches and mangers scattered everywhere in cities and towns near and far away.

Everyone who happens to worship on Epiphany has their own idiosyncratic story to tell concerning their pathway to the manger. Some may have no idea who lies there. Others have mistaken ideas about the swaddled child. Nevertheless, all are present due to the prompting of God, who initiates our asking, our seeking, and our finding. Presenting this story with openness and integrity requires pastoral interpreters to trust that God's truth ultimately triumphs, regardless of the trappings of culture, training, or piety. This is an awesome and simultaneously unsettling proposition that seems to match our cultural moment exactly. The magi's journey to Bethlehem exposes God's intention to welcome everyone "into the joy of [God's] home not made with hands, but eternal in the heavens,"[2] and, remarkably, on earth as well.

STEPHEN BAUMAN

---

2. St. Leo the Great, *Sermons*, trans. J. P. Freeland and A. J. Conway (Washington: Catholic University Press, 1996), 133–34.

1. Augustine, *Confessions*, trans. F. J. Sheed (New York: Sheed & Ward, 1942), 3.
2. "A Service of Death and Resurrection," in *The United Methodist Hymnal* (Nashville: United Methodist Publishing House, 1989), 872.

Exegetical Perspective

trip to Bethlehem, and bypass Jerusalem on their return journey.

There are a number of anomalies in this narrative. The story shows no awareness of the bitterness that existed between Herod and priests or that the Sanhedrin was not at Herod's beck and call. That the birthplace of the Christ was to be Bethlehem here seems esoteric knowledge, but in John 7:42 the whole crowd knows of this tradition. A pathologically suspicious Herod makes no attempt to follow the magi or to discover the house where they saw the infant Jesus. Josephus does not mention any slaughter of children in his detailed account of the horrors of Herod's rule, nor is "all Jerusalem" being aware of the magi's presence reflected in later accounts of Jesus in Jerusalem.

Some have suggested that the outlines of the story were taken from the story of Balaam (Num. 22–24), a seer from the east who saw David's star rise (Num. 24:17), resisted the efforts of an evil king to destroy his enemy, and instead blessed the enemy, thus thwarting the evil king. The magi story was then filled out in light of Isaiah 60:1, 5–6, where Israel's light has arisen and representatives of the nations bring frankincense and gold.

Whatever its source, the account of the magi announces at the beginning of Matthew's story of Jesus that he is the king of the Jews (v. 2), the Christ (v. 4), and the promised ruler of Israel (v. 6). The assembling of the Sanhedrin here anticipates such action on the part of Jesus' enemies at the time of his passion (26:3, 57; 27:17, 27, 62) and serves with the Great Commission (28:16–20) to bracket the story of Jesus with the acknowledgment of his universal import. Astrologers from a foreign land are the first to acknowledge Jesus as God's anointed king, and the final command of the risen Jesus is to carry the gospel to all nations, including them via baptism into God's new chosen people.

PAUL J. ACHTEMEIER

Homiletical Perspective

coming of this Messiah and to foreshadow the comprehensiveness of the coming kingdom he will one day proclaim.

The theological concept of epiphany provides another opening on the text, especially here at the beginning of the season of Epiphany. Preachers whose congregations are tuned to the church calendar may explore the visit of the wise men as a preview of all the biblical epiphanies to come, from Jesus' baptism (next Sunday) to his transfiguration (on the last Sunday before Lent). What do such epiphanies have in common? What is their purpose? Are there any differences between the theophanies of the First Testament and epiphanies of the Second?

Perhaps most importantly of all, preachers may explore with their congregations whether epiphanies are things of the past—always introduced by "once upon a time"—or whether such manifestations of the Divine go on happening even now. Preachers who choose this tack will spend a generous portion of their preparation time sitting in their chairs without any books open in their laps. There they will ask the Holy Spirit to enlighten them, helping them recall the ordinary and extraordinary ways in which the light of Christ has appeared to them in their own lives and the lives of those they love. They might also think of four or five people they would like to ask the same question: by what light do you see God? The church has a word for this. When we tell the stories of our encounters with God—in community, in nature, in relationship, in the chambers of our own hearts—we give testimony to the ongoing revelation of the Word made flesh.

Preachers who decide to stay in the narrative mode will deal carefully with the miraculous features in today's story. It is not necessary to try to explain the guiding star in scientific terms, any more than it is necessary to assert that the star is a metaphorical device. This rich story deserves a preacher's best storytelling response, full of faithful imagination and a trusting heart.

BARBARA BROWN TAYLOR

BAPTISM OF THE LORD
(FIRST SUNDAY AFTER THE EPIPHANY)

Isaiah 43:1-7

¹But now thus says the LORD,
　he who created you, O Jacob,
　he who formed you, O Israel;
Do not fear, for I have redeemed you;
　I have called you by name, you are mine.
²When you pass through the waters, I will be with you;
　and through the rivers, they shall not overwhelm you;
when you walk through fire you shall not be burned,
　and the flame shall not consume you.
³For I am the LORD your God,
　the Holy One of Israel, your Savior.
I give Egypt as your ransom,
　Ethiopia and Seba in exchange for you.

Theological Perspective

This particular Sunday raises a number of christological questions, of course. If Jesus was in fact wholly God, why did he need to be baptized? What does his baptism mean, and why was he baptized? However, those are not the issues that present themselves in this reading from Isaiah. Isaiah, writing for a people in exile, invokes promises of redemption for Israel in a creative way.

The passage begins with a reference to creation ("the LORD . . . who created you, O Jacob, . . . who formed you, O Israel") moving immediately to language of redemption ("Do not fear, for I have redeemed you"). In this way, Isaiah joins creation and redemption before we leave the first verse. Although we often associate God the creator with power, sovereignty, and providence, and God the savior with love, grace, and mercy, in fact the creating and saving acts of God are intimately linked in God's relationship with creation. Creation is a deeply loving act of God; redemption is an event of great sovereign power.

The Bible points the believer in this direction repeatedly. Isaiah 51:9–10 asks: "Was it not you who cut Rahab in pieces . . . ? Was it not you . . . who made the depths of the sea a way for the redeemed to cross over?" (Verse 2 of our reading for today echoes that water imagery.) The Christ hymn of

Pastoral Perspective

A new student looks out on a sea of strange faces in the high school cafeteria, wondering where he should sit, which group he should join, how he will be received.

A woman walks down the hall in her empty house to look at her daughter's bedroom. The bedroom contains pictures and souvenirs of childhood and high school, left behind when this youngest daughter set off for her first year of college. Now the mother wonders what lies ahead—not just for her daughter but for herself, suddenly cut adrift.

An older man groans in his sick bed. Retirement from his successful law practice had not been that difficult. But now he has been felled by chronic illness that leaves him lethargic, with nothing to show for his days. He feels worthless.

A younger man drives toward his hometown. He has been away for two years in a minimum-security prison for misappropriating money at work. His time in prison has ended, but he wonders if the true penalty he must bear for his wrongdoing is a lifetime sentence.

Who am I? Where do I belong? What makes me worthy? These questions, which come to the forefront in adolescence and young adulthood, never really go away. Whether we ask them explicitly or only subconsciously, we often look for the answers in

⁴Because you are precious in my sight,
   and honored, and I love you.
 I give people in return for you,
   nations in exchange for your life.
 ⁵Do not fear, for I am with you;
   I will bring your offspring from the east,
   and from the west I will gather you;
 ⁶I will say to the north, "Give them up."
   and to the south, "Do not withhold;
 bring my sons from far away
   and my daughters from the end of the earth—
 ⁷everyone who is called by my name,
   whom I created for my glory,
   whom I formed and made."

Exegetical Perspective

Although Second Isaiah writes for exiles in Babylon, this lyrical text also carries quintessential claims that Christian baptism will later make on believers. The text speaks of passing through deadly waters, of being loved and ransomed by God, and of living as a people named by God for the sake of God's glory. All of its promises seek to reverse the deep fear of a people on the precipice of extinction under Babylonian domination, a people whose future is in grave doubt and whose God seems to have abandoned them (or lost the war to the gods of Babylon). Isaiah reassures these abandoned ones by reasserting divine presence and power among them.

The voice of God unifies the passage because God is the only speaker. Divine declarations appear in a long, rhythmic string of "I" statements. These, in turn, receive an internal frame from the divine command, "Do not fear" (vv. 1, 5). The addressee of God's speech is Jacob/Israel, the father of the nation, who stands in the role of the whole community. Although the poem is a monologue, it uses direct address to create the impression that readers are overhearing one side of an intimate conversation. God addresses the whole nation, but in second-person-singular verb forms, as if speaking to each member of the community.

Terms of divine address are personal and revelatory, because in them God discloses the divine

Homiletical Perspective

Life's Hard Places. Some texts scream "universal" in the way they grab us. Who among us does not know what it feels like to be overwhelmed and underprepared for life's hard places? Though the text clearly is directed at the covenant people of the ancient text—Jacob, the ancestral foreparent; Israel, the chosen nation—churches and individuals want to hear "Do not be afraid" as a sure word from God.

Expressionist painter Edvard Munch, most famous for his painting "The Scream," captures the angst that fear produces, modernity's fear that war will alienate all humanity from itself. In our postmodern world, we know the emotion expressed in "The Scream," where the sky is bloodred. We are baptized in fear, forgetting everything in the paralysis of the moment: our names, our heritage, our purpose, and our resources. Ancient Israel, as a worshiping community and as a nation-state in exile, knew intimately the force of fear. They no doubt felt abandoned, and what faith they had was threadbare as the story of their chosen status unraveled seam by seam. How would they believe that God, YHWH, was "the Holy one of Israel," that is, uniquely connected to them? How could they trust that they would not be ransomed away like slaves; that another nation had not taken their place in God's heart?

Isaiah 43:1-7

Theological Perspective

Colossians says that "in [Christ] all things in heaven and on earth were created. . . . and through him God was pleased to reconcile to [God's] self all things" (Col. 1:16, 20). Perhaps most famously, John tells us in his prologue that "all things came into being through [the Word], and without [the Word] not one thing came into being" (John 1:3). When this Word became flesh, to all "who received him, who believed in his name, he gave power to become children of God" (John 1:12). Clearly, the Bible posits a strong connection between the creating and saving acts of God.

Theologians make the connection by positing creation as an act of the triune God. The three persons of the Trinity exist in loving relationship. Desiring to express love beyond God's own self, God's Word (or, to stay with OT imagery, God's Wisdom) moves outward to create a world external to God. That world becomes the object of God's love and exists in union with God. Creation, rather than being simply an act of power on the maker's part, manifests itself as an act of love. One already sees the pattern for the world's redemption anticipated in that act. In salvation, God again goes outward in love, assuming human life in Jesus and remaining active in the Holy Spirit, this time to recreate the world that is estranged from God and to restore the broken harmony that results from sin. Creation and redemption flow from the same gracious essence of God, joined just as intimately as Isaiah makes them here in 43:1.[1] Transcendence and immanence coexist in God, not in tension but in balance.

That is why the creative redemption of Israel takes place via the elements and events of the created order. Passing through water and fire cannot hurt the people—these elements are used by God for our benefit to cleanse and purify. (Isaiah 43:2 says, "I will be with you"; the believer recognizes "Emmanuel.") The end of the Babylonian captivity and the return of the people to Judah under Cyrus take place in the course of the world's political and military machinations, in which the actors have no awareness of the result that God is accomplishing through them. Even the superpowers of the day serve God's redemptive purpose: "I give Egypt as your ransom, Ethiopia and Seba in exchange for you" (v. 3). Salvation takes place not outside of creation but in the course of life in God's providence; redemption may come from

Pastoral Perspective

the wrong places: in our roles, our work, our peer groups, or our accomplishments and acquisitions. Ultimately, none of these can deliver what we need. What we need, according to the prophet, is to hear how God gives us identity and value.

In Isaiah 43, the prophet speaks to a people bloodied, bruised, and beleaguered. As punishment for Israel's arrogance and disobedience, God has permitted Israel to be conquered by the Babylonians and thrown into exile. Before this passage, Isaiah had words of judgment; now he has words of comfort and hope. The tender words of Isaiah 43 remind these exiles who they are and whose they are, despite their sins.

Who They Are. The central verse of this passage is also the center of the prophet's message here: "Because you are precious in my sight, and honored, and I love you, I give people in return for you, nations in exchange for your life" (v. 4). As Claus Westermann notes in his commentary on this passage, if the exiles were to take an honest look at themselves, they would see "a tiny, miserable, and insignificant band of uprooted men and women" standing on the margins of a hostile empire.[1] But the prophet declares that this people have a new and different identity: they are a people valued and honored by God.

Whose They Are. "Do not fear, for I have redeemed you; I have called you by name, you are mine" (v. 1). What is Israel's comfort and hope? The One who made them has not turned away from them. Instead, God still claims Israel and holds on to them. Israel belongs to God as sheep belong to a shepherd. Therefore, Israel need not fear their plight or their foes, the chaos of the waters, or the dangers of the fire.

Despite Their Sins. Isaiah 43 cannot be separated from the angry words of divine disappointment and judgment in Isaiah 42:18–25. Without Isaiah 43, Israel would not know that God's words of comfort and restoration are greater than Israel's sins and defeat. Despite Israel's sins, God will not let the rivers overwhelm Israel or "the flame . . . consume you" (v. 2). Yet, without the reminder of Isaiah 42, Israel might be tempted to think that divine assurance is the same as divine license, that God's election of Israel is the occasion for self-indulgence.

---

1. For a concise and helpful presentation, see Bradley C. Hanson, *Introduction to Christian Theology* (Minneapolis: Fortress Press, 1997), 68–70.

1. Claus Westermann, *Isaiah 40–66: A Commentary*, trans. David M. G. Stalker (Philadelphia: Westminster Press, 1977), 118.

character, as if meeting listeners for the first time. God is the creator, not here of the whole world, but the creator of Israel. The implication of this announcement is that if God created the nation once, God can do it again in their present scattered, fractured state. The command to cast out fear comes with the reason fear is unnecessary: "I have redeemed you" (v.1). To put aside fear must seem impossible for exiles deported from their land, but the fearless future that God opens for them does not rest upon the people's own strength or political and military wisdom. Fear should be gone because God has already claimed them and redeemed them.

To be redeemed according to Israel's law means to be bought out of human bondage by one's kin, a close member of the extended family (Lev. 25:47–49). This means two things. When God redeems Israel, God does not redeem the nation from its sin but from slavery to Babylon, from the sinful conditions of another nation's aggrandizement; and when God redeems Israel, God asserts close kinship, family relationship, with them. Through deadly perils, through waters that overwhelm, and through flames that consume, God promises to be with them. They will survive these devastations because "I have called you by name;" because "I will be with you" (43:1–2).

God's self-declarations, the repetitive "I" statements across the poem, reveal by function and action who this Redeemer is. "I am the LORD your God, . . . I give Egypt as your ransom. . . . I love you, I give people in return for you. . . . I am with you" (vv. 3–5a). These first-person announcements have immense power, not simply because they reveal divine strength or because they convey God's emotional, familial connection to the people. These statements have startling authority because they also establish the nation's relationship with God through a legal exchange of cosmic dimensions. God buys them back from slavery, but the currency of exchange is neither money nor property; it is with other nations that God pays their ransom. "I give people in return for you, nations in exchange for your life" (v. 4). The national enslavement to Babylon will be the subject of a giant, global transaction because the Redeemer is the governor of the world.

After this exchange, their Redeemer promises, with still more" I" affirmations, to bring them back to the land, to their true identity, and to their God. "I will bring your offspring" from every corner of the earth, from the east, the west, the north, the south, "everyone who is called by my name" (vv. 5–7a).

Sure, they had been in waters that went over their heads and had been delivered; in fact, they had seen their enemies drown in the very waters that had saved them. They had stories of deliverance from fiery furnaces, and a pillar of fire was part of their redemption in the wilderness. But how could they trust that those once-saving flames would not consume them? How could they know that a baptism of fire would not singe their souls?

We Belong to God. By the time Isaiah's prophetic community speaks and records these words, these questions are thickening the air like locusts. So the word comes, reportedly direct from God: "I created you; I formed you," the Deity declares (v. 1). The direct and emphatic words are clear: God makes a claim that is based in God's responsibility for the nation's existence. God is creator and birth mother for them. How could a mother forget her children? How could an inventor abandon his invention? Such thoughts are as absurd as thinking God could forget God's people. We are appalled when we learn that a parent has been abusive or neglectful. We recoil at the notion. In the same way, we ought to recoil, the prophet suggests, at the notion that God would abandon us.

"I have redeemed you."

"I have called you by name."

"You are mine." Possessive and protective, God acts, the prophet says. We abandon fear because we have not been abandoned.

For a people in exile, these words must have been hard to hear. If God is with us, they must have wondered, how did we end up in Babylon? We too may find ourselves wondering about God's behavior (or lack of it). If God is with us, why are we so besieged by crime, war, poverty, and hunger? If God is with us, why do we continue to feel alienated and isolated? If God is with us, then why . . . ?

Every affirmation God makes on our behalf, through prophets and their kind, can be met with a question. We may feel as if we are between a rock and a hard place or, in a colloquialism of the Deep South, "between the devil and the deep blue sea." But the prophet will continue to answer our questions with assurance that no matter what—fire or flood, wind or relationship distress, war or famine—God is with us.

What Price for Freedom? Do we want others to suffer so we can be free? The deity is willing to ransom every other nation for this one, to sell off the children, women, and warriors of Egypt, Cush, and

Isaiah 43:1-7

Theological Perspective

beyond the created order, but in Christ Jesus it does not come apart from that order.

To return to our beginning, perhaps that is the import of the baptism of the Lord. By receiving baptism, Jesus bears witness in himself that the transcendent, creating God is present in the world, sharing our lives to achieve our reconciliation. As John asserts, one sees the creating and saving nature of God united in this Jesus of Nazareth. His baptism is not just an example for the church—it is that; but even more, it is the first step that puts him on the path to the cross, where he can say of both creation and redemption, "It is finished."

In addressing this theme of creation-redemption, the preacher may want to note another element of this passage: universality. Although Isaiah wrote to the people of Israel, the Christian may correctly apply the gift of liberation to all people. The divine message, says verse 7, is for "everyone who is called by my name, whom I created for my glory, whom I formed and made." All creation, and therefore all people, is the result of God's love. It only follows that God's saving acts are also meant for all people.

Christians should resist the tendency to exclude others from God's love, whatever personal, social, or theological differences may divide us. Differences are real and important and should be admitted. The message of the Bible is that in God those differences are transcended—not eliminated—in the gracious power of love. It is no accident that verses 5–6, in which God promises to bring the people from all points of the globe, anticipate the eucharistic liturgy that proclaims, "People will come from east, and west, and north, and south, and sit at table in the kingdom of God." We do well to remember that our boundaries are not God's.

RICK NUTT

Pastoral Perspective

In the wrath of Isaiah 42 and the grace of Isaiah 43, "faith recognizes the presence of the God who wills only to love and be loved in return."[2]

Who are we? Where do we belong? What makes us worthy? Isaiah 43 speaks not only to us as individuals but also to us as communities of faith. The prophet reminds us that our core identity lies not in our roles as individuals, or in our relative size and wealth as congregations, but in God's identification of us as "precious in my sight, and honored." Our sense of belonging comes not from the acceptance of our peers or the status of our communities but from the One who claims us and will never let us go. What makes us worthy is not our individual achievements or the size of our congregational budgets but God's gracious love.

God calls Israel precious in God's sight, despite Israel's sins. Therefore, when we fail and fall, as we inevitably will as both individuals and congregations, we can take comfort in the realization that our failures do not prompt God to quit loving us or laying claim to us. We can trust and hope in the God who is with us and will protect us, even in the midst of the floods of chaos caused by our irresponsibility as both individuals and communities.

This passage is paired with Luke's description of Jesus' baptism in the revised common lectionary. The pairing is an apt one, because in the waters of baptism, we understand that God marks us and claims us as God's children. In the waters of baptism, God seals God's love for us, no matter what we might have done and what might happen. In the waters of our baptism, God gives evidence of what God says to Jesus in Luke 3:22: "You are my [child], the Beloved; with you I am well pleased."

The comforting and hopeful words of Isaiah 43:1–7 are easier to read and write about than they are truly to hear and believe. This is a passage we need to return to over and over, just as we need to be reminded of our baptisms. Words this good—love this uncommon—take time to be believed and absorbed.

W. CARTER LESTER

2. Paul D. Hanson, *Isaiah 40–66* (Louisville, KY: John Knox Press, 1995), 60.

Exegetical Perspective

This ingathering of the nation draws them back to their land and to the relationship for which they were created in the first place—to life with the God who loves them, honors them, and holds them "precious." It is they whom "I created for my glory" (v. 7). For these reasons, for the sake of this vision about to be realized just over the horizon, God commands them, "Do not fear" (v. 5).

Second Isaiah's poem is a vision of re-creation. It tells of the "new things" God is doing for an enslaved, despairing people left for dead at the hand of their conquerors. Like the eloquent preacher he is, Isaiah dips deeply into the national story and its creation traditions to startle and provoke his audience into a renewal of life with God.

This poem eminently suits the feast of the baptism of the Lord because all the divine promises articulated by Second Isaiah receive a new layer of meaning in Jesus' baptism. In that New Testament event, Jesus passes through the waters and comes fully to his identity. He becomes the ransom for many. He brings new life for people lost to enslavement. He reveals God's love for the people, the new Israel, gathered anew from the four corners of the earth for the glory of God.

In the sacrament of baptism, Christians too pass through the waters like the Israelites in the exodus and like the captives in Babylon. Christians too receive the promise of new life that does not exempt them from suffering but assures them, "I have called you by name," "I am with you," "I will ransom you," "I am the LORD your God." It is these promises that impel Christians to fearless lives of fidelity, called together in God's name for the sake of God's glory.

KATHLEEN M. O'CONNOR

Homiletical Perspective

Seba for Israel (v. 3). The Holy One will, for love of this one nation-state, "sell off the whole world" and "trade the creation" for them (v. 4 *The Message*). To poor exiles, languishing far away from their ancestral land, these words must have sounded like good news. The scattered children gathered for a great reunion (vv. 5–7). It was a family reunion, one of all those called by God's name. That is the only distinguishing mark—"called by God's name"—not skin color, gender, or nationality (though this text does in fact refer to Israel). But for us, and for our posterity, the boundaries are swept away. For who is not God's own?

"When you pass through the waters, I will be with you" (v. 2). These words had a historic ring to the ears of the exiles, for God had been with them, already, through the waters of the Jordan and the Reed Sea. God had made a path. This promise is not foreign to them, nor is the promise of a nonconsuming fire. Had not Moses stood before a bush and watched it burn and not be consumed?

Precious in Your Sight. A woman sits in a restaurant with her daughter, son-in-law, and only grandchild. The granddaughter plays in the lap of her grandmother, the grandmother enthralled by the child's every move. This baby girl, just barely two years old, is precious in the older woman's sight. Observers see it in their interaction. This delight must give us some glimpse of what the prophet means by God's love and delight in the people Israel and in us—unabashed desire that moves God to compassion and action. How can God leave the people languishing in exile, with a lost identity and diminished hope? A God who honors and loves would not do that, the prophet says. In fact, God's voice is carried on the wind, north and south, from Babylon to Egypt: "give them up." God's voice demands a return, a remnant, a rescue. Sons and daughters, created in God's image and for God's glory, hear the call.

We are those children, listening and responding in the light of God's grace. We are those who belong, baptized by water and by fire. We are the kin-dom, in the glow of God's glory.

VALERIE BRIDGEMAN DAVIS

Psalm 29

¹Ascribe to the LORD, O heavenly beings,
  ascribe to the LORD glory and strength.
²Ascribe to the LORD the glory of his name;
  worship the LORD in holy splendor.

³The voice of the LORD is over the waters;
  the God of glory thunders,
  the LORD, over mighty waters.
⁴The voice of the LORD is powerful;
  the voice of the LORD is full of majesty.

⁵The voice of the LORD breaks the cedars;
  the LORD breaks the cedars of Lebanon.

Theological Perspective

Originally redacted to be a psalm of theonomy that exalts the power of God in the face of the claims of rival indigenous Canaanite belief,[1] Psalm 29 serves the church today in two ways very similar to its original function. In the first instance, it calls the church's attention to the reality that there are forces at work within our world born of indigenous belief and that even these are subject to the power of God. In the second place, the psalm calls to our memory the power of God's voice in the face of these powers specifically, but also as a force within creation more generally.

As we reflect on the first dimension of this psalm's usefulness for the contemporary church, we do well to recall how variant translations can open a text to new meanings and new understandings. This is clearly the case with Calvin's commentary on this psalm. Where many commentators have clearly identified the initial addressees of the psalm as either "sons of gods," "heavenly beings,"[2] or some variant thereof, Calvin translates the verse as "ye sons of the mighty."[3] From

---

1. Arthur Weiser, *The Psalms: A Commentary* (Philadelphia: Westminster Press, 1962), 260–61; Hans-Joachim Kraus, *Psalms 1–59: A Commentary*, trans. Hilton C. Oswald (Minneapolis: Augsburg Publishing House, 1978), 346–47.
2. Charles Augustus Briggs, *A Critical and Exegetical Commentary on the Book of Psalms* (New York: Charles Scribner's Sons, 1906), 251; Wayne A. Meeks, ed., *The Harper Collins Study Bible: New Revised Standard Version with the Aprocryphal/Deuterocanonical Books* (London: HarperCollins Books, 1993), 824.
3. John Calvin, *Commentary on the Psalms*, vol. 1, trans. James Anderson (Grand Rapids: Eerdmans, 1949), 475.

Pastoral Perspective

Baptism does not prevent us from entering into troubling waters. Some of the troubles we bring upon ourselves, while others just seem to find us. It would be a naive understanding of faith to think that because we have been baptized we will be exempt from life's hardships. Luke records, for example, that after Jesus was baptized he was immediately led into the wilderness (4:1–11). Perhaps Jesus was so overwhelmed by the experience of his baptism that he sought a secluded place to further clarify to what (and to whom) he was dedicating his life. Regardless of what motivated him to go into the wilderness, he was challenged there to discern the values by which he would live.

Many of the psalms were written to be recited or sung by people gathered for worship. We assemble in worship to experience God. When we gather to share our journey of faith, drawing strength from one another, we are transformed from a meeting of faithful people into a congregation of faithful believers.

The voice of God in Psalm 29 is symbolized by the sound of thunder and associated with the power of the strong winds and rain of a serious storm. The psalmist attempts to assure the gathered people of God's care of them during their wilderness places and all the storms of life. He declares that "the LORD

⁶He makes Lebanon skip like a calf,
and Sirion like a young wild ox.

⁷The voice of the Lord flashes forth flames of fire.
⁸The voice of the Lord shakes the wilderness;
the Lord shakes the wilderness of Kadesh.

⁹The voice of the Lord causes the oaks to whirl,
and strips the forest bare;
and in his temple all say, "Glory!"

¹⁰The Lord sits enthroned over the flood;
the Lord sits enthroned as king forever.
¹¹May the Lord give strength to his people!
May the Lord bless his people with peace!

Exegetical Perspective

This hymn in praise of God is placed between an individual's plea for God's help (Ps. 28) and an individual's psalm of thanksgiving for help received (Ps. 30). The hymn has a central theme: God's awesome power over the whole of creation. The psalmist uses the imagery of the clap of thunder in a violent storm to depict God's coming to the aid of the community, ruling as sovereign over all creation. Seven times we hear "the voice of the Lord" sounding forth with terrifying power. The culmination of this familiar nature imagery takes place in the temple, when the assembled congregation shouts "Glory!" (v. 9).

Early Israelite poetry depicts God through the imagery of nature's upheavals, especially the windstorm's violent thunderclaps and flashes of lightning. See the Song of Deborah (Judg. 5:4–5). The appearance of God to Moses on Mount Sinai makes use of storm and earthquake (Exod. 19, 24; contrast 1 Kgs. 19). Reconstructions of the worship of Israel in the temple give a regular place to so-called theophany hymns such as this one. At the appropriate time in acts of celebration, especially during the major festivals, people and chorus would recite one of these hymns, vividly announcing that God had once again come to the holy center, ready to sweep away every enemy and bring deliverance to

Homiletical Perspective

Psalm 29 is appropriately appointed for the First Sunday of Epiphany, when the church has traditionally marked Christ's baptism in the Jordan. This text is an apt choice for this day, as it sets baptism within the context of God's claim on all creation. God's voice spoke all this into being; it is a voice both present and powerful in the water, the fire, the trees, and the very foundations of the earth.

The images conveyed include descriptions of a broad range of events in the natural world, encompassing familiar experiences and their causes, explained only by divine power. The psalmist associates God with big things, for God is a big God, with power manifest in the natural elements themselves. God's voice is "full of majesty," capable of shaking the foundations of the earth, laying the forests bare, setting fire to the world.

The preacher might paint a vivid picture, taking listeners back to the ancient world, when thunder represented the mightiest of sounds, when the natural elements constituted the most fearsome of perils. When we hear of God shaking the wilderness, we are reminded of the times when the ground beneath us shakes as thunder rumbles through the sky. God reigns over all this. When the earth shakes, when the fires burn, when the waters rise, God reigns. The power of God is evident in the power of nature.

Psalm 29

Theological Perspective

this translation he then proceeds to read the address as being directed not to the celestial creatures, but rather to haughty humans. As he puts it, David directs this psalm to "great men, who excel in rank." This particular turn of Calvin's creates a significant moment to recall that earthly power can in many ways be an impediment to recognizing the true power of God.

While some might see Calvin's translation as being influenced by the challenges to literalism that were growing in the era on the cusp of modernity, I think it is rather the case that he wanted to call attention to the reality that frequently humans come to view themselves, their works, and their organizations as being of the majesty of the cedars of Lebanon. They masquerade as the giants of creation, if you will. This is the stuff of which nationalism, ethnocentrism, and many other "isms" are made. Calvin's point is that the *words* and voice of God strip away the pretense of omnipotence with which these ever-present idols parade.

It is here, with Calvin's reading of the second clause of the first verse, that we find the continuing value of this psalm for the church in our age. For is it not the case that every people in every time find something about themselves to exalt in the face of others—including God? By elevating dimensions of their particular finitude (e.g., nationality or race) these groups create an indigenous faith no less foreign to the worship of the God of Israel than the Canaanite worship of Baal. Whether that indigenous faith is the German Christian Movement or the Christian Dominionist movement in our time, Psalm 29 calls to our remembrance that it is *the Lord* who reigns in all creation, not our little tribal gods— no matter how "godly" they may seem.

While clearly using the imagery of a thunderstorm, the psalmist does more than reinforce the ancient idea that atmospheric turbulence is a sign that God is at work. Hearkening to the Genesis account of creation (v. 1), the psalmist identifies God's voice as that which hovers over the waters displaying God's glory and majesty (vv. 3–4). Giving different dimension to the power of God evident in the mighty cedars of Lebanon (cf. Judg. 9:14–16; Isa. 14:8), the writer of this psalm identifies the voice of God as the power that bends and breaks these giants of creation. It is the voice of God that sweeps across the face of creation with power and majesty (vv. 7–9).

In many Christian traditions the preacher is thought of as the "mouthpiece of God." Put another way, Christian proclamation in all of its forms can be

Pastoral Perspective

will give strength unto his people [and] bless [them] with peace" (v. 11 KJV).

I recently visited with a group of people, many of whom are living in poverty, in a small South African township. They meet regularly to give one another support as people infected or affected by HIV and AIDS. One of their activities is to break into small groups and formulate their own interpretation of a biblical passage. Recently they composed their own version of Psalm 23:

> The Lord loves and protects us even though we are HIV-positive.
> The Lord is Alpha and Omega.
> ARVs [antiretroviral drugs] do not work because we are clever, but with the grace of God.
> The situation we are in, it shows that God will take us to green pastures.
> Even though we are HIV-positive, we will not fear death.
> He prepares even when neighbors look at you through their windows saying: "when are you dying?"
> He gives us strength to go on.
> Even if the going gets tough, he is our shelter.
> Through God, everything is possible.

This interpretation of the Twenty-third Psalm expresses the courage and faith of ordinary people who live every day under conditions of poverty and poor health unimaginable to many. The inspiration of Psalm 29, like that of Psalm 23, flows down through the ages, connecting the spirits of people whose faith and courage remind us that the same spirit lives in us all.

The baptism of Jesus signaled the beginning of his long journey of becoming for us the strength and hope we need for the path we travel. It is reassuring to know that we can find direction in a wilderness and that peace will follow a storm. God is the creator and sustainer of all things, including human life.

In worship we praise God for who God is and for who God has become to us. The psalmist (traditionally believed to be David) seems to have a keen understanding of this, as well as of our human need to connect with God. God was personal to David. So much teaching and preaching about the Christian life makes faithful living seem joyless and full of struggle. The spirit of faith conveyed in David's writings reflects his personal experiences, growth, and theological insights about how to discover the mercy and goodness of God. He strove to share his faith with those who worship God.

Exegetical Perspective

the people. The God of the natural order was also powerfully in control of history, ready to save.

The opening of the psalm reveals a characteristic understanding of how ancient Israelites understood their acts of worship. The imperative "ascribe" or "give" is more than a call to the community to acknowledge that God is glorious and powerful and thus entitled to praise. It means that the community is called on to *bestow* honor and strength upon God through its utterance of the hymn of praise. God's glory exists independently of Israel's declaration, of course, but Israel's praise makes all the more real the glory and strength of the Deity. Created in the divine image and likeness, human beings (according to Israelite understanding) may, by their deeds and by their worship, enhance God's glory.

The cosmology reflected in the psalm is familiar from many biblical texts (Gen. 1, Ps. 104, etc.). The vault of heaven holds up and back the heavenly waters while the earth rests upon the lower waters, anchored by mountains whose peaks reach through earth's surface and tower above. Some stars are fixed in the vault of heaven, while others move across the heavens on their regular rounds. Heavenly windows open or close at God's bidding, and the winds and storms mysteriously come and go, also at the will of their creator and master.

Israelite cosmology also allows for heavenly beings (literally "sons of the gods") who surround the divine throne and do God's bidding. A vivid picture of this court of God is found in 1 Kings 22:19–23. That vision of the prophet Micaiah pictures heavenly beings discussing with God what to do about the evil King Ahab. One of the beings proposes to go and be a lying spirit in the mouth of all Ahab's prophets, a suggestion that God accepts. Later Jewish writings outside the Bible carefully note that these heavenly beings are of course created by God and not to be considered lesser gods, as was true among Israel's neighbors.

So powerful is this cosmic voice that even the virtually indestructible cedars of Lebanon and Mount Hermon itself (Sirion is another name for the mountain) dance and skip before God. The voice is so devastating that even the wilderness is not spared. It too is set in motion, its small but sturdy trees uprooted and the land itself shaken.

The center of the psalm, however, appears in verse 9b: "and in [God's] temple all say, 'Glory!'" This clause confirms the use of the psalm in the temple on the great festival days. The people gather at the holy place, sing God's praises, and offer their

Homiletical Perspective

Today's listeners may struggle with the descriptions that the psalmist presents to us. Having seen the waters rise, and the enormous consequences of a storm such as Hurricane Katrina, we have our doubts about a God who controls the waters. Can we shout "Glory!" to God who "sits enthroned over the flood" in the wake of such an event?

The answer is not a simple one, even in this jubilant psalm of praise. In presenting these images of the created world, the vastest images that the psalmist can conjure, we sense the poet's desire to guide the worshiper to an understanding of God's greatness. When the psalmist tells us that "the God of glory thunders . . . over mighty waters," we understand the waters to signify chaos, the powers of undoing, the great unknown deep, both physical and cosmic. The images called to mind in Psalm 29 bring us close to the limits of our understanding, to that which the original listeners would have been unable to explain, such as the wilderness shaking, the great waters rising, and towering trees shattering to splinters.

Psalm 29 is clearly intended for worship, to bring honor to God, to describe God's great glory. In the context of worship, the psalmist was able to make some sense of God at work in the world, even in the midst of otherwise inexplicable phenomena. The question becomes not why but where. God is here in the midst of these earth-shattering events, the psalmist tells us. God is here, engaging with chaos, bringing order to it, making it right. When God's people come together to listen for God's voice after the wind has torn through, the beams of houses have been splintered, and floods have carried homes away, they will find that God is there, brooding over the chaos, opening the way of peace.

The psalmist points to God's power as the basis for true peace. This peace reaches to the center of our existence, encompassing vast oceans and tiny molecules. It is a gift from the one who laid the foundations of the world. God's peace is a gift to all creation, not something that humans can bring about. It is not even something that humans can fully grasp, but we can rest in its promise and look for God at work in the world, seeking occasions to cry out, "Glory!"

We find one such occasion in baptism, where the chaotic power of water, the great deep that could completely swallow us, becomes for us a sign of pure, clear grace. In the waters of baptism we find not destruction, but forgiveness and hope. As we enter the water, we die with Christ, but in the chaos

Psalm 29

Theological Perspective

understood by the church as being a voice of God, doing the work of God in creation. Where other psalms point to the heavens or creation as exemplars in their witness to God, here we might understand the voice of Christian proclamation as being exemplary of God's power in the face of human hubris and arrogance. Read in this way, the psalm speaks powerfully to any moment in which idolatry replaces the true worship of God, creating *sons of the gods* and—more importantly—it speaks to the power of faithful proclamation to tear these idols apart as God's voice breaks the mighty cedars of Lebanon. One is put in mind of figures such as Martin Luther King Jr., who understood the church's voice to be an expression of God's voice—a powerful force at work within creation to engage injustice rooted in idolatry and unfaithfulness founded in hubris.

Psalm 29 is of enduring value to the church because it not only captures our attention when we may be captivated by the *sons of the gods* of our age; it also reminds us of the primacy of our vocation as *a* voice of God within creation and the power of that voice. Is this not what we see in Christ, who after his baptism announced that he had come to preach the acceptable year of the Lord, freeing the captives and binding up the brokenhearted?

STEPHEN G. RAY JR.

Pastoral Perspective

God's love has, for the Christian community, become present through Jesus Christ. By the resurrection of Christ from the dead, God assures those who believe that we need not fear death or those things that remind us of our mortality. Wanting to be genuine people and wanting to live meaningful lives are universal human desires. We may proceed through our lives trusting in the One who has become our Way, Truth, and Life. Believing this can transform us and give us a new direction and purpose for living.

Grief, mourning, separation, awe, and joy are all realities of life. Sometimes we may feel that we have too many losses, too much sadness and separation in our lives. When we gather to worship God, we are seeking confirmation that things will be well. This is especially true if we have just experienced or anticipate facing a storm in our lives. Confirmation often comes through our commitment to give witness, as best we can, to what we believe it means for us to be Christians. At some point, faith requires that we embrace and trust the God whom the Christian community has witnessed in Christ. Hope emerges from the texture of our experiences and gives wings to our dreams, integrity to our actions, strength and substance to our efforts to be witnesses and agents of God in the world.

As Christians, we learn from Jesus what we know about God. God does not render us unknown, unfulfilled, and separated from God's love. Whatever lies ahead of us, there is also the God who promises to be with us always. This faith is not ours to possess alone, but by serving others we also share the hope of Christ.

Congregations hope for us, pray for us, and believe for us when we feel that we can no longer do these things for ourselves enough to rejoice in God's name. They remind us through honest worship that during moments of fear, anguish, and doubt we are not alone. The presence, blessing, and peace of God celebrated in Psalm 29 were announced again at the baptism of Jesus and accompanied him on his way. By faith they can be with us as well.

FREDERICK J. STREETS

Exegetical Perspective

pleas for help. At the right moment the priests and choirs lead the people in reciting a theophany hymn such as this one, describing the coming of God from the heavenly throne to the Holy of Holies in the temple, where the Deity stands, invisible but unmistakably there, atop the "mercy seat," with the cherubim standing on either side. While God is always present throughout the universe, God is purposefully present uniquely in the temple, ready to receive the praises and petitions of the people.

The closing lines of the psalm complete the picture. God is at once enthroned in the upper heavens (see Ps. 104 for particulars) and ruling in Zion as king of the universe. Again, we can see how the Israelite community recognized the weight and value of its acts of worship. The acts of worship do not compel God to come to Zion, but they invite, even entice, the Deity to do so. The last sentence of the psalm can be translated as the NRSV translators have rendered it: "May the LORD give strength to his people! May the LORD bless his people with peace!" They may, however, be translated as declarations, not wishes: "The LORD gives strength to his people. The LORD blesses his people with peace!" Israel's worship was understood to change things, to effect what was prayed for, since the community understood worship to be a joint act of God and people, each essential to the outcome. Such an understanding carried dangers, of course, which is why some of Israel's prophets on occasion would denounce the notion that God in any way depended on Israel's responses to the Deity. See, for example, Amos 5:21: "I hate, I despise your festivals, and I take no delight in your solemn assemblies," and Isaiah 1:14: "Your new moons and your appointed festivals my soul hates."

Such denunciations of Israel's worship, however, almost certainly were not calling for Israel to abandon the worship of God. The prophets understood well that love of God and love of neighbor go together, but acts of worship can never substitute for acts of faithfulness to God in public and private life.

WALTER J. HARRELSON

Homiletical Perspective

God finds us and raises us to new life. In baptism, God's voice, the same great voice that thunders throughout the earth, gently names us as God's beloved. God's claim on all of creation now extends specifically to us, the water marking us and remaking us as we glory in God's amazing grace.

In the setting of people gathered for worship, the preacher might look for ways to describe God's glory, helping listeners identify the ways that God is working in our midst. Where do we hear God's voice, loud as thunder? In this modern, networked world, where thunder is just one of many sounds that clamor for our attention, do we hear God's voice in other ways? Where do we experience the fire of the Spirit? Where is God stirring the waters of our baptism so that we might live more fully into God's call? Where do we sense God shaking our core? Where do we find glimpses of the eternity that is God's peace?

The lections for the first Sunday after Epiphany call us to reflect on Jesus' baptism and thus on our own baptism and call to ministry as people who understand who Christ is and live as his disciples. For many Christians, this day is also the first Sunday they are back in church following Christmas, when we celebrate the miraculous gift of God born among us. Epiphany season is a time of discovery, a time for being intentional about opening our eyes to catch glimpses of God at work, a time for opening our hearts to the light of God's truth. Psalm 29 provides substance for reflection in this season, reminding us that it is God's voice that we hear as "heaven and nature sing" and that it is God's peace that came to dwell among us in great power in the person of Jesus Christ.

APRIL BERENDS

Acts 8:14-17

¹⁴ Now when the apostles at Jerusalem heard that Samaria had accepted the word of God, they sent Peter and John to them. ¹⁵The two went down and prayed for them that they might receive the Holy Spirit ¹⁶(for as yet the Spirit had not come upon any of them; they had only been baptized in the name of the Lord Jesus). ¹⁷Then Peter and John laid their hands on them, and they received the Holy Spirit.

Theological Perspective

The book of Acts' jubilant narrative of the church as a Spirit-filled community has often generated heated and sometimes bitter controversy. This brief passage has contributed to the church's perplexity, raising questions about how reception of the Spirit relates to the ritual of baptism by water. However, read carefully in light of other passages in Acts, these verses can help foster a growing consensus concerning what a truly "spiritual" church should look like.

The context is established by Philip's proclamation of the gospel in Samaria, which eventuated in a spate of baptisms. In verse 14, the focus abruptly shifts away from Philip's successful evangelical activity to Peter and John's mission in Samaria. These two apostles pray and lay hands on new converts who then receive the Holy Spirit. The vexing issue that informs this passage's drama is the previous absence of the Spirit among the newly baptized Samaritan Christians.

Through the centuries, the distinction between water baptism and baptism by the Spirit has captured the church's theological imagination. In the church's history, different Christian groups have explained this seeming differentiation of water and Spirit baptisms in diverging ways. Some, including most evangelicals, have held that baptism by the Holy Spirit occurs for all believers at conversion, subsequently witnessed to by

Pastoral Perspective

The Context. In the eighth chapter of Acts, the apostle Philip travels into Samaria, preaching the good news and working miracles. This is the first missionary outreach of the church beyond its Jewish roots and the first time the message of the coming of the Messiah is offered to the wider, religiously pluralistic world. In Acts 8:14–17, the story of the results of Philip's missionary work offers certain theological and exegetical challenges, as Philip baptizes Samaritan converts in the name of the Lord Jesus, but they do not receive the Holy Spirit until some time later, when Peter and John come to Samaria, pray, and lay hands on these new Christians.

Implications for the Life of Faith. From a pastoral perspective, this brief story offers rich and useful insights into the life of faith, both of the individual and of the community of the baptized. For as this story shows, the relationship between the moment of baptism and the lifelong journey of faith is a complex one that cannot be reduced to a predictable, linear system of cause and effect. People in churches today represent a wide variety of faith experiences: baptized as infants and as adult believers, raised as Christians and coming into the faith community later in life, having uninterrupted relationships with

Exegetical Perspective

The story of Acts is related by Luke through an expanding geographical progression of God's providential work via the Holy Spirit, starting in Jerusalem, ending up in Rome, and infiltrating many places in between (see 1:8). The section (6:8–9:31) that contains the focal passage for this Sunday features the work of Stephen and Philip—two Hellenists who were appointed by the disciples to "wait on tables" (6:2–5)—in Judea and Samaria and highlights the responses of three significant figures: Simon the magician (8:9–25), the Ethiopian eunuch (8:26–40), and Saul of Tarsus (9:1–9). More immediate to 8:14–17, the work of God is marching forward into Samaria, ironically (and providentially) resulting from the scattering of the followers of Jesus due to the persecution that broke out after the stoning of Stephen (8:1b). Therefore, Philip finds himself in Samaria, where he encounters a magician named Simon.

The two-part story of Simon the magician (8:9–13, 18–24) provides the immediate context in which 8:14–17 finds its meaning and significance. Luke identifies Simon as one who captivated and gained a following among the people of Samaria due to his practice of magic. The high esteem in which the Samaritans hold Simon is evident in that he is called "great" (*megas*), speaking of him not only in

Homiletical Perspective

Alongside the prophetic assurance of the Old Testament reading, the poetic glory of the psalm, and the vivid imagery of the Gospel, this reading from Acts seems very ordinary. Prosaic in its language, it is a straightforward and notably brief account of one event in the life of the early church. The chapters preceding and following it are far more dramatic (and far easier to preach), full of dialogue and detail. Consequently, this passage's significance is easy to overlook—but it remains a pivotal passage, describing a significant event in the unfolding of the story of the book of Acts.

There are (at least) three ways of preaching this passage. The first is to focus on the giving of the Holy Spirit as an essential part of the process of becoming a Christian. The idea of receiving the Holy Spirit makes many people uncomfortable; sometimes we end up worshiping and experiencing God as Duality ·rather than Trinity. This is an excellent opportunity to talk openly about the essential place of the Holy Spirit in our lives, although there are no details within the text itself about how the presence of the Holy Spirit was expressed in the lives of the Samaritans.

This passage has frequently been used to support a two-stage process of Christian initiation: first, one is baptized, and then, second (often at a later date

Acts 8:14-17

Theological Perspective

water baptism. Others, particularly the Pentecostal traditions, have insisted that there are indeed two different baptisms, a baptism by water and a later baptism by the Spirit. Wesleyan holiness movements have linked the "second blessing" with assurance of salvation and complete sanctification. For Roman Catholics, the initial gift of the Spirit at baptism is completed by a second gift of the Spirit at confirmation, which fosters Christian maturation. Other traditions have conflated the two, insisting that baptism for forgiveness and the conferring of the Spirit are aspects of a single phenomenon. Reformed theology has generally resisted the separation of baptism by water and baptism by the Spirit, regarding the water baptism as an outward sign, not only of the washing away of sins, but also of the inward giving of the Spirit.

In spite of the controversies, a convergence of ecumenical opinion develops when the passage is read in light of other episodes in Acts.[1] Three points become clear. First, the Spirit's operation cannot be neatly comprehended or controlled. Different patterns of relating the bestowal of the Spirit to the ritual of water baptism are evident in Acts. This passage implies that water baptism can exist without the conferral of the Holy Spirit, while Acts 10:44–48 suggests that the Holy Spirit can be given without water baptism. On the other hand, Acts 2:38 implies that water baptism is followed by the reception of the Holy Spirit. Similarly, Acts 19:1–6 implies that water baptism, the laying on of hands, and the conferral of the Holy Spirit, form one unit.

Considering the testimonies of these passages together, it seems that according to Acts the Spirit is free to act before, during, or after baptism. There is no monolithic pattern linking the reception of the Holy Spirit, water baptism, and the laying on of hands. Optimally, baptism and the bestowal of the Holy Spirit belong together.

Perhaps this insight has been preserved in the Reformed tradition's distinction between the "ordinary" means of grace and the "extraordinary" means of grace. God has covenanted with humanity to make God's grace available through certain practices, including baptism. However, God is not restricted to acting in these ways alone. Huldrych Zwingli, more than any other reformer, emphasized this freedom and sovereignty of the Spirit.[2] Although

Pastoral Perspective

the church and going through periods of inactivity or even estrangement.

This passage in Acts does not say how much time elapsed between Philip's baptism of the Samaritans and John and Peter's laying on of hands, but the simple fact that baptism and the reception of the Holy Spirit were not simultaneous for the Samaritan Christians affirms that the life of faith is a process that follows an unpredictable path of spiritual growth. "The Holy Spirit is at work in the lives of people before, in, and after their baptism. . . . [Baptism] marks them with a seal and implants in their hearts the *first installment* of their inheritance as sons and daughters of God."[1]

When considering the connection between baptism and the reception of the Holy Spirit, we assume that there will be a time of growth and maturation in faith after the baptism of a child. However, the same is true in the case of believers' baptism, that "baptism is related not only to momentary experience, but to life-long growth into Christ."[2] Baptism is the beginning of the journey, not the end.

Shaping the Liturgy. There are many ways that this can be reflected in the worship life of a congregation. In most churches, the Lord's Table is always visible, even set, on any Sunday morning, whether the Lord's Supper is to be celebrated or not; but in many of the same churches, the baptismal font is in evidence only if a baptism is scheduled. Otherwise it may be standing off in a corner of chancel or nave, or stored in another room until it is needed. How much more meaningful as a continuing transformative force in the community's life this symbol of baptism would be if the font stood in a prominent place every Lord's Day. It could be visibly and audibly filled with water every Sunday, perhaps at the same time that candles are lit or bread and wine are brought to the Table, as a constant reminder to all present of their baptism and an invitation to reflect on its meaning as they prepare for worship.

John the Baptist stood by the Jordan River preaching a "baptism of repentance for the forgiveness of sins" (Luke 3:3). As a sign of the ongoing need for repentance and forgiveness, the one presiding in worship could stand at the font as he or she leads the people in the prayer of confession. This is also an appropriate location for any call to commitment, mission, stewardship, or service to the church

1. See World Council of Churches, Faith and Order Commission, *Baptism, Eucharist and Ministry* (Geneva: World Council of Churches, 1982), 2.
2. See Huldreich Zwingli, "An Account of the Faith," in *The Latin Works of Huldreich Zwingli*, trans. Samuel M. Jackson (Philadelphia: Heidelberg Press, 1929), 2:46–47.

1. World Council of Churches, *Baptism, Eucharist and Ministry* (Geneva: World Council of Churches, 1982), 2; italics added.
2. Ibid., 3.

human terms (v. 9) but also in divine terms (v. 10). In typical Lukan fashion, Simon's acts are presented via a comparison and contrast to Philip's miracles. Both are able to perform amazing acts, and both gain a following because of them. Yet only Philip has an accompanying proclamation (v. 5), and only Philip's wondrous deeds are identified by Luke as "signs" (*sēmeia*; 8:6, 13; cf. John 2:23; 3:2; 6:2; 9:16), thus pointing beyond themselves to the content of his messianic proclamation. By contrast, Simon's acts in verse 11 are identified as "magic" (*mageia*), deeds performed through the invocation of unseen spirits and powers, which—with the lack of an identifiable source of power behind them—end up pointing back to Simon himself. In the end, the Samaritans and even Simon follow Philip, a recognition of the superior power evident in Philip's miraculous acts. The Samaritans believe and are baptized, as is Simon, who now constantly shadows Philip in awe (and envy?) of the miracles he is able to perform.

Simon's fascination with the miraculous deeds and power of the followers of Jesus, now Peter and John, continues in the latter part of the story (vv. 18–24). Upon witnessing the reception of the Holy Spirit by the Samaritans via the laying on of hands by Peter and John, Simon seeks to purchase this ability and power. What follows are Peter's harsh rebuke of Simon, identifying his heart as not being "right before God" (v. 21), and Simon's request for prayer from Peter and John so that nothing of this judgment will happen to him. Acts is silent on Simon beyond this.

In the focal passage for this Sunday (vv. 14–17), the apostles in Jerusalem have heard of the positive response of the Samaritans to the proclamation of Philip, and Peter and John are commissioned to go to them. Though some have argued for this visit to be understood as an effort by the Jerusalem church to check up and report on the situation, or even formally to approve or disapprove of it, such an interpretation lacks force, since the text makes no explicit statement on their precise motive. What is clear, though, is that Peter and John do not undo or redo what Philip accomplished among the Samaritans. Peter and John do not initiate a reproclamation of the messianic message, nor do they rebaptize the Samaritans. Rather, they pray for and lay hands on them so that they may receive the Holy Spirit. Peter and John, therefore, come as participants in the larger work of God, offering support for and extending what Philip had already accomplished.

associated with confirmation), one receives the gift of the Holy Spirit through the laying on of hands. There is no doubt that this is the pattern we see here; however, there is nothing in the text to indicate that this particular incident, isolated from the other stories of baptism and reception of the Holy Spirit in Acts, should be seen as paradigmatic for the church. Repentance, baptism, forgiveness, and the gift of the Holy Spirit belong together (2:38). The order they come in varies (for example, Acts 10:44–47). Likewise, while in this case the laying on of hands is the occasion on which the Holy Spirit is given, elsewhere the Spirit is given when the gospel is preached. This is one story of the gift of the Holy Spirit; we need the witness of other parts of Acts, and indeed of the Scriptures, to develop a full picture.

The second way to preach this text is to explore its immediate context. Chapter 8 of Acts focuses the story of the conversion of the Samaritans on the encounter with the magician Simon, who wants to buy the gift of the Holy Spirit. Exploring this makes clear that the Holy Spirit comes as a gift and not as something any of us can control. Philip the evangelist preached and baptized, but the Holy Spirit was not within his power to give. The apostles had to arrive in order for the Spirit to come. Furthermore, it is clear in the narrative that the Holy Spirit is far more powerful than Simon's magic; this is an issue worth addressing in a world where some people read their horoscopes daily, seeking guidance through tarot cards, crystals, and other "spiritual" sources.

The third approach, which is richest and does most justice to the text, takes account of both the wider context and the unique content of the passage. Stephen has just been martyred; the persecution of Christians has escalated, and they have been scattered far and wide, with only the apostles remaining in Jerusalem. These scattered Christians have taken to preaching wherever they find themselves. For Philip, that is Samaria, where he proclaims Jesus as Messiah and accompanies this proclamation with miracles. The Samaritans respond with faith, and he baptizes them.

But the believing Samaritans do not receive the Holy Spirit through Philip. This raises a whole host of questions. Was Philip's baptism second class? Or was it because they were Samaritans? It is not until the Jerusalem apostles arrive that they receive the Holy Spirit.

Although brief, the power of this story is revealed when we look at it from the perspective of the Samaritans. Historically, there had been great

Acts 8:14-17

Theological Perspective

the grace of regeneration through the Spirit is promised at baptism, the Spirit's operation is by no means limited to baptism. We can boldly trust that spiritual regeneration is promised with our baptism, but we need not despair that God's Spirit cannot work in any other way.

Secondly, the passage highlights the fact that the reception of the Spirit is not a bonus supplement to the Christian life but is absolutely essential to it. In this passage, John and Peter must complete the baptismal act initiated by Philip, for the forgiveness of sins and regeneration by the Spirit are correlative. The Christian life would be fatally deficient and deformed without renewal by the Spirit. The bestowal of the Spirit is not an optional second blessing intended for a spiritual elite but is a blessing granted to the whole church. Without the enlivening power of the Spirit, there can be no church. The Spirit that primordially blew over the waters must now breathe new life into God's people. An individual cannot be a member of the ecclesial community without sharing the Spirit that sustains the community's very existence. Accordingly, Luther associated the work of the Spirit with sanctification—the application of the benefits of Christ, including justification, to the believer.[3] Reformed theologians even more emphatically regarded sanctification as the necessary complement of justification.

A third crucial feature of the Spirit's operation is suggested by the cultural setting of the passage. It is telling that the scene is a city of the Samaritans, a people related to the Jews but despised by them as being religiously aberrant. By evangelizing this region, Philip had transgressed the boundaries of race and religion. This episode functions as one more step on the journey of the inclusion of both Jews and nonJews in the people of God. A primary characteristic of the Holy Spirit is its power to forge unity in the midst of cultural, ethnic, and ideological difference and tension. The Holy Spirit is an inclusive Spirit that fosters fellowship and communication across human boundaries.

LEE C. BARRETT

Pastoral Perspective

and the world, as an invitation to consider the many ways Christians live into their baptismal vows. If the font is movable, it could be placed in different locations around the sanctuary: by the entry doors to symbolize baptism as the means of incorporation into the Christian community, in the center aisle to show its centrality in the life of the faith community, or at the foot of the cross as a sign of our dying and rising with Christ in baptism.

Services for the renewal of baptism would also be appropriate any time this text is preached. Pastorally, there are several specific occasions or transitions in the life of a congregation or the lives of individual members that could be the focus of such a service. An entire congregation could be invited to renew their baptismal vows; traditionally this would take place as part of an Easter vigil, but it would be equally appropriate any time a congregation has experienced a major transition, a change of mission focus, or even an upheaval in its corporate life. Similarly, when a person or persons who have been estranged from the church are restored to the community, a public service of renewal of baptism could be accompanied by the laying on of hands for healing and blessing. This would encourage the entire congregation to reflect on the variety of paths the journey of faith may follow and the constant need for God's grace as they travel. In the same way, marriage ceremonies, reception of new members into the church, and funeral services also are opportunities for renewal of baptism and speaking of the ongoing (and ultimate) fulfillment of those vows.

The Holy Spirit moved in Samaria. The good news was preached, and a whole new community embraced the message of salvation. Philip baptized the new believers into the name of the Lord Jesus; Peter and John prayed and laid hands on them, bestowing blessing, healing, and commission as they received the Spirit. The way may not follow a particular formula; it may be circuitous and unpredictable, but "the whole Christian life is lived out of baptism, and growth is expected."[3]

KAREN STOKES

3. See Martin Luther, *The Large Catechism of Martin Luther*, trans. Robert Fischer (Philadelphia: Fortress Press, 1959), 59–64.

3. Presbyterian Church (U.S.A.), *Holy Baptism and Services for the Renewal of Baptism* (Philadelphia: Westminster Press, 1985), 72.

Exegetical Perspective

In variation from the more common order in Acts—receiving the Spirit just after, or even simultaneous with, water baptism—Luke's explanatory note in verse 16 clearly indicates that for the Samaritans the former had yet to occur following their water baptism. Though it is tempting to read various contemporary conceptions about the sequencing of water baptism and the reception of the Holy Spirit into this passage, no such normative pattern is to be found in Acts. As Ben Witherington notes, "the Spirit comes sometimes with apostles present, sometimes without (cf. 9:17); sometimes with the laying on of hands, sometimes without (cf. 2:38); sometimes very close to the time of water baptism, sometimes not; sometimes before water baptism, sometimes after (as here)."[1] The primary emphasis of the passage, then, is not on the sequence or order of actions.

Rightly to capture the thrust of this Sunday's focal passage, Simon must be brought back into play. In the larger account of Philip and Simon, Luke does not draw primary attention to the awe-inspiring acts themselves. Rather, he underscores the *source* of the power by which these acts are performed and from which the Holy Spirit is received. It is this power that elicits the allegiance of the Samaritans and captures the attention of Simon. In proper recognition and response, the Samaritans believe, submit to baptism, and later receive the Spirit as a gift from God. By contrast, though Simon believed and also submitted to baptism, he was so captivated by the miraculous acts themselves (so much so that he sought to buy the power) that he did not acknowledge the source behind them and seemingly did not receive God's Spirit. To put it baldly, the Holy Spirit is *God's* "gift" (*dōrea*, 8:20; cf. 2:38; 11:17), not a commodity to be purchased or owned, and God is giving it freely to those who will receive it as such. Keeping in mind the context of first-century Judaism, it is not unimportant that God is giving the gift here even to the Samaritans, which may have surprised or even angered some who heard of it. God's salvation knows no national boundaries, outsiders, or enemies . . . and neither does God's gifting of the Holy Spirit. This is the good news of Acts!

TROY MILLER

Homiletical Perspective

animosity between Jews and Samaritans. At best, they had regarded one another as second class. Even in the Gospels, the portrayal of the Samaritans is mixed. In Matthew 10:5 Jesus told his followers not to visit their villages, yet he himself spoke with the woman at the well in John 4, staying at her village for two days. Jesus healed a Samaritan leper (Luke 17:16), and a Samaritan was the hero in one of his parables (Luke 10:30–37). Philip came to preach the gospel, and the Samaritans believed, but they may well have been unsure about how welcome they would really be among Jewish Christians. That uncertainty may have been confirmed when they were not blessed with the gift of the Holy Spirit.

But then Peter and John came from Jerusalem. They were leaders among the apostles. Along with James, they had been with Jesus at the transfiguration. They were the ones sent to prepare the meal that we know as the Last Supper. In the early chapters of Acts, they healed and preached and were clearly the leaders of this newborn Christian faith. Their presence and subsequent laying on of hands with the giving of the Holy Spirit validated the Samaritans as full members of the newborn Christian church. This was one church, composed of Jew and Samaritan alike, whose former hostility turned to unity through the gift of the one Spirit.

Furthermore, in Acts 8:25, we hear that as Peter and John returned to Jerusalem, they preached to other Samaritan villages. Thus the apostles' ministry continued to embrace both Jew and Samaritan.

Seen from this perspective, this text marks a turning point. It contains good news for all, not just for the insiders. The gospel is proclaimed for strangers and aliens, for those who are typically perceived as second class. The text models a church that reaches across boundaries of nation and ethnicity, of tradition and heritage. We are inheritors of that gospel, called to continue that pattern of inclusion. Our faith, generations and centuries later, is as valid as the faith of the first Christians in Jerusalem and Samaria.

RAEWYNNE J. WHITELEY

1. Ben Witherington III, *The Acts of the Apostles: A Socio-Rhetorical Commentary* (Grand Rapids: Eerdmans, 1998), 288.

Luke 3:15-17, 21-22

15As the people were filled with expectation, and all were questioning in their hearts concerning John, whether he might be the Messiah, 16John answered all of them by saying, "I baptize you with water; but one who is more powerful than I is coming; I am not worthy to untie the thong of his sandals. He will baptize you with the Holy Spirit and fire. 17His winnowing fork is in his hand, to clear his threshing floor and to gather the wheat into his granary; but the chaff he will burn with unquenchable fire." . . .

21Now when all the people were baptized, and when Jesus also had been baptized and was praying, the heaven was opened, 22and the Holy Spirit descended upon him in bodily form like a dove. And a voice came from heaven, "You are my Son, the Beloved; with you I am well pleased."

Theological Perspective

Among the theological questions that this passage raises is a particularly thorny one: when John's baptism is so clearly tied to judgment and repentance, why does Jesus get baptized? Up to this point Luke has gone to extraordinary literary measures to establish Jesus' holiness, which he later reiterates in the temptation scene; so why does the voice from heaven declare a baptism of repentance to be a pleasing gesture?

The narrative of Jesus' baptism comes before Luke's genealogy and his account of Jesus' temptation in the wilderness. It is easy to pass over the seemingly banal genealogy that directly follows the baptism, but it holds a clue to our question. Luke's genealogy (3:23–38) begins in ambiguity and culminates with tragic paradox. The lineage starts with Jesus both joined to ("son of") and separated from Joseph ("so it was thought," v. 23 NIV); it ends with the leap from Seth, the son of Adam, to Adam, the son of God. Along the way, Jesus' religious and royal lines are established, but not without residual traces of tragic choices and destructive actions. In fact, Seth's location in the genealogy causes these traces to linger. Seth is the son born to Adam and Eve whom tradition considered a replacement for Abel, killed by his brother Cain (Gen. 4:25). Jesus stands in a stream of men (Luke, in contrast to

Pastoral Perspective

With many words Luke has told us of the births of John the Baptist and Jesus. Now with very few words Luke will transition from the end of John's preaching mission to the beginning of Jesus' public ministry. The necessary hinge is Jesus' baptism. The people are wondering if John might be the Christ, but John lets them know that one more powerful is coming, one empowered by the Holy Spirit. John's ministry of preparation for the Messiah is ending with his imprisonment by Herod. The beginning of Jesus' ministry is marked by his baptism, not described here but merely reported in one-half of one verse: "When all the people were being baptized, Jesus was baptized too" (Luke 3:21a NIV).

According to Luke, all we know about the baptism of Jesus is that it was with "all the people"— but maybe that is what the church has sometimes forgotten. Jesus presented himself for baptism as an act of solidarity with a nation and a world of sinners. Jesus simply got in line with everyone who had been broken by the "wear and tear" of this selfish world and had all but given up on themselves and their God. When the line of downtrodden and sin-sick people formed in hopes of new beginnings through a return to God, Jesus joined them. At his baptism, he identified with the damaged and broken people who needed God.

Exegetical Perspective

The Hebrews expected a Messiah to come and save them from destruction, leading the nation into a new political and religious future. John the Baptist, who was already preaching, baptizing, and collecting many disciples, was considered to be a logical candidate (John 1:35–38). But then came Jesus—also preaching, teaching, and baptizing. Behind the self-abnegating voice of John the Baptist rehearsed in the Gospel narratives is a swirl of intrigue and controversy. Leadership of this radical movement must be clearly identified: Will the real Messiah please stand up!

An obvious problem exists. If the adage is true, "where there is smoke, there must be fire," then the protests of John, clearly stating his inferiority to Jesus, must reveal that someone from somewhere thought that John was superior to Jesus. All four evangelists are compelled to define the relationship between John the Baptist and Jesus, attesting to the leadership conflict that was stirring in the background and giving witness to the final outcome (see Matt. 3:11–12; Mark 1:7–8; John 1:26–27, 33).

The Gospel of John describes the shift in leadership. John the Baptist is traveling with two of his own disciples when Jesus appears on the scene (John 1:35–39). John sees Jesus and declares him to be the "Lamb of God." John's disciples defect and

Homiletical Perspective

Baptism of the Lord Sunday comes abruptly each year to kick off the season of Epiphany. In our yearly liturgical journey we suddenly leap forward from the stories surrounding the birth of Jesus to his baptism in the Jordan as a thirty-year-old adult (Luke 3:23). The three-year lectionary cycle rotates between the accounts of Matthew (3:13–17), Mark (1:4–11), and Luke (3:15–17, 21–22). Paying careful attention to the particularities of the way each evangelist tells the "same" story adds freshness and depth to the proclamation.

Luke's account has a number of significant particularities worth exploring.

First, there is Luke's evocative introductory phrase "the people were *filled with expectation*" and "*questioning* in their hearts concerning John, whether he might be the Messiah" (3:15, italics mine). The hope for someone who can lead the people out of their current difficulties is a recurrent theme in human experience and history, especially when elections are at hand, economies are down, or nations are at war. What expectations are people filled with today? What are they looking for in a leader? How can they discern whom they should trust and support?

Second, there is Luke's insertion, immediately before the baptism, of verses 19–20, which tell of John's imprisonment by King Herod. This does two

Luke 3:15-17, 21-22

Theological Perspective

Matthew, does not include women in his genealogy) with great courage, personal flaws, competing interests, and fragile heroism.

Jesus was born *from* as well as *into* a world of systemic sin, and his baptism is a signal that he understood the full implications of the incarnation. He was not merely identifying with or showing solidarity with the human world; he was fully acknowledging its tragic structure. There are no innocent, no perfect, no unambiguous, no controllable, indeed no sinless, choices in this world. All choices must be made within a context of a system that precedes and impinges upon them.

Marjorie Suchocki's treatise on sin, *Fall to Violence*, is helpful here. Suchocki opens the book with reflections on her experience serving as jurist in a case where the defendant was found guilty. Although she believed that the individual committed the crime for which he was convicted, after the trial was over she began to reflect on her own place in the system that formed and eventually indicted this man. As a member of this interrelated system, she felt she had some relation to the man's crime.

> The sorry world of the crack house . . . had seemed so distant from my world as the academic dean of a theological seminary. But in truth, that "other" world was only a few miles from my home. Where did that world start, and where did it stop? "My" world was geographically close, but had I ever intentionally done anything at all to touch the lives in that "other" world? Was I only involved to judge its inhabitants? Or was there not a sense in which I was a participant in that world as well as mine, even if that participation were as an absentee neighbor?[1]

In fact, Suchocki has reframed the concept of "original sin" as that "which precedes us bending us willy-nilly against inclusive good."[2]

Here we come to a point of theological nuance and possible variation in the tradition. It is arguable that the writer of the Gospel of Mark thought Jesus did not escape the bending of his will against inclusive good; certainly Jesus' interaction with a Syrophoenician woman in Mark 7:24–30 allows us this theological reading. Jesus, shaped by his social and historical context, appears to respond "against inclusive good" to this woman's plea to heal her

1. Marjorie Hewitt Suchocki, *The Fall to Violence: Original Sin in Relational Theology* (New York: Continuum, 1994), 11.
2. Marjorie Hewitt Suchocki, *Divinity and Diversity: A Christian Affirmation of Religious Pluralism* (Nashville: Abingdon, 2003), 105.

Pastoral Perspective

It is a question worth asking whether our churches truly identify with sinners and are willing to get in line with them, to welcome and work for them as brothers and sisters in Christ. The church may say all the right words, declaring that we are hospitals for sinners and refuges for those who have lost their way, but too often we may send the message that respectable, successful folks are the ones we need to build up our communities. Time and again people who encounter difficulties in life drop out of our churches, seek help from other caregivers, and return to church only after they feel they can be recertified as respectable, churchgoing people. Jesus got in line with sinners and was baptized with them. That might be worth knowing and remembering.

Luke does not have Jesus say a single word out loud at his baptism, but after he is baptized, Jesus prays. Jesus is not only coming to us sinners; he is coming to God in prayer. He will not undertake his public ministry of teaching and healing in his own power and abilities. The source of his strength will be beyond himself. The Holy Spirit will encourage him all the way, even when the way becomes difficult. The disciples will learn this posture of prayer from Jesus, as the Spirit will give them the stamina and patience to love and love again in faithful ministry.

Again, it is worth asking whether our churches depend upon the Holy Spirit and our connection to God in prayer for the spiritual stamina to go into the world and make a difference in people's lives through Christ. This connection remains the lifeline of every disciple, every congregation, and every ministry. It is significant that this intensely spiritual experience following Jesus' baptism happens while he is in the posture of prayer. James Weldon Johnson prays that the church will never forget how to bend toward God for its strength:

> O Lord, we come this morning
> Knee-bowed and body-bent
> Before thy throne of grace.
> O Lord, this morning
> Bow our hearts beneath our knees
> And our knees in some lonesome valley.
> We come this morning
> Like empty pitchers to a fountain full.[1]

Identifying with sinners in the waters of baptism and holding onto God in prayer, Jesus will now be

1. James Weldon Johnson, "Listen, Lord—A Prayer," in *God's Trombones* (New York: Viking Press, 1927), 13.

began to follow Jesus. The message is clear: Jesus is the new Messiah, not John the Baptist.

Luke 3:17 establishes the locus of power using the words of John the Baptist: Jesus holds a "winnowing fork . . . in his hand, to clear his threshing floor." This common agricultural illustration was frequently used in the biblical world (Ps. 1:4; Prov. 20:26; Isa. 41:15f.; Jer. 15:7). The harvested grain is taken to the threshing floor and cleaned. Toss a portion of the harvested grain in the air with a winnowing fan, a fork-like shovel, then let the wind do the work. The wind takes control of the process, separating the wheat from the chaff, a mixture of heavy husks and straw. The wheat falls away from the chaff. The chaff is collected and burned, and the wheat remains safely stored in the barn.

Gospel writers promote both John and Jesus and their ability to bring listeners to judgment, "preaching a baptism of repentance for the forgiveness of sins" (Luke 3:3). The illustration of wheat and chaff (Luke 3:17), however, reveals that the most active agent is the wind. The agent that does the separating of good and evil, the righteous from the unrighteous, is the Spirit. John the Baptist and Jesus both preach and baptize, but the Spirit, like the wind in John 2, separates the righteous from the unrighteous. The light of truth, or the movement of the wind, exposes the unrighteous. Jesus holds the shovel, and the Spirit does the work.

The placement of the story of Jesus' baptism is significant in Luke's Gospel (3:21–22). Luke's story of Jesus' baptism occurs after the elaborate birth stories of John the Baptist and Jesus (Luke 1–2). A comparison of the stories of Jesus' baptism in the other Gospel narratives (Matt. 3:13–17; Mark 1:9–11; John 1:29–34) reveals that Luke gives a secondary place to this important event. In Matthew's Gospel we are given clear and specific details of the baptism. Jesus comes to John asking to be baptized. Dialogue between Jesus and John is recorded. The ritual in Matthew's Gospel provides the inauguration for Jesus' ministry (Matt. 3:16–17). The Gospel of Mark, in contrast, reports the baptism without the explicit dialogue between John and Jesus as recorded in Matthew, focusing attention on the Spirit of God, who is "well pleased" (Mark 1:10–11). The baptism, for both Matthew and Mark, appears as an important beginning of Jesus' public ministry. The Gospel of John, however, simply implies that this baptism occurs. No detailed report of the event is provided, just an indirect report in the voice of John the Baptist (John 1:32–34).

things. It serves to get John off the stage of history before Jesus is baptized and begins his ministry. John's work is done; Jesus' is just beginning. But the arrest of John also adds a somber note to the joyful epiphany that follows. Jesus receives his revelation, "You are my Son, the Beloved; with you I am well pleased" (v. 22), even as "all the evil things that Herod had done" (v. 19) reach a new level of depravity in the imprisonment of John, God's prophet (1:76). Rulers have violently resisted (and will continue to do so in the future) "the good news" as proclaimed first by John (3:18) and soon by Jesus (4:18). There is a personal cost to be paid by those who proclaim the good news. John's arrest thus foreshadows the eventual arrest and crucifixion of Jesus. Unfortunately, Luke's literary foreshadowing is erased when the lectionary leaves out verses 18–20. A sermon might reflect on how our understanding of baptism and life is enriched by reincorporating and reflecting on these excluded verses.

A third Lukan distinctive is that he does not show the reader the actual baptism of Jesus, but only the events *after* "all the people," including Jesus, have been baptized. Luke may have done this to avoid the question that apparently troubled Matthew, why Jesus would submit to a baptism of repentance by John, especially if John is "not worthy to stoop down and untie the thong of his sandals." But more positively, Luke adds to Mark's account that it is while Jesus "was praying" that "the heaven was opened, and the Holy Spirit descended upon him." This shifts the experience of the epiphany from the act of being baptized to the practice of prayer.

Throughout his Gospel, Luke shows us Jesus praying. Jesus prays before he calls his disciples (6:12), before asking them who he is (9:18), at the time of his transfiguration (9:29), before teaching his disciples how to pray (11:1), on the night of his arrest (22:41), and at his death (23:46). For Luke, what is characteristic of Jesus will also be characteristic of the church. In the Acts of the Apostles, Luke shows us the church in prayer as they wait for the promised coming of the Holy Spirit (Acts 1:8, 14). And after the promised Spirit comes upon them at Pentecost (with wind and fire!), they continue the regular practice of prayer (Acts 2:42; 3:1; 4:31; 6:4; 12:5, 12; 13:3; 14:23; 20:36; 21:5). What is begun in baptism is lived out through the practice of prayer by which one receives the Holy Spirit. Just as Jesus was empowered for and guided in his ministry through prayer, so too are his followers, down to this day.

Luke 3:15-17, 21-22

Theological Perspective

daughter when he says to her: "Let the children be fed first, for it is not fair to take the children's food and throw it to the dogs" (v. 27).

The story of the Syrophoenician woman, however, is one of Luke's selective omissions from the Markan material upon which he drew. Luke, perhaps in distinction from Mark, wants readers to know that the condition leading to Jesus' baptism is not related to his personal human will. In fact, in the symbolic depiction of the temptations, Luke has taken the reader out of history to show a stylized controlled experiment. The devil manipulates a factor, and Jesus responds. This temptation scene shows us that if there is only one variable to test Jesus' will, then he is able to make a sinless choice.

In a world with uncontrollable variables and overdetermined outcomes, however, Jesus' will is part of a larger nexus of tragedy and sin. Thus, by placing the baptism and the genealogy alongside the temptation, Luke wants his readers to understand both that Jesus' will is aligned with God's and that Jesus cannot escape the tragic structure of the world. He is, indeed, "the son of Adam, the son of God" (v. 38).

Whether we lean toward Mark or Luke (as interpreted here) on the issue of Jesus' will, we can agree that Jesus lived within a bent system. We cannot claim that Jesus made choices in a moral vacuum; the most that even the highest Christologies can affirm is that Jesus made the best choices possible within the systemic injustice that surrounded him.

Luke himself partakes of the ambiguity to which he points. He has a particular concern for the poor, and he gives more space to women than the other Gospels (forty-two passages, twenty-three of which are unique to Luke)—and yet Luke has no women who compare in assertiveness to the Syrophoencian woman of Mark 7.

John the Baptizer understood that Jesus would surpass him, and so he did. By accepting John's baptism, Jesus refuted John's dualism between the wheat and the chaff (v. 17). In fact, this led to accusations of his being a glutton and a drunkard, a friend to tax collectors and sinners (Luke 7:34). Perhaps this is a major sign of holiness: that we see ourselves as part of an interconnected web and that we are accused of being deeply enmeshed in that web.

CAROL LAKEY HESS

Pastoral Perspective

claimed as God's Son. As Clarence Jordan renders it: the sky split, the Holy Spirit in the shape of a dove came down upon him, and a voice came from the sky saying, "You are my dear Son; I'm proud of you."[2] At his baptism, Jesus is ordained as Messiah by a God who loves him and tells him so. This powerful affirmation, this calling from God, will sustain Jesus through a time of temptations in the desert and then through the joys and trials of faithful ministry.

Yet again, it is worth asking whether the church is sustained by knowing that God claims us as his children and is proud of us for bringing God's love to all people. John Leith, a Presbyterian professor and theologian, liked to say that every human life is rooted in the will and intention of God: "In baptism the child's name is called because our faith is that God thought of this child before the child was, that God gave to this child an identity, an individuality, a name, and a dignity that no one should dare abuse. Human existence has its origin not in the accidents of history and biology, but in the will and the intention of the Lord God, creator of heaven and earth."[3]

We need to hear this affirmation from God, and we need to hear it from each other. These are life-giving words that every human being upon this earth should hear: "You are my child, whom I love; with you I am well pleased." When Jesus heard those words, they changed his life forever. They will do the same for our children, our neighbors, our spouses, our church members, and, Jesus promised, even our enemies.

Luke uses very few words to share with us the baptism of our Lord. But those few words lead us to very deep wellsprings of joy in the faithful ministry. To identify with all people, to depend upon God in prayer for the strength to live and to love, and to hear the affirmation of your God as the source of your calling and purpose in life are the most enduring joys of life. These are the blessings of our life together in Christ as the church.

ROBERT M. BREARLEY

2. Clarence Jordan, *The Cotton Patch Version of Luke and Acts* (Chicago: Association Press, Follett Publishing Co., 1969), 23.
3. John H. Leith, "An Awareness of Destiny," in *Pilgrimage of a Presbyterian* (Louisville, KY: Geneva Press, 2001), 126–27.

Exegetical Perspective

In Luke's Gospel, Jesus' baptism clearly takes place after other people have been baptized: "Now when all the people were baptized. . . ." (3:21). No special ritual designed just for Jesus happens here. He stands in line with the others patiently waiting for John to baptize all of them with water. Also absent in Luke's account of Jesus' baptism are the ideas of judgment, fire, and righteousness. The baptism is uniquely characterized by prayer and a heavenly declaration, clearly marking the end of the ministry of John the Baptist and a new beginning for Jesus, but without the great fanfare seen in the accounts of Matthew and Mark.

That Jesus' baptism is an important story for the early church is attested by the presence of shared material in all four Gospel accounts. The specific details of the story, however, which vary with each Gospel presentation, reveal that each of the four Gospel communities understood Jesus' baptism in a different manner. Jesus' baptism in Luke's Gospel does not set him apart from the others; rather the act of baptism underscores the popularity of John's ministry and the willingness of Jesus to belong to the actions of the larger group.

Luke's special focus, however, is on prayer. Luke carefully notes that Jesus prays after he is baptized (3:21). Luke intentionally adds this important feature to the baptism ritual, which is missed by the other Gospel writers. For Luke the act of prayer will be the most important feature of the baptism and will clearly indicate the presence of the Holy Spirit in the life of Jesus and ultimately, the believer. In other places of Luke's Gospel, prayer is the focus of Jesus' ministry (5:16; 6:12; 9:18, 28ff.; 11:1; 22:41; 23:46). The power of Jesus' baptism as an important inauguration ritual, so important to the Matthean and Markan communities, loses energy in Luke's Gospel. Likewise, the heavy tones of the leadership debate between the followers of John the Baptist and Jesus are toned down in the Gospel of Luke. For Luke, prayer is all that matters.

LINDA MCKINNISH BRIDGES

Homiletical Perspective

A final Lukan distinctive is his addition of "in bodily form" to Mark's descending of the Holy Spirit on Jesus "like a dove." Through this addition Luke is emphasizing the paradoxical *reality* of this spiritual experience; it is tangible ("in bodily form") yet elusive and indefinable ("like a dove"). When heaven opens up, something real descends and enters earth. This is the inbreaking of the new age. The Spirit is loose in the world in and through Jesus, who will baptize his followers, not with water alone, but with the Holy Spirit and fire.

While the epiphany itself is christological, Luke's setting during prayer opens up questions about the nature of prayer and religious experience that could fruitfully be explored in a sermon. What is our experience of prayer? What about moments of epiphany? How are we called into ministry and empowered, first through our baptism, but then through prayer?

As for the revelatory message of the voice from heaven, Luke follows Mark's wording exactly, "You are my Son, the Beloved; with you I am well pleased" (3:22). This message is directed to Jesus himself, rather than to the listeners in the crowd (as in Matt. 3:17). It is about his self-understanding as God's Son. "This heavenly attestation combines Ps. 2:7, used at the coronation of Israel's king as son of God, and Isa. 42:1, a description of the servant of God," writes Fred Craddock. "The two texts join sovereignty and service."[1] A sermon could explore with examples from Jesus' ministry how he lived out those two aspects of his identity.

The preacher could also fruitfully explore the power of such affirmations in our lives: "You are my son, my daughter." "You are Beloved." "I am well pleased with you." When we experience this kind of honest affirmation from a parent or other significant person in our lives, we are strengthened in identity, will, and ability to act from that secure identity. Without it, most persons will struggle with low self-esteem. The good news is that in Christ we are all the Beloved.

ERNEST HESS

---

1. Fred Craddock, *Luke* (Louisville, KY: John Knox Press, 1990), 51.

Isaiah 62:1-5

[1]For Zion's sake I will not keep silent,
  and for Jerusalem's sake I will not rest,
until her vindication shines out like the dawn,
  and her salvation like a burning torch.
[2]The nations shall see your vindication,
  and all the kings your glory;
and you shall be called by a new name
  that the mouth of the LORD will give.
[3]You shall be a crown of beauty in the hand of the LORD,
  and a royal diadem in the hand of your God.
[4]You shall no more be termed Forsaken,
  and your land shall no more be termed Desolate;
but you shall be called My Delight Is in Her,
  and your land Married;
for the LORD delights in you,
  and your land shall be married.
[5]For as a young man marries a young woman,
  so shall your builder marry you,
and as the bridegroom rejoices over the bride,
  so shall your God rejoice over you.

Theological Perspective

Theology of Liberation. The dominant concept of Isaiah's exilic writing is liberation from captivity. God will soon take steps to end the Babylonian exile of Israel. Isaiah reminds the people of God's saving activity in the exodus, providing a basis on which to trust the promises of God to act similarly in the present. Consequently, one should avoid making the message of redemption so individualistic or other-worldly that this dimension lacks emphasis. The image of God's liberating involvement in history has fueled the imagination of many religious movements in history, including the Puritans, who understood their flight from the bondage of England, through the Atlantic waters to the promised land of New England, as a new exodus given by a providential God.

A more recent application of the redemption of Israel out of Egyptian slavery and Babylonian captivity is made in theologies of liberation. At the level of individual salvation from sin, God's redemption is for all, equally and without distinction. However, inasmuch as salvation includes a call for believers to work for justice in life now, one can see in Scripture God's preferential treatment of the poor (as liberation theologians have expressed it). The people of Israel were an oppressed people, captive in a foreign land. Not only would God bring about the redemption of

Pastoral Perspective

Isaiah 62:1–5 shines with good news about God's vindication of Jerusalem. Paired on this Second Sunday after Epiphany with the Gospel of John's account of Jesus turning water into wine at Cana, it is easy to consider this passage to be a straight-forward Epiphany text that focuses on yet another dramatic manifestation of God's power. But Isaiah 62 does not end where it begins. Before the good news of changed names and weddings, there is a call by the prophet for God to set things right. These five verses begin as a lament.

In chapters 40–55 of Isaiah, the prophet announces God's intention to bring about the defeat of the Babylonians and the return of the exiles. In chapters 56–66, those events have taken place, but all is still not right. The Babylonians may be defeated, but the restoration and rebuilding of Jerusalem have met obstacles and delays. In Isaiah 62, the prophet is addressing a people who have been full of hope but now must battle the deteriorating morale caused by broken dreams and crumbling faith. The people wonder if God is powerless to fulfill the promises made during the era of exile—or if God is indifferent to the plight of God's people.

In this context, the prophet does not announce another promise or declare another good news headline. The prophet's first audience is not Israel; it

Exegetical Perspective

Third Isaiah, the anonymous prophet writing after the exile (Isa. 56–66), draws on the long prophetic tradition of Israel/Jerusalem as God's wife. She first appears in Hosea 1–3 as the northern kingdom, cast off for her harlotrous idolatry. Jeremiah picks up her story and expands it (Jer. 2:1–4:2) to tell of the nation's fall to Babylon as a family breakup, again because of the wife's infidelity. Although God casts her off reluctantly, the divorce stands for rupture between God and Judah during the Babylonian period. Lamentations, in turn, draws on this tradition to present the forlorn, cast-off wife weeping and bewailing her fate. She first accepts the interpretation that the collapse of the relationship is her fault (Lam. 1), but then the text shifts the blame to God (Lam. 2). It is her story that names and interprets Judah's fall as the disintegration of a once loving family. In the process, the tradition defends God, whose own reliability has been sorely challenged by historical events. Not only is the survival of the nation up for grabs at this time, but God's own being faces radical doubt among survivors of this catastrophe.

When the book of Isaiah picks up the poetic figure of God's wife, Second Isaiah (Isa. 40–55) revives her as a symbol of the broken nation. In three poems (Isa. 49:13–50:3; 51:17–52:12; 54:1–17), God promises to bring her back, restore her

Homiletical Perspective

As a lectionary choice, Isaiah's intercessory pronouncement is paired with the wedding at Cana (John 2:1–11) and the psalmist's declaration that God's "steadfast love" extends beyond the known boundaries of heaven or earth (Ps. 36:5–10). Preachers may home in on several themes: the role of prophetic intercession; what it means to shine as nations, groups, or individuals; how to recognize God's view of us versus an identity battered by loss; how to excavate a metaphor weighted with demeaning implications; and the importance of reveling in God's delight over God's people.

For Zion's Sake. What happens when we stand up on behalf of a people (in this case, the prophet pleads on behalf of Zion/Jerusalem)? Poet and feminist activist Audre Lorde once proclaimed that our silence will not save us. Lorde spent her life calling marginalized people, especially lesbians, from the corners and closets to speak the truth. This example may seem far-fetched, but surely the prophet cries out in a climate of despair and disbelief, one that does not expect God to change things. Silence usually accompanies such feelings, but the prophet sets an example for us. He declares, "For Zion's sake I will not keep silent, for Jerusalem's sake I will not remain quiet, till her righteousness shines out

Isaiah 62:1-5

Theological Perspective

Israel, but God would seek in the Torah to provide means for protecting the most vulnerable in society: the poor, the widow, the orphan, the resident alien, and so on (see, for example, Exod. 22:21–27 and the provisions for the jubilee and Sabbath years in Lev. 25 and Deut. 15). God desires justice in this world, not only salvation in the next, and works to establish it.

Justice requires liberation for the oppressed, the poor, and all those marginalized by systems that favor some through the exploitation of others. The exodus was long the dominant biblical theme in African American church life, as the people worked toward justice from the days of slavery through the nadir under Jim Crow to the American civil rights movement. Whether in Latin America or South Africa, in feminist or womanist theology in the United States, liberation has been understood as the means to end oppression and establish justice. Liberation promises that those who benefit from injustice will lose power. Thus, Isaiah begins today's reading by pointing to Israel's vindication (vv. 1–2).

In anticipation of vindication, the oppressed must cling to the conviction that—contrary to what the oppressors may say—they are valuable to God and do not deserve the treatment they receive. "You will be a crown of beauty in the hand of the LORD, and a royal diadem in the hand of your God" (v. 3). One can almost hear in those words the self-affirmation of base communities in South America or the chant "I am Somebody!" that has risen from the African American community in the United States.

Liberation theology is no longer the prominent theological movement it once was. Injustice and oppression remain, however. How and where are we involved in God's promised work of liberation that is good news to the poor?

God's Surprise. The vindication of the oppressed comes as a surprise to those who fail to see that God is about a new work—especially those who now lose their status and power. "The nations shall see your vindication, and all the kings your glory," observes verse 2. It is surprising because the change is thoroughgoing and radical: Israel will receive a new name from God, which means a new identity and new relationship with God. The people have been called "Forsaken," and Judea called "Desolate," but now they have "My Delight Is in Her" and "Married" for new names (v. 4). A great new day will dawn through God's redemptive power, initiating a drastic reversal of the present order that vindicates Israel and manifests the Lord's delight in the people.

Pastoral Perspective

is God. The prophet begins by demanding that God do something about the situation: "For Zion's sake I will not keep silent, and for Jerusalem's sake I will not rest, until her vindication shines out like the dawn, and her salvation like a burning torch" (v. 1).

Part of the power of the Bible is the good news it has to offer to people who desperately need to hear such news, but the other part of the Bible's power is its ability to name the reality that people are facing. For example, a young but wise priest visited one of her parishioners in the nursing home where he lived. He did not speak or look at her. He simply stared straight ahead. Instead of trying to chat with him, she went straight to the Psalms. When she read one of the laments there, his face softened and he looked at his visitor for the first time: "Finally, somebody knows how I feel."[1]

Someone knows how we feel: this is the power of Isaiah 62:1 for the discouraged returnees and for anyone dealing with the feeling that God has turned away in indifference. To follow the prophet's example, we need to acknowledge the reality faced by those dealing with defeat and broken dreams before we move to words of hope and new beginnings. Otherwise, the good news we bring them can feel empty and even untruthful.

Isaiah 62 also gives us a model for honest prayer when life is difficult and God seems distant, if not indifferent. We dare to emulate Isaiah's lament and bold protest because those are elements of the prayers of God's people just as much as words of thanksgiving and praise. Isaiah's protest to God reminds us that in our prayers "[t]here is nothing out of bounds, nothing precluded or inappropriate. Everything properly belongs in this conversation of the heart. To withhold parts of life from that conversation is in fact to withhold part of life from the sovereignty of God."[2]

Isaiah's lament and protest in chapter 62 cannot be ignored, but neither can it properly be seen as Isaiah's last word. There is good news here—very good news, made explicit in a change of names.

Names in the Old Testament offer clues to the character of the person named. A change in name can represent a change in character, such as the new name of Israel given to Jacob (Gen. 32:28). Here in Isaiah 62 the name change does not just describe the change in Israel's character; it also describes the change in God's relationship with Israel and in

---

1. Ellen F. Davis, "Like Grass, I'm Dried Up," *Living Pulpit* 11, no. 4 (2002): 11.
2. Walter Brueggemann, *The Message of the Psalms: A Theological Commentary* (Minneapolis: Augsburg Publishing House, 1984), 52.

disappeared children to her, and resume their relationship, even confessing to have abandoned her. "For a brief moment I abandoned you, but with great compassion I will gather you" (Isa. 54:7). It is this story of the nation's fall and promised renewal that Third Isaiah revisits in speaking to the exilic people regathered in Jerusalem. They are divided into factions: those who stayed in the land, those who have returned from exile, and those born later. Power struggles are massive and poisonous, and God's fidelity is again in question as the people try to rebuild and begin life together anew.

In Third Isaiah's poem, God speaks about speaking, as if to surprise readers who expect only divine silence, expect no response, anticipate no vivid interaction between them. "I will not keep silent . . . I will not rest" (v. 1). The reason God moves to speech and action is not for God's own honor but to vindicate Zion, the broken, defeated, God-abandoned city-woman. God's speech will make her vindication burst out and her salvation become "a burning torch." That new event will create global awareness of the city's glory. Her emergence will be like an epiphany revealing her beauty, her royal stature, and her new identity because God will give her a new name (vv. 2–3). She will be a crown and a royal wreath in God's own hand. God will receive honor and glory on account of her.

Zion's new life will stand in marked contrast to her previous experience. "You shall no more be termed Forsaken, and your land shall no more be termed Desolate" (v. 4). With these words, Third Isaiah recognizes the historical devastation of the community, the city's suffering, and the long time of despair in which they have lived. For Zion to be vindicated means, at the least, that the reality of past horrors be acknowledged for what they have been, that the experience of divine abandonment be recognized as true. But now everything is to change, and the change rests not in anything she must do, but in God's enduring love for her. No longer will she be desolate, lost, and forsaken; now she "shall be called My Delight Is in Her" (v. 4). God announces a reunion of the broken household, a remarriage in which God delights in her and her land shall be married.

The couple's reunion will be as tender and delightful as the honeymoon (Jer. 2:15), as when "a young man marries a young woman" (v. 5). That is how God who has built her, created her, and formed her will marry her again. Like the bridegroom rejoicing over the bride, "so shall your God rejoice

like the dawn, her salvation like a blazing torch" (v. 1 NIV).

Zion's light is dim in the world, decimated by exile. The only thing that can uncover Zion's ability to shine is to hold God accountable. The notion of "holding God accountable" makes many of us squeamish. Elie Wiesel, in "The Trial of God," accuses God of being absent from the horrific genocide of the Holocaust. While we will never know how brutally the nations of Judah and Israel came to their ends, the biblical texts point to something like the Holocaust. In Isaiah's time, some of Judah's people have settled into exile, living as aliens in Babylon; others, such as the poor or infirm, have been left on the land. It is not hard to imagine that these two populations experienced the exile differently. In our day, there is similar difference between watching an event on the news and living deeply in it. The event may be the same, but the two vantage points are very different.

Until She Shines. The goal, according to the prophet, is to restore "shine" to Judah, represented by Zion in the text. What does it mean to "shine," as a nation and as a person? How do we recover from devastating and debilitating events in our lives? In this case, Isaiah speaks to what happens when a nation-state's identity has been stripped by war, when its best and brightest have been carried away to a foreign land, when those who once saw themselves as God's chosen lose their luster.

Identity is sometimes located—or at least revealed—in the way we name ourselves. In the text, Israel considers herself "deserted," "despised," and "divorced." YHWH has been her consort, her husband, but abandoned and left to languish in a strange land, she feels the absence of a God she sang would always be with her. The prophet must reawaken her sense of being special without arousing her arrogance. Imagine, if you can, how refugees from the Sudan must feel. How do you reclaim your identity when you feel "lost"?

A New Name. The prophet says it is time for a naming ceremony: "you shall be called by a new name." Naming is powerful. What someone calls you defines you. In the 1970s epic television series, Alex Haley's *Roots*, a scene about naming is especially poignant. After several failed attempts to run away, the African Kunta Kinte has his foot chopped off. One would think the foot-chopping incident was the most brutal part of the scene, but no; the beating he

Isaiah 62:1-5

Theological Perspective

The surprising work of God marks a common theme of Scripture. YHWH chooses a ragged, not particularly moral, seminomadic clan as God's special people ("How odd of God to choose the Jews," quipped the humorist Ogden Nash). The Magnificat, Hannah's great prayer of thanksgiving at the birth of Samuel, which is repeated by Mary in Luke 2, reiterates that theme of surprising reversals of fortunes: God has "scattered the proud in the thoughts of their hearts"; "brought down the powerful from their thrones, and lifted up the lowly"; "filled the hungry with good things, and sent the rich away empty" (Luke 1:51–53). Jesus, himself born in humble conditions, often made the point. Not only did Jesus' fraternization with the marginalized of his society demonstrate God's surprising work, but parables such as the Laborers in the Vineyard (Matt. 20:1–16, ending with "The last will be first, and the first will be last") bear witness to it also.

Clearly Isaiah's message of return from exile in 62:1–5 reflects the long biblical tradition of God's promised liberation of the oppressed with the unexpected vindication of Israel that recreates them with a new identity in God.

Covenant. The naming of the land Beulah (Married) in verse 4 and the image of marriage in verse 5 ("For as a young man marries a young woman, so shall your builder marry you") remind the reader that God's liberating activity grows out of God's covenant promise to Israel—for marriage always evokes ideas of covenant. The gods of the ancient world were often capricious; one could not know when favor or disfavor might be forthcoming. YHWH, on the other hand, imposed limits on God's own freedom to exercise power. In the covenant, God promised steadfast love—*hesed*—as the basis of the relationship with the people, and in return the people promised to love and serve God. Judgment may come, but it will always be on the basis of the covenant—and because of the covenant, restoration will always follow. Liberation renews Israel's relationship with God to wholeness, because God will be true to covenant.

RICK NUTT

Pastoral Perspective

Israel's future. Instead of being called "Forsaken," Israel can be called "My Delight Is in Her." Instead of the land being called "Desolate," the land may be called "Married" (in Heb., *be'ulah*), a name that signifies God's commitment to Israel and Israel's good future.

Name changes also can signify a change in relationships and in the future. When a husband and wife hyphenate their names, or more traditionally, when a woman takes her new husband's last name, the change in names is intended to symbolize the new relationship and the new future for each partner. When a neglected child goes through the foster system and is then adopted by parents ready to love her as their very own, then her change of surname is good news signifying a priceless gift of love and a new future.

What the prophet announces to the people of Israel, God has revealed to us in Jesus Christ. We "who once were far off have been brought near by the blood of Christ" (Eph. 2:13). We, who may properly be designated "sinners," have been renamed as God's "beloved children." We too have received a priceless gift of love and a new future.

The prophet begins these five packed verses with a bold protest against how God appears to have turned away from God's people. The prophet ends with names signifying how God has turned toward God's people—and with the image of a wedding. God has not turned reluctantly to face us; God comes toward us with all of the delight and joy that a bridegroom has for his bride. What a startling image of God's grace this is, full of attraction to and love for us.

Everyone loves a good wedding. Pastors can use the Isaiah and John passages to signify the joy of our relationship with God. While we may never witness the changing of water into wine at our weddings, as the people do at Cana when Jesus performs his first "sign," we do get a glimpse through the bridegroom and bride of God's great and personal love for each one of us.

W. CARTER LESTER

Second Sunday after the Epiphany

over you" (v. 5). This is her vindication, her restoration, and her salvation.

Isaiah's poem, like the poetry of prophets before him, takes historical circumstances and transposes them into the smaller story of a couple and their household. The poetry moves between language about an ancient city and the life of a bride. It attends to and gathers up the suffering of generations by using imagery of a woman cast off and abandoned. In ancient Israel such a woman faced life-threatening peril, because she could not survive without family to support and protect her.

This poem reframes her prospects. Not only will she be safe and protected; she will be raised up and singled out from among the nations to be God's wife, the one in whom God delights above all others. In this poetic world, Isaiah turns the family story firmly in the new direction begun earlier in the book. Here God reiterates the promise to take her back and restore the household in tender love and affection, in terms designed to persuade the unpersuaded audience of their call to live anew in this family. For the community struggling in conflict over how to rebuild city walls, how to rebuild the temple, how to govern themselves, how to decide who belongs among them, this text is a kind of epiphany. It reveals God in their midst, defending, protecting, and insisting on their special beauty. This God will not relent until the city is vindicated.

This God is the God of the poor, afflicted, enslaved, and downtrodden. This God tells them they are chosen, singled out, selected from all the earth's people as God's beloved bride. Isaiah's passage supports divine election not to buttress the contented, to uphold the secure, the confident, or the arrogant. Isaiah's theology of election is rhetoric of immense power because it tells the poor, the second-class nation, the excluded and cast-off women of this world, that God takes immense delight in them.

KATHLEEN M. O'CONNOR

endures is punctuated by a painful ending in which Kunta Kinte finally succumbs to the slave master's designation for him, "Toby." The glory of his heritage and the splendor of his name disappear in that moment. His name suffers a profound death. During the showing of *Roots* and for years afterwards, many people reported being irrevocably changed by this scene.

How do once-proud and self-knowing people reclaim their identity? How do they rename themselves? Exile has beaten them into resigned submission. Silence gives testimony to their loss. Who speaks for the people whose light has been extinguished, whose glory has been dimmed?

A Covenant with One's Maker: Marriage Made in Heaven. Many of us reject marriage as it functioned in ancient Near Eastern culture (and in some cultures today). We reject marriage that demeans and devalues women and does not see them as full and equal partners in the relationship. In the marriage metaphor of the biblical text, no such relationship exists. The husband is "lord" over everyone in his household, including the wife or wives he "owns." This metaphor resonated with biblical listeners because it reflected their view of the Deity's power—only greater and more ironclad. When preaching this text, then, preachers must make every effort to avoid ascribing textual values that are not liberating for twenty-first-century readers. The point, of course, is that God loves so deeply and so completely that though God may have been the reason for the loss of identity, God wants to restore and revive God's people. What kind of relationship must we preach between deity and people if we believe in God's sovereign nature and humanity's radical freedom? Is it possible to do both?

A Rejoicing God. No matter how problematic the marriage metaphor is, the prophet focuses on the feeling of a new and giddy marriage, at least for the husband. The husband, representative of the Deity, sings and dances for joy. Ancient Israelite men would no doubt have understood the power of the role of protector and redeemer. So would women, who depended on this protection in a precarious world. The nation, as God's wife, would experience God's joy as evidenced in their return to their homeland, their sense of belonging, and their hope of never again being banned from all that was dear to them.

VALERIE BRIDGEMAN DAVIS

Psalm 36:5-10

⁵Your steadfast love, O Lᴏʀᴅ, extends to the heavens,
 your faithfulness to the clouds.
⁶Your righteousness is like the mighty mountains,
 your judgments are like the great deep;
 you save humans and animals alike, O Lᴏʀᴅ.

⁷How precious is your steadfast love, O God!
 All people may take refuge in the shadow of your wings.
⁸They feast on the abundance of your house,
 and you give them drink from the river of your delights.
⁹For with you is the fountain of life;
 in your light we see light.

¹⁰O continue your steadfast love to those who know you,
 and your salvation to the upright of heart!

Theological Perspective

This part of Psalm 36 follows an account of the ways of the wicked person (vv. 1–4). The person who takes joy in plotting mischief is described as listening to the voice of sin in his or her heart. The psalmist seems intent upon reckoning with the knowing doer of wrong. With verse 5 there is an immediate shift to a reflection on the goodness and righteousness of God toward those who incline their hearts to God. It is the juxtaposition of these two reflections that makes this text an important aid in thinking about the importance of this season of Epiphany.

It is a cardinal rule within the broad stream of the Augustinian tradition that fully to understand and appreciate the expansiveness of God's grace, it is important to have some clear sense of the depths of human sinfulness. While the writer(s)[1] of this psalm are more intent on contrasting the ways of the conscious evildoer and the ways of the God of grace, thinkers in the Augustinian tradition—particularly its Reformed branch—have observed the propensity

1. Several commentaries note the distinct possibility that the two distinct sections of this psalm (vv. 1–4, 11–12, and vv. 5–10) may actually have been two separate meditations that were fused together at some point in the redaction of the book of Psalms. If this is indeed the case, then clearly the final redactor's aim was to contrast the lament in the face and experience of evil with the hope borne of God's grace. See Hans-Joachim Kraus, *Psalms 1–59: A Commentary*, trans. Hilton C. Oswald (Minneapolis: Augsburg Publishing House, 1978), 397–98.

Pastoral Perspective

Some people comprehend the essence of something that is presented to them more readily than others. Gaining insight and perspective from our experiences can be a slower process for some of us and is a part of our natural maturation. During the seasons of Christmas and Epiphany, we are presented with images and stories of God from narratives of the infant Jesus. There are ways God may be understood that are not initially apparent to us when we read and hear these stories. God-among-us represents a truth about us and God that is important for us to recognize on our journey of faith.

The Christian witness begins with what people say about a baby named Jesus. Later in his ministry, Jesus will refer to children as models for the attitude that opens us to the meaning and power of faith. Sin, it seems, is a loss not of innocence but of our ability to see and trust God as a child might trust a parent. Our dependence upon God is not a sign of weakness, any more than it marks the absurdity of having faith in God. It is instead a mark of wisdom born from our recognition that the spiritual quality of the life we seek is not found totally in our own strength or understanding of life. It is found in our acceptance of responsibility for the life we create, even as we acknowledge our limits.

Exegetical Perspective

Surrounded by a long and plaintive lament of an individual hounded by enemies (Ps. 35) and a classic wisdom poem (Ps. 37), this psalm opens with a wisdom poem (vv. 1–4) and closes with a lament (vv. 10–11). The most prominent section (vv. 5–9), however, is a beautiful hymnic portrayal of God's grace and mercy, which is boundless and beyond comparison. To be in God's loving presence is like enjoying a sumptuous banquet.

The wisdom poem (vv. 1–4) opens with personified Evil addressing evildoers, encouraging them to believe that their evil deeds will go unnoticed even by God. For them, evil deeds have become a way of life, and the path of goodness is alien to them. Not even during the night's rest does their thirst for destruction subside; even as they sleep, they plot their next step in taking advantage of others. One thinks of those who expend enormous amounts of energy plotting how to evade just laws designed to protect the community from predators.

The opening wisdom text connects with the following hymn in one powerful way. The contrast is not drawn, as in Psalm 1 and frequently in the Psalms, between evildoers and the righteous. The contrast is rather between those whom Evil has corrupted, who now know nothing else, and those

Homiletical Perspective

Throughout the centuries, the Psalms have served as the prayer book of the church, reflecting every sort of human emotion and predicament and portraying the range of conditions in which we find ourselves in relationship to God. The church would do well to pray often these verses from Psalm 36, as they speak in powerful, beautiful language of God's great love and our call as God's people.

The psalmist praises God, whose abiding love and faithfulness stretch to the skies above. God's justice, strong as the mountains, reaches into the depths of all that is. As the mountains keep the land from succumbing to the chaos of the sea, so God's love keeps creation from plummeting into the deep. The nature of God's love and faithfulness is woven into the very fabric of the universe; the whole of the world is dependent upon it. Humans too have a place in this love, described poetically as being under the shadow of God's wings.

We find in these verses a radical, joyous, inclusive vision of God's great love. The psalmist exalts—how wonderful it is, O God, that you draw us in, all your creatures, folded under your wings and seated at your table. Though the psalmist does not explicitly bid us to do so, the preacher might invite the congregation to reflect upon what such a gathering might look like. What does it mean for us to be

Psalm 36:5-10

Theological Perspective

of all people to harbor a *manufactory of sin* in their hearts. This is especially the case when that sin is related to the construction of idols.[2] It is in the building of these idols that the wicked are most clearly heeding the voice of sin in their hearts.

Moreover, the NRSV translation suggests that through self-flattery the wrongdoer is made blind to her or his own sin. In sum, we have the picture of someone to whom evildoing is an exquisite pleasure. It is further made clear that the writer of this psalm suffers because of the evildoing of the wicked. Against this backdrop the psalmist(s) draws a picture of God as the protector of the weak—"the children of human beings" (v. 7b, my trans.)—and the "light" of the pious. It is here as well that we find the great value of this psalm for the church.

Human history is replete with the laments of persons and peoples who have suffered because of the evildoing of the wicked. Perhaps more distressing is when the evil that is inflicted becomes an almost "exquisite pleasure" for those inflicting it. One has but to reflect on stories that emerge from every holocaust in history to see this reality. What one can find as well in many of these stories is the dogged dedication of those enduring the wrath of evil in the conviction that God is their protector who will finally make things right.

The superlative example of this in the North American context is the witness of the enslaved African American Christian community of the antebellum United States. Theirs was a faith built entirely on the experience of God's nourishing presence in the midst of a "weary land." The spirituals born of their faith and the narratives that are their lingering witness all point to the God who was the final protector of their children when law and custom were not, the host of the one place and table at which they might find their full humanity—that is, the church—where their hope and wisdom were sustained by the one who was forever faithful. In all of this, their faith was not confirmed by their immediate circumstance—for they remained chattel in the eyes of many—yet their faith was greater than their circumstance. Theirs was a faith born and nurtured in a world that, while seemingly the same, had changed fundamentally and inalterably because of the presence of God.

This presence created a space in which they and their children could experience their humanity as

2. John Calvin, *Institutes of the Christian Religion*, ed. John T. McNeill and trans. Ford Lewis Battles (Philadelphia: Westminster Press, 1960), 1.1.8.

Pastoral Perspective

In Psalm 36 David affirms that God shows us kindness, even when we are most foolish and trusting in our own abilities. He fears that those who do not fear God will reap the results of their rejection. David refers to the kindness of God with gratitude and prayerfully requests that God extend kindness to those who trust God. He believes that those "who do put their trust under the shadow of [God's] wings" (vv. 7–8, my trans.) will be rewarded.

Cornelia (Corrie) Schumann, a friend of mine, told me a story from her childhood that beautifully illustrates this reality, which I share here with her permission. "My father grew up on a wine farm and was a high school scholar," she said. "He became a professor in chemistry at the University of Pretoria. I adored my father. I liked to sit on his lap, hold his hand when we walked, sit close to him when he cut his roses in the garden, and stand next to him when he fed the day-old chicks. I liked the smell of his white laboratory coat in which there were small holes caused by chemicals.

"We had a small room at the back of our house, and against one wall my father and mother's trunks were put on top of each other. Every morning before my father went to work he went into this little room and stayed there for a while. One day I peeped through the keyhole and saw him kneeling at the trunks. He was praying. Next day I dared to tiptoe towards him when he was kneeling, very much unsure if I would disturb him. The next moment he turned his head and with his eyes still closed he put out his arm to welcome me to kneel next to him. Immediately I knew my father had asked Jesus if he wanted me there too!

"When I knelt down my father's strong arm was around me. Jesus loved my father and I knew Jesus loved me. How absolutely wonderful! My father loved Jesus and from that day I too loved Jesus. Every morning since then the circle was completed. The circle of love and peace and joy in the heart of Jesus was in the heart of my father and was in the heart of a four-year-old girl named Corrie. Often when I think of my father I remember that day as if it was yesterday."

It is not always easy to trust in God or to sing praises to God as David did. He must have been a pleasure to worship with and to be around because of his exuberant expressions of faithful joy. Like Corrie and David, we wait to be embraced and invited into our own epiphany of God's presence and love. We cannot just think our way into the heart of God. Arriving there requires that we be

Exegetical Perspective

who have received the grace and mercy of YHWH, which issue only in joy and delight.

Verses 5–9 vividly and powerfully depict God's steadfast love (*hesed*), faithfulness (*'emunah*), righteousness (*tsedaqah*), and judgment (*mishpat*) by means of a series of images: These divine qualities extend into the heavens, reaching the clouds. They bear comparison with mighty mountains and the great deep (*tehom rabbaʻ*). Psalm 103 uses similar images: "For as the heavens are high above the earth, so great is [God's] steadfast love toward those who fear him; as far as the east is from the west, so far he removes our transgressions from us" (Ps. 103:11).

"You save humans and animals alike, O LORD" (36:6c). The poet claims not only that God the Creator cares for animal life, along with the rest of creation (see Ps. 104), but also that God's steadfast love, faithfulness, righteousness, and judgment enrich both animal and human life.

The closing lines of the hymn (vv. 7–9) bear comparison with other psalms portraying God's intimate love and presence (see Pss. 23, 73, 139). The steadfast love of God is "precious" (*yaqar*) or highly prized. Proverbs 3:15 declares Wisdom to be more highly prized, or rarer, than jewels, beyond all other possessions in value. God's love is likewise beyond compare. God's love provides security for all people (*bene 'adam*) under the shadow of God's wings. Psalm 17:8 connects the two thoughts found here in 36:7: "Guard me as the apple of the eye; hide me in the shadow of your wings." See also Psalms 57:1 and 63:7. The wings of God bore the Israelites from Egypt across the dreaded desert to God—"to me" (not Mt. Sinai but to God; Exod. 19:4). Jesus' lament over Jerusalem shows the same degree of intimacy conveyed by a similar expression: a mother hen gathering her brood under her wings. (See Matt. 23:37 and Luke 13:34.)

In the following verse (v. 8), this intimacy between God and the human community appears in the imagery of food and drink. The use of the term "all people" (*bene 'adam*) in verse 7 means that eating and drinking at God's table is not a direct reference to the worship of God in the temple, as some commentators have suggested. The imagery is broader: God's love extends to all; God's protection is for all, and all have access to the table God spreads.

"For with you is the fountain of life; in your light we see light" (v. 9). This line, familiar from the prayers and liturgies of the church, sees God not only as the Creator. God continues to give life and

Homiletical Perspective

together at God's table, to feast together in God's house? What is our most hopeful vision for such a gathering? As we taste God's sweet goodness, we see God's light reflected on the faces of those around us, on all the people who take refuge there. Might we be surprised at what we see?

These lovely verses comprise the core of a longer psalm, the rest of which describes the persistence of the wicked in trying to undo God's work and God's people. The psalmist responds by looking to God and reminding the people of God's steadfastness. In the midst of threatening opposition, mischief makers, and evildoers, God persists in love, calling us always home to the joy that comes when we are gathered together, drinking from the river of delight. In the face of persistent arrogance, deceit, and ways that are not God's ways, the psalmist praises God, rejoicing in the fact that "all people may take refuge in the shadow of your wings" (v. 7). This prayer includes not only the people who have it all figured out, but all people seeking sanctuary from the things that threaten to undo us.

In the book *Traveling Mercies,* writer Anne Lamott explains why she makes her young son Sam go to church. "I want to give him what I found in the world, which is to say a path and a little light to see by." [1] In the same book, Lamott describes a woman named Ranola, a devout pillar of the church. Ranola was weary of Ken, a gay man who was a member of the church. She had been raised to believe that his life was not pleasing to God. Ken was dying of AIDS. He had been too ill to make it to church, but one Sunday he returned to worship, though he was unable to stand for the hymns. During the singing, Ranola watched Ken with a cool eye, his face contorted in a combination of illness, pain, and joy. Then suddenly, Ranola's face assumed the same expression as Ken's, and she went to his side, lifting his body up next to hers, his weakness resting on her strength, and vice versa. Ranola's fears melted, as both she and Ken began to cry. [2] In that moment, they found shelter and hope, resting together in the shadow of God's wings, drinking from the fountain of life.

This is but one example of how we might glimpse God's steadfast love, a love so great that it stretches to the depths of the earth, yet so gentle that it folds us under its wings. It is always present, holding together the depths of creation and the core of our being. When we gather as God's people, we commit

---

1. Anne Lamott, *Traveling Mercies: Some Thoughts on Faith* (New York: Pantheon Books, 1999), 99–105.
2. Ibid., 63–66.

Psalm 36:5-10

Theological Perspective

more than suffering and a veil of tears. They could see through to eternity and with *that* vision claim a sense of "somebodiness" that no whip or auction block could finally destroy. While most enslaved African Americans lived their entire lives in slavery, they were able to pass along a hope to each succeeding generation that would not wane in the face of segregation, lynching, and decades of oppression, precisely because its bearers understood that they were not trapped in the momentary reign of evil.

In our contemporary context it is not uncommon for many in the church to proceed as if, in the face of the wicked, God is not enough. They seek to control the levers of powers politically, economically, and militarily in the hopes that the creation of a "Christian" nation, society, or culture will ensure their flourishing and guard against their being stepped on by the proud or the wicked. Time and again, however, we have seen that it is precisely this tendency that has led the church and good Christian folks to visit wickedness on others. It is this need for "more than God" that has always led to the manufacture of idols to serve as proxies for God—flags, images, certain translations of Scripture.

We have learned from history that all of this inexorably comes to naught. For in the end, the only proxy for God is God, the God whom we see in the face of Christ and experience in the power of the Holy Spirit. As we move on through this season of Epiphany, let us recall the wisdom of the redactor of this psalm: namely, that the wicked will do what they do, finding exquisite pleasure in it, but that God is the only answer to their works and our only protection.

STEPHEN G. RAY JR.

Pastoral Perspective

open to seeing, feeling, hearing, and being touched by God through our experiences and the story of God's presence among us.

Spiritual experiences cannot be controlled or predicted. We can prepare ourselves to receive them by being open to them at times other than when we are in crisis. We prime ourselves for this to happen through our prayer and meditation life, by trusting God and using this confidence to take risks and serve others. The discipline of prayer keeps our hearts open to the mysterious ways of God, calling us to discipleship and not just to worship God for God's goodness toward us.

It seems that David imagined himself beyond what he knew himself to be. This is the hope expressed in the Psalms and echoed in the miraculous story of Christ coming among us as a child. Being childlike is not the same as being a child. The childlike willingness to learn—like the honesty and humility of the psalmist—leads us to our spiritual transformation. Dare we ask God for an awareness of God, a consuming sense of God's love that holds us in the midst of life's contradictions? Do we have the courage to ask God for the divine light that exposes the unity and wholeness of things that appear to us to be unrelated and broken? What would happen if we understood a deep sense of our oneness (with each other, nature, and God) to be a sign of our maturity?

The psalmist rejoices that those who know and adhere to the true voice of God, as a child recognizes the voice of her loving parent, are richly blessed. On this Second Sunday after Epiphany we come to see Jesus with the awe and wonder as a child being exposed to that which gives the child delight and life.

FREDERICK J. STREETS

Exegetical Perspective

light at every moment. Psalm 104:30 has a similar assertion. Human breath depends on God's breath or spirit. Should God's spirit be withdrawn, death follows, but God's spirit recreates the self over and again. Continuous creation! Light here means life (see Job 3:16; 33:28; and Ps. 49:19).

Verses 10–12 are a prayer or lament of an individual for deliverance from enemies. The universal themes of the hymn are forgotten. Here an individual prays to God to be gracious to those who know the Deity, to those who are upright, such as the one who prays. The prayer for deliverance from enemies is widespread throughout the book of Psalms. Enemies often acted out of a spirit of malevolence, perhaps possessed and controlled by dark powers (see Ps. 41:8). Psalmists prayed for God to break the hold of evil and evildoers and free the worshiper once again.

The three parts of the poem actually work together well. The beautiful Psalm 73 has as its basic theme the prosperity of the wicked in the world at the expense of the righteous, but the poet's distress over injustice in the world leads to a hymnic utterance of extraordinary beauty and power. "Whom have I in heaven but you? And there is nothing on earth that I desire other than you" (Ps. 73:25). And the glorious Psalm 139 ends with a plea that God rid the earth of evildoers, the psalmist's inveterate enemies (Ps. 139:19–24).

Israelite poets and prophets recognized that the presence of evil in the world was an acute theological problem defying adequate explanation. Wisdom teachers who insisted that evildoers were marked for divine judgment and the righteous for sure divine rewards could not convince those who pondered the world's pain and suffering and who looked deeply within their own souls. And it is often just those poets and prophets who are drawn to recognize just how close they are to God's intimate love and care. Knowing and sharing earth's pain may be a precondition for knowing and feeling the depth of God's love.

WALTER J. HARRELSON

Homiletical Perspective

ourselves to seeking out that love and letting it shine through us.

The psalmist articulates our dependence on God. We rely on God for the water of life and for the food at the table. We depend on the light of God to keep seeing the way. We need this light so that we may continue to see our neighbors as God's beloved and share God's shelter with those who have been battered by the storm. God's light is what enables us to flourish. It is the sun that allows us to see and makes us grow.

The preacher might explore how the psalmist's vision takes root in the congregation and community. From what do we take refuge? What are the things that threaten to undo us? In the given context of the gathered community, what does it mean to feast on the abundance of God's house? What is God calling us to share? We have been promised plenty of room under the shadow of God's wings. Do we need to move over to make room for someone else? What delights us? Where do we see light?

The psalmist describes the power of God's grace as it unfolds in community. As we find our safety, our home, in God, we enter a process of discovery. The love that sustains us continually illuminates the world around us. Each time we take a sip from the fountain of life, we are reminded of God's faithfulness, abundance, and gracious embrace. We are at our best as God's gathered people, guests at God's banquet, drinking together from the river of God's delights. The psalmist's prayer for the continued outpouring of this steadfast love thus becomes the prayer of all who seek refuge under God's wings.

APRIL BERENDS

1 Corinthians 12:1-11

¹Now concerning spiritual gifts, brothers and sisters, I do not want you to be uninformed. ²You know that when you were pagans, you were enticed and led astray to idols that could not speak. ³Therefore I want you to understand that no one speaking by the Spirit of God ever says "Let Jesus be cursed!" and no one can say "Jesus is Lord" except by the Holy Spirit.

⁴Now there are varieties of gifts, but the same Spirit; ⁵and there are varieties of services, but the same Lord; ⁶and there are varieties of activities, but it is the same God who activates all of them in everyone. ⁷To each is given the manifestation of the Spirit for the common good. ⁸To one is given through the Spirit the utterance of wisdom, and to another the utterance of knowledge according to the same Spirit, ⁹to another faith by the same Spirit, to another gifts of healing by the one Spirit, ¹⁰to another the working of miracles, to another prophecy, to another the discernment of spirits, to another various kinds of tongues, to another the interpretation of tongues. ¹¹All these are activated by one and the same Spirit, who allots to each one individually just as the Spirit chooses.

Theological Perspective

First Corinthians is Paul's impassioned plea for unity in the church. Throughout the letter, Paul responded to a dizzying variety of dissentions, including the manifestation of "spiritual" phenomena in worship and the broader community life. To deal with this issue, Paul stressed the multiplicity and complementary nature of spiritual gifts. All of his intricate rhetorical strategies were intended to counteract self-centered and divisive understandings of spiritual capacities, reframing them in light of the need to edify the entire church.

The immediate catalyst for Paul's intervention seems to have been the claims of certain members of the Corinthian church to preeminence based on their special spiritual capacities, possibly speaking in tongues. What troubled Paul was the tendency of the spiritual adepts to use their alleged religious attainments to assert their own power and status in the community. According to some interpreters, the tongue-speakers may have been more affluent or enjoyed a higher social status than other members in the congregation.[1]

Significantly, Paul does not seek to discredit the authenticity of these spiritual experiences. Rather, he

---

1. See Dale Martin, *The Corinthian Body* (New Haven, CT: Yale University Press, 1995), 87–92.

Pastoral Perspective

The Christian congregation in Corinth is often lifted up as a prime example of the remarkable diversity that could be found in the early church. Worshiping together were Greeks and Jews, slaves and free people, men and women, rich and poor, united only by their shared confession of Jesus as Lord. Yet the diversity of the first-century Corinthian church is striking, not so much in its *contrast* to churches in the twenty-first century, but to its *similarity*— particularly as we explore varieties of spiritual gifts from a pastoral perspective.

In today's society, when someone is called "gifted," it usually refers to an ability that lifts the individual above the rank and file, implying greater promise and potential for success in that area of expertise or innate talent. The gifts that are affirmed reveal what society values most, such as intellectual prowess, athletic skill, or leadership potential. Paul's assertion runs counter to that cultural definition: he says that everyone is gifted.

In the Corinthian church, the spiritual gift that was most valued and honored was that of ecstatic speech. This was not surprising, considering the fact that the church was made up primarily of Gentile converts who would have placed high value on prophesying and speaking in tongues, due to the pagan practices common at that time. This emphasis

Second Sunday after the Epiphany

Exegetical Perspective

Paul's transition to a new topic in the letter at 12:1 is signaled by his use of the phrase "Now concerning" (cf. 7:1, 25; 8:1), which introduces the subject of "spiritual things" (*pneumatikōn*), one of the issues related to communal worship that has arisen in Corinth (chaps. 11–14). Grammatically speaking, while this term can legitimately be understood as masculine ("spiritual persons") or neuter ("spiritual things"), the ensuing discussion of the gifts of the Spirit supports the latter option. In fact, a number of English translations, including the NRSV, use the contextually driven translation of "spiritual gifts" here, even though the Greek term is not that narrowly focused.

Spiritual utterances were not something that the Corinthians were unaccustomed to. With a bit of a sarcastic edge, Paul indicates that he does not want the Corinthians to be "ignorant" (*agnoeō* 12:1; NRSV utilizes "uninformed"), not because they are entirely unfamiliar with the subject, but because in his eyes they lack wisdom in knowing what is truly spiritual. Evidence for this is found in the Corinthians' following after mute idols (v. 2); now this supposed knowledge and wisdom in spiritual matters has bled over into their spiritual practices as followers of Christ. Gordon Fee considers this passage, and really the entirety of chapter 12, to be the most significant

Homiletical Perspective

Spirituality is a popular topic. Many people seem to have an unquenchable thirst for it. For some, it takes the form of dabbling in New-Age practices or paganism; for others, a return to the mystic and liturgical traditions of the past; for yet others, an absorption with nature. What all of these paths have in common is that they are concerned with spiritual things. So a text that begins "Now concerning spiritual things . . ."[1] is particularly apt for our society and our churches, especially when it ties spirituality down to very concrete things: the gifts of the Holy Spirit and their relationship to God and to the church.

Whether or not this section was written in response to a query from the church at Corinth, it is clear that the issue of spiritual things was—and still is—problematic. We like the Holy Spirit as long as we can imagine it as some sort of nebulous, comforting force field. As soon as we begin to talk about it manifesting itself in tangible ways, we get into trouble. Churches divide over whether tangible manifestations have any place in the public worship of the community, developing internal hierarchies based on who has or has not "got the Spirit." In today's text we have some basic principles—some

---

1. The majority of commentaries argue that this is a better translation than "spiritual gifts" or "spiritual people."

1 Corinthians 12:1-11

Theological Perspective

responds only to the disruptive and self-aggrandizing uses to which the experiences are put, employing a variety of strategies to do this. First, his repetition of the word "gifts" (*charismata*) makes it clear that the source of any genuine spiritual phenomenon is not the self but the Holy Spirit. Spirituality is not an innate human capacity simply waiting to be activated by a little individual effort. Our piety, no matter how impressive, is not a natural endowment, like an aptitude for playing the piano, or the product of resolute willpower. Calvin, following Augustine, cited this passage in his polemic against all efforts to regard self-cultivated human capacities as the ground of growth in the Christian life.[2] Our seeming aptitudes for certain types of ministries, our putative spiritual profundities, and our alleged religious accomplishments, no matter how spectacular, can only be ascribed to the initiative of God. Because we can take no credit for our spiritual gifts, they cannot be used as rationale for high status in the church.

Second, Paul emphasizes the sheer variety of these capacities, thereby expanding the concept of "spiritual gift" that he had introduced. As liberation theologians have recognized, this expansion has an egalitarian thrust. All Christians receive gifts, not just an elite few. The Christian life and Christian ministry are not the personal property of an exclusive class of spiritual superheroes. Paul's extensive list of gifts implies that all of them, not just the sensational ones that attract the most notoriety, are valuable. The specific nature of the gift is no grounds for claims to superiority. The fact that all such gifts are rooted in the same Spirit and serve a common purpose rules out malign calculations of relative value.

Third, the gifts have a definite purpose: the edification of the entire community. A genuine spiritual gift is not granted to individuals for their own private spiritual delectation. Genuine spirituality is not the cultivation of private emotional highs, mystical thrills, or an exclusively individual serenity. Christianity is not a religion of spiritual Lone Rangers or narcissists. Rather than fostering a purely private ecstasy, the gifts are bestowed in order to build up the church. They are intended to be publicly communicable, publicly shared, and publicly enjoyed.

Paul also suggests that the plural nature of these gifts is not accidental. The church can never be

2. See John Calvin, *Calvin's Commentaries: The First Epistle of Paul the Apostle to the Corinthians*, trans. John Fraser (Grand Rapids: Eerdmans, 1960), 9:258–61.

Pastoral Perspective

on inspired speech had set up a hierarchy within the church where those who had those particular gifts were more honored than those without. As a consequence, division and conflict arose within the community around the issue of spiritual gifts. In this letter, Paul addressed the issue by making three powerful points. First, he claimed that every person who confessed Jesus as Lord was gifted by the Holy Spirit; second, that all of those spiritual gifts were to be used for the good of the whole community; and third, that all gifts were equally activated by the grace of God. The diversity of gifts in the early church is still in evidence in the church today.

There are varieties of gifts, there are varieties of service, and there are varieties of activities, all given by the same Spirit in the service of the same Lord. Pastoral work in the church today can be informed by this assertion, and Paul offers insight into what that pastoral work might look like within the faith community. This passage invites reflection on what gifts are valued (and devalued) in the culture of a particular church. Who gets invited or nominated to certain positions and roles in the church, and who does not? How are they identified and by whom? How can the full range of gifts be lifted up, supported, and welcomed into service of Christ, his church, and the world?

Ultimately, this is a task of discernment on the part of both the pastor and the congregation as a whole. The members of the church can also help each other to discern their gifts by noticing and nurturing the potential in another, of which that person might not even be aware. The pastor, as one who is "in but not of" the local congregation, has a unique perspective on the culture of that particular church and may be able to see and understand dynamics that those more intimately involved in the daily life of the congregation may miss. Which gifts *are* more valued, and why? Which are lying fallow, waiting for a word of encouragement or a shift in the church's mission? Who has obvious skills that are being put to good use, but who may have some less noticeable skill that could be given a chance to flower in the church? For example, how many professional teachers end up in the Sunday school and business people on the finance committee, when they might be encouraged instead to sing with the choir or visit shut-ins? And the more problematic question: who needs to be invited to step aside from a particular form of service, either because their gifts are not in that area or because someone else might grow in

in the entire letter, because, as he contends, "here in particular the differences between him [i.e., Paul] and them [i.e., the Corinthians] come to a head, especially over what it means to be 'spiritual.'"[1] Paul's extended address of the topic (chaps. 12–14) adds additional weight to Fee's contention.

As he does elsewhere in the letter (e.g., chap. 8), Paul begins chapter 12 in an indirect fashion. He first establishes the confessional framework into which his later instruction fits. For Paul, vital to the determination of whether something is genuinely spiritual, that is, from the Holy Spirit of God, is its direct linkage to the confession "Jesus is Lord" (v. 3). This simple statement is commonly understood to be the earliest Christian confession of faith, one that represented a radical commitment of exclusive allegiance to Christ. Since the Holy Spirit is the only source from which such singleness of allegiance would be uttered, any accompanying utterances are authentically spiritual as well. Counter to this, if someone's spiritual utterance stands apart from or in opposition to the confession of Jesus' lordship, then the persons, instructions, and/or utterances are not of the Holy Spirit and are not truly spiritual. Notably absent here is any significance given to the messenger through whom the utterance comes.

The idea that governs the remainder of the passage (vv. 4–11) is the need for and value of a diversity of spiritual gifts, though still within a unity. Prior to moving into a more detailed explication of this diversity and unity, though, Paul establishes the theological context in which his teaching is grounded. For Paul both the *unity* of source and purpose and the *diversity* of expression for spiritual gifts come from the Godhead, which he distinctly articulates in Trinitarian form. God is diverse and the diversity of the "gifts" (*charismata*, v. 4) given by the Spirit testify to that. Likewise, the diversity of "services" (v. 5) and "activities" (v. 6), emanating from the one "Lord" and one "God" respectively, also testify to this diversity of God's character. While some have offered more detailed interpretations for the three distinct terms Paul associates with the members of the Godhead, their primary significance is still to be found in their parallelism, testifying in triplicate to the diversity within the character of God. Accompanying each identification of the diversity of God in these verses is Paul's consistent monotheistic emphasis. The oneness of God here

ground rules, if you like—for the role of the Spirit in the ongoing life of the church.

First, the Spirit is part of the life of *every* person who confesses Jesus is Lord. It does not matter what your background is, Jew or Gentile. It does not matter whether you have some of the fancier gifts or not. What matters is your response to Jesus. "Jesus is Lord" is the earliest Christian confession, and to confess it is evidence of the Holy Spirit at work in your life. This balances a reading from the previous week, Acts 8:14–17, where a distinction was made between the profession of faith that resulted in baptism, and the giving of the Holy Spirit. Here in 1 Corinthians Paul makes is clear that no one can make such a profession of faith in the absence of the Holy Spirit. If you confess "Jesus is Lord," the Holy Spirit dwells in you. This is an important assurance for Christians who feel somehow second class. The faithful in the pews, Sunday by Sunday, are as much inheritors of the Spirit as those of us who are called to preach or speak in tongues or have gifts of healing.

Second, the Holy Spirit gives gifts—but the Spirit is not some adventuring stepchild, working in one corner independent of the rest of the Godhead. Gifts, service, activities—all we do in the name of God—come from the fullness of God. It is tempting here to take verses 4–6 as an early Trinitarian formula, but that would also mean reading the Council of Nicaea back into the text. This passage is not about attributing the genesis of the things we do in God's name to different parts of the Godhead; rather, it reminds us that just as there is diversity in the Godhead, there is diversity in spiritual gifts as well, but all have their source in God. Paul's use of three different words—gifts, services, and activities—does, however, point us toward the latter part of the chapter, where the gifts of the Spirit will include not just the so-called charismatic gifts of verses 8–10, but also the more ordinary gifts that we might otherwise think of as everyday skills, such as teaching, leading, and helping others. These, along with many gifts mentioned elsewhere in Scripture (e.g., generosity, compassion, evangelism, administration, encouragement, service, mercy, hospitality, worship, and prayer) are the practical gifts of the Spirit that undergird the life of the church and its work in the world.

Third, simply confessing "Jesus is Lord" is not all that the Holy Spirit has in store for us. The Holy Spirit gifts each person—not for individual glory but for the common good. For clergy, this is a timely

---

1. Gordon D. Fee, *The First Epistle to the Corinthians*, New International Commentary on the New Testament (Grand Rapids: Eerdmans, 1987), 570.

1 Corinthians 12:1-11

Theological Perspective

monolithic or homogenous. The differentiation of talents and experiences in the Christian community is absolutely necessary. The sanctifying agency of God is so rich, so multidimensional, that it requires a variety of expressions. In verses 4–6 the same Spirit, Lord, and God are manifested in the multiplicity of gifts, services, and activities. The church, in reading this text, has discerned a Trinitarian structure in these verses.[3] The triune Deity who is Spirit, Lord, and God is a prototype of the unity-in-diversity reflected in the life of the church. It is only to be expected that the graces of God, who is no static monolith, would be manifested in the temporal sphere through a dynamic kaleidoscope of phenomena.

Finally, Paul insists that the work of the Spirit cannot be disassociated from the person of Jesus Christ. Paul reminds the Corinthians that it is the Spirit who enables the confession that Jesus is Lord. Echoing this motif, Reformed theologians have emphasized the close connection between Jesus Christ and the Holy Spirit, maintaining that the Spirit works to illumine the Word and to promote the union with Christ that issues in faith and growth in Christ. Because the work of Christ and the work of the Spirit cannot be separated, a christological confession such as "Jesus is Lord" functions as a criterion for authentic Christian spirituality. Conversely for Paul, no one filled with the Spirit can say, "Jesus be cursed." Those who truly are in the Spirit will speak and act in ways congruent with the life, death, and resurrection of Jesus. Paul suggests that the Holy Spirit is not some generic mystical principle. The message of 1 Corinthians has nothing to do with diffuse New-Age religious experience. The reference to the phrase "Jesus is Lord" points to Paul's reliance on the simple and most essential confession of the early church. Because Jesus alone is worthy of trust and obedience, no other political, cultural, or religious lords can be the focus of the Christian's spiritual interest. All who can confess that Jesus is Lord do indeed share this indwelling of the Spirit. Because the persons of the Trinity always act together, where the second person is, so too is the third person.

LEE C. BARRETT

Pastoral Perspective

their own spiritual life if given that opportunity to serve?

The pastor also needs to be willing to relinquish some power, or the desire to be admired, or the need to be needed, in order to make room for others in the church to exercise their gifts. David Steele, a Presbyterian pastor and columnist, wrote this axiom: "The key to ministry: knowing what not to do and not doing it."[1] It is helpful to note that Paul's letter says wisdom is given to *one*, while knowledge to *another*; faith, healing, prophecy, all to *others*, and all by the Spirit's own free choice. The role of minister in a modern congregation can become impossibly complex: preacher, teacher, CEO, scholar, administrator, therapist, spiritual guide, organizational expert—the list can be endless and the risk of burnout obvious. Less obvious is the potential for disempowering the people of the congregation in the exercise of their own gifts for ministry, gifts allotted to them by the Spirit to be given back to God in service. Knowing what not to do and then not doing it involve careful and prayerful discernment of one's own strengths and weaknesses, followed by a willingness to let go of those roles or tasks that would be better done by other people whom the Spirit has chosen to bless with other gifts.

All of this discernment, all of these gifts, services, and activities are activated by God for a purpose. Each person, Paul says, is given a manifestation of the Spirit to be used for the *common good*. In the culture that surrounds the church today, and often even within the church, individualism has been exalted to such high status that the phrase "common good" has nearly vanished from the lexicon. Paul's words offer a refreshing, even shocking reminder that faith, while personal, is never private, and that the gift each person has been given is meant to be shared.

KAREN STOKES

---

3. See Miroslav Volf, *After Our Likeness: The Church as the Image of the Trinity* (Grand Rapids: Eerdmans, 1998).

1. R. David Steele, "Axioms," in *Tuesday Morning: Musings and Meditations of a Parson* (Spokane: KiwE Publishing, 2002), 61.

Exegetical Perspective

stands in stark contrast to the Corinthians' multiplicity of idols (v. 2) and gods that stood prominent in their spiritual matters.

In the final movement of the passage (vv. 7–11), where Paul begins to turn to the gifts themselves, he sustains the emphasis on diversity within unity. The initial and final verses here are used as bookends iterating that the gifts of the Spirit are distributed in diverse ways. In the intervening list of spiritual gifts (vv. 8–10), a couple of interpretive points are prominent. First, the list is not meant to be exhaustive. Paul's preoccupation here is not to spell out a comprehensive list of the gifts of the Spirit but rather to illustrate them. The lack of uniformity in Paul's lists of spiritual gifts in his letters lends support to this. Second, it is highly unlikely that Paul ordered each single item in the list to serve a unique function. Arguments of this sort end up appearing intentionally or unintentionally contrived. In contrast, the most convincing proposals have paid attention to the distinct groupings within the list and offered explanations for how they support Paul's overall argument. The first two items, "wisdom" and "knowledge," commonly have been noted as two things the Corinthians prided themselves in, as well as two problems that are prominent in the first part of the letter (see especially chaps. 1–4). Similarly, the final items in the list, "tongues" and "interpretation of tongues," are contextually driven, as they lay at the heart of the Corinthian problem with spiritual things. This is supported by the appearance of tongues in key places (i.e., heading or ending) in each list of spiritual gifts in the letter (12:10, 30; 14:6; see also 13:1). The remaining five items that stand between these others are best understood as comprising a random list of prominent spiritual gifts that, when held up to the two that head and end the overall list, would highlight the Corinthians' absurd touting of any gifts to the exclusion of others. In the end, Paul communicates that the prerogative for such spiritual gifting lies entirely with the Holy Spirit (v. 11) so that the Spirit may be made visible (v. 7).

TROY MILLER

Homiletical Perspective

reminder that our own gifts, publicly affirmed by our congregations and denominations, are not ours alone but for the benefit of the whole community of faith. *All* Christians are given gifts to use for the common good. What that means is that all of us are (or are called to be) involved in ministry; ministry is not something to be left to the paid staff, but the work of each and every Christian. Sometimes our preaching needs to be explicit: "The Holy Spirit has given you gifts. Yes, *you*! Let's work together to find out what those gifts are and how you can use them for the common good."

All spiritual gifts, whether charismatic or prosaic, are given by the Spirit with all the wisdom of God. In our individualistic society, where we tend to think of gifts (or in the case of the less charismatic gifts, what we might call skills or strengths) as things we possess—signs of individual piety or holiness—this text reminds us that we have not done anything to deserve them. Gifts are not merit badges for holiness or a signs of approval from God, but God's response to the needs of our communities.

This list of gifts is just a beginning place. It is not exhaustive. The point here is not to catalog all possible gifts; indeed, it is not even precisely clear how some of these gifts can be distinguished. The focus is on their common source, the Holy Spirit.

Many of our churches struggle with issues of unity and diversity. This text addresses one aspect of diversity, that of the gifts exhibited in a community. Such gifts can be a source of disunity when they become the criteria for determining different ranks in the church, leading to a hierarchy of holiness. Here we are reminded that because the gifts have a single source, they are meant to be things that unite the community of faith. Gifts are used for the common good.

RAEWYNNE J. WHITELEY

John 2:1-11

[1]On the third day there was a wedding in Cana of Galilee, and the mother of Jesus was there. [2]Jesus and his disciples had also been invited to the wedding. [3]When the wine gave out, the mother of Jesus said to him, "They have no wine." [4]And Jesus said to her, "Woman, what concern is that to you and to me? My hour has not yet come." [5]His mother said to the servants, "Do whatever he tells you." [6]Now standing there were six stone water jars for the Jewish rites of purification, each holding twenty or thirty gallons. [7]Jesus said to them, "Fill the jars with water." And they filled them up to the brim. [8]He said to them, "Now draw some out, and take it to the chief steward." So they took it. [9]When the steward tasted the water that had become wine, and did not know where it came from (though the servants who had drawn the water knew), the steward called the bridegroom [10]and said to him, "Everyone serves the good wine first, and then the inferior wine after the guests have become drunk. But you have kept the good wine until now." [11]Jesus did this, the first of his signs, in Cana of Galilee, and revealed his glory; and his disciples believed in him.

Theological Perspective

The story of Jesus' sign at the wedding in Cana of Galilee is one of the most familiar passages in John, if not the Gospels as a whole (although it appears only in John). Commentators often remark on the extravagance of the miracle, and surely the reader was meant to notice this—in the midst of a spare narrative style, the writer details for us that the water jars were many in number and large in volume.

Even though the narrative's climax is divine generosity "filled to the brim," this passage is a troubling, even scandalous text for today's world. The stumbling block for the modern mind is not so much the hint of magic; it is the glitch in the flow of the narrative: "What concern is that to you and to me?" This is *the scandal of divine reluctance*. Why does God the incarnate one hold out?

Surely we can give good reasons for Jesus' reluctance in this passage. More wine at a wedding party that may contain a lot of drunken guests seems frivolous; alternatively, the expectation that Jesus be a cash and goods dispenser is both ridiculous and corrupting. Or we may read this reluctance in light of the Johannine emphasis on divine control of timing—"my hour has not yet come." There is a plan, and everyone must be patient as it unfolds.

Yet just as the mother of Jesus saw her son as one who could—and should—meet need, so do many

Pastoral Perspective

Weddings are accidents waiting to happen. Something almost always goes wrong at a service of holy matrimony. Something is going wrong at this wedding in Cana of Galilee.

In those days, the bride and groom celebrated the marriage not with a honeymoon but with a seven-day wedding feast at the groom's home. This celebration is in trouble, because the wine is giving out before the party is over. The situation constitutes a crisis for the family who shoulders the responsibility of hospitality. It is the mother of Jesus who notices. She provides the leadership for this miraculous sign by observing the difficulty and taking action to help. Jesus hovers in the background as one who also had been invited and seems content to keep his distance at first. When his mother tells the servants to do whatever Jesus says, Jesus performs one of his most understated mighty acts, "Fill the jars with water. . . . Now draw some out, and take it to the chief steward" (vv. 7–8). The best wine is now served to keep the party going. The servants know what has happened, the steward is amazed, and the disciples believe in Jesus. How is that for a happy ending? Everyone seems to sense that the joyous feast has been saved.

Sometimes the church has forgotten that our Lord once attended a wedding feast and said yes to

Exegetical Perspective

The story of the wedding at Cana is not a simple tale of a supermiracle exposing Jesus' supernatural power of turning water into wine, framed with a happy nuptial background. Deeper, more symbolic meaning awaits the attuned reader. In this story, the identity of Jesus and his ministry is introduced with important symbols: a joyous wedding, six Jewish ritual pots, thirsty wedding guests, and an abundance of wine.

Jesus' ministry begins in this blissful setting of great joy and abundance, in a seemingly insignificant place called Cana. Cana, less than ten miles north of Nazareth, not mentioned in the New Testament except in John's Gospel, becomes the site of Jesus' first miracle, or *sign*, as termed in the Gospel of John. This important section (chaps. 2–4) begins in Cana and ends in Cana of Galilee (4:46), forming an interesting narrative surrounding this ancient and seemingly insignificant city.

In chapters 2–4, with the village of Cana as bookends to the larger narrative block, Jesus turns water into wine, explains that his body is the new temple (2:13–25), challenges Nicodemus to be born from above (3:1–21), offers living water to an unnamed woman at a well (4:1–45), and returns to Cana to give life to the son of a royal official (4:46–54). Jesus clearly fulfills the promise of the

Homiletical Perspective

Two common human themes provide an initial point of contact between the world of today's text and our lives. The exposition of these common themes can draw readers and listeners into the story where they may see and experience the more challenging and disrupting aspects of the text.

First, there is the familiar setting of a wedding. While wedding customs differ widely through history and across cultures, and such differences should be explored, most readers can connect to the problem of running short of refreshments for a wedding. In today's text the shortfall is that "the wine gave out," but we can imagine, or perhaps have actually experienced, many other ways that a wedding celebration can be ruined and the party cut short. These images of social disaster, whether actual or imagined, evoke within us strong, primal, human emotions of anxiety, shame, and compassion, leading us to ask: What can be done to alleviate this painful situation of human need?

Here is where the mother of Jesus (Mary is never referred to by name in John's Gospel) steps in. "They have no wine," she tells Jesus. The implication is that he can and should do something about it. The mother-adult son relationship is another of the common, even archetypal, human themes that we necessarily bring to our interpretation of this text. So

John 2:1-11

Theological Perspective

followers of Jesus. We see a world in need, and we believe in one who claimed to bring abundant life to those in need. In a world where for so many there is no clean water—let alone fine wine—where is the extravagance of God? In a world where children play in bomb craters the size of thirty-gallon wine jugs, why the divine reluctance? In a world where desperate mothers must say to their small children, "We have no food," why has the hour not yet come? No matter how we rationalize divine activity, we still want to tug at Jesus' sleeve and say: "they have no wine."

It may seem like a travesty to turn a narrative about divine abundance into a trial of God, and yet it is passages like this one about divine extravagance that make God's absence in the face of poverty, suffering, and evil stand out. How do we reconcile a story of potent generosity with a world of tremendous need? If God is both generous and able, then apparently God continues to express Jesus' attitude: what is that to me? Because we trust that God wants abundance (plentiful wine and lavish food are common symbols of God's grace in both the Hebrew Bible and the New Testament), we follow in the footsteps of the mother of Jesus by prodding God for divine compassion and generosity.

The reluctance of Jesus in this story is only half the scandal. Here is the rest of it: the mother of Jesus (never named in John) is a catalyst to Jesus' extravagant generosity. In fact, the need in this passage is a "concern" to her before it is to Jesus. In the history of interpretation, commentators have denied that Jesus' mother advanced his, and surely in Johannine thought "the Father" is in control of all events. Yet the structure of the text leaves traces:

"They have no wine."
"What concern is that to you and to me?"
"Do whatever he tells you."
"Fill the jars with water."

The text will not let go of this subtheme. The prodding of the mother of Jesus endures; the traces were not and cannot be erased.

Theologians who grapple with theodicy, justifying God's goodness in face of suffering and evil, come to various conclusions. Some say that it is not yet God's hour; others say God relies on human compassion to do the will of God. Still others dare to argue that God continues to need the heirs of Jesus' mother to go on prodding divine generosity.

John Roth, with his vigorous "theodicy of protest," represents the last group. Roth writes, "If God's power is bound only by God's own unnecessitated will, as I believe, then God's ways can change.

Pastoral Perspective

gladness and joy. Prompted by his earthly mother, Jesus turned water into wine to point us to his heavenly Father, a God who loves to hear the laughter of people celebrating people. Sometimes the church has forgotten to live the joy of such revelation.

James McBride Dabbs, an author and Presbyterian elder, remembers religion as the opposite of life in rural South Carolina: "Religion was a day and a place: religion was Sunday and the church: almost everything else was life. Religion was a curious, quiet, and inconsequential moment in the vital existence of a country boy. It came around every week, but it didn't seem to have much to do with the rest of life, that is, with life."[1] The sign at Cana tells us that Jesus served a God who puts joy into life, who thinks it is worth a miracle to keep the party going as we celebrate people.

God does not want our religion to be too holy to be happy in. Throughout his life and his ministry, Jesus of Nazareth celebrated people—people getting married, people being healed of disease and deformity, people enjoying meals together. He carried a spirit of celebration with him wherever he went as he proclaimed a God of mercy and peace and joy. This joyous feast at Cana is still a sign to the church that we are to rejoice in the people of God and to toast the world with the amazing good news of grace.

David Steele, a Christian pastor and author, refers to this spirit of celebration as "Cana-Grace," the knack for throwing parties that combine food, decorations, music, and laughter to create an atmosphere of welcome, well-being, and love. Just like Jesus, Steele learned this grace from his mother and thanked God for this gift of celebration many times in his ministry. He even coined a beatitude: "Blessed is the pastor whose church has a real tenor or plumber. But doubly blessed is the pastor whose congregation knows Cana-Grace."[2] Our joy flows from knowing our God. University of Chicago theologian Robert Hotchkins remarks that "Christians ought to be celebrating constantly. We ought to be preoccupied with parties, banquets, feasts, and merriment. We ought to give ourselves over to veritable orgies of joy because we have been liberated from the fear of life and the fear of death. We ought to attract people

---

1. James McBride Dabbs, *The Road Home* (Philadelphia: Christian Education Press, 1960), 25.
2. David Steele, "Cana-Grace," in *Presbyterian Outlook* 174, no. 14 (April 13, 1992): 6.

Exegetical Perspective

Gospel narrative: "these [things] are written so that . . . you may have life" (20:31). Symbols such as water, temple, wind, birth, and old wells are given new meaning as Jesus proclaims his life-giving powers.

The symbols of the wedding reveal that the old religion lacks hospitality and vigor. The six ritual pots of water signify the old order. Jesus, however, provides overflowing vats of wine that never run dry. From the poetic hands of the evangelist and the hearts of a believing Johannine community, this is not your everyday miracle story.

On the third day (2:1), the wedding celebration begins. Why on the third day? Several options are available.[1] Some suggest that the numbering is related to the chronology of the narrative; the wedding day comes after the first day mentioned in John 1:35, the second day in John 1:43. Others suggest that the third day is used as a symbolic representation of the resurrection, implying that the event that will be described is a third-day kind of happening, a rebirth of possibilities in a post-Easter perspective. The symbolic nature of the number three, added by a post-Easter narrator, suggests that this story is another type of resurrection story, offering new birth and life from death.

Jesus, his mother, and the disciples are present (v. 2). When the wine supply is low, mother Mary feels responsible. She turns to her son Jesus for help. Reluctantly, Jesus responds, "My hour has not yet come" (v. 4). This statement is repeated by Jesus throughout the Gospel as he prepares for his death until finally in chapter 17 Jesus admits that his "hour has come" (17:1). At this wedding, however, he is just beginning. John's Gospel presents an omniscient Jesus, who knows his end from the beginning. His self-revelation and eventual death unfold slowly, leaving time for Jesus' teaching and deeds to take root in the lives and hearts of the disciples. Jesus is at a party. His mother needs a miracle. He is reluctant to reveal that part of himself to the wedding guests, but this is his mother, and he obeys. He turns the water into wine.

Six water pots, used for ritual cleansing, are available. These are not just simple clay pots when the evangelist tells this story. These are symbols that point to the emptiness of the traditional religion. The six pots, while used for religious purposes, are still not complete. Read Mark 7:3–4 for an explanation of Jewish rituals. The pots contain only

---

1. See survey of options for interpreting "third day" in Raymond Brown, *The Gospel according to John I–XII,* Anchor Bible (New York: Doubleday, 1984), 97–98.

Homiletical Perspective

it is jarring and disorienting to hear Jesus reply to her, "Woman, what concern is that to you and to me? My hour has not yet come." This sounds unnecessarily rude. Why is he talking this way to his mother?

Gail O'Day notes that although these words "sound harsh to the modern ear," they are "neither rude nor hostile." However, they do "create a distance between Jesus and his mother by downplaying their familial relation." O'Day continues, "The expression translated 'what concern is that to you and me?' like 'woman,' is a formula of disengagement, not rudeness."[1] The point is that Jesus must be guided by his inner calling from God (i.e., his "hour") and not by any human claim or authority, not even his mother's. Ultimately this is true for all of us, and a sermon could profitably develop this point.

Jesus' mother affirms his independence of thought and action when, without any further comment, she tells the servants, "Do whatever he tells you." It is not clear what moves Jesus to act, since he has said that his "hour has not yet come." This is one of the unexplained mysteries in this text. Although Jesus acts freely, with divine sovereignty, the text implies that his mother's statement of human need *has* influenced the timing of his hour. Can our honest statement of human need to God in prayer influence the course of events? Can a measure of what will come to fulfillment only in the eschatological "hour of glorification" be drawn into the time of present need? The text suggests that this is a possibility.

The miracle of turning water into wine is problematic to many modern readers. It is not part of our common human experience in the modern world to have situations of scarce physical resources solved by a miracle. For example, none of us seriously believes that our current shortage of oil will be solved by miraculously turning water into oil. It will not do, however, simply to assume that back then people believed in miracles, but we do not today. Notice that the chief steward, when he tastes the wine, does not say, "Good, some miracle worker has turned water into wine. That happens a lot!" His assumption is that the host of the party has brought out some wine that he had in storage, although he is puzzled as to why this wine is so much better than the wine served earlier. Only Jesus' disciples know that Jesus has produced this good wine, and recognizing this miracle as a revelation of his glory, they

---

1. Gail O'Day, "John," in *New Interpreter's Bible,* vol. 11 (Nashville: Abingdon, 1995), 536.

John 2:1-11

Theological Perspective

Moreover, if the biblical narratives can be trusted at all, God's activities do form changed ways from time to time."[1] Roth further contends that it is the conviction that God acted in events such as the exodus and Easter that stands in stark contrast to both history (especially recent holocausts and genocides) and the world around us.

In Toni Morrison's masterpiece *Beloved*, a white mountain girl named Amy Denver aids pregnant Sethe as she escapes slavery. Seeing Sethe's bloody back torn from the whip and astonished by the degree of her mutilation, Amy utters, "Come here Jesus . . . Wonder what God had in mind."[2] John 2, however, reveals what God *has* in mind—abundance, and the mother of Jesus nudges us to ask what God *had* in mind—during slavery, the genocide of Native peoples, the Holocaust. And Amy Denver does here what the mother of Jesus does in John 2—she poses the question and nudges the Divine.

This troubling text invites us to trust so much in God's generosity and abundance that we, like the perceptive mother of Jesus, nudge God with our observation: they have no wine. This is not fully satisfying, for as Roth states: "Religious vitality depends on more than one way of encountering the divine. None lacks risks and problems, but a religious perspective that allows room for quarrelsome protest against God can, in fact, be an asset and not a hindrance to moral commitments."[3]

The mother of Jesus figures again in John's Gospel when Jesus is on the cross. Jesus' final action is to join his mother and the disciple whom he loved into a new family (John 19:26, 27). Let us not lose the witness of the mother of Jesus, for the writer of John keeps her witness as a thin but long thread through the Gospel.

CAROL LAKEY HESS

Pastoral Perspective

to the church quite literally by the fun there is in being a Christian."[3]

The church needs to remember how the mother of Jesus swung into action to keep a party going in Cana and how her son determined that it was time after all for the water to be turned into wine, all so a wedding feast could continue. What a way for Jesus to begin his public ministry in John's Gospel! It is called Cana Grace, and it is worth a miracle because it manifests the glory of God—the very God who wants even now for the community of faith to be a celebration of people. Brothers and sisters in Christ eating barbecue on the back porch and laughing until the sun goes down; Christian women turning the church gymnasium into a festive tea party as they share gospel and good food together; a new members' dinner at someone's home that ends with folks hugging one another and giving thanks to God for the welcome they have received at church—it is called Cana Grace. Give thanks for everyone in your church and in your life who has the knack for throwing a party. What a way to begin a ministry!

ROBERT M. BREARLEY

1. John Roth, "A Theodicy of Protest," in *Encountering Evil: Live Options in Theodicy,* ed. Stephen Davis (Louisville, KY: Westminster John Knox Press, 2001), 34.
2. Toni Morrison, *Beloved* (New York: Alfred A. Knopf, 1987), 81.
3. Roth, "Theodicy of Protest," 35.

3. Robert Hotchkins, quoted in Brennan Manning, *The Ragamuffin Gospel* (Sisters, OR: Multnomah Publishers, 1990), 143–44.

water. Soon Jesus will fill them with eschatological wine, a rich symbol in the biblical tradition inferring prosperity, abundance, good times; the wine will overflow the water pots. Their true purpose will be fulfilled, not simply to hold ritual water. Now they will hold fine wine for the wedding guests, provided by Jesus in order for the party to continue. Changing the pots of water into pots flowing over with good wine becomes a metaphor for Jesus' ministry as he brings vitality to the ancient religion.

The abundance of good wine is a shock to the wine steward. Wedding etiquette in ancient Palestine advocated serving the good wine first, then the inferior wine later in the evening when the intoxicated guests are less likely to distinguish the quality of the wine. Alan Culpepper writes, "The wine, of course, had not come from the host but from Jesus. Jesus' coming as the fulfillment of Israel's hope and eschatological expectations is therefore reflected in the provision of a bountiful amount of good wine, 'kept until now,' at a wedding."[2]

The miracle at Cana was Jesus' first sign, or symbolic action (v. 11). In the Gospel of John, Jesus will perform seven signs; however, only two signs are numbered—the turning water into wine (2:11) and the raising of the royal official's son (4:54). These symbolic actions are unique to John, not repeated in the Synoptic accounts, which suggests that the evangelist may have had access to a book of signs, or a signs source. The purpose of Jesus' miracles, or signs, is to reveal the person of Jesus. The result of the sign will be that some who see the sign will understand it and some will reject it.

John 2:11 clearly states the purpose in summary fashion, "This, the first of his signs, Jesus did at Cana, in Galilee, and manifested his glory; and his disciples believed in him" (my trans.). Jesus' face is reflected in the pools of flowing wine being poured out for the laughing, happy wedding guests who are present to celebrate life. In those same vats of wine, the faces of the believing disciples are also seen. Because of this sign, the disciples "believed in him" (2:11).

LINDA McKINNISH BRIDGES

believe in him (v. 11). This is, in fact, the purpose of such "signs" (the term John uses for miracles in his Gospel), of which this is the first, *to point beyond themselves to what is being revealed through them.*

What is being revealed, according to O'Day, is the "fulfillment of OT eschatological hopes." This first of Jesus' signs is the "inaugural act of God's promised salvation." O'Day stresses that *extravagant abundance* characterizes this miracle, abundance both in the outstanding quality of the wine produced and the astonishing quantity (120–180 gallons!). She connects this to OT prophecies in Amos 9:13 and Joel 3:18 where "an abundance of good wine is an eschatological symbol, a sign of the joyous arrival of God's new age."[2]

Like all biblical texts that proclaim present eschatological fulfillment and the pouring out of abundant blessings, the question, where is it in our lives? needs to be honestly addressed. In a world where many suffer from poverty, disease, injustice, and hunger, how do we understand this story of extravagant abundance? These are important questions without simple answers. However, the text suggests that our three-dimensional understanding of life in this world, with its painful limitations, has been unpredictably invaded by grace and that when this happens, we may not recognize it.

In our text the chief steward recognizes the excellence of the wine when it is brought to him, but he does not know its source in Jesus, or its meaning as a sign pointing to God's grace. We are often like that, recognizing good gifts without recognizing their source in the Creator's love. The steward also notes that the ability of people to discern even what is good wine is typically impaired when they are drunk. Both literal drunkenness (alcoholism may be a serious problem in many congregations) and, more profoundly, drunkenness as a metaphor for all the ways we dull our physical and spiritual perceptions, could be explored in a sermon on "Recognizing the Good Stuff." By this I mean recognizing and choosing not just the better things in life, but the One who is the source of all these things.

ERNEST HESS

2. R. Alan Culpepper, *The Gospel and Letters of John*, Interpreting Biblical Texts (Nashville: Abingdon, 1998), 131.

2. Ibid., 538.

Nehemiah 8:1-3, 5-6, 8-10

¹All the people gathered together into the square before the Water Gate. They told the scribe Ezra to bring the book of the law of Moses, which the LORD had given to Israel. ²Accordingly, the priest Ezra brought the law before the assembly, both men and women and all who could hear with understanding. This was on the first day of the seventh month. ³He read from it facing the square before the Water Gate from early morning until midday, in the presence of the men and the women and those who could understand; and the ears of all the people were attentive to the book of the law. . . . ⁵And Ezra opened the book in the sight of all the people, for he was standing above all the people; and when he opened it, all the people stood up. ⁶Then Ezra blessed the LORD, the great God, and all the people answered, "Amen, Amen," lifting up their

Theological Perspective

Jewish people mark the last day of the observation of Sukkot, or Feast of Booths, with the celebration known as Simchat Torah—Rejoicing in the Torah. That day ends the annual cycle of the reading of the Torah in the synagogue, and the people read the opening of the book of Genesis to begin the process again. As the name of the festival suggests, the events reflect great joy that God has given the law to Israel.[1] Some Christians may find that an odd practice, given the traditional idea in Christianity that the gospel supersedes the law, but perhaps a more positive view of the law is in order. This story of the reading of the law upon the return of the people from the Babylonian exile may help Christians recapture an appreciation for the law and remind them that the law is a gift from God.

The church has long recognized the importance of a natural law that all people know through the conscience. Among the many reasons to acknowledge the presence of that law, one of the most compelling for Christians is Paul's observation in Romans 2:15 that "what the law requires is written on their hearts, to which their own conscience also bears witness." Clearly, a sense of right and wrong is

1. For a quick description of the festival, see "Simchat Torah," in *Encyclopedia Judaica* (Jerusalem, Israel: Keter Publishing House, 1971), 14:1571–72.

Pastoral Perspective

While the Bible is full of sermons, prophetic speeches, and prescriptions about how worship of God *should* take place, it is relatively rare to get a picture in the Scriptures about how worship *actually* takes place. On this Third Sunday of Epiphany, we get two such glimpses, in Nehemiah 8 and Luke 4. Nehemiah 8 in particular is rich in possibilities for teaching and preaching about worship. It is also a text to be considered by anyone who plans a worship service.

What do we learn about worship here?

First, worship is something that all of the people of God do together. "All the people gathered together into the square before the Water Gate" (v. 1). The place is significant; the square in front of the Water Gate was a place where everyone could be present, even those who were ritually unclean. In verse 3, the author of Nehemiah is explicit that Ezra spoke to a gathering that included men, women, and children "who could understand." The unity of God's people is emphasized by the number of times that "all" appears in this text and by Ezra's instructions to the people as they leave: those who have brought food and drink are to share them with those who have brought nothing (v. 10). Nehemiah 8 brings to mind the admonitions for inclusivity in passages such as Deuteronomy 12:12 and 14:26–27.

hands. Then they bowed their heads and worshiped the LORD with their faces to the ground. . . . ⁸ So they read from the book, from the law of God, with interpretation. They gave the sense, so that the people understood the reading.

⁹And Nehemiah, who was the governor, and Ezra the priest and scribe, and the Levites who taught the people said to all the people, "This day is holy to the LORD your God; do not mourn or weep." For all the people wept when they heard the words of the law. ¹⁰ Then he said to them, "Go your way, eat the fat and drink sweet wine and send portions of them to those for whom nothing is prepared, for this day is holy to our LORD; and do not be grieved, for the joy of the LORD is your strength."

Exegetical Perspective

Ezra and Nehemiah preside over a community in severe conflict, dispute, and fragmentation. The book tells about returnees from exile in Babylonian, led by Nehemiah and Ezra among others, who attempt to rebuild Jerusalem and restore Judah as a worshiping community. The future of the people is in serious doubt. Enemies attack from outside, but even more disruptively internal disagreements threaten to undermine the community's future. The people form factions arguing about who is in and who is out, who should govern, how the temple can be rebuilt, how Jerusalem can be reestablished in safety and peace.

The question of whether or not the Jews can revivify life together and reclaim their identity as a worshiping people is an urgent matter of life and death. Like all communities that undergo military invasion and cultural breakdown, their identity has come unraveled. To rebuild their faith and their cultural life requires recovery of their pre-Babylonian worldview, yet they must reimagine it for the new situation, because their history has undermined their faith. Ezra and Nehemiah's actions in today's reading provide one way the community can reestablish itself in continuity with the past and in unity and hope for the present. Although today's passage looks like a factual account of a worshiping assembly, it is a

Homiletical Perspective

The book of Nehemiah narrates Nehemiah's return to Jerusalem to rebuild the city and its wall. As King Artaxerxes' cupbearer, Nehemiah receives news that the city is ruined. Known to have a good disposition, he becomes depressed. So the king releases him to help restore his homeland. By the time of our text, the work is complete. Now it is time for the people to experience the word of God read and explained. Additionally, these verses give preachers an opportunity to explore worship in its various forms, from lifting hands and hearts, to bowing to the ground in reverence, to standing as the word is read. Those who proclaim may explore with worshipers how they experience the reading of biblical texts.

An Open Book for Everyone. The egalitarian phrases "all the people" and "both men and women" show up in five verses approximately eight times (vv. 1, 2, 3, 5, and 9). Though we might lament the patriarchal impulses of the Law of Moses, Nehemiah's book tells us that "all" the people who could understand gathered to hear and listen for an interpretation.

Have you ever been in a foreign country where you could listen to natives speak the language? You have taken the language for years in a class setting; but on the streets of that country, the words bump up against you and you panic. Nothing sounds

Nehemiah 8:1-3, 5-6, 8-10

Theological Perspective

important to human beings as they live together in community. Most people can agree on that, and such natural law was never the meaning of "law" that the church—not even those Reformation giants Martin Luther and John Calvin—rejected.

What they rejected is called the "moral law," that is, the Torah given to Israel or any other set of works designed to make a person righteous. The problem with the moral law is that the human bent to self-reliance may lead one to think that she can achieve salvation through observing it. The reformers charged the church with teaching such a doctrine, and so wrote vehemently against the moral law. Even so, they did not embrace a completely negative understanding of the law, for it retained helpful purposes.

Both Luther and Calvin held that the Word of God is partially made known in the law, for it contains God's eternal will for creation and is a gift of love. As such, the law serves a dual role. First, the law restrains evil in the world and preserves order (this especially applied to the social realm through the rule of government). That is, the law serves as a deterrent to wrongdoing and, failing that, punishes the transgressor through its application by proper authorities. Second, the law exposes sin in the world and the life of the believer. This is how the law becomes perceived as the wrath of God. So wrote Paul: "Yet, if it had not been for the law, I would not have known sin. . . . [A]nd I died, and the very commandment that promised life proved to be death to me" (Rom. 7:7,10). One might call these two purposes of the law negative; that is, they show our weakness and improper relationship with God and neighbor but do not correct them.[2]

John Calvin had a third, positive use of the law that may help Christians identify more closely with the reading from Nehemiah. In Book 2.7.11 of his *Institutes of the Christian Religion*, Calvin referred to the law as a "tutor," commenting on Galatians 3:24, in which Paul calls the law *paidagōgos* (custodian, or guide, the term used for an adult assigned to assist a child into adulthood in Greek society). The law is a teacher, preparing believers to understand God's will once we receive saving grace in Christ Jesus—the "best instrument for them to learn more thoroughly each day the nature of the Lord's will to which they aspire, and to confirm them in the understanding of it."[3] No longer need the law scare or condemn those

Pastoral Perspective

This passage speaks a countercultural word to the individualistic West. While private spiritual disciplines and practices are important, there is no substitute for God's people gathering together to worship. As someone has said, there are many things we can do on our own, but being a Christian is not one of them. Together, we are the body of Christ. In our life together, we should seek to share and to be inclusive, so that all parts of the body feel welcomed and valued.

Second, the people know that they have entered the presence of the living God. The people do not ask Ezra to speak *about* God. They ask him to read the Word *of* God. When Ezra opens the Torah, he prays, and the people prostrate themselves with their faces to the ground in response to God's living presence.

God is not just the *object* of our worship; God is also the *subject* our worship, the living, Holy One whom we encounter in our worship. Does our worship convey that? We may well work hard to express through our worship the friendliness, hospitality, and grace of God's immanence. Do we work equally hard to convey the holiness of God's transcendence, that is, "the *awesomeness* of God . . . the *overpoweringness* of God . . . the *energy and urgency* of God . . . the *mystery* of God . . . and the *fascination* of God?"[1]

The writer Annie Dillard colorfully describes what worship might look like if we approached it as the people in Nehemiah 8 did:

> Does anyone have the foggiest idea what sort of power we so blithely invoke? . . . It is madness to wear ladies' straw hats and velvet hats to church; we should all be wearing crash helmets. Ushers should issue life preservers and signal flares; they should lash us to our pews. For the sleeping god may wake some day and take offense, or the waking god may draw us out to where we can never return.[2]

Third, the worship led by Ezra centers on the Word. Worship in Nehemiah 8 is simple and straightforward: Ezra steps up on a wooden platform made for the occasion and reads directly from the Torah. Then, certain named Levites present with Ezra interpret the Scriptures, either by translating the Hebrew into the Aramaic language more

---

2. See Paul Althaus, *The Theology of Martin Luther*, trans. Robert C. Schultz (Philadelphia: Fortress Press, 1966), 251–55, for a summary of Luther's understanding of the law.

3. John Calvin, *Institutes of the Christian Religion*, ed. John T. McNeill, trans. Ford Lewis Battles (Philadelphia: Westminster Press, 1960), 360.

1. Albert Curry Winn, *A Christian Primer: The Prayer, the Creed, the Commandments* (Louisville, KY: Westminster/John Knox Press, 1990), 37–38.

2. Annie Dillard, *Teaching a Stone to Talk* (New York: Harper & Row, 1982), 40–41.

highly symbolic narrative, dividing into three closely connected parts: Ezra Reads Torah (vv. 1–2); The Whole Community Assents to Torah (vv. 3–8); The People Celebrate Torah on a Holy Day (vv. 9–10).

Ezra Reads Torah (vv. 1–2). The passage makes a deliberate effort to present Ezra as a new Moses who reestablishes the Torah. The Torah is the law of Israel, found in the Pentateuch, the first five books of the Bible. It is not primarily a legal system but instruction about how to live as God's covenant community. After the people have settled in towns, they gather in solemn assembly at one of Jerusalem's city gates. The gates of a city are significant in the ancient world, because they are places of deliberation and judgment. The assembly commands Ezra the scribe to bring the book of Torah before them. Ezra, now identified as priest, brings the book before everyone, "men and women and all who could hear with understanding" (v. 2).

The Whole Community Assents to Torah (vv. 3–8). The text ties this solemn event to history by reporting date and time. On "the first day of the seventh month," Ezra began reading the Torah early in the morning and did not finish until noontime. Meanwhile all the people—identified again as men, women, and everyone who could understand—were "attentive to the book of the law" (v. 3). The narrative takes every opportunity to underscore the unanimity of the people in responding to Ezra's reading.

The lectionary omits two verses (vv. 4, 7), probably because they list names of attendees who might hold little interest for modern readers. But for the Jews, these lists have immense importance, because they name witnesses and supporters of Ezra present at the reading. Although the reading seems to be over in verse 5, the text revisits it, as if it has not yet happened. Ezra proclaims the Torah like Moses. He does not speak from Sinai but from a platform raised above the people (v. 4), a point reiterated, "for he was standing above all the people" (v. 5). The phrase "all the people" appears three times in this verse to emphasize that Ezra oversees the renewal of God's covenant with all Israel.

The renewal ceremony comes to a climax when "all the people answered, 'Amen, Amen,'" agreeing to the terms of covenant like the people in the wilderness (v. 6). But the most significant aspect of this renewal occurs next. Another list of names identifies members of the community sent to help the assembly understand the Torah. This means that the

familiar, even though you have studied. Confusion shows on your face, and finally someone recognizes the look. The speaker slows down, asks whether you speak German, Swahili, Wolof, or French—whatever language is under negotiation. You say "a little bit" in the native's tongue. Now, for the first time, you will hear the language with someone who will help you understand what you are hearing.

Imagine. These ancient peoples have been so long away from their homeland. They may have heard the Law of Moses read in the shadow of Babylonian temples or even in synagogues. But here, in its native place, the Law looms large, and it needs an interpretative voice.

In African American churches, it is common to see members stand when the preacher says something that rings true to them. It is part of the call-and-response heritage in black churches. "Say that, preacher!" This phrase and others like it say we know when something sounds like the truth. Whether from pulpits, in classrooms, or over coffee, each new context demands that words be not only read but also discussed, argued for and against, and made sense of. If nothing else, this reading shows us what it means to listen for understanding.

With Interpretation. In the movie *Amistad*, written in 1997 by David Franzoni and directed by Steven Spielberg, there is a scene where the characters played by Morgan Freeman and Matthew McConaughey search among New Haven's crowds of slaves for anyone who speaks Mende. As they search, they count in Mende, the language of Cinque, the free man who led the revolt of the slaver ship *Amistad*. They are searching for someone who can understand them and understand Cinque. What they know, as they seek to help the mutineers, is that understanding requires interpretation. They count in Mende, in hopes that someone who speaks English will recognize the language and interpret for them.

There is a language barrier that must be crossed in reading the Bible too. We lose many metaphorical nuances across the divides of time and culture. And so we "count" in order to find someone who can help us make sense of what we hear. This counting takes the form of listening and asking questions, reading from different translations of the biblical text, consulting commentaries, and putting the biblical text in dialogue with other cultural artifacts, to name just a few practices.

Nehemiah 8:1-3, 5-6, 8-10

Theological Perspective

in Christ, for it now becomes our helper. Believers see the law for the gift—the revelation of God's will—that it is and rejoice.

Returning to Nehemiah, the reader sees among the people a pattern similar to the one outlined above. Ezra, who has returned from exile with the "book of the law of Moses" (v. 1), stands before the people of Israel and reads it to them. Notice that the peoples' first reaction to the law is to cry out in repentance for their sin: "'This day is holy to the LORD your God; do not mourn or weep.' For all the people wept when they heard the words of the law" (v. 9). However, beyond that initial reaction comes the realization of the law as the revelation of God to the people for their benefit, not their condemnation. They are told to celebrate: "Go your way, eat the fat and drink sweet wine . . . and do not be grieved" (v. 10). Verse 12, beyond the lectionary selection, says the people did eat and drink and made "great rejoicing." Simchat Torah!

Christians, then, while denying the law or any system of works as a way to salvation, can embrace the law for the purposes it serves: restraining evil, convicting of sin, and aiding our understanding of God's will. Because we know the law as gift from God, we understand that the entire law can be summarized positively as loving God and loving one's neighbor. Christ becomes for us not the rejection or abrogation of the law but its telos, or fulfillment. No longer can Christians, as we are prone to do, simply think of the OT as containing the law and, therefore, telling of a God of judgment, while we now worship a God of love and mercy. The law remains, in a sense, in the gospel, and it continues to serve us. In that we can rejoice.

RICK NUTT

Pastoral Perspective

commonly spoken by the people or by explaining the sense of the Torah to the people, passage by passage.

Much has been written in recent years about the need for "seeker-friendly" churches and the importance of applying marketing principles to understand a congregation's "targeted audience." To be sure, good preaching and good pastoring require that the Scriptures read in worship are translated and interpreted with words that the people of God can understand. Good preachers and pastors also seek to understand the questions and concerns of their people. But there is great danger if we lose sight of the primacy of the Scriptures in worship. As William Willimon has pithily put it: "At the heart of preaching is either a God who speaks, and who speaks now . . . or preaching is silly."[3]

Finally, what we see in Nehemiah 8 is worship that transforms lives. After Ezra completes his reading, all of the people weep (v. 9). Why? We are unsure. Perhaps they are overcome with regret for the loss of the Torah during the exile. Perhaps they have been reminded of how far short their actions have fallen from God's expectations of them. Or perhaps their tears are tears of joy, for the recovery of the Torah and for a sense of God's abiding presence and providential care.

God's Word can do all of that, because the Scriptures give us a lens to look at this world and our lives through God's eyes. We are reminded of God's presence and love when we otherwise might feel alone and abandoned; we are pierced with words of judgment when we might otherwise be puffed up with arrogance and self-satisfaction.

When we gather together as God's people, when we are conscious of coming into the presence of the living and holy God, when we center our worship on God's Word, when we offer all of ourselves to God, we cannot help but be changed over time. We gather to give glory to God and to have God make a difference in us so that we can be sent to make a difference in God's world. When all of that happens, we have reason to follow the example of the people on this special day in Nehemiah 8 who ate and drank together and made "great rejoicing" (v. 12).

W. CARTER LESTER

---

3. William Willimon, *Proclamation and Theology* (Nashville: Abingdon Press, 2005), 2.

Exegetical Perspective

Torah is not self-explanatory, that its interpretation changes as the circumstances of the people change. "They read . . . from the law of God, with interpretation. They gave the sense, so that the people understood the reading" (v. 8).

For a people seeking to renew themselves as a community, this passage solemnizes and proclaims that their unity rests in the law of Moses, the Torah that "gives light to the eyes" and is a "lamp to the feet" (Ps. 119). Given at the nation's beginning, the law of Moses guides them in their identity as worshipers of God. But that law requires interpretation, updating, understanding anew in light of the new situation of believers. This reading about the reading of Torah does not inflict the rigid orthodoxy of the past on the gathered people but urges them to meet God anew in the changing times in which they find themselves.

All the People Celebrate Torah on a Holy Day (vv. 9–10). Nehemiah joins Ezra, identified now as both priest and scribe, along with the priestly tribe of the Levites, to preside over the recovenanted community in a fuller liturgical response to the Torah that was just read to them. When Nehemiah urges them neither to weep nor to lament, the text implies that they have forgotten God's law. Rather than grieving their infidelity, they are to feast on fat and sweet wine, and to send some to those who do not have any. "The joy of the LORD is your strength" (v. 10).

The covenant renewal of all the people calls them to unity and invites them to renew life in their God. Rather than seeing divine instruction as cramping, restricting legislation, the Jews, then and now, recognize Torah as a compassionate guide, a pathway, a set of wise instructions about how to live together in justice and joy. But that guide and that path have not been sealed forever in concrete at Sinai. Instead, they must be reinterpreted to show the path to community and to joy, as the people worship the God who renews their life. In the season of Epiphany, Ezra reminds us that we too are recipients of divine instruction, a people called to continual renewal and reinterpretation of God's word among us. That word is alive and ever new in the power of the Spirit among us.

KATHLEEN M. O'CONNOR

Homiletical Perspective

Eat, Drink, and Be Merry. Where did we ever get the notion that merriment is antithetical to holiness? We probably can blame Puritans and the Protestant work ethic. In this text, holiness is connected to eating fat and drinking sweet wine. Life in God should produce gladness, especially in the context of listening for and living out God's word.

In *Babette's Feast*, that luscious book made into a film that hides grace in one final and prodigal meal prepared by the title character, food becomes a gateway to redemption and reconciliation. Set in late nineteenth-century Denmark, the movie describes the culinary artistic extravagance of a woman exiled because of war from her beloved France. When given a chance to return home because of a lottery winning, she instead prepares a feast. The meal, meant to celebrate the one-hundred-year memory of a now-dead founding pastor, represents an extravagance that borders on sin. But Babette knows, as does the declaration in Nehemiah 8:10, that food and drink appreciated and relished may be the best witness to grace. After hearing the word and understanding it, what more is there to holiness but to enjoy the life God has given?

That notion is what the writer of Ecclesiastes suggested in 2:24, declaring "there is nothing better for mortals than to eat and drink, and find enjoyment in their toil." These pleasures, according to Ecclesiastes, are the heritage of those who please God, with wisdom and knowledge thrown in. God's precepts, expressed in the law, make the heart rejoice (Ps. 19:8a). In the parable of the rich fool (Luke 12:13–21), Jesus does not chastise the man for saying, "Eat, drink, and be merry." Rather, the challenge is that the man in the parable ignored what comes after "eat the fat and drink the sweet wine," that is, "Send portions of them to those for whom nothing is prepared" (v. 10). Holiness includes enjoying God's gifts and extravagance as well as sharing what one has with those "for whom nothing is prepared." It is a balancing act. Too much play might make us self-indulgent and self-centered; too much looking beyond enjoyment might make us dour, like the sisters in *Babette's Feast* who try to keep their father's memory alive.

In the end, this text is rich with sensual, embodied encounters—hearing, bowing, eating—that lead us carefully into deep relationship with God.

VALERIE BRIDGEMAN DAVIS

Psalm 19

[1]The heavens are telling the glory of God;
   and the firmament proclaims his handiwork.
[2]Day to day pours forth speech,
   and night to night declares knowledge.
[3]There is no speech, nor are there words;
   their voice is not heard;
[4]yet their voice goes out through all the earth,
   and their words to the end of the world.

   In the heavens he has set a tent for the sun,
[5]which comes out like a bridegroom from his wedding canopy,
   and like a strong man runs its course with joy.
[6]Its rising is from the end of the heavens,
   and its circuit to the end of them;
   and nothing is hid from its heat.

[7]The law of the LORD is perfect,
   reviving the soul;
the decrees of the LORD are sure,
   making wise the simple;
[8]the precepts of the LORD are right,
   rejoicing the heart;

Theological Perspective

This psalm takes us through the three distinct moments that are, in the psalmist's view, central to the worshipful life. In the first moment, we are invited to recall the witness given to God's splendor by the textures and glory of creation (vv. 1–6). The second moment reminds us of the significance and wonder of God's law (vv. 7–10). Finally, the psalmist calls us to the humble recognition of human frailty and limitation in the face of these majestic glories, and the need for God's grace (vv. 11–14). The psalm ends with, and in form exemplifies, what has become a central framing for public and private prayer in the church.

Psalm 19 is a particularly elegant example of what some commentators have identified as doing God's work of leading humanity to perfection through forms of speech. That is to say, the Psalms exemplify words and speech as a medium through which God "speaks" into creation, and how creation through its very character "speaks" as a witness to God. This dimension of Psalm 19 led Calvin to refer to the heavens as "preachers" of the glory of God.[1] Understood in this way, the psalm is an important reminder of two facets of the relationship between

Pastoral Perspective

The Psalms endure because they resonate with our human experiences and quest for God. On this Third Sunday of Epiphany we hear one of the seventy-five psalms traditionally ascribed to David, listening from his experience for what John Edgar Wideman refers to in his book *Fatheralong* as a "moment of freedom, of self-revelation in [David's] accounts when self merges with something greater than self."[1]

David's writings seem to be part private diary and part public liturgy. He expresses his adoration of God with passion and honesty. His utmost want is to please God, and his greatest fear is that he will fail to do so. Sharing with us both his struggle and his witness, he grapples with the fact that some of his desires conflict with his expectations of himself and the expectations of his faith. This complexity helps us to see him as more than a one-dimensional person. As David writes of his experience with the sensitivity of a poet and musician, he describes our own experience as well.

The last verse of this psalm has almost become a mantra for preachers who recite it before delivering a sermon: "Let the words of my mouth, and the meditation of my heart, be acceptable in thy sight, O LORD, my strength, and my redeemer" (KJV). It

---

1. John Calvin, *Commentary on the Psalms*, vol. 1, trans. James Anderson (Grand Rapids: Eerdmans, 1949), 309.

1. John Edgar Wideman, *Fatheralong* (New York: Vantage Books, 1995), xxi.

the commandment of the LORD is clear,
    enlightening the eyes;
[9]the fear of the LORD is pure,
    enduring forever;
the ordinances of the LORD are true
    and righteous altogether.
[10]More to be desired are they than gold,
    even much fine gold;
sweeter also than honey,
    and drippings of the honeycomb.

[11]Moreover by them is your servant warned;
    in keeping them there is great reward.
[12]But who can detect their errors?
    Clear me from hidden faults.
[13]Keep back your servant also from the insolent;
    do not let them have dominion over me.
Then I shall be blameless,
    and innocent of great transgression.

[14]Let the words of my mouth and the meditation of my heart
    be acceptable to you,
    O LORD, my rock and my redeemer.

Exegetical Perspective

This complex hymn in praise of God the Creator and of the Torah is set between two hymns in praise of King David. Psalm 18, which finds an almost exact replica in 2 Samuel 22, records David's devotion to God and celebrates God's many interventions to protect and save the king. Psalm 20 is a hymn in praise of King David, one of several such hymns. No close literary connections with Psalm 19 are evident.

The psalm divides into three parts. Verses 1–6 praise God the Creator and celebrate the praise of God uttered (without a sound) by the heavenly bodies. Verses 7–11 celebrate the equally glorious way in which God's Torah reflects God's glory. The psalm closes with the prayer of an individual (vv. 12–14) asking God to assist the psalmist to be a faithful follower of Torah.

One translation difficulty was encountered long ago. In verse 4, the Hebrew term *qawwam*, literally "their line," is translated in both the Septuagint and the Vulgate as "their sound" or "their voice." That translation may be correct: the original Hebrew may have been *qolam*, "their voice." Another translation difficulty appears in the same verse. The Hebrew reads, "In them he has set a tent for the sun." Both the Septuagint and the Vulgate read, "In the sun he has set his tabernacle." Most translators read, as in the NRSV, "In the heavens he has set a tent for

Homiletical Perspective

"Let the words of my mouth and the meditation of my heart be acceptable to you, O LORD, my rock and my redeemer." These words comprising the last verse of Psalm 19 are often the first words uttered by a preacher prior to delivering a sermon. They are a prayer for the act of proclamation and for the act of listening. The prayer becomes even more meaningful when viewed in the context of the psalm from which it originated. The heavens tell the glory of God, the firmament proclaims God's work. The whole world rejoices night and day, God's voice echoes throughout all of creation, and we pray this simple prayer: let the words of my mouth, O God, let the thoughts of my heart, be acceptable to you.

The psalmist reminds us that we are a small part of a big world. Our words and thoughts are even smaller pieces of this intricate universe held and kept by God. The author bids us to look beyond our own small selves to discover how God is at work. The heavens and the earth tell us something about God, whose work stretches to the ends of the earth and beyond to the skies. As the creator of all things, God's activities extend to the farthest reaches. This elemental yet profound concept provides the basis for understanding our relationship to God.

Creation bears witness to God's glory by living out its created goodness, each element giving praise

Psalm 19

Theological Perspective

revelation and Scripture. In the first place, the psalm helpfully recalls the fact that God's voice has not been locked up as prisoner in the print of Scripture. In times of rampant bibliolatry and the attendant idolization of the solitary reader as biblical interpreter, this is a reminder that God is still speaking through the majesty of creation—both "nature" and humanity—with words of blessing and judgment.

Beyond drawing us to appreciate the power of creation to bear witness to God, this psalm also entreats us to see the law of God as a thing of beauty and sweetness. While the psalmist had Torah in mind, Christian interpreters might think of the broad stream of Christian wisdom encompassed in the tradition and practices of our faith communities. This might create dissonance for preachers and commentators who hear the words of Paul echoing in our ears—"the letter killeth" (2 Cor. 3:6 KJV)—but Calvin again provides a helpful way to work through this dissonance when he counsels "that we give ourselves up to be guided and governed by the word of God, we are in no danger of going astray, since this is the path by which he securely guides his own people to salvation."[2]

When God's word is understood in the generous sense offered by the psalmist, we are drawn beyond understanding law as rule and invited to understand law as direction. Too often, legalists of every age seek to make the law something onerous—as when it is reduced to a selective reading of Scripture and then used as a cudgel in culture wars. Here the psalmist invites us to another understanding, namely, of the law of God as the way-making and sense-making word of guidance. This word of God, while borne witness to by the majesty of the heavens and all of creation, is never reducible to any "thing" in creation. So the church, its traditions, and its Scripture must always be understood as parts of God's address to us, but never confused with that address in its totality. For even while God is revealed to us in Christ's epiphany, even then God still speaks though the majesty of creation. Each time Christ draws attention to something within creation (e.g., the sparrow) to exemplify God's love and presence, he is bearing witness to this fact.

To this point we have a poetic psalm that places spectacles on our face that we might see in the majesty of creation a witness to God. The psalmist goes on to observe how human frailty and weakness

2. John Calvin, *Commentary on the Psalms*, vol. 1, trans. James Anderson (Grand Rapids: Baker Book House, 2003), 309.

Pastoral Perspective

suggests that David had a significant meditation and prayer life through which he sought to please God while acknowledging God as the source of his strength and redemption. By speaking these words, the preacher conjures David's personality, vicariously identifying with it and inviting us to do the same. This theme of David's intimacy with God (Ps. 139) is a strong characteristic of the psalm and something for which we too may yearn.

David's portal to God was partially through his respect for and adherence to God's laws and statutes as he understood them. The words of God are life itself given by God to the believer who commits to a lifelong study of God's laws and practice of faith. David knew this, even as he struggled with bringing its truth to bear on his life. Like him, we wish to "declare the glory of God" as we continue our Epiphany reflection on and celebration of the divine nature of Christ and his coming into the world. We too aspire for some manifestation of God's presence in our lives. Yet it is only by an act of faith that we claim to have some sense of apprehending God's presence in the world through Jesus Christ.

Suffering can affect our understanding and faith in God. A very bright twenty-five-year-old woman living in poverty, who contracted HIV, the virus that causes AIDS, two years earlier when she was twenty-three years old, said to me, "In my most difficult moments living with this disease I wonder why God does not like me." She said, after a few seconds of silence, "But I know that is not true and that I am going to make it." I think part of what she was wondering about was why God did not help her to make a better choice than the one that resulted in her current condition.

Many of us have had similar thoughts when we have made the wrong decisions. Our personal sense of God and the things that happen to us can mutually influence each other. Some people feel drawn closer to God through their hardships while others may feel estranged from God by those same experiences. David gives us the impression in the Psalms that he adores God and through his experience of suffering he finds strength in God that turns his "mourning into dancing" (Ps. 30:11). His hurts and dependence upon God open his soul to us, showing us how he saw the heart of God.

Our experiences with both success and pain can make it difficult for us to trust and feel the presence of God. Success can give us a false sense of what it means to be secure as human beings living in a world over which we have little control. Our painful

Third Sunday after the Epiphany

the sun." Clearly, the sun is the subject of the next two verses.

The unevenness in the text may support the view that an ancient hymn in praise of the sun has been incorporated into the psalm.

The poet's thought, even so, seems clear and striking. The author of Psalm 8 exults that God's "excellent name" is proclaimed throughout the universe by frail human beings who cannot bear comparison with sun and moon and stars. Here, the heavenly bodies silently proclaim God's glory as they make their appointed rounds. The heavens are speckled with the stars, some of which are fixed to the hard firmament overhead, like a vast inverted bowl. Others, like the giant sun, move in stately rhythm across the sky.

Uniquely, for the poet, the great sun rises in the east, dances across the heavens, and returns to the tent God has pitched for it in the high heavens. As it rises, the poet tells us, it is like a bridegroom emerging from the marriage bed, boldly challenging all other heavenly bodies to compete with it or match its heat.

Many have pointed out that the order, complexity, and beauty of the universe do not "prove" the existence of God. Our poet, however, is not seeking to prove that God exists. The psalmist is caught up in exultation and praise of One to whom he attributes such glory and beauty and order.

Abruptly the subject shifts in verse 7 to God's Torah, God's teaching. This part of the psalm may be from an entirely different author than verses 1–6. If that is not the case, the poet must be drawing a direct parallel between the silent praise of God "voiced" by the heavenly bodies and the silent praise uttered, also without spoken words, by the Torah. The point is the same, whether made by one poet or by two poets whose separate works are now joined.

The poet uses six terms for the Torah in verses 7–9, each followed by a description of Torah's excellence. Torah is "perfect," "sure," "right," "clear," "pure," and "true and righteous altogether." God's Torah, in short, bears comparison with the gift of God's steadfast love (Ps. 36:5–9), our psalm for the Second Sunday of the Epiphany. This section of the psalm closes with a statement of two "uses" of the Torah, as Christians have pondered the Law's value for them. It warns one of the dangers of sin (v. 11a), and it positively keeps those who are faithful on a life that brings daily benefits (v. 11b).

Three psalms in the Psalter sing the praises of Torah. Psalm 1 counts happy and blessed all those

by being what God made it to be. So it is with God's people. Living according to God's laws enables us to live as God made us to live, taking our place in the created order with eyes opened to God's glory.

How do we move from the heavens to our hearts? The psalmist takes us on a journey of faith from praise of God's glory in nature to praise of God's law to a description of our relationship with God. God's law is the link between the cosmos and our inmost thoughts, reviving the soul and helping us to see God at work in the world. The heavens tell the glory of God. As the energy of the sun shines light upon the world, bringing growth and sustenance, so does following God's commands for God's people. Heaven and earth are at once ordered dynamically and in harmony with their source, exemplifying a relationship of dependence that reflects the glory of the Creator. The preacher might expand upon this, reflecting on the marvels of the created world and God's attributes revealed in nature.

The law helps to shape our limited selves into redeemed creation, calling us to bear witness to God's goodness. The psalmist's prayer is a hymn of the heart, moving from the farthest objects beheld by the human eye to our most intimate thoughts.

The preacher might challenge the congregation to consider how our own lives are shaped to reveal God's glory. The psalmist describes God's law as soul food of the most gratifying kind, sweeter than honey. When we live according to God's desire we are satisfied at our core, and we taste deep gladness. The law "enlightens our eyes" (v. 8), like the aperture of a camera lens opening up to let in more light, giving us power to understand more fully this world and the God who has given it into our care.

"Clear me from hidden faults" (v. 12), the psalmist prays, reminding the listener that violation of God's law consists of not only the sins we have actively committed, but also hidden sins, our sins of omission. This provides a vast territory for the preacher to explore, especially in light of the creation imagery found in this psalm. Whereas the earth itself behaves in ways that are consonant with God's will, humans have found ways to tear it apart with very little conscious effort. Where God's creation is concerned, it is entirely possible that human sins of omission have caused more harm than deliberate acts of exploitation. We squander the resources of God's good creation without even so much as a thought. The patterns of our daily lives drain resources and pollute the earth; our leaky sinks and overflowing landfills may well be signs of leaky souls and empty

Psalm 19

Theological Perspective

impede our knowledge of God and the wisdom to contemplate how we might please God. In identifying these frailties, the psalmist takes the important step of naming the faults that are secret, or invisible to us (v. 12)—the sins that emerge from presumption—as sins of the first order, from which God's protection is needed. In our contemporary context, these sins might be thought of as distorted worldviews or misguided cultural practices and beliefs (i.e., ethnocentrism, classism, and sexism). On the psalmist's account these frailties make us vulnerable to the dominion of evildoers.

Beyond the invisible sins of custom and common sense, the psalmist also reflects upon the sins of willfulness and self-centeredness. Several translators read the psalmist as naming this as the path to the "great transgression,"[3] which we might read as living our lives under the dominion of any but God. It is here, with the identification of our willfulness in the face of this display, that the psalmist invites us to see how our failure to see and hear God in creation ultimately leads to our downfall. It is entirely possible to read this caution as prophetic in an age of environmental degradation. Our incapacity to understand creation as both a witness to God and a medium of God's speech is imperiling us in significant ways. Led by the psalmist, we must ask, Are we destroying the first and final witness to God? Would we give so little attention to the well-being of all, if we understood? It is this lack of understanding that requires God's grace and help.

On this Third Sunday of Epiphany it is all the more important to remember that when the Word took on flesh, it was precisely the flesh of creation that was taken on. So, far from relativizing or discounting creation, we have all the more reason to experience the Divine flowing through it.

STEPHEN G. RAY JR.

Pastoral Perspective

experiences can erode our confidence in our own abilities and cause us to distrust ourselves, others, and even God. David seems to have had his faith in God strengthened by both his disappointments and his achievements.

The various rituals, symbols, and celebrations of the seasons of Advent, Christmas, and Epiphany remind us of God's endearment to us. Our preparations for observing the coming of Christ, our joyful worship announcing his arrival, and the church's emphasis upon God being with us are attempts to point us toward something that goes beyond our worship services themselves. Such services are invitations for us to experience afresh—or perhaps for the first time—our own spiritual awakening to the presence of God and how this awareness may affect the way we live. The culture's materialistic promotions of these occasions add to our challenge to see beyond their hype and to open ourselves to the wonder and awe of God loving us.

We, like David, have a mixture of what makes us feel ashamed and proud to be who we are. The Psalms gives us a sense of how David was set free by his faith in God. His praise of God (cf. Pss. 107:32; 149:3; 150:4) was not in the abstract. His gratitude and trust in God reflected what he had been through in his life, including the wars he had fought, his marriages and betrayals, and the death of his son Absalom. Still he felt God bless him. It was difficult for him to be released from attitudes that would have otherwise limited him from having a larger view of himself, God, and God's mercy, yet this was and is the essence of experiencing the presence of God that goes further than dogma, doctrine, and rituals can carry us. Beyond our own sin and triumphant and tragic experiences of life, we are still a part of God's grander vision for God's creation. This gives us, as it did David, hope.

FREDERICK J. STREETS

---

3. John R. Kohlenberger III, ed., *The NIV Interlinear Hebrew-English Old Testament*, vol. 3 (Grand Rapids: Zondervan Publishing House, 1982), 365; Samuel Terrien, *The Psalms: Strophic Structure and Theological Commentary* (Grand Rapids: Eerdmans, 2003), 206.

Exegetical Perspective

who live their lives in accordance with God's Torah, while pointing out how far from happy and blessed are those who ignore Torah. Psalm 119 provides eight lines, each with a different name for Torah, in twenty-two separate stanzas, for a total of 176 verses in praise of Torah. "Oh, how I love your Torah!" the poet exclaims in 119:97. If we had only these three poems in the Hebrew Bible in praise of the glory of God's gift of Torah, they surely should suffice to correct the Christian notion that God's Torah, God's Law, was viewed in ancient Israel as a burden to be borne. Torah was a loving gift from a loving God. Even the Ten Commandments are set in the context of God's gracious act of deliverance of Israel from slavery in Egypt. Indeed, the first of the Ten Commandments for the Jewish community is "I am the LORD your God, who brought you out of the land of Egypt, out of the house of slavery" (Exod. 20:2).

The poem closes with a prayer of petition in two parts. Verses 12–13 acknowledge that it is no simple matter to be faithful to Torah, despite the great blessings that follow from doing so. The prophet Jeremiah acknowledged (17:9), "The heart is devious above all else; it is perverse—who can understand it?" Our poet also knows that human beings who love God and God's Torah still turn from both. Moreover, those who flaunt the Torah and its precepts can influence those who seek to be faithful. Verse 13 may be speaking of evildoers or of the sins they commit. Either and both can lead one astray.

The closing petition brings to an end this remarkable tribute to the testimony of the heavenly bodies and of the Torah to the glory of God. It is a suitable closing benediction for any prayer, any act of worship.

WALTER J. HARRELSON

Homiletical Perspective

hearts. Many of the stars that sparked the psalmist's praise are now lost to our vision, dimmed by the haze that shrouds our cities and the lights that consume energy all night long.

Yet the psalmist professes confidence in God's ability to reshape our lives. The law provides a way for God's people to reenter their relationship with the Creator, the means by which our relationship with God is restored, and thus the means by which our relationships with our neighbors and with our environment are fashioned anew.

Psalm 19 helps to contextualize the Gospel and Epistle lectionary texts for the Third Sunday after the Epiphany in lectionary year C. Luke's Gospel recounts Jesus' reading of the scroll in the temple, proclaiming, "The Spirit of the Lord is upon me." He uses the language of fulfillment to declare that he has come to proclaim good news to the poor and bind up the brokenhearted. The fulfillment of the law involves restoring relationships, bringing life to the chasms that lie between us. In 1 Corinthians, we hear the language of the body, with many members and many gifts offered together for God's purpose, greater than any one of us. Psalm 19 affirms our place in this divine pattern, as joyful participants in the goodness of creation, as people in relationship with the one who made us.

Psalm 19 offers a helpful guide for the life of prayer, emphasizing a desire to align ourselves with the law of love that governs our existence. Lifting a voice with all of creation, the psalmist prays that the thoughts of our hearts may be so set on God that we may know what God desires for us and for this world. As nature tells the glory of God, making God's work so plain and so easy to observe, so too the psalmist prays that our words and thoughts may belong to God, in whom our lives are grounded and who leads us into life.

APRIL BERENDS

1 Corinthians 12:12-31a

¹²For just as the body is one and has many members, and all the members of the body, though many, are one body, so it is with Christ. ¹³For in the one Spirit we were all baptized into one body—Jews or Greeks, slaves or free—and we were all made to drink of one Spirit.

¹⁴Indeed, the body does not consist of one member but of many. ¹⁵If the foot would say, "Because I am not a hand, I do not belong to the body," that would not make it any less a part of the body. ¹⁶And if the ear would say, "Because I am not an eye, I do not belong to the body," that would not make it any less a part of the body. ¹⁷If the whole body were an eye, where would the hearing be? If the whole body were hearing, where would the sense of smell be? ¹⁸But as it is, God arranged the members in the body, each one of them, as he chose. ¹⁹If all were a single member, where would the body be? ²⁰As it is, there are many members, yet one body. ²¹The eye cannot say to the hand, "I have no need of you," nor again the head to the feet, "I have no need of you." ²²On the contrary, the members of the body that seem to be weaker are indispensable, ²³and

Theological Perspective

Today's text develops one of the most famous metaphors in the history of Christianity. To elaborate his overarching exhortation for unity in the church, Paul introduces his celebrated analogy of the church as human body. Since then, understandings of the Christian community as a type of organism have periodically come to the fore in ecclesial reflection. Even the most extreme understandings of the church as a voluntary society of autonomous individuals have been tempered by the memory of Paul's organic metaphor.

The comparison of a human community to the physical body was certainly not original with Paul. The trope already enjoyed a long history in classical literature. However, Paul gave it a revolutionary new twist. Previously, the comparison had reinforced hierarchy, suggesting that the lowly workers, the drones, should obey and support their military, mercantile, and political leaders. Those at the bottom of the social ladder should stay put and be grateful for the guidance and protection of their natural superiors. After all, in the body, the brain that makes crucial decisions is more critical than the lowly organs that sustain routine daily functioning. Even today, the analogy retains a seductive plausibility. Our culture assumes that a talented CEO is worth more than a janitor and should be remunerated accordingly.

Pastoral Perspective

The playful charm of this passage makes it one of the most memorable of Paul's teachings. Yet underneath the amusing imagery of talking feet and self-deprecating ears is the profound statement of unity that is the essence of the church: "Now you are the body of Christ and individually members of it" (v. 27).

This metaphor of individual members together comprising one complete body offers rich possibilities for reflection on how churches function as people come together for worship, education, fellowship, and mission. It particularly raises the question of balance, that is, how pastors can help foster communities where there is a healthy balance between the need for connection and for a clear sense of oneself as an individual. To paraphrase Paul, how can the ear maintain and value its essential "earness," even as it participates in the functioning of the whole body? The family systems model is a useful tool for understanding and encouraging this process. It speaks to the importance of "differentiation" within a family or congregation, which Edwin Friedman defines as "the capacity to be an 'I' while remaining connected."[1]

---

1. Edwin Friedman, *Generation to Generation, Family Process in Church and Synagogue* (New York: Guilford Press, 1985), 27.

those members of the body that we think less honorable we clothe with greater honor, and our less respectable members are treated with greater respect; [24]whereas our more respectable members do not need this. But God has so arranged the body, giving the greater honor to the inferior member, [25]that there may be no dissension within the body, but the members may have the same care for one another. [26]If one member suffers, all suffer together with it; if one member is honored, all rejoice together with it.

[27]Now you are the body of Christ and individually members of it. [28]And God has appointed in the church first apostles, second prophets, third teachers; then deeds of power, then gifts of healing, forms of assistance, forms of leadership, various kinds of tongues. [29]Are all apostles? Are all prophets? Are all teachers? Do all work miracles? [30]Do all possess gifts of healing? Do all speak in tongues? Do all interpret? [31]But strive for the greater gifts. And I will show you a still more excellent way.

Exegetical Perspective

The passage for this Third Sunday after the Epiphany is located within a larger grouping of texts concerning disturbances within the worship context (chaps. 11–14) and, more immediately, within Paul's address of spiritual gifts (chaps. 12–14). The present verses (vv. 12–31a) reinforce and extend the emphasis in verses 4–11 on the need for a diversity of spiritual gifts, which emerge from and mirror the diversity of God's character. Dominating this section is Paul's use of the body (*sōma*) image, which was often employed in other ancient writings as a reminder to those of low social and/or political status of their place in society, namely, in a position of subservience to those of higher standing. In light of this, Paul's usage stands out as unique. He employs the image to emphasize the *importance* of the seemingly less important, less prominent, or less significant parts, lifting up the "least" of the members and calling the "greater" parts to pay attention to and even honor these others.

Additionally, this is not the first instance in the letter where the body image comes up. It is featured earlier, in 10:17, where the unity of those in the body is emphasized through the "bread" of the Lord's table. Yet, the use of the body metaphor here in 12:12–31 varies from its use in the previous text. Here (v. 12), the necessity of diversity within the body is a presupposition for Paul and therefore is not

Homiletical Perspective

The human body has 206 bones, 639 muscles, and about 6 pounds of skin, along with ligaments, cartilage, veins, arteries, blood, fat, and more. Every time we hear a sound; every time we take a step; every time we take a breath, hundreds of different parts work together so that what we experience is a single movement, our minds and bodies working as one unit. Even the greatest engineers struggle to achieve anything like it in mechanical form. The human body represents one of the most complex systems in existence.

That is why the body is one of the most powerful images for the church offered in Scripture. The metaphor conveys both complexity and organic unity. Often people find it difficult to name their place in the church, but asked to envision themselves as a part of the body, children and adults of all ages have little difficulty identifying themselves as hands, feet, brains, and funny bones! Preaching on this passage offers our hearers insight into how the church is structured, as well as their own places within it.

We Belong to the Body. We come to the water of baptism as individuals, independent and relatively self-contained. We come out of that water changed. Our identity is no longer solitary; we can no longer

1 Corinthians 12:12-31a

Theological Perspective

Similarly, congregations often shower the homiletically gifted senior pastor with accolades and allow the director of Christian education to languish unacknowledged in the shadows.

Paul inverts the force of the metaphor, as many liberation theologies have emphasized. Rather than arguing for hierarchy and subordination, Paul uses the figure of the body to advance a rationale for diversity and interdependence with a strongly egalitarian thrust. According to Paul's analogy, the assertion of superiority is ridiculous, for it implicitly reduces the church to one body part and its function. In reality, however, "privileged" congregants are so intimately bound to their lower-status brothers and sisters in one body that the entire notion of status is subverted. Higher-status Christians need lower-status Christians, and vice versa.

In the human body, the head cannot claim that it does not need the feet (v. 21). The eloquent preacher could not be heard if the sound technician did not ensure the proper operation of the microphone. The force of Paul's analogy points to the equally essential nature of all functions. Consequently, the church should not just tolerate a plurality of capacities and experiences but should actively cultivate a spirit-breathed synergy. The radical interdependence that Paul portrays requires radical diversity of gifts, all necessary for the common good. The differences in gifts should not become the foundation for hurtful comparisons.

In fact, in Paul's trope society, a "natural" scheme of values is turned upside down. The apparently lower-status members play an indispensable role in the community. The purpose of Paul's reference to the less honorable members of the body (presumably sexual organs) that are treated with more honor is to suggest that those persons who would be the most disdained according to ordinary social standards should actually be treated with the most respect in the Christian community. Some theologians have extended the trajectory of this theme, suggesting that even the politically marginalized, the disabled, the uneducated, and the ugly have gifts of superlative value to offer the community, for they reflect the weakness of Christ.[1] Those odd folks sitting in the back pews with their disheveled clothes and questionable hygienic habits have just as much worth as do the more respectable and well-groomed members of the congregation.

---

1. Jürgen Moltmann, *The Source of Life: The Holy Spirit and the Theology of Life* (Philadelphia: Fortress Press, 1997), 66–68.

Pastoral Perspective

The inviting church is a tangible expression of the hospitality of God; people come in search of meaning in their lives, spiritual growth, deeper relationship with Christ, opportunities to be of service in the world. They also come in search of authentic community, a place where they are known and accepted and where they can experience a sense of belonging. The challenge is to build a community where "there may be no dissension within the body, but the members may have the same care for one another" (v. 25). There will always be differences within a congregation—differing opinions, experiences, priorities, needs—and it is dangerous to try to play down those differences in the interest of some superficial harmony. When this natural diversity within a congregation is not allowed to be expressed openly, subtle judgments are communicated: when the ear gets the message that it would really be better if it were an eye, when the foot realizes that the community values hands more highly.

This is the dynamic that Friedman refers to as "togetherness pressures," when the positive desire for closeness and connection is turned into pressure to conform in some false unity. In systems theory, this pressure makes the congregation very vulnerable to anxiety when there is any kind of change. Changes in leadership, in membership (increase or decrease), in the buildings or the surrounding neighborhood, can make individual members of the church anxious. When there is excessive closeness or pressure to conform within the congregation, the anxiety of a few members can cause anxiety within the rest of the "system," bringing about conflict and dissension. Anxiety lessens one's ability to be imaginative, creative, and self-reflective, and instead causes reactivity, defensiveness, even paranoia. Conversely, in a church where individuality and closeness are well balanced, the eyes, ears, hands, and feet can maintain their own identities, vision, and loyalty to the Head without succumbing to "togetherness pressures." Then tensions within the church family, which are a normal part of life together, can be navigated with compassion and care for one another.

The role of the pastor is an essential part of a healthy "body." When conflict and tension arise within the congregation, it is the pastor's task to be a nonanxious presence; calm, clear and creative, not defensive or reactive. Too often, afraid of losing those most anxious people, pastors and other leaders in the church lean too far in one direction or another: becoming "peace-mongers" and avoiding conflict at all costs, or becoming excessively

Exegetical Perspective

something that he "will argue for but argue from."[1] The body of Christ is and needs to be diverse.

Prior to articulating various aspects of his teaching on the diversity of spiritual gifts in the body, and possibly as a safeguard against an overemphasis of it, Paul first communicates how the unity of the body of Christ was established and is sustained. The Corinthians' (and others') common reception and experience of the Holy Spirit is the single source for this oneness. As is also stressed in Ephesians 4, Christian unity has not been (and cannot be) *attained* by the members of the body; it is yet another gift of the Spirit to be received and *maintained* "in the bond of peace" (Eph. 4:3). Gordon Fee, a leading scholar on Pauline pneumatology, notes that "for Paul the reception of the Spirit is the *sine qua non* of the Christian life. . . . Thus it is natural for him to refer to their unity in the body in terms of the Spirit."[2] This unity—a unity that is not overcome by any social, religious, or ethnic variations in the Corinthian body—does not nullify the need for diversity within the Spirit. In fact, "unity" is coherent as a concept and reality only amid diversity. Therefore, for the remainder of the passage, Paul turns to the needed diversity in the Corinthian body.

The teaching that Paul delivers on the necessity of diversity in the body comes in two structurally parallel units: verses 15–20 and verses 21–26. In each of these there are (1) a personification of parts of the body; (2) a series of rhetorical questions or observations that highlight, through absurdity, a misguided understanding of the identity and value of members within the body; and (3) a final application to the body itself. Additionally, both stress the vital importance of each member of the body, thus highlighting the utter need for diversity. Distinct in the first unit, though, is Paul's emphasis on God's arrangement of all of the members of the body. As Richard Hays notes, "the body is internally differentiated in accordance with the design of God (v. 18); without such differentiation, the body would be grotesque and helpless (v. 17), all eye or all ear. For that reason, no member of the body (church) should ever think that he or she is worthless or unimportant (vv. 15–16)."[3]

The second unit (vv. 21–26) continues the emphasis on diversity seen in the first, but also

---

1. Gordon D. Fee, *The First Epistle to the Corinthians*, New International Commentary on the New Testament (Grand Rapids: Eerdmans, 1987), 602.
2. Ibid., 603.
3. Richard B. Hays, *First Corinthians*, Interpretation Series (Louisville, KY: John Knox Press, 1997), 215.

Homiletical Perspective

truly be known without reference to that community into which we have been incorporated: the body of Christ, the church. After baptism, we are more than just ourselves; we are by definition beings-in-relationship. Where the spirit of God once moved over the face of the deep and brought life to the world, the Spirit of God remains the source of the life, the breath of the church, moving among us and within us.

One of our human needs is the need to belong. We want to have a place in this earth. We want significance. Belonging is the gift of baptism, the gift of the Spirit.

And yet there is a tension here. Some people want to belong without belonging. They are the ones whose obituaries read, "Dorothy was a lifelong member of St John's Church"—except that no one at St John's can ever remember meeting her, although ninety-three-year-old Mrs. Smith thinks that maybe Dorothy was once in a wedding she attended, and there is an entry for her in the baptism register, though nothing after that.

As far as 1 Corinthians is concerned, there is no such thing as belonging without participating. That abrogates the nature of the body. A body does not work when one part checks out for a few years; not only will its function be unfulfilled, but the rest of the body will be thrown out of balance. Belonging is not a one-sided affair. We are given the gift of belonging at baptism, but we are also signing up for the responsibility of functioning as part of the body of Christ.

Belonging Means Participating. Every member of the church is given gifts, to be exercised for the common good (12:7). One of the tasks of the community is to discern these gifts—many of which are named in this chapter—and to provide ways in which they may be used. Preaching about gifts needs to be accompanied by naming practices of discernment within our churches, along with the structures that ensure such gifts are used and valued. Many churches have a practice of thanking people for the contributions they make to the life of the church, sometimes with special honors for those who have served long and faithfully. A culture of thanking can build up the community and encourage people to use their gifts, but it can also carry implicit messages that run counter to the messages we preach from the pulpit. Rewarding those who have exercised their gifts, we imply that this is something special, above and beyond the call of duty, and that the only

---

1 Corinthians 12:12-31a

Theological Perspective

Paul emphasizes that his valorization of the interdependence of the community members and his subversion of hierarchies of value extend to leadership functions, not just to spiritual capacities and experiences. It is not clear that Paul is enumerating discrete offices in the church in his list of "apostles," "prophets," "teachers," and so forth, but he certainly is referring to a variety of essential activities in the church and the persons who exercise them. The dramatic and potentially status-conferring gift of tongues is merely one type of ability among a host of necessary gifts for leadership. Consequently, this passage has often been used by reform movements within the church, like the Spiritual Franciscans and the Quakers, who have sought to counteract the growth of clericalism or any other attribution of superior worth to certain members of the Christian community. This egalitarian force of Paul's metaphor lies behind the tendency of the early evangelicals to hail all believers, no matter what their role in the church, as "sisters" and "brothers."

By the end of this passage it becomes clear that the church as the body of Christ is not just a rhetorical device but points to real participation in Christ. The members of the church are enlivened by the same Spirit bestowed by Christ to do Christ's work in the world. Through the mutually shared union with Christ, the organic bond is so real that individual members share one another's sufferings and joys. Of course, different Christian traditions have understood the church as the body of Christ in different ways. For some it suggests a unity closely associated with the church's sacramental life. For others it suggests a oneness born of common religious experience, for others a solidarity rooted in a shared participation in Christ-like action, and for yet others a unity linked to a common confession of faith or witness. However different these emphases may be, they all presuppose that the church's bodily character is the product not of its sociological structures or institutional arrangements but of its relation to Jesus Christ.[2] As Paul proclaims toward the end of this passage, "Now you are the body of Christ and individually members of it" (v. 27). In Christ, the church is already a unified body, even if that unity is not being adequately expressed. Its organic oneness is a gift of grace. The Christian community simply needs to enact what it already is.

LEE C. BARRETT

Pastoral Perspective

controlling. When this happens, the most anxious and reactive members hold the church hostage as the leaders' own anxiety infects the rest of the body.

Again, the main point here is balance. A healthy church invites and enables its members to find their own answer to the question, "How can I be who I am and stay connected to you?"[2] Paul writes that, when this body is functioning in accordance with God's design, "if one member suffers, all suffer together with it; if one member is honored, all rejoice together with it" (v. 26). The integrity and value of the individual are honored, yet in a context of compassion and mutuality. Members of the body can feel compassion for another's suffering without becoming responsible for it; they can rejoice when another receives honor without envy or bitterness.

This is a particularly challenging balance for pastors to achieve. There is great temptation and pressure to allow oneself to be defined by the community—by their needs, wants, and expectations, which are often conflicting and ultimately impossible to fulfill. Couple this with Paul's encouragement to maintain a clear sense of one's individual identity, and the daily necessity of handling tensions and conflicts in the life of the church and the quest for balance can seem impossible.

Peter Steinke gives specific guidance to pastors on how to attain and maintain this balance, by developing "the capacity to self-manage: to think before we act; to observe ourselves; to define ourselves by saying, 'I think' or 'I believe'; to resist cutting off from or giving in to others, to focus on our own behavior."[3] It is a challenge, but a worthy one, one that leads to the fullest expression of Christian identity. As Paul writes, God has made each one indispensable to the whole—hand, foot, ear, eye—and given each an essential role: apostle, teacher, leader, healer, and so on. Our individual and corporate health as the Christian community is to be found in fully embracing both within the context of the body of Christ.

KAREN STOKES

---

2. Peter Steinke, Workshop, San Francisco Presbytery Council, Alamo, CA, March 13, 2008.
3. Peter Steinke, *Congregational Leadership in Anxious Times* (Herndon, VA: Alban Institute, 2006), 155.

2. Karl Barth, *Church Dogmatics*, IV/1, ed. G. W. Bromiley and T. F. Torrance (Edinburgh: T. & T. Clark, 1936–62), 663–64.

extends it by specifically highlighting the necessity and value of the seemingly less significant parts of the body. Here the "weaker" members, possibly a reference to internal organs, are identified as being vital not just to the body as a whole but also to each of the more prominent members individually. The weaker members are "indispensable" or "necessary" (v. 22) to the whole. This is the case because "God has so arranged the body" (v. 24), resulting in a lack of any basis for internal dissension and emphasizing instead the need to offer care for all members. Suffering on the one side and honor on the other, therefore, become a collective (rather than individual) experience of the body due to this interdependence. In these final verses, the occasion to which Paul is applying this metaphor seems to bleed over directly into it. The absurdity of "dissension" among parts of the human body leads the interpreter to see this comment as more concretely directed at the Corinthian situation of conflict over spiritual things.

Paul concludes the passage with a more overt application to the Corinthians (vv. 27–31a). They are the single, unified body, and likewise they are the individual, diverse parts that compose it. The list inserted here is more varied than the previous ones. It includes a series of gifted persons, a set of gifts, and finally two acts of service. The passage also includes a sequence of rhetorical questions that magnify the absurdity of uniformity in the body of Christ, highlighting the Corinthians absurdity of overemphasizing the significance of tongues within the range of spiritual gifts (v. 30). Instead, Paul urges them to seek "the greater gifts" (v. 31a), which is seemingly not a reference to certain other gifts— this would be contradictory to Paul's overall argument!—but a lead-in to the final bit of his argument on spiritual gifts found in chapter 14, all of which are to be expressed in the "way" (v. 31b) of love (chap. 13).

TROY MILLER

valuable ministries are those that receive public thanks. As we preach about the body of Christ and each person's place within it, we need to be constantly aware of how our practices reinforce—or undermine—our message.

One of the strengths of the image of the body is that it provides an opportunity to speak about the place of those who are not normally valued in our society. This text suggests that every single person in the church matters—the housebound elderly, babies, those with disabilities, as well as the generous givers and hard workers. This is a reality we can name, which has less to do with equality than with wholeness. Only with all of our members can the body of the church be whole.

Being a Community in Christ. Verses 25–26 talk about suffering and rejoicing with one another. This is more than making casseroles for someone in need or throwing a party for someone celebrating. It is about being a community that shares its life. Many of us rarely experience this kind of community. Too many of our relationships are functional, existing in order to do or to achieve something. But our relationships in Christ in a sense have no purpose beyond themselves. They exist as the visible expression of the love of God, a love that simply takes delight in the presence of the beloved. As part of the body, we share each others' lives, in good times and in bad. As we do, we become a tangible expression of God's care. We know God loves us when we are held in a community of love.

This is a vision of church: not a building, but a body of people, caring for one another, sharing the work of God in the world. But lest this passage be heard as placing yet another burden on already overburdened people of faith, it is important to remind our hearers that this all is made possible by the gifts of the Spirit, who works in and through each of us. All of us who are part of the body belong to Christ, and we depend on the Spirit, who is life.

RAEWYNNE J. WHITELEY

Luke 4:14-21

[14]Then Jesus, filled with the power of the Spirit, returned to Galilee, and a report about him spread through all the surrounding country. [15]He began to teach in their synagogues and was praised by everyone.

[16]When he came to Nazareth, where he had been brought up, he went to the synagogue on the sabbath day, as was his custom. He stood up to read, [17]and the scroll of the prophet Isaiah was given to him. He unrolled the scroll and found the place where it was written:

[18]"The Spirit of the Lord is upon me,
  because he has anointed me
    to bring good news to the poor.
  He has sent me to proclaim release to the captives
  and recovery of sight to the blind,
    to let the oppressed go free,
[19]to proclaim the year of the Lord's favor."

[20]And he rolled up the scroll, gave it back to the attendant, and sat down. The eyes of all in the synagogue were fixed on him. [21]Then he began to say to them, "Today this scripture has been fulfilled in your hearing."

Theological Perspective

Whether or not we Christian readers/interpreters acknowledge it, we bring an overarching preunderstanding of the gospel to each encounter with particular biblical texts. This preunderstanding comprises our sense of how the good news coheres, our sense of the center of the biblical message. Every part of the Christian canon is thus interpreted in light of this sense of coherence of the whole. Furthermore, when we acknowledge, articulate, and critically assess our overarching theological criterion, we open up the possibility for the center to speak *to* and sometimes even *against* parts of the canon that obstruct the gospel. Thus, when preaching or teaching a text, we may bring the central view of the gospel to bear on and reinterpret other portions of the canon.

According to *The New Interpreter's Bible*, Jesus' reading and interpretation of the words of Isaiah in this scene function "as a keynote to the entire ministry of Jesus, setting forth the perspective from which it is to be understood."[1] Luke 4:14–21 offers us a sense of the center of the gospel, something like an overarching theological criterion. Luke implies that Jesus himself chose to read this part of Isaiah and that he drew selectively on the tradition to

1. R. Alan Culpepper, "The Gospel of Luke," in *The New Interpreter's Bible*, vol. 9 (Nashville: Abingdon, 1995), 102.

Pastoral Perspective

Later, Luke will tell us in the early chapters of Acts how the Holy Spirit came upon the believers at Pentecost and launched the church in witness. Now he is telling us of the Holy Spirit's involvement in the life of Jesus as he steps forth in public ministry. Even Jesus is not self-sufficient. He is dependent upon his God for life, faith, and mission. Our text, which finds Jesus reading from the scroll of Isaiah in the synagogue in Nazareth, is preceded by the brief story of Jesus' baptism and the somewhat longer account of his temptations in the wilderness. For Luke, all three episodes are Holy Spirit stories as the Spirit claims, tests, and empowers Jesus for the ministry that lies before him. The Holy Spirit descends upon Jesus like a dove while he is praying after his baptism and speaks the claiming word of affirmation. Then the Holy Spirit fills and leads Jesus into the wilderness for a time of testing as Jesus refuses the pathways that are the wrong choices for his servant ministry. Now as Jesus returns to Galilee, the Holy Spirit will fill him with power for ministry as he reads a text that will be his mission statement as Messiah.

Luke wants us to know that it is the Holy Spirit who leads Jesus in saying no to false options in the temptation story and saying yes to a mission that is given to him by God. When Jesus reads Isaiah 61:1–2 in the synagogue in Nazareth, he is declaring that his

Exegetical Perspective

The introductory section, verses 14–15, serves an important introductory function. Jesus is introduced as a teacher (*didaskalos*) who teaches in various synagogues around Galilee. Luke tells us that Jesus had positive response from his teaching: "he was glorified by all" (v. 15, my trans.). This summary affirms the peripatetic teaching ministry of Jesus and the wide and positive response he received—at least for a while.

Then Jesus arrives in Nazareth (v. 16). This is his childhood home, where he played and worshiped. Jesus enters the familiar synagogue, where he has attended with his family as a young child. He knows the people; he knows their faces. He can call many of them by name. Perhaps they are even aunts and uncles, cousins, and dear family friends in the small, local synagogue of his hometown. In contrast to the positive introductory summary in verses 14–16, this event in his home synagogue brings rejection (vv. 22–30). When Jesus speaks on this particular Sabbath, the listeners are filled with wrath. They throw their own beloved homegrown son out of the synagogue (14:29–30).

The ordinary day in the synagogue becomes a very extraordinary day when Jesus comes to town. Ordinary synagogue worship practices included the following elements: (1) recitation of the Shema

Homiletical Perspective

All three of the Synoptic Gospels (Matt. 13:54–58; Mark 6:1–6a; Luke 4:14–30) recount the story of Jesus teaching in the synagogue in his hometown of Nazareth and being rejected by the people, but Luke's much fuller account is distinctive both in his placement of the story at the very beginning of Jesus' public ministry, immediately following his baptism and temptation, and in giving the content of what Jesus read and said. Both of these distinctives, in placement and content, are significant. As Fred Craddock notes, "Luke places the Nazareth visit first because it is first, not chronologically but programmatically. That is to say that this event announces who Jesus is, of what his ministry consists, what his church will be and do, and what will be the response to both Jesus and the church."[1]

Thus, while it may be inviting to preach this story as an example of the perennial human story of the young man who has grown beyond the community that birthed and raised him, and is therefore rejected by the hometown folks who cannot value what he has become, this approach risks missing the more significant and *challenging* meaning of the text in Luke. The challenge comes from the *content* of the Scripture that Jesus chooses to read when he is

1. Fred Craddock, *Luke* (Louisville, KY: John Knox Press, 1990), 61.

Luke 4:14-21

Theological Perspective

emphasize his ministry to the poor. (Significantly, Luke quotes Isa. 61:2a, "to proclaim the year of the Lord's favor," but leaves out 2b, "and the day of vengeance of our God.") From the beginning of his Gospel (1:52, 53) Luke emphasizes that Jesus' work was to bring good news to the poor. Luke's portrayal of Jesus' reading and exposition signals that concern, for the liberation of the impoverished and oppressed was of paramount importance to Jesus' ministry.

Whatever we take to be the heart of the gospel will be the central shaping force in our life of faith; the author of Luke instructs readers to place this text as the central concern and even plumb line of Jesus' teaching. In today's passage we learn what Jesus came to do; insofar as we measure our lives against this, we are following Jesus' ministry.

The implication of this text is that if we are going to study, interpret, and follow the gospel, we should keep *coming back* to this text to measure our work. Here the context of this passage is important, as it follows the story of temptation where Jesus has refused to be lured by power and spectacle. Jesus was "full of the Holy Spirit" and "was led by the Spirit in the wilderness" just before our text; in this passage he returns to Galilee "in the power of the Spirit" and reads from Second Isaiah that "the Spirit of the Lord is upon me."

It is easy to get sidetracked from the central message of the gospel. The prophets often had to remind the people about God's main purposes. Thus in Isaiah 1 the Lord is reported to have asked: "What to me is the multitude of your sacrifices?" (v. 11). The Lord indicates there has been "enough of burnt offerings" and that there is no divine delight in blood sacrifice. "When you come to appear before me, who asked this from your hand? . . . Bringing offerings is futile; incense is an abomination to me" (vv. 12–13). The Lord commands that the people, "Trample my courts no more" (v. 12c), and that they "learn to do good; seek justice, rescue the oppressed, defend the orphan, plead for the widow" (v. 17).

Luke, in the traditions of First and Second Isaiah as well as the wider prophets, deemphasizes ceremonial displays of righteousness, underscoring acts of human compassion and social justice instead. The primary question is not so much, what does God demand for righteousness? It is, rather, who needs attention and compassion?

It is interesting to put this narrative of Jesus' "keynote" alongside John Updike's novel *In the Beauty of the Lilies*. This novel is the tale of a turn-of-the-century minister, Clarence Wilmot, who lost

Pastoral Perspective

ministry in the Spirit as Messiah of God calls him to be an agent of mercy to the downtrodden in this world: he will be good news to the poor, release to the captives, sight for the blind, freedom for the oppressed, and new beginnings for all who have failed. Luke rearranges Mark's chronology of Jesus' Galilean ministry in order to move this mission statement to the front and center of the public ministry. It is a defining moment in the Spirit.

The Rev. Joan Gray, moderator of the 217th General Assembly of the Presbyterian Church (U.S.A.), has commented, "When you really think about it, this *dunamis* of the Spirit is the only thing the early church had going for it. It had no buildings, no budget, no paid staff, and very few members."[1] The opposite situation may face us: we have buildings, budgets, staff, and members, but do we have the power of the Holy Spirit? How can we know if we have it?

The Holy Spirit gives us something to do for God. Everyone seems to want to know these days, "How are we doing as a church?" The real question is, "As a church, what are we doing for God?" Jesus steps forward in Nazareth and declares the truth about his life: he has been filled with the power of the Spirit and anointed to bring good news to the poor. To know our mission and to understand what God has given us to do are as important to us as they were to Jesus. Tom Harvey, a Presbyterian missionary in Singapore, preached these words: "Mission catches you up in the life and vitality of God, for it is God who relentlessly draws men and women to himself in love and compassion. Moreover, when we step away from mission, there is a corresponding depletion of the life and vitality in the church."[2]

How can we know that we have the power of the Spirit? We know because the Holy Spirit gives us something to do for God, and a time to do it. There is a sense of urgency in Jesus' mission. He finished reading, rolled up the scroll, gave it to the attendant, sat down, and with all eyes upon him said, "Today this scripture has been fulfilled in your hearing." The time of God's Holy Spirit is today, right now. It is the Holy Spirit speaking when you hear God whisper to you: "Child of God, live this day as if it were your first day, as if it were your last day, as if it were your only day."[3]

1. "Come Holy Spirit," in *The Presbyterian Outlook* 189, no. 20 (June 4, 2007): 16.
2. From a sermon preached at Myers Park Presbyterian Church, Charlotte, NC, and quoted by Dr. Ernie Thompson in *First Presbyterian News*, First Presbyterian Church of Wilmington, NC, vol. 12, issue 22, p. 1.
3. Walter J. Burghardt, "What We Don't Have Is Time," in *Best Sermons*, vol. 3 (New York: Harper & Row, 1990), 57.

Exegetical Perspective

(Deut. 6:4–9; 11:13–21; Num. 15:37–41); (2) praying while facing Jerusalem; (3) the "amen" response from the gathered congregation; (4) reading from sections of the scrolls of the Torah and of the Prophets; (5) a sermon; and (6) benediction.[1] Any male could volunteer or be asked to pray or read portions from the Torah or the Prophets. Likewise, any male could also be asked to give the sermon (Acts 13:15, 42; 14:1; 17:2). Readers were appointed before the service began.

On this particular Sabbath, however, Jesus volunteers to read the section from the Prophets.[2] He stands to read on a special platform, as was the custom. Jesus most likely was given the scroll that he requested—the scroll of Isaiah (4:17). Jesus unrolls the scroll, finds the place, and begins to read: "The Spirit of the Lord is upon me, because he has anointed me to preach good news to the poor. He has sent me to proclaim release to the captives and recovering sight to the blind, to set at liberty those who are oppressed" (Isa. 61:1ff.). This passage, already in circulation, was used in the Qumran community as an important reference to the work of the Teacher of Righteousness (IQH 18:14). These words had been attached to the description of the Messiah who was to come; and they were waiting.

The messianic job description, already familiar to the synagogue worshipers as messianic expectations of the Coming One, is reinterpreted before their very eyes. In a dramatic moment, Jesus rolls the scroll, returns it to the attendant, and sits down. "The eyes of all in the synagogue were fixed on him" (v. 20). Then Jesus speaks from his place of sitting: "Today this scripture has been fulfilled in your hearing."

To read these words aloud before your own relatives in your hometown synagogue required much courage. In reading this portion of Hebrew Scripture, Jesus is saying that his life work will be to (1) heal the brokenhearted; (2) announce the release of prisoners of war; (3) recover sight to the blind; (4) announce the acceptable year of the Lord (vv. 14–19). Jesus' announcement says that they can no longer see him simply as a village carpenter or as Mary and Joseph's boy. He is the one that they have been waiting to come all of their lives, and their grandparents' lives, and the generations before them. The carpenter's son is the Messiah.

Homiletical Perspective

handed the scroll from the prophet Isaiah (vv. 18–19) and from his comment, "Today this scripture has been fulfilled in your hearing" (v. 21).

Jesus' Mission. Jesus presents these verses from Isaiah 61:1–2 and 58:6 as a description of who he is and what he is about. They form his *purpose* or *mission statement* or *agenda* for his ministry. This latter term was coined in the curriculum *The Agenda: 8 Lessons from Luke 4,* published by the Baptist Center for Ethics in 2007. In the introduction Robert Parham writes that "Luke 4:18–19 is one of the most ignored, watered down, spiritualized or glossed-over texts in many Baptist pulpits, evading or emptying Jesus' first statement of his moral agenda." He goes on to summarize that in these verses "Jesus said the gospel was for the poor and oppressed, speaking to those at the margins of society. Jesus was announcing that he came to liberate from real oppressive structures the marginalized—the impoverished, the war captives, the poor in health, the political prisoners. Jesus came to turn the economic structures upside down, instituting the year of Jubilee when crushing debts were forgiven and slaves were freed."[2]

All of this is very challenging for those of us who are not among the poor, marginalized, oppressed or imprisoned of our society to hear. It is threatening to contemplate the turning upside down of economic structures from which we benefit; but we need the moral courage to listen to the intention of God for humanity as Jesus proclaims it in Luke 4, and we can be opened up by hearing accounts of how persons who are in those very situations hear with joy and renewed hope this good news of social transformation. Perhaps too we can be encouraged by noting that when Jesus proclaimed this prophetic text that is so challenging for those in positions of privilege, he left out Isaiah 61:2b, "and the day of vengeance of our God." Jesus' focus was on bringing healing and justice, not vengeance.

The way in which Jesus combines the spiritual and the social/political in his teaching and ministry, beginning with this text from Isaiah, should also be noted. The Spirit that descended upon Jesus at his baptism while he was praying (3:22), led him into the wilderness to be tested by the devil (4:1), and now empowers his ministry in Galilee (4:14), has "anointed" him "to bring good news to the poor" along with release, healing, freedom, and justice. A

1. E. Yamauchi, "Synagogue," in *Dictionary of Jesus and the Gospels,* ed. Joel B. Green and Scot McKnight (Downers Grove, IL: InterVarsity Press, 1992), 782.

2. According to I. Howard Marshall, this passage, Luke 4:16–21, is "the oldest known account of a synagogue service" (*The Gospel of Luke: A Commentary on the Greek Text* [Grand Rapids: Eerdmans, 1978], 181).

2. Robert Parham, *The Agenda: 8 Lessons from Luke 4: Students Guide* (Nashville: Baptist Center for Ethics, 2007, accessible through www.ethicsdaily.com), 3, 4.

Luke 4:14-21

Theological Perspective

his faith in the God he was taught in seminary. The God Wilmot was taught—rationalistic, all powerful, and in control—made no sense in light of the poverty he was seeing around him. His seminary teachings were like the "twigs of an utterly dead tree," such "sad sap," "paper shields against the molten iron of natural truth."[2]

Wilmot concluded that his genteel professors had sold him on a message that was half wishful thinking, half self-promoting lies. "The doctrine had for these years past felt to Clarence like an invalid, a tenuous ghost scattered invisibly among the faces that from sickbeds and Sunday pews and oilcloth-covered kitchen tables of disrupted, impoverished households beseeched him for hope and courage, for that thing which Calvin in his Gallic lucidity called *la grace.*"[3]

At one point in his ministry, Wilmot decided against expanding the church buildings; he could not justify adding underused ecclesiastical structures when poor immigrants down the street slept six to a room. Apparently his education did not provide him the wherewithal to see in that decision any link either to his faith or to his ministerial calling. He considered a turn to the poor to be a turn away from the all-powerful God. The moderator of the presbytery identified his problem as having been shaped by a conservatism that would not adapt to the vicissitudes of life and history. Having studied the two Hodges and Warfield, theologians who could not bend, Wilmot's faith shattered when the storms of life overwhelmed his doctrine.

The moderator was correct, but too late. The litany "*There is no God*" kept repeating in Wilmot's head. He never saw an alternative to the God of the inflexible doctrines he learned. Wilmot ended up peddling encyclopedias to people who could not afford them (but bought them anyway), mirroring the doctrinal peddling he was trained to do as a minister.

Wilmot, steeped in authoritative Christologies, somehow missed Luke's Jesus. If only Wilmot and his professors had opened Luke and found the place where it was written: "The Spirit of the Lord is upon me, because he has anointed me to bring good news to the poor."

CAROL LAKEY HESS

Pastoral Perspective

Luke wants us to know how Jesus' ministry began upon this earth. It began when the Holy Spirit claimed him in baptism, tested him in the wilderness, and filled him with power for an urgent ministry of grace to the downtrodden in this world. The Holy Spirit came and taught Jesus what was real: to say no to the false options and temptations in this world and yes to God's good purposes for all people; to say no to self-glory in all its forms and yes to helping the poor and the captured of all kinds; to say no to trying to get your God to work for you and yes to working for your God with urgency and compassion.

The Holy Spirit comes when we have something to do for God and a time to do it. Following this Jesus means accepting his mission and his time. What would change in our lives and in our churches if we stood in the pews on Sunday morning and declared to God and to one another, "God gives us no other day than today to bring good news to the poor, release to the captives, sight to the blind, freedom to the oppressed, and new beginnings to all who have failed"? Jesus went forth in the power of the Spirit as an agent of God's mercy to the downtrodden, and so do we.

ROBERT M. BREARLEY

---

2. John Updike, *In the Beauty of the Lilies* (New York: Fawcett/Ballantine Books, 1996), 20.
3. Ibid., 13.

Exegetical Perspective

In this stunning moment of reinterpretation, an ancient and well-respected prophetic passage has just been turned upside down. Jesus announces that he has come to proclaim the good news to the poor. No longer do they need to wait. His message will bring much needed healing among the people. In addition, Jesus has come to bring forgiveness, to release those who have been imprisoned. To those eyes who have been blinded to the reality of God in their midst, Jesus will provide sight. Finally, Jesus has come to announce the year of forgiveness, the acceptable year. Jesus announces that his ministry will be like the year of jubilee. Every fifty years, the fields rested and were reinvigorated for future harvests. In this jubilee year, debts were forgiven. People returned home. Slaves were set free. Some scholars speculate that the very year that Jesus appears in the Nazareth synagogue may have been the year of jubilee, around 26–27 CE.[3] The scene has particular potency, if Jesus is standing before his hometown crowd in the year of jubilee, announcing the beginning of his ministry. No wonder the crowd is stunned (v. 20).

These four points not only describe the work of Jesus; they also outline the message of the Gospel of Luke in a nutshell. Jesus' life can be described in all these terms: an eschatological prophet, a kingly Messiah, and a wounded healer. In this one moment in the synagogue, all of these important roles become merged into one person.

The response of the people to this bold act is fascinating. Something clicked. The crowd realizes something unusual has just happened. They cannot take their eyes off him. He leaves the reading platform, sits down with the congregation. They are still staring at him. Perhaps Jesus feels compelled to say aloud what the worshipers are thinking silently. So he declares while sitting on the floor of the Jewish synagogue among his family and kin in his home village of Nazareth, "Today this scripture has been fulfilled in your hearing" (4:21).

LINDA MCKINNISH BRIDGES

Homiletical Perspective

sermon could explore how Jesus was guided by and lived out the various points of this mission statement in his ministry as described by Luke and the other Gospel writers.

The Church's Mission. At the time of this writing, it is quite popular in American culture to lift up the importance of knowing and clarifying one's purpose and consciously working toward fulfilling that purpose. There are best-selling books of advice on this subject that focus on business, sports, politics, relationships, and religion; there are even "life coaches." One of the biggest sellers is *The Purpose-Driven Life*[3] by Rick Warren, pastor of Saddleback Church in Orange County, California, one of the most influential megachurches in America. Citations from Scripture fill this book, dozens in every chapter, which makes it even more surprising and troubling that Luke 4:14–21 is never quoted. Apparently, this succinct and powerful statement of Jesus' own purpose is not considered relevant for informing a Christian's "purpose-driven life."

For me it is axiomatic that a Christian's understanding of his or her purpose, and the church's understanding of its purpose and mission, should be informed by Jesus' understanding of his purpose and mission. For this, today's passage from Luke is essential. A sermon could profitably compare and contrast Luke 4:18–19 with a congregation's or denomination's mission statement, budget, commitments, priorities, and activities. Statements or actions from outside the church—from business, entertainment, and politics—could similarly be compared and contrasted with Jesus' statement of purpose.

Today. When Jesus announces that "Today this scripture has been fulfilled in your hearing" (v. 21), he proclaims that the promised liberating work of the Spirit of God is now present through him. Luke traces that continuing fulfillment in his Gospel and through the book of Acts. That same fulfillment of eschatological hope enters into our present again and again through the Word and Spirit. A sermon could show examples where the promises of Luke 4:18–19 have been or are being fulfilled in the present, recognizing that there is much more to be done.

ERNEST HESS

3. Ibid., 183.

3. Rick Warren, *The Purpose-Driven Life* (Grand Rapids: Zondervan, 2002).

Jeremiah 1:4-10

⁴Now the word of the LORD came to me saying,
⁵ "Before I formed you in the womb I knew you,
and before you were born I consecrated you;
I appointed you a prophet to the nations."
⁶Then I said, "Ah, Lord GOD! Truly I do not know how to speak, for I am
only a boy." ⁷But the LORD said to me,
"Do not say, 'I am only a boy';
for you shall go to all to whom I send you,
and you shall speak whatever I command you.
⁸ Do not be afraid of them,
for I am with you to deliver you,
says the LORD."
⁹Then the LORD put out his hand and touched my mouth; and the LORD
said to me,
"Now I have put my words in your mouth.
¹⁰ See, today I appoint you over nations and over kingdoms,
to pluck up and to pull down,
to destroy and to overthrow,
to build and to plant."

Theological Perspective

Both this reading from Jeremiah and next Sunday's from Isaiah narrate God's call to prophets, providing an opportunity to address the meaning of Christian calling, or vocation, more generally. What does it mean to be called by God? What does God generally call people to do? To whom does God issue this call? Do only ministers and priests experience vocation, or is it an essential part of every Christian's religious life?

One of the challenges presented by the story of Jeremiah's calling is that it tempts us to think of vocation as something reserved for great figures of religious history—prophets, evangelists, and missionaries. The task for the preacher is to "democratize" Jeremiah's experience, to emphasize that God calls every Christian to live the radical gospel of Christ through faithful obedience in the world. For some, that faithful obedience may require grand utterance, heroic measures, or world-changing actions. For others of us, it is in fulfilling the tasks of our social, political, and familial roles that we stand as prophets in the cultural wilderness, testifying to God's intentions for the world in the way we live our lives.

The Swiss theologian Karl Barth (1886–1968) defined vocation as "the event in which [persons are] set and instituted in actual fellowship with Jesus Christ, namely, in the service of His prophecy, . . . and therefore in the service of God and [their fellow

Pastoral Perspective

Imagine Jeremiah being a candidate to be pastor of your church. If asked for his qualifications to serve as a pastor or preacher, he would say he was chosen in the womb for this opportunity. He would say that he tried as a young boy to make a career change, but that God said he would give him the words he would need, thus explaining his lack of a seminary degree. The interview ends and Jeremiah, as a pastoral candidate, would disappear. Jeremiah might be muttering on his way out the door about plucking up and pulling down, adding the message to destroy and overthrow. The search committee would be thinking that is the last thing we need to hear. They would never even hear Jeremiah talk about building up and planting.

Calls from God are scary. Tell someone God spoke to you, and you might be locked up. Maybe your call is not exactly a voice. It could be a thought you cannot shake—an idea that seems crazy or irrational. You try to ignore it, but it seems to be there again and again. The owls that bring Harry Potter invitations to attend Hogwarts School of Witchcraft and Wizardry are like a call from God. Harry's less-than-kind foster parents try, as best they can, to destroy the invitations. They even try escaping to a remote cabin on an island. Finally the umpteenth letter arrives personally delivered by an

Exegetical Perspective

In the book of Jeremiah this report of the prophet's call is preceded only by an extended superscription (1:1–3) that identifies the prophet and his date. The location of the vocation report suggests that the designation of the prophet took place in the thirteenth year of the reign of Josiah, that is, 627 BCE. The superscription presumes the activity of Jeremiah into the fifth month of the captivity of Jerusalem (587 BCE). Therefore, as in the other prophetic books, the vocation story would have been supplied by later editors of the prophetic words.

The calls of prophets and other servants of God are very private matters. That is especially true of Jeremiah, who reveals throughout his work so much of his personal turmoil. It is all the more remarkable, therefore, to learn that Jeremiah's report of his call has a great many features in common with other Old Testament vocation reports. These include the reports of the calls of Moses (Exod. 3:1–4:17), Gideon (Judg. 6:11–24), Isaiah (Isa. 6:1–13), and Ezekiel (Ezek. 1–3). All these report an encounter with God, a commission to do the Lord's will or speak the Lord's word, and a ritual act or sign symbolizing the designated role. In all cases except Ezekiel, the one who is called objects to the vocation, and then is reassured. We may conclude from the persistence of this feature in vocation reports that

Homiletical Perspective

Before we who preach can preach on this account of Jeremiah's call to preach, we would be wise to own the memory of our calling. None of us will ever attain the rank of a Jeremiah, but we too were called once upon a time. How long ago was that, not merely in years but in the heart? Has the raging fire dwindled to a mere ember?

Do we not preach to people who themselves harbor the memory of youthful passions tamed? In high school she dreamed of changing the world but now feels stuck; he fantasized he would serve God nobly but settled in to some other life. Or perhaps the arrow of time is reversed: they wonder if they will ever hear from God, or they have heard but are holding out for a more convenient time. Jeremiah's call was remembered not merely as a shimmering moment of intimacy between God and a hero of old. His call suggests that God still calls, God's mission is not yet accomplished, and even the jaded, weary ex-idealist can still be hauled by God into a fresh place, a renewed discipleship.

The preacher could examine the common pattern in Scripture: God interrupts someone, issuing marching orders; the recipient resists (usually for very good reasons); God insists, reassures, and empowers. But the sermon can never veer into wrist-slapping, scolding spiritual dolts for failing to hear,

Jeremiah 1:4-10

Theological Perspective

human beings]."[1] In other words, Christian calling is not just reserved for those asked to do mighty things. It is the invitation to every Christian to witness to the gospel by investing with radical grace whatever worldly roles God opens to us. John Calvin assured, "No task will be so sordid and base, provided you obey your calling in it, that it will not shine and be reckoned very precious in God's sight."[2] As Martin Luther famously said about parenthood, when understood as Christian vocation, even changing dirty diapers is done for the glory of God!

Jeremiah's response to his call is particularly noteworthy. Many Christian theologians have taken the prophet's reference to his youth as metaphorical; Jeremiah was emphasizing his inexperience and unsuitability for this kind of charge. Whether or not we read his objection in verse 6 as an accurate reflection of his chronological age may not matter much. What is important is that Jeremiah resisted the call of God because he believed himself not up to the task. Jeremiah's reaction contrasts with the response of Isaiah, who after a momentary declaration of unsuitableness, embraced divine forgiveness and enthusiastically accepted his commission ("Here am I, Lord; send me!"). Isaiah's response reflects the courageous enthusiasm we expect from heroes and saints, whom we distinguish from ourselves. By his misgivings—which continue throughout the book of Jeremiah—Jeremiah is the "everyman's" prophet; he shows us that fear, anxiety, resistance, inadequacy, even resentment are understandable reactions to the call to represent God in the world, and these feelings do not disqualify us from serving God's intentions.

Neither our achievement nor our confidence qualifies us to answer the call of God. Instead, it is *God* who prepares us to live out the vocation for which we were created. Verse 5 makes this claim poignantly. God's insistence to Jeremiah that "before I formed you in the womb I knew you" is often cited in the abortion debate as scriptural evidence that even embryos have souls and a relationship with God. While the verse might lend itself to that interpretation, the question of when personhood begins is not the point of the passage. Instead, God's statement testifies to divine providence and election, in which the idea of vocation is rooted. Jeremiah's selection as prophet has nothing to do with his

1. Karl Barth, *Church Dogmatics*, IV.3.2 (Edinburgh: T. & T. Clark, 1962), 482.
2. John Calvin, *Institutes of the Christian Religion* (Philadelphia: Westminster Press, 1960), 3.6.10.

Pastoral Perspective

angry giant of a man named Hagrid. God's call was like this for Jeremiah—it was relentless and inevitable.

The prophet Jeremiah speaks to something many of us know; we do not choose God; God somehow mysteriously and even against our will chooses us. Jeremiah says that he heard the word of the Lord. The real sense of the passage is that the word of the Lord *happened to him*. This was an event. Not only has God followed him like a spiritual detective from the beginning, but with God's awesome command of logic there is a response to every objection. Jeremiah was not going to slip out into the night undetected and go on his merry way. It was an event and God had him. Maybe that is what God has in mind for each person—some moment, some awareness, when we say yes to God.

Acceptance or resignation usually happens only after struggle, and that is true in this story. Jeremiah is not easily cornered, especially not after being asked to be a prophet to all the nations, a terrifying idea at any time. The Hebrew word for nations, *goyim*, referred in the natural discourse of that day to the enemies of Israel, to those who sought its destruction. God's vision for this job was about as difficult as any sane Israelite could imagine.

Jeremiah was so desperate to wiggle out of this call that he tried the strategy first attempted by Moses, who said he could not speak. Making excuses really is not new. It goes all the way back to Adam and Eve and continues today. "Oh, I could not do that. I'm just a layperson. I never went to seminary." "I don't have very much to give. I'm not very good with kids." "I am too new to this church to help much." We sound like Jeremiah all over again, even though the stakes for him were enormous.

Actually the reasons for not doing something that relates to God's work are often reasonable and justifiable. Most of us are not trained for these tasks, or if trained, we are ill prepared. Yet if God's call is about skills or experience, God does not tell this to Jeremiah. God does not say, "Don't worry, I have a trade school for prophets. You will get it all there." Instead, God says, "Do not be afraid," which just happens to be an angelic message rather common in the biblical story.

"Fear not" is an offer of salvation and a promise of protection. God's promise was to shade or guard Jeremiah. At the heart of this call, and maybe of every call, is the Twenty-third Psalm all over again. "Yea, though I walk through the valley of the shadow of death, I will fear no evil." That means God will

resistance is not linked so much to individual personalities as it is to the very experience of standing in the presence of the Holy One and being called as God's servant. It goes with the office to feel unworthy or inadequate.

Nor do the similarities of the vocation reports suggest that Jeremiah's was not a real or a personal experience. Rather, the parallels of form indicate that both the role and the call to that role were parts of an institution, that of prophecy. Therefore, not only reports but also behavior and experience were shaped by the traditions of that institution.

Although the vocation reports in the OT have many features in common, there are important differences. The vocation reports of Isaiah and Ezekiel are highly visual while Jeremiah's is aural. The visual and visionary reports (see also 1 Kgs. 22:19–22) give accounts of experiences before the Lord's heavenly throne. The closest parallels to Jeremiah's vocation are those of Moses (Exod. 3:1–4:17) and Gideon (Judg. 6:11–24). Jeremiah's report focuses upon the encounter with the word of God, as verse 4 explicitly states. If this experience is viewed as an epiphany, the Lord appears fundamentally through his word, in speech. There is, of course, the ritual of the hand of the Lord (v. 9), but even that focuses on speech. The Lord touches the prophet's mouth and puts words in his mouth, powerful words.

The report is organized as a dialogue between YHWH and the prophet. The initial divine speech (v. 5) announces past events. Even before Jeremiah was formed in the womb, he was known by YHWH, consecrated and appointed "a prophet to the nations." This was his destiny. Jeremiah's response (v. 6) is a twofold objection: he does not know how to speak, and he is too young. YHWH then reacts to both the objections (v. 7), but addresses one more seriously than the other. He brushes aside Jeremiah's complaint that he is only a boy by telling him not to say such a thing. In answer to the question of speaking ability, the Lord announces that he will command Jeremiah to speak, and what to speak. Then YHWH utters a promise of deliverance to an objection that had not been voiced, fear of opposition: "Do not be afraid of them" (v. 8).

This sentence is an important clue to the purpose of the vocation report and its circumstances. This is a first-person report, that is, in autobiographical form, but its function is not autobiographical in anything like the modern sense. The purpose is not to give information about or insight into the author.

much less do, what God requires. The call is enveloped in love, and the primal response in all human beings to any kind of change is fear. That is the tenderness and power in this text: God notices young Jeremiah's fear, and God reissues the Bible's most frequent commandment: "Fear not."

Fear isn't infidelity or evil; we have good cause to be afraid. Scott Bader-Saye nailed the issue: excessive fear is "when we allow the avoidance of evil to trump the pursuit of the good. . . . Our overwhelming fears need to be overwhelmed by bigger and better things."[1]

Jeremiah is ushered into something bigger and better, into God's truth and a life of service to the Almighty. Perhaps this is the edge young people have: they are not too big themselves just yet, either physically or in the soul. Jeremiah's solid excuse for why he cannot speak God's word is that he is "only a youth"—as if grownups know how to speak of God! Never do we speak of God capably. We try, we mumble impotent sounds; but does this not happen with babies who coo or with young lovers? The most eloquent words we can muster seem ridiculously inadequate, and the stammer voices the truest affection.

The preacher could explore the advantages the young and small enjoy, and would thereby stand in good company (recalling that Jesus not only spoke of the virtue of childlikeness, but came as a child himself). The peril is that the sermon can then become sentimental.

Jeremiah is lucky. God does not say, "Go think up a sermon." Instead God tells him precisely what to say. A good commentary will tell us that Jeremiah (God actually) employs a poetic craft called *chiasmus*: "pluck up" is countered by "plant" and "break down" by "build," and if diagrammed, they crisscross, a chi (*x*). An interesting literary technique—but what is the crisscross but a giant X-mark, a red stroke from the teacher's pen, a firm "No!" Life as we know it is corrupt, off-key, upside down, out of sync with God. We get everything backwards, and nothing is left but for it to be x-ed out, turned inside out.

The order is everything: before building and planting, you break down and pluck up. Spiritually we prefer just some building addition, some planting to spruce up the place a bit, so that we can hang on to what we already have: we are attached to it, we earned it. But when the gospel dawns, the whole

1. Scott Bader-Saye, *Following Jesus in a Culture of Fear* (Grand Rapids: Brazos, 2007), 56, 60.

Jeremiah 1:4-10

Theological Perspective

capabilities for the job (as Jeremiah himself repeatedly attests), but is made prior to his exhibiting any prophetic "qualities." God declares that the assignment of Jeremiah's role was made before he was able to do anything to merit his selection. As the English Puritan William Ames remarked, our calling "does not depend on the dignity, honesty, industry, or any endeavor of the ones called, but only upon the election and predestination of God."[3]

Does this mean there is no correspondence between God's intentions for our lives and the abilities and predispositions we develop? The experience of prophets like Jeremiah (Moses also comes to mind) suggests not, but something is lost in assuming that God always calls us to be and do what does *not* come "naturally" to us. While God sometimes asks us to take up roles and responsibilities for which we may at the advent feel ill suited, often enough God prepares us for our calling *through* the interests and abilities we cultivate. Rather than insisting on a single form for divine calling, Jeremiah's story simply reminds us that both the calling to serve and the capacity to fulfill that calling come from God. Verses 7–9 make this point vividly; God is acknowledged as the sudden source of Jeremiah's capability to fulfill his vocation.

Verse 10 ends the reading with the specifics of Jeremiah's commission, to speak a word of judgment to Judah in the shadow of international threats. In our time, a couple of things are important about this commission. Against a view of religion as essentially a private matter, God puts words into the mouth of the prophet that give him authority "over nations and over kingdoms." The word of God is thus a dynamic force that at times stands in opposition to the inertia of culture and politics. Finally, while the overall tenor of Jeremiah's commission is judgment, the destructive imperatives are followed by a constructive pair; Jeremiah is appointed not only "to pluck up and to pull down" but "to build and to plant." Here we see the necessary cooperation between judgment and good news, essential to the gospel. Jeremiah is commissioned to take to God's people the message of death *and* rebirth—so that even in the forecast of judgment lies the promise of new life.

JAMES CALVIN DAVIS

Pastoral Perspective

shadow me, not death. That is God's promise to Jeremiah and to each of us as well. No matter how far we may go from the call of God, no matter how many reasonable excuses we may offer, God is there watching out for us and even giving us words to say.

In Jeremiah's case the words touch his lips. At another point he eats the word of God. We may not frame it exactly like that, but we talk about not being able to escape some word or some truth. We talk about having a story inside of us. We say we live with a certain hope or faith. Jeremiah might tell us that is what he meant.

Finally, the Lord tells Jeremiah that he is appointed as a prophet. I was told by a friend of mine who is a Hebrew scholar that the verb translated as "appoint" really means "put into office." There is just no career track. Jeremiah gets the corner office right away: his prophet nameplate is on the door, his calling cards are printed, his wardrobe chosen. In this regard, we are probably the lucky ones. As baptized Christians no one can identify us by what we wear. Our faith is evidenced by what we do and what we say. Our call to serve the God who shadows us is to speak a word of truth in daily life. We are asked to respect the dignity of every human being. Hardest of all, and easily the riskiest road we dare, is the road that seeks justice and counters evils, letting the face of Christ emerge in love of neighbor. Sometimes we must even speak a word of judgment or just say no. This calling will never be easy if it is the calling of God. To do these things is to recognize those holy moments and touches of grace that really do plant and build up.

GEORGE H. MARTIN

---

3. William Ames, *The Marrow of Theology*, trans. John Dykstra Eusden (1629; reprint, Grand Rapids: Baker Books, 1997), 157.

Exegetical Perspective

"Do not be afraid of them" indicates the prophet faced opposition, as set out in detail later in the book. In the face of opposition, the purpose of the vocation report is to justify Jeremiah's office and message, to lend authority to the mission and message because they are set in motion by God. Prophets report their vocations in order to establish their authority to speak (cf. Amos 7:10–17).

At this point the dialogue is over, and the ritual of ordination begins. As befits designation for the prophetic role (see Isa. 6:5–7; Ezek. 2:8–3:3), YHWH touches Jeremiah's mouth and establishes his office "over nations and over kingdoms" and gives him the message he is to deliver (vv. 9–10). If one thinks of the experience of a call as an inner experience, here it quickly moves out into the world of international politics. God means to shape the history of nations through the word of a solitary human being. The voice of God through Jeremiah is to actually bring about destruction, and then rebuilding.

One of the most important aspects of this report concerns the meaning and authority of the prophetic word. In the first place, the words of the prophet are to be those the Lord gives him. That self-understanding persists not only in Jeremiah but in all the other Old Testament prophets: they are messengers bearing revelations from their God. Over and over again their speeches begin or end with expressions such as "thus says the Lord," or "This is what the Lord has said." Secondly, it is equally clear that the prophetic words are not idle talk but powerful (see Amos 1:2). In fact, the Lord does not actually tell Jeremiah what to say but what to do. To have the words of God in one's mouth is to be "set . . . over nations . . . to pluck up and to break down" (v. 10 RSV). As in Genesis 1, when God speaks, it is so. Small wonder that anyone called by God to speak such a word would be reluctant to take on the task.

So in addition to reflecting on vocation, this text is an invitation to reflect on the power of words to shape the future, even in modern culture.

GENE M. TUCKER

Homiletical Perspective

structure has to be ripped out, every growth in the garden plowed into fresh dirt so the gardener, the builder, can start over. Woody Allen once said, "I would prefer to achieve immortality without dying," but no good life from God can grow without our dying to our old self, as old, bogus priorities are tossed aside, the house of cards cast down. Seeing the baby Jesus, Simeon spoke prophetically that the child was set "for the falling and rising of many in Israel" (Luke 2:34). In our world, civilizations rise and fall; but in God's kingdom it is always fall and only then rise.

Interestingly, Jeremiah uses four verbs for this deconstruction (break down, pluck up, overthrow, destroy, v. 10 RSV), but only two for the new creation. Is the deconstruction harder labor? New life is God's proper work: so is it easier, less painful for God, even swifter, once the demolition is done? The chi is the first letter in Christ, who was crucified on a chi, a cross, not a piece of jewelry or an amulet, but a gnarled question mark, the known world nixed. This was the *breaking down* of the old temple, the *plucking up* of all smug self-righteousness, the *overthrow* of sin, the *destruction* of death; then the new planting began in a garden, the building up of the heavenly city that is our destiny.

If a bevy of other sermons have covered the basics thoroughly, and if there is much love and trust between pastor and congregation, the sermon can probe the stunning truth that Jeremiah and therefore all of Scripture and the church itself have been "set over the nations." Nobody is over the nations! And surely not a young preacher! Church and state are to be safely separated, right? Separated perhaps—but with the Word of God in the lofty seat of judgment over nation. To speak of such things requires a deft pastoral touch to express love while exposing how the powers flex their might and begin to strut like deities, prideful, self-sufficient. Empires do not know it, but they need a Jeremiah, somebody small, perhaps the youth, maybe a weary preacher or a cynical parishioner, willing to stick close to the chi, the cross, the hope.

JAMES C. HOWELL

Psalm 71:1-6

¹In you, O LORD, I take refuge;
   let me never be put to shame.
²In your righteousness deliver me and rescue me;
   incline your ear to me and save me.
³Be to me a rock of refuge,
   a strong fortress, to save me,
   for you are my rock and my fortress.

⁴Rescue me, O my God, from the hand of the wicked,
   from the grasp of the unjust and cruel.
⁵For you, O Lord, are my hope,
   my trust, O LORD, from my youth.
⁶Upon you I have leaned from my birth;
   it was you who took me from my mother's womb.
   My praise is continually of you.

Theological Perspective

The Hebrew perception of divine presence is a visceral one. God not only acts as sovereign and lawgiver but also is perceived to be physically involved with the people, as the psalmist boldly reminds YHWH in this lament. For the Hebrews, hell is the absence of God. The reverse of hell, however, is more than a mere comforting awareness of God's presence. It is the physical experience of being handled by God. Throughout Psalm 71, it is clear that the relationship between God and God's people is immediate and hands-on.

This psalm is said to be the lament of an elderly man looking back on God's presence in his life and asking God to rescue him from his enemies.[1] The description the psalmist gives for God's presence in the past is beyond mere companionship along the road of life. Modern translations of the psalm have abstracted the bodily imagery that portrays God's relationship with humankind. The original Hebrew gives more vivid descriptions of how God has reached out for the psalmist in very physical and not necessarily tender but always loving ways.

Beginning the lament with a statement of trust in God, the psalmist explains how God can reciprocate

1. Herbert May and Bruce Metzger, eds., *The New Oxford Annotated Bible with the Apocrypha: Revised Standard Version* (New York: Oxford University Press, 1977), 708.

Pastoral Perspective

In this lectionary entry, we are considering only the first six verses of Psalm 71, but the key elements of the lament form are present. The Hebrew lament addresses the pastoral situation where something is amiss in faith and life. The normal structures are skewed. Threats are perceived. Anxiety is increasing. Here, the dis-ease is being provoked by the "wicked," a group who were characterized as "chaff," as nothing, in the introduction to the Psalter in Psalm 1. Now things appear turned on end, and the "wicked" are asserting themselves against the psalmist with a "cruel" and "unjust" power. Rather than the "wicked," it is the "righteous" who may be blown away. Not only is the life of the psalmist in jeopardy; God's promises are also under assault and suspicion. A crisis is brewing.

Such crisis experiences represent a "boundary situation"—an unsettling and troubling place. Questions and uncertainty abound. Beliefs and patterns of living are pushed and pulled and bumped and poked. At such times, it is hard to get one's bearings. Disorientation, distress, and vulnerability are commonplace, and we come face to face with our finitude and powerlessness. It is a critical time, when structures of safety and security are crumbling. In such times, the mind and soul can become traumatized. Indeed, at the heart of psychological and

Exegetical Perspective

Lacking attribution, Psalm 71 has traditionally been ascribed to David, because Psalm 70 is credited to him and because Psalm 72 (the last psalm of Book 2) concludes, "The prayers of David son of Jesse are ended." In reality, we cannot know to whom we should credit the psalm.

Verses 1–6 provide an introduction to the whole of Psalm 71, which is a lament. In the introduction, the author expresses a lifelong confidence in God. Verses 7–11 detail current distress; enemies declare of the author, "Pursue and seize that person whom God has forsaken." In the following section (vv. 12–16) the psalmist pleads that God remain close and put the accusers to shame; then the psalmist, finally, declares God's righteousness. Verses 17–21 celebrate God's wondrous deeds from the time of the psalmist's youth and assert that God will continue to act beneficently until the author's old age. The section concludes with the declaration that God "will revive me again; from the depths of the earth you will bring me up again" (v. 20). The final section (vv. 22–24) praises God's faithfulness in delivering the psalmist from the enemy.

Like all laments, Psalm 71 wavers between declarations of confidence and the unsettling current reality of suffering. Indeed, this characteristic of the lament genre can be understood as a variation on a

Homiletical Perspective

Most commentators understand Psalm 71 as a psalm of individual lament, but Mowinckel interprets the psalm as a poem about protection.[1] The psalmist seeks protection not so much from past calamities but from pending future ones. Certainly a cursory reading of the passage will reveal that both themes are present. There are three characters interacting in the psalm: (1) YHWH, (2) the psalmist (Protagonist), and (3) the enemies of the psalmist (Antagonist). The preacher can pin each of these characters against each other and create an engaging, theologically rich, and responsible sermon. However, there are other dominant themes in the pericope, namely, God our protector (vv. 1–4); God our sustainer (vv. 5–6); the immanence of God (vv. 2–3); and the righteousness of God (v. 2).

Protagonist vs. YHWH. The Protagonist is a mature worshiper of YHWH and recognizes that their very existence is dependent upon the gracious sustaining work of God (v. 5). God has brought them forth from their mother's womb, and in turn the psalmist lives in reliance and confidence in God. This is a wonderful encouragement to all believers to focus their faith and hope in God. A lifetime of

---

1. Sigmund Mowinckel, *The Psalms in Israel's Worship* (Nashville: Abingdon Press, 1962), 1:220.

Psalm 71:1-6

Theological Perspective

that trust. The first verse is a challenge along the lines of, "Do not make me end up being ashamed for believing you will be there for me." Instead, the psalmist pleads for God to reach down and snatch the psalmist away from threatening forces. The verb used in the second verse, usually translated "deliver" (*natsal*), means to snatch away, to tear from, or to physically remove in a forceful manner. This is not a request for God to be rooting for someone from the sidelines. It is a hope on the part of the psalmist to be grabbed bodily by God from the clutches of the enemy.

In verse 4, we learn that the psalmist needs God's hands for deliverance, because the psalmist is trapped in the hands of evil people and powers. To stress the point, the psalmist reiterates that it is unjust and cruel people, rather than God, who currently clutch the psalmist—but this has not always been the case. During younger days, God held the psalmist up. Even earlier, God took the psalmist out of the womb. The psalmist vividly reminds God that "you are the one who cut me out of my mother's bowels" (v. 6, my trans.). At the present moment, the psalmist feels tossed out of God's hands into evil hands and longs to be back in God's embrace.

Remembering how God has held on in the past, the psalmist concludes the passage by reassuring God of constant praise. This promise is an echo of an earlier remark in verse 3, where the psalmist asks God to be a sturdy home "into which I can always come" (my trans.). The psalmist is offering to reciprocate God's firm grasp. The intended message is, "If you keep me in your arms, I will keep you in mine." The psalmist feels that God wants and needs human presence and touch just as much as humans crave God's.

As exemplified by this psalm, Hebrew faith centers on belief in a God who is present in a physical way with people. This is a God who parts waters to open a path out of oppression; who engages in an all-night wrestling match; who speaks in a whirlwind; but who also, according to today's psalmist, holds on to us from birth until death and hopes for us to hold on to God as well. The Hebrew people felt that they had a physical relationship with their God, described by the psalmist as being held, pulled, snatched, protected, and nurtured by and in God's hands. They also believed strongly that God wanted them to reciprocate by holding on to God just as forcefully.

The deepest expression of Christian theology is the physical presence of God on this earth in Jesus Christ. Because we as Christians tend to limit God's

Pastoral Perspective

spiritual trauma is the loss of faith in the order and continuity in life. Trauma can occur when one loses the sense of having a safe place to retreat within oneself or outside of oneself to deal with frightening emotions and experiences. In chaotic times the alternative is either heroically to turn inward, taking matters into one's own hands, seeking frantically to create this safe space, or to recognize one's needs and limits and seek refuge outside the self. The pastoral task of the Hebrew lament is to lead the reader outside the self to a conversation with God and, further, to a new and deeper understanding of the self and its relationship to God. It provides a laboratory for discovery.

Psalm 71 frames a safe space that is bounded on both sides and furnished throughout with trust in God. In this space, God is regarded as a refuge, a deliverer, a rescuer, a rock, a fortress—One to be leaned on and praised. Pastoral psychotherapy uses the metaphor of the "frame" to imply a space where different therapeutic conditions exist within the frame than are present without. A holding environment is created within the frame that is safe and secure against the threatening outside world. The person is freed in this safety zone to speak more freely, reveal the self more candidly, grieve more fully, listen more acutely, and embrace a deeper understanding of self, others, and God. Repressed and hidden parts of the self are invited into consciousness, where the person gains a more detailed picture of who and whose he or she is. The lament form provides a similar frame—a sacred space or a sanctuary where nothing is to be hidden and everything is invited into the open. In this sacred space, some of the lament psalms display deep disappointment, anger, and contempt toward God and speak of darkness, affliction, and agony. Psalm 71 is more restrained. Whether it be from long years of life experience or wisdom or both, there is a steadiness with the psalmist which tips neither toward bursts of passion nor ecstatic experiences.

Distinctive to Psalm 71 is a movement between descriptions of trouble and supplications on the one side, and declarations of trust on the other. In the final tally, a confidence in God's providence outweighs a concern for trouble. The sacred space carved out by the lament form here provides the context for an experiential process of learning that moves gradually from disorientation to a new orientation of faith and life. The psalmist reminisces across a lifetime. Through flashback images and reconstructed memories, life is again gathered

Exegetical Perspective

major theme of the Hebrew Bible. The persistent declaration of God's faithfulness, in the face of evidence to contrary, is a theme that runs through all three divisions of the Hebrew Bible. Much of Genesis is occupied with narratives that revolve around the anxiety best described as the promise in peril. Abraham no sooner gets to the promised land than he is forced, by famine, to leave it (Gen. 12). As if it were not enough that the promise of land is in doubt, even his chances for having descendants are in jeopardy in Genesis 15–22. Obviously Genesis ends with Israel in Egypt and the promise once again delayed. One can see, in the way the Torah (Pentateuch) ends, something of the same anxiety as Moses, the great leader of his people, is left on the east side of the Jordan as the Israelites enter the promised land. In many ways, the historical books (especially Judges, Samuel, and Kings) can be understood to treat the tension that arises from concern over God's faithfulness. That the Deuteronomic Historian has couched the discussion in language of Israel's faithfulness merely serves to assuage anxiety over God's ability to protect the people. Clearly, many of the prophets (esp. Ezekiel) engage similar dilemmas, if with different rhetoric. Finally, many of the texts in the Writings, the third division of the Hebrew Bible, deal precisely with the crisis of the destruction of the first temple and Jerusalem. Job seems to have given up on the notion of simple justice, and in the book of Esther God never makes an appearance. In these latter texts, God's people must rely on their own cleverness and resources! During the Second Temple period, the great challenge was to understand Israel's history of long suffering in light of God's righteousness, the problem of theodicy.

Within the context of this larger theme of the promise in peril, the passage for today is especially intriguing. In particular, verses 5–6 employ language that helps to bring into greater focus the tension that our passage shares with so much of the Hebrew Bible. For those who know Scripture well, the language of verses 5–6 likely has a familiar ring: "For you are my hope, Lord God, my trust from my youth (*min'uray*). Upon you I have leaned from the womb (*mibeten*), from the belly (*mim'e*) of my mother you severed me. In you is my praise always" (my trans.). The language and imagery here is remarkably resonant with the call of Jeremiah in Jeremiah 1:5–6. Here we translate only the pertinent parts of that section, "Before I formed you in the womb (*babeten*) I knew you, and before you came forth from the womb (*merekhem*) I sanctified you" (my trans.). In

Homiletical Perspective

dependence upon God gives us a mature foundation in which to "lean" upon God (v. 6). A past recognition that God has breathed life into us grants us a sure and certain hope that God will sustain us in the future. This is a provocative reminder that our "life does not consist in the abundance of possessions" (Luke 12:15) or that we may gain the world and yet lose our lives (Matt. 16:26). One of the continuing modern tensions we face is that our excesses lead to independence from God, but our deep need as human beings builds dependency on God. Even though there is the clear delineation between the righteousness of YHWH (v. 2) and the vulnerability of the psalmist, there is a deep intimacy between the two. Five times in the NRSV the writer uses the possessive "my" to refer to God.[2] This reiterates that God does not remain aloof but in his sovereign freedom is active and engaged in our lives, being an ever present help in times of trouble (Ps. 49:5). Conversely we must remember the creation/ Creator distinction that generates a crisis in the voice of the psalmist. The inability of the Protagonist to overthrow the Antagonist raises the opportunity for a calling on the name of the Lord for divine intervention. How important is this comfort for each of us who face our own dark days (Eccl. 11:8). God is our rock and fortress during difficult times in our lives. This conjures up the image of the Rock of Gibraltar or the Fastnet Rock off the coast of Ireland. We can call on the creator and the sustainer of the universe to bear our daily problems no matter how trivial or tragic.

Protagonist vs. Antagonist. Life does not transpire in a vacuum or in a utopia. Just as the psalmist lives in a fallen and broken time and place, so do we. Either way a cry goes forth to be delivered, rescued, and saved from the "hand of the wicked . . . the grasp of the unjust and cruel" (v. 4). Certainly this refers to a person like Saul, who stood opposed to David and sought to snuff out his life, but it is well within the preacher's arsenal to expand the Antagonist to include anything that stands against the will and the kingdom of God and God's beloved. This psalm is a great comfort for those fighting a terminal illness, struggling with financial difficulties, having relational problems, experiencing grief, loss, and so on. This psalm is appropriate following a national or natural disaster. Because the Lord is our "rock of

---

2. "My rock" (v. 3); "my fortress" (v. 3); "O my God" (v. 4); "my hope" (v. 5); and "my trust" (v. 5).

Psalm 71:1-6

Theological Perspective

physicality to a first-century Palestinian man, it is helpful for us to be reminded by the psalmist that God is still with us today, holding us, pulling us, snatching us, protecting us, and nurturing us, not just spiritually but in the most physical of ways. The psalmist presents us with vivid imagery for the providence of God, the doctrine that speaks of God's upholding, sustaining, governing, and directing of our lives. God is always there, holding out God's hand in an offer of pure love. We are to take hold of that hand and reciprocate the love that God has so graciously shown us.

To engage in an embrace with God means to celebrate the physicality of our existence. This does not mean that we indulge cravings or neglect our health. It means that we appreciate the miracle that is life by savoring the beauty of this world and enjoying the bounty God has given us. But it also means not being afraid to face the ugliness of this physical world; to stand up to those who would abuse God's creation and help them and ourselves to be better stewards of it; to reach out to those who do not fit the latest social standards, and to hold their hands. In other words, it means to live as Jesus did: to be labeled a drunkard and a glutton for taking pleasure in God's good gifts, but at the same time to break bread with those whom the world rejects.

The psalmist makes it clear that holding hands with God is not always comfortable and relaxing. In these six short verses, there is quite a bit of being pulled out and snatched away and generally being tossed around. But as long as it is God's hands that are doing the pulling and snatching, the psalmist may hold on tightly to God, assured of safety; of having hope, and refuge, and trust; of being released from the clutches of evil; and of being free to come and go within God's safe and secure home.

REBECCA BLAIR YOUNG

Pastoral Perspective

around God's *hesed*. Within the frame of this psalm, the supplicant explores the mystery of God more profoundly, connects with the presence and reality of God more firmly, and trusts in God more fully.

Central to the psalm is the bold claim, "You, O Lord, are my hope, my trust" (v. 5). Notice how the construction of the sentence makes "my hope" the predicate of the subject "Lord". The Lord is not simply to be hoped for, but is experienced by the psalmist as present in "my hope." The psalmist earlier sees God as "my rock and my fortress" and implores God to act now in that way—to "be that rock of refuge" (v. 3). Because God is perceived as a rock close at hand, not simply a hope out there on the horizon, God can be regarded as a powerful refuge and deliverer here and now, in and through the hoping of the psalmist! Within the holding environment of the psalm's sacred space, there is a heightened awareness of God's Spirit, even though outside that space, appearances may be to the contrary. Such is the transformative and therapeutic character of the lament form. Moving through the distress of the crisis process, the psalmist discovers a newness of life gifted by God. This is why the lament has been a powerful pastoral tool for healing in the ministry of the church.

The literary structure of the Psalter as a whole weighs the first half of the book more heavily with lament psalms and the last half of the book with a preponderance of psalms of praise. Psalm 71, situated near the end of the first half of the book, is an interesting and unique interplay of lament and praise. The path of the righteous, grounded in hope and trust, yields bumps and potholes. Our understanding of faith and life and conceptions of God will be stretched, challenged, and changed. The Hebrew lament is testimony to this process. Yet what emerges on the other end of the lament is a new appreciation for God's leading that calls out a deeper and more enthusiastic praise. What at the outset of the Psalter is a recognition that the righteous are blessed to delight in God's leading becomes, in the latter part of the Psalter, a lived reality effusive with experienced joy and praise.

CHARLES M. MENDENHALL

Jeremiah's famous response he demurs by claiming, "I don't know how to talk, for I am only a youth (*na'ar*)" (my trans.). Jeremiah shares with Psalm 71 an awareness of the difficulty in being God's chosen. While Jeremiah likely appreciates his special status, he remains hesitant. Jeremiah's hesitance seems justified when we consider his own lament in Jeremiah 11:19, "But I was like a gentle lamb led to the slaughter."

Another passage that resonates with both Psalm 71 and Jeremiah 1 is found in Job 3. In Job's initial complaint, he declares his resentment toward the day he was born. While we could focus on a number of verses in chapter 3, verse 11 is especially intriguing. Here we read, "Why did I not die from the womb (*merekhem*), from the womb (*mibeten*) come forth and perish?" (my trans.). Clearly Job's language is closer to Jeremiah's, but all three passages use strikingly similar language and imagery. Note that Jeremiah, like Psalm 71, not only emphasizes the length of God's relationship with the believer, but also reflects an awareness of the cost of discipleship. Job, on the other hand, reflects an entirely different perspective. No longer confident in a traditional piety that presumes that justice prevails, Job uses the language of the womb, not to describe a long relationship with God, but to articulate his death wish. Still, we may be meant to understand that, in using this language, Job has more trust in his God than it first appears. The texts from Jeremiah and Job reflect the tension that gave rise to the lament of Psalm 71. The long history of the relationship between God and believers is one often marked by disappointment but equally by the recollection of that very history and the hope that is implied in it.

LARRY L. LYKE

refuge" and our "strong fortress," God provides a safe haven from the malevolence and injustice of this life. The preacher can develop this tension to create a crisis in the individual parishioner in which the only solution is God. There is a wealth of movies and novels that utilize this classic tension in epic conflicts between good and evil (e.g., *Lord of the Rings*).

Antagonist vs. YHWH. Whereas there is a clear distinction between Creator and Protagonist, there is also a clear separation between Creator and the Antagonist. This time the contrast is stark, because the Antagonist is wicked, cruel, and unjust and stands opposed to the will of God. We have already pointed out that the Antagonist can be a personified disease, suffering, or social ill, as long as it is clearly something or somebody that defies God or the one who cries out to God in distress. The key teachable element of this struggle is that the psalmist does not take matters into his own hands. He is not vengeful or vindictive. Her hope and trust is in God her rock and fortress, and God alone is her advocate and judge. We need not worry about balancing the scales of justice, and we need not avenge ourselves. This is reserved for God alone (Deut. 32:35; Rom. 12:19). When the people of God come to grips with this truth in freedom, they can turn their cheek to their enemy (Matt. 5:39–41). Jesus says it so well, "Love your enemies and pray for those who persecute you" (Matt. 5:44). It is important for congregants to understand that this does not mean that our lives will be comfortable and cushy. Our "leaning" upon God and relying on God's righteousness means that we may postpone immediate vindication from "the hand of the wicked," knowing that God's justice will prevail. Our hope and trust in God projects us into the future: justice may not come until the end of days. Conversely, moments of difficulty or tragedy create opportunities for us to praise continually (v. 6) because we believe that God will not let us "be put to shame" (v. 1).

ROBERT M. LEACH

1 Corinthians 13:1-13

¹If I speak in the tongues of mortals and of angels, but do not have love, I am a noisy gong or a clanging cymbal. ²And if I have prophetic powers, and understand all mysteries and all knowledge, and if I have all faith, so as to remove mountains, but do not have love, I am nothing. ³If I give away all my possessions, and if I hand over my body so that I may boast, but do not have love, I gain nothing.

⁴Love is patient; love is kind; love is not envious or boastful or arrogant ⁵or rude. It does not insist on its own way; it is not irritable or resentful; ⁶it does not rejoice in wrongdoing, but rejoices in the truth. ⁷It bears all things, believes all things, hopes all things, endures all things.

⁸Love never ends. But as for prophecies, they will come to an end; as for tongues, they will cease; as for knowledge, it will come to an end. ⁹For we know only in part, and we prophesy only in part; ¹⁰but when the complete comes, the partial will come to an end. ¹¹When I was a child, I spoke like a child, I thought like a child, I reasoned like a child; when I became an adult, I put an end to childish ways. ¹²For now we see in a mirror, dimly, but then we will see face to face. Now I know only in part; then I will know fully, even as I have been fully known. ¹³And now faith, hope, and love abide, these three; and the greatest of these is love.

Theological Perspective

How surprised the apostle Paul would be to discover that this most challenging and grace-filled ode to love has become a staple of secular and quasi-religious marriage ceremonies! No wonder, given the absence of any reference to God or Jesus Christ in the text itself. If we are to get at its theological meaning, we must place it back in Paul's letter and remind ourselves of the author's intention in addressing these words to the church in Corinth.

Apparently Paul has heard that some members of the Corinthian congregation are trying to enhance their status on the basis of their particular spiritual gifts. Sound familiar? In 1 Corinthians 12, Paul counters this by asserting that all spiritual gifts are manifestations of the Spirit of God. He likens the church to a body of diverse members, each playing an essential role for the good of the whole. Then in 1 Corinthians 13, lest there be any lingering doubt about the folly of taking pride in one's knowledge or one's capacity to speak in tongues or to prophesy, Paul claims that love trumps all such gifts.

"If I speak in the tongues of mortals and angels, but do not have love, I am a noisy gong or a clanging cymbal" (v. 1). The same sentence structure, turning on the phrase "but do not have love," is repeated in verses 2 and 3. Read outside the context of Paul's entire letter, it might seem that love is simply the

Pastoral Perspective

Some texts have such a well-established setting in the life of the community of faith that it is hard to dislodge them from their ritual captivity or see them with fresh eyes. It is difficult to hear 1 Corinthians 13 without thinking of white dresses, rented tuxedos, bouquets, unity candles, and all the other practices and paraphernalia that the culture uses to prop up its romanticized notions about marriage. Yet this stunning word on the nature and practice of Christian love needs no human props to speak powerfully to many other pastoral situations in the life of the church. These words come to life when one remembers that they arose out of a pastoral crisis in the Corinthian church. The Corinthian Christians are abusing their freedom, refusing to share, scorning their neighbors' spiritual gifts, boasting in their own gifts, seeking recognition for themselves, and jockeying for position in the church. The problem is not the lack of spiritual gifts, but the ways in which these gifts are exercised. Every pastor knows that these struggles are as common today as they were in the time of Paul.

In his pastoral role, Paul admonishes and exhorts the Corinthian Christians with a simple command: practice love. Love is not another spiritual gift, but the way in which God intends us to practice all of our gifts. In this passage, Paul speaks about the primacy of love, the character of love, and the endurance of love.

Exegetical Perspective

Structure. The chapter unfolds in three sections. Three rhetorical questions underscore love as the essential element that animates all acts of religious devotion (vv. 1–3). A description of love (vv. 4–7) is then placed in eschatological perspective (vv. 8–13).

Literary Context. It would be tempting to build a sermon around sentimental illustrations of verses 4–7. But the astute preacher should consider the context of chapters 12–14. Love is the "more excellent way" (12:31), and Paul urges his readers to "pursue love" (14:1). Further, the gifts mentioned in 13:1–3 echo the lists in chapter 12: tongues (12:10, 28, 30), prophecy (12:10, 28–29), knowledge (12:8), and faith (12:9). But now tongues and prophecy move to the top of the list and become the focus through chapter 14, which suggests that they were sources of trouble in the Corinthian assembly.

In 13:4–7, Paul describes love in ways that correspond to issues he discusses throughout the letter. Love does not envy (13:4), but envy and strife characterize the Corinthians (3:3). Love does not boast (13:4), but the Corinthians do (4:7; 5:6). Love is not puffed up (13:4), but the Corinthians are (4:6, 18–19; 5:2; 8:1). Love is not shameful (13:5), as Paul teaches (7:36). Love is not self-seeking (13:5), as Paul models (10:33). Love does not delight in injustice

Homiletical Perspective

Sometimes familiarity breeds not contempt but challenge. That is true with 1 Corinthians 13. Virtually everyone loves these words, virtually everyone thinks they know what they mean, and it often seems virtually impossible to find anything new and different to say about them. The familiarity of these verses, however, also encourages us to dig deeper and seek new perspectives on God's word for us. Here are some possibilities.

A Conflicted Church. Certainly one of the easiest ways to subvert the tendency to reduce Paul's ode to God's love in Christ to a series of platitudinous aphorisms is to focus on the conflict of the Corinthian church. They were doing real and potentially destructive battle with each other over a number of issues. Paul inserts this passage in his letter not to offer a pious reflection on the way things should be, but rather to call the Corinthians to account for their behavior. Everything he says love is not, they are; everything he says love is, they are not. Not unlike the congregation in Nazareth at the beginning of Jesus' public ministry, those who heard these words more likely responded with gasps of shock and anger than ahs of affirmation and delight. This is provocative writing, that all but demanded the Corinthians take a look at the less than positive

1 Corinthians 13:1-13

Theological Perspective

foremost in a list of virtues, yet another talent one might try to perfect; but read within the context of the letter, this love is a state of being. It constitutes that fundamental relationship to God without which "I am nothing" (v. 2). Paul is writing to a community of people to whom God's love has been revealed in Jesus Christ. Their love is a response to God's gracious love, and it is from this relationship of love that all their spiritual gifts spring.

The explicit theological foundation for the love Paul writes about in 1 Corinthians 13 is laid out at several points earlier in the letter. For example: God "is the source of your life in Christ Jesus" (1:30); "So neither the one who plants nor the one who waters is anything, but only God who gives the growth" (3:7); and "Yet for us there is one God, the Father, from whom are all things and for whom we exist, and one Lord, Jesus Christ, through whom are all things and through whom we exist" (8:6). The love Paul has in mind in today's text is the reality of God's presence in our lives and the very basis of our humanity.

For Paul, our capacity to flourish as human beings is realized to the extent that we can live in the love of God revealed in the cross of Jesus Christ. The concrete reality of this divine love is present in our lives as described in verses 4 through 7, where love is the subject, actively expressing itself in patience and kindness, rejoicing in the truth, and bearing, believing, hoping, and enduring all things. This love is not envious, boastful, arrogant, rude, irritable, or resentful, nor does it insist on its own way. Is such love humanly possible? As an individual character trait or a personal attitude, *no*; but as the presence of God's love in Christ crucified and in a community of believers that live in that love, *yes*. To belong to God's church in Corinth is to be an agent of God's love in the world, not seeking one's own advantage, but working on behalf of others.

That this is no ordinary love, that it is not simply on a par with the spiritual gifts, is evident in the permanence Paul claims for it in verses 8 through 13. Prophecy, speaking in tongues, and knowledge not only bear the imperfection and partiality of the present age; "they will come to an end" (v. 8). But "Love never ends" (v. 8); in its present reality it manifests the age to come. This eschatological contrast is sharpened with respect to knowledge, spoken of first as a spiritual gift that will come to an end and then as something at the core of our ongoing relationship with God. "For now we see in a mirror, dimly, but then we will see face to face. Now

Pastoral Perspective

In every congregation and in every human life, there are spoken and unspoken assumptions about what is most important. The church is full of diverse theological viewpoints, programs, small groups, organizations, missions, and specialized ministries. For much of the time, there is room in the church for this diversity to coexist peacefully. When resources of space, time, and money are scarce, tensions can arise, and unspoken assumptions are sometimes verbalized in hurtful and divisive ways. Social and cultural concerns press upon the church and lead some within the church to insist on their own way. When this happens, Christians seem to have a special gift for cloaking self-interest with self-righteousness.

These words on the primacy of love can help the church in conflict understand that there are some things more important than being right or powerful or honored. If those within the church do not do what they do in a spirit of love, then all religious talk, knowledge, piety, and sacrificial giving add up to nothing. Without love, Christians are like the salt Jesus described as having lost its savor and not good for anything except being "thrown out and trampled under foot" (Matt. 5:13). Those who think they have gained everything by standing on principle, dominating others, or by being right, have lost it all.

Paul also speaks about the character of love. Christians are bombarded every day with countless and often conflicting images and ideas of love. Perhaps it is helpful to remind the congregation that Paul is speaking about *agapē*, the love embodied most visibly in God's love for humankind in the life, death, and resurrection of Jesus Christ. This love is not in the first instance a feeling, but an action. This love seeks not its own good, but the good of the one who is loved. Paul defines this love in a series of words that depict what love is and what love is not. Both the negative and the positive descriptions of *agapē* convict those with ears to hear of their lack of love, misunderstanding of love, and corruption of love. Paul's description of the character of love awakens believers to the transformation and renewal of love in the body of Christ.

In light of Paul's compelling description of love, it would be helpful to explore how the church carries out its ministry of pastoral care, its mission in the community, and its organizational leadership. As the church engages in pastoral care, do pastors, officers, and members become irritable and impatient when those receiving care do not change or conform to the "caregiver's" expectations? Well-meaning but

Exegetical Perspective

(13:6), but some Corinthians manipulate unjust courts (6:7–8). Thus, love is an antidote to many of the problems that plague the community, not only those in chapters 12–14.

The exercise of spiritual gifts as proxies for status conflicts in Corinth[1] can provide useful analogies for modern congregations trying to negotiate worship wars, social tensions, and similar issues.

The Argument. In 13:1–3, Paul writes in the first person, offering himself as an example, since he speaks in tongues (14:6, 18), is a prophet (2:7–10; 7:40; Gal. 1:15–16), fathoms mysteries (2:1, 7; 4:1; 15:51) and knowledge (2:12), performs miracles (2 Cor. 12:12), and lives self-sacrificially (4:9–13; 9:12, 15; 2 Cor. 6:4–10; 11:23–29).[2]

Each rhetorical question builds toward increasingly lofty gifts. If a miraculous ability to communicate in human languages (Acts 2) is impressive, how much more an ability to communicate with God in ecstatic language (14:2)? If prophecy is good, how much more an understanding of all mysteries? Better still would be omniscience or even mountain-moving faith (Matt. 17:20//Mark 11:23//Luke 17:6). If it is good to dole out all one's possessions to feed the poor (Matt. 6:20; Luke 12:33; Matt. 19:21//Mark 10:21//Luke 18:22), how much more to sacrifice one's body like Jesus? Yet all such actions are empty apart from love.

In 13:8–13, love is the greatest of those things that endure (13:13), even when such spiritual gifts as prophecy, tongues, and knowledge pass away (13:8), or when the *teleion* comes (13:10). The adjective *teleios* is usually translated "complete" (RSV, NRSV) or "perfect" (KJV, NAS, ESV), because it stands in contrast to "incomplete" or "partial" (13:9–10). But the word also carries an overtone of the "end" (NLT) or "end time." Elsewhere Paul contrasts the "mature" (*teleioi*, "end-times oriented") with the "rulers of this age" (2:6). As long as we remain in "this age" with human limitations, then, even with the aid of the Spirit, we know and prophesy only in part (13:9). Our understanding is no clearer than a reflection in a mirror (13:12). Ancient mirrors were polished bronze, but even in modern, plate-glass mirrors we see ourselves in reverse, never quite as other see us. When the *teleion* comes (13:12) when God's reign is

1. Dale B. Martin, "Tongues of Angels and Other Status Indicators," *Journal of the American Academy of Religion* 59 (1991): 547–89.
2. Carl R. Holladay, "1 Corinthians 13: Paul as Apostolic Paradigm," in *Greeks, Romans and Christians: Essays in Honor of Abraham J. Malherbe*, ed. D. L. Balch, E. Ferguson, and W. A. Meeks (Minneapolis: Fortress Press, 1990), esp. 80–98.

Homiletical Perspective

side of their community life. When this context is acknowledged, these words become a standard against which every congregation can be judged and found wanting. None of us reach the heights of love that Paul describes. All of us have room to grow. The standard is, after all, set by God and made real in Christ. Yet these qualities of love are also present to some extent in most congregations in real and life-giving ways. A sermon that holds these verses up as a plumb line for a community of faith can be one that both affirms and challenges.

Nothing without Love. Since Paul knew the Corinthian church well, we have every reason to believe that he selected his list of gifts carefully. If, as some maintain, the gifts Paul names in verses 1–3 were ones the Corinthians particularly valued in themselves, then these verses open the door to a discussion of those elements of ministry that are cherished in a congregation. Is it a great choir, service in the community, an array of small-group offerings, contemporary worship, a deep commitment to mission? All congregations can point with justifiable pride to certain aspects of their life and ministry. Quite often their identity is shaped by these things they do well. The question this passage raises is, "Are these things done with love?" Or perhaps it could be phrased, "How might they be done with greater love?" The gong may not yet be noisy and the cymbal not yet clanging, but how might these things a congregation does well be enhanced with love?

A Personal Dimension. While some see the gifts that are named in verses 1–3 as ones valued by the Corinthians, others take a more personal perspective, arguing that they are gifts for which Paul himself was noted. Paul then is doing what he often does: using himself as an example of faithfulness or, in this case, an example of what can happen if love is lacking. While there is always an element of danger in using oneself as a sermon illustration, Paul's approach here offers a possibility. In a setting in which the pastor-congregation relationship is healthy, in which qualities of the pastor are widely acknowledged, it might be possible to follow Paul's lead here. Some personal reflection on a growing sense of how love is shown (and can be shown more fully) in these qualities can offer a model for others as they consider their own growth in living as disciples. This need not be limited to the pastor, however. It might be that several in the congregation

1 Corinthians 13:1-13

Theological Perspective

I know only in part; then I will know fully, even as I have been fully known" (v. 12). Here Paul is making a radical theological claim. Having told us, especially those of us who are preachers and teachers, that "knowledge puffs up, but love builds up" (8:1), he now tells us that our dim, mirrorlike sightings will one day become face-to-face visions, that our partial knowledge will become full. Paul makes this claim in the context of God's love. If our quest for knowledge, whether through science or theology, is rooted in that love, then the knowledge we seek is of the one who already knows us fully. "Anyone who claims to know something does not yet have the necessary knowledge; but anyone who loves God is known by him" (8:2).

The love described in 1 Corinthians 13 is a love we experience as God's unshakable grasp upon our lives. It is the source of our greatest security and, thus, our freedom to actually be *patient* and *kind*, to *bear all things* and not *insist on our own way*. In his book about ethics in the age of genetic engineering, Harvard professor Michael Sandel writes eloquently about the giftedness of life and the dangers that come with our heightened sense of mastery.[1] Paul is raising similar issues in the church in Corinth, as we must in our own churches and in the larger world, where insisting on our own way wreaks havoc with other peoples, not to mention the natural environment. Lest our efforts be additional acts of human willfulness, let them spring from the love of God, that love which distinguishes 1 Corinthians 13.[2]

JERRY IRISH

Pastoral Perspective

misguided individuals often think they know what is best for others and become frustrated when others do not immediately respond to their suggestions and plans. Do congregations involved in community and global missions press their own agenda on those they serve, or do they truly join in a respectful partnership with others as they listen together for the Spirit's guidance and leading? Are officers trained to exercise leadership in a spirit of love that seeks the good of all and rejoices when the broadest understanding of truth is reached? There is nothing sentimental about the image of love that Paul sets before the church. Such love is active, tough, resilient, and long-suffering.

Paul ends his pastoral words about love with a picture of the endurance of love. Every spiritual gift will end. All the monuments humans create will crumble away. Even human life will come to an end. In this life, human beings are given the opportunity to grow in love, from childhood to adulthood and from immaturity to full spiritual maturity. There is a beautiful irony in the fact that the one thing that lasts forever is the love that is given away. Even though no person can make complete sense of all of his or her experiences in this world or see clearly what lies beyond this world, each person can trust in the permanence and persistence of divine love lived and experienced in human life. In Christ, believers are known and chosen by divine love. In an anxious world that grasps for the permanent, the eternal is given through the experience of love. When the church gathers to celebrate the resurrection at the time of death, the pastor and people have the opportunity to witness to the truth that the legacy that matters most is love. The faithful life is one that gives testimony in word and deed to the primacy of love, the character of love, and the endurance of love.

LEWIS F. GALLOWAY

---

1. Michael Sandel, *The Case against Perfection* (Cambridge, MA: Harvard University Press, 2007), 85–100.
2. See Victor Paul Furnish, *The Theology of the First Letter to the Corinthians* (Cambridge, UK: Cambridge University Press, 1999) for an excellent analysis of 1 Corinthians.

Exegetical Perspective

"finally" and fully realized, then "we shall know fully" (13:12). That is, we may know the mysteries of God perhaps, but also we shall know ourselves. More to the point, we may know fully the people whom we find disagreeable now. Paul wants the Corinthians to think eschatologically, to be end-times oriented in their relations to one another (cf. 14:20), to love one another now in ways that reflect the love of Christ and not the sort of things that pass for love in this age.

Cultural Context. Exploring cultural context can help bring the Corinthians to life so we can imagine how/why they misunderstood Paul. Regarding "tongues," the Corinthians may have assumed the sort of ecstatic speech associated with the oracle of Apollo at Delphi (Plutarch, *On the Oracles at Delphi*, Moralia 397A, 404EF). Interestingly, Plutarch goes on to modify this understanding of ecstatic speech in terms similar to those Paul uses in chapter 14. Regarding "mysteries," the Corinthians may have presumed something similar to worship of Isis (Apuleius, *The Golden Ass*, Book 11) or Demeter (*Homeric Hymn to Demeter*), since archaeological evidence shows that these mystery cults were active in Corinth.

Textual Problem.[3] An interpretive issue in verse 3 has to do with the reason Paul gives for the hypothetical "if I give my body." English texts traditionally read "that it may *be burned*" (KJV, NAS, NIV), but the earliest and best NT manuscripts read, "that I may *boast*" (NRSV). Paul wrote this letter about 54 CE, and we know of no Christians who were burned before 64 CE, in Rome under Nero (Tacitus, *Annals* 15.44). Paul may be tweaking the Corinthians' boasting (4:7; 5:6) as improper motive for their religious practices. Reflection on the logic of Paul's rhetoric of boasting might sharpen the point of a sermon.

CHRISTOPHER R. HUTSON

Homiletical Perspective

would be willing to share about their growth in making love the guiding force in their lives, especially in those areas where others consider them strong and able.

Essential, Effective, Eternal. While Paul himself was not married and these words were not intended for weddings, it is perhaps an overreaction to dismiss their use in this way out of hand. Without oversentimentalizing, it is possible to relate these words to love in our relationships with others. Even if they hold out a somewhat abstract and unobtainable picture, it is one worth keeping in mind as we face the challenges of maintaining and enriching relationships. A sermon that takes this approach could focus on the way in which these verses describe a love that is essential (vv. 1–3), effective (vv. 4–7), and eternal (vv. 8–13). Certainly such a love is worthy of a significant investment of time and energy.

What Did Jesus Do? The juxtaposition of this passage with the Gospel lesson for the Fourth Sunday after Epiphany (Luke 4:21–30) offers an opportunity to explore the application of these words to a real-life setting. A sermon could explore ways in which these qualities of love are or are not demonstrated in the story of Jesus returning to his hometown of Nazareth. Do his former neighbors treat Jesus with this kind of love? It is not difficult to say they do not. The more difficult question is, does Jesus treat his former neighbors with this kind of love? On the surface it does not appear so, and yet this is Jesus, who is for us the exemplar of love in all situations. The dilemma this incident presents opens the door to a discussion of the ways in which love shows itself, if love is always the same as being nice or kind or accepting, and of the ways in which love might confront and provoke. The somewhat harsh reality of this story provides an effective counterpoint to the beauty of Paul's words, offering the opportunity to probe the meaning of love more deeply.

JEFFREY D. JONES

---

3. See J. H. Petzer, "Contextual Evidence in Favour of *kauchēsōmai* in 1 Corinthians 13.3," *New Testament Studies* 35 (1989): 229–53.

Luke 4:21-30

²¹Then he began to say to them, "Today this scripture has been fulfilled in your hearing." ²²All spoke well of him and were amazed at the gracious words that came from his mouth. They said, "Is not this Joseph's son?" ²³He said to them, "Doubtless you will quote to me this proverb, 'Doctor, cure yourself!' And you will say, 'Do here also in your hometown the things that we have heard you did at Capernaum.' " ²⁴And he said, "Truly I tell you, no prophet is accepted in the prophet's hometown. ²⁵But the truth is, there were many widows in Israel in the time of Elijah, when the heaven was shut up three years and six months, and there was a severe famine over all the land; ²⁶yet Elijah was sent to none of them except to a widow at Zarephath in Sidon. ²⁷There were also many lepers in Israel in the time of the prophet Elisha, and none of them was cleansed except Naaman the Syrian." ²⁸When they heard this, all in the synagogue were filled with rage. ²⁹They got up, drove him out of the town, and led him to the brow of the hill on which their town was built, so that they might hurl him off the cliff. ³⁰But he passed through the midst of them and went on his way.

Theological Perspective

God—ever present, everywhere present, universal—is also and always in the particularities.

Jesus' announcement that the powerful text of Isaiah is fulfilled, coupled with his recitation of God's presence through Elijah and Elisha, points to and underscores this reality. But that startling, yet "gracious" announcement points as well to the reality that God is unfolding new narratives in the strangest of places, in the midst of outsiders to the established community of faith.

Elijah's journey at God's behest to "a certain widow" at Zarephath of Sidon, coupled with God's healing of Naaman the Syrian through Elisha, gives witness to this seeming paradox: the dramatic unfolding of God's omnipresence in the singular lives of outsiders. In a drought-stricken, famine-ridden land of many widows, God designated but one, a nonbeliever, to make known both God's presence and God's power. In the life-giving healing of the widow's son, God far surpasses the miraculous, life-giving food provided the widow, her family, and Elijah, and thereby prompts the joyous exclamation of her belief.

Likewise God's healing of the Syrian Naaman's leprosy—again, in the midst of many who likewise suffered in Israel—manifests this pattern, this presence of particularity. The commander of the

Pastoral Perspective

This text cannot be appreciated without reference to the preceding passage concerning the jubilee. It is a message of hope and vindication to the marginalized, to the disadvantaged in this world, and to those whose hope and confidence rest in God. It is a realized eschatology announcing to those who have lived under the power and control of oppressive systems and rulers that the bonds of oppression are now being broken.

This text addresses God's concern for persons and God's liberating activity in very concrete sociological categories. Luke's beatitudes and his corresponding woes are expressed in concrete and precise ways in Luke 6. The poor, the hungry, those who weep, and so forth include the underprivileged and marginalized of society. The preacher may seek to lift up this message of hope to these very concrete sociological categories in a world where so many Christians have a primary focus on inner spiritual peace, while looking askance at the world of human suffering all around.

The opening verse of this passage, "Today this scripture is fulfilled in your hearing" (v. 21 NIV), challenges the preacher and the individual members of the Christian community to hear the imperative: Pay attention to these persons who are of special concern to God! Pay attention in both a prophetic

Exegetical Perspective

Jesus captured the attention of all in the synagogue—their eyes were fixed on him. Empowered by the Spirit, he read words from the prophet Isaiah that serve as the springboard for his ministry. He had come to bring good news to the poor, to proclaim release to the captives, recovery of sight to the blind, freedom for the oppressed, and the acceptable year of the Lord's favor (Luke 4:14–20; cf. Isa. 61:1–2; 58:6). After taking his seat, he pronounced, "Today this scripture has been fulfilled in your hearing" (v. 21).

Those in the synagogue of Nazareth were initially amazed and impressed by these grace-filled words of Jesus and proceeded to discern who he was and why he had come to dwell among them. Their amazement is reflected in the question in verse 22: "Is not this Joseph's son?" Both Matthew and Mark record the crowd having a more negative response to Jesus: "They took offense at him" (Matt. 13:57; Mark 6:3). Yet for Luke the clarifying question about the identity of Jesus has special rhetorical value, and such questioning is not unfamiliar in his writings. In Acts 21:38, for example, he places a question on the lips of a tribune who is trying to verify the mistaken identity of the apostle Paul: "Are you not the Egyptian?" Just as Luke wanted to demonstrate that it would have been inconceivable that Paul would be

Homiletical Perspective

Luke was a master storyteller who was interested in the complexity of stories. He "thought pictorially and was interested in people and places . . . but he was not simply an innocent and plain teller of tales."[1] In the year of Luke, the preacher should be attentive to the layers of this Gospel, and so be challenged to employ new images, pictures, and stories that enable twenty-first-century congregations to hear narratives that have lost their power through superficial overfamiliarity.

This text is a case in point, and we are not helped by the lectionary, which places us in the synagogue in the middle of the action. Therefore the preacher will have to remind the congregation of the context, lest the integrity of Scripture be lost in the liturgy. This pericope also reminds us that we must always make sense of God, life, and the important issues before us, even though we usually begin *in the middle of things*. Rarely do we start at the beginning of any story, even our own, and rarely do we see a story to the end. Seeing things whole is a divine, not a human, perspective; and still we are not absolved of our own responsibility *to try to make sense*.

---

1. J. L. Houlden, "Luke, Gospel of, and Acts of the Apostles," in J. L. Houlden, ed., *Jesus: The Complete Guide* (New York: Continuum, 2003), 558.

Luke 4:21-30

Theological Perspective

army of Syria, a "mighty man of valor," learned of Elisha from a young woman he had captured from Israel to serve his wife. With a cache of silver and gold, and preceded by a kingly letter for safe passage, he "stood at the door" (2 Kgs. 5:9 KJV) of Elisha's house only to be rebuffed by a messenger telling him to wash seven times in the Jordan. Angered, and then cajoled by his servants, Naaman relented, bathed, was healed, and was won over to God.

The recitation of these ancient stories provoked the temple crowd that moments earlier had spoken well of him and wondered at his gracious words. The crowd was likewise stirred by Jesus' interlude regarding his acceptability by his own people, and incensed that one of their own had the audacity to sit among them and intimate that they would not be the vessels for the unfolding of God's new narrative. Here, now, was the insider who suddenly becomes the outsider. Here, now, was God acting in the particularity of Jesus of Nazareth. Here, now, was the beginning of a new narrative out of the ancient narrative, out of and dramatically beyond the solid foundations of the people of faith upon whose ears it fell.

This is God at work, as God has been at work across the millennia, as God is at work even now—unfolding new narratives with, through, and among particular people, who are often outsiders to the assumed faithful. The good news that God bears through Jesus is concurrently jarring news, infuriating news to the temple stalwarts who push him, rush him out of the city to throw him headlong down the hillside. The good news is not the narrative they were used to, not what they expected from the living God, who had come once again to break through their calcified ways.

So it is with new narratives born of God. In the midst of the global complexities of this era, this century, the church faces the daunting possibility—indeed, the reality—that God is unfolding a new narrative through the particularities of "outsiders," of edge-people who come to God and bear witness to God through God's actions in edge-places, and occasionally in temple settings. Deserts. Drought-wracked lands. Famine. Struggling widows. Dying children. Disbelieving commanders. Servants. Isaiah. Elijah. Elisha. Jesus.

The God we proclaim and worship will not be domesticated, "homebound," shut in, confined by our temples, and stagnated by our stories. God does not quietly accept our own well-worn narratives, smoothed over and sweetened by complacency and

Pastoral Perspective

sense and in terms of the exercise of mission in and to the world! Consider how this Scripture might be fulfilled in the hearing of today's congregation as the preacher highlights the plight of the homeless, the poor, and those without access to adequate medical care, housing, and education. In addition, one can look at the impact of globalization on the people of both developed and developing societies, as the gap between the rich and the poor widens in unprecedented ways. The millions of uprooted and displaced people all over the world, whose only sense of stability and hope is to be found in God, may also be the subject of consideration at this point.

The preacher may focus on the work of individuals and relief agencies who have committed themselves to the relief of the homeless and asylum seekers fleeing oppressive governments and starvation as part of God's work of liberation. The preacher may also support and encourage members of the community of faith to study and to pursue ways in which they can be a part of the global enterprise for the liberation of oppressed and marginalized people.

Jesus, the son of the community, has achieved some notoriety in other places and word of this has reached back to the home village. One can just imagine the pride that fills their eyes when he begins the reading. Then suddenly expressions begin to change. Jesus' selection of the Isaiah passage and his interpretation of it is a clear declaration that he has received the Spirit of God and is the fulfillment of prophecy. This son of Joseph and Mary whom they know must certainly have lost his way or his sense of propriety somewhere along the way, as far as they are concerned. The pride of identification now turns to anger. Jesus is too local to be heard.

The preacher may seek to focus on the subtle contrast Jesus creates between this circle of the gathered home folks and the picture of God's inclusive household that he is seeking to proclaim. Jesus perceives that they are now expecting him to do some of the works of wonder that they have heard are being done in Capernaum and among Gentiles, of all people. Surely the very people of God, the children of Abraham, are deserving of such a display. Jesus voiced their covert expressions of rejection: "Surely you will quote this proverb to me: 'Physician, heal yourself! Do here in your hometown what we have heard that you did in Capernaum'" (v. 23 NIV). Jesus declares that they will not receive the manifestation that they are seeking and provides precedence for what he has done among the

Exegetical Perspective

associated with the Egyptian who was known for stirring up riots,[1] he also wanted to show that it would have been inconceivable for the son of Joseph, born of such humble circumstances (Luke 2:1–7), to speak with such authority among the people in the synagogue. Luke demonstrates that Jesus clearly challenged the preconceived assumptions of those in the synagogue.

This initial acceptance and amazement, however, was quickly put to the test as Jesus appealed to three rather disconnected sayings that eventually stirred the crowd to anger and unrest. First, he appealed to a saying attested in both Jewish and Greek writings: "Doctor, cure yourself!" (v. 23). Its use in this context appears out of place since Jesus had not made any attempts to heal or identify any sicknesses. The saying may be a way of anticipating that Jesus should deal with his own shortcomings before attempting to speak of the shortcomings of others. The second saying, "Do here also in your hometown the things that we have heard you did at Capernaum" (v. 23), is actually misplaced, since Luke has not at this point in the narrative described the encounters of Jesus in Capernaum (Luke 4:31; cf. Mark 1:21 and 6:1–6). Unlike the first saying, which was registered with no response, Jesus responded directly to the second saying with a third familiar expression, "No prophet is accepted in the prophet's hometown" (v. 24). At this point Jesus moved to what is the climax of this discourse recorded in verse 25. Here, Jesus declared what is ultimately at stake in this encounter, that is, the truth (*alētheia*). And this truth is revealed in the ways in which unexpected outsiders figure so prominently as models of faith in Israelite history.

At this point Jesus recalled two examples that hearken back to earlier prophets—Elijah and Elisha—who reached beyond the people of Israel to welcome those who were most representative of the marginalized "Gentiles" (vv. 25–27). Elijah went to the unnamed poor widow at Zarephath in Sidon, and Elisha healed the Syrian leper known as Naaman. The widow was obedient and faithful to God, willing to give the last of what she had in order for her household to receive a blessing from God (1 Kgs. 17:1–16). She endured the severe famine in the land and did not allow the apparent lack of resources to interfere with her relationship with Elijah. Naaman, who was initially resistant to Elisha's prophetic instructions, eventually immersed himself seven times in the Jordan and was healed of his leprosy (2 Kgs. 5:1–14).

1. Josephus, *Antiquities* 20.8.169–72.

Homiletical Perspective

Commentaries often identify the question "Is not this Joseph's son?" as the point at which the scene goes from approbation to criticism. This is not self-evidently the case. Jesus' words "Today this scripture has been fulfilled in your hearing" do not provoke anger, but wonder. These are "gracious words." The inquiry "Is not this Joseph's son?" might well be understood in the light of what *precedes* it, and so be heard as a compliment (rather than with what *follows*, and be heard as an attack). It may not be the case that the people are angry with Jesus because he has done no miracles among them. They have asked for nothing.

What *is* clear is Jesus' confrontation of the congregation in the next verse. It is Jesus, and not the congregation, who changes the tenor of the encounter. Why this antagonistic posture? Why is he anticipating objections that have not been spoken? The congregation is filled with rage only after Jesus gives them a tongue-lashing out of left field. Who could blame them?

Once we start asking questions like this, instead of assuming that we know how the story goes, we allow Scripture to speak. We have "heard" this story in a particular way over and over; now we see it from a different angle (with Jesus, not the crowd, as the protagonist), and our assumptions are called into question. Like the congregation in Nazareth, we may be filled with assumptions, but in the presence of Jesus they are shown to be unexamined assumptions. We may have many questions, but when Jesus is the preacher, our self-serving answers will not do. We have no access to what was in Jesus' mind, and from the distance of two millennia it may be just as hard to understand why Luke tells the story as he does. But the question, "What is going on here?" still begs to be asked.

Another approach to the text may be through the second reading from 1 Corinthians. How might we hear one passage in the light of the other? How do Jesus' words and actions fulfill the demands of love in 1 Corinthians 13? In discussing these texts, the preacher might take the Lukan theme of the inclusive nature of God's embrace. It will take some work to bring the congregation into the force of this text in a way that is neither trite nor superficial. In many congregations talk of inclusion can very quickly descend into self-congratulatory pabulum focused on one issue only.

But how inclusive are we *really*, and whatever do we mean by this? If talk about God's inclusive embrace—rather than (or as well as) his general

Luke 4:21-30

Theological Perspective

comfort. Jesus comes into our midst and declares that the Scriptures have been fulfilled in him, through him. Then he goes on to create a new narrative that is ours to follow *and* to re-create. This is a dynamic, raucous God who jars us to wrath or to faithfulness, and who simultaneously provides us the opportunity to partner in the creation of a new narrative, woven with edge-people in edge-places, and in the particularities of daily living and daily people. Indeed, new narratives *are* unfolding in our midst, in some of the most peculiar places, where God continues to act, far outside our holy walls.

In this brief text Luke has passed on the history of God, as well as indicators for the new and renewing narratives that God is unfolding with or without us, and usually in spite of us. God gives us opportunity to respond. We can listen but not hear, hear but not respond, respond but not follow. We can be filled with wrath, as were those in the temple who heard the young, upstart Jesus when he came home and spoke of the new narrative. We can be quietly indifferent. Or we can—indeed we are called to—follow, and by following contribute to that renewing, redeeming narrative that is God's relentlessly powerful story, come alive on the edges of the human family and the faith community.

To follow and to participate in the unfolding of that narrative is also to be open to its costs. It is to be with and to become the outsider. It is to live with the puzzling particularities and with the edge-people through whom God is manifest. It is to risk the journey in the desert, the trek to the Jordan, the headlong plunge down the hillside, the journey to Jerusalem, and the cross.

In our creative participation in framing this new narrative we also know the fullness of life, the depth of God's promise spoken through Isaiah, Jeremiah, and Jesus, and all those who have had the audacity to believe that God is indeed creating a new narrative of hope and justice. It is to know the fullness of the love of God and the overwhelming power of God's narrative even in our own time.

DAVID L. OSTENDORF

Pastoral Perspective

Gentiles. Jesus cites the case of the widow of Zarephath, showing that God has acted in the past through the prophetic tradition in reaching out to non-Jews, thereby providing for the inclusiveness of his mission to embrace the Gentiles.

The preacher may develop the theme of the inclusiveness of the mission of Jesus and of his church, and may also explore this in terms of interfaith dialogue in a world that is becoming increasingly polarized around religious, political, and economic agendas.

The messianic hope anticipated the end of oppression, injustice, and exploitation and the inauguration of a new age. These were central tenets of the faith and life of Israel. If faith is not merely wishful thinking, then there comes a moment in human history when God acts to fulfill what God has promised. It is the realization of this hope that Jesus announces as being fulfilled in him. In so doing, Jesus introduces a radical element to a limited faith perspective, the element of potency and the broadening of horizons. By making the hope present and real, it is no longer fascinating, intriguing, consoling, and comforting, but explosive. So riled up is his audience in response that they attempt to kill Jesus. The preacher may therefore want to look at the ways in which Christians make of the faith and their discipleship something that is sterile and impotent, while ignoring the imperatives and the broader horizons of the faith.

Change is a dynamic that is most unsettling and is usually resisted in preference for the old, the familiar, and the routine. Jesus' audience opts precisely for this choice. Not only do the religiously committed resist change, but they also see their resistance to change as a protection of the divine interest. The preacher may need to raise up this issue by exploring the strength and basis of the rejection of Jesus in the passage.

The twenty-first-century mind may have questions about how Jesus escapes from this hostile gathering, yet the preacher may choose to highlight the interest of the writer of the Gospel to show that rejection does not bring an end to this project of God in Jesus Christ, but only serves to further it.

HOWARD K. GREGORY

Exegetical Perspective

As a leader in the Syrian army, he epitomized a tangible threat to Israelites. Both of these examples represented the extreme "other" to those in the synagogue crowd, and they served to drive home the point that the good news Jesus proclaimed was intended for Jew and Gentile alike.

Indeed there were many widows and lepers in Israel, yet Jesus stated that "none of them" (i.e., none of the hometown Israelites) received assistance from Elijah or Elisha. The repetition of this phrase "none of them" stirred the ire of the crowd (v. 28). They could now see that the message of Jesus was not simply a seal of approval, but rather a message that threatened to dismantle the status quo and the stereotypes that defined the religious and social boundaries of those in the synagogue. Their initial astonishment with the words of Jesus had now turned to anguish. The comfortable assumptive world of those in the synagogue was challenged, as Jesus had now moved from declaring the acceptable year of the Lord's favor to calling judgment on those who were not willing to accept "the least of these."

The crowd, in their anger, drove Jesus out of town and even desired to hurl him off a cliff (v. 29). But Luke does not end the story here! Jesus—who brought a message of freedom for the oppressed, hope to the poor, and release to the captives—passed through this encounter (v. 30), providing a symbolic image of his prophetic teaching about transgressing boundaries. This lection shows that the fulfillment of Scripture is challenging and frightening to those who are incapable of including and identifying with marginalized outsiders. Yet, the fulfillment of Scripture is also liberating and healing to those who are able to keep their eyes fixed on Jesus and model his example of engaging the "other" and moving beyond prescribed roles and expectations.

GAY L. BYRON

Homiletical Perspective

upbraiding of the group—infuriated Jesus' first hearers, how can the preacher open up what this might have been like? Are there experiences and complexities with which a twenty-first-century congregation might be familiar? Exclusion is an individual experience, but it is also a collective one. As Peter Gomes has remarked, "the people take offense not so much with what Jesus claims about himself, as with the claims that he makes about a God who is more than their own tribal deity."[2]

The preacher might put us in the place of the congregation who first heard Jesus speak. After all, they had certain (reasonable) expectations of God, learned over generations. All of a sudden Jesus turns those expectations on their head. Let us remember again that they are not initially antagonistic: "The eyes of all . . . were fixed on him" (v. 20). If we criticize them for rejecting what Jesus had to say, might they remind us that, like them, we should be eagerly expectant of the word of God? What capacity do we have for hearing the "new things" of God in our midst?

A third approach to this passage, one that would have delighted patristic writers, involves an exploration of the imaginative intertextual connection between the "pinnacle of the temple" and "brow of the hill." The devil's temptation of Jesus to "throw [himself] down," confident in God's safekeeping (4:9–10), coincides with Jesus being chased to the "brow of the hill . . . in order to throw him down" (4:29 NIV). Both the devil and the people of the synagogue were disarmed by Jesus.

Finally, as John Drury notes in his thought-provoking book *Tradition and Design in Luke's Gospel*,[3] the word "today" has great force for Luke. This is a reminder that Jesus stands before us not just yesterday, or in some longed-for tomorrow, but *today*. The preacher may, if she has not done so in previous stories, use *today* as the theme for a sermon on the living of the faithful life.

PETER EATON

2. Peter J. Gomes, *The Scandalous Gospel of Jesus: What's So Good about the Good News?* (New York: HarperOne, 2007), 39.
3. John Drury, *Tradition and Design in Luke's Gospel* (London: Darton, Longman & Todd, 1976), esp. 70f.

Isaiah 6:1-8 (9-13)

[1]In the year that King Uzziah died, I saw the Lord sitting on a throne, high and lofty; and the hem of his robe filled the temple. [2]Seraphs were in attendance above him; each had six wings: with two they covered their faces, and with two they covered their feet, and with two they flew. [3]And one called to another and said:

"Holy, holy, holy is the LORD of hosts;
the whole earth is full of his glory."

[4]The pivots on the thresholds shook at the voices of those who called, and the house filled with smoke. [5]And I said: "Woe is me! I am lost, for I am a man of unclean lips, and I live among a people of unclean lips; yet my eyes have seen the King, the LORD of hosts!" [6]Then one of the seraphs flew to me, holding a live coal that had been taken from the altar with a pair of tongs. [7]The seraph touched my mouth with it and said: "Now that this has touched your lips, your guilt has departed and your sin is blotted out." [8]Then I heard the voice of the Lord saying, "Whom shall I send, and who will go for us?" And I said, "Here am I; send me!" [9]And he said, "Go and say to this people:

'Keep listening, but do not comprehend;
keep looking, but do not understand.'

Theological Perspective

Like last Sunday's Old Testament reading, this one features the call of a prophet, and the preacher of this story may be well served to revisit the text from (and commentary on) Jeremiah 1 (pp. 290–95). The account of Isaiah's call includes elements similar to Jeremiah's: the invitation to represent God to the world, an uncertain response from the would-be prophet, a tangible sign of empowerment (i.e., "touching the mouth" of the prophet), and the commission to proclaim a specific word to God's people. However, Isaiah's story follows a different sequence than Jeremiah's.

The first (and most obvious) difference between last week's reading and today's is that Isaiah's story begins with a theophany, an appearance of God. God appears to Isaiah in regal brilliance, seated in the temple and attended by heavenly creatures. There is a certain appropriateness to this reading falling early in the season after Epiphany, when many Christians celebrate not only the arrival of God in the person of Christ but also the quintessential theophany of the Triune God at the baptism of Jesus. The appearance of God to Isaiah obviously stresses the awesome nature of God, a worthwhile theme to emphasize in a Christian culture that too often "domesticates" God, in service to self-fulfillment. But even in this display of divine glory, God is portrayed as

Pastoral Perspective

There are certain events in life where time seems to stop still. There are moments that divide time: what was before is changed and is no more. On the national level, Americans experienced September 11, 2001, like that. Many of us said on the day that things might never be the same again. Our prophetic awareness seems to have come true in the daily news that has followed ever since.

Isaiah had one of those moments. It defined the rest of his life. It was almost as if he was born anew on that day in the temple when he saw God in such immensity that the hem of God's garment filled the entire temple. If only the hem, then how much more was there that could not be seen? We are left with a slim picture of the transcendence of God, and that is as it must be.

That awesome presence defined consecration and dedication, and it was the moment of call. Not only did he witness the glory of God and feel engulfed in the song of holiness praising God from that mysterious swirl of the birdlike creatures called seraphim, but his lips were touched with a burning coal. It was a decisive moment. He could no longer talk about the weather or the latest gossip on the streets. One writer perceptively reminds us that to consecrate someone or something is not simply to transfer that person or object into the safe world of

¹⁰Make the mind of this people dull,
    and stop their ears,
    and shut their eyes,
so that they may not look with their eyes,
    and listen with their ears,
    and comprehend with their minds,
    and turn and be healed."
¹¹Then I said, "How long, O Lord?" And he said:
"Until cities lie waste
    without inhabitant,
and houses without people,
    and the land is utterly desolate;
¹²until the Lord sends everyone far away,
    and vast is the emptiness in the midst of the land.
¹³Even if a tenth part remain in it,
    it will be burned again,
like a terebinth or an oak
    whose stump remains standing
    when it is felled."
The holy seed is its stump.

Exegetical Perspective

Like the Old Testament lesson for last Sunday, Jeremiah 1:4–10, this text from Isaiah reports the prophet's vocation. These are appropriate readings for the season of Epiphany because they describe epiphanies—encounters with the God of Israel. Isaiah's report begins with the dramatic affirmation: "I saw the Lord," and then sets out the details of the encounter.

The location of Isaiah's report of his call in the book of Isaiah is unusual. Those of Jeremiah and Ezekiel are found more logically at the very beginning of the books. This chapter begins a collection of materials (6:1–9:7), mainly narratives about Isaiah's activities, that interrupts a previously established collection of the prophet's speeches. It seems likely that the vocation report once stood at the beginning of an early collection of traditions concerning the prophet. Many of these accounts share the historical horizon of the so-called Syro-Ephramitic war of 735–732 BCE (see Isa. 7:1–9).

The vocation report begins with a date formula that also sets the mood. "The year that King Uzziah died" could have been as early as 742 or as late as 736 BCE, but that king's death signaled the end of an era of relative independence for Judah. Tiglath-Pileser III came to power in Assyria in 745 BCE and after consolidating his power in Mesopotamia began

Homiletical Perspective

Through the 2,000-year history of the church, preachers have probed and pulled on this text to expound theological notions like the doctrine of the Trinity, the mystery of election, and God's incomprehensibility. Although we know Isaiah was utterly unaware of the full explication of these ideas, we can say that his encounter with God is a rather dramatic window into the wonder of God's revelation. Even with the benefit of passing centuries, we comprehend God far more dimly than Isaiah did.

Most preachers need a constant reminder: the text, and therefore the sermon, is primarily about God, not me or us or our spirituality. Isaiah is magnificently overshadowed by the massive yet personal presence of God; he happily recedes into the background, preferring to be a docent who points to the beauty of God, instead of drawing attention to himself. In a way, Isaiah's vision is kin to what catapulted each preacher today into the pulpit: it was God who called, no rational career choice was settled upon, and the preacher might prefer something easier to do for a living. Isaiah 6 doesn't say to the laity, "You too can speak directly with God!" For this narrated vision tells us that the book of Isaiah has the authority of God stamped upon it; to the laity this vision says "You are privileged to converse with God through the pages

Isaiah 6:1-8 (9-13)

Theological Perspective

condescending to the needs of the human. Aware that human beings are incapable of handling an unadulterated view of the Divine, God communicates through angelic mediators. John Calvin saw in this passage a confirmation of two themes that factored prominently in his own theology: (1) the mystery of God, an appreciation for which Calvin frequently commended, in response to theologies he thought excessively speculative and insufficiently respectful of the limits to human knowledge; and (2) God's willingness lovingly to condescend to us, for our edification—through Scripture, the sacraments, and most importantly, the incarnate Christ.[1] Isaiah's experience emphasizes both the unapproachable glory of God and God's provision of the means by which we might access that glory.

Another difference between Jeremiah's prophetic call and this one is that, unlike Jeremiah's, Isaiah's insistence on his unworthiness is not *elicited by* God's appointment of him as a prophet, but *anticipates* it. That is, Isaiah's uncertainty comes not as a response to the invitation to be a prophet but as a reaction to a prefatory display of divine power. Isaiah's doubt does not seem to be rooted in feelings of inadequacy so much as in *guilt*. He identifies himself as "a man of unclean lips . . . among a people of unclean lips," and in doing so gives voice to the problem of individual and social sin to hearing and responding to the call of God. In response to Isaiah's insistence on unworthiness comes a physical sign of empowerment and the bestowal of authority. Through an angelic agent, God touches the mouth of the prophet with a coal from the altar and cauterizes it, removing his guilt and enabling him to take up his vocation as God's prophet. Calvin saw here a sacramental dimension to the prophet's encounter with God. The coal mediated grace; it served as a "visible sign of an invisible grace," to adopt (as Calvin did) Augustine's understanding of a sacrament.[2] To follow Calvin's reading of this passage may lead to an interesting exploration of the connection between sacramental worship and the discernment and fulfillment of Christian vocation. At the very least, sacramental worship provides a context and community in which to experience that encounter with grace that beckons and empowers us to serve God's reign.

One final important difference between Jeremiah's call and Isaiah's is to be found in the response. Whereas Jeremiah responds to his

Pastoral Perspective

what is holy. On the contrary, there are lasting consequences to consecration. "To consecrate means . . . to derail from normalcy."[1] The whole action inside that temple for Isaiah is decisive and life changing.

Yet the drama for Isaiah was not simply in what he saw; the drama was contained in what he was called to say. His understanding of God's world and his commission would set him apart as a prophet and witness for God (vv. 9–13). He was sent with a particular message—a message that perplexes and confuses, rather than clarifies and explains. How strange this must seem to our ears, or maybe it is not so strange. We are accustomed to experts who can explain everything, who make sense of the evening news—except when they are often wrong. We expect our doctors to diagnose our every illness correctly, but then discover in the hardest of ways that disease is often more mystery than science to them.

The most perplexing language of all remains the language of parables. That was how Isaiah was told to speak for God. "Make the heart of this people calloused; make their ears dull and close their eyes" (v. 10 NIV). How strange is that? Imagine telling teachers to teach so the children all fail, or imagine a world where we expect traffic cops to create congestion and cause accidents. Try to imagine a coach instructing his players on how not to tackle or when to drop the ball, rather than how and when to catch it. This is the kind of world into which Isaiah is pulled.

Most amazing of all, perhaps, this is where Jesus lived. In the thirteenth chapter of Matthew, in fact, Jesus quotes the same passage about calloused hearts, deaf ears, and blinded eyes.

Why? That is the hard question to answer, and yet it is the reality known to people of faith. You walk in the way of the Lord, and others seem to walk in a different direction. We live among people who want to hate their enemy, and yet we hang on to a message about loving not just your neighbor but your enemy as well. We live in world of wars and rumors of wars, and yet we have a Lord who suggests that when we are weak we are strong. We live in a world that measures success by the size of our possessions, and yet we are a people who share a common meal, just a small piece of bread, as if that were sufficient for a meal, and then we have a small sip from a cup, as if that would slake our thirst.

---

1. John Calvin, *Commentary on Isaiah 1–32* (Grand Rapids: Baker Books, 2003), 200.
2. Ibid., 210–12.

1. Ronald Rolheiser, *The Holy Longing: The Search for a Christian Spirituality* (New York: Doubleday, 1999), 123.

to expand his empire to include the small states in Syria and Palestine. His successors would continue his military and political policies. During most of Isaiah's lifetime Judah lived under the threat of Assyrian domination, and the prophet regularly addressed the political issues facing king and country.

This chapter is a fully self-contained unit, a report by the prophet of what happened to him, what he saw and heard, and what he said. So it is a story, and as such has a plot and characters. The main ones are the prophet and God, but there are others, including the seraphs, the heavenly court, and, of course, offstage, "this people" (v. 9) to whom Isaiah is sent. The account, consisting mainly of dialogue, is continuous and complete, and its main parts recognizable on the basis of shifts of genre, speaker, and contents. Broadly, the elements include the vision and audition (vv. 1–4), the prophet's reaction (v. 5), the ritual of purification (vv. 6–7), YHWH's question and Isaiah's response (v. 8), YHWH's commission to the prophet (vv. 9–10), and Isaiah's objections with the Lord's response (vv. 11–13).

Isaiah's defining encounter with the Lord of hosts would have been a personal and private experience. Why is the prophet—as well as those who subsequently passed down his words—telling us about it? If we stop with the dramatic words at the end of the recommended reading in verse 8 ("Here am I, send me!"), we will have some understanding of the purpose of the report, but we will have missed the main point. After offering to be the Lord's messenger, Isaiah is given a harsh and uncompromising message to deliver, one that would prevent repentance and set judgment into motion. Frequently the authority of prophets to speak was challenged (see Amos 7:10–17; Jer. 1:6–8), especially when they proclaimed judgment. Since prophets in Israel had no "official" standing comparable of that of, for example, priests, their right to speak in the name of the Lord was open to question. The vocation reports were their responses to such challenges. They were not only entitled but also compelled to speak, because God had called them to do so; they had not sought the role, but it had been thrust upon them. So the purpose of Isaiah 6 is to authenticate both Isaiah as the Lord's messenger and his message ("keep listening, but do not comprehend . . ." vv. 8–10) by reporting his vision of the Lord on a throne.

One clear theme of this text for preachers and their congregations centers on vocation in general and the prophetic vocation in particular. Who can

of this inspired book, and indeed through all of the Bible."

How can this passage be preached? Happily, Isaiah 6 affords us the opportunity to anchor Scripture in history: "In the year that King Uzziah died." He was a real king; we know the date of his death, the political consternation, the memorable, real-world historical arena into which God's word inserted itself. God happens in space and time, in the corridors of power, in the impact of governments on obscure people in the hinterlands; God is not boxed into a little private chapel of spirituality inside my own soul.

God is inexpressibly huge; even a slight brush from the mere hem of God's garment (what a trenchant image!) would bowl us over. Yet the beginning of this God's revelation is a conversation. God does not simply thunder, but God asks, invites, listens, urges, waits, pushes a bit harder. Isaiah is obviously unable to fulfill God's task. But who is? The best knowledge of God people in the pews will ever have is dumbfounded puzzlement; the best eloquence the preacher will ever muster is a stammer, with "uh" and "oh my" and "hmm" pauses pregnant with awe. As Karl Barth truly said, we must speak of God, but we are unable to do so, and it is in trying and failing that we give glory to God.

God is not just a big conversationalist. God is holy—not a singular "holy" but a thrice-repeated "holy, holy, holy." The classic hymn by that name (sung to the tune Nicaea), and more contemporary praise music declare repeatedly that God is "holy." We, sadly, are not "holy," although we should be, we could be, at least in some measure.

Isaiah confesses that he is "lost," his lips are "unclean"—but it's not merely personal. He is sucked into the vortex of a culture lost and unclean, and today's preacher need not mince words: we are lost, we are unclean, however nice or pleasant we may think ourselves to be. Notice the grace in God's holiness and in our abysmal failure to be holy: God bothers speaking with us about the matter, and God provides the means to remove the guilt. Sermons must negotiate the way to name our personal, common guilt, the cavernous distance between ourselves and God, in order to celebrate the grace, the healing power of God's presence. Isaiah does nothing to heal himself; he doesn't screw up his courage and try harder to be good. He simply is healed by a power beyond himself.

Healed, he hears God's need for some help. How startling! God, the ominous, robe-clad, glorious one,

Isaiah 6:1-8 (9-13)

Theological Perspective

prophetic appointment with misgivings, Isaiah enthusiastically volunteers for the assignment. If Jeremiah reassures us that the feelings that come second nature to him—fear, inadequacy, resentment—do not disqualify him (or us) from divine service, Isaiah presents more of an ideal response, one of energetic obedience. The challenge for the preacher is to hold up this response as a laudable ideal without implicitly judging as deficient those whose response to God's call is more like Jeremiah's.

Despite the attention given by most classical Christian theologians to Isaiah's personal encounter with God, some modern biblical scholars suggest that the commission in verses 9–13 is at least as important to the meaning of this selection as the call itself in verses 1–8.[3] If they are correct, then the common lectionary's inclusion of the later verses only parenthetically is unfortunate. The biggest hurdle for a modern reading of these verses is the strong insinuation that the prophet will be used intentionally to prevent the people from hearing and accepting God's message. The preacher will have to consider carefully how to navigate this confusion of divine intention and human culpability, resisting the temptation to resolve it too easily (as too much of the tradition has), in favor of either a heavy view of predestination or a theologically illogical insistence on God's simple "foreknowledge" of human refusal. The more certain point to take from God's instructions to Isaiah is this: the refusal of the people to heed the prophet's warning is not a failure on Isaiah's part. Witnesses to the gospel need to know that their words and deeds may not have the desired effect of turning people immediately to God, and in fact they may have the opposite effect. This text reminds us not always and immediately to judge the faithfulness of our efforts by the results, a particularly important reminder in a culture that demands just that. For in the end, the success of grace is assured not by the striving of God's witnesses but by divine power, in the promise of renewal (the "holy seed") at God's appointed time.

JAMES CALVIN DAVIS

Pastoral Perspective

Dare we ever speak up in this world? Some of us wonder if we have a right to speak. The answer may be that none of us has the right to speak. Even Isaiah was a man of unclean lips—but God called upon him to speak. God may call upon us as well, even to say things that may be filled with truth but may not make much worldly sense. That is what Paul said about the cross. It was a stumbling block to the Jews and foolishness to Gentiles (1 Cor. 1:23).

Isaiah was called to proclaim a word of judgment that was also a word of promise. He was called to persevere and endure, even though the outward picture of things might become dark and bleak. He was to know that even though the last tenth (the tithe) might be laid waste, there was yet a holy seed or a stump left. Not much, but enough. That is a parabolic faith if ever there were one. It is the same faith that has been given to us. By faith we are given light and hope in the darkest of times. Paul said that others might think we are dying "and yet we live on; beaten, and yet not killed; sorrowful, yet always rejoicing" (2 Cor. 6:9–10 NIV). Such is the cross-based faith of Christianity.

As Christians we live in a world marked by so many things that remind us of the cross, including that fateful day called simply 9/11. Knowing the perplexing parabolic message of Isaiah, we have to wonder what he might have said in its aftermath. You have seen violence; now walk in the way of peace. You have heard vindictive speech; now practice forgiveness. We would have had trouble, naturally, seeing his vision or hearing his message. It is sobering to realize that God still calls prophets to speak the prophetic word the world most needs to hear.

GEORGE H. MARTIN

---

3. See, for instance, Christopher R. Seitz, *Isaiah 1–39*, Interpretation Series (Louisville, KY: John Knox Press, 1993), 53.

Exegetical Perspective

hear Isaiah's "Here am I; send me!" (v. 8) and not be challenged? But this brave response must be heard in its context. Isaiah's initial response to the vision is fear and resistance: "Woe is me! I am lost" (v. 5). He does not volunteer until he has confessed his inadequacy and uncleanness, and then had his lips purified by a burning coal from the altar.

Nor can one use Isaiah's call to drive a wedge between prophetic and priestly roles, between concerns for justice and concerns for religious piety. This prophet's encounter happened in the temple, where he heard the hymn of praise, saw the smoke of the offering, and was the subject of a ritual of purification.

A more difficult theme for preacher and congregation is the message Isaiah was given to deliver to his people. This command to prevent hearing, to "make the mind of this people dull," has long been a problem for readers, but its meaning is unmistakable. Many prefer to interpret even the prophetic announcements of disaster as warnings, to encourage repentance and thus avert the announced judgment. Here the prophet is to *prevent* repentance: "so that they may *not* look, . . . listen, . . . comprehend, . . . and turn and be healed."

To be sure, this message needs to be interpreted in its wider context in Isaiah 1–39, the entire book of Isaiah, indeed the biblical tradition as a whole. This is neither the only word nor the last word, but readers, and especially modern readers, tend to move over it too quickly. Is it ever possible that the word of God, the truth for the present and future, is the proclamation of judgment? The word of God is not a dogma, requiring the same proclamation in all times and places. Thus there is a time and occasion for judgment, but also for salvation. Could we miss the yes because we have not heard the no?

Do circumstances have to get worse before they can get better? Something like that is suggested in the final form of Isaiah 6. With that glimmer of hope in the final line, "The holy seed is its stump," the editors of the text did not deny the announcement of disaster—in fact, they may have experienced it—but they could see beyond judgment.

GENE M. TUCKER

Homiletical Perspective

needs something. Isaiah doesn't unfurl a resume, but raises his hand, offering not cleverness, but his humble willingness to be used: "Here am I, send me." The popular hymn by Dan Schutte voices this pledge of faith in lovely ways. Perhaps our singing, the poetry and harmony of praise, is our best witness. Talk is cheap, talk underestimates the grandeur of God; so we sing. The best sermon isn't a clattering of words, but the pregnant silence between the words, a rest in the musical score, and we draw our breath to intone our only sensible reply, "Here I am, Lord."

All this takes place, not in the woods or in front of the computer screen. Isaiah was in the temple, richly decorated with symbols evoking the divine presence. God is everywhere, but this God seems to want to be encountered in a holy place. Some of our sanctuaries will offer a fledgling glimmer of such symbolic power, whereas a storefront church might have to rely on the faces of fellow worshipers who, unbeknownst to themselves, flawlessly exhibit the image of God. In the holy place we learn reverence, which is the staircase into a conversation with God that is not a silly idol or a monologue with nothing but my own bias. For Isaiah, the temple was a copy of the unimaginably stupendous courts in heaven, a pale imitation, just as our work mimics in laughable ways the labor of Christ. But isn't imitation the sincerest form of flattery?

The sermon happens in some place you can at least pray might become holy. In that place, the preacher had better watch out, and alert those who come for worship: God might just show up. Or better: Isaiah showed up, and perhaps he wanted the Lord to intrude into his world, to say or do something; but Isaiah accidentally stumbled through some hidden doorway into the heavenly realm, and before he and the people knew it, God was manifest, God was sending him and them out with impossible tasks; and in their very inability to do what God asked, they mirrored to the world and back to God the stunning yet tender greatness and love of God.

JAMES C. HOWELL

Psalm 138

¹I give you thanks, O LORD, with my whole heart;
  before the gods I sing your praise;
²I bow down toward your holy temple
  and give thanks to your name for your steadfast love and your faithfulness;
 for you have exalted your name and your word
  above everything.
³On the day I called, you answered me,
  you increased my strength of soul.

⁴All the kings of the earth shall praise you, O LORD,
  for they have heard the words of your mouth.

Theological Perspective

One of the limitations of the English language is the slipperiness in the meaning of the word "pride." The positive form of pride finds expression in the synonyms dignity, self-worth, and self-esteem. However, there is also the pride of arrogance, egotism, and vanity. Psalm 138 speaks to both forms of pride. It has a clear message to practitioners of the latter form, and the message is not reassuring. Those who find their worth in God, however, have a right to pride by association. The psalm also differentiates between God's form of self-pride and that of human beings.

The psalmist begins the hymn with an expression of thanksgiving to God that infuses the emotions as well as the entirety of one's intellect and will. In other words, the act of thanksgiving itself is a form of submission to God. To reinforce this understanding of thanksgiving as subjugation to God, the psalmist states that all the other lesser gods will be witness to the psalmist's act of praise. In the second verse, the submission of the heart and mind leads to an act of submission of the body, as the psalmist prostrates the body in homage to God. It is a physical as well as spiritual and intellectual yielding to YHWH.

Then the next verse speaks to the way in which God exalts Godself above all else. Being all-powerful, God has the right to pride in Godself as no one else

Pastoral Perspective

Psalm 138 is written for people like us who seek to worship and praise God in the post-9/11 age. Its praise and thanksgiving are set within a world where God's saving work has clearly been seen, felt, and thus trusted. Yet it is also a world in which threat and insecurity continue to haunt the lives and memories of the redeemed. Ours is a world where terrorist attacks are headline news in every sector of the globe, a time in which a spectrum of threat levels color our individual and collective anxieties. For the most part, we and those with whom we worship have long ago passed a quiet and muted "blue" and "green" (guarded or low risk of terrorist attack) concern. We now sing praises in the bright spotlight of "yellow" or "orange" (elevated or high risk) apprehension both here and abroad. We lived in the "age of anxiety" before 9/11. Now that anxiety has metastasized and flirts with trepidation in the deep recesses of our minds and souls. In so many conscious and so many more subconscious ways, we like the psalmist "walk in the midst of trouble" (v. 7).

So we bow down to sing the Lord's praises as the psalmist does here—reclaiming our core sacred story by thinking back to the day when we called and God answered mightily. Indeed, the origin of this psalm is most likely the postexilic period, about the time the Psalter was edited in its current form. Memories of

⁵They shall sing of the ways of the Lord,
    for great is the glory of the Lord.
⁶For though the Lord is high, he regards the lowly;
    but the haughty he perceives from far away.

⁷Though I walk in the midst of trouble,
    you preserve me against the wrath of my enemies;
    you stretch out your hand,
    and your right hand delivers me.
⁸The Lord will fulfill his purpose for me;
    your steadfast love, O Lord, endures forever.
Do not forsake the work of your hands.

Exegetical Perspective

Psalm 138, a psalm of thanksgiving (*todah*), is ascribed to David and celebrates God's might, kindness, and faithfulness. Perhaps the best way to understand Psalm 138, and the genre of thanksgiving psalms as a whole, is to see the ways in which they echo some of the oldest material in the Hebrew Bible. In particular, the resonance of our passage with Exodus 15:1–18, known as the Song of the Sea or the Song of Moses, is as remarkable as it is revealing. Thought to have been composed around 1000 BCE, the Song of the Sea is among the most famous passages in the Hebrew Bible, and many texts that came after it resonate with and perhaps purposely echo its language and themes. This is easy to explain, given the nature of the Song of the Sea. It likely became well known as the most stirring account of God's power to redeem.

Here we will follow the order of Psalm 138 and consider its connections to the Song of the Sea as we progress. A strange harmony emerges when we consider that Psalm 138 is understood first to have been uttered by David but, because it has become Scripture, has been recited or sung by countless believers ever since. This is a diachronic analogy to the event at the Sea of Reeds when Moses and all his followers spontaneously sing their song of thanksgiving and redemption. This genre lends itself, at one

Homiletical Perspective

There is some disagreement among exegetes whether Psalm 138, a psalm of thanksgiving, is intended for individuals or for community. Mowinckel suggests that the psalm is a "royal psalm of thanksgiving" sung for both the individual and community.[1] Most likely it was used for the communal liturgy after the return from Babylonian exile. Thinking individually, the psalm could more likely be used after a worshiper has recovered from a life-threatening illness. Either way, the phrase "I give you thanks, O Lord, with my whole heart" sets the homiletical tone for the entire passage. Embedded in the first two verses of the psalm is a miniliturgical order of worship stated in the first person: I give thanks, I sing, I bow down, I give thanks again.[2] Again, this can be both an individual liturgy for thanksgiving and praise and also a community order of worship. Is there any higher purpose in worship than exalting God's name above everything in heaven and on earth? This psalm leads us in that awesome endeavor.

The antidote for life in a culture of narcissism, vanity, and egocentrism is a heart and mind that are thankful to God. Thoughtful preachers will bring

---

1. Sigmund Mowinckel, *The Psalms in Israel's Worship* (New York: Abingdon Press, 1962), 2:32.
2. Walter Brueggemann, *The Message of the Psalms* (Minneapolis: Augsburg, 1984), 134.

Psalm 138

Theological Perspective

does. Indeed, royalty throughout the world will recognize the greatness of the glory of YHWH. Not only will they praise God, but they will also sing about God's wonderful ways. Singing is a form of personal submission to God. Spoken words of praise can be repeated by rote without much feeling. Singing, however, requires an outpouring of one's breath, one's spirit, and one's wind (*ruach*) in a deeply felt form of adoration. Although one is hard-pressed to envision members of the House of Windsor bursting into spontaneous praise hymns, the image of contemporary monarchs revealing feelings of awe toward their Creator through music is a powerful one.

The psalmist praises God's great kindness and faithfulness, and declares that God is greater than all other gods and deserves the full adoration of the greatest peoples of the earth. Such praise is common from an appreciative underling toward an authority figure. The distinction comes when the psalmist turns to God's attitude toward that underling, and herein lies the heart of the psalm and its most intriguing message. This God is like no other in regard to the company God keeps.

The psalmist is clearly an ordinary person rather than royalty. The psalmist faces many troubles and has enemies with harmful intentions. In spite of this seemingly hopeless situation, the psalmist also knows that God is on the side of the common person. This fact is what makes God the greatest of all. Human leaders do not consort with hoi polloi, but God does. Most gods prefer to mingle with other gods, but YHWH reaches out to the poor and lowly. "Sublime as he is, Yahweh looks on the humble" (v. 6 NJB). Even more telling, God distances Godself from the proud and the haughty. God wants nothing to do with people who exalt themselves for their own sake.

With God on the side of ordinary people, they have justification to be prideful. God's act of hearkening to the psalmist's cry emboldened the psalmist to act "stormily, boisterously, arrogantly"[1] (*rahab*). This is a good kind of arrogance, because it is an arrogance that stems from having God paying heed and responding to the call of someone who is considered insignificant in worldly affairs. The God who is the subject of the songs of world leaders nonetheless makes time for the forgotten of this earth. Because of God's faithfulness, those forgotten folk can think highly of themselves. Not only can

1. Francis Brown, ed., *The Brown-Driver-Briggs Hebrew and English Lexicon* (Peabody, MA: Hendrickson, 1999), 923.

Pastoral Perspective

captivity in an alien culture and even the threats and hardships of returning to a sometimes inhospitable homeland are still very real. Psalm 138 provides a therapeutic as well as liturgical form—a theologically and psychologically healthy way to live and give thanks fully, in spite of the haunting memories and lingering threat and crises.

Narrative theory understands the nature of crises as a disruption in the flow of a person's core life story. Such transient crises create an environment like that of the psalmist, in which we are vulnerable to despair. The therapeutic move is to reach back into our past and to vision ahead to the future as a way to reconnect with the whole of our sacred life narrative. The liturgical move is to ground ourselves in the wider sacred story through singing praise in the community of faith. Here, the gratitude of the psalmist is actively expressed by thanking, singing, bowing down in both the heavenly court and the earthly courtyard of the temple. It starts with the grateful response of an individual who reaches back to recall the day upon which he/she called and God answered, but quickly expands to include the praises of others who resonate with the way God's intervention has strengthened their souls. This combination of individual and communal praises glorifies the Author of the saving narrative of God's people and reaffirms and reinforces each individual's place in that narrative. Liturgical hymn and therapeutic narrative responses thus intertwine and reinforce each other.

The central hymn of praise in verses 4–6 reveals the distinctive astounding core of the saving narrative. God is placed at the very highest of the high here. Members of the heavenly court and earthly kings both recognize and praise the greatness of God's glory. Yet highness alone is not what elicits the depth of praise. The universal chorus of praise is rooted in an astonishing, even scandalous, twist of what might be expected. God does a very unregal and ungodly thing. God, the very highest of the high, attends to the helpless and vulnerable—those on the margins of faith and life! This is extraordinary. The high and mighty simply do not do this sort of thing. They are too far removed to consider the plight of those who are distressed, weak, insecure, low, and in jeopardy. Yet here the tables are completely turned. The psalmist suggests that the very height of highness and glory are attributed to God, not because God aspired to these things, but because God stretched out a divine right hand to reach low to deliver the lost and downcast. This

Exegetical Perspective

and the same time, to both personal and public celebration.

The most compelling part of verse 1 is in its second half where the NRSV translates, "before the gods I sing your praise." In Exodus 15:11 the Israelites declare that none of the gods is like theirs. Many parts of the Hebrew Bible represent such early stages of the development of the religion of Israel that they do not presume monotheism. Something closer to monolatry or henotheism prevailed at early stages of Israelite religion, and Psalm 138 seems to share with the Song of the Sea this perspective.

Verse 2 begins, "I bow down toward your holy temple (*hekhal qodshekha*) . . ." The Hebrew verb translated "bow down" (*'eshtakhaveh*) comes from a root that often suggests ritual and cultic action; as a result, we likely should see in this verb a description of something beyond merely kneeling. For instance, Genesis uses this verb to describe what Abraham and Isaac will do when they reach the top of Moriah in Genesis 22:5. More to the point, the reference in Psalm 138:2 to the temple in the midst of thanksgiving is reminiscent of the multiple references to the sanctuary and temple in the Song of the Sea, which culminates in verse 17: "You brought them in and planted them on the mountain of your own possession, the place, O LORD, that you made your abode, the sanctuary (*miqdash*), O LORD, that your hands have established." One would think that the mountain to which God had brought the Israelites is Sinai, but here it is described in language that brings to mind Zion, the temple mount. There is a good chance that this reference in Exodus 15:17 is a later addition, but it is significant because Sinai and Zion, the two mountains of God, became interchangeable in ancient Israelite religion. More to the point, Psalm 138 can be understood to reenact, at the mountain of god, a timeless celebration of redemption that began at the very origin of the Israelite relationship with its God in the exodus.

It is hard to miss the resonance of verse 7, "Though I walk in the midst of trouble, you preserve me against the wrath of my enemies," and the imagery at the heart of the Song of the Sea. In fact, it was precisely by leading the Israelites through the midst of the Sea of Reeds that God preserved the Israelites from their enemy, the Egyptians. Verse 7 concludes with imagery even more closely connected to the Song of the Sea: "you stretch out your hand, and your right hand delivers me." Hebrew poetic parallelism in part explains this double reference to God's hand, but Exodus 15:6, "Your right hand, O

Homiletical Perspective

their congregations back to the place of gratitude on a regular basis, changing the spectacles on the eyes of God's worshipers to see all the goodness, faithfulness, and steadfast love (*hesed*) of God (v. 1). This does not come easily for most churchgoers, but Psalm 138 gives us a platform from which to declare "before the gods I sing your praise" (vv. 1, 5). The use of *hesed* draws our attention back to the book of Hosea, which is an analogy for God's unfailing love for Israel. The tradition is that God called Hosea to pursue his wife Homer, who had abandoned him for a life of harlotry. Although Hosea had every justification to divorce his wife, nonetheless Hosea with steadfast love found his wife and purchased her (redeemed) back into the covenant of marriage (Hos. 2:19–20). This story models for us the rock solid love that God has for us irregardless of our desire to separate ourselves from God. God's faithfulness and love breed in us a heart of gratitude and thanksgiving so that we may prostrate our wills in God's temple, praising God's holy name.

Nobody can escape trying moments in life. It may be divorce, a serious illness, a death of a child, or even a near-death experience. When God walks us through these crises we emerge on the other side, sometimes tattered and scared, but with a renewed appreciation of God's steadfast love. Peter Seary waddled up to the bow of the Yendys sailboat in the midst of a gale during the 1998 Sydney-Hobart race. He forgot to clip his safety harness just as a wave washed over the bow and threw Seary into the Tasmania Sea. The crew did not realize what had happened. Seary clawed at the side of the Yendys but she was slipping away out of his reach. Before he could even realize the severity of the situation, another rough wave hit the side of the yacht and lifted Seary up and back into the cockpit.[3] Thank God he was safe! Realizing God's faithfulness and goodness to save us in times of trouble elevates us to give thanks, exalt God's name, and sing of the ways of the Lord.

Often we are unable to see the ways in which God extends God's right hand and delivers us in times of trouble (v. 7–8). The right hand of God is illustrative of God's power and might. The right hand extends blessings (Gen. 48:17; Ps. 16:11), crushes the enemies of Israel (Exod. 15:6ff.), and tenders strength to the weak (Ps. 18:35).

Finally, notice the psalmist's use of "word" (*ma'mar*) (v. 2) to describe the theological experience

---

3. Robert Mundle, *Fatal Storm: The Inside Story of the Tragic Sydney-Hobart Race* (Camden, ME: International Marine, McGraw-Hill, 1999), 64–65.

Psalm 138

Theological Perspective

they think positively about themselves, but they can even act boldly and insolently, with flamboyance and fierceness.

Seen in the context of this day's readings in the lectionary cycle, Psalm 138 is particularly fitting. While it may be hard to imagine contemporary monarchs lending their voices to a choir, it is extremely easy to imagine Isaiah, Peter, or Paul belting out Psalm 138 with particular relish. Each one of these servants of God finds himself in a position of humility before God, only to be exalted by God to unimaginable heights. Isaiah protests that he is unclean and lives among the unclean, yet he has seen the Lord of Hosts (Isa. 6:5); his exaltation by God gives him the courage to heed God's call. Peter, in awe of Jesus' miracles, asks Jesus to leave him alone because he is a sinful man (Luke 5:8), but Jesus responds to his request by anointing him as a disciple. Among the three, Paul makes the most blatant use of God-inspired pride in himself; having identified himself as the "least" and unfit to be an apostle (1 Cor. 15:9), in the very next verse Paul seems to be leaning toward vanity ("I worked harder than any of them"), but then redeems himself by adding "though it was not I, but the grace of God that is with me."

Christians are proud in the knowledge of being exalted through the resurrection of the savior, Jesus Christ, who showed the ultimate sign of humility in Godself by becoming human. Fellowship with Christ in the Holy Spirit gives one the courage to boast, as Paul so eagerly declares. We remember, however, that the concept of God as one who stoops to the level of the poor of this earth is not exclusive to the New Testament, but has deep and solid roots in the Hebrew Scriptures, as is reflected in this rousing hymn of praise to YHWH. Knowing this consistent attribute of the Creator toward common folk grants one ample excuse for pride.

REBECCA BLAIR YOUNG

Pastoral Perspective

concern with the lowly, those who are marginalized, helpless, and needy is a unique concern of the God of Israel and therefore the faith of the Hebrew people. Incorporated in Hebrew law were specific provisions for the welfare of those whose physical, economic, or social circumstances put them in weak, low, needy, or life-threatening situations.

The Gospels carry this regard for the lowly even further. The way one is instructed to demonstrate love and praise for God is through caring for "the least of these." Indeed, God in Christ took this regard for the lowly to the point that God "being in the form of God did not count equality with God a thing to be grasped, but became empty, taking the form of a servant, being born in human form" (Phil. 2:6–7, my trans.). Such is both a cause for reveling in the grace-filled power of our sacred stories and an impetus for our own efforts to reach out to those whose lives have been broken, whose spirits are in anguish, and whose life stories have reached a low and desperate point.

We know, as well as the psalmist, that life is an unsolvable problem. Our life stories will continue to entail precarious chapters. Trouble, distress, and pain remain. None of us is immune. Yet the actions of the One whose *hesed* steadfastly and decisively embraces all of us at each point in our lives can resurrect in each of us the core life themes of courage, hope, and strength of heart. It can give voice to enthusiastic praise; and it can instill in us the passion to embrace those whose voices are muted, whose spirits are frayed, and whose hope is dim. Such is the nature of the community of faith whose chorus of praise continues to grow and resonate throughout the world, enfolding the terrorized and terrorists alike into the sacred saving story and reminding all that God will "not forsake the work of [God's] hands."

CHARLES M. MENDENHALL

Exegetical Perspective

LORD, glorious in power—your right hand, O LORD, shattered the enemy," resonates remarkably well with our passage. The psalmist here might be understood to be engaging in a typical rhetorical move, found in many places in the Hebrew Bible, whereby the author gently reminds God of his ability to intervene in Israel's behalf. By a subtle allusion to the most famous of God's acts of redemption, the psalmist seems to remind God of God's power to save.

Reinforcing such a reading, Psalm 138:8 says, "The LORD will fulfill his purpose for me; your steadfast love, O LORD, endures forever. Do not forsake the work of your hands." Here we have in microcosm a standard motif, declaring God's faithfulness while admitting of a degree of anxiety. Especially intriguing in this last verse is the call, "Do not forsake the work of your hands." This likely has multiple registers against which it can be understood, but two are especially important. First, the psalmist likely has the temple in mind as the work of God's hands, given the reference in the beginning of our psalm to that edifice. Recall Exodus 15:17: "the sanctuary, O LORD, that your hands have established." Secondly and more significantly, it is precisely the work of God's hands in bringing Israel out of Egypt that seems to be echoed here.

Whether or not the psalmist intentionally makes reference to the Song of the Sea, by hearing the echoes of that song in Psalm 138, we recognize that any instance of thanksgiving in the Hebrew Bible has its origins in that primal moment when God first redeemed Israel. That later tradition should resonate with that most famous of events is hardly surprising.

LARRY L. LYKE

Homiletical Perspective

of God's very word being mediated not only to Israel but to humanity in general. The other readings for this day can be woven into your sermon to develop a theology of the word of God. Isaiah 6:1–8 is the call of the prophet Isaiah to be sent by God with clean lips to proclaim the word of the Lord to Israel. Likewise in 1 Corinthians 15:1–11 Paul reminds the Corinthians of the "good news" that was proclaimed to them and received by them. Paul admonishes the church, therefore, to "hold firmly to the message" (v. 2). The apostle goes on to describe the wonderful message of the gospel so their belief is not "in vain," but, rather, by the sheer grace of God their belief will be valuable and effectual.

The preacher only needs to look toward the Gospel reading (Luke 5:1–11) for the day to be encouraged that the word of God we preach is not in vain. A crowd "pressed in on [Jesus] to hear the word of God" (v. 1). We may simply surmise that if we preach the same word and message of Jesus, a crowd will press into the sanctuaries of our God to hear and be filled with his word. In other words, it is our task as preachers to be responsible and faithful to that word. After a wonderful object lesson about fishing from our Lord, Peter hears the urgent word from Jesus that he will now be "catching people." How will he accomplish that purpose? By faithfully reciprocating the words of Jesus to others (cf. Acts 1:15; 10:34ff.). The point is that the fundamental task of the church of Jesus Christ is to exalt the name of God and God's word above everything (Ps. 138:2) because we earnestly believe that when the kings of the earth hear the word of God's mouth, they will praise him (v. 4). Worshipfully, they will "sing of the ways of the LORD," for they have seen and experienced the "glory of the LORD" (v. 5).

ROBERT M. LEACH

1 Corinthians 15:1-11

¹Now I would remind you, brothers and sisters, of the good news that I proclaimed to you, which you in turn received, in which also you stand, ²through which also you are being saved, if you hold firmly to the message that I proclaimed to you—unless you have come to believe in vain. ³For I handed on to you as of first importance what I in turn had received: that Christ died for our sins in accordance with the scriptures, ⁴and that he was buried, and that he was raised on the third day in accordance with the scriptures, ⁵and that he appeared to Cephas, then to the twelve. ⁶Then he appeared to more than five hundred brothers and sisters at one time, most of whom are still alive, though some have died. ⁷Then he appeared to James, then to all the apostles. ⁸Last of all, as to one untimely born, he appeared also to me. ⁹For I am the least of the apostles, unfit to be called an apostle, because I persecuted the church of God. ¹⁰But by the grace of God I am what I am, and his grace toward me has not been in vain. On the contrary, I worked harder than any of them—though it was not I, but the grace of God that is with me. ¹¹Whether then it was I or they, so we proclaim and so you have come to believe.

Theological Perspective

First Corinthians 15 aims to counter the belief, apparently held by some members of the church in Corinth, that there is no resurrection of the dead. Paul employs the entire complex chapter to demonstrate that believing in the resurrection of the dead is both necessary and plausible.[1] Today's reading introduces that demonstration and provides its first step.

Paul reminds the Corinthians whence they received the gospel (v. 1) through which they are being saved (v. 2). He then summarizes the good news that he himself has received: "that Christ died for our sins in accordance with the scriptures, and that he was buried, and that he was raised on the third day in accordance with the scriptures, and that he appeared to Cephas, then to the twelve" (vv. 3–5). This earliest canonical witness to the Easter event asserts the death of Jesus Christ and also his resurrection as confirmed in his appearances to the disciples. By citing the Easter tradition and extending the list of appearances (vv. 6–8), Paul calls the Corinthians back to the fundamental ground they share with him, that God did indeed raise Christ from the dead. This is the basis for the next step in his argument, which comes in next Sunday's reading (v. 12).

Pastoral Perspective

What does it mean to be a witness? In 1 Corinthians 15:1–11, Paul speaks of how he came to be a witness to the gospel. As a witness, he handed on to the Corinthians what he also received. Paul describes the heart of the gospel as the death and resurrection of Jesus. His death was confirmed by his burial; his resurrection is confirmed by the many people to whom the risen Lord appeared. Through the testimony of Paul and these witnesses, the Corinthians have come to believe the gospel of Jesus Christ.

First of all, to be a witness, one has to receive within one's own being the good news. A person cannot witness to what he or she has not experienced in the heart and mind to be true. Paul says that the Corinthians have received the gospel; they stand in the gospel; and they are being saved by the gospel. A task of the pastor is to help the congregation understand that the good news of Jesus' death and resurrection is not one more piece of information to add to the information overload from which many people suffer. Receiving the gospel is not simply giving assent to the articles of a creed. Receiving the gospel is not a matter of accruing one more good thing to a life that is already full of good things. Receiving the gospel is discovering in Christ a new center of existence, a new power for living, and a new perspective from which to view all things.

1. Victor Paul Furnish, *The Theology of the First Letter to the Corinthians* (Cambridge, UK: Cambridge University Press, 1999), 109.

Exegetical Perspective

Chapter 15 comprises the last major section of the letter. This opens Paul's discussion of the resurrection, which extends through the whole chapter.

Structure. The passage is bracketed on one end by "the gospel" (v. 1, my trans.) that "you believed" (v. 2) and on the other by "so we preached, and so you believed" (v. 11). These rhetorical bookends (*inclusio*) define the contents of the passage.

The heart of the passage is the creedal statement about Christ (vv. 3b–4). Paul introduces this as a traditional formulation of the gospel that he had first proclaimed at Corinth (vv. 1–3a). Each element of the creed begins with "that," so one must decide whether "that he appeared to Cephas" (v. 5) is part of the tradition that Paul received and passed on. If so, then where does the traditional creed end? Verse 8, at least, must be Paul's own addition, and perhaps it is best to take all of the appearances (vv. 5–8) as Paul's addition. Finally, Paul defends his right to call himself an apostle (vv. 9–11), explaining why he was "last" (v. 8) and "least" (v. 9).

The Argument. Paul returns to a basic statement of the gospel that he proclaimed when he first came to Corinth. Paul never tells about Jesus' birth, miracles, or parables. Paul says he proclaimed the death and

Homiletical Perspective

Going back to the basics is essential—especially in times of uncertainty and conflict. As Paul dealt with the conflict in Corinth, he found it necessary to remind them of where and how it all began. In today's church this back-to-the-basics (or perhaps more appropriately forward-to-the-basics) movement is also essential. We live in a time when the old ways of being and doing church no longer communicate the faith effectively, especially to this generation. The old answers do not work anymore. In fact, in many cases the old questions are not even being asked anymore. Yet the basic message that has been entrusted to the church from the beginning (vv. 3b–4) is never old. Therefore in this time it is essential to remind the community where it came from, what it believes, and how it all began. This passage provides the opportunity not only to do that, but also to affirm the essential importance of doing so. It encourages thoughtful reflection on the key dimensions of our belief and the ways in which they impact our faith.

An Affirmation of Common Ground. Paul is continuing to deal with conflict in the Corinthian church. Previously he has dealt with sexual conduct, worship, the eating of meat offered to idols, and the use of gifts. While these were all issues of

1 Corinthians 15:1-11

Theological Perspective

The simple and essential statement of the gospel in verses 3–5, really the heart of today's reading, makes theological sense in the eschatological context assumed throughout Paul's letter to the Corinthians. Operating out of the Jewish apocalyptic tradition from which he came, Paul understands the end of this age to come about through a radical transformation that will include our resurrection, of which Christ is the firstfruits. "And God raised the Lord and will also raise us by his power" (1 Cor. 6:14); "for as all die in Adam, so all will be made alive in Christ" (1 Cor. 15:22). Paul discusses the nature of resurrection more fully in verses 35–55. The point here is that the gospel Paul proclaims to the Corinthians is a theological call to action, to a new way of living in the present age, that is rooted in a hope for the age to come.

That "Christ died for our sins" (v. 3) has been the subject of numerous theological interpretations, many of which turn on the notion that only the death of God's Son could atone for the injustices we have committed. In this particular Pauline letter the theological message is much less abstract. Some in the Corinthian church are exploiting the gifts of the Spirit to enhance their status within the congregation and tailoring their beliefs to coincide with those of their fellow citizens outside the church. In short, they are not living in the love of God and neighbor so powerfully described in 1 Corinthians 13. The "sins" of these Corinthians may sound trivial by twenty-first-century standards, but they are symptomatic of what biblical scholar Marcus Borg describes as conventional wisdom with its system of social rewards and punishments, by which we measure our performance and deepen our self-preoccupation. Like the apostle Paul, Borg sees the marriage of conventional wisdom and Christianity as the source of internal divisiveness and a subtle merit-based understanding of God's forgiveness.[2] It is precisely this conventional scheme of things from which we are liberated by the love of God revealed in Christ's death.

How Christ died for our sins is of crucial importance to Paul as a revelation of the nature of God's wisdom and power. Earlier in 1 Corinthians he writes, "For the message about the cross is foolishness to those who are perishing, but to us who are being saved it is the power of God" (1:18), and "we proclaim Christ crucified, a stumbling block to Jews and foolishness to Gentiles, but to those who

Pastoral Perspective

An important pastoral act is helping believers articulate how the gospel has changed them and continues to change them. The gospel *is* Jesus Christ, the risen Lord present with the church. Many Christians are timid and uncertain about expressing their experiences of Christ's presence in their lives. In the worship of the church, a part of the preacher's work is giving worshipers images of how the gospel transforms lives and the language through which they can express their own experiences of transformation. There may also be opportunities in response to the preaching of the word for worshipers to share their own witness.

A second pastoral dimension to Paul's testimony is the way in which the gospel tradition is passed from one generation to the next. As evidence of the resurrection, Paul speaks of all those to whom the risen Lord appeared. The list builds from Cephas to the Twelve, from the five hundred to James, and from all the other apostles to Paul himself. All of these witnesses proclaimed the gospel of the death and resurrection of Jesus for the forgiveness of sins and the salvation of humankind. Each believer stands as a link in the transmission of the gospel. Believers are not called to invent the gospel or embellish the gospel. They are called to proclaim what they have received. The living witness of the church is manifest in the continuing worship of the church, the story of the Scriptures, the creeds of the church, and the ongoing story of God's people today. Believers receive with gratitude the word of life and offer this same word of life to others.

The transmission of the gospel brings to life a third aspect of Paul's testimony. As the gospel is shared, it becomes incarnate in the particular life of each new believer. The gospel today is the same word of salvation that Paul proclaimed, but it may be expressed in fresh ways as it becomes embodied in other lives. The gospel has a way of letting the light of Christ shine in unique ways through each believer. Paul spoke of himself as "one untimely born" (v. 8). It is difficult to understand what Paul intended by this unusual expression, which usually referred to a premature birth. He could have meant many things, but quite possibly he was thinking of his encounter with Jesus on the road to Damascus as a difficult, unexpected birth. His former life as a persecutor of the church led him to think of himself as "the least of the apostles" (v. 9). This was not a display of false modesty. The sense that he had so much to overcome led Paul to strive even harder for the gospel. Yet in all his labors he came to

---

2. Marcus J. Borg, *Meeting Jesus Again for the First Time* (New York: HarperCollins, 1994), 75–80.

resurrection of Jesus, and now he calls the Corinthians to recalibrate their faith to that story (cf. 1 Thess. 1:9–10).

What Paul passed on "first" (v. 3a) could imply of first importance (NRSV, NAS) or first in time (KJV). There is little practical difference, but the temporal connotation fits the context in which Paul is recounting his early preaching in Corinth.

The creedal formulation is traditional. The language of receiving (*paralambanō*, vv. 1, 3) and passing along (*paradidōmi*, v. 3) links the Corinthians through Paul back to the earliest Christian testimony about Christ. For similar uses of this language, see 11:23; Philippians 4:9; 1 Thessalonians 2:13. Similar confessional statements can be found elsewhere (Phil. 2:5–11; 1 Tim. 2:5–6; 3:16; Titus 3:4–7). Such traditional formulations preserve a common understanding of basic tenets of the faith.

Christ died "for our sins" (v. 3a; cf. 1:13; 11:24). But this is not a simple payment of debt, since Paul finds analogy in the Passover lamb (5:7), not in the Day of Atonement sacrifices (Lev. 16). "Our sins" are mere symptoms of a larger problem of the tyranny of death, which was defeated by Christ's resurrection (15:20–28; cf. Rom. 6–7).

The Greek perfect tense in "that he has been raised" (v. 4) implies not only that Jesus was raised from the dead but that he remains alive. A simple past tense ("was raised," NRSV) loses the point. One could say "he was raised" about Lazarus (John 11) or the widow's son at Nain (Luke 7:11–17). But Jesus "has been raised." He *is* risen. In the rest of the chapter Paul will elaborate the theological meaning of that resurrection.

In verses 5–8, Paul offers his only proof that the resurrection occurred. The rest of the chapter is not about proving that the resurrection happened so much as explaining its theological significance. Here Paul lists numerous eyewitnesses, most of whom were still available for cross-examination when Paul wrote, if any of the Corinthians had cared to find and question them. At least one of those eyewitnesses—Cephas—had visited Corinth. But this proof loses its force for modern readers, since the witnesses are no longer available to us.

Paul's self-description (vv. 9–11) is calculated to defend himself as a legitimate apostle against some factions that rallied around other teachers and questioned Paul's apostleship (1:11–12; 2 Cor. 11). The designation apostle here is not an office or rank but a function. The word means, literally, "missionary" or one who is "commissioned." Paul is an apostle because

appropriate behavior (How is a Christian to act?), this issue is one of appropriate belief (What is a Christian to believe?). Paul begins this discussion by reminding them of what they all believe and so establishing the common ground on which they stand. Next Sunday's passage, verses 12–30, will explore the differences in belief. Here it is important to begin with the affirmation of what is shared. This is the message he "proclaimed," they "received," and in which they "stand." It is what holds them together as a community. Even though they are divided by conflict, even though they don't treat each other in the way one would expect Christians to treat each other, this is something all of them affirm. As such, it provides the beginning point for any discussion of their differences.

The three words "proclaimed," "received," and "stand" offer entry points into the common ground of every congregation. What is the word proclaimed to us—from our beginning to now? How have we received it—openly and eagerly or guardedly and with reservation? What does it mean for us to stand in that word—how does it shape who we are and how we live our faith? Is this word the same for us as it was for Paul and the Corinthians? Is there something more than this (or less) that provides our common ground? This search for common ground can be a challenging task, especially in a conflicted congregation. It is the preacher's joy and burden to find the language that makes that common ground apparent, so that it can serve as a positive force in affirming the church's unity and managing conflict that arises.

The Relationship of Belief and Action. In saving the controversy about belief to the end of his letter, Paul is affirming its importance. What we believe shapes the way we act. Our theology shapes our ethics. Paul is saying that when you get this part right, the other pieces will fall into place more easily. Much that is written today in the area of congregational renewal talks about the importance of determining and stating core values and bedrock beliefs. When those are clear, it is possible to turn people loose for ministry without the traditional board and committee systems that tend to stifle effective and vibrant mission. When the beliefs are clear, the actions follow naturally and appropriately. This echoes Paul's approach to the Corinthians. A sermon that takes this approach to the passage could raise important questions about the beliefs and values that are held by the congregation and ways in which they shape action and mission.

1 Corinthians 15:1-11

Theological Perspective

are the called, both Jews and Greeks, Christ the power of God and the wisdom of God" (1:23–24). The crucifixion is, paradoxically, the triumph of conventional wisdom and, simultaneously, its most radical subversion. The one who healed the sick, fed the hungry, and befriended the outcast, the one who lived by love rather than the sword, got what he deserved from the arbiters of conventional wisdom. He was a threat to their system, so they executed him. And yet, according to Paul's gospel, after his death and burial, Christ was raised and "appeared to Cephas, then to the twelve" (15:5). Whatever else those appearances may have been, and however long the list of such appearances has become, they affirm God's wisdom and power contrary to that of the powers that be. Dietrich Bonhoeffer, Martin Luther King Jr., and Oscar Romero, like so many others who have been killed in their fight for the poor and disenfranchised, illustrate the same notion that "God's foolishness is wiser than human wisdom, and God's weakness is stronger than human strength"(1:25). The meaning and inspiration of their lives and, yes, their deaths live on in our minds and hearts. To say that they are "Christ figures" is to say that they challenge us to live the gospel we too have received.

The eschatological context in which Paul's gospel makes theological sense is as relevant to Christian churches today as it was to the church in Corinth. Whatever our particular apocalyptic scenario, we are confronted with the world as it is, torn asunder by human arrogance and greed, and the world as we hope it may become, one in which all its inhabitants can share the gift of life in love for one another. We live in a tension between conventional wisdom and the wisdom of God. Paul tells us that Christ's death and resurrection reveal the way to live in this tension. If we "hold firmly" to this gospel message, it is the way we are "being saved" (15:2), which is to say, most simply, the way we are living now in response to God's love revealed in Christ Jesus.

At the end of today's reading, Paul himself becomes an example of living out the gospel message. After acknowledging that he has become an apostle by God's grace, he writes "I worked harder than all of them—though it was not I, but the grace of God that is with me" (v. 10). He concludes, "so we proclaim, and so you have come to believe" (v. 11). Have we?

JERRY IRISH

Pastoral Perspective

understand that it was all grace; it was God's work in and through him. What mattered was not personal acclamation, but that Christ was proclaimed through him. Paul expressed a profound moment of self-understanding when he said, "By the grace of God I am what I am" (v. 10).

It can be an intimidating experience for Christians to hold their religious experiences up to the light of Paul's encounter with the risen Lord on the road to Damascus. Paul knew that his experience was unique; he did not intend for his experience to be normative. Christians come to faith in different ways. A pastoral task is to present Paul's experience in a way that does not shut off conversation or end personal reflection about one's own experiences of grace. Perhaps the preacher can use the very uniqueness of Paul's experiences to affirm the uniqueness of each person's spiritual journey. Just as Paul did not hide his past, stifle his personality, or suppress his anxieties, so Christians today can recognize that they are who they are by the grace of God. Each person's struggles, pains, joys, accomplishments, and dreams are stories of the gospel that can light the way for others. Tom Long writes:

> Christians are on the witness stand to tell that story, not because it is a likely story or an advantageous piece of testimony, but because it is true. We know it is true because we ourselves have experienced it and witnessed its truth. That is why we are on the witness stand and have taken the oath to tell the truth "so help us God."[1]

Whenever Christ turns a life around, heals a marriage, transforms a bitter heart, forgives a sinner, teaches a fearful person to love, or shows a greedy person how to give, there is a witness ready to take the stand to tell the good news of God's grace.

LEWIS F. GALLOWAY

---

1. Thomas G. Long, *Testimony: Talking Ourselves into Being Christian* (San Francisco: Jossey-Bass, 2004), 29.

Exegetical Perspective

he accepted and carried out the mission that was given to him by God's grace.

Theological Emphasis. Those who look for proofs that the resurrection occurred risk becoming like the "debaters of this age" who expect to know God "through wisdom" (1:18–25). They will be disappointed. Paul's eyewitnesses are not an adequate proof for modern believers. Nor should we twist the repeated phrase "according to the scriptures" (vv. 3b–4) into a "proof." This is no facile proof based on prediction and fulfillment. Rather, it is a claim that the messiahship of Jesus, as God's fullest and most definitive self-revelation, is consistent with the grand sweep of God's previous self-disclosures as attested in Scriptures about God's mighty acts in history, about the worship of Israel, and about the theological critiques of historical events by the prophets of old.

We could easily compile a list of texts that Paul and other NT writers interpret christologically, but it would be fruitful to focus on passages quoted or alluded to in chapter 15:

"As in Adam all die" (15:22< Gen. 3).
"He has put all things in subjection under his feet" (15:25, 27 < Ps. 8:6).
"Let us eat and drink, for tomorrow we die" (15:32 < Isa. 22:13).
"The first man, Adam, became a living soul" (15:45 < Gen. 2:7).
"Death is swallowed up on victory" (15:54 < Isa. 25:8).
"O Death, where is your victory? . . . where is your sting?" (15:55 < Hos. 13:14).

All of these verses, read in their contexts, can shed light on how God relates to the world and by analogy on how God has acted in the cross and resurrection of Christ.

There is one other possible allusion in our specific passage. Paul says he was "like *the* stillborn infant" (v. 8), which suggests that he had some story in mind about some specific stillbirth. He may be alluding here to Numbers 12:12, in which Miriam is stricken with leprosy after she and Aaron challenge Moses's authority.[1] Aaron compares her with a stillborn infant. Miriam's plight would resonate with Paul's awareness of his own rebelliousness against God, and a sermon that correlated the two passages might shed light on Paul's self-presentation.

CHRISTOPHER R. HUTSON

Homiletical Perspective

The Continuing Story. Paul's discussion of the appearances of Jesus offers an opportunity to begin a conversation on the ways in which we encounter the risen Lord in our lives. The story of the appearances had been passed on to Paul—Cephas, the Twelve, the five hundred, James, all the apostles. This is the story Paul received, but before passing it on to others he added to it: "Last of all, as to one untimely born, he appeared also to me" (v. 8). With these words Paul invites all of us to consider the ways in which we are a continuation of the gospel story, the ways in which the risen Christ has appeared to us and transformed our living. It might be possible to continue the story by including others in the faith, in the denomination, or in the congregation whose lives were clearly shaped by an experience of the risen Lord. With this as background the sermon could then raise the question of how listeners place themselves in the story: How has Jesus appeared to you? In what way has that appearance transformed you? In what way has it shaped the way you live? Inviting several members of the congregation to reflect on these questions could enhance the power of this sermon and relate the passage even more directly to the lives of listeners.

A Story to Share with Others. It is not enough, however, simply to place ourselves in the story, as important as that may be. This is a story to share, as Paul shared it with the Corinthians. There is something about our own experience of Christ that leads us to share with others. Tom Bandy, who speaks and writes about congregational transformation, regularly reminds his listeners that the key question for church members to consider is "What is there about my experience of Jesus Christ that this community cannot live without?" How can your experience provide insight for the way in which others might experience the good news? How can the difference Christ has made in your life be made a real and compelling story for others that touches their own deepest needs? The story Paul shared with the Corinthians did that. Our own stories of life and faith should do the same.

JEFFREY D. JONES

---

1. N. T. Wright, *The Resurrection of the Son of God* (Minneapolis: Fortress Press, 2003), 328–29.

Luke 5:1-11

¹Once while Jesus was standing beside the lake of Gennesaret, and the crowd was pressing in on him to hear the word of God, ²he saw two boats there at the shore of the lake; the fishermen had gone out of them and were washing their nets. ³He got into one of the boats, the one belonging to Simon, and asked him to put out a little way from the shore. Then he sat down and taught the crowds from the boat. ⁴When he had finished speaking, he said to Simon, "Put out into the deep water and let down your nets for a catch." ⁵Simon answered, "Master, we have worked all night long but have caught nothing. Yet if you say so, I will let down the nets." ⁶When they had done this, they caught so many fish that their nets were beginning to break. ⁷So they signaled their partners in the other boat to come and help them. And they came and filled both boats, so that they began to sink. ⁸But when Simon Peter saw it, he fell down at Jesus' knees, saying, "Go away from me, Lord, for I am a sinful man!" ⁹For he and all who were with him were amazed at the catch of fish that they had taken; ¹⁰and so also were James and John, sons of Zebedee, who were partners with Simon. Then Jesus said to Simon, "Do not be afraid; from now on you will be catching people." ¹¹When they had brought their boats to shore, they left everything and followed him.

Theological Perspective

The life-altering power of God's word—spoken, heard, and heeded—is dynamically evident in this story of call. The church has claimed from the beginning that the word spoken in the beginning, the word that became incarnate in the fullness of time, is the consistency and constancy of God at work in the world. "God said" and there was light and all creation. "God spoke" and Moses led the people of Israel out of bondage. "The word of the Lord" came to the prophets and prompted them to call the people back. "A voice from heaven" proclaimed the Beloved Son on whom God's favor rests.

Prior to Jesus' call to Simon, James, and John as their fish-laden boats groaned toward land, the allure and appeal of Jesus' expression of the word of God brought the people to the lakeshore. His reputation had spread rapidly, widely. His recent healing of the possessed man in Capernaum amazed the people and drove them to ask "what is there in this man's words?" (4:36, my trans.). And so they "pressed in on him to hear" and thereby moved him to the sanctuary of Simon's boat. Even there, from the emptiness of the boat, he continued to teach—he continued to draw the people to listen to his compelling word.

What set Jesus' words apart? In Capernaum he had "astounded" the people "because he spoke with

Pastoral Perspective

This passage introduces us to Luke's account of the call of the first disciple, Simon, and needs to be explored on its own merit and with its own integrity. In this account, Jesus encounters fishermen who had an unfruitful night on their fishing expedition and who are now cleaning their nets before putting them away. Into this context, where men and women come face to face with their limits and give up, Jesus enters and asks the men to push one of the boats away from the beach.

Jesus initiates the relationship by asking a small favor of them, putting himself as it were into their debt. This encounter has overtones of Jesus' encounter with the woman at the well of whom he asks a drink of water (John 4). A seemingly insignificant encounter between two persons opens up possibilities certainly not envisaged at the time by Peter. It all begins with a risk on Jesus' part as Peter could reject his initiative. For the preacher, reflection on this account of Jesus' encounter with Simon could lead to a consideration of the way in which God in Christ takes the initiative and the risk as he beckons us into a relationship with himself. As for Simon, a positive response brings with it a challenge to be a part of this movement of God in reaching out to others. Like Peter's call to fish for persons, the outcomes are unpredictable when people risk encountering each other across cultures, groups,

Exegetical Perspective

At first glance Luke 5:1–11 is difficult to classify. It is generally considered a call narrative, similar in some respects to the stories of Moses (Exod. 3), Gideon (Judg. 6), and Isaiah (Isa. 6). In the parallel accounts in Matthew and Mark, Jesus says quite explicitly, "Come, follow me" (cf. Matt. 4:18–22; Mark 1:16–20). Yet Luke is much more subtle, using the terse phrase "they left everything and followed him" (v. 11). This passage is also considered a miracle story, given the abundant outcome manifested at verse 6: "they caught so many fish that their nets were beginning to break." And because of its similarities to another fishing story associated with the appearance of Jesus along the Sea of Galilee described in John 21:1–14, it is also considered a resurrection narrative. These options offer viable entry points for interpreting this text, yet the theme of discipleship provides a theological anchor for this story about the fishermen and their experience with Jesus.

Discipleship, which is central for those would-be followers of Jesus, is best understood as the act of teaching and learning, leading and following. It is a two-way process that involves an invitation *and* a response. In several places throughout the Gospel, Luke discusses the characteristics and costs of discipleship (9:23–27; 9:57–62; 14:25–33; 18:22–30), best summarized through these direct words of

Homiletical Perspective

In his excellent book *The Meaning in the Miracles*,[1] priest and New Testament scholar Jeffrey John reminds us that the miracle stories in the Gospels are about more than an astonishing event. Miracle stories say something about Jesus' mission and, more often than not, concern people who are outside the accepted social and religious structures.

Clearly this story and the story of the miraculous catch of fish at the end of John's Gospel (21:3–11) are related. In Luke, the miracle brings Peter to his knees in repentance (a favorite Lukan theme); however, Peter's response, not the miracle itself, is the crux of the matter. The preacher can say much about our response of repentance in the face of God's presence in our lives, especially in a time when many believe miracles are a reward for religious behavior and in a church where many have forgotten the spiritual practice of repentance. Nor should we forget that those who heard this account of the call of Peter and his confession of sinfulness at the Gospel's beginning would immediately recall Peter's dramatic denial of Jesus at its end (22:54–62).

More than a "nature miracle," the catch of fish is also layered with eucharistic allusions. Fish mean

---

1. Jeffrey John, *The Meaning in the Miracles* (Norwich: Canterbury Press, 2001).

Luke 5:1-11

Theological Perspective

authority" (4:32 NRSV). From town to town and in the synagogues of Judea the people were given hope because Jesus proclaimed the "good news of the kingdom of God" (4:43–44). The reports of the demonstrable healing power of the word that cured Simon's mother-in-law and many others compelled the crowd to the water's edge to hear, to listen.

God's word lived among them. In this account of crowd and call, in this summoning of Simon, God moves again, as God had moved previously among and with the people of Israel, toward new and boundless horizons. Here God beckons; here God's anointed reveals and lives and makes real God's word for the people to hear and see and experience. The word has come to dwell in the midst of everyday lives and everyday fishermen. The word begins to move *horizontally*—outward and outbound from Jesus. It falls on the ears of crowds hungry for that word; it falls on the ears of Simon and James and John, afraid, amazed, attracted, and ready. Not knowing what lay ahead on that open and uncharted journey from their familiar fishing boats, "they left everything and followed him," unbound, outward-bound, horizon-bound, captured by a word that they would, in turn, carry "on the ground" among people waiting for it, listening for it.

God's living word cuts through the din of pressing crowds and the lives and labors of common people. It shapes the sweep of the human story. It alters the lives of those who hear and heed.

God's living word cuts through daily life with the gift of freedom—the radical, radicalizing freedom that enables one to leave everything, to follow to the fullest.

God's living word draws people in. It calls and pulls and then pushes people out—Simon and James and John, who could scarcely believe their net-bulging catch from deep, empty waters. They were amazed and yet afraid. The word came to them, captured them. They left boats and nets. They left the old way and followed.

Heard and seen and heeded, God's living word demands our decision—it lays upon us the choice of staying on the boat or leaving everything and following, of moving through that transformative moment to the fullness of life, when ears and eyes and hearts are truly opened and we cannot turn back. For followers of the living word, life is never and can never be the same. It is altered forever.

Hearing the living word is not enough—*acting upon it* is its inherent, paradoxical invitation *and* demand (6:46–49). Jesus was clear about those who

Pastoral Perspective

and traditions, thereby moving beyond the stereotypes they have embraced. This passage could also lead to an exploration of the power of seemingly gentle ways to engage and transform human lives. Additionally, one may also consider the implications for evangelism, especially so in the light of those who believe that the way to go about the engagement of persons is with a tract in hand and a Bible-thumping, overbearing approach.

At the end of his engagement of the crowd, Jesus invites Simon to put out into the deep and once more cast those nets that he had just finished cleaning. Perhaps there is a look of incredulity coming from Simon on hearing Jesus' words. Simon protests, saying, "Master, we toiled all night and took nothing!" (v. 5 RSV). Yet there is something about this man Jesus that compels Simon to stop washing his net and let Jesus have the use of one of the boats. How strange this must have felt to a rough and tough fisherman!

The invitation to put out into the deep for a catch provides a sharp contrast to our human penchant for the predictable and the routine. It is an invitation to venture into new ground or new depths, but it also points to new challenges in mission and ministry for the church in every generation. We are challenged to respond to the urgings of God breaking into human lives. In the case of Simon, as for the Christian faced with such a command, there is the realization that the most profound and significant experiences of God and life are not to be found in the safe ways and places. Simon obeys the instruction and is surprised by a catch so huge that assistance had to be sought to rein it in!

Here the nature of religious experience and the interpretation of these experiences may be a theme for the preacher to explore. It is clear to Simon that something out of the ordinary has happened. He knows that he is standing in the presence of someone who mediates the immediacy of the divine presence. This profound religious experience has put his life under a new spotlight and set in motion a path toward transformation. Simon becomes aware of his unworthiness and diminutive stature in the presence of the Divine; so he underscores his sinfulness and asks that Jesus depart from him, "Depart from me, for I am a sinful man, O Lord" (v. 8 RSV). Rather than writing him off, Jesus now reveals to him the potential that resides in him through a participation in the work of God, "Do not be afraid; from now on you will be catching people" (v. 10 NRSV).

Exegetical Perspective

Jesus: "If any want to become my followers, let them deny themselves and take up their cross daily and follow me" (9:23). Yet Jesus is not always so direct in his teachings about discipleship, as this text in Luke demonstrates. Moreover, discipleship calls for obedience to and recognition of a divine power and source of authority beyond human strength, knowledge, and will. The encounter between Jesus and Simon indicates that discipleship is risky business with great rewards.

The Sea of Galilee (Lake of Gennesaret) was a busy hub for local fishermen. After a long night on the water with nothing to show for it, the fishers were ready to clean their nets and to return to their respective homes. Luke uses this ordinary circumstance to situate Jesus not as a teacher in the traditional setting of the synagogue (e.g., 4:15), but rather as one who taught the crowds in the metaphoric setting of Simon's boat (v. 3). It was not unusual for Jesus to teach from a boat as a way of gaining some distance from the large crowds who were following him (e.g., Matt. 13:1–2; Mark 4:1), yet the boat of Simon, who would become one of Jesus' closest disciples, is particularly instructive in this narrative.

Jesus asks Simon to go a short distance from the shore for his first round of teaching. Luke does not provide the content of the teaching in this brief verse; instead, the reader is to focus on what happens *after* the instruction when Simon is summoned to "put out into the deep water and let down your nets for a catch" (v. 4). These are clearly hard words for Simon to hear after an unproductive night of fishing. He offers a brief retort, reminding Jesus of the obvious: "Master, we have worked all night long but have caught nothing" (v. 5; cf. 8:24, 45; 9:33, 49; 17:13 for other references to "Master"). Yet Simon submits to the request as an act of obedience and a humble acknowledgment of the one who is clearly no ordinary man in this circumstance.

This tangible sign of obedience leads to miraculous results—an abundance of fish that cannot be contained in their nets and boats. Indeed, the results are so overwhelming that it nearly causes a mishap in the midst of the water, which leads Simon and his fishing partners James and John to call for help (vv. 7, 10). In this great sea of overwhelming abundance Simon—now referred to as Simon Peter—is able to recognize the presence and power of God (v. 8). This recognition leads to Peter's bold acknowledgment: "Go away from me, Lord, for I am a sinful man!" (v. 8). He and all those who witnessed this miraculous event are astonished and amazed by the catch

Homiletical Perspective

food, and wherever we read about fish in the Gospels, we are reading about the miracle of sustenance for the new community that Jesus is creating in the call of the first disciples. Therefore the call of the disciples in the wake of this eucharistic miracle is another fruitful avenue of exploration. Disciples are not simply called in the midst of and away from their "ordinary" work. Faithful discipleship makes ordinary work itself the vehicle of Jesus' real presence in the life of the world.

In the third place, the preacher might tease out one of the many key phrases in this passage. The NRSV rendering "catching people" masks a dynamism in the Greek that is lost in translation. Jesus is saying to Peter that he will be "taking" or "saving men and women *alive*" for the kingdom. "To take men and women alive" is a very different image from simply catching them as though they are food to be consumed. As John Drury reminds us, the verb is "used in the Septuagint to denote rescue from peril of death, not the capture of animals—and so [it is] as inappropriate to fishing as it is appropriate to the Christian mission which it initiates."[2] The kingdom requires not dead fish, but human beings fully alive—not creatures writhing in the last gasps before death, but people living the life of the good news in all its fullness.

This is still a tricky subject, and it is the able preacher who can plot a course between the force of the language and the appropriate desire to avoid any notions that evangelism might involve some sort of entrapment. To make disciples is a legitimate (indeed *necessary*) business. But *how*? How do we nourish without force-feeding? How do we rescue persons from the peril of death, and then allow them to live in liberty? That is the hard part.

Before there is talk of "taking men and women alive" for the kingdom in Luke, there is an advance warning for would-be disciples about the perils of following Jesus (see 4:14–30). There is talk about him, gossip about who he might be. Simon, James, and John do not encounter Jesus cold, as the apostles do (apparently) in Matthew and Mark, and perhaps also in John. In Luke they know about him; Simon has even met him.

Here may be a way to speak about both discipleship and evangelism that can have some

2. John Drury, *Tradition and Design in Luke's Gospel* (London: Darton, Longman & Todd, 1976), 67. The understanding of the force of "catching men (and women) alive" is found in some older commentaries, e.g., Clarke's Commentary, vol. 5 (reprinted by Abingdon Press); see also among modern commentaries I. H. Marshall, *The Gospel of Luke* (Grand Rapids: Paternoster Press, 1978), 205f.

Luke 5:1-11

Theological Perspective

heard but did not act: the word of God is not to be taken lightly. Hearing and acting upon the living word is not simply about "catching others," as etched in childhood song. Call has consequences. Following has price.

The pressing crowds dissipated, and Jesus and his first three followers began their journey from the lakeshore to the cities and countryside and cross. As that journey unfolded, it slowly became clearer to Simon, James, and John that the living word with whom they walked was indeed the living Child of the God who had created the world they traversed and the peoples they encountered. This was the God who came to Abraham and Sarah, to Moses and Esther, to the prophets and the people of Israel. And this was the God who had now become flesh and was leading them away from their boats.

God's word is like that—in the past, the present, the future. We live in a cacophonous time, when it is difficult to hear the word, or to see it made manifest in movement or miracle. The crowds do not always press eagerly in to hear and then act. Lives, nations, and cultures seem empty. The workers are not always ready to leave everything and follow Jesus to the ends of the earth, or even into the neighborhood. We who proclaim the word do not always believe fully in its power. We ourselves are not free of clogged ears or closed hearts, and may not be ready to heed fully the living word's radical, radicalizing call to freedom—a call that compels us to turn away from accommodation to all the worldly ways that lure and enwrap us.

And yet God remains faithful. God declares God's word. To the crowd by the Lake of Gennesaret. To Simon and James and John. To generations before them, to us. From the creation to the people wandering in the wilderness to Jesus to now. Calling, pulling, pushing us outward toward new and boundless horizons. Freeing us from our nets.

DAVID L. OSTENDORF

Pastoral Perspective

Perhaps the preacher may want to focus on the real manifestation of the profundity of the experience for Simon, which is evidenced in the change that it brings to his life. Having hauled in this huge catch of fish, having been given the opportunity to make a good return, thus reversing the earlier fruitless expedition, Simon now does the strangest thing. He pulls ashore his boat, with the catch, and walks away from it, livelihood and all. Many persons may identify with this change of vocation and values, especially those who in midlife find it necessary to make vocational changes. Some do so because of redundancies at the workplace and in an effort to make themselves more marketable, but others sense the pull of a higher calling. Indeed this is the source of many religious vocations across denominational lines.

This change of life course is not restricted to Simon. The members of his party also join Simon on the mission. Yet Simon is mentioned as the leading actor throughout. Only at the end do the others figure in the picture. This detail no doubt signifies that Simon is the one around whom things revolve. He uses his ability and influence as a leader to good effect. This offers a useful springboard from which the preacher may choose to explore the nature of leadership in the various areas of life, including the church.

While one may see in this passage the call to discipleship that came to those designated apostles, nevertheless, obedience and commitment are the appropriate response to Jesus' call to discipleship for all who would respond. It is clear that there is a cost to discipleship, with its claim upon the life of those who would respond. It involves putting God in Christ at the center of one's life, even if this involves a change of vocation. One does this, not because one is being forced to do so, but because like Simon one has experienced the grace of God in a moment of revelation and can do no other.

HOWARD K. GREGORY

of fish and realize that it is more than a stroke of luck. At this point Jesus speaks again with words of assurance: "Fear not, for from now on you will become catchers of people" (v. 10, my trans.). The big catch of fish symbolizes the multitude of people whom the disciples will eventually catch through the teachings of Jesus. Thus, instead of a direct "call" to Peter and the other fishermen in the boats, the presence of the Divine provides an abundant "invitation" to discipleship.

The two-way encounter of teaching and learning, leading and following, is obvious. Simon is obedient in his response to Jesus because of the authority of this teacher. He does not necessarily understand all of the details of the encounter, yet he is willing to trust and follow Jesus in this situation and learn more about his power and authority. As a true follower and learner (*mathētēs*), Simon Peter responds with great faithfulness and receives a great commission.

Central to this lection is the theme of recognition and astonishment that is revealed when Simon refers to Jesus as "Lord" and acknowledges his sinfulness. This amazement affected not only Simon Peter but also his fishing partners, James and John, and all who were with them. The lection ends with the theme of renunciation, indicated by the terse statement, "they left everything and followed him" (v. 11). This is the heart of discipleship. For Luke, it includes the denial of family, friends, and physical possessions (5:28; 9:57–62; 14:33; 18:22–23). Not only are the disciples to leave the big catch of fish they have just hauled in; they are also to renounce and leave everything else, to embark upon an incomprehensible mission. With the presence of God and the willingness to trust wherever this "Master" and "Lord" who orchestrated the great catch may lead, Simon Peter and the other disciples are ready to embark upon the journey. This abundant invitation to discipleship requires an obedient and repentant heart, a persistent and fearless response, and a willingness to renounce everything to follow Jesus.

GAY L. BYRON

traction for twenty-first-century listeners. It is no real secret in our day who Jesus is. If by comparison with the Jesus of Scripture and the rich tradition of the church, popular knowledge of Jesus even among regular worshipers may be poor or inadequate, Jesus is unlikely to be a complete stranger. So how can the preacher and the community of the body of Christ make Jesus real for others and for ourselves in ways that are both true and genuinely compelling? How can the preacher take the insufficient rumors of Jesus that are already out there, use them, and build on them?

Eduard Schweizer tells us that faith "does not come as assent to statements previously preached, but as trust in Jesus' call to try once more, contrary to all dictates of reason." More recently, Rowan Williams said the same thing in rather a different way: to say that we believe in Jesus is the equivalent of saying that we have confidence in Jesus above all things; Jesus is where we belong, the one to whom we belong.[3] To know ourselves as those who belong to Jesus before we belong to anyone or anything else is the beginning of a right understanding of discipleship.

There is one final, incontrovertible truth that this passage drives home. So often the cost of discipleship does not come off the top; it is demanded of us after we have given everything that we can give. Jesus did not show up after a good night's sleep and a hearty breakfast. He came to find these men at the end of a long working day, after backbreaking labor, and he told them to keep on working. He does the same to the preacher of this passage, and to all of us.

PETER EATON

---

3. See Eduard Schweizer, *The Good News according to Luke* (London: SPCK, 1984), 106, and Rowan Williams, *Tokens of Trust: An Introduction to Christian Belief* (Louisville, KY: Westminster John Knox Press, 2007), esp. chap. 1.

Jeremiah 17:5-10

⁵Thus says the LORD:
  Cursed are those who trust in mere mortals
    and make mere flesh their strength,
    whose hearts turn away from the LORD.
⁶They shall be like a shrub in the desert,
    and shall not see when relief comes.
  They shall live in the parched places of the wilderness,
    in an uninhabited salt land.

⁷Blessed are those who trust in the LORD,
    whose trust is the LORD.
⁸They shall be like a tree planted by water,
    sending out its roots by the stream.

Theological Perspective

This psalm-like utterance attributed to the prophet Jeremiah highlights what we might call two "foundations of piety." The first is that blessedness consists of radical trust in and dependence upon God. The second is that the true locus of piety—and of its opposite, sin—is the heart.

In verses 5–8, the prophet declares that trust in God distinguishes those who are truly pious (and thus truly happy) from those who are not. This theme of radical trust in God, over and above dependence on human means of achievement or security, is deeply rooted in Christian theology. A radical trust in God lay at the heart of the conversion of Augustine and the same trust prompted an epiphany for Martin Luther that sparked the Protestant Reformation. Reformer John Calvin agreed that true knowledge of God ultimately consisted of trust in and reverence for God as "the fountain of every good."[1] And the medieval theologian Thomas Aquinas wrote that "it is evident that nothing can bring the will of man [*sic*] to rest except the universal good. This is not found in any created thing but only in God. . . . Therefore man's [*sic*] happiness consists in God alone."[2] Trust in divine

Pastoral Perspective

Jeremiah stood in the midst of a time of transition. His career as a prophet began in the shadow of the Jewish temple in Jerusalem. It ended in a time of exile. Having lost his home along with others when the holy city was conquered and destroyed by the Babylonians, he was finally forced to flee to Egypt, likely against his will, by those who had remained to the end in Jerusalem. Jeremiah had seen it all coming and counseled the people to surrender or be destroyed. Now in these verses he preached a different and equally troubling message: exile was to be the new normal. How would the people of God respond? As if they lived in a desert? Or would they be planted in this strange world like trees rooted next to flowing river? Only one response would indicate faithfulness and trust.

In times of great change and transition, though, it is not always easy to remain faithful. Jeremiah spoke about those whose hearts would turn away from the Lord. His metaphor for the unfaithful was that they would be like a shrub in the desert, constantly searching for water that could not ever be found. You have to wonder if we are not in the same bind, though our problem instead may be the flood of things we own and the abundance of choices we face in daily living.

Even though we live with seeming prosperity, we also live in a world that does not always feel right. It

---

1. John Calvin, *Institutes of the Christian Religion* (Philadelphia: Westminster Press, 1960), 1.2.1.
2. Thomas Aquinas, *Treatise on Happiness*, trans. John A. Oesterle (Notre Dame, IN: University of Notre Dame Press, 1964), 26 (Q2, A8).

It shall not fear when heat comes,
    and its leaves shall stay green;
in the year of drought it is not anxious,
    and it does not cease to bear fruit.

⁹The heart is devious above all else;
    it is perverse—
    who can understand it?
¹⁰I the LORD test the mind
    and search the heart,
to give to all according to their ways,
    according to the fruit of their doings.

Exegetical Perspective

This text from Jeremiah is included among the readings for this day because it is parallel in form and, to some extent, in content to the blessings and woes in the Gospel lesson. Reading Jeremiah 17:5–10 in this context reveals the roots of these blessings and woes in Old Testament wisdom sayings as found in Proverbs and Ecclesiastes and scattered throughout other books. These roots apply to the Beatitudes (Matt. 5:3–12) as well, although they have only blessings without the woes.

The immediate context of our lesson is Jeremiah 17, a collection of quite different materials. It begins with a prose sermon (vv. 1–4) very similar in style and substance to the book of Deuteronomy. These verses would have been included in the developing book of Jeremiah by the same circles responsible for the final form of Deuteronomy and for the history of Israel found in Joshua through 2 Kings. Our reading is part of the second section of the chapter, verses 5–11, sayings in the style of proverbial wisdom. (It is unclear why v. 11, a comparative saying on the folly of amassing wealth unjustly, was not included in the lesson.) The next unit, verses 12–13, praises the temple in Jerusalem and pronounces curses upon those who forsake it, turning away from the Lord. The final section (vv. 14–18) is one of Jeremiah's many complaints, similar to the individual laments in the Psalter.

Homiletical Perspective

No preacher relishes the thought of expounding a text that begins with the Lord hurling a curse. Mind you, at times the preacher is frustrated, exasperated, or wounded by the people, and the temptation to vent in the voice of God's word is not easy to resist.

The particular curse Jeremiah voices is intriguing: "Cursed is the man who trusts in man," in the RSV, or as the more inclusive NRSV phrases it (transmuting the singular into a plural!), "Cursed are those who trust in mere mortals." How do we make sense of the idea that people should be anti-people? This feels like politicians saying, "I am anti-government." Don't trust people? It is people who then do not do the trusting.

All a man has is man; all a woman has is woman. And isn't the church always pressing us to use our abilities, to strive for holiness, to be generous stewards, to labor in God's vineyard?

Jeremiah seems bent on a subtle but crucial nuance in the way we think about life. Is it about me? Or is it about God? Do I find meaning in or outside myself? Charles Taylor has explained history's primal turn to the "secular age": "We have moved from a world in which the place of fullness was understood as unproblematically outside of or beyond human life, to a conflicted age in which this

Jeremiah 17:5-10

Theological Perspective

benevolence rather than human sources of power or fulfillment is equally important as we navigate Christian existence in our contemporary world. Military power, technological innovation, social status, and economic achievement all tempt us to see them as ultimate sources of security and personal meaning. By contrast, today's lesson suggests that reliance on these apparent sources of power and control renders us insufficiently rooted for the trials that confront us. Taken in the right context, these expressions of human accomplishment might serve as penultimate goods, but misplaced confidence in them will eventually prove to be shallow and unsatisfying, compared with the "blessedness" of keeping God the object of our ultimate loyalty and trust.

One problem for the preacher, however, is that the empirical evidence may not appear to validate the declarations of this text. The prophet insists that those who trust in human assertions of power will suffer in hard times, while those who trust in God possess the deep resources necessary to flourish, even in times of drought. In reality, however, we know that the self-indulgent often seem blessed by their narrow preoccupation. The politically or economically powerful routinely make out pretty well, while the pious frequently do not enjoy discernible reward—and in fact can be penalized—for the priority they place on God. The challenge of this text is to make it resonate with hearers who may be living faithful but still difficult lives, and to do so in a way that avoids platitudes. One strategy may be to point out the expansive understanding of "blessedness" and "curse" in this passage, that turns our attention away from the immediate and materialistic preoccupation of our culture and toward more ultimate notions of human happiness and fulfillment.

The last two verses of this passage deal with the human heart as the reservoir of sin and, by extension, piety. With a nod to what classical Calvinists called "total depravity," the prophet emphasizes that the roots of sin extend deeper than the simple commission of bad actions. Sin is a matter of the heart, and the human heart is often more "devious" and "perverse" than we are willing to fathom. Sin is a heartfelt turn from God, just as piety is an equally heartfelt turn to God. The importance of the heart to good religion is a prominent theme in the book of Jeremiah. See, for instance, the significant declaration of "a new covenant" that God promises to write "on their hearts" in Jeremiah 31:33.

This emphasis on the heart as the locus of sin and piety also was an important theme for the

Pastoral Perspective

is as though the threat of being an exile hangs over all our heads. The plight of exiles from war-torn parts of the world is daily news. The homeless are exiles in our own cities. The jobless are exiled from meaningful employment. To face a serious illness means being exiled from health. None of us is immune from some threat of exile. The only question for Jeremiah was, which path were the exiles to follow? Living as if life were a desert and therefore a desperate struggle? Or living as if rooted by a flowing river, even though we were being tested and tried?

Jeremiah knew about living with difficult choices. He painted word pictures of impending doom and gloom. No one would be excluded from dealing with difficult decisions. In that light he declared, "The heart is devious above all else" (v. 9). The root of the Hebrew word for "devious" is related to the name of Jacob. Therefore Jeremiah's story and all our stories are somehow connected to those ancient stories about Israel—the name Jacob was eventually given. In matters of the heart much is complicated and convoluted.

Jeremiah's prophecy concerns the hearts of all in Judah, and not just the hearts and minds of those holding political and religious power. While other prophets may have railed against the structures and systems that represented idolatry and faithlessness, Jeremiah saw the issues of his day in far more personal terms. The problem between God and the chosen people would not be resolved simply in palaces or by armies. On the contrary, the path to wholeness and to the restoration of a relationship with the holy would begin inside each person—deep down in the heart. Jeremiah said that it was the Lord who would "test the mind and search the heart" (v. 10).

How do we hear this prophetic call? Are we ready for God to test our minds and search our hearts? How do we hear this on the personal level and in terms of our faith? As good news or as a threat? It is easy for us to be deceived about ourselves. We each carry inside things that we wish were different. There are the unfinished parts of our selves. We are a work in progress, we say at times. That could mean that now is not the time for this test or for our heart to be searched.

Jeremiah proclaimed that God is constantly testing our minds and searching the hearts. No one is excluded from this examination. Even the prophet is tested. A few chapters later Jeremiah lamented his lot and then said, "O Lord of Hosts, you test the

Exegetical Perspective

The authorship and historical circumstances of Jeremiah 17:5–10 are uncertain and disputed. The chapter as a whole does not develop a consistent theme but includes diverse materials, some of which (vv. 14–18 in particular) correspond to Jeremiah's thought and language. The concern with the heart in vv. 9–10 is consistent with Jeremiah's concerns. In terms of form and style, these verses are unusual in the book of Jeremiah, which consists mainly of prophetic addresses in poetry, prose speeches, and narratives about the life and work of the prophet. Wisdom sayings typically are anonymous, polished by being passed from hand to hand, and validated because they correspond to human experience: Everyone knows that "Haste makes waste" and "A soft answer turns away wrath, but a harsh word stirs up anger" (Prov. 15:1). Such sayings appear in prophetic books, and scholars have linked some prophets to popular or folk wisdom, but such sayings are unusual in Jeremiah. However, there is nothing in these lines that is explicitly contrary to the prophet's views.

Our reading contains a set of wisdom sayings, verses 5–8 and 9–10, or a collection when verse 11 is considered. The first part begins with an introductory messenger formula, "Thus says the Lord," but what follows is neither prophetic address nor divine speech; rather, the Lord is spoken of in the third person. The messenger formula introduces a neatly balanced and concise wisdom speech, extended sayings giving the two sides of a coin. The first (vv. 5–6) points out that "those who trust in mere mortals," who turn away from the Lord, are cursed. It then compares them to a shrub in the desert, alone and without relief from drought. The second (vv. 7–8) gives the antithesis. Those who trust in the Lord are blessed, like a tree planted by the water. Remarkably both those who trust in mere mortals and those who trust in the Lord experience drought. The difference is that the latter thrive because they send out their roots toward the stream, and therefore develop green leaves and produce fruit. The parallels of this section to Psalm 1—both in form and contents—are strong and obvious. Most scholars argue that Psalm 1 is later than and dependent upon this passage, but both could just as well derive from a common wisdom tradition.

The second section (vv. 9–10) also contains two parts, the first a proverblike saying on the human heart as "devious" and incomprehensible, and the second a divine speech in which YHWH affirms that he knows the heart and gives to every one according to their ways. Divine speech in such a context is

Homiletical Perspective

construal is challenged by others who place it within human life."[1]

Jeremiah is thinking political strategy, and we need to do so as well. But there is a deeper principle at stake, one that affects everything that goes on, including the preparation and delivery of sermons. What is the sermon about? Sadly, not many sermons are actually about God. Instead, we speak of me and my faith, my spiritual seeking, my doing good for the poor, my mood of gratitude. Yes, God gets stitched onto the fabric somewhere, but perhaps in a merely decorative way. Jeremiah pronounces a curse on those who focus on the human, who trust in what we are able to do, who take their cues from personal desire.

While I cannot escape being myself, I have to trust myself to foil God's threatened curse against me for trusting myself, by harboring a hermeneutic of suspicion toward my thinking and toward the world constructed around us. Likewise, preachers must nag their church families constantly to be wary of themselves, wary of the conventional wisdom of the world, wary of what titillates but is hollow. Jeremiah claims that the human heart is "fickle" (v. 9, my trans.). The Hebrew original is *'aqobh*, reminding us of Jacob (*ya'aqobh*), the deceiver, who takes advantage of other people, who will stop at nothing to get what he is after.

This fickleness, this deceitful capacity of the human heart, feeds ominously into the most perilous phenomenon the preacher battles: BS. (We could spell out the full eight-letter word but there is no need!) BS has been analyzed wonderfully by the Princeton philosopher Harry Frankfurt. The BSer isn't a liar. To lie, you have to care enough about truth to know what is not true. The BSer simply says whatever he thinks you want to hear; the BSer will say anything to talk you into what he wants you to do.

Obviously in our culture BS is everywhere. People are accustomed to BS from politicians, advertisers, their boss, even friends and family. Not only do we produce much BS, we have BS filters in our ears; we tend to twist whatever we hear into whatever we want to hear.

Even in church, there is plenty of BS—preachers, authors, and experts who say precisely what people want to hear—but none of it is of God. Just because we talk a pious game and use religious jargon does not mean we are saying anything true or meaningful about the living God.

---

1. Charles Taylor, *A Secular Age* (Cambridge: Belknap, 2007), 15.

Jeremiah 17:5-10

Theological Perspective

eighteenth-century American evangelist and theologian Jonathan Edwards. Like the prophet, Edwards insisted that "true religion" was a matter of the heart. "If the great things of religion are rightly understood, they will affect the heart," Edwards wrote.[3] He believed that our true nature is determined by the ultimate loyalty of our heart, and that the "affection" of our heart—what constitutes our greatest love—determines how (and for what) we live. The emphasis in this Sunday's biblical text is on the negative, but the implications hold for the positive too. Both sin and piety root deeply and complexly in the fundamental allegiances of our hearts in ways that are often too subtle for us to understand, in ourselves or in others.

The last half of verse 10, however, suggests how the measure of the heart's affections might be taken. These verses draw a direct connection between the virtue or vice of the heart and its manifestation in acts and practices. The ultimate loyalties of persons correspond directly with "the fruit of their doings." For good or ill, our actions betray our fundamental allegiances. As Edwards put it,

> godliness in the heart has as direct a relation to practice, as a fountain has to a stream, or as the luminous nature of the sun has to beams sent forth, or as a life has to breathing, or the beating of the pulse, or any other vital act. . . . Christian practice or a holy life is a great and distinguishing sign of true and saving grace. (Edwards, *Treatise*, 165)

Against simplistic moralism that too easily excuses bad actions as anomalies of a good heart—that is, against excessive optimism in "good people who do bad things"—this passage suggests that our actions normally reflect our fundamental loyalties, loves, and dispositions accurately—perhaps more than we would like to admit.

JAMES CALVIN DAVIS

Pastoral Perspective

righteous, you see the heart and the mind" (20:12). Perhaps that verse lies behind the collect for purity that addresses God in this way, "to you all hearts are open, all desires known, and from you no secrets are hid," and then makes this petition: "cleanse thoughts of our hearts . . . that we may perfectly love you and worthily magnify your holy Name."[1]

At times we are all tempted, of course, even as Jeremiah must have been tempted—or tested, to use his language (17:10)—to invent a second self, a self that dreams of a life without worries and challenges. It was God's word that called Jeremiah back to the reality of his world. One way or another we all get called back to face the reality of our world and our need to be honest about ourselves. Jeremiah's vision meant accepting the challenges of change and maybe even of exile, with faith (trust) in the God who sees deep within our hearts. The God who would test the heart was not to be feared, but only to be trusted.

We must not forget that Jeremiah finally had a vision of a time when God would give the people a new covenant. This time God would not use stones that could be broken. If people in the time of Jeremiah thought their hearts were beyond saving, soon they would hear of God's grace given them in a new covenant that would be written on their hearts. At the Last Supper, Jesus recalled this vision of Jeremiah as he held the cup in his hands and said it was a sign of the new covenant. Jeremiah's vision lives in our common life and worship. Even those in exile can take bread and drink from a cup, and remember not only God's love in Christ Jesus, but the affirming message of Jeremiah, who said God searches our hearts. If God searches the heart, let us pray that by God's grace, God will choose to dwell there as well.

GEORGE H. MARTIN

---

3. Jonathan Edwards, *A Treatise concerning Religious Affections* (1746), in *A Jonathan Edwards Reader*, ed. John E. Smith, Harry S. Stout, and Kenneth P. Minkema (New Haven, CT: Yale University Press, 1995), 148.

1. *Book of Common Prayer* (New York: Seabury Press, 1979), 355.

Exegetical Perspective

unusual. It seems likely that verse 10 is a prophetic interpretation of and a sermon on a traditional saying. The point is clear: The human heart may be devious and almost impossible to understand, but the Lord tests it and gives to everyone according to their "ways," their actions.

A number of themes or issues present themselves for homiletical reflection:

1. As in other Old Testament prophetic and Wisdom literature from the time of Jeremiah onward, the focus is upon the inner life of the individual. God is concerned with the heart, the thoughts and beliefs of the person. However, the passage concludes by pointing out that the Lord looks also "to the fruit of their doings" (v. 10), to what emerges from that inner life.

2. Perhaps the key word in this text is "trust" (vv. 5, 7). This trust does not mean belief in propositions, but commitment, devotion. The verb must have an object, and that is the decisive point: to trust in what is human or to trust in God, that is the question. Trust in the Lord, even when the rain does not come. Trust in the Lord gives deep roots and will bear fruit.

3. Both sections of this reading (vv. 5–8 and 9–10) raise the question of divine retribution, as does the reading from Luke. *Does* God give to everyone according to what they have done? One who preaches on such texts is obligated in the first instance to let the text have its say. Here that would include reflection on the context of the verses, which suggests that those who trust in what is human and those who trust in God have their reward. To do the one is to live an arid life; to do the other is to live the abundant life. Having examined the perspective of the text, one might reflect on the extent to which the viewpoint corresponds to experience and to the rest of the biblical canon. Experience confirms that in many but not all instances, actions have predictable consequences. In the canon as a whole, divine retribution is not the only or the last word.

GENE M. TUCKER

Homiletical Perspective

The alternative to the deceitful heart is a tree. To biblical people desperate for water, the tree was symbolic of life that could withstand drought and storms. We see trees, their trunk, branches, and leaves: but the secret to the life of a tree is not what we see, but what we cannot see: the roots, thirsty tentacles reaching deep into the earth where even a hard shovel cannot penetrate, finding hidden moisture. Life happens in a subterranean place, in the dark. The fruit of marvelous processes that operate in dark, hidden recesses comes to light, and we find shade, beams to build a house, fruit to refresh our bodies, nests for birds, the dazzling array of color as the seasons come and go.

A sermon on the tree happily runs the risk of psychologizing or allegorizing, because Jeremiah hardly wanted us to think of him as an arborist. Trees can teach us about life with God. The tree is no independent force; the tree does not decide, "I'll go be a tree in that other field for a few weeks"; the tree is not in a big rush to flit off with sparrows or people, wherever they might be going. No, "a tree gives glory to God by being a tree."[2]

Although a modern-day historical critic would issue a stern reprimand if you plunge further, Christendom's greatest preachers—Chrysostom, Luther, Spurgeon—provide good company. The tree is the image of humanity gone awry, for it was a tree's fruit that tripped up Adam and Eve. But the tree is also the fulcrum of our salvation, of our rescue from the curse. Jesus bore the curse of crucifixion on a tree so we could be grafted onto the tree of God's people, so we might eat from the tree in paradise forever, when there will be no more BS and no more wars, the secular will be a dim memory, and everything will always be about the glory of God. Such is the hope the preacher dangles before the congregation, offering them the very heart of God, trusting its allure over what people can find in their own hearts.

JAMES C. HOWELL

---

2. Thomas Merton, *New Seeds of Contemplation* (New York: New Directions, 1961), 29.

Psalm 1

¹Happy are those
  who do not follow the advice of the wicked,
 or take the path that sinners tread,
  or sit in the seat of scoffers;
²but their delight is in the law of the LORD,
  and on his law they meditate day and night.
³They are like trees
  planted by streams of water,
 which yield their fruit in its season,
  and their leaves do not wither.
 In all that they do, they prosper.

⁴The wicked are not so,
  but are like chaff that the wind drives away.
⁵Therefore the wicked will not stand in the judgment,
  nor sinners in the congregation of the righteous;
⁶for the LORD watches over the way of the righteous,
  but the way of the wicked will perish.

Theological Perspective

A cursory glance at Psalm 1 leads one to conclude that life has two clear choices with distinct outcomes. Those who choose good will be rewarded—and happy!—while the bad will be miserable; but human experience does not correspond to this oversimplification. Many of the so-called bad people appear to have a pleasant and prosperous existence, while those who seek to live a decent life face nothing but struggles. There is no easy way to rectify this inconsistency except a deeper investigation into whether the meaning of this psalm is indeed so straightforward.

The key to understanding Psalm 1 comes from the very first word, "happy." Happy are those who do not follow the way of the wicked, the psalmist instructs. Happiness in a post-Enlightenment, consumer-driven world consists of an abundance of material goods, instant access to cyberspace, and the entire catalog of our favorite movies a click away. It is highly unlikely that this is the type of happiness the psalmist had in mind. The most fundamental definition of happiness in the psalmist's day would have been being in the presence of God.

The second aspect of happiness would be the ability to study the Holy Scriptures. Because the struggle for daily survival was the predominant factor in most people's lives, it was luxury to have time to meditate on the Torah. The image of Tevye's

Pastoral Perspective

Those of us who open the Psalter anticipating the rich tradition of liturgical hymns and prayers that have graced worship in the church since ancient Hebrew times are in for a surprise when we start with Psalm 1. What is an instruction guide on law and lifestyle doing at the beginning of a worship book? It is like signing up for a liturgics course and finding yourself walking into an ethics or Christian education seminar. Yet from a pastoral perspective the preface provided by Psalm 1 is an important prerequisite for understanding, interpreting, responding to, and appropriating the whole of the Psalms and life in general. The Psalter is full of the highs and lows, hopes and fears, despairs and aspirations, agonies and joys of the people of faith. It is a roller-coaster ride through the "stuff of life."

If one were to move through it with blinders, focusing only on what is immediately present in a piecemeal fashion, it would be easy to get lost in the myopic moment. Our own current world situation lends itself to such a reading. We live in a time when we have access to more information than ever before—so much information that we cannot process it all. We are constantly bombarded by images of earthquakes, tsunamis, tornados, genocide, terrorism, domestic and community violence, disease, and death. These threats take their toll,

Exegetical Perspective

Psalm 1 is known as a torah psalm, which is a sub-division of the larger genre of wisdom psalms. Many believe that our text was placed at the beginning of the book of Psalms in order to guide the way one reads the whole book. This compelling argument suggests that just as the wise one who studies the teaching (torah) of God has a rich and full life, so too will the thoughtful reader of the Psalms. In particular, this theory depends on the notion that we are meant to read carefully and ruminate on the Psalms. Most intriguing about Psalm 1 is its place in an emergent tradition that saw in wisdom and torah the intimate presence of God. To reveal how this tradition evolved, it is best to detail how Psalm 1 relates to it.

In verses 1–2 the psalmist tells us that happiness comes not from following the fool but from taking delight in meditating on God's instruction (torah). In our psalm the term "torah" simply means instruction, but it is likely that those who compiled the book of Psalms understood it to be a reference, at least in part, to Torah, or the first five books of our Bible. Clearly, the history of interpretation of Psalm 1 came to understand precisely the same thing. Torah, in this the most restricted sense, occupied an inestimable place in Judaism. It was seen as God's perfect and precious gift to the

Homiletical Perspective

As the preacher approaches this wisdom psalm, it is important to keep two perspectives in mind. First, this psalm serves to introduce readers to the Psalms as a whole. In other words, Psalm 1 is an interpretive rubric for the chapters that follow. It has been suggested that the structure of Psalm 1 provides a table of contents, so to speak, for the entire 150 psalms.[1] Second, the psalm is not simply an exegetical key to the rest of the Psalms, for it is a psalm in its own right and therefore has a message, a word from God, for the church today. This psalm affords the preacher a wonderful opportunity to teach interpretative skills. The sentence "Happy are those [whose] . . . delight is in the law of the Lord" is a metatheme for all the psalms.

Most preachers and parishioners will certainly be tripped up over the use of "law" (torah) in this passage. Does not Paul tell us that we are "justified by faith" apart from the law (Rom. 3:28; Gal. 2:16)? Therefore, to soften the blow many preachers will be tempted to interpret torah not as "law" in the legal sense, but as "instruction" in the didactic sense. Exercise caution here. Jesus reassures us that he did not come to abolish the law, at least not until heaven

1. J. Clinton McCann Jr., *A Theological Introduction to the Book of Psalms* (Nashville: Abingdon Press, 1993), 27.

Psalm 1

Theological Perspective

song in *Fiddler on the Roof* comes to mind: "If I were rich I'd have the time that I lack to sit in the synagogue and pray. . . . And I'd discuss the holy books with the learned men, several hours every day, and that would be the sweetest thing of all."[1]

The third and crowning element to happiness is to apply what one has learned by living a life in obedience to God. With this third step toward happiness, one responds to God's loving presence by making oneself obedient to God's law, bringing oneself back to God's side.

Trying to convince twenty-first-century society that these three things are the basic building blocks of a happy life seems an irreconcilable anachronism. Yet the wisdom in the psalm resonates, because humans do seek happiness and ponder its illusiveness. Most people at some level acknowledge that having possessions does not constitute happiness—except perhaps those wicked people themselves, who revel in their ill-gotten gains. Many seek a more meaningful existence and do subject themselves to discipline in order to achieve it: a 12-step program, a strict diet, yoga classes, an attempt to read classic books, and so on. Meditating day and night on God's law rarely falls into contemporary categories of popular disciplines.

The Torah may not appear on many nightstands these days, but this psalm's imagery of the difference between a happy and an unhappy life can ring true to present-day ears. The first verse of the psalm explains that happy people will never walk, stand, or sit with the unhappy ones. Already one recognizes that the unhappy life consists of constant movement: walking here, standing there, sitting a moment, then jumping up and starting over again. In other words, the unhappy lack groundedness. Engaged in constant movement, nothing ever satisfies so they are always seeking the next thing, the new contact, or the greater high. In verse 4, the wicked are compared to the chaff of wheat blown about by the wind, too light and useless to be worth keeping and so allowed to drift away.

The happy ones, however, are the trees beside the river. What a stark difference between a minuscule piece of chaff and a magnificent tree. Deeply rooted in the earth, trees are the opposite of constant movement. They stand firm and tall, and never lack for water because of their far-reaching roots. They do not thirst for shallow pleasures of life, but are

1. Sheldon Harnick, "If I Were a Rich Man," *Fiddler on the Roof* (Los Angeles: Metro-Goldwyn-Mayer Studios, 1971).

Pastoral Perspective

shaking the foundations of our faith and assumptions about life. They appeal to and engender in us frenetic, self-centered coping behaviors. Psalm 1 prepares us for such an onslaught and provides an alternative response grounded and firmly rooted in God's law.

What emerges here and weaves its way throughout the Psalter is a lifestyle whereby reflecting on and adhering to God's law is more than a simple obedience to rules and regulations. It is a deep, continuous steeping of oneself in God's word, trusting in God's leading, seeking God's counsel, and learning to live, survive, and prosper by turning again and again to the source of life. To delight in this law is to experience the joy of lifetime learning. The Psalter is a how-to book for meaningful living in a world where threat and promise, joy and sadness, despair and hope dot the didactic landscape. "Law" as it is presented here foreshadows the Reformer's third use of the law—as guidance in living. It becomes a life coach for those who take refuge and seek to thrive in God's kingdom. Psalm 1 invites us to lean eagerly into each psalm that follows, reflecting on the way God instructs and guides.

The initial psalm is starkly clear. There are two pathways, and only one of them leads to life. Life throws a lot our way. Where we step and how we sift through, make sense of, and act on the vicissitudes of life are critical to our psychological, physical, and relational well-being. The obvious choice for the psalmist is the path that is informed and guided by meditation on God's law and leading. People on this journey not only survive but flourish! They are fortunate, happy, and blessed. The metaphor of the tree planted in rich nurturing soil near vital flowing waters is a vivid visual symbol of this. Such a tree, placed carefully by a skilled arborist, anchors its roots in life-giving nutrients. It grows strong, tall, and productive. Winds may blow its leaves and sway its branches, but it stands firm. In the same way, the righteous are characterized by a steady, grounded persistence and focus. This enables them to bear fruit even in the confusion of life—to walk, sit, and stand in good company with hope in a world of despair, embracing the mystery of life where others see only messiness. The alternative is much less desirable. It is the path of the "wicked." This whirlwind route is a frenetic roller-coaster ride. Travelers are like fragile chaff—grounded and rooted only within themselves and therefore not at all—subject to being blown hither, yon, and away.

Exegetical Perspective

Israelites and the source of their sustenance and survival. That the editors of the book of Psalms have placed our psalm first indicates that torah could apply to more than the first five books of the Bible, and indeed in Jewish tradition the term can apply to the whole of the Hebrew Bible as well as the Talmud and other early rabbinic texts.

The imagery in verse 3 is especially important in tracing the history of the rise of the status of early written traditions. In declaring that the wise "are like trees planted by streams of water, which yield their fruit in its season," the psalmist associates the wise with fully fertile and verdant trees and likens torah to the fresh running water that sustains them. To understand fully this verse, we need to consider other places in the Hebrew Bible that rely on similar imagery. In parts of Proverbs 1–9, Wisdom is personified as a woman who consistently cries out to those who will listen. In Proverbs 5:15 a father gives advice to his son: "Drink water from your own cistern, flowing water from your own well." The next five verses continue to elaborate in fecund language the joys of this intimate relationship. While it remains unclear, it seems that this woman, described as "the wife of your youth" (v. 18), is Wisdom. In other words, a rich and full life belongs to one who remains devoted to Wisdom.

In Proverbs 8:22–31 Wisdom makes an astonishing claim. Verse 22 records Wisdom's voice: "The LORD created me at the beginning of his work, the first of his acts of long ago." The following nine verses describe the early stages of creation in a sequence and language that brings to mind Genesis 1. In verse 30, Wisdom declares, "Then I was beside him, like a master worker; and I was daily his delight, rejoicing before him always." From early in its reception, this passage in Proverbs 8 spurred speculation. That the word in verse 22 translated beginning (re'shit) appears as the first word of Genesis (bere'shit), albeit with a preposition, suggested to early readers that Wisdom was God's first creation. Given the lack of an explicit statement to this effect in Genesis 1, interpreters sought subtle suggestions in that text that might confirm Wisdom's claim.

Sirach 24 reveals the results of decades, even centuries, of rumination on the relationship of Proverbs 8:22–31 to the creation accounts in Genesis. Here, as in Proverbs, Wisdom calls out but adds specificity, "I came forth from the mouth of the Most High, and covered the earth like a mist" (Sir. 24:3). For Sirach and the tradition of interpretation it represents, Wisdom comprises God's speech in creation. She comes forth from God's mouth and

Homiletical Perspective

and earth pass away (Matt. 5:17–18). Certainly our Lord did not reduce the entire Pentateuch to "instruction." Rather, the Sermon of the Mount is an exposition of the proper interpretation and application of the Torah. To "delight" in God's law is to find happiness in the precepts, even further, in the very word of God as it was mediated to Israel. We must remember that in our preaching and teaching we are modeling for our listeners this act of delighting, or partaking, in all that God has brought to bear on our life and work through Scripture. Therefore we wholeheartedly agree with Paul when we say "we uphold the law" (Rom. 3:31). We do not delight in the law divorced from our Lord. Rather, we worship the one who composed the law and the one who offers grace and mercy when we are unable to measure up to the law.[2]

Saint or Sinner? The psalm offers some very stark and glaring contrasts. The first is between the wicked, sinners, and scoffers and those who find happiness meditating on God's precepts following the path ("way") of the righteous (vv. 1–2; 5–6). (Note the chiastic structure of the psalm and the use of antithetical parallelism as a means for building a thesis/antithesis in the mind of the listener.)

This is posed as a choice for each of us, a fork in the road, a decision to walk by the Spirit or by the flesh (Rom. 8:5). Those who choose to delight in the contemplation of God and his law are like the healthy and lush tree that grows along a stream in a dry and weary land (Ps. 63:1; Isa. 32:2). Although this is no promise of living a comfortable and cushy life, this is the way of prosperity (v. 3) and the path of the kingdom of God.

Those who choose differently become the opposite of a fruitful tree; they are "chaff," the waste of threshed wheat. Again, pay attention to the contrast of metaphors. In one hand is the promise of being a firmly rooted tree, established in a place with the necessary resources for growth and vitality. In the other hand, we have the option of being chaff, which has no foundation, is ungrounded and disconnected, and is left at the mercy of the wind (cf. Eph. 4:14).

Even in the midst of horrendous circumstances, we must direct our minds toward the mind of God. Natan Sharansky, a Russian Jew and advocate for human rights for Russians, was in 1977 arrested by

---

2. Walter C. Kaiser Jr., *Preaching and Teaching from the Old Testament* (Grand Rapids: Baker, 2003), 143–45.

Psalm 1

Theological Perspective

satisfied by the steady currents of the river flowing past. One is reminded, perhaps, of a rabbi who sits comfortably in the synagogue and entertains questions from the many wandering seekers who pass by. The rabbi is adept at responding in wisdom to a gamut of questions from the young and the old, whether of contemporary events or of things long past, yet is content to stay rooted in one place, drawing sustenance from a well that never runs dry.

Furthermore, the firmly rooted trees always bear fruit in season and have leaves that never wither. In contemporary society, happiness is a factor of what one is allowed to take from the world's bounty. The happy person, according to Psalm 1, does not take from the world but contributes to it, bearing fruit for the sustenance of other beings and leaves for their breath and shade. The fruit and leaf bearing happen only in season, however. The psalmist is not saying that the tree must give ceaselessly and in all manner of gifts. There is no place for martyrdom in this analogy. God has created each to bear fruit according to its particular species and its due season. Each person has a different type of fruit to offer and a different time line.

The conclusion of the psalm reassures us that God will be present along the way with those who take God's law to heart and follow it. The curse for the wicked is that they will blow here and there, without the comfort of God's presence. Life does offer opposing choices: to indulge in what the world has to offer for pleasure, or to dig deep and quench one's thirst for happiness by connecting with the Maker. Meditation on God's law day and night becomes the better option, because it teaches that the things of this world are fleeting and will never bring peace. Reluctance to do so may come from a human inclination to reject imposition of the rules of law. God's law, however, is not a tedious list of rules. It is the law of love, of a Creator who cares deeply for the created and wants each one to be happy, grounded, and present with God.

REBECCA BLAIR YOUNG

Pastoral Perspective

These two paths confronted the shapers of the Psalter in the postexilic period as the Hebrew faith was rerooted in the promised land. Returning exiles encountered despair, disillusionment, uncertainty, danger, and religious laxity. It was a crucial time. At stake was no less than the continued survival of Hebrew faith and life. At such a time, Ezra pointed to God's law. Haggai pointed to the temple. Psalm 1 and the Psalter orient faith and life down this same life-giving path and away from the helter-skelter of each one for himself or herself.

There is a sense in which individuals and the whole human community can be broken into these two groups traveling these two paths. "Righteous" and "wicked" may assume other names, but the characteristics are the same. On the one side is contentment, even a spirited gladness. There is a conscious and comfortable awareness of finitude, boundaries, limits, shortcoming, possibilities, and talents. Life draws its élan from the outside. It is not a law unto itself, but is grounded in God's eternal law, upon which it reflects and in which it seeks to discover new insight and strength every day. Lives are not self-owned or contained or gratified, but live in every phase of existence to glorify and enjoy God. On the other side is anxious self-protection and suffi- ciency. Life is self-ruled, self-grounded, self-centered. It is free-floating and unattached. It concocts and owns the truth, and the truth is its own.

In our world, religious factions rigidly defend their interpretation of divine law with contentious- ness and violence. Narcissism and misery have increased in the Generation Me by 30 percent over the past twenty-five years.[1] But for those dwelling between these two extremes, there is clearly room to "find delight in God's law." It is no accident that Psalm 1 opens with "happy," a word that begins with the first letter, and ends with "perish," the last letter of the Hebrew alphabet. This is the stuff of life. It is all here in Psalm 1. It is where we begin our walk down an elucidating and promising path.

CHARLES M. MENDENHALL

---

1. See Jean Twenge, *Generation Me: Why Today's Young Americans Are More Confident, Assertive, Entitled—and More Miserable—Than Ever Before* (New York: Free Press, 2006).

Exegetical Perspective

partakes in establishing the created order. This line of interpretation likely associates Wisdom with "enlightenment" and has in mind that God first creates light in Genesis 1:3. Furthermore, that Wisdom covers the earth like a mist probably makes reference to Genesis 2:6, where this source of moisture is the origin of life. Wisdom continues to describe her role in creation and then in the life of God's people. We even hear of her role in ministering to God in the tabernacle and temple (Sir. 24:10–11). In Sirach 24:13–22 Wisdom describes herself in luxuriant and fecund language that brings to mind the garden of Eden, and she beckons, "Come to me, you who desire me, and eat your fill of my fruits" (v. 19). Finally, in verse 23, Sirach identifies Wisdom as none other than "the book of the covenant of the Most High God, the law that Moses commanded us." He next links it with several rivers that include the four that emerge from Eden. This tradition that envisaged the origins of Wisdom/Torah at creation has its influence on the New Testament in the prologue to the Gospel of John, where the Word takes on so many aspects of the history of interpretation we have traced above.

Wisdom's career is remarkable, and in this interpretive history we can gain insight on how Psalm 1 came to be understood and why it might have been placed at the beginning of the book of Psalms. In the context of the association of Wisdom with Torah, the claim that happiness comes to those dedicated to torah in verses 1–2 takes on new and fuller meaning. Read in this light, Psalm 1 seems to suggest that reading the Psalms, as part of the whole of Torah, will lead to a fecund, full, and blessed life.

LARRY L. LYKE

Homiletical Perspective

the KGB for treason. His wife, Avital, gave him a book of Psalms while he was incarcerated. Sharansky shares that his meditation on the psalms gave him the strength to withstand brutal conditions for nine years.[3] Upon his release, Sharansky found himself without his book of Psalms. The psalms had had such a tremendous impact on his life that he refused freedom by lying down in the snow until the KGB returned his beloved Psalms. That is the power of God's word to bring us emotional and spiritual strength through trials.

Content or Condemned? The path of righteousness leads to success and prosperity in the eyes of God (v. 3); the other path, the path of the wicked and scoffers, leads to spiritual malfunction (v. 4). Obviously it is the task of the preacher to convince the listener to choose wisely. Sometimes it is better to use sugar than salt. It may be more effective illustrating the benefits of being content with God and standing in the assembly of the righteous, rather than the pain of being apart from God or being the object of God's judgment. Those who find themselves alienated from God can always choose a path of restoration and renewal (cf. 2 Chr. 7:14). Here the preacher is focusing on the internal peace (e.g., "happy") of the believer who "delights" in the law of God. Some like to think that peace is the absence of conflict. Quite the contrary, peace is the security to endure conflict. There will always be a seat in the assembly of scoffers and the worn-out path of sinners. However, when we latch onto God, meditate on God's precepts, and follow them in obedience, then comes the internal peace in a world of external depravity.

ROBERT M. LEACH

---

3. Natan Sharansky, *Fear No Evil* (New York: Random House, 1988), 400ff.

1 Corinthians 15:12-20

¹²Now if Christ is proclaimed as raised from the dead, how can some of you say there is no resurrection of the dead? ¹³If there is no resurrection of the dead, then Christ has not been raised; ¹⁴and if Christ has not been raised, then our proclamation has been in vain and your faith has been in vain. ¹⁵We are even found to be misrepresenting God, because we testified of God that he raised Christ—whom he did not raise if it is true that the dead are not raised. ¹⁶For if the dead are not raised, then Christ has not been raised. ¹⁷If Christ has not been raised, your faith is futile and you are still in your sins. ¹⁸Then those also who have died in Christ have perished. ¹⁹If for this life only we have hoped in Christ, we are of all people most to be pitied.

²⁰But in fact Christ has been raised from the dead, the first fruits of those who have died.

Theological Perspective

Today's reading is the second step in Paul's assertion that belief in the resurrection of the dead is a necessary tenet of faith for the church in Corinth. It follows on Paul's reminder that the Corinthians share with him the gospel of Christ's death and resurrection (vv. 1–11). Put most simply, if one believes that Christ was resurrected, one must also believe in a more general resurrection of the dead. "But in fact Christ has been raised from the dead, the first fruits of those who have died" (v. 20). Looking beyond today's text, we see in Paul's comparison of Christ and Adam a still more precise connection between Christ's resurrection and our own: "For since death came through a human being, the resurrection of the dead has also come through a human being; for as all die in Adam, so all will be made alive in Christ" (vv. 21–22).

Before leaving this quasi-logical connection between Christ's resurrection and a more general resurrection of the dead, it is worth noting that in 1 Corinthians 15 Paul gives no conclusive credence to the theological claim that God ultimately raises from the dead only Christian believers. Verses 23–24 in Paul's brief apocalyptic sketch following on today's reading have provoked considerable debate on this matter. Yet verse 26, "The last enemy to be destroyed is death," would seem to be a decisive

Pastoral Perspective

A faithful pastor listens carefully to the concerns, doubts, and struggles of the congregation in order to let the needs of the people shape the preaching, teaching, and pastoral care of the church. In his correspondence with the Corinthians, Paul has learned that some within the church doubt the truth of the resurrection. Others are worried about what has happened to those who have died before the return of Christ. For Paul, everything stands or falls on the resurrection. Their disbelief in the resurrection of the dead runs directly counter to the heart of his proclamation. Paul has inextricably linked the resurrection of Jesus Christ with the general resurrection of the dead. If there is no resurrection of the dead, and if Christ has not been raised from the dead, then the faith of the church is empty and without meaning.

It is common in the church today for people to question, doubt, and even disbelieve the resurrection of the body. Paul wrote to the Corinthian church some twenty years after the death and resurrection of Jesus; those twenty years have become twenty centuries, and there is still no sign of the return of the risen Lord.

In this scientific age, people know all about the processes of nature. On television and computer screens everyone can watch the cycle of natural life

Exegetical Perspective

Literary Context. Having affirmed the centrality of the death, burial, and resurrection of Jesus to Christian faith, and having offered a list of eyewitnesses to substantiate his claim (vv. 1–11), Paul now turns to those who doubt that Jesus was raised from the dead. Beginning in verse 12, his aim is not to prove that the resurrection happened (as in vv. 5–8) but to explain what the idea of resurrection means theologically.

The lectionary does a disservice to Paul in that it skips over his lengthy discussions in the rest of the chapter. An astute preacher should take some notice at least of Paul's primary theological rationale for the resurrection in verses 21–28.

Historical and Cultural Context. Paul says that "some" in Corinth say there is no resurrection from the dead (v. 12). It is not clear whether this was an organized faction, like those mentioned in 1:12, but it is likely that skepticism about resurrection from the dead arose among some Gentile Christians, because most Greeks and Romans assumed a sharp distinction between body and soul. It was common to describe the body as a prison of the soul, as the first-century Stoic philosopher Seneca wrote,

> For this body of ours is a weight upon the soul and its penance; as the load presses down the soul is

Homiletical Perspective

Last Sunday's Epistle reading affirmed the common ground; this Sunday's confronts the conflict head-on. Preaching on this passage necessitates making an essential decision about what to discuss and what not to discuss. The central argument Paul makes in these verses is that if you do not believe in the resurrection of the body ("corpses" is perhaps a more literal translation), your faith is a sham. Here is the problem. Today's congregations are filled with folks who, despite what the creeds say, do not believe in the resurrection of the body at the end of time. They have opted instead for a view of resurrection in which one's soul goes to heaven at the time of death. Since this may, in fact, have been one of the views of resurrection that Paul was arguing against, these verses have the potential to create a firestorm in a congregation. So there is a choice to be made: will the sermon deal with this issue or not? It might be that this is better left to a classroom setting, that it can be handled more effectively in teaching than in preaching; and yet a sermon on this passage may be a way to help the congregation understand the challenges of biblical interpretation, as well as raise the possibility of an even more radically powerful understanding of the resurrection.

The Resurrection of the Body. If the decision is made to address the issue of Paul's understanding of the

1 Corinthians 15:12-20

Theological Perspective

underscoring of the "all will be made alive" in verse 22.[1]

Given the importance of resurrection in today's reading, we do well to remind ourselves that the term in question, derived as it is from the same apocalyptic tradition Paul draws on throughout 1 Corinthians 15, does not mean the resuscitation of a dead body. The empty tomb narratives in later canonical texts are of no concern to Paul. As is clear from verses 35–49, the resurrection bodies Paul has in mind are spiritual bodies resulting from a radical transformation analogous to the simultaneous continuity and discontinuity between a seed and a full grown plant. Likewise, there is no place here for a disembodied immortal soul. The resurrection Paul would have the Corinthians anticipate on the basis of Christ's resurrection will come when God's reign is complete. Christ's resurrection is the "first fruits," the initial instance, of that reign. It establishes the eschatological tension in which all those who believe in the gospel must live their lives.

This theological point has profound ethical implications. If the Corinthians cannot hope in the fulfillment of God's love in the age to come, all their striving in the present age to order their lives in accordance with that love would seem to be in vain; thus, verses 14, 17, and 19. Put positively, not even the death-dealing forces that presently obscure God's wisdom and power can finally separate us from God's love. This is the meaning of the resurrection without which the birth of Christianity cannot be conceived.

It is clear from 1 Corinthians 1–11 that the appearances of Christ to the disciples and then, according to Paul, to many others are understood to substantiate Christ's resurrection. How do those appearances square with the understanding of resurrection as something other than the resuscitation of a dead body? It helps to understand that the word "appeared" in Greek is used elsewhere to mean visionary experience.[2] That is certainly an appropriate way to describe Paul's own experience of the risen Christ cited in Acts 9, 22, and 26. Such experiences of Christ's presence vary from individual to individual, depending on their particular associations with Jesus. This accounts for the variety of appearance narratives that develop in the Gospel accounts. Despite their sometimes contradictory details, these narratives all report the

Pastoral Perspective

from birth to death and from death to decay. Modern medicine can resuscitate a body in certain circumstances, but no one has ever seen anyone raised from the dead who does not die again. People know the philosophical arguments against life after death; in this context, the testimony of the church can seem like a quaint myth leftover from a former age. In addition, bodily existence is a problem for many people. Like some of the Corinthians, escape from this bodily existence for some higher disembodied afterlife sounds like a good idea. How much more pleasant it is to contemplate the immortality of the soul than this messy business of bodily resurrection.

People come to worship with open wounds and unresolved grief over a miscarriage, the death of a child, the suicide of a mother, or the death of a life partner. Beyond the personal experience of death, instant communications have made almost everyone keenly aware of the vast scale of human tragedies in our local communities and in the world. Can God truly value physical existence when so many people die of abuse, random violence, genocide, and famine?

There is every reason in the world to question, doubt, and disbelieve the resurrection, except one: "But in fact Christ has been raised from the dead, the first fruits of those who have died" (v. 20). Since the resurrection of the body stands at the core of the Christian proclamation, the implications of this belief touch every area of congregational life and ministry.

First of all, the belief in the resurrection is an affirmation of the whole life of Jesus. Without the resurrection, the Christian faith can be reduced to little more than a moral code to guide well-meaning people about how to live their lives. How could anyone know that what Jesus said and what Jesus did are worth following? It is the resurrection that makes sense of the life and teachings of Jesus. Only in the light of the resurrection can believers understand the paradox of saving one's life by losing one's life. Only in the light of the resurrection does it make sense for followers of Jesus to stand with the poor, the outcasts, and the oppressed. The doctrine of the resurrection invites people to join Christ in providing care and seeking justice for the most vulnerable people in our society and trusting that God will bless these efforts, even when the results cannot be seen. The resurrection gives the faithful the freedom to live their lives in the shadow of the cross, as Jesus did. The hope of the church is not confined to this world.

---

1. See Victor Paul Furnish, *The Theology of the First Letter to the Corinthians* (Cambridge, UK: Cambridge University Press, 1999), 111f., for a fuller discussion of this issue.
2. Paul J. Achtemeier, ed., *Bible Dictionary*, rev. ed. (San Francisco: HarperCollins, 1996), 927.

crushed and is in bondage, unless philosophy has come to its assistance . . . so the soul, imprisoned as it has been in this gloomy and darkened house, seeks the open sky whenever it can, and in the contemplation of the universe finds rest.[1]

For Seneca it was not hard to imagine the soul living on after death. After all, the soul was the real "you," and the body was expendable. This way of thinking is still present in many Western Christians today. Modern people tend to focus on the afterlife of the soul and think of the body as irrelevant.

By contrast, Paul follows the Jewish idea that the real "you" is an inspired body, into which God breathed the breath of life (Gen. 2:7). What is more, Paul follows the ancient Jewish apocalyptic belief that in the end time God will resurrect all the bodies of the dead for judgment (v. 52; Rev. 20:11–15; cf. *1 Enoch* 51). So Paul uses an agricultural metaphor to say that the resurrection of Jesus was the "first fruits" (v. 20) of a general resurrection to follow. But there is a twist. For many Jews, the idea of a crucified messiah was a "stumbling block" (1:23). It is a distinctly Christian claim that the cross is an eschatological event. In the cross and resurrection of Christ, the end time has already begun.

The Argument. Paul's response in verse 12 to the denial of resurrection is a logic problem that stands like a row of dominoes. One thing leads to another, and if you knock down the first domino by denying the possibility of bodily resurrection (v. 13), then pretty soon you are standing there a pitiful sinner with nothing to believe in (vv. 17–19). This is no proof that the resurrection happened; rather, it is a restatement of the question. In verses 12–19, Paul asserts that Christian theology does not hang together as a coherent system of thought apart from belief in the resurrection. To put it another way, it is strange for a Christian to affirm that God raised Jesus' body from the grave and deny that he will raise ours. If we agree that God *can* raise the dead and that he *has* done so, how can we deny that he *will* do so again? Our hope is that what God did for Christ God will also do for those who are in Christ (cf. Rom. 6:4–5, 8–9).

The heart of Paul's theological explanation of the resurrection is in the next paragraph (vv. 20–28), where he describes the death of death. This is the real theological rationale for why Jesus died. First,

resurrection of the body, here are some thoughts that might shape that sermon: (1) None of us knows for certain precisely what the resurrection entails—either immediately following death or at the end of time. (2) Paul in this passage uses the image of the resurrection of the body to explain what is essentially unknowable. (3) Since Paul also believed that the end of time would occur shortly, perhaps within his own lifetime, even he did not have a complete understanding of the way in which the resurrection would become real for those other than Jesus. (4) Paul later in this chapter talks about the resurrection body being different from our earthly bodies, which reminds us that the nature of the resurrection body is something we cannot grasp in this life—our experience, even our imaginations, are too limited. (5) The image of the resurrection of the body reminds us once again that ours is an incarnational faith, that it is lived out in an embodied form. The resurrection is not about some ethereal happening; it is an incarnate resurrection. Its precise form is something we cannot imagine, but it is embodied in a real, tangible way. And its power is to be experienced both in this life and in the life beyond.

The Resurrection of the Dead. Most translations of this passage use the phrase "resurrection of the dead." Most people assume this means life continuing in some form after a person dies. Thus it is possible to avoid the problems inherent in the passage without undue difficulty and focus the sermon on the relationship between Christ's resurrection and our own. If the danger of the first approach is creating conflict, the danger here is reducing the sermon to little more than pious platitudes about heaven. That is to be avoided at all cost!

The problem for many of the Corinthians was difficulty believing, not so much in Christ's resurrection, as their own. In many ways this seems the reverse of the situation many find themselves in today. They are willing (perhaps eager) to believe in life after death, but find the idea of Jesus' body rising from the tomb and appearing to his disciples difficult to accept. The great insight of this passage is that the two are intimately linked together. Belief in Christ's resurrection provides reason to have faith in our own. Faith in our own resurrection provides reason to believe in Christ's. There is something other than a rational argument at work here, for the very nature of resurrection defies reason. It is, rather, an experientially based conviction. Whether we start with Christ's resurrection (as the Corinthians did) or

1. Seneca, *Moral Epistles* 65.16–17, trans. R. M. Gummere, Loeb Classical Library (Cambridge: Harvard University Press, 1917), 453–55.

1 Corinthians 15:12-20

Theological Perspective

unmistakable presence of the postcrucifixion Jesus. To call the crucified Jesus the Christ or Messiah, against all expectations of that figure in Jewish apocalyptic literature, must have been rooted in a profound existential awareness. That awareness entailed a commitment to Jesus' message that God's wisdom and power were of a radically different order than that of the ruling political and religious hierarchies.

The commitment in question here, rooted as it is in the experience of the risen Christ, is far more than allegiance to an ideology. It is a deeply personal response to the love of God revealed in the life, death, and resurrection of Jesus Christ. So 1 Corinthians 15 is best read alongside 1 Corinthians 13. The latter evokes the love that must have overwhelmed the disciples, and certainly the apostle Paul, when Jesus appeared to them as the risen Christ. It is a love that is always incarnate, embodied in our world today as it was two thousand years ago. Paul's list of appearances in 15:5–8 has not come to an end. It has been added to through the centuries, right up into our own time. Jesus Christ is no less a presence in our world than in Paul's, but are we aware of that presence? Can we abandon our multitude of distractions, many of them rooted in the same status seeking that plagued the church in Corinth, long enough to experience God's love and live our lives in response to that love? As in today's reading, Paul's theology always couples death and resurrection, Christ's and our own. Marcus Borg writes that "death and resurrection become a metaphor for the internal spiritual process that lies at the heart of the Christian path."[3] That process entails the death of our self-seeking ego, that stake some Buddhists say we are tied to, like a dog running in circles but never free. With that death comes a resurrection, a gift of new life empowered by God's gracious love. As Paul writes elsewhere, "It is no longer I who live, but it is Christ who lives in me" (Gal. 2:20).

Addressed to a church two millennia ago, today's reading may be even more relevant in our ultraindividualistic age. For Paul, the internal transformation characterized by death and resurrection is not a private affair. The life in Christ is made real in the life of faithful communities as well as faithful individuals.

JERRY IRISH

Pastoral Perspective

The belief in the resurrection of the body is an affirmation of the significance of human life as a part of the created world. Human existence is bound up in the life of the material, visible world. God has a plan not only for the resurrection of humankind, but also for the redemption of creation. In truth, human beings know no other kind of life except bodily existence. Even if the most sophisticated dissecting tools imaginable could be fabricated, the soul could not be teased out of the body. The human creature is an indivisible unity of body, soul, mind, and spirit. The pastor can help individuals struggling with issues of self-worth or self-image to come to value their bodies and their lives because God values each human life. It is a pastoral task to help people see that how they live their lives, use their bodies, spend their time, and care for creation can be a testimony to their belief in the resurrection of the body.

The resurrection of the body also speaks to the anxieties people have about sin, death, and eternal life. Without the resurrection, Paul says, "Your faith is futile and you are still in your sins. Then those who have died in Christ have perished" (vv. 17–18). In other words, the resurrection of Jesus confirms the truth of his words that sin is forgiven. In the prayer of confession and the assurance of pardon, in the proclamation of the word and the hymns of the faith, and in the sharing of bread and wine, the risen Lord meets troubled hearts with the promise, "Your sins are forgiven." The resurrection also tells us that death is not the end of life. Jesus is the "first fruits of those who have died" (v. 20). Human destiny is bound to the Christ's destiny. The affirmation of the resurrection by a pastor who is sensitive to the emotional and spiritual struggles of the congregation can bring hope and healing to those who have watched the dying process, received the ashes of a loved one, or participated in the burial of a friend. The resurrection stands over the whole of the Christian life, giving birth to faithful mission, grace-filled pastoral care, and vital worship.

LEWIS F. GALLOWAY

---

3. Marcus J. Borg and N. T. Wright, *The Meaning of Jesus: Two Visions* (San Francisco: HarperCollins, 1999), 139. This is a superb resource for contrasting theological interpretations.

Exegetical Perspective

Paul argues that the bodily resurrection of Christ foreshadowed the resurrection of all the dead at the end time (vv. 20–23). Christ was the "first fruits" (vv. 20, 23), which implies that a harvest is coming (cf. Col. 1:18; Rev. 1:5). Second, Paul establishes an analogy between Adam and Christ, between creation and new creation (vv. 21–22; 45–49, cf. Rom. 5:12–21).

Third, Paul views the cross and resurrection in apocalyptic categories as an attack on the tyranny of death (vv. 23–27; cf. Rom. 6–7). Notice the apocalyptic themes in this paragraph: "coming" (v. 23), "end" (v. 24), "kingdom/reign" (vv. 24, 50), and "last" (*eschatos*, vv. 26, 52). In the end time, *every* rule, authority, and power is destroyed. There is no room in Paul's theology to assume that God favors any nation or earthly power over others. The reign of God transcends all earthly powers. The reign of God is not about defeating sinful people, who are mere symptoms; rather, it is about defeating death itself, the root motivation for sin. Fear of death causes us to rationalize preemptive strikes, to hoard money, to overreact against real and perceived threats, to behave against one another in so many destructive ways. But the resurrection of Christ demonstrates that death holds no power, and this frees us to love our enemies, even at the risk that they might take advantage and kill us. The dead will be raised, and then where will be death's victory (vv. 52–55)?

Theological Connection. The Corinthians' assumption that the dead do not rise is much like modernist assumptions along the same lines. There is no scientific basis for any such thing; so modern people who rely on empirical evidence and the scientific method as the arbiter of all truth tend to struggle with the idea of resurrection. It is true that science is the best set of tools we have for explaining natural events, but the resurrection is by definition a supernatural event. One cannot prove it scientifically. One must test that proposition theologically, and this is what Paul does.

CHRISTOPHER R. HUTSON

Homiletical Perspective

with belief in life after death (as many today would), faith in that conviction moves us to the other. We believe, not because of any inherent logic, but because our acceptance of that conviction opens us to the wonder and power of God at work. It moves us beyond the rational and scientific so that we begin to see with eyes of faith.

Another approach to this passage would focus on the power of the resurrection to impact both the present and the future. Paul acknowledged the legitimacy of both when he described the consequences of there being no resurrection as "you are still in your sins" (v. 17) and "those also who have died in Christ have perished" (v. 18). Paul's declaration in verse 19, "If for this life only we have hoped in Christ, we are of all people most to be pitied," also affirms that both the present and the future are shaped by the resurrection. It is not either/or, but both/and. Paul wrote to a people who questioned the power of the resurrection to impact their future. Today, when the import of the resurrection has shifted to a focus on life after death, he might well have written, "If for the next life only we have hoped in Christ, we are of all people most to be pitied." A sermon might explore the legitimacy of such a comment for people today. The power of the resurrection is the power to transform this life and bring us to eternal life. Once again, the two are intimately connected. The reality of one assures us of the reality of the other. A helpful way to explore this might be to look at the use of both "abundant" and "eternal" to describe the life that Christ offers to us and that God intends for us. Another way might be to consider how our ethics are shaped by our eschatology.

JEFFREY D. JONES

Luke 6:17-26

17He came down with them and stood on a level place, with a great crowd of his disciples and a great multitude of people from all Judea, Jerusalem, and the coast of Tyre and Sidon. 18They had come to hear him and to be healed of their diseases; and those who were troubled with unclean spirits were cured. 19And all in the crowd were trying to touch him, for power came out from him and healed all of them.

20Then he looked up at his disciples and said:

"Blessed are you who are poor,
  for yours is the kingdom of God.

21 "Blessed are you who are hungry now,
  for you will be filled.

"Blessed are you who weep now,
  for you will laugh.

Theological Perspective

This is the raw, unvarnished, faith-rattling declaration of the realm of God.

To "a great crowd of his disciples" Jesus speaks unequivocally of God's blessing on the poor, the hungry, the reviled and, conversely, God's judgment on the rich, the sated, the comfortable. This is the God of Isaiah whose prophecy Jesus read aloud in the Nazareth synagogue (4:16–20), announcing that he had been sent by God to bring good news to the poor, release to the captives, sight to the blind. Now Jesus lays out what the fulfillment of that text means in terms and tones that are direct and terse, pointed and searing. The God of the prophets is speaking and creating a new, unsettling, upsetting order.

The depth and impact of this new order, this realm of God, has always been difficult for the church to fathom, and easy for it to neutralize. Ever since Matthew spiritualized the poor in his Sermon on the Mount (5:1–12), the inclination has been to domesticate the radical pronouncement so that it comfortably fits "us" who by no means meet its criteria. Surely we are all "poor in spirit." We hunger for right to prevail. Perhaps we have even been reviled. Over generations in hallowed sanctuaries the prophetic word became hollow and even more watered down than Matthew had rendered it.

Pastoral Perspective

The Great Sermon on the Plain as presented in Luke is delivered on the plain where the people are gathered to hear Jesus and to be healed of their various infirmities and afflictions. Yet the sermon seems to be addressed not to the people in general who have gathered around him, but to the disciples in the presence of the large gathering—to the church. Pastorally this highlights the fact that the very nature of the sermon, the values and ethics that it expresses, are apparently not intended to be a moral code binding on the society in its widest sense. Rather, it is for those who have made a commitment to follow Christ.

At the same time, the fulfillment of the demands of this sermon will not be the outcome of personal effort and resources, but of divine grace. There are many who are attracted to Jesus as a great teacher and think that if we just adhered to the teaching of Jesus, then the world would be a better place. The good news is that our fulfillment of the demands of the sermon is the enabling work of the gift of grace, the gift of the Spirit.

Popular preaching on television often portrays the call to Christian discipleship as the call to a life of constant blessing and a materialistic prosperity. Luke's Sermon on the Plain does not provide us with anything that could be classified as the success-and-blessing theology of the televangelists, even though it

²²"Blessed are you when people hate you, and when they exclude you, revile you, and defame you on account of the Son of Man. ²³Rejoice in that day and leap for joy, for surely your reward is great in heaven; for that is what their ancestors did to the prophets.

²⁴ "But woe to you who are rich,
    for you have received your consolation.
²⁵ "Woe to you who are full now,
    for you will be hungry.
"Woe to you who are laughing now,
    for you will mourn and weep.
²⁶"Woe to you when all speak well of you, for that is what their ancestors did to the false prophets."

Exegetical Perspective

This text, part of Luke's Sermon on the Plain (6:17–49), is often overshadowed by the longer, more developed Sermon on the Mount in the Gospel of Matthew (Matt. 5–7). Luke's version is a mere 32 verses compared to the 107 verses in Matthew. Yet the Lukan account includes significant teachings in the activities that take place before the sermon and in the sermon itself, especially the probing affirmation and visionary challenge recorded in what is generally considered the "beatitudes" (Luke 6:20–26; cf. Matt. 5:3–11).

At the outset it is important to clarify to whom this sermon is addressed. It follows the narrative describing the twelve disciples whom Jesus chose after a night in prayer to God on a mountain (Luke 6:12–16). Jesus comes down from the mountain with these disciples (more specifically known as apostles) and finds gathered on the plain "a great multitude of people from all Judea, Jerusalem, and the coast of Tyre and Sidon" who had come to hear him and to be healed of their diseases (vv. 17–18a). There were also gathered among the crowd those who were "troubled with unclean spirits" (v. 18b). All were trying to touch Jesus to receive his power and experience healing from their afflictions (v. 19; cf. Luke 4:14; 8:46; Matt. 14:36; Mark 3:10). After healing them all, Jesus "raised his *eyes*" (v. 20, my

Homiletical Perspective

Like Matthew's Sermon on the Mount, Luke's Sermon on the Plain is full of traps for the unwary preacher. Indeed the whole of chapter 6 is hard going!

First, the poor have Luke's special attention. He is among the clearest of the New Testament writers on the power that wealth wields to isolate us from God and from the rest of the human community. In these verses, Luke picks up again the images that he painted so powerfully in the Magnificat (1:46–55).

But Luke does not consider those with wealth to be beyond salvation. There are "success stories" about the wealthy in Luke (see Zacchaeus, 19:1–10; Joseph Barnabas, Acts 4:36–37; Cornelius, Acts 10:2; and perhaps also Lydia, Acts 16:14). So although the beatitudes and woes in Luke tend to remind us immediately of the story of the rich man and Lazarus (Luke 16:19–31), the preacher will need to be attentive to Luke's subtleties in this matter.

Second, it is significant that these words are addressed to the disciples and not to the crowd, that is, to the church and not, in the first place at least, to the wider world. According to Eduard Schweizer, the "Sermon on the Plain is a call to action . . . not a theologically conceived attempt to summarize the Christian message in its entirety," but "a call to the

Luke 6:17-26

Theological Perspective

In Luke, God breaks down the doors, splinters them, and in Jesus boldly proclaims to the disciples, the crowds, the church the coming of a dramatically different realm. Here Jesus stands "on a level place" *with* the disciples and the multitude, not on a mount above them. He declares to those who have left everything to follow him that theirs is the kingdom of God, regardless of how reviled and defamed they might be. And he warns those who do not follow in this way that their lives will be woeful. God is turning the world upside down, and taking discipleship far beyond a simple "follow me" to a level of sacrifice that is nothing less than daunting.

In this world, however, even poverty does not translate into blessing. New Testament scholar John Dominic Crossan distinguishes between the pauper/peasant and the destitute/beggar. He asserts that "Jesus declared blessed, then, not the poor but the destitute, not poverty but beggary."[1] God's blessings do not fall on "the poor" simply because they are poor. The utterly reviled and expendable of the human family, the wretched of the earth, are the favored of God's blessings.

If so, this is not the "good news" we expected to hear. No wonder the watered-down, spiritualized version of these beatitudes is preferable and more comfortable. It is unlikely that even those who flocked around Jesus that day realized the cost of discipleship. Like us, they probably heard Jesus' words—God's blessings—being showered on them simply because they had gathered around him or because they presumed their inclusion in his litany of the blessed.

But no! God asks for—indeed demands—our all. Everything. Material goods and money are but a part of what God expects us to give up and give over. God wants the entirety of our lives. The destitute poor have nowhere to turn but to God. God watches over them and blesses them abundantly in God's way, not the way of the world: they will be filled, and they will laugh, and they will inherit the kingdom of God. To be disciples is to follow in this way. To be blessed of God is to have nothing but God.

As if such demands alone were not enough, God also makes clear that those who remain well off and full and self-satisfied—those for whom God is an afterthought, if at all—will reap woe upon woe. Woe be unto us "when all speak well of you," as those in the past spoke well of "false prophets"—searing

Pastoral Perspective

is punctuated with constant references to the "blessed." The Great Sermon is the call to a radical way of discipleship that turns the way of the world upside down.

Those who are willing to suffer so that the will of God may be accomplished are blessed. To these persons Jesus offers the assurance that the rule of God will come and the things for which they have longed, the hope they have nurtured, will be realized. We all have people in our congregations who live with great suffering; we hear of the displacement and uprooting caused by war and famine. Whereas in former times war usually involved combat between armies, today much of the violence is directed at civilians and is played out in our city streets. It is estimated that millions are internally displaced within their countries' borders and millions of others move on to become refugees in other countries. These are people who know what it is to be poor, to hunger, to weep, to be excluded, and to look to God for vindication. The preacher may choose to highlight the predicament of these millions, most far away and some near at hand.

Luke's Great Sermon is characterized by four beatitudes followed by four woes, each beatitude having its corresponding woe. His beatitudes and woes have a sociological dimension that is expressed in very concrete and pointed ways. He speaks of the poor and the hungry without the qualifying references of Matthew to the "poor in spirit" and those who "hunger for righteousness." The preacher cannot escape reflecting on the issue of whether blessedness resides in the sociological experiences of the people or in the relationship they share with God. Here the preacher may need to wrestle with God's "preferential option for the poor" that has been a significant claim of liberation theology. In addition, the preacher may explore poverty, hunger, and disease as preventable conditions in a world that would have enough food and resources for all to enjoy a better life, were it not for economic systems, systems of governance, and global spending on military armaments that condemn millions to a life of hunger and poverty.

The poor and the hungry know the reality of their situation. They are totally dependent on God and therefore are disposed to entrust themselves to God's care and mercy, which is the foundation of grace and a right relationship with God. The rich, on the other hand, are disposed to take comfort in themselves and their resources, thereby finding it more difficult to trust themselves to the mercy and grace of God.

---

1. John Dominic Crossan, *The Historical Jesus: The Life of a Mediterranean Jewish Peasant* (San Francisco: HarperSanFrancisco, 1991), 272 ff.

trans.) on his disciples (presumably "the Twelve" whom he had called) in preparation for delivering the heart of his message. Though his attention is directed at the disciples at this point (as is the case in the Matthean version; cf. Matt. 5:1), those who had been touched by him and those who had gathered to hear him would have been in the purview of this message.

In Matthew, Jesus simply opens his mouth (*stoma*) and begins to teach the disciples (Matt. 5:2). For Luke, Jesus focuses his eyes (*ophthalmoi*) on the disciples *after* the healing excursion in verses 18–19. The reference to eyes in this passage (v. 20) should not be glossed over as insignificant. It is here and also in *what is missing* after the preceding healing section that we find the theological import for this epiphany passage. The parallel account describing the healing of those who were troubled with unclean spirits (Mark 3:7–12) indicates the following: "Whenever the unclean spirits saw him, they fell down before him and shouted, 'You are the Son of God!'" (v. 11). Luke does not include this acknowledgment of the Divine in the Sermon on the Plain; rather, it is placed in an earlier healing story during Jesus' stay in Capernaum whereby the "demons" acknowledged that Jesus was the Son of God (Luke 4:38–44, esp. 41). This strategic ellipsis, calling attention to the lack of recognition of—or inability to see—the Son of God, makes the fact that Jesus is gazing at the disciples all the more poignant. It is not so much that the people are able to see God in this encounter with Jesus. The subtle undercurrent and the word of hope in this passage is how the disciples (and presumably all those would-be followers of Jesus) are *seen by God*! So the raising of the eyes by Jesus is a symbolic metaphor for the watchful eyes of God, who is ultimately responsible for the blessings and curses that are at the heart of this sermon.

Central in this text are four "blessings" or beatitudes (*makarioi*) with corresponding curses or "woes" (*ouai*) organized in a systematic manner to emphasize their importance for Luke's understanding of the kingdom of God (vv. 20–26). The poor are contrasted with the rich (vv. 20, 24). The hungry are contrasted with the full (vv. 21a, 25a). The weeping are contrasted with the laughing (vv. 21b, 25b), and the hated and marginalized are contrasted with venerated false prophets (vv. 22, 26). Luke does not mention four additional blessings that are included in Matthew: "Blessed are the meek," "Blessed are the merciful," "Blessed are the pure in heart," and "Blessed are the peacemakers" (Matt. 5:5, 7, 8, 9).

life of discipleship."[1] Luke is drawing a comparison of the life of the disciples with the life of Jesus. We are called to be the women and men that God has created us to be. Nothing less. In this pilgrimage, we shall follow Jesus, who is our unique example. The life of faith is so difficult precisely because there is no avoiding this individual responsibility. Luke's beatitudes and woes state baldly something of what that commitment will mean for us.

Third, the preacher might want to experiment by writing beatitudes and woes that accurately reflect the point of the originals but in language that speaks to our time; or even better, invite the congregation to do so. The beatitudes and the woes challenge us to ask what it is that we value and what it is that we reject, in relation to faithful Christian living. The effective sermon will enable the community to see not only that the kingdom enshrines values different from the world's, but also that it is possible for the community and its members to live those values "now" (6:21).

Fourth, consider the close association of poverty with shame in Jesus' time and our own. It is one thing to think of this in relation to the homeless beggar; it is quite another to try to understand that discipleship for us means a participation in this same shame and disgrace. In a contemporary popular religious culture that equates wealth with divine approbation, here is Scripture telling us exactly the opposite.

Fifth, while in Matthew Jesus teaches on a mountain, in Luke Jesus is "on the level."[2] He is speaking not just "on the plain," but *plainly*. If the truth is to be trusted, then this is the best news of all. We can trust Jesus to be absolutely "on the level" with us every step of the way, telling us the truth of our lives as he sees us, rather than as we portray ourselves at parties. There comes a time in most lives when this sort of truth is the only truth that is worth the candle. We hear this truth only through our participation in a community—the community of lifelong partnerships and families, the community of the eucharistic fellowship, the community of those who pray and discuss the Scriptures together, the community of service, the community of mutually committed members.

Sixth, Jesus' words are cast in the second person plural. Once again, this is not to lessen individual

---

1. Eduard Schweizer, *The Good News according to Luke* (London: SPCK, 1984), 117–18.
2. I owe this thought to Phyllis Kersten, "Shrubs and Scrubs," *Christian Century*, Jan. 31, 2001, 10.

Luke 6:17-26

Theological Perspective

words that cut to the core of our being and belief and assault deeply held notions of our faith and faithfulness. Are we not the bearers, the teachers, the preachers of God's word? Are we not the body of Christ, the church? Are we not the living witnesses to God's love made manifest through Jesus Christ?

Indeed we are, and therein is our woe. God does not take kindly to halfheartedness. God does not bless us as we maintain the status quo, reaping the accolades of those who hear us and follow us. God does not bless us as we bathe in respectability in the eyes of the world. God does not bless us as we quietly maintain tradition and gloss over or ignore prophetic voices calling us back to God—in the church and in the world. God does not bless us as we protect and build institutions and empires. God does not bless us, well off, full, comfortable, hearty, and well spoken of.

The realm of God rests among those who have nothing but God.

Jesus' Sermon on the Plain—these wondrous yet stark beatitudes—jar us out of our faithful complacency. The God Jesus speaks of is not always the God we proclaim. Our human inclination is to fit God into our own small definitions, cultures, and places. But God is always breaking down the barriers we construct to keep God in or out. Here, once again, God is calling us back. God is always reminding us that we must empty ourselves, turn away from the ways of the world, and then—and only then only by God's grace—receive the fullness of blessings God offers to the utterly destitute, the marginalized, the expendable.

A great crowd of his disciples and a great multitude of people came to hear him. Power came out from him. The power of God among the peoples of God. What they heard and what they saw is what is and will always be heard and seen when God's word is truly unleashed and God's work is truly done—the upbuilding of the realm of God with and among the blessed.

DAVID L. OSTENDORF

Pastoral Perspective

One of the things that surprises Christians from developed countries who visit the church in the global South is the way in which people who live in poverty and substandard conditions can be so firm and vibrant in their faith and Christian witness. The preacher may want to challenge her or his hearers to engage persons across sociological barriers. To experience their stories of faith just might transform the life of those in privileged circumstances.

The preacher will no doubt find it easier to preach on the blessings than on the woes. Several approaches are possible to those who will experience the "woes." One approach is to challenge the privileged to a simplicity of living as an imperative of the gospel. This would constitute a rejection of the unbridled materialism and consumerism that characterize much of Western society. But it would also constitute an expression of solidarity with those whose life has been determined by others to be one of poverty and want, even as the same life has been "blessed" by God.

The "woes" deal with those who are preoccupied with how they look in the eyes of others. Jesus says in this sermon that how one looks in the eyes of persons and how they speak of you are not important considerations or criteria: "Woe to you when all speak well of you, for that is what their ancestors did to the false prophets" (v. 26). The preacher may choose to raise the challenge posed by this statement of Jesus in light of a culture of consumerism in which so much is spent on appearance and making a good impression.

In a similar way, the Great Sermon sets out for the Christian an ethic of Christian discipleship that is contrary to the way of the world. To take the beatitudes seriously is to go against the grain of the world, to ride against the tide.

HOWARD K. GREGORY

Exegetical Perspective

"Blessed" (*makarios*) does not simply describe a state of happiness or bliss. Rather, it refers in a theological sense to ones standing before God (Deut. 33:29; Pss. 1:1; 40:4). Likewise the woes, though not as piercing as the pronouncements against the scribes and Pharisees in Matthew 23, are characteristic of oracles of prophetic judgment (Isa. 5:8–23; Amos 6:1; Hab. 2:6–19). Luke's use of such warnings in other parts of the Gospel (Luke 10:13; 11:42–52; 17:1; 21:23; 22:22) indicates that he was familiar with this genre of speech and its effectiveness for adding a layer of prophetic challenge, as compared to Matthew's spiritualized words of comfort (Matt. 5:3–11).

All of this material is set in an eschatological framework that contrasts the *now* and the *not yet*—the present reality and the vision for a better future. Luke emphasizes this when he highlights "you who are hungry *now*" and "you who weep *now*" (v. 21). This eschatological frame of reference is one of the most challenging aspects of this text, for on the surface it appears that the reward is a future reward in heaven (v. 23). Yet for Luke, "behold, your reward *is* great in heaven," implies a present reward in "heaven" as understood in the realized reversal of the social, economic, and political conditions of the poor, hungry, downcast, and marginalized. Matthew's Beatitudes, in contrast, focus on what *will* become a reality or reward in the "kingdom of heaven" (Matt. 5:3). Indeed a great reversal is suggested in both passages, but for Luke these beatitudes and woes are not to be interpreted as a type of endorsement of suffering and persecution for the sake of a heavenly pie-in-the-sky reward in the eternal hereafter, or simply understood as general ethical prescriptions or impossible spiritualized mandates. Rather, they should be looked upon as a direct pressing challenge for the disciples (and all followers of Jesus who can hear these words) to reorient relationships and reverse social, economic, and political injustices so that they gain right standing in the eyes of God.

GAY L. BYRON

Homiletical Perspective

responsibility in the moral realm; rather the second person plural emphasizes that the moral realm is a community concern and that individual and corporate conversion are inextricably intertwined. The beatitudes and the woes (indeed all of chap. 6) are addressed to the disciples and therefore by extension to us, their successors in the apostolic community. This week the preacher can continue to build on the theme of discipleship we noticed in last Sunday's Gospel reading, reminding the congregation that it is impossible to separate our reading today from the great commandment of love and its consequences (6:27–49).

William Willimon once wrote that a "sermon is a sermon when it is about God. We learn implications for human behavior only after we learn who God is and what God is up to."[3] When preaching, it is never a bad thing to begin with God! What do we mean by a God who is defined by the values of the beatitudes and the woes, and what does it mean to worship a God whom Schweizer has called the "powerless omnipotent"?[4]

Our God is the God of those who have nothing *but* God. That actually includes us too, even if our need of God is masked in part by our comparative prosperity. In the final analysis, we are as naked as the poorest of the poor, and our possessions are no tabernacle for everlasting. To paraphrase Johnny Cash, we must not be so heavenly minded that we are of no earthly use; but conversely we must not be of such earthly use that we are no longer heavenly minded. Right at the beginning of the journey of discipleship, Jesus tells us the truth, plainly, of what faithful living is going to be like. We cannot say after today that we have not been plainly advised.

PETER EATON

---

3. See *Christian Century*, February 10, 2004, 18. Metropolitan Anthony of Sourozh described a similar focus of attention when he wrote, "It is not the constant thought of their own sins, but the vision of the holiness of God, that makes the saints aware of their own sinfulness" (*Living Prayer* [London: Darton, Longman & Todd, 1966], 11).

4. See the immensely helpful Eduard Schweizer, *Luke: A Challenge to Present Theology* (London: SPCK, 1982), esp. chap. 6, "God's Presence in Jesus Christ."

Genesis 45:3-11, 15

³Joseph said to his brothers, "I am Joseph. Is my father still alive?" But his brothers could not answer him, so dismayed were they at his presence. ⁴Then Joseph said to his brothers, "Come closer to me." And they came closer. He said, "I am your brother, Joseph, whom you sold into Egypt. ⁵And now do not be distressed, or angry with yourselves, because you sold me here; for God sent me before you to preserve life. ⁶For the famine has been in the land these two years; and there are five more years in which there will be neither plowing nor harvest. ⁷God sent me before you to preserve for you a remnant on earth, and to keep alive for you many survivors. ⁸So it was not you who sent me here, but God; he has made me a father to Pharaoh, and lord of all his house and ruler over all the land of Egypt. ⁹Hurry and go up to my father and say to him, 'Thus says your son Joseph, God has made me lord of all Egypt; come down to me, do not delay. ¹⁰You shall settle in the land of Goshen, and you shall be near me, you and your children and your children's children, as well as your flocks, your herds, and all that you have. ¹¹I will provide for you there—since there are five more years of famine to come—so that you and your household, and all that you have, will not come to poverty.'" . . . ¹⁵And he kissed all his brothers and wept upon them; and after that his brothers talked with him.

Theological Perspective

The liturgical feast and ensuing season of Epiphany marks the public "manifestation" or "appearance" (*epiphaneia*) of God in Jesus Christ. In the West, the Epiphany is associated primarily with the visit of the magi, and thus in a broader sense with the making known of Christ to the Gentiles and their acknowledgment of him. In the East, the primary association is with the baptism of Jesus in the river Jordan and with the public disclosure to those witnessing it (the descent of the dove, the voice from heaven) that this one is the beloved Son of God. Jesus' miraculous provision of wine at the wedding at Cana—the "first of his signs," that "revealed his glory" (John 2:11)—is also recalled in this connection, along with other occasions representing the showing forth of the identity of Jesus Christ.

The lectionary texts for this season generally bear, or bear on, this theme of manifestation in one way or another. In approaching them, then, it might be well to ask how this is. Where and how is epiphany occurring in this passage?

In the present case, we may not have far to look. There is an explicit disclosure of identity, initiating the dramatic climax of the Joseph story: "I am your brother, Joseph" (45:4). With this, everything changes. Not only is Joseph's identity revealed; what God has been doing in the whole succession of

Pastoral Perspective

This dramatic scene follows the stories of Joseph's growing up, his being sold into slavery, his becoming a dream interpreter for the Pharaoh, his ruling over all the land of Egypt, and his confronting of his brothers. Now the drama turns on Joseph's reconciling act. "I am Joseph," he says to his astonished brothers. They cannot speak.

What happened to Joseph over these years is what today we call psychological growth. Joseph was an arrogant young man. His self-importance angered his brothers so much that they had sold him into slavery. From this pit of despair, Joseph did rise with wisdom. Revenge was replaced with compassion. Growth is now offered to his brothers, as well. They have all been humbled by the trials and tribulations of life that have brought them closer to their true, whole selves.

Humility is the virtue that may come when one's pride (egocentricity) is confronted. Joseph has to devise a way for his brothers to surrender to him and receive forgiveness. Surrender is a painful, personal process in our relationships, our faith communities, and our country. To surrender humbly to a higher good does lead to new life, love, and a deeper joy. Moreover, joy is a sign of reconciliation! As the brothers are brought into the presence of the living Joseph, they face their real guilt. Joseph says, "Do not be distressed, or angry with yourselves, because you

Exegetical Perspective

Love Your Enemies. Genesis 45 is perhaps the most affecting scriptural scene of forgiveness and reconciliation, a most compelling text for preaching. Rapprochement and harmony blossom forth here at the climax of the Joseph novella (Gen. 37, 39–50), right at the point of Joseph's revelation of himself to his brothers. They have hated him, sold him into slavery, and given him up for dead; but all that now becomes a thing of the past.

True reconciliation is demanding. Joseph's hard efforts begin with creating a safe space for the work to be done (v. 1). Attentive to his brothers' dismay at his epiphany before them (v. 3), he responds patiently to each of their hesitations and fears. He makes repeat moves to bridge his family's estrangement, twice identifying himself (vv. 3 and 4), twice weeping before his brothers (vv. 2 and 16). He draws his siblings near to him (vv. 4a); he recalls their common story (v. 4b).

Joseph sets aside his trappings to meet his brothers where they are. He proves willing to let go of the past and share a new perspective from God with his kin. The brothers respond with fellowship and intimate conversation (v. 15). The alienation of Genesis 37:4 is finally reversed.

Getting Personal and Vulnerable. Healing the breach with his brothers requires Joseph to tear away all

Homiletical Perspective

Years have passed since ten jealous brothers abandoned Joseph to slavery. Now, in one of Scripture's most poignant narrative moments, Joseph comforts the culprits: "Do not be distressed, or angry with yourselves, because you sold me here; for God sent me before you to preserve life" (v. 5). Joseph forgives his brothers their vicious betrayal and then secures their future by virtue of his powerful position in Egypt. The tale is soaked in divine irony, as the wronged one ensures the safety of those who endangered him. By responding faithfully to his brothers' treachery, Joseph rescues Israel from a killing famine and so ushers forward the larger purposes of God.

It's a wrap! All is well. Cue the schmaltzy music. All that remains for the preacher is to offer the attendant assurance, "All things work together for good," or the obvious exhortation, "Forgive as Joseph forgave." But when she speaks these words, her congregation is left, mouths open, before a reality not their own. In their worlds, part of the story goes mysteriously missing. The dramatic tale of Joseph's reunion with his sibling malefactors powerfully pairs forgiveness with a strong confidence in God's providential hand in history. But picture the scene absent such obvious providence—in a prison cell rather than a palace boardroom, with Joseph still

Genesis 45:3-11, 15

Theological Perspective

events involving Joseph is also announced. This is given first in capsule form—"God sent me before you to preserve life"—and then in more detail, as encompassing both the saving of the people of Egypt from famine and the preservation of Jacob's family through the same difficult times.

Christian readers of these lines have rarely been content just to let Joseph's self-disclosure and his theological interpretation of events stand. They have added their own interpretations to his, usually in the conviction that in doing so they are simply bringing out the real meaning, helping to make manifest what is already there. To John Calvin, for example, Joseph's declaration in 45:8 "shows us how we are to think of God's providence and how we are to profit from it." "I ask you to note how often God not only resists the malice of those who desire to harm us but also turns their evil efforts to our good!"[1] For Calvin, our text thus gives us a short course in the doctrine of providence.

Despite the legitimate observation of Claus Westermann that "[t]he Joseph story knows nothing of a concept of this kind,"[2] issues associated with the traditional doctrine of providence are bound to be raised in the minds of many present-day readers and hearers of this text. Does God indeed enact all the ills that befall us, for some good purpose? Does God not merely "permit" but actually will and bring about, in every particular, the suffering, destruction, and loss that is so much a part of human and creaturely experience? It might be wise to join Westermann in resisting the tendency of many interpreters to read more into Joseph's testimony than is warranted. At the same time, reading closely what *is* there might spark some healthy reorientation in our thinking about God's involvement in human affairs.

The key verse for that purpose might be verse 5: "And now do not be distressed, or angry with your-selves, because you sold me here; for God sent me before you to preserve life." The last phrase, "to preserve life," is an effort to render a simpler (as usual) Hebrew construction that might also be rendered as "to save lives" or "for sustenance." How-ever, it may be that the Septuagint version and its literal English counterpart, in their stark simplicity, make the point best: "God sent me before you for life [*eis . . . zōēn*]." Joseph's testimony is that, whatever

Pastoral Perspective

sold me here; for God sent me before you to preserve life." Reconciliation is possible because in facing our own frailties, vulnerabilities, and even hostilities, we come to understand that divine purposes were at work.

It always gives us pause to declare the ways that God is working out God's purposes. To name God's ways as our ways leads to arrogance. Not to name the presence of God in our human affairs leads to an emaciated faith. In looking back on his own life, Joseph discerns that the hand of God has woven things together for good. Even those things that are hard, difficult, and perhaps even evil have come under the aegis of God's activity in human history. This declaration goes to the heart of the gospel where the question of theodicy, how God and evil can share the same space, is addressed.

The English mystic Julian of Norwich lived at the end of the fourteenth and the beginning of the fifteenth century. During those years the Black Death was the most devastating pandemic in human his-tory, killing seventy-five million people. Julian was a Benedictine nun who herself was mortally ill. During her illness she had visionary experiences. Recording these visions, she wrote the first book by a woman in English. "And so our good Lord answered to all the questions and doubts which I could raise," she wrote, "saying most comfortingly: I may make all things well, and I can make all things well, and I shall make all things well, and I will make all things well; and you will see yourself that every kind of thing will be well."[1] This is not cheery optimism, or smiley-button faith. Rather, it is an affirmation of the mystery of God's love in all things, in all circumstances, even in the midst of personal and enormous human trage-dies. With the perspective of God and God's own love being present in all things and through all things, Julian was able to live fully and faithfully. Like Joseph, Julian was in the stream with those who have come to see the pattern of divine love woven into life, bringing good out of evil.

This pattern was also elucidated by the late John Sanford. "When the pattern of our lives becomes clear to us, even the darkness and pain can be seen to have its proper place. In Joseph's case, the evil the brothers intended against him was intended by God for the purification of his soul, the destruction of his egocentricity, and for a way to bring him to Egypt where he would perform a great work."[2] Joseph

---

1. The quotations are from an abridged version of Calvin's commentary in modern English: John Calvin, *Genesis*, ed. Alister McGrath and J. I. Packer (Wheaton, IL: Crossway Books, 2001), 340–41.
2. Claus Westermann, *Genesis 37–50: A Commentary*, trans. John J. Scullion Jr. (Minneapolis: Augsburg Publishing House, 1986), 143.

1. Julian of Norwich, *Showings* (New York: Paulist Press, 1978,) chap. 31, p. 229.
2. John Sanford, *The Man Who Wrestled with God* (New York/Ramsey: Paulist Press, 1974), 78–79.

Exegetical Perspective

facades. Dismissing all attendants and courtiers, he steps out of his official role (v. 1). Inquiring whether his father Jacob is really still alive (see Gen. 43:27–28), he invites his family to get real with him (v. 3). Drawing everyone close (v. 4), he bids them see for themselves that it is he. It is his mouth speaking (v. 12). Joseph realizes that transformation will be possible for this family only if they find a way to encounter each other in true subjective authenticity.

The quality of Joseph's speech to his brothers further reveals his determination to push aside pretense. Gone is the bratty, self-absorbed dreamer of the novella's beginning (see Gen. 37:5, 8, 10). God's work is now front and center in Joseph's perspective (vv. 5–8). He makes no claim of private wisdom, but seems just as confounded as his brothers at the disclosures of verses 5 and 8. God is probably granting him revelations on the spot, as cross-reference to Proverbs 16:1 suggests. As the proverb declares, what comes out of our mouths in the heat of the moment may turn out to be an illuminating fresh word from God.

Joseph not only humbles himself, connecting with his brothers in true subjectivity, but also opens his soul to them. His work of rapprochement begins and ends with unrestrained weeping (vv. 2 and 15). His tears confirm a deep humanity and openness to transformation. They reveal a Christlike self-giving love willing to become vulnerable amid estrangement and hostility.

The ancient Christian expositor Caesarius, renowned bishop of Arles (ca. 470–543), emphasized the powerful reconciling effect of Joseph's emotional availability. His tears prove to be a balm of healing and harmony. Joseph "tenderly kissed each one of [his siblings] and wept over them individually," Caesarius notes. "As Joseph moistened the necks of his frightened brothers with his refreshing tears, he washed away their hatred."[1]

Offering a New Perspective. A twice repeated, attention-grabbing phrase, "but now" (Heb. *we'attah*), alerts us to a powerful turn in Joseph's rhetoric of reconciliation (vv. 5 and 8). To the entire family's surprise, Joseph's past misfortune turns out to have been a work of divine initiative. God was behind it all, scripting everything; the brothers need not despair or turn on each other. A new perspective

1. Caesarius, Sermon 90.4, quoted in Mark Sheridan, ed., *Genesis 12–50*, Ancient Christian Commentary on Scripture: Old Testament, vol. 2 (Downers Grove, IL: InterVarsity, 2002), 292.

Homiletical Perspective

doing time for chasing the boss's wife (Gen. 39:6b–20) and the brothers caught red-handed with food they had stolen to survive. Picture the scene in the pediatric cancer ward or the domestic violence shelter or just in the middle of a life that seems not to have added up. In the story, the magnanimous one has risen from abject slavery to great power in a great land, but we preachers journey to Joseph in company with many endings that are not yet happy—maybe never will be. So what if providence frowns? "Sure Job is righteous," says Satan in the prologue. "Everything's going right (Job 1:9–11)!" If there's no happy ending, though—then will Joseph forgive?

Access is a preacher's central question in the Joseph narrative. How do I build a story world that my whole congregation can enter? And this question swings on how we imagine God's activity in the world. The Joseph story has it that "the LORD was with [Joseph], and . . . the LORD caused all that he did to prosper" (Gen. 39:3), but that is certainly not the way all faithful or faith-seeking people experience their lives or their God. Discussions of why bad things happen to good people fill church parlors and classrooms, because in them we raise hard questions about how we can imagine God's activity in a flawed world. If God is the divine bellhop, acknowledged only when the parking space comes open at the right time or when the marriage works, the suffering half of our lives and our congregation's stands knocking outside the door. On the other hand, if we render God the absentee landlord who leaves humanity to fend fully for ourselves, we lock our whole congregation out of meeting Joseph's living and active God.

To make matters worse, the preacher and congregation who venture to imagine together the active hand of heaven present in the ups *and* downs of history get no immediate help from Torah. God next appears when a bush burns in Horeb (Exod. 2), to liberate Moses's enslaved generation from their dire oppression. What of the intervening four hundred years of slavery under pharaohs who knew not Joseph or Moses? What was the hand of God doing with Israel then? Some of our people live in those twenty generations—the unspoken, uncharted territory of suffering and the sense of purposelessness that can haunt it. How does one preach this passage to a congregation that rightly does not share our narrator's confidence that God will ultimately prosper them?

Access is the key, and if contemporary Christians cannot easily connect with Joseph's prosperity, his

Genesis 45:3-11, 15

Theological Perspective

may have been the intentions of his brothers or anyone else involved, God has been acting in these events for life. The epiphany here, incorporated in and carried by Joseph's self-disclosure, is an epiphany of the God of life.

Just as Calvin's remarks on our text alert us to its connections (both problematic and promising) with the theological theme of God's providential involvement in events, Martin Luther's commentary opens another rich theological topic. Luther offers a thoroughly (but not exclusively) christological reading of the Joseph story, seeing Joseph as a figure of Christ. Joseph was betrayed, mistreated, handed over to death; unexpectedly revealing himself as alive, he offers forgiveness and a new beginning. What his brothers had intended as an end to Joseph, God has turned into "the salvation and life of Egypt and of the whole world."[3] With characteristic intensity and insight Luther dwells on the transformative impact of this evangelical message of forgiveness and grace upon the brothers, and even ventures an imaginative exploration of the different way each brother might have responded, depending on each one's particular character and experience.

Just as reading a doctrine of providence into the text is best avoided, "figural" christological interpretation along the lines Luther pursues here is best avoided if one's aim is to understand the text in its early historical setting, or in a number of other legitimate ways more recent biblical scholarship has enabled us to pursue. However, in the context of Christian worship and proclamation, the interplay of text, tradition, and contemporary struggles is always complex and generally unruly. Rightly handled, this text can provoke some fresh questioning, and perhaps some fresh insight, concerning the shape of God's involvement in the events of our lives and of our history and concerning the ways that the decisive manifestation of the divine reality in Jesus Christ helps us to understand this.

CHARLES M. WOOD

Pastoral Perspective

came through the dark night of the soul, where his attitude was shaped to see a pattern in his life. Finding meaning woven into the fabric of one's life gives shape and substance to living and allows engagement with others in a conscious and honest way. So it was with Joseph and his brothers. So it is with us and with those we are called to serve. Sanford continues, "Evil remains evil until man's consciousness grows because of it. Then God can use it for good" (Sanford, *The Man*, 79).

In our own spiritual journeys, we remember those times where we too were harsh, vengeful, unforgiving, or indifferent. In our relationships with our children, our spouse or partner, our church community, and our neighbors and colleagues, if we reflect long enough, we can recall such hurtful encounters. Brought to our knees and humbled by acknowledging our own egregious deeds, God comes inviting us to receive divine compassion in our brokenness. Looking back, we see how God has been at work within and among us and offering strength and meaning for our present and the future. All that Joseph's brothers have done comes into their awareness and in the light of Joseph's compassion, they embrace. Reconciliation happens. Sanford concludes that the brothers have undergone "psychological development in the only way it is ever possible: painful self-confrontation, a reckoning with the past, and a willingness to give up egocentricity in order to serve God" (Sanford, *The Man*, 79).

The work of Archbishop Desmond Tutu in the South African Truth and Reconciliation Commission was aimed at that, as well. It allowed those who had committed egregious acts during the time of apartheid to confess what they had done, come to terms with their past, and then be restored to their humanity by the forgiveness of the human community.

Divine love transcends and conquers all when we surrender our own egocentricity. That surrender may come through the shattering experiences that we do not welcome, but that reveal God's presence for our growth.

ALAN JOHNSON

3. Martin Luther, *Lectures on Genesis, Chapters 45–50*, ed. Jaroslav Pelikan and Walter A. Hansen (St. Louis: Concordia Publishing House, 1966), 29.

Exegetical Perspective

is available to them that reframes the past and paves a wonderful new way forward.

Joseph's powerful oratory in verses 5 and 8 at first seems to relieve his brothers of all responsibility for past wrongs. His intention, however, is not to deny or trivialize human agency, which clearly has played its role in the Joseph story (see Gen. 50:20). In stressing "*not you . . . but God,*" Joseph is rather employing a powerful Hebrew rhetorical technique of *dialectical negation* (see the same technique in Ps. 51:16–17; Hos. 6:6), which pushes hearers to embrace the more profound of two truths in tension.

Joseph's language is parallel to that of the character Len in C. S. Lewis's story *The Great Divorce*.[2] In this story, the ghost of Len, a past murderer, urges his former boss (now also deceased) to give up the sense of grievance that has built up inside him over time. He must stop allowing his preoccupations to matter, fretting about his lot and going on and on about fairness and just deserts. There is no need to bother about all that, Len implores. The old boss will be pleased about everything presently. He need only come to understand God's larger picture.

Unfortunately, Len's boss is simply unable to let go of his hang-ups, and refuses to accompany Len into heaven. He reveals to Len just how *stuck* he is when he declares, "I'm not making pals with a murderer, let alone taking lessons from him."[3] Paradoxically, the past *does* turn out to matter for the boss, because he will not let go of it.

Len's story is the opposite. He experienced a new beginning after his act of murder. The deed forced him to own up to everything he had become and to let it all go, putting his old self behind him. Now safe in God's embrace, he no longer bothers about past history. "It is all over now," he rightly affirms. Joseph's hope for his brothers in Genesis 45 is that they may embrace the selfsame healing perspective as Len. That they do in fact begin to do so is a model for us all.

STEPHEN L. COOK

Homiletical Perspective

experience of being wronged *is* universal. In the story, forgiveness is crucial to God's providential movement in the world. Earlier we asked whether Joseph's forgiveness may be conditioned on happy providence. But is not Joseph's forgiveness really a vehicle of providence here, and not simply the outcome of it? More than occasionally the Josephs of our world use their power to pay back those who wronged them on the way up. The nerd in the bad comedy wins the day and then embarrasses the prom king who used to make sport of him. After election day, the victorious political candidate sets out to reward supporters and punish opponents. We see things like this happen all the time. Now imagine that *lex talionis* had reigned in our story's Egypt, with the powerful one justly selling his sellers into slavery themselves, or simply sending them away empty to perish from the famine. If Jacob's sons do not survive, God's promise to Abraham (Gen. 12:1–3) fails. This moment of reconciliation is crucial to the larger movement of God through Genesis and Exodus and beyond, and it never could have happened if Joseph had not forgiven his brothers.

Our congregations can enter that world. Joseph's story has space for us because, however different our people's reality is from Joseph's, God's reconciling movement in the world still and always hinges on forgiveness. Everyone has access, because the dramatic moment of Genesis 45 longs to be played out again every time someone is wronged. A pope steps into an Italian jail cell and forgives his would-be assassin; a grieving mother walks across a tense courtroom to embrace the man whose drunk driving snatched away her son's life; in South Africa, race inconceivably forgives race. Joseph's God lives on in a new form. A wife forgives her husband, a friend forgives his friend, an enemy forgives enemy—reconciliation breaks out in these moments, and suddenly the position of the victim has radically changed. In the moment of forgiveness, the wronged one is transformed from critic of the world as it is to cocreator with God of a brand-new world. And in that new creation, a light comes on: maybe our world is not so different from Joseph's after all. Maybe forgiveness and reconciliation are God's true prosperity.

ALLEN HILTON

---

2. C. S. Lewis, *The Great Divorce* (New York: Macmillan, 1946), 31–36.
3. Ibid., 35.

Psalm 37:1-11, 39-40

¹Do not fret because of the wicked;
 do not be envious of wrongdoers,
²for they will soon fade like the grass,
 and wither like the green herb.

³Trust in the L<small>ORD</small>, and do good;
 so you will live in the land, and enjoy security.
⁴Take delight in the L<small>ORD</small>,
 and he will give you the desires of your heart.

⁵Commit your way to the L<small>ORD</small>;
 trust in him, and he will act.
⁶He will make your vindication shine like the light,
 and the justice of your cause like the noonday.

⁷Be still before the L<small>ORD</small>, and wait patiently for him;
 do not fret over those who prosper in their way,
 over those who carry out evil devices.

Theological Perspective

Introduction. The overarching season of Epiphany frames this psalm pericope, which emphasizes various aspects of God's perpetual faithfulness. Set within the tradition of Wisdom literature, the writer has structured the entire psalm as an acrostic, each section starting with a different letter of the Hebrew alphabet. This aid to memorization invites the reader to look at the many manifestations of God's presence and promises. Selected verses for this Seventh Sunday after the Epiphany focus on several of these themes: the struggles of faith in trusting God; God's commitments to those who believe; the nature of an interim faith and God's final vindication of God's people.

Uneasiness to Trust (vv. 1–4). Psalm 37 reads like an impassioned conversation. One can imagine the questioner raising various existential issues to which the psalmist responds. These appointed verses progress by discussing the tensions between the reality of life experiences and God's proclaimed intentions toward the righteous. Clearly the audience to whom the psalmist speaks has felt the disjuncture between their struggles as believers and those who commit acts of wrongdoing against the faithful. The psalmist begins with an injunction to forgo concerns over the actions of wicked. "Do not fret . . . do not be envious of wrongdoers." This is more than advice

Pastoral Perspective

In an age of plagues, wars, and schisms, Julian of Norwich declares, "All shall be well, and all shall be well, and all manner of thing shall be well." Her statement of faith collides with an old truth: Things go badly. People misuse power. Children die of curable diseases. Soldiers and civilians fall. When we dare to listen to the news of our day, we know that all is not well.

The author of Psalm 37 understands. Writing in the evening of his life (v. 25), the psalmist has seen too much to deny that ancient truth. In particular the author acknowledges the handiwork of "wicked" people, those who "carry out evil devices" and "prosper in their way" (v. 7). Beyond the scope of today's pericope, we hear of people who "plot against the righteous" and "draw the sword and bend their bows to bring down the poor and needy" (vv. 12, 14). And yet the psalmist offers a far-reaching and faithful word. Do not worry. Trust in God. That exhortation springs from neither innocence nor naïveté but from a hard-won faith that God is God and shall be God and all shall be well.

The architecture of the psalm supports the wide sweep of its message. Psalm 37 is an acrostic composition; in this case, every other line begins with successive letters of the Hebrew alphabet. The form of the psalm matches its function, insofar as it

⁸Refrain from anger, and forsake wrath.
   Do not fret—it leads only to evil.
⁹For the wicked shall be cut off,
   but those who wait for the L<small>ORD</small> shall inherit the land.

¹⁰Yet a little while, and the wicked will be no more;
   though you look diligently for their place, they will not be there.
¹¹But the meek shall inherit the land,
   and delight themselves in abundant prosperity.

. . . .
³⁹The salvation of the righteous is from the L<small>ORD</small>;
   he is their refuge in the time of trouble.
⁴⁰The L<small>ORD</small> helps them and rescues them;
   he rescues them from the wicked, and saves them,
   because they take refuge in him.

Exegetical Perspective

Psalm 37 is a wisdom psalm that follows the pattern of an alphabetic acrostic. Our lectionary text takes us from the letter *aleph* in the acrostic to *waw* and then picks up the last letter, *taw*.

The psalm begins with an injunction from a traditional proverb, one that we find with a slightly different ending in Proverbs 24:19. This traditional saying is the theme of the poem: "Do not be angry at the wicked. // Do not envy those who commit iniquity" (v. 1, my trans.). Throughout, Psalm 37 reiterates familiar themes known from the Bible's wisdom books as to how the wicked will receive their just deserts and the righteous will prosper. What tempers this optimistic outlook is the recognition that the wicked may indeed prosper for "a little while" (v. 10) and might be envied for their apparent success (vv. 7, 12, 14, 16). The counsel of the psalm is against preoccupation with the successes of the wicked, recognizing that outrage against them is the result of envy. The poet works out this theme in today's lection (vv. 1–11). That point made, the writer next explains the ultimate fate of the wicked (vv. 12–22) and, finally, counsels against fear of the wicked, because the Lord will protect the righteous (vv. 23–40).

There are parallels between Psalm 37 and Isaiah 58:6–14 (Third Isaiah), especially in verse 6, where the poet uses light symbolism in a way similar to

Homiletical Perspective

Preachers sometimes suffer from the ailment of providing answers to questions that no one is asking. When they do, they are accused of being out of touch with the exigencies of living in the "real" world. Those who choose to preach from Psalm 37 need not fear this ailment or the resulting accusation, because this psalm comes right out of the "real" world, a world where the wicked get wealthy and the righteous look at all their struggles to live faithful lives and wonder, "What's the point?"

Before preaching Psalm 37, there is an ethical question to answer: is it right to preach someone else's sermon? For those who preach on this psalm are not simply reading some provocative ancient poetry; they are preaching an ancient sermon. Like much of the wisdom tradition, Psalm 37 wrestles with the apparent deficiencies in God's just design of the world. The advice the psalmist gives to those who strive to lead a righteous life is captured in contemporary slang by the expression "chill out." The psalmist's refrain "do not fret" suggests that this psalm is addressing people who are fretting, in particular about why the wicked enjoy such a good life.

Preachers of Psalm 37 will soon encounter the same challenge that the psalmist faced. How do you convey the call to live in accord with God's just view of the world when people witness the wicked

Psalm 37:1-11, 39-40

Theological Perspective

merely to ignore what is happening. It is also a reminder to God's people that they may fall victim to the temptation of not trusting in God's faithfulness. What then should supersede the gnawing anxieties wickedness causes believers? Verses 3 and 4 invite the believer to a multitude of responses: trust, doing good, enjoyment of God's security, and delighting in the certainty of God's blessings. Verse 4 is also the first of three references to land in this pericope. The well-being of God's elect may indeed wait spiritually for the fulfillment of God's promises, but God's actions also have a material dimension in which the goodness of the earth itself serves as affirmation of God's faithfulness.

God's Commitments to Us (vv. 5–7). The promise of God's faithfulness is reiterated again in these three verses. The content of God's responses is enumerated in two particular ways. The faithful will experience God's justifying actions on their behalf in a public and significant fashion so "your vindication [will] shine like the light" (v. 6). Furthermore, believers will also have their actions justified in terms of their intentionality and motives, since "the justice of your cause" will be revealed to all. Christians will hear resonance in the psalmist's words with two New Testament passages; from the Sermon on the Mount (Matt. 5:3–12) and the Sermon on the Plain (Luke 6:20–26). If God's people encounter life as unjust or under assault from those who commit wrongful actions against them, God's faithfulness will prevail. Like both New Testament texts, these verses persuade the believers to trust not in the evidence of daily life, however tragic or difficult, but in the faithfulness of God's future forms of vindication. The psalmist also addresses a nagging reality in verse 7. Not only do evildoers act against the faithful; they also seem to "prosper in their way." Who cannot sympathize with any believer who feels the sting of watching someone get away with doing wrong and even doing well in the process? In the face of such insult, the psalmist urges the believer always to focus and refocus on what is important. "Be still before the LORD."

Interim Faith and Final Victory (vv. 8–11). The psalmist addresses the *effects* of the fretting of the faithful, which he has mentioned twice in verse 1 and 7. Allowing the wrongful acts of others to gnaw at one can lead to "anger" and "wrath." Such responses are not only fruitless, but believers could potentially fall into the same ways as wrongdoers. Being upset over the actions of others leads only to evil.

Pastoral Perspective

reads as a primer on the importance of Israel's hope in God's faithfulness. From A to Z, from *aleph* to *taw*, from beginning to end, God's care for the faithful is to be trusted. The opening verse of Georg Neumark's hymn "If You but Trust in God to Guide You" rises in agreement:

> If you but trust in God to guide you
> And place your confidence in him,
> You'll find him always there beside you,
> To give you hope and strength within.
> For those who trust God's changeless love
> Build on the rock that will not move.[1]

Upon the rock of God's trustworthiness, the psalmist instructs Israel not to worry. The psalmist urges three times in eight verses, "Do not fret" (vv. 1, 7, 8). Such repetition may be, in itself, cause for concern. As a pastor, when I hear a church member say three times in a single conversation, "I'm fine," I have reason to wonder. As a student of Psalm 37, I also have reason to agree. I can affirm the parishioner's hope for wellness, because God's faithfulness is sure. The future of the righteous will be secure.

Throughout Psalm 37, nearly every reference to God's saving work and to the good fortune of Israel is expressed in the future tense. In the context of pastoral ministry, an unknowable tomorrow tests today's faith. You visit a church member and his family in the oncology unit. The patient's condition declines. In the midst of a fury of fretting, a family member utters a statement of faith that echoes today's psalm. She says, "Because God is God, I will not let go of my hope for his recovery." Waiting for a sign of improvement, a turn for the better, is an exercise in trust.

In the waiting rooms of this life, trust calls for an active hope. Every morning, a soldier's loved ones hope for a homecoming. Every day, a senior hopes her neighborhood will be redeemed from a growing threat of violence on her street. Every Saturday night, a parent hopes his daughter will walk through the door. The trust we observe in the people of our congregations, the trust of which the psalmist writes, is a living hope—a hope that beats at the center of today's psalm.

With the assurance that God holds our tomorrows, the psalmist calls the faithful to "do good" and "commit your way to the LORD" (vv. 3, 5). The author points to the importance of living in ways that glorify God, even when those good deeds

---

1. *Lutheran Book of Worship* (Minneapolis: Augsburg Publishing House, and Philadelphia: Board of Publication, Lutheran Church in America, 1978), #453.

Exegetical Perspective

Isaiah 58:10. In Isaiah 58:14 the writer writes, "Then you shall take delight in the LORD," using the same verb as does the author of Psalm 37:4, "Take delight in the LORD." The same verb with the same meaning is, however, also found in Job 22:26 and 27:10, allowing us to draw no conclusions about literary dependence, not even allowing us to say that the author of Psalm 37 knew Isaiah 58:6–14.

The interpreter's solution of certain translation ambiguities will affect the understanding of the text. Miles Cloverdale, for instance, rendered the thrice-used expression *al-titkhar* (vv. 1, 7, 8) as "Fret not thy self," and the AV, RSV, and NRSV maintain this translation. This colorless translation does not suggest the full sense of anger or heated competition the verb suggests in other contexts. The same reflexive verb in Jeremiah 12:5, for instance, suggests competition: "If you have raced with foot-runners and they have wearied you, how will you *compete* with horses?" (emphasis added.) The connotations of competition, jealousy, and anger all attach to this verb and heighten the poet's warnings about anger against the success of the wicked.

Faith in Psalm 37 has fascinating aspects and implications. Verses 3–6 read like a list of metaphors for faith. We hear an echo of the Deuteronomist when the author tells us that we should trust in the Lord so that we may settle in the land and "enjoy security" (v. 3). In verse 4, the author enjoins the reader to "take pleasure" in the Lord. Finally, the author uses the vivid idiom "roll to/upon the LORD," with the meaning "commit to," a usage otherwise limited to Ps. 22:9; Prov. 16:3; and Sir. 7:17. The composite figure is one of a faith in God built of confidence, delight, and commitment.

The promises in return for such faith include settlement in the land of Israel, security there (v. 3), vindication, and (favorable) judgment. Tenure on the land will also be a result of being quiet (v. 7) and waiting expectantly for the Lord (v. 7, 9). The poet uses the expression "inherit the land" in both verse 9 and verse 11, as well as in verses 22, 29, 34 to refer to God's promise of untroubled existence for God's people in the land of Israel. The repetition of the phrase "inherit the land" is not an example of bad writing but a measure of the importance of the promise.[1]

Biblical acrostics (Nah. 1:2–8; Lam. 1–4; Pss. 9–10, 25, 34, 37, 111, 112, 119, 145; Prov. 31:10–31)

---

1. The Septuagint's translation of Ps. 37:11 (Ps. 36:11 LXX) forms the basis of Matthew's third beatitude (Matt. 5:5): "Blessed are the meek, for they will inherit the earth."

Homiletical Perspective

prospering? To hear that the advantages of the wicked are fleeting, "like the grass" (v. 2) may have a fine poetic ring, but it is a tenuous argument and ultimately unconvincing, even to the righteous.

A common problem that preachers face in sorting through this psalm is the temptation to equate wealth with wickedness, as if wealth is a sign of a wicked life and poverty is a sign of piety. As James Luther Mays reminds careful readers about wealth and the wicked in this psalm, "They are not wicked because they are wealthy but wealthy because they are wicked."[1] Wealth gained through wickedness is not to be envied, says the psalmist, because the wicked, even those who are wickedly wealthy, will eventually answer to the just ways of God.

The just ways of God are certain in Psalm 37, if not necessarily imminent. In God's good time, the righteous will "inherit the land" (v. 9), a promise not unlike the promise of Jesus to the crowd, "The meek shall inherit the earth" (Matt. 5:5). In an instantaneous society, where we can access information in a microsecond, there is not a high premium on waiting. Americans in 2007 saved less than 0.8 percent of their income. We want what we want, and we want it now. The preacher of Psalm 37 faces the daunting task of inviting anxious and busy, poor and struggling people to wait on the justice of God, "For the wicked shall be cut off, but those who wait for the LORD shall inherit the land" (v. 9).

A related challenge that the preacher of Psalm 37 will confront is people's anger at the prosperity of the wicked. This anger is often interpreted as "righteous anger" by those who wait for God to make "vindication shine like the light, and the justice of your cause like the noonday" (v. 6). The psalmist writes about what any preacher knows well, the spiritual danger of being consumed by anger, righteous or not, and by envy of those who succeed despite their total ignorance of God.

The psalmist's sermon ends with words of wisdom that set the theological struggles of the righteous in context, "The salvation of the righteous is from the LORD; he is their refuge in the time of trouble. The LORD helps them and rescues them; he rescues them from the wicked, and saves them, because they take refuge in him" (vv. 39–40). Because salvation comes from no other source than God, those who trust in God can "chill out," put

---

1. James Luther Mays, *Psalms,* Interpretation Series (Louisville, KY: Westminster John Knox Press, 1994), 160.

Psalm 37:1-11, 39-40

Theological Perspective

Land is mentioned twice in these verses, this time in relationship to the cessation of the wicked. They will be "cut off," with the result that those who are waiting for God "shall inherit the land." To present-day listeners, any mention of land in a sermon is certain to elicit a number of associations. The psalmist's reflections on the struggles for a peaceable place of one's own are reflected in the heartbreaking, life-destroying reality of today's world. Nations and people are racked with border disputes and crossings, land grabs, occupations and invasions of one another's land. Reminders of such bitter encounters are found in the struggle between Palestinians and Israelis and the issues many nations face related to immigration and refugees.

The theme of land taken from the wicked and given to the righteous continues in verse 10. God will so completely erase the sources of wrongdoing and evil that if the righteous wonder how the land came to be theirs, they will see the wicked "will not be there" (v. 10). In an echo of Matthew 5:5, verse 11 describes the land passing into the inheritance of "the meek."

Salvation's Triumph (vv. 39, 40). The wording of the last two verses summarizes all that has gone before. God is the source of salvation, the faithful are rescued from the wicked, and God is the ultimate refuge. The words of assurance stand against the fact that advising the faithful to wait for a better day is one of the most difficult homiletical and therefore pastoral acts. Enduring suffering at the hands of the wicked leaves open the possibility that believers may suffer not only physical death but the death of hope itself. Human-rights violations today continue to witness globally to the concerns this psalm discusses.

Conclusion. This psalm's perspectives reinforce the paradoxical nature of God's actions. God's power shows itself in great reversals. If the righteous experience the loss of peace of mind, justice, and land, God will finally restore everything to them no matter what daily experience says to the contrary. Certainly this is what Christians confess in the reality and triumph of the cross.

SUSAN K. HEDAHL

Pastoral Perspective

are overshadowed by all that threatens our well-being. The need for the faithful "to do justice, and to love kindness, and to walk humbly with your God" (Mic. 6:8) abides, despite thin evidence that all is well in the present day.

William Sloane Coffin too recognized the active nature of faith. In *Credo* Coffin writes:

> It is terribly important to realize that the leap of faith is not so much a leap of thought as of action. For while in many matters it is first we must see, then we will act; in matters of faith it is first we must do then we will know, first we will be and then we will see. One must, in short, dare to act wholeheartedly without absolute certainty.[2]

For Coffin, like the author of Psalm 37, a living faith perseveres when things go badly, when signs of life are hard to find, when the future looks dim. The people of Israel and the people in our congregations may struggle under the thumb of uncertainty, but our witness in word and deed to God's faithfulness is grounded in a belief that the future tense is authored by God.

In North Philadelphia, a group of neighbors demonstrate a living faith. The Norris Square Neighborhood Project aims to transform derelict lots into green space, gardens that bear fruits and vegetables and offer sanctuary to neighbors.

The street scenes beyond the gardens' chain-link fences challenge the notion that a new and brighter day will dawn there. Drunkards sit on the stoops of bars in the midday heat. Teens on the corner exchange drugs and money. Sirens careen back and forth on the avenues.

The sowers and reapers of Norris Square could fret with good reason. The women in those gardens not only know of the wrongdoing in their neighborhood; they know many of the wrongdoers by name. Despite the abundant evidence of urban violence and blight, they refuse to let anyone compromise their steadfast commitment to improving their neighborhood. A faithful few continue to plant and prune, water and weed. They go about their good work quietly, trusting that what they do will make a difference, that God will give them "the desires of [their] heart," that there is "posterity for the peaceable" (v. 4, 37). They trust like the psalmist, the medieval mystic, and the fiery preacher. Their faith—our faith—is an active hope in the faithfulness of God.

ANDREW NAGY-BENSON

2. William Sloane Coffin, *Credo* (Louisville, KY: Westminster John Knox Press, 2004), 7.

Exegetical Perspective

are all alphabetic acrostics in which each line, each strophe, or each line of each strophe begins with a successive letter of the Hebrew alphabet. Psalm 37 is a strophic acrostic in which the first line of each strophe begins with the next Hebrew letter of the alphabet.

Are Hebrew acrostics mnemonic devices, as some claim? Probably not. Ancient Assyrian also boasted acrostics; but in Assyrian, cuneiform signs often represent more than one syllable, rendering Assyrian acrostics more visual than auditory in nature. Consequently this acrostic feature could not help the ear in memorization. Likely this was true of the biblical acrostics as well.

The category "wisdom psalm" itself is currently under scholarly discussion, as well as the setting of these psalms within the life of the community. The usual view is that these psalms come from wisdom teachers who composed them both as instruction and as artistic creations. Some have recently attempted to portray the wisdom psalms as having a setting in the communal prayer of Israel, perhaps in liturgies of the early synagogue. The wisdom concepts and vocabulary in the wisdom psalms, however, do not differ significantly from the other examples of Hebrew wisdom in the Bible, most of which are not liturgical. In this vein, the reader should note that prohibitions in Psalm 37 begin with the suggestive and relatively weak *'al*, common in Wisdom literature, not the strong prohibitive *lo'* of biblical commandments and liturgical speech.

In favor of a communal interpretation is the fact that the ancient promise of inheriting the land is the principal promise in Psalm 37. Further, the promise of salvation at the end of the psalm reads less like the Wisdom literature's emphasis on the power of righteousness to save an individual from trouble (as in Prov. 11:6) and more like the Psalter's cries for and promises of salvation for God's people.

FRED L. HORTON

Homiletical Perspective

their anger and envy in context, and have confidence that the just ways of God will prevail.

Those who trust God's just promises know that they will "live in the land," a powerful metaphor for living life that Jesus would later expand upon when he declared that the reign of God is at hand (Mark 1:14–15). Clinton McCann provides a feast of images for preachers as they reflect upon trusting in the sovereign goodness of God, a trust revealed in the life and teaching of Jesus. "For Jesus," writes McCann,

> the reality of God's rule turned worldly values upside down. Because God rules the world, "the meek . . . will inherit the earth" (Matt 5:5; see also Ps 37:11a). Because God rules the world, "those who hunger and thirst for righteousness . . . will be filled" (Matt 5:6; see also Ps 37:19). Because God rules the world, there is a source of joy and an experience of peace greater than the world can give (see John 14:27; see also Ps 37:11b). Because God rules the world, "life does not consist in the abundance of possessions" (Luke 12:15; see also Ps 37:16). Because God rules the world, "it is more blessed to give than receive" (Acts 20:35; see also Ps 37:21, 26). Because God rules the world, there is no need to "worry about your life" (Matt 6:25; see also Ps 37:4).[2]

Psalm 37 is not simplistic about the human struggle to trust in God when those who do not seem to be faring so well. It is a psalm that assumes a community of the faithful that emboldens each other to trust in God and to challenge each other not to give in to anger or envy when justice lags. Some preaching texts challenge preachers to demonstrate their relevance to the "real" world. Psalm 37 is written to challenge its readers to distinguish what will be "real" in God's just time from what they see in the time being.

GARY W. CHARLES

2. J. Clinton McCann, Jr., "Psalms," in *The New Interpreter's Bible*, vol. 4 (Nashville: Abingdon Press, 2001), 830.

1 Corinthians 15:35-38, 42-50

³⁵But someone will ask, "How are the dead raised? With what kind of body do they come?" ³⁶Fool! What you sow does not come to life unless it dies. ³⁷And as for what you sow, you do not sow the body that is to be, but a bare seed, perhaps of wheat or of some other grain. ³⁸But God gives it a body as he has chosen, and to each kind of seed its own body.

⁴²So it is with the resurrection of the dead. What is sown is perishable, what is raised is imperishable. ⁴³It is sown in dishonor, it is raised in glory. It is sown in weakness, it is raised in power. ⁴⁴It is sown a physical body, it is raised a spiritual body. If there is a physical body, there is also a spiritual body. ⁴⁵Thus it is written, "The first man, Adam, became a living being"; the last Adam became a life-giving spirit. ⁴⁶But it is not the spiritual that is first, but the physical, and then the spiritual. ⁴⁷The first man was from the earth, a man of dust; the second man is from heaven. ⁴⁸As was the man of dust, so are those who are of the dust; and as is the man of heaven, so are those who are of heaven. ⁴⁹Just as we have borne the image of the man of dust, we will also bear the image of the man of heaven.

⁵⁰What I am saying, brothers and sisters, is this: flesh and blood cannot inherit the kingdom of God, nor does the perishable inherit the imperishable.

Theological Perspective

First Corinthians 15:35–50 contains Paul's most extensive description of a key Christian doctrine that still causes confusion in the church: bodily resurrection. Immediately before this pericope, Paul presents his defense of the resurrection of the dead against those who, like the Sadducees, "say there is no resurrection of the dead" (15:12). He then turns his attention to those who would deny the resurrection of the *body* or who question, "With what kind of body do they come?"

The relationship between the body and salvation was a source of tension in the Corinthian congregation. Those believers known as "enthusiasts" or "spiritualists" were abusing their bodies through debauchery (6:12), gluttony (6:13), and sexual immorality (6:15–20) under the cover of a misinterpretation of grace. They claimed that because they were already justified by grace (thus essentially *already* resurrected), what they did in their temporal bodily state did not matter. It may be this same group that was questioning the logic of embodied resurrection. In his response to this attack on bodily resurrection, Paul uses the metaphor of a seed to address two misconceptions that continue today: a reductionistic materialism (reducing humans to their bodies) and an anthropological dualism.

Pastoral Perspective

One can almost see the veins throb at Paul's temples, hear his teeth grind. The quill snaps and ink spatters the parchment and his hand. "Fool!" he scrawls—not the first listing in almost any pastoral lexicon. But as he does in the Galatian correspondence, here Paul imprecates those among whom he has labored and whom he still loves (see 15:1), lambasting their fecklessness and vain imaginings. He screams that they have syncretized received doctrine with the "knowledge" of the day (*gnōsis*; see 8:1). In Paul's agitated judgment the Corinthians teeter on the precipice of both disintegration and perdition.

Today's lection is one part of a much broader and more comprehensive debate. Reading snippets can blunt its rapier edge, because for Paul literally everything is at stake: the gospel he had preached in all of its particularity, the call these believers had answered in all of its urgency, the communal life that had set them apart from their pagan context and solidified their faithfulness with *koinōnia* (fellowship).

By the time we get to chapter 15, Paul's language is feverish and apprehensive, tightly reasoned and passionately expounded. Perhaps that is because Paul's argument with the Corinthians begins in chapter 1. It gains stridency across the epistle as Paul decries the ways in which the body of Christ in Corinth is being

Exegetical Perspective

Paul was no advocate of abstract or disembodied spirituality. First Corinthians 15, with its varied but connected arguments, shows that Paul expected even the afterlife to be embodied. At verse 35 he quotes "someone," a hypothetical interrogator, posing a pair of questions. "How are dead bodies (*nekroi*) raised? With what kind of body (*sōma*) do they come?" Some scholars have suggested that a faction at Corinth believed they had already experienced a spiritual resurrection and therefore rejected Paul's view of a future resurrection (see 2 Tim. 2:17–18). This passage, however, suggests a controversy not over *future* resurrection, but over *bodily* resurrection.[1]

Posing and answering questions is a frequent marker of Paul's style and of an ancient form of argument called the diatribe. In this passage, whose position might these hypothetical questions represent? First Corinthians gives varied evidence for church factions, but repeatedly names a divisive group Paul terms "the strong," who claim superior knowledge, status, and giftedness. "The strong" might well have held a sophisticated intellectual view that coarse material flesh simply cannot become immortal, and therefore *bodily* resurrection is inconceivable, even

1. Dale Martin, *The Corinthian Body* (New Haven, CT: Yale University Press, 1995), 105–6.

Homiletical Perspective

In my fifteen years of ordained ministry, I cannot think of a text that has elicited such confused responses from parishioners as this pericope from Paul's First Letter to the Corinthians. Maybe it is because, while church folks know a bit about seeds, we know very little about resurrection of the dead. Our faith compels us to believe, but reality causes us to be uncertain.

What were the issues in the Corinthian community that compelled Paul to write about resurrection of the dead, and to do so in terms of what is perishable or imperishable? Clearly people were asking, "How are the dead raised?" and "With what body do they come?" They also had exchanged Paul's original response to these questions for answers that departed significantly from the gospel. The Corinthian Christians not only were fledgling in their understanding of Christ's resurrection; they also were wrong! Paul seeks once again to invite the Corinthians to hear the gospel and to help those who, though they have heard his preaching of Christ crucified and Christ resurrected, still do not grasp the message. The preacher would do well to identify the misunderstandings of today's congregation and invite them anew to hear the gospel they have yet to grasp. Paul's argument suggests an outline for our own.

1 Corinthians 15:35-38, 42-50

Theological Perspective

First, Paul rejects any simplistic materialism that would claim that the exact same earthly body that dies is resurrected. Because of sin, this earthly body is weak and dishonorable and therefore doomed to perish. The rotting corpse in the grave is certainly not the resurrected body.

While Paul rejects the notion that the same physical body that believers possess on earth is raised, he is even more insistent that humans are raised with some type of body. Paul rejects the sharp spirit/body dualism of Platonism and later Christian Manicheism, which denigrated embodiment. Paul clearly does not see the body as inherently evil. In 1 Thessalonians 5:23 Paul entreats believers concerned about the delayed Parousia, "May your spirit and soul and *body* be kept sound and blameless at the coming of our Lord Jesus Christ." And to the Corinthian "spiritualists" he said, "glorify God in your *body*" (1 Cor. 6:20).

How then do we understand his claim that "flesh and blood cannot inherit the kingdom" (15:50)? It is too simplistic to say, as some commentators do, that "flesh" represents the physical, sensual part of humanity that does not enter the kingdom while "body" represents the wholeness of our being that does enter the kingdom. The better distinction is between life according to the flesh and life according to the spirit. "[I]f you live according to the flesh (*kata sarka*), you will die; but if by the Spirit (*de pneumati*) you put to death the deeds of the body, you will live" (Rom. 8:13). Embodied life is not evil. What is evil is life according to the flesh/sinful nature (Gk.: *sarx*), a life in opposition to God's will, one that places confidence in earthly things and human achievements. (Paul contrasts a life according to the flesh with a life according to the Spirit in Gal. 5:19–26.) So when Paul says that "flesh and blood cannot enter the kingdom," he is saying that an attitude *kata sarka* (according to the flesh) has no place in the presence of a holy and righteous God. "Of the dust" and "of heaven" represents a similar distinction, not between the spiritual and the physical, since both Adam and Christ are embodied beings, but between Adam who follows the sinful nature (*sarx)* and Christ who follows the way of the Spirit.

Paul adamantly rejects the idea that the body is inherently evil and thus cannot be resurrected. God, who created all things, can redeem the body "as he has chosen." Embodiment is a good thing. Christ, the *logos*, became embodied and walked among us (contra docetism); and contrary to the heretical line

Pastoral Perspective

dismembered by petty squabbles. Some of the controversies are, on the face of them, silly and very much like the kinds of arguments contemporary pastors might hear (even be wounded by) in everyday church life: which (former) preacher was the best, whose baptism or worship leadership was the more meaningful (see 1:12–16), who is the ensign of the congregation's life and thought. For Paul, of course, the answer to all these questions is Christ (today's pastors do well to take note and comfort).

Some of the Corinthian debate, however, is more substantive. In chapter 15 there is genuine and acrimonious theological controversy. Paul aims special disparagement at one particular member of the community (or at a few) who had received the gospel as Paul preached it but now, over time and in his absence, have materially redefined its terms, especially as regards the doctrine of the resurrection.

Or perhaps there is no "one" teacher Paul identifies in Corinth. The NIV translates the adjective *aphrōn* (v. 36) impersonally rather than vocatively, leaving Paul to voice his ire at a theological position rather than its holder: "How foolish!" With this reading Paul's rhetoric is pastoral strategy: he grants his reader-listeners room to recognize the absurdity of the argument without immediately personalizing his attack. A direct assault on one or some of their own might well have prompted the Corinthians to close ranks and defend the error and/or its proponent(s).

The redefiners do not seem to doubt the resurrection *of Christ*. They may, however, consider Easter to be a unique occurrence in the life of God and the history of the world. Most likely they advocate some form of spiritualized or "realized resurrection" or contend that *they* in fact have already experienced this resurrection and the spiritual gifts they manifest are proof.

Paul is horrified. Accordingly, the NRSV renders Paul's Greek as a withering vocative. In this reading Paul appears ready to part with the one(s) who have reconfigured the gospel, knowing that common cause was no longer possible when such a fundamental truth was sacrificed. In fact the community is already broken, for the gospel is a specific hope, and the church is a community of that specific hope. Only the comprehensive gospel as Paul had presented it could unite and drive the community.

Where these teachers got their ideas is anyone's guess—perhaps from Gnosticism and perhaps not—but the tendency to alloy received doctrine with other, lesser doctrines is an ongoing challenge for churches. The history of theology may be read as an attempt to

Exegetical Perspective

offensive, conjuring ghoulish specters of resuscitated corpses. Whoever the questioner represents, Paul responds vehemently: "Fool!" (v. 36).

As he argues for an expectation that cannot be tested by ordinary experience, Paul weaves together images of plants, animals, stargazing, and more that help "naturalize" his views, carry them forward by the power of association more than logic, yet also convey intellectual credibility.

Paul begins with images of sowing. The germination point of seeds is like the transition point of death, he suggests, making death the precondition for being made to live (*zōopoieitai*) (v. 36). Seed-to-plant transformations show that bodily forms may change radically, yet be in continuity. Indeed, God's creativity in plant forms opens more flexible ways to contemplate "the body that is to be" (v. 37).

Although the lectionary omits verses 39–41, they are integral to Paul's reasoning. Skipping them may obscure how Paul describes embodiment across a continuum and overstress his later more dualistic language. These verses also help clarify how Paul is using three key terms, flesh (*sarx*), body (*sōma*), and glory or splendor (*doxa*), whose meanings depend heavily on context. Flesh (*sarx*) in this passage indicates the basic stuff of which living beings are made, and Paul emphasizes its variety. From human, to animal, to bird, to fish (v. 39), his list may move in order of decreasing refinement, but may just highlight difference. Bodies (*sōmata*) (here not a synonym for "flesh" but a term for "structured forms") also vary, as shown by glancing from terrestrial to celestial bodies, with their differing splendor, glory, or radiance (*doxa*) (v. 40). Though glorious and distant, they remain perceptible as bodies.

From such images, Paul draws human correlates: "So it is with the resurrection of the dead" (v. 42). He pairs the verb "raise" from the opening question (v. 35) with the now familiar "sow." If "sowing" leads naturally to "raising," then raising of the dead might not seem so strange. Paul insists that resurrection reverses the human experience of impermanence, susceptibility, and frailty (vv. 42–44).

At verse 44, two more key terms appear, derived from nouns usually translated "life" or "soul" (*psychē*) and "spirit" (*pneuma*). As Paul uses their adjective forms to modify "body" (*sōma*), his language is intriguing: how does one construe *sōma psychikon* and *sōma pneumatikon*? Some translations offer "physical body" and "spiritual body" (RSV, NRSV), but "physical" unfortunately implies a contrast

Homiletical Perspective

Paul proclaims the gospel of Christ's resurrection so that people will be enabled to live in the face of death without fear and will be empowered to live in the world as those who believe death no longer exercises dominion. Paul lays out his argument to make certain that the Corinthians will not, cannot, miss the discrepancy between how they are living, and what God has done in Christ's resurrection. Paul insists that an understanding of the resurrection will lead to a change in their behavior and in their lives.

Paul affirms here what we Christians know to be true. What we believe has a direct impact on how we behave and the ways that we behave reflect what we believe.

So it is that "a fool" is introduced in this letter, letting Paul once more address this issue that is of such central importance to him and to his mission. He has compassion on the Corinthian people, who just do not seem to get it yet. How many times does Paul have to explain this necessary concept of faith? He will try again, of course, answering the question of a "fool" without making it feel to the readers in Corinth that he is talking about them, even though he might well be.

It is interesting that Paul ignores the first question posed. Perhaps that was just a way to get the community's attention. Who after all does not wonder from time to time about the resurrection of the dead? It will be the second question, "with what bodies do they come?" that Paul attempts to answer.

A basic biology lessons begins. I imagine my ninth-grade daughter's biology teacher standing in front of her students beginning the class for the morning. The bodies of things differ. There are seeds that become plants. Then the plants die and become seed. Bury the seed, give it care, and a new plant grows. There can be no new plant life unless the old plant dies, turns to seed, and is replanted. The Corinthian crowd, an agrarian community, understands this concept well.

Paul moves on to the flesh. While the dying plant provides for the new plant to take life, it is God who raises the imperishable from the perishable human being. Paul perhaps goes farther than we might in insisting that there is dishonor in the human body by its very origin. God transforms this dishonorable body, raising God's own children in glory. Though the human body knows weakness in our current incarnation, it will be raised with power. The new creation in Christ, says Paul, is spiritual. Yet it is clear that for Paul, spiritual still means bodily!

1 Corinthians 15:35-38, 42-50

Theological Perspective

of preaching that endures in Christianity, salvation does not involve redemption *from* the body but redemption *of* the body.

How then do we understand the strange oxymoron used to describe our resurrected bodies—spiritual bodies (*sōma pneumatikon*)? Just as it is erroneous to think of flesh merely in terms of physicality, so it is a mistake to think of spirituality as signifying incorporeality. Spirit is a way of living, a way of relating to God and neighbor. "The *sōma pneumatikon . . .* is to be understood not as one which consists of *pneuma* [spirit], but as one which is controlled by *pneuma*."[1] In our resurrected beings, we will be completely moved by and in conformity with the Spirit of God (Rom. 8:11).

So while it is not the body in the grave that is resurrected, what is resurrected is not completely unconnected with the earthly bodies we possessed. There is continuity between the bodies we possess on earth and our new, resurrected bodies. Our bodies are not mere husks covering the essential "spiritual" self; a person's body is part of that person's identity. Paul also wants to emphasize the discontinuity between the body that is sown "in dishonor" and the body raised "in glory," so he uses the metaphor of a plant and its seed. The plant dies but a seed from that plant continues on. The "bare seed" is not identical with the plant but contains all that the plant is and can be again.

Christ is the model for believers' resurrection. Christ's resurrected body is both like and unlike his earthly body, recognizable to believers but also transformed. Similarly, the resurrected bodies of believers will be identifiable but transformed, from the image of Adam to the image of Christ. Christ is "from heaven"; Adam is "from the dust." Again, this is not a contrast between embodiment and disembodied spirituality, but between ways of living. Just as Adam represents a life lived according to the flesh, Christ models the fruits of the Spirit. Believers simply partake of Christ's resurrection. "Just as we have borne the image of the man of dust, we will also bear the image of the man of heaven" (v. 49). We "put on" Christ (Rom. 13:14) and are "conformed to the body of his glory" (Phil. 3:21). Just as we are the body of Christ on earth, at death we shall put on the imperishable and immortal body of Christ.

KYLE FEDLER

Pastoral Perspective

hold fast to the faith once delivered to the saints and concurrently determining what exactly that faith is. Contemporary pastoral ministry may be interpreted as the struggle to counter the corrupt and idolatrous refiguring of the gospel in terms of political ideology or success (the Corinthians are not the only ones to imagine they were living their best life now!).

The *results* of the Corinthian controversies are, to Paul the pastor, as troubling as the subjects are to Paul the theologian. This "new" Corinthian theology (analogous to the TV gospel with which we are familiar) did nothing more than reify the class distinctions and divisions that already characterized the pagan world. Table fellowship, a mark of Jesus' own ministry and the touchstone of Christian *koinōnia*, was splintering (see 11:17–34). There was litigation, moral laxity, condescension, competition—in sum, all manner of division.

By contrast, the gospel Paul announced, with the cross at its heart, served to obliterate the cultural and social distinctions that could only paralyze and ultimately disintegrate the Corinthian church. They still do. And so (whether his invective is personal or rhetorical) he maintains that "holding fast" to the original terms of the gospel by which the Corinthians were summoned to a shared life is crucial.

With many other moderns, Christian leaders and people sometimes construe congregations as but one more of our many voluntary associations, outward and visible clusterings of persons around one or more shared interests or goals. Like-mindedness is sacrificed for common cause. Accordingly, doctrinal affirmations and even confessional traditions are regarded as "opinions," expendable for the sake of relationships. Conversely, some imagine "doctrine" as a deep moat surrounding ancient castles of theological tradition. Its near edge proves the far shore of inclusion, its far edge the nearest precincts of exile and exclusion. In such tribes nothing matters more than uniformity of doctrine.

In either view, what might be called true doctrine and true community are independent of each other. For Paul, however, authentic community and particular "doctrinal" confessions of the gospel are interdependent. The church is not a group of volunteers who have chosen Christ, but saints chosen by Christ—called and given identity through a particular confession and hope (1:26–30). The origin and arc of the gospel proclamation (see 15:3–8) remain the foundation and nerve of authentic and lasting community life.

THOMAS R. STEAGALD

---

1. Gerhard Kittel, *Theological Dictionary of the New Testament* (Grand Rapids: Eerdmans, 1971), 421.

Exegetical Perspective

between material and immaterial entities, which is inconsistent with Paul's sustained argument. Better is the translation of "natural body" and "spiritual body" (NIV, NJB, KJV). The Jerusalem Bible (as Richard Hays comments[2]) renders verse 44 in particularly lovely and perceptive language: "When it is sown it embodies the soul, when it is raised it embodies the spirit. If the soul has its own embodiment, so does the spirit have its own embodiment" (JB).

Life or soul (*psychē*) and spirit (*pneuma*) remain key terms as Paul then develops a compressed first-and-last-Adam comparison (see also 1 Cor. 15:22; Rom. 5:14). Closely echoing the Greek version of Genesis 2:7 (adding the words "first" and "Adam"), Paul contrasts the first human, who became "living," with Christ, who is "life-making" or "life-generating" (*zōopoioun*, echoing v. 36). Whereas the first Adam was a "soul" or "natural being" (*psychē*), the last is "spirit" (*pneuma*). Clearly, Paul notes, "natural" precedes "spiritual" (v. 46). The Adam images also extend his earlier distinction between earthly and heavenly: humans are not merely earthy but "of the dust"; Christ elevates believers not toward the stars but toward God (v. 47). Paul assures his hearers, bearing Adam's image, that they will ultimately resemble Christ (v. 48); resurrection will recapitulate creation.

Verse 50 closes the lectionary passage. Now addressing "brothers and sisters," Paul offers one negative answer to "someone's" questions. However the dead are raised, and with whatever body they come, resurrection will not involve "flesh (*sarx*) and blood," those lower levels of the stuff of life. Perhaps on this point Paul and his opponents agreed. But for Paul, embodied life is reducible neither to flesh (*sarx*) nor to natural existence (*psychē*). The lasting commonwealth of God may exclude that which is coarsely material and perishable, but there are bodies (*sōmata*) that give form to glory (*doxa*) and especially to spirit (*pneuma*), as his web of creative analogies and arguments has shown.

After Paul, other views of the afterlife also developed in Christian tradition. Yet Paul's insistence that our futures are sown in our present lives and that the life of the spirit is fundamentally embodied (now and forever) holds deep ethical and communal resonance. We benefit too from lingering over Paul's conviction that God's creative and transformative acts revealed all around us and in Christ are a reliable guide for anticipating God's actions in the imperceptible and distant reaches of time and experience.

B. DIANE LIPSETT

Homiletical Perspective

We are well beyond the biology classroom now. Believers are willing to live and to believe on the levels of both physical science and theological truth. Indeed, who would ever claim that mortal flesh can inherit the realm of God? The perishable has no business with the imperishable.

Yet Paul wants us to understand that our bodies are necessary to resurrection. While we live in the world with one, we are given eternal life with the other. In both mortal life and eternal life, we are given a body, but a change will take place to transform us from one into the other. For Paul, that transformation is the work of God's grace.

Paul's questions are appropriate for us as well. If we are a resurrection people, we too must wonder about what the resurrection means in theological terms and in personal terms. Perhaps we need not be tied to Paul's biology lesson as we ponder this text today. We know so much more now about life and about death; and, to be honest, we worry less about what happens to our physical bodies at the point of death. Perhaps it is enough for us to believe that resurrection happens. We live as a people of the resurrection. So today's preacher might well ask "How are we to realize resurrection in our day, our time, our lives? How are we to live into that resurrection?"

We surely see resurrection every time we see the struggle for justice prevail. We see signs of resurrection every time we engage another in reducing the pain and hurt in the world. We move closer to the hope of resurrection when we show compassion, and recognize that that compassion is God's movement in our very lives.

Hard though this passage is, one might well want to engage Paul in the weeks following the birth of Jesus and just before Lent, offering a good word about life after death, a word that will be most welcome in a world where signs of death are too evident. Here and now the hope of resurrection is sorely needed.

MARIA LASALA

2. Richard Hays, *First Corinthians* (Louisville, KY: John Knox Press, 1997), 272.

Luke 6:27-38

27"But I say to you that listen, Love your enemies, do good to those who hate you, 28bless those who curse you, pray for those who abuse you. 29If anyone strikes you on the cheek, offer the other also; and from anyone who takes away your coat do not withhold even your shirt. 30Give to everyone who begs from you; and if anyone takes away your goods, do not ask for them again. 31Do to others as you would have them do to you.

32"If you love those who love you, what credit is that to you? For even sinners love those who love them. 33If you do good to those who do good to you, what credit is that to you? For even sinners do the same. 34If you lend to those from whom you hope to receive, what credit is that to you? Even sinners lend to sinners, to receive as much again. 35But love your enemies, do good, and lend, expecting nothing in return. Your reward will be great, and you will be children of the Most High; for he is kind to the ungrateful and the wicked. 36Be merciful, just as your Father is merciful.

37"Do not judge, and you will not be judged; do not condemn, and you will not be condemned. Forgive, and you will be forgiven; 38give, and it will be given to you. A good measure, pressed down, shaken together, running over, will be put into your lap; for the measure you give will be the measure you get back."

Theological Perspective

In this segment of the Sermon on the Plain, Jesus prescribes an ethic of generosity for Christians living in a hostile world. He calls his listeners to love their enemies, to bless and give even to those who curse and take. His hearers are taught to behave in a way considered imprudent by many, sowing generosity where nothing is expected to grow. Jesus rejects the advice that would have been more common, that one should give to those who will respond appropriately. Even sinners do such things. Jesus challenges the listener to a higher standard.

A theological problem of the passage is that it can encourage a passive response to violence and evil. The heart of the problem is verse 29: "If anyone strikes you on the cheek, offer the other also; and from anyone who takes away your coat do not withhold even your shirt." When the perpetrator does not understand his or her actions as wrong, turning one's cheek may send the message that the violence is justified. It might appear to the striker as admission or acceptance of guilt, or approval of the punishment given. Likewise, the offer of a gift to someone who steals condones the act of violence. The successful thief may be encouraged to steal again. In some situations, "turning the other cheek" is a prescription for perpetuating abuse. In teaching these things, does Jesus call the listener to endless

Pastoral Perspective

In this Sermon on the Plain, Luke reminds us that the coming of the Christ into the world makes a difference. In fact, the inbreaking of God into human history makes all the difference in the way we respond to other people.

Of the four canonical Gospels, Luke gives us the fullest account of the birth of Jesus. Characters are fleshed out. The parents of John the Baptist are named. Elizabeth and Mary, though separated by age, are joined together in the excitement of sharing the birth of their children.

The account of the birth of Jesus in Luke 2 is reproduced in Christmas pageants across the world. Against the backdrop of the threat of Emperor Augustus and the Roman power structure, we are moved by the fact that a baby is born and then in his birth, God has come to us. Luke wants us to know that Christmas is an event in history.

Is that all there is to the celebration of the coming of the Christ? Do we live on the fond memories that once in time God came to us? Yes, at least in part we do! Memory is important. That God really came to us at the center of human history is important. The Gospel of Luke takes seriously a God who uses people, events, and all of the components of history to reveal God's purposes in history and God's love for the created world. God works in time, and every

Exegetical Perspective

The writer of the Gospel of Luke is, among other things, a storyteller. He is a storyteller who sets out to tell the truth concerning a man's life, but not just any man. This man Jesus is, among other things, a prophet. Beginning with an expansive birth narrative, the evangelist tells of the coming of John the Baptist, the baptism of Jesus, and the sending of Jesus into the wilderness. In this Gospel the very first public act of Jesus, when he returns from the wilderness, is to go to the synagogue and read aloud from Isaiah (4:14–30). Luke's Jesus is introduced at the beginning of his ministry as the anointed prophet in the synagogue. This prophet does not necessarily foretell the future, but enacts the future that is the kingdom of God, where all are equal. The prophet in the pericope considered here preaches a sermon. Jesus, the great equalizer, begins his ministry reading aloud in the synagogue. He heals, teaches, calls the twelve disciples, then goes up to pray on the mountain. Then, *having come down (katabas)*, he stands on a *level place (topos pedinos)*, in order to preach a sermon to the disciples that he means for all people to hear and heed.

Matthew's Jesus preaches from the mountain. Luke's Jesus comes down from the mountain and preaches on the plain. There is a great leveling, a great equalization, of many things in Luke: the

Homiletical Perspective

Congregations respond to this text in the same way my children respond to seeing cooked spinach on their plate at dinner. No matter how much I explain the nutritional value, no one around the table really wants to dig in. I suspect preachers are not terribly different. Even though we know enough to understand how texts can be bound by culture and time, we also know this text goes down hard, no matter when or how it is served. Perhaps we should not be surprised that professionals and neophytes in scholarship and faith struggle to swallow what Jesus served us in this text. Maybe he would have had an easier time of it if he had left this item off the menu. Goodness, Jesus, who wants to love an enemy?

Congregations fill stadiums to hear sermons on "Three Easy Steps to Love" and "Five Paths to a Better Life." If Jesus had preached either of those sermons on the mount, Constantine would have been born into a Christian home and baptized as a child. Jesus focuses, however, on the real problem with nutrition; there is a vast difference between what we want and what we need. All who dare prepare a sermon with the ingredients Jesus offers will do well to remember that tension.

No one comes to church on Sunday already thinking, "I would really like a challenge today; perhaps I will be asked to love my enemy."

Luke 6:27-38

Theological Perspective

cycles of violence? Should the faithful allow evil deeds to flourish—not only against oneself but against others? How would such a message be "good news to the poor" (4:18)?

The message of these verses looks very different when viewed from the theological vision of the Sermon on the Plain. Jesus speaks to "you that listen" (v. 27), that is, to those disciples who have already heard the beatitudes and woes proclaimed in verses 20–26. These are the people to whom Jesus has declared, "Blessed are you who are poor, for yours is the kingdom of God" (v. 20). The inbreaking kingdom of God already belongs to these listeners. Luke portrays the disciples both as poor and as those who truly possess a superabundance, who have been given all the good things of God's reign. They can expect to be treated unjustly by the world (v. 22), yet they are to respond as those who are already shaped by their new identity as children of God (vv. 35–36).

The knowledge that "yours is the kingdom of God" transforms the disciple's actions from compliance to resistance in the face of evil. First, Jesus gives the listeners new lenses through which to view their situation. Even though they are hated and insulted (v. 22), from Jesus' perspective the disciple is the one who is "blessed." The reversal of the blessings and woes puts the listener in a position of power—not a worldly power, to be sure, but one that shares in the power of the kingdom of God. The listener's generosity is modeled after the mercy of God (v. 36), and comes out of the same abundance. As one who belongs to God's kingdom, she can "afford" to give even to those from whom no positive response is expected. She gives not from the position of one who is oppressed, but as one who already shares in the riches of God's kingdom. This does not mean that the disciple's actions do not have personal costs. However, redefining the disciple's perspective on her position can also redefine the meaning of her actions in that context.

Second, the act of giving by the disciple breaks the expected cycle of retribution. In a social context of reciprocal gift giving, the act of giving one's cloak or lending without hope of return is not a futile action. The actions commanded here go against common wisdom, but they still reflect the social norms of giving and receiving that were common in the ancient world. Relationships were built on exchanges of gifts. Friendships were forged between peers who could evenly reciprocate each other's gifts. While gifts were freely given, the bond of friendship created a desire to respond in kind to the generosity

Pastoral Perspective

week preachers come to the pulpit with the task of trying to see God in the times of our lives.

However, Luke is not content with leaving the birth of Jesus only as an event to be remembered. What about our lives now? Is the Christ who was really born in a manger born also in us, so that we come to live in a new, more compassionate way?

"Do to others as you would have them do to you," Jesus said (v. 31). The Golden Rule! It is not unique to Jesus or even to Luke. Matthew has its version of the rule. Philo, Homer, and others articulated the idea and reminded us that treating others as we wanted to be treated was a "golden rule."

Despite the fact that others advocate treating others as we want to be treated, the Gospel of Luke calls for a radical new interpretation of this rule. Jesus talks about loving our enemies and doing good to those who hate us, curse us, and even strike us on the cheek. In other words, our response to others is not predicated on their behavior. Our response, in fact, is diametrically opposed to the way others treat us. Jesus' response is to do good to those who do bad to us.

These words cut across the grain of the natural response to perceived enemies or those who may curse what we value. "Do to others as they do to us" may not be golden, but in reality it is the rule by which life should be lived.

Here is the dilemma. How do we move from the natural instinct to match blow for blow and word for word? To put it another way, how do we live our lives responding with grace and kindness, instead of reacting with words or actions that seek to answer hurt with more hurt?

According to Luke, Jesus indicates that followers of Christ remember how God responds to us. "Be merciful," Jesus states, "just as the Father is merciful." Examples are powerful. Over time, examples create images that fashion a person's approach to life. "I was raised in a violent, dysfunctional home," he said. I was his pastor. This was his image for reacting to those he professed to love. The balled fist of his father was the image. Could he change the image to a welcoming hand? Images that guide behavior are hard to change.

Yet Jesus was more than an example or a new image. Jesus revealed the merciful God. In him we see that the very nature of God is to be merciful. The next time we want to react, we both imagine God and also live as a people to whom God has shown mercy! Some people are fortunate to have mercy and kindness as examples. Watch children with parents

mountain becomes the plain, you who are poor receive the riches of the kingdom, you who weep will laugh (6:20–23). The leveling continues in the Sermon on the Plain's middle section, which is the text for this Sunday. Enemies are not only to be forgiven, but, like friends, are to be loved, blessed, and prayed for. Enemies are on equal footing with friends. Turn your cheek, give your coat, hand over your shirt, to anyone, for all are equal, enemies and friends.

In Luke's Gospel, Jesus speaks rhythmically and repetitively, so the hearer has no opportunity to miss the point: "If you love those, . . . If you do good, . . . If you lend to those . . ." A modern-day preacher might heed this homiletic style, for exactly the same reason, so the hearer has no opportunity to miss the point. Form follows function for the preacher on the plain. The words are repeated as the deeds they describe are to be enacted repeatedly, spoken or performed not once, but over and over again, shaping lives, speaking a rhythm of love and forgiveness and generosity throughout every moment of every day.

It is important when the rhythmic words are spoken, when the good deeds are done, that the preacher or the doer not be too impressed with herself, lest she begin to think that she is indeed unequal to, better than, the hearers. The gospel preacher in Luke, indeed, reminds the preacher or the doer that he is ungrateful and wicked and that God will be merciful none the less, that God's mercy is the reward for the children of the Most High. Here Luke's Jesus necessarily forsakes a focus on equality, to declare that there is one who is unequal, there is one alone who is God.

The rhythm continues: "Do not judge, . . . do not condemn, . . . Forgive, . . . give." For all are equal, all things are equal and measured fairly. The wheat or the oil is pressed down. Every grain, every drop that can be given is equally given by the one who is unequal. Every good measure is given by God.

The writers of Matthew and Luke probably had a copy of Mark's Gospel in front of them as they wrote. Material found in Matthew and Luke, but not in Mark, probably came from another common source. Scholars have named this source, of which there are no extant copies, "Q", for the German word *Quelle*, which means "source." The verses considered here are Q material. The words in Matthew and Luke are similar enough that it is likely the writers used the same source for the Sermon on the Mount in Matthew (5–7) and the Sermon on the Plain in Luke

Nevertheless, that is what Jesus demands. Look at this text for what it is. Jesus offers this ridiculous teaching to his closest followers. Remember that anyone else who heard it probably laughed out loud and with good reason. This clarion call is to swim upstream. It asks the disciples to break conventions, to stand out in a crowd, to find fulfillment in going a second, third, and seventy-seventh mile. Consequently, expect the congregation to look at you as if you just asked them to love some scoundrel. Imagine Jesus today serving us "the good thief," "the good batterer," or "the good molester." Anyone need an antacid? This text is gospel for the committed. Anyone who hears this text with a low level of commitment will think this "good news" is "bad advice."

If we are honest, the history of the church offers examples where our preaching about love and grace is overshadowed by immorality, corruption, and exclusion. The critics of the church are right: far too often there is a vast difference between what we say we believe and what we do. Therefore, as preachers we will do a complete and utter disservice to our congregations and the gospel if we do not tell the truth that this teaching, and much of the gospel itself, is hard. What Jesus offers his followers in this text is not a recipe for self-help, intended to make us feel better (although that is not out of the question); it is a recipe for disaster, because the very idea of forgiveness is radical and powerful. It runs against our thinking, our inclinations, our desires, and our will.

A temptation might be to read this text and settle on the words "Your reward will be great." What we want to hear is that if we love that rascal down the street, then Jesus will love me all the more, and my "reward will be great." Going that direction sermonically has two sad outcomes. First, it will reinforce the kind of gospel sunshine for which the nonreligious have rightly critiqued the church through the centuries. That direction will place us all back in the courtroom scene with Job, where the accuser as prosecuting attorney asks the hard question, "Do we love God and others only because it gets us good rewards?" (Job 1:9–10; 2:4–6).

Second, this direction negates the idea of grace, because it assumes the claim that God "loved us while we were yet sinners" (or better yet, that God "loved us while we were *enemies of God*") is a lie. Despite our failure to love our enemy, God loves us anyway. We need the kind of revelation with this text that came to Flannery O'Conner's character Ruby Turpin. Ruby believed that God loved some better than others and that she could tell the difference by

Luke 6:27-38

Theological Perspective

of the other. Seen in this light, the actions suggested by the passage most closely resemble those of the wealthy patron. The wealthy gave gifts to their friends, but would also give to those who could not reciprocate in kind. In this case such gifts were often a way of fostering loyalty or gratitude in the recipient. The social norms were such that the act of giving obligated the recipient to reciprocate, even if he or she could not do so in kind. It was always possible that the recipient might not reciprocate the gift, in breach of social conventions. Yet initiating the benevolent action may awaken in the other a similar response.

Third, the listener gives with full expectation of repayment—from God, rather than the recipient. The expected result is a reward: "a good measure, pressed down, shaken together, running over, will be put into your lap" (v. 38; cf. v. 35). The abundance of God's kingdom ensures that the disciple's good action will be returned. From the logic of those who exclude and revile the disciple, the actions described here make little sense. Resources are finite and should not be squandered on those who will not appreciate them. But from the perspective of one who has experienced the kingdom drawing near (Luke 10:9, 11; 11:20; 17:20–21), a different logic prevails. This one gives out of a great storehouse and expects good things in return.

When the teachings of the Sermon on the Plain are not grounded in the disciple's identity as God's child, they become an onerous list of ethical demands that do not further justice and wholeness. When the disciple understands his actions as flowing out of God's abundance, to which he belongs and which belongs to him, turning the other cheek becomes an act of resistance to evil that has the power to transform others and the world.

SUSAN E. HYLEN

Pastoral Perspective

who give them unconditional love. Watch people in a church who hear the pastor speak about a merciful God. For the most part, we see children and congregants who practice the example and who have also internalized the goodness and mercy of God that has been mediated to them through those whose lives have cradled the Christ.

So back to Christmastide and to Epiphany for a moment. On the Seventh Sunday after Epiphany, the church still remembers the coming of Christ. From Matthew's Gospel we recall the wise men who made the journey to see the holy child but returned with an experience of the Holy One that transformed their lives. What God has done in history, God has made real in their lives, so that their lives became the mangers in which Christ was born.

The admonition of Luke to love even our enemies is not just a good idea where we try our best to make it happen. It is not a call to grit our teeth and make a resolution to be nicer even to those who are not nice to us. Rather, the call of Luke is to live in a way contrary to our human nature, a way that is possible only as we "live out" of a new power born from above.

In none of the four Gospels in our Bible is the term "Christianity" used. Luke wants us to see that faith in Christ is far more than giving cognitive assent to doctrines. Rather, this faith is a way of life, a way that is contrary to our own inclinations. To answer hurt with forgiveness is plausible only because the Christ is our strength.

CHARLES BUGG

Exegetical Perspective

6. In the text under consideration, there are specific differences between Matthew and Luke that reveal the deeply compassionate nature of Luke's Jesus. Matthew's Jesus preaches righteousness. Cheeks are turned, coats given away, beggars given alms. Enemies are loved and prayed for. Luke's Jesus affirms these behaviors and attitudes, but preaches that enemies, thieves, and beggars are, as well, to be *blessed (eulogeō)*, a word not used in the parallel passage in Matthew.

Matthew's Jesus concludes this section of the sermon by requiring that hearers "must be perfect as your heavenly Father is perfect." Luke's kinder, gentler Jesus promises that good behavior and attitude will be rewarded by the Father, who is kind and merciful. Matthew's God the Father is perfect; Luke's God the Father is kind and merciful. The writer of the Gospel of Luke consistently softens the demands of righteousness found in Matthew's interpretation of Q.

The writer of Luke seems to summarize the message of his Jesus in verses 35 and 36. The eloquent preacher gives instructions, proclaims how hearers ought to live. The kind and gentle teacher promises great and unexpected reward. The great equalizer points out that all are equal, all are children, of the Most High. The compassionate healer of this Gospel attributes kindness and mercy to God the Father. The anointed prophet summarizes the message of mercy for all in verse 36. Luke's Jesus seeks to bring forth the kingdom of God and persuasively invites hearers to live into the future to which God calls them.

Preaching Luke, especially when contrasted with Matthew, allows the preacher to emphasize God's grace, while still proclaiming God's call to live righteously. The anointed prophet of the synagogue, the preacher on the plain, seeks to shape the future, to bring about the kingdom of God, not by demands and threats, but by gentle persuasion. Luke's Jesus models in word and deed the compassion of a loving God for all people.

DENA L. WILLIAMS

Homiletical Perspective

their dress, stature, and place in life. In "Revelation," she discovers she is wrong. Ruby discovers that, whether we like it or not, God loves us all, not because of what we have done, achieved, or claimed, but solely because of who God is.[1]

Where then could a sermon on this text go? Perhaps a fruitful horizon will be to focus on the grace and transformation necessary for us to live out the radical faith Jesus demands. In other words, the "great reward" we receive is not full pockets, garages, or self-esteem, but who we become in the process. Jesus knows full well that we will never love our enemies without an amazing grace that transforms us and makes us different than we are. Like the musician, the academic, or the athlete, who train body, mind, and spirit and become what they need to be to practice their craft, we too can become more than the sum of our parts. Yet the hard truth is that practice may make us better, but it will not make us Christian. What changes us and allows us to love is a grace greater than our sin, our best intentions, or even our hard work.

Consider forming a sermon that details how grace transforms us, even as we resist. This sermon offers opportunity to say to the congregation that while the gospel may be "good news" for us all, it is not always "easy news" for those called to follow. In this text, Jesus points his followers then and now toward a narrow and difficult path illuminated only by grace, but it is one that rewards us in ways we can hardly imagine.

VAUGHN CROWE-TIPTON

---

1. Flannery O'Conner, "Revelation," in *The Complete Stories* (New York: Farrar, Straus & Giroux, 1971).

Isaiah 55:10-13

^{10}For as the rain and the snow come down from heaven,
and do not return there until they have watered the earth,
making it bring forth and sprout,
giving seed to the sower and bread to the eater,
^{11}so shall my word be that goes out from my mouth;
it shall not return to me empty,
but it shall accomplish that which I purpose,
and succeed in the thing for which I sent it.

^{12}For you shall go out in joy,
and be led back in peace;
the mountains and the hills before you
shall burst into song,
and all the trees of the field shall clap their hands.
^{13}Instead of the thorn shall come up the cypress;
instead of the brier shall come up the myrtle;
and it shall be to the LORD for a memorial,
for an everlasting sign that shall not be cut off.

Theological Perspective

These verses should be read in continuity with the preceding two, with which they are connected by the "For" that begins verse 10. In this prophet's estimation, one of the things that distinguishes God's ways and thoughts from the ways and thoughts of mortals is precisely the integrity of God's word, its unique reliability and power. Second Isaiah thus ends, as it began, with a sharp contrast between the word of the Lord and "all flesh." From Isaiah 40 (cf. v. 8: "The grass withers, the flower fades; but the word of our God will stand forever") to these lines in Isaiah 55, the unique character of the word of God is for this prophet an overarching consideration and a firm ground for hope and joy. God's word establishes reality, both in the sense of bringing it about and in the sense of making clear what is truly real; by it the reality of all else is to be measured. Our own human efforts to establish what is real—in either of these senses—generally fall far short of this mark.

Our efforts fall short in two different ways, for two different reasons. The contrast between the word of God and the thoughts, words, and ways of humankind is a twofold contrast. There is, first, the basic ontological distinction between God and creatures. We are finite, fallible, frail; our creaturely life is good, but our strength is nothing like God's, and inevitably we wither and fade, while God "abides

Pastoral Perspective

Many of us have experienced the "trust walk." In a youth group or an adult retreat, people are paired off. One is invited to put on a blindfold. The other, sighted person leads the blindfolded person. The guide may say words like, step to your right, or step up, or whatever is needed to make it safe for the person who cannot see to move. It is called a trust walk since the person who cannot see does not know where he or she is going. The blindfolded person has to trust the person who can see. Words alone are spoken to protect the blindfolded person.

Several questions come up with this exercise. Is the guide trustworthy? Can one trust the words that the guide offers? Will the people who are being led around allow themselves to be led? Do the people doing the leading know where they are going?

This trust experience is analogous to the situation of the people of Israel who are hearing these words from Isaiah 55. They have been led—or rather been captured and taken—to Babylon, where they are exiles. They do not see hope for their future and in fact have bemoaned their fate being uprooted from their homeland. Isaiah prophesies with hope that they shall return to where they had been before they were made captives. Is this too good to be true? How are the Israelites to believe that the God who had supposedly been with them before they were taken

Exegetical Perspective

The two poetic stanzas of Isaiah 55:10–13 conclude a section of Scripture known as Second Isaiah (Isa. 40–55). A community of exiled priests, sons of Aaron, was responsible for this part of Isaiah, and they emphasized a theology of *reverence*.[1] In reverence theology, God's towering mystery dwarfs humanity and draws us to recognize our finitude, frailty, and dependence on God and each other. How poignant to find an affirmation of God's mystery and hiddenness during the dark era of Babylonian exile, amid deep wrestlings with God's apparent absence! Verse 9 flips the crisis of God's hiddenness on its head: "As the heavens are higher than the earth, so are my ways higher than your ways and my thoughts than your thoughts."

Our surest path to real joy, reverence theology asserts, is to abandon all of our claims to self-sufficiency and control. Forsaking our pride, we must align ourselves with God's word and ways, which provide the only solid foundation for human living. Here at Second Isaiah's close, our passage sums up this theme with rich poetry. Spectacular

---

1. On the authorship and provenance of Isa. 40–55, see Stephen L. Cook, *The Apocalyptic Literature*, Interpreting Biblical Texts (Nashville: Abingdon Press, 2003), 111–18; Robert R. Wilson, "The Community of the Second Isaiah," in Christopher R. Seitz, ed., *Reading and Preaching the Book of Isaiah* (Philadelphia: Fortress Press, 1988), 53–70.

Homiletical Perspective

The brilliant words of Isaiah 55 speak of God's sturdy trustworthiness and Israel's bright and promising future of joy, peace, and cosmically accompanied song. According to this vision, the word of God is sound and trustworthy, and all Israel will flourish again when it "listen[s], so that [it] may live" (v. 3). But this beautiful poetry of promise is spoken to exiles whose circumstances may not allow them to imagine the ultimate fulfillment of God's bright promise. In this way, the words of Isaiah 55 speak across the ages to all of us who need occasionally to be wooed back to trusting an unpredictable God.

Context. The preacher arrives at Isaiah 55:10–13 with a twenty-first-century interpretation to address. In our time, these four verses find their way into most conservative Christian apologetic teaching about Scripture's authority. They are quoted from pulpits and memorized by the faithful as proof that Scripture is inspired and infallible. So many of the people in our pews will have first encountered our text in the context of a modern battle over the Bible, in which one side especially has equated "my word" with the Holy Bible and its "purpose" with all the ends Scripture names for itself in all its pages.

It is important, then, for our congregations to understand that the promising "word" of Isaiah 55

Isaiah 55:10-13

Theological Perspective

forever." This Creator-creature distinction is the main difference upon which Second Isaiah dwells in these lines and throughout. A second contrast, a second reason for our falling short, is also acknowledged, both here and more pervasively in the book of Isaiah as a whole: we are sinners. We are heedless of God and busy carrying out our own plans (30:1, 9–11).

These two features of our existence should not be conflated. Creatureliness is our proper status. The good future envisioned and promised in verses 12–13 of our text is not a nullification or overcoming of creatureliness, but rather its flourishing. Being "flesh" in the sense of our text is not a bad thing and should not be confused with the "fleshly" dispositions, actions, and so forth to which Paul (here using a different sense of "flesh") refers disapprovingly. These distortions of created good do need to be overcome, as counter to our creaturely well-being; and the good news common to Paul and Second Isaiah is that the word of God is able to overcome them.

The prophetic reminder of the character of the word of God, and especially its assurance that the word of God will indeed do its work, are apt for the season of Epiphany but not out of place in any season of the church's life. God's word has its own life and life-giving strength. It is persistent, and it will accomplish its purpose. Christians, and perhaps particularly Christian theologians and preachers, have not always shared the prophet's confidence on this point. They have sometimes felt compelled, rather, to come to the aid of God's word—perhaps by attempting to justify or vindicate what they take to be the substance of that word by showing how well it fits in with the reigning paradigm of knowledge and with the values and sensibilities of intelligent people of the present day. Or they attempt to defend God's word by launching a wholesale preemptive attack against those same values and sensibilities and demanding a *sacrificium intellectus* as a condition of genuine faith. Neither strategy puts much faith in the capacity of God's word to take care of itself by demonstrating its own sense-making power.

Hans Frei has written memorably about the "reversal in the direction of interpretation" that took place in Western culture around the first half of the eighteenth century. Prior to that time, people tended to try to make sense of their world and their experience by interpreting them in the light of a common, "strongly realistic" reading of the Bible; after the reversal, many people began trying to make sense of the Bible by interpreting its concepts and stories in the light of modern knowledge, which had come to

Pastoral Perspective

away was now to return them to their home? Throughout the prophet's words we read, "Do not fear, for I am with you; do not be afraid, for I am your God" (41:10). In their terrifying experiences in exile, they are hearing the words of Isaiah, which are words of comfort, guidance, and strength. "I have taken you by the hand and kept you" (42:6b). God promised they will be a light to the nations, a people who will spread compassion and live with justice.

This new exodus from Babylon means homecoming. They had been led into the wastelands and felt abandoned. Now this God will again lead them home. Can this word be trusted? Isaiah says the word "shall accomplish that which I purpose, and succeed in the thing for which I sent it" (55:11b). Is the One who offers this word to be trusted? This gets down to the bare bones of faith. Is the God we have experienced and known worthy of our trust?

We know there have been holocausts in human history, and in particular the extermination of more than six million Jews and others in the Nazi death camps. What is the word that is going out from God and what is it that is being accomplished? Can one hold onto trust in this God while in the concentration camps? Can one trust in a God who would allow the slaughter of the innocents in war? It takes more than a leap of faith to hold on to the hand of the One who has promised to accompany us on our journey of faith. On the other hand, is it that God holds onto our hand as we walk, as if blindfolded, through the turmoil and the tragedies of human life, or have we God's word alone?

Henri Nouwen told of his experience following the Rodleigh Brothers, the flying trapeze artists, through Europe. Henri was fascinated with the courage of the person who would fly into the air and then let go of the bar to wing their way across space in the circus tent. When Henri told the father of the Rodleigh family of his admiration for the flying trapeze artist, the father responded that it is all about the catcher. That is where you ought to look, he suggested. It is up to the catcher to time the catch and be right there when the flyer comes. "Trust the Great Catcher," he wrote.[1]

As people seek to interpret their experiences and weave their woes and joys into a framework of meaning, it is crucial that one realizes the presence of the mysterious guide on their journeys. The One who is the catcher can be trusted. As surely as water

---

1. Henri Nouwen, *Bread for the Journey: A Daybook of Wisdom and Faith* (San Francisco: HarperSanFrancisco, 1997), January 11.

poetry such as this has the capacity to reach deep into our guts, rekindling the embers of reverence in our souls. It makes the depth of things resound.

God addresses us directly in the first stanza (vv. 10–11), declaring the firm reliability of God's word. In the second stanza (vv. 12–13), we hear Isaiah's dramatic persona proclaiming the overpowering vibrancy of salvation. The images of both stanzas get us thinking. Shaping our imaginations to envision the wonder of God, our poems kindle our desire to seek the Lord and find true, fail-safe joy.

Getting in Sync with God. Verses 10–11 use an illustration of rain and snow showers to help us imagine the quality of God's direction of life and history on earth. Water from heaven falls from the clouds, irrigates the earth, and wondrously supports the miracle of agriculture. Such water efficiently accomplishes God's good intentions. It is a sure witness to God's wondrous ordering of creation and providential care of the world. This natural system of precipitation is a particular blessing to farmers, automatically meeting their irrigation needs.

With the comparison to water from heaven, our poetry envisages God's word as something objective, even physical (v. 11). God's reality is neither airy nor dreamy, but bracing, like cold rain or snow. What is more, the poetry personalizes God's word. It reveals a divine game plan for existence reflective of God's unique way of working. The word of God speaks to us of God's personal, programmatic intention for us.

Beyond being programmatic, the game plan of God for history is fail-safe. Like the sprouting of healthy crops after seasonable weather, the effectiveness of God's word is assured. God speaks words that work, on which we can base our lives with confidence. After all, God is the speaker!

Using the key word *succeed* (Hebrew *tsalakh*), the end of verse 11 describes how God's word gets results and achieves abundance. Like natural precipitation, it is fully effective apart from human stress and strain. Given its guarantee of success, it would be foolish not to align our lives with it. God is directing history, and we should get with the program.

Imagining the Wonder of Salvation. Verses 12–13 shift our attention to imagine the wonder of God's promised restoration. Their homecoming procession underway, God's marchers set their sights on new lives in accord with assured divine intentions. The magnitude of what is happening hits us through the power of poetic personification. Mountains and hills

was a word of specific covenant promises spoken by God to ancient Israel through prophets, and that its ancient audience may have had their doubts. The exiles likely alternated between guilt for causing God's anger by their disobedience, and anger at God for breaking promises. On the one hand, their prophets had hammered them with God's righteous anger. But, on the other, trusted voices long ago assured them that David's dynasty would be eternal (2 Sam. 7:16); and some who were standing among them had to watch as Babylonian armies burned beloved Jerusalem's palace and temple to the ground.

Text. Into this complex psychology of the ancient exilic community, Isaiah speaks of a God whose love and care are not undermined by but anchored in history. God renews the covenant with Noah (and all the world) by assuring Israel that the divine anger that led to defeat and exile has now and forever turned back into divine love (54:9–10). Then God extends the sure (and reinterpreted) covenant with David (55:3–4) to all the people of Israel and all foreigners who obey God (56:3–7). But this God has credibility problems. So in the middle of the covenants, into the midst of exiles, Isaiah 55:10–13 speaks out the trustworthiness of God's word:

> As the rain and the snow come down from heaven,
> and do not return there until they have watered the earth,
> making it bring forth and sprout,
> giving seed to the sower and bread to the eater,
> so shall my word be that goes out from my mouth;
> it shall not return to me empty,
> but it shall accomplish that which I purpose,
> and succeed in the thing for which I sent it.
> (vv. 10–11)

To paraphrase the poetry, God's promising word works. It does what it was sent out to do. And if that is true, this current prophetic word will restore Israel's hope that beloved Judea and Jerusalem, hundreds of miles distant and last seen in the smoldering flames of destruction, will one day teem with new growth, as mountains "burst into song" and the new growth trees of the field "clap their hands" in time with Israel's praise. This vivid imagery of flourishing, heard by rememberers of distant ashes, will have nothing of thorn and brier. "All will be well and all manner of thing will be well," as Julian of Norwich one day put it.

The Crisis. There is one problem. In this passage, God's promised good is envisioned in space and time. Even Second Isaiah imagines Israel's defeat and exile

Isaiah 55:10-13

Theological Perspective

constitute a more plausible frame of reference than this realistic reading of the Bible itself.[1] Lest anyone be overcome by nostalgia for the days before this reversal, it is well to remember some of the less admirable features of that earlier era in the Christian West, and to acknowledge the great positive gains that accompanied this changed approach to Scripture, as people were able to apply critical resources to examine and challenge received truths in every area of human knowledge and experience. This reversal did, however, seem to narrow the hermeneutical options for Christian interpreters of Scripture. Some theologians and preachers responded to this new situation by trying to assimilate the Christian message to modern knowledge. Others responded by trying to discredit modern knowledge and to isolate Christian truth from it. Neither group recognized sufficiently the power of the message itself to transform our understanding.

Vital theology and preaching in our own time have often come about when we have rediscovered the promise of our lectionary text and have glimpsed the capacity of God's word to manifest itself and, in doing so, to disclose the reality of things. In his classic *The Meaning of Revelation*, H. Richard Niebuhr offers a good way of thinking about this. He speaks of a revelatory event, such as the event of Jesus Christ, as an "intelligible event which makes all other events intelligible." The revelatory occasion is "intelligible in itself," but, more than that, it "illuminates other events and enables us to understand them."[2] When it is proclaimed and apprehended in the power of the Spirit, the word of God does not need to shout, or to apologize. It does not need our defense. It makes itself known.

CHARLES M. WOOD

Pastoral Perspective

nourishes the seed that yields bread, so the word of God will do what it is intended to do. Even the whole creation will rejoice, and the promise of new life will not be cut off. People in the direst of situations need to hear this word of comfort, promise, and strength. While it seems bleak, there is hope. The good news is that the bad news is never the last news before becoming good news again.

In the play *For Heaven's Sake* by Helen Kromer, one of the characters talks about "The Word." The character expresses that seeking to understand what God is saying to people can be like a small child hearing the words "This is your foot, so walk." It does not happen. However, if we say, "Here, let me hold your hand and let's practice walking," eventually, the word "walk" takes shape with the action. Kromer writes that when God wants to communicate with us, we do not always know what is meant. Therefore, God showed us the meaning of the word by becoming Jesus. We see the word in him so that we might one day live that word in our lives.[2]

In Isaiah, the word does work. When the people experience their return from exile, they "see" the word at work through them. They trust, since the One whose word is given is trustworthy. I remember a sermon in which James Forbes said all that each of us is given is a piece of the puzzle. That piece does fit into the large puzzle. However, we cannot always see the whole picture. We have to trust that what we have is sufficient, is enough for us to realize that we are part of the whole. God knows the whole thing and sees the whole thing. Though we are not blindfolded, we can trust in what we do not yet know, for the guide is our God, whose word leads and is not empty but yields abundance.

ALAN JOHNSON

1. Hans W. Frei, *The Eclipse of Biblical Narrative* (New Haven, CT: Yale University Press, 1974), 1–9.
2. H. Richard Niebuhr, *The Meaning of Revelation* (New York: Macmillan Co., 1941), 93, 109.

2. Helen Kromer, *For Heaven's Sake* (Baker's Plays, 1963).

Exegetical Perspective

welcome the parade of God's people with jubilant rejoicing. Then applause is heard from the open country. It is the trees clapping their hands with exuberance. Nature itself clearly wants in on the festivities and is supplying the fanfare to prove it.

With the jubilant songs of mountains and hills reverberating in their souls, the marchers join their own human voices together in wondrous accord. Truly "led back in *peace*," they sing with one voice. They feel *shalom* (v. 12). Their new harmony stems from being in tune with God's word and ways, and from supporting each other in the endeavor. They have adopted lifestyles in tune with God's life-giving, life-nourishing words. Adapting our lives to God's game plan makes for natural, efficient living. Why exhaust ourselves rowing through life, when God's wind is available for our sails? Or, to return to the agricultural metaphor, why dig irrigation ditches, when we can count on water from heaven?

Fecundity is the hallmark of the new world of *shalom* toward which the marchers press forward. Thistles, thornbushes, and other emblems of barrenness now become things of the past. Instead, evergreens and firs sprout up as permanent monuments to salvation (v. 13). It is hard not to be reverent in the presence of such stately and majestic trees, which arise so inexplicably in what was previously a wasteland. Their towering grandeur unites God's people in shared feelings of humility and finitude, reinforcing communal bonds of mutuality and caring. Beyond doubt, virtue will come naturally and effortlessly from now on.

Consider further the virtue-inspiring wonder of the new promised land. Naturally fecund, this self-producing world flourishes of its own accord. In the Hebrew of verse 13, the cypress and myrtle trees are the active subjects of the verbs. They control the action! Plant life flourishes effortlessly, but does so on its own terms and schedule. Humans will have to adjust. In this world, then, the order of the day for humankind is active respect.

The pattern will spill over from the agricultural realm into human community. In the promised land, a state of *shalom* will reign, in which everyone and everything will necessarily interact in a mode of patience, balance, and mutual giving. As a result, efficient, joyful living will reign supreme.

STEPHEN L. COOK

Homiletical Perspective

as God's abandonment and wrath at the nation's disobedience (54:7). And if the past is mapped as a report card of Israel's faithfulness, the future is also mapped out in terms of faithfulness—Israel's faithfulness and God's as well. In fact, it is only a new expectation of faithfulness during this heady exilic moment that has God promising,

No weapon that is fashioned against you shall prosper,
and you shall confute every tongue that rises against you in judgment.
This is the heritage of the servants of the LORD and their vindication from me, says the LORD.
(54:17)

The prophet seems to be calling Israel to the same Deuteronomic schoolroom that preexilic Israel attended, in which God's grade for Israel can be discerned by looking at circumstances. Obey and you will be politically successful; disobey and you are doomed. And so even the splendid history imagined in 55:12–13 is conditioned on divine mercy purchased with human faithfulness.

Do our people want to sign up for this course? Should they? How can undying divine love be spoken on those historical and circumstantial terms? How can the word of God be trusted under these conditions? Good people get sick. Faithful people get abused. One later day the faithful Israelites who lived under Antiochus Epiphanes in second-century BCE Jerusalem would realize that their atrocious suffering was not God-sponsored—that it had nothing to do with their obedience or disobedience. And so they looked for God's answer to their faithfulness beyond history, in a time beyond time when "the holy ones of the Most High shall receive the kingdom and possess the kingdom forever—forever and ever" (Dan. 7:18).

Preacher and people must similarly image together a form of divine blessing that is not circumstantially delivered. The effective word of God to which Isaiah points in 55:10–11 must instill a confidence in God's good (vv. 12–13) that cannot be shattered when the political or physical or meteorological winds blow another way. It may be a vision of internal peace and joy in the here and now, or it may be the consolation of a final peace and joy beyond time. Only then can the divine word really be counted on really to work.

ALLEN HILTON

Isaiah 55:10–13   391

Psalm 92:1-4, 12-15

¹It is good to give thanks to the LORD,
  to sing praises to your name, O Most High;
²to declare your steadfast love in the morning,
  and your faithfulness by night,
³to the music of the lute and the harp,
  to the melody of the lyre.
⁴For you, O LORD, have made me glad by your work;
  at the works of your hands I sing for joy.
. . . .
¹²The righteous flourish like the palm tree,
  and grow like a cedar in Lebanon.
¹³They are planted in the house of the LORD;
  they flourish in the courts of our God.
¹⁴In old age they still produce fruit;
  they are always green and full of sap,
¹⁵showing that the LORD is upright;
  he is my rock, and there is no unrighteousness in him.

Theological Perspective

Introduction. The assigned portion of this psalm exhibits an exuberant, robust trust in God. Within the psalmist's framework, individual thanksgiving reflects theological motifs such as the worshiper's joy in the presence and works of God. The psalmist rejoices too that God is one who remains constant in God's love for humanity. The psalm's emphases include praise, unrelenting belief in God's sustenance, and acknowledgment of God's graciousness toward the believer. These themes can point the preacher to an exploration of the role and manifestations of God's providence toward humanity in both Old and New Testaments.

In order to give the fullest picture of the psalm's proposals and conclusions, the preacher may invite listeners to speak the entire psalm, including the omitted verses 5–11, which provide examples of *why* the psalmist is giving praise and what this praise reflects about the nature and works of God. Even without these additional verses, however, the preacher can point to the fact that God's righteousness and redemption are hallmarks of the psalmist's praise focus.

Creator of All (vv. 1–4). The lyricism of these opening verses depicts the individual believer doing

Pastoral Perspective

Epiphany is a season for seeing. We read accounts of Christ's life that reveal the identity of Christ and the nature of discipleship. In today's Gospel passage, Jesus offers wise words on the practice of seeing clearly. On this Eighth Sunday after the Epiphany, we will do well to *listen* too. In the opening verses of Psalm 92, we hear music playing and voices singing.

Psalm 92 is a song of praise that underscores the importance of music in the worship of God. Here we hear not only voices lifted in praise but the accompaniment of lute, harp, and lyre. This song of the Sabbath day is a celebration of "the works" of God's hands set to music; in the psalmist's words "it is good" (v. 1) to give thanks to God in this way.

As pastors we know of such goodness. We recognize the ways a hymn or musical composition can elevate our congregation's experience of God's divine presence. The baptismal hymn "I Was There to Hear Your Borning Cry" moistens the eyes of many. An ensemble of oboe, cello, and violin at a Good Friday service expresses a depth of emotion beyond words. A choral anthem completes the preacher's message and draws the congregation deeper into the Word. Like the psalmist we know how sacred music amplifies our praise on the Sabbath.

Exegetical Perspective

Since the lectionary reading does not include the central section of the psalm (vv. 5–11), it lacks what some would find to be the basic theme of the psalm, namely, God's condemnation of the psalmist's wicked enemies and exultation of the (righteous) poet. This omission can make the remainder of the psalm seem disjointed, reading like a hymn in verses 1–4 and like a wisdom psalm in verses 12–15.

In his *Introduction to the Psalms,* written with Joachim Begrich, Hermann Gunkel, the father of form criticism in the Psalms, set Psalm 92 squarely among the thanksgiving psalms of the individual, but the psalm's affinities with hymns and wisdom psalms have conspired to make it difficult to categorize. While scholars have recognized all three elements in Psalm 92, there is no agreement among them about its genre or form. Samuel Terrien, for instance, labels it a "hymn" in general but recognizes within it strophes of personal thanksgiving, trust, and meditation. Erhard Gerstenberger entitles it a "hymnic prayer" and then later "a kind of confessional declaration." Hossfeld and Zenger insist that hymn, wisdom psalm, and thanksgiving are three equally important "levels" of the

Homiletical Perspective

The first decision for the preacher of Psalm 92 is to accept or reject the unfortunate limits imposed on this text by the lectionary. While the lectionary verses capture the theme of our timeless joy in giving God thanks and praise, the lectionary omits key verses that amplify and enrich the texture of this governing theme.

Whatever decision is made, the psalmist insists that the preacher remember that Psalm 92 is a "song for the Sabbath," the only one of the 150 psalms to be so notated. Long before the first lectionary, the community had set aside Psalm 92 to be sung on the Sabbath.

Western Christians living in the third millennium who preach this psalm as a "Sabbath song" do so in a social context with significant parallels to that out of which this psalm arose. Most likely, Psalm 92 was first sung on foreign soil by displaced Jews taunted by their Babylonian conquerors. It was sung by those trying to hold on to the notion of a Sabbath in an alien culture, trying to hold on to a fragile faith when many around them thought that faith in YHWH was impotent or ludicrous.

This ancient Sabbath song teaches believers a chorus to sing, even in fear-laden times: "It is good to give thanks to the LORD, to sing praises to your name,

Psalm 92:1-4, 12-15

Theological Perspective

what is core to faith: "to declare your steadfast love." In making these worship declarations, this predominant theme of thanksgiving to a loving God serves as the backdrop for the major theme: thankfulness for creation and an ever-creating God. In the opening verses, the psalmist praises God, in part, because God has brought the believer to another day. Just as the passage of the days in the Genesis creation stories reflects God's action and creative hand in the world, so too each new day for the believer is cause to rejoice in God's willingness, love, and ability to re-create the believer anew. Indeed, the psalmist's gratitude demands music (v. 3) most powerfully to express this joy of creation.

Flourishing (vv. 12–15). The personal pronouns that open the psalm turn to the corporate inclusion of all who are true worshipers of God. These final verses are a picture of those who have withstood the evils they have confronted in life and have found their refuge in God. In fact, they have not simply endured but "the righteous *flourish.*" The themes of growth and creation are sounded here as the psalmist hymns a God whose gift of salvation creates change in the believers.

The images used in these final verses are organic in nature. Like the opening verses, these closing ones are full of life and confidence in God. The believers are compared to a palm tree that has the growth and strength capacities of an even larger tree, the cedar of Lebanon. Such trees have always been highly significant in the economies of the ancient world for their various ways of sustaining life in agriculture and architecture. These symbols connote long life and blessing for the righteous. A number of details are offered with this analogy. These trees are planted under the aegis of God, "in the house of the LORD." Such trees are bound to receive the perpetual care of those in whose precincts they are planted! They are also fruitful "in old age." There is a further corporate detail: such trees grow in groves, even forests. The magnificence of such types of trees is documented in history and the biblical record. Longevity, fruitfulness, loving care are all signs of the creator God's blessing of the righteous.

Certainly many who hear these marks of God's care, symbolically portrayed, may be struggling with what they consider the *lack* of noticeable signs of God's care in their lives. How is the preacher to respond to this fact? Using the tree analogy, the proclaimer may describe the often imperceptible but real growth of trees, the length of time needed to

Pastoral Perspective

The superscription (not included here) of Psalm 92, "A Song for the Sabbath Day," occurs only here in the Psalter. That music and song are appropriate expressions of worship resonates with our weekly attempts to make a joyful noise to the Lord. Still, a question remains: Why is this psalm, in particular, designated for Sabbath worship?

The language of Psalm 92 suggests two reasons why this song is especially appropriate for the Sabbath. First, this song celebrates the Creator's handiwork. The opening words of Psalm 92—"it is good"—echo the language of the first creation narrative. At the end of the sixth day, "God saw everything that he had made, and indeed, it was very good" (Gen. 1:31). In this light the psalm's opening declaration and later references to "the works of your hands" call to mind God's activity in creation. Thus, as God considers the work of creation on the seventh day, the congregation of Israel assembles on the seventh day to remember with thanksgiving all that God has made.

Second, while the psalm celebrates God's hand in creation, the references to God's "work" and "works" also point to God's saving acts in Israel's history. In the context of worship, Israel gathers on the Sabbath to recall the stories of deliverance and homecoming throughout their history (see Deut. 32:4; Josh. 24:31; Judg. 2:7; Pss. 33:4; 44:1; 90:16; 95:9; Isa. 5:12).

In the concluding verses, this remembrance of God's past provision for Israel flows into the promise of God's present and future care for the faithful. While it is difficult to reconstruct the psalm's historical context, the author acknowledges that "enemies" and "evildoers" sprout like grass (vv. 7, 9). And yet, while "the wicked" flourish today (v. 7), the psalmist proclaims that "the righteous" ones flourish and will bear fruit even in "old age" (v. 14). Such a statement of faith belongs to a worshiping community that gathers together to celebrate God's past actions and to strengthen their resolve in God's eternal faithfulness. Sung praise for the God who saves—in the past, present, and future—is the taproot of Israel's Sabbath worship.

As we consider the reasons we gather on the Sabbath to worship God, we find ourselves rooted in similar ground. On our Sabbath day, we sing to the Creator of "all things bright and beautiful." We sing "the mighty power of God that made the mountains rise." We also sing of God's faithfulness: "All I have needed your hand has provided; Great is your faithfulness, God, unto me!" Those hymns of remembrance and assurance are songs for the

Exegetical Perspective

psalm and would not place Psalm 92 in any single category.[1]

This psalm lacks the convention of repeating or paraphrasing the prayer for deliverance the poet previously prayed (Pss. 18:3–6; 30:8–10; 34:6; 41:4; 66:17; 116:4; 118:5; 138:3); but this omission is not unprecedented among the individual thanksgivings. For instance, Psalm 40 also lacks the same feature. What is unusual is that the psalm lacks any specifics of the distress that preceded the psalmist's deliverance, an element of a thanksgiving Gunkel called the "narrative." At best, verses 5–11 only obliquely suggest persecution by opponents. Despite the lack of specifics, however, verses 5–11 stand in the place of Gunkel's "narrative," giving the psalm formal correspondence with the structure of individual thanksgivings.

The introduction to the psalm, verses 1–3, establishes the cultic setting of the psalm where one offered such prayers of thanksgiving, along with whatever thank offerings might be appropriate. The introduction sets the reader/hearer within the temple worship by putting "give thanks to the LORD" in parallel with "sing praises to your name" (v. 1; see Pss. 7:17; 9:2; 61:8; 66:4; 68:4). The poet follows with mention of the morning and nighttime offices of the temple as the occasions for singing the psalm (v. 2). Finally, the liturgical stringed musical instruments appear in verse 3 ('*asor*, Pss. 33:2; 144:9; *nevel*, Amos 5:23; 6:5; Pss. 33:2; 57:8; 71:22, etc.; *kinnor*, Pss. 33:2; 43:4; 49:4; 57:8; 71:22; 81:2, etc.).

Verse 4 provides transition between the introduction (vv. 1–3) and the "narrative" of the poem. The parallel between "make happy" and "sing for joy" is like the parallel between the same roots in Psalm 5:11 and continues the worship motif. Use of "sing with joy" as an element of worship is shown in Psalm 132:9, 16. The verse also points us forward to the middle section (vv. 5–11) by reference to the Lord's "work" (v. 4a) and "deeds" (v. 4b).

The works that gratify the psalmist include the destruction of the foolish wicked (vv. 6–9), who are, indeed, enemies of God, as well as enemies of the psalmist. The didactic language of verse 6 criticizes the enemies as brutish (*ba'ar*) and fools (*kasil*) because they are incapable of perceiving God's great acts and deep thoughts (v. 5). While they may be as

1. See Samuel Terrien, *The Psalms: Strophic Structure and Theological Commentary* (Grand Rapids: Eerdmans, 2003), 653–54; Erhard Gerstenberger, *Psalms, Part 2 and Lamentations*, Forms of the Old Testament Literature, vol. 15 (Grand Rapids: Eerdmans, 2001), 168–69; and F.-L. Hossfeld and Erich Zenger, *Psalms 2*, trans. L. M. Maloney, Hermeneia (Minneapolis: Fortress Press, 2005), 436–68.

Homiletical Perspective

O Most High; to declare your steadfast love in the morning, and your faithfulness by night, to the music of the lute and the harp, to the melody of the lyre. For you, O LORD, have made me glad by your work; at the works of your hands I sing for joy" (vv. 1–4).

Third-millennium Sabbath in America, when it is celebrated at all, is celebrated in a thoroughly secular, Homeland-"Insecure" color-coded-fear society where God is an afterthought for most—anything but "a very present help in trouble" (Ps. 1:46). Given this social situation, Psalm 92 could well be the anthem for believers living in the twenty-first century. It is a fiery protest song that flies in the face of the prevailing reality of its day.

Christians and Jews who try to live Sabbath-centered lives in the third millennium do so not only in a culture of fear, but in a largely apathetic society. Retail stores do not close for the Sabbath, and sporting events do not adjust their weekend schedules so the Sabbath may be observed, be it at Friday sundown, Saturday night, or Sunday morning. To sing a Sabbath song—especially a fiery protest song—in a secular land is something Psalm 92 invites the preacher to consider.

Psalm 92 also invites believers to sing to God's glory every morning and every night. John Calvin offered this reason for such ceaseless praise:

> It might seem a strange distinction which the Psalmist observes when he speaks of our announcing God's goodness in the morning and his faithfulness at night. His goodness is constant, and not peculiar to any one season, why then devote but a small part of the day to the celebration of it? And the same may be said of the other Divine perfection mentioned, for it is not merely in the night that his faithfulness is shown. But this is not what the Psalmist intends. He means that beginning to praise the Lord from earliest dawn, we should continue his praises to the latest hour of the night; this being no more than his goodness and faithfulness deserve.[1]

Calvin does not address the difficulty for believers to sing God's praise with timeless regularity in a secular, fear-driven culture. Psalm 92 pushes believers to sing God's praise even in times when many challenge God's existence and/or God's benevolent purpose at all. "As much [as] or more than any generation before in the history of the world," writes Clinton McCann, "we are inclined to trust our own intelligence, strength, and technology

1. John Calvin, *Commentary on the Book of Psalms* (Grand Rapids: Christian Classics Ethereal Library, 2004), 1:585.

Psalm 92:1-4, 12-15

Theological Perspective

flourish, the possibility that we may not "see the forest for the trees!" In other words, the lives of the righteous are nourished by the creator God in ways that may be more subtle than obvious.

Conclusion. This is the only psalm designated in the superscription as "A Song for the Sabbath Day." Its motifs of praise and creation make this a premier liturgical work in Israel's life. The psalm links the individual to God and to the corporate well-being of God's people. It demonstrates many theological links to the doctrine of creation, prefigured in the Genesis story and reenacted every seven days on Israel's Sabbath and ours. The historical dating of this psalm carries an underlying message as well. Many commentators suggest that its joyous thanksgiving to God is a rebuke to all who believe that God had abandoned Israel during the difficulties experienced in the exile. The psalm's assertions clearly state that such is not the case. God prevails as the one bringing love, life, and flourishing to Israel.

Few listeners will have trouble personalizing this psalm—for a number of reasons—if it serves as a preaching text. Specifically, the final comparison of the righteous to palm trees that "in old age . . . still produce fruit; they are always green and full of sap" is a reminder to a generally aging American population that God is present and supportive throughout one's life span. Little is said from the pulpit, often by way of corporate denial, about aging. This psalm gives opportunity to speak of the God who is involved with loving supportiveness in the lives of all the righteous, regardless of age.

Additionally, the themes of thanksgiving and the expressions of God's care challenge the evils of the world directly with the message of God's care. The psalmist's words provide proof of the enormous relief and joy that come as a result of understanding that God remains active in creation and the sustenance of the righteous. The psalm is a witness to anyone who encounters these realities.

Epiphany is the season for discerning the presence of God among us in Jesus Christ. This psalm plays a central role in providing demonstration of the works and intentions of a God who redeems and sustains regardless of circumstances. It invites the listener, like the psalmist, to respond with joy and thanksgiving.

SUSAN K. HEDAHL

Pastoral Perspective

Sabbath day. Like Psalm 92 they celebrate God's works in creation and champion an abiding faith in God's provision. Those songs, like today's psalm, are rooted deeply in us—sometimes surprisingly so.

Years ago a fellow seminarian led a weekly prayer service in the dementia unit of a nearby health-care facility, as part of his "supervised ministry" internship. Early on, members of that Sunday afternoon congregation stared blankly during the reading of the Word. Others dozed off during the homily. The pastor-in-training quickly realized that his well-intentioned aim missed the mark.

One day the student brought his acoustic guitar to the chapel service, and something surprising happened. As he strummed the introduction of a familiar hymn, the congregation became newly engaged. Some looked up attentively. Others smiled. Everyone started to sing. These worshipers, many of whom could not remember the names of loved ones, recalled verse after verse of well-known hymns.

For the length of that service, and for the balance of that year, the dementia patients became a choir. Each week, they joined their voices in off-key praise. Each week, they poured themselves into Sabbath songs. Each week, the eyes of the choristers filled up, as if in tearful recognition of the psalmist's words: "It is good to give thanks to the LORD, to sing praises to your name, O Most High" (v. 1). In the company of those righteous men and women, one could hear with new clarity the psalmist's song. Indeed, "in old age they still produce fruit; they are always green and full of sap" (v. 14).

Epiphany is a season for seeing more clearly the person of Jesus Christ and the way of discipleship. This is also a time for singing praises, for the sound of gratitude in our sanctuaries. With the psalmist we give thanks—with instrument and voice—for all that God has made, for the faithfulness of God, and for the promise of new growth in the house of the Lord.

ANDREW NAGY-BENSON

Exegetical Perspective

numerous as blades of grass and flourish in their wrongdoing for a time, they are nevertheless doomed to destruction (v. 7). God, on the other hand, is eternal in the heights of heaven (v. 8). God's enemies and all their iniquitous deeds will be scattered (*yitpardu*, v. 9; Ps. 22:14; Job 4:11; 41:9).

God has, on the other hand, exalted the poet's "horn" (*qeren*, v. 10) in the presence of these enemies, a double entendre that compares the horn of a "wild ox" with the "horn" that stands as a symbol of power (Jer. 48:25; Zech. 2:1–2). In addition to the psalmist's public vindication, God has let the writer see the punishment of the enemies (v. 11).

The last major section of the psalm (vv. 12–15) reverts to wisdom language to celebrate the flowering (vv. 12–13) of the righteous in an extended natural metaphor. The righteous are like a palm tree and a cedar of Lebanon (v. 12). They grow in the sacred precincts of God's house (v. 13). The Wisdom literature's promise of long years for the righteous comes out in this figure as old trees that are still green, full of sap, and bearing fruit (v. 14). Hossfeld and Zenger, on the other hand, do not find the metaphor merely "natural" but, rather, a reference to the lush temple gardens of Mesopotamian rulers, seeing this motif as connecting with the cultic setting envisaged in verses 1–3.[2]

Conventionally, the English versions render the Hebrew imperfect of the verbs in this section with the present tense. Since, however, by its nature, the imperfect refers to action that is not yet complete, the vision of verses 12–15 is also a vision of the psalmist's future.

The psalm's concluding verse declares the Lord "straight" (*yashar*) and without iniquity. These are qualities of God's actions in favor of the psalmist rather than abstract qualities of God.

The superscription of Psalm 92 labels it "A Psalm. A Song for the Sabbath Day," a designation shared by no other psalm in the Psalter. Because this heading is later than the psalm, however, it is impossible to connect its contents definitively with Sabbath worship in the temple.

FRED L. HORTON

Homiletical Perspective

more than we trust God or each other. From the perspective of Psalm 92, the irony is that the more sophisticated and self-sufficient we think we are, the more stupid and more insecure we actually are."[2] Psalm 92 sounds a bold note of confident praise despite cajoles of a dubious, dismissive, or downright "stupid" crowd.

Preaching Psalm 92 in its entirety forces preachers to wrestle with an issue that leads many people to refuse to sing and even to exit the body of believers: why do evil people prosper? Not unlike what the prophet proclaims in Isaiah 40:7, the psalmist pleads with believers not to base their faith in God on appearances. "Though the wicked sprout like grass and all evildoers flourish," contends the psalmist, "they are doomed to destruction forever, but you, O LORD, are on high forever" (vv. 7–8). The psalmist acknowledges the apparent inequity when the wicked prosper, but he goes on to shout with proleptic confidence that while the wicked "sprout like grass," those who trust in God's justice will "flourish like the palm tree" (v. 12).

For the preacher to teach this ancient Sabbath song to the congregation will produce at least two results that no community of believers can live well without. It will prevent believers from sucking the joy right out of the Sabbath—a temptation that believers have given in to for centuries—by making it some sort of obligatory day of rules and regulations that one needs a scorecard to manage.

Singing this Sabbath song will also prevent believers from being seduced by the sirens of secularity and will prevent them from exhibiting a tepid faith, lest they look too religious in a society that is largely not. Singing this song will invite others into a life that does not give up on God, even when God seems painfully absent, and does not give up on the just ways of God, even when it looks as if only the unjust prosper.

Consider all this, and it makes perfect sense why the psalmist declares Psalm 92 as "a song for the Sabbath."

GARY W. CHARLES

2. Hossfeld and Zenger, *Psalms 2*, 440–41.

2. J. Clinton McCann Jr., "Psalms," in *The New Interpreter's Bible*, vol. 4 (Nashville: Abingdon Press, 2001), 1050.

1 Corinthians 15:51-58

[51]Listen, I will tell you a mystery! We will not all die, but we will all be changed, [52]in a moment, in the twinkling of an eye, at the last trumpet. For the trumpet will sound, and the dead will be raised imperishable, and we will be changed. [53]For this perishable body must put on imperishability, and this mortal body must put on immortality. [54]When this perishable body puts on imperishability, and this mortal body puts on immortality, then the saying that is written will be fulfilled:

"Death has been swallowed up in victory."
[55]"Where, O death, is your victory?
Where, O death, is your sting?"
[56]The sting of death is sin, and the power of sin is the law. [57]But thanks be to God, who gives us the victory through our Lord Jesus Christ.

[58]Therefore, my beloved, be steadfast, immovable, always excelling in the work of the Lord, because you know that in the Lord your labor is not in vain.

Theological Perspective

Today's text is the culmination of Paul's proclamation on resurrection. There are two eschatological issues raised in this text: the nature/timing of the resurrection and the defeat of death. Paul claims that with the Parousia (second coming) all will put on imperishable, eternal bodies—both those already dead and those still living. For those Corinthian "spiritualists" who saw embodied existence as repugnant, "the idea that the body would be raised would have been anathema."[1]

This text points to an ongoing debate about the timing and nature of bodily resurrection. Some Christians claim that our *souls* are "raised with Christ" and only reconnected with our *bodies* upon Jesus' triumphant return. Others claim that believers are *immediately* resurrected in bodily form. The first interpretation is too dualistic for Paul, as if bodies and souls existed independently; and the idea that believers are *immediately* resurrected in bodily form is refuted by this passage and 1 Thessalonians 4:13–18. Rather, Paul states that only upon the "final trumpet" (v. 52, NRSV "last trumpet," a Jewish apocalyptic image for the final victory of God—see Joel 2:1) will the dead be bodily raised into the kingdom, along with the living.

Pastoral Perspective

One of the most basic definitions of ongoing pastoral practice is "the care of souls." How Christian caregivers define "soul," and indeed how they might delineate or incarnate the actual "care" of such, are matters of continuing interrogation and reflection. Still, it may be observed that, from the first, the church has taken as one of its most important pastoral ministries the preparing of believers for a faithful death. Dying faithfully, whether at the hand of persecutors or otherwise, was considered a form of testimony, a grace afforded by prayer, the sacraments, and, perhaps especially, the promises of the gospel. If we hold those doctrines, we are prepared to die well and, Paul would argue, live well.

The text before us, often read at funerals, is on the face of it a pastoral word. It is Paul's word of preparation and comfort to those who are facing the reality of death. It becomes a word of preparation and comfort to the people under our own care as we come to understand Paul's argument. In terms and tones somewhat reminiscent of 1 Thessalonians 4:16c, Paul affirms that there will come a day when there is no more "victory" for death, but instead victory for believers "through the Lord Jesus Christ" (v. 57). Until then, the faithful are to live well, remain "steadfast, immovable, always excelling in the

1. Gordon Fee, *The First Epistle to the Corinthians* (Grand Rapids: Eerdmans, 1987), 715.

Exegetical Perspective

Everyone loves a good mystery, right? At the close of 1 Corinthians 15, Paul lets readers in on one. For us, "mystery" might suggest an enigma, puzzle, or intriguing problem, perhaps a crime, arousing suspense until a reasoned solution can be teased out. For Paul, *mysterion* refers, rather, to the hidden counsel or purposes of God, knowable not through reasoned problem solving, but through revelation, proclamation, or fulfillment (see also Rom. 11:25; 16:25; 1 Cor. 2:1, 7). Throughout chapter 15, Paul argues for the bodily resurrection of the dead, convinced that Christ's resurrection was not an exception but the crucial precedent for believers. At one point, his perspective is cosmic, surveying eschatological events leading to Christ's defeat of all powers hostile to God (vv. 24–28). At another, he underscores the personal consequences if there were no resurrection: "If for this life only we have hoped in Christ, we are of all people most to be pitied" (v. 19). "We" language returns in verses 51–58 as Paul proclaims the *mystery* of believers' ultimate release from mortality.

Interpreters sometimes pause over, "We will not all die, but we will all be changed" (v. 51b), wondering whether Paul thought he or some of his hearers would be alive when Christ returned (see 1 Thess. 4:17). Perhaps he did. Paul may also have

Homiletical Perspective

When I became a mother, a friend sent me a card that included a sentence from the King James Version of this day's reading from Paul's first letter to the church in Corinth: "Behold, I shew you a mystery; We shall not all sleep, but we shall all be changed."

In the weeks that followed, my husband and I got little sleep and did a good deal of "changing." However, the text also had a deeper resonance. In this text Paul presents the Christian hope of resurrection in the face of the inevitability of death, and for a parent holding a vulnerable newborn, the question of life and death, of mystery and miracle, is ever present.

We no longer pay much heed to the King James's "shew" of a mystery. In fact, the now-familiar New Revised Standard Version of this text uses the word "die" in place of "sleep." In part, this may be because we want to face the reality of death, leaving euphemisms aside. In part, it is because in the light of Christ's resurrection we *can face the reality of death—courageously, faithfully.*

At this point we might use our sermon to recall Jesus' response to Jairus, the ruler of the synagogue, who thought his daughter dead. Jesus said, "Do not fear, your daughter is not dead but sleeping." Those around Jesus think him cruel to taunt Jairus in such a way, but Jesus knows better. He knows that the line between this mortal life and eternal life in God is

1 Corinthians 15:51-58

Theological Perspective

When Christ returns and the physically dead and the spiritually dead put off perishability, decay, and sin and put on the imperishable body of Christ (vv. 53–54) then death will be totally "swallowed up in victory." This reference to the eschatological expectation of Isaiah 25 is the only time that Paul quotes an unfulfilled prophetic vision, but so sure is he that in the new creation death has been decisively defeated on the cross that he taunts the "final enemy" by asking, "Where, O death, is your victory? Where, O death, is your sting?" (v. 55). He answers his own taunt with a line that will command our attention for the rest of this essay: "The sting of death is sin."

The proper exegesis of this verse depends on one's understanding of the nature of death. Some commentators claim that Paul is saying that physical death is the result of sin; that humans were intended to live forever but sin introduces death to an otherwise immortal creation. But this is not the way in which Paul views death. To understand what Paul means when he says that death has "lost its sting" or that the "wages of sin is death" (Rom. 4:23), we must first understand Paul's dialectical view of death.

For Paul, two views of death stand in tension: death as natural and death as final enemy. First, death represents the natural end of human life. Death is the termination of our lives on this earth. We are mortal beings, never intended to live forever, "like grass that is renewed in the morning; in the morning it flourishes . . . in the evening it fades and withers" (Ps. 90:5–6). Death may be a cause of regret for the dying and a source of mourning for the survivors, but it is not evil; it is simply the intended ending point of our creaturely lives (Heb. 9:27).

Paul claims, though, that "the last enemy to be destroyed is death" (1 Cor. 15:26). How do we make sense of this twofold vision, that death is both natural and an enemy to be overcome? To do so, we must understand what death means. Death entails alienation or separation on three planes: from our bodies, from other human beings, and from God. Life means unity with self, neighbor, and God. Death threatens separation in all of its stark, horrific manifestations.

Thinking of death in terms of separation helps us understand how the two conceptions of death—as natural and as final enemy—are connected. In a world without sin, death is simply the natural end of human life, the closing of the first act of human existence. This should be followed by eternal life with God, because sin has not separated us from God. Because of sin, however, physical death

Pastoral Perspective

work of the Lord, because you [plural] know that in the Lord your labor is not in vain" (v. 58).

Our lection, not unlike our pastoral care, is challenge as well as comfort. Paul encourages Corinthian (and subsequent) believers to retain the hope of Christian faith in the terms by which he preached it—that at the "last trump" (v. 52 KJV) every faithful believer will be raised to share in a resurrection like that of Christ. "We will all be changed," he writes, in the "twinkling of an eye" (cf. Phil. 3:20–21). Paul had proclaimed Jesus' resurrection as a precursor, a prefiguring of a promised resurrection for all the faithful.

In eschatological, even apocalyptic terms, Paul advanced the doctrine of the resurrection as essential, not only to the life and missional work of Christian communities, but also for a faithful understanding of the ultimate salvation of Corinthian believers. The faithful are "being saved," but the final form of that salvation will be completed only at the last (see Phil. 1:6). Paul maintains that the Corinthians must not relinquish either the specific orientation or the obligations that hope in the resurrection demands (15:2). This particular eschatology proves the only true and lasting foundation for both this life and the life to come.

The comfort Paul offers his reader-listeners, then, is not a "general" palliative but, instead, a specific encouragement to a particular way of thinking/believing. His pastoral word is in fact a prophetic word (the speaking of God's particular truth into a particular moment). His prophetic word is pastoral (the speaking of God's abiding promises in the gathered community of faith). The exhortation to "hold firmly" (15:2) to faith in the gospel's promised coming resurrection is itself a balm to those "stung" by death. Comfort comes to those who do not let go of this gospel.

What becomes clear is that the Corinthians (one? a few? many?) have done just that, have, one way or the other, redefined "resurrection" as Paul had preached it. Exactly what the reinterpreters are teaching is not clear. Perhaps they contend that Christ alone experienced resurrection, a reality unique and unrepeatable in the life of God. His resurrection effected changes in those who believe through the conferring of *charismata*, or gifts. If so, these teachers are advancing a kind of spiritualized or realized eschatology, with "this life," now, as the sphere where believers experience victorious living.

This "new" teaching disintegrates Christian discipleship as Paul understands and lives it. The

Exegetical Perspective

used "we" more flexibly to include both present and future believers, holding that Christ's return would interrupt human history sooner or later.[1] Clearly, however, transformation is promised equally to the living and the dead.

Change will be sudden, happening in the smallest conceivable bit of time—as fast as the glance or sparkle or blink or quiver of an eye (all possible alternatives to "twinkling," v. 52). Yet a deliberate signal will announce it: a trumpet sound. In other biblical passages, trumpets may signal God's rescue or judgment (Isa. 27:13; Joel 2:1; Zeph. 1:14–16) or a new stage in an eschatological scenario (Matt. 24:31; 1 Thess. 4:16; Rev. 8:2ff.). Here it proclaims resurrection.

Paul has already argued that the resurrected body will be made of more refined "stuff" than corruptible flesh and blood, and that even in radical transformation there is continuity (vv. 39–50). Verses 53–54 extend those views. That which is perishable (*to phtharton*), subject to decay and destruction, and that which is mortal (*to thnēton*) must put on, like clothing, imperishability and immortality. What one has previously been is not annihilated, but subsumed into a state of being without previous vulnerabilities. Even Paul's repetition of "this" subtly communicates continuity: *this* entity that humans now are will both persist and change.

In that transformation, a saying of Scripture will be fulfilled. In verses 54–55, Paul actually merges *two* brief quotations from prophets, both about death. He begins by echoing Isaiah: "Death has been swallowed up in victory" (v. 54b). Paul's wording differs somewhat from both the Hebrew text of Isaiah 25:8a—"He will swallow up death forever" (NRSV)—and from the Septuagint (the Greek translation of the Hebrew Bible)—"Death in his strength has devoured." Despite the altered phrasing, Paul is true to the vision of Isaiah 25: a joyous banquet in the presence of God, during which God swallows up death and wipes tears from all faces (see also Rev. 21:4).

Paul immediately juxtaposes questions from Hosea: "Where, O death, is your victory? Where, O death, is your sting?" Interestingly, Paul inverts the force of this saying in its original context. In Hosea 13:14, God calls upon death and the place of the dead to help bring judgment on God's people: "O Death, where are your plagues? O Sheol, where is

1. Anthony Thiselton, *The First Epistle to the Corinthians*, New International Greek Testament Commentary (Grand Rapids: Eerdmans, 2000), 1293.

Homiletical Perspective

thin indeed, that the distance separating any of us from the eternal realm can be crossed in a moment, in the twinkling of an eye (Mark 5:35–40).

We run into difficulty, Paul proclaims, when we close ourselves off from the power of God's love to work miracles in our lives—especially the miracle of resurrection, life brought out of death.

Those who are closed to resurrection will surely feel as if they are sleeping through life. Those who are closed off will either live in fear of death or, denying the reality of death, simply cling frantically to the present. Those who are closed off from the hope of the resurrection will know none of the wonder in the moments of our living, none of the possibility that God has placed in the midst of our very human experience. They might as well be dead.

In the life that is steadfast and immovable in the face of death, in the living that excels in the work of the Lord because one need not fear the grave, a purpose is given, the gifts of God are used fully, and, as Paul puts it, our "labor is not in vain" (v. 58).

Some have no interest in such a revelation. As you prepare a sermon on this text, you might try to gather a group of church folks to talk about the way in which the reality of death and the hope of resurrection bear fruit in their own lives. You may well find people who would rather talk about alienation and exhaustion than finitude and death. Alienation and exhaustion seem almost manageable. Not so death. Even though people come to church in hopes of finding meaning in their lives because the labor of their death-denying days is without such meaning, they like the Corinthians before them would rather not go there, that is, to the grave.

As you preach this sermon, note that Paul has good news for the Corinthians in this passage that brings to a conclusion his proclamation about resurrection. Paul has good news for us as well. Just as those first disciples were transformed from being terrified members of a failed movement, cowering behind closed doors, into women and men emboldened to proclaim the good news of a God whose power is in humility, whose life is known even in the midst of death, all believers have the chance to experience a similar transformation.

Resurrection talk surely reflects the Jewish culture of Paul the Pharisee, and probably of Jesus as well. Pharisaic Jews shared a belief in a messianic expectation, an age when the world would experience a real change.

Amy-Jill Levine suggests that for such Jews "the messianic age would witness a general resurrection of

1 Corinthians 15:51-58

Theological Perspective

threatens eternal separation from self, community, and, worst of all, God. Death is not something that happens only at the end of our physical existence. Because sin disrupts relationships, even though we are physically "alive," we are dying. The alienation of spiritual death is a potential precursor to the final separation upon physical death. It is in this spiritual sense that Paul talks of being "dead through [our] trespasses and sins," separated from God and one another (Eph. 2:1).

The relationship between death as natural and death as the final enemy is now clearer. It is not that, with sin, previously immortal beings become mortal but, rather, that sin causes death to be a terror, threatening us with eternal separation. Without sin, death has no "sting"; it is simply a transition to eternal life with God.

Death may be the final enemy but it does not have the final word. If sin and death represent separation from God and neighbor, Christians believe that in Jesus Christ death has been defeated. As a result of taking upon himself the result of sin, namely, death, we are spared that final separation from God. "Just as sin came into the world through one man, and death came through sin, . . . so one man's act of righteousness leads to justification and life for all" (Rom. 5:12, 18). Therefore Paul no longer fears physical death, since it has "lost its sting" of separation. In fact, Paul says that he even desires physically to die, because he has already been raised to new life. "Living is Christ and dying is gain. . . . I do not know which I prefer" (Phil. 1:21, 22). Here we see the clearest expression that death is no longer an enemy, once our relationship with God has been restored through Christ's "victory."

Paul reminds us that we can be physically alive but spiritually dead. More importantly, we can attain eternal life, not just when we physically die, but here and now. If spiritual death means separation, eternal life is the life of fellowship and love of God and neighbor. This is such good news that Paul breaks forth in doxology in verse 57: "Thanks be to God" that death, both the Redeemer's and the believers', has been defeated, "swallowed up" by Christ's victory on the cross.

KYLE FEDLER

Pastoral Perspective

notion that believers receive the benefits of resurrection presently refigures not only apostolic doctrine but Christian life and ministry. Gone for these reinterpreters is the urgency Paul feels for preaching and mission. Gone is the rationale for sacrifice and suffering. Gone, as well, is the community of hope and faith, the particular and unique identity of the congregation as hopefully cruciform.

Paul preaches resurrection, Christ's and that of those who believe—a promise for all who in spite of suffering remain faithful. Paul also preaches Christ and him crucified—a sacrificial challenge to life and ministry. As Paul can clearly see, to lose this basic shape of the faith—not only "once delivered" to the saints in Corinth, but indeed delivered over and over again—is to lose community, sound doctrine, and therefore Christian identity.

Paul contends elsewhere in the letter that this "spiritual" teaching, this redefined resurrection, has left the Corinthians as fractious as the society at large (see 11:18–19). The community of faith itself is wounded, perhaps fatally, if their faith continues off course. Those who accept this "new teaching" are materially altering the terms of the gospel as it had been preached even before Paul, and the consequences are dire.

The word of "comfort" in verses 51–58 is, of course, a piece of a tightly packed and theologically urgent altercation comprising all of 1 Corinthians 15, Paul's longest discourse on resurrection. The chapter in toto is his challenge of the "new" in favor of his original proclamation. He does not so much argue for believers' resurrection as announce it, point to it as undeniable truth. The life to come is the heart of the present life. The present life is a time to be faithful to that hope. Hope prompts and rewards faithful ministry.

The community of faith, in Corinth and elsewhere, is for Paul fueled by the faith's particular hope. That unique confession is two-edged, pastoral and prophetic, and reinforces awareness that true comfort, like true community, is never the product of abstract truth—there is no balm in vague appeals to common experience. Instead, the affirmation of the gospel prompts us to live as those who are prepared to die, and prepares us to die as those who go forth to live.

THOMAS R. STEAGALD

Exegetical Perspective

your destruction?" (Hos. 13:14c, d). Hosea's "where" implies "bring them here"; Paul's "where" conveys a mocking "nowhere." Paul's wording is closer to the Septuagint version: "Where is your penalty, O Death? Where is your sting, O Hades?" Rather than Sheol or Hades, Paul addresses personified death twice, with intensified effect. He changes "penalty" to "victory" (*to vikos*) and retains "sting" (*to kentron*), sometimes used for a goad for driving herds, but here for a sting like an insect's or scorpion's. Paul taunts death, the once powerful foe, now defeated.[2]

A pithy epigram follows, commenting on death's former or apparent power (v. 56). Although "law" is not a primary topic in 1 Corinthians and has not yet been mentioned in chapter 15, Paul's compressed remark hints at views he elaborates in Galatians 3 and Romans 4–7 regarding the complex interplay of sin, death, and law. Having declared death's defeat, Paul exclaims: "Thanks be to God!" (v. 57). For at the end of mortal existence, who (or what) wins? Not death, according to Paul, or the sin-law-death triad. Not even Christ, simply. Rather, through Christ, God gives the victory to "us."

For Paul, anticipating ultimate release from death's threat has strong consequences for present living. In verse 58, he draws emphatic ethical conclusions from his eschatological argument. He began the chapter with an appeal to brothers and sisters (*adelphoi*) to "stand" in the gospel and "hold firmly" to the message (vv. 1–2). Now he ends by urging "my *beloved* brothers and sisters" (*adelphoi mou agapētoi*) to be steadfast and immovable. Earlier Paul referred to the value of work for the Lord, particularly his own (vv. 10, 30, 32); now he urges his hearers always to excel or abound or overflow (*perisseuō*) in the work of the Lord. Throughout the chapter, he has also explored conditions under which believing in Christ might or might not be vain or futile, when God's grace and the gospel might even come to nothing (vv. 2, 10, 14, 17). Now he affirms forcefully, "You know that in the Lord your labor is not in vain."

Given death's defeat, life calls for a surpassing investment and steadiness. Work has meaning. The promise of bodily resurrection confirms that what we do with our bodies matters. Paul's tight treatise on resurrection is no exercise in mere speculation; rather, it undergirds a call to effort and excellence in present Christian life.

B. DIANE LIPSETT

Homiletical Perspective

the dead, as parents and children, patriarchs and matriarchs together with their descendants would feast at the final banquet and there would be no more reason to pray, 'give us this day our daily bread.'"[1]

More than 2,000 years have passed, and we have surely discovered that our lives have meaning, not because of popularity contests or television talent shows, but because of a God who commands us to stand against every evil and every hurt, with the assurance that the one who has shown us the way and the truth and life will finally prevail, in our own lives and in all the world eternally.

This passage invites the preacher to proclaim just how it is that a people of God excel in the work of the Lord, how it is that we daily encounter the risen Christ and find that our lives are transformed. The body of Christ, alive in this world, becomes ever more like Jesus, speaking truth to power, healing the broken, lifting up those whose lives are in the depths of despair, and preaching a word of forgiveness to a battered world.

Is Paul's challenge too great for us to accept? The earliest followers of Jesus, Jews like him, believed that Jesus was God's chosen one, the Messiah, and they believed that he had been resurrected from the dead. As they went about proclaiming the good news, they became a changed people. No longer were they afraid and uncertain. In fact the resurrection of Jesus, whom they proclaimed as Messiah, compelled them to preach about a world yet to come, which would be not only different from but also other than the world where death appeared to be the victor. "Death has been swallowed up in victory." A mystery to proclaim indeed. And all will be changed.

MARIA LASALA

---

2. See Richard Hays, *First Corinthians* (Louisville, KY: John Knox Press, 1997), 276.

1. Amy-Jill Levine, *The Misunderstood Jew* (New York: HarperCollins, 2006), 57.

Luke 6:39-49

[39]He also told them a parable: "Can a blind person guide a blind person? Will not both fall into a pit? [40]A disciple is not above the teacher, but everyone who is fully qualified will be like the teacher. [41]Why do you see the speck in your neighbor's eye, but do not notice the log in your own eye? [42]Or how can you say to your neighbor, 'Friend, let me take out the speck in your eye,' when you yourself do not see the log in your own eye? You hypocrite, first take the log out of your own eye, and then you will see clearly to take the speck out of your neighbor's eye.

[43]"No good tree bears bad fruit, nor again does a bad tree bear good fruit; [44]for each tree is known by its own fruit. Figs are not gathered from thorns, nor

Theological Perspective

Jesus continues teaching his disciples in a series of three parables. They address questions the listener might have about the life of discipleship. All three segments grow out of the subject matter of the Sermon on the Plain, and all focus on the activities of Jesus' disciples. The metaphorical terms of each parable are very different and at certain points may seem contradictory. Yet taken together, they may also be understood as complementary. The disciples' actions are presented both as a natural outgrowth of discipleship and as hard work; they are both interior and exterior actions. The three parables are a rich source for contemplation on the active life of discipleship.

The first parable (vv. 39–42) focuses on the listener's need for self-examination. While Jesus has just cautioned the hearer regarding judgment of others (v. 37), this parable makes it clear that disciples are meant to serve as guides or teachers of others. However, judgment of oneself is necessary for the disciple who is fully taught. He must eradicate his own faults before assisting others, or he will be unable to see to help them. The parable draws on two conventional metaphors: "seeing is understanding," and "understanding is a journey." The disciple must remove the log from his own eye in order to be able to lead others toward greater

Pastoral Perspective

On this Eighth Sunday after Epiphany, it is good to remind ourselves what the Epiphany represents. While the Gospel reading for the Epiphany usually centers on the wise men and their journey to see the Christ, Epiphany is really about all of us and our journeys of faith. What capacity do you and I have to bring our gifts to the One God sent to us, and what capacity do we have to live the gift of life that we receive from our encounter with this incarnate God?

In the sixth chapter of Luke, Jesus teaches his disciples about the implications of our encounter with the Holy One. The writer of Luke is clear. An experience with the Christ results in a new way of living. Jesus speaks plainly: "Why do you call me 'Lord, Lord,' and do not do what I tell you? I will show you what someone is like who comes to me, hears my words, and *acts* on them" (vv. 46–47, emphasis added).

The method Jesus uses to teach this truth is a series of pithy parables and sayings. Jesus speaks about the blind leading the blind, specks and logs in people's eyes, good and bad trees, and houses that are built on foundations and those that are not.

The underlying theme is that our experience with Jesus results in a life that is changed for the good. This is a particularly needed word for our day. Many people are looking for some kind of remarkable

are grapes picked from a bramble bush. ⁴⁵The good person out of the good treasure of the heart produces good, and the evil person out of evil treasure produces evil; for it is out of the abundance of the heart that the mouth speaks.

⁴⁶"Why do you call me 'Lord, Lord,' and do not do what I tell you? ⁴⁷I will show you what someone is like who comes to me, hears my words, and acts on them. ⁴⁸That one is like a man building a house, who dug deeply and laid the foundation on rock; when a flood arose, the river burst against that house but could not shake it, because it had been well built. ⁴⁹But the one who hears and does not act is like a man who built a house on the ground without a foundation. When the river burst against it, immediately it fell, and great was the ruin of that house."

Exegetical Perspective

Luke's Jesus has come down from the mountain to the level plain, where he has healed, blessed, declared woes, preached love of enemies, and called his disciples. Now he concludes the Sermon on the Plain by telling a series of "parables." A parable is usually a narrative metaphor of some length, at least several sentences, as in the stories of the sower (8:4–8), the rich fool (12:16–21), the lost sheep, coin, and son (15:4–32), the widow and the unjust judge (18:1–5). This Gospel writer uses the word "parable" (*parabolē*) several times (4:23; 5:36; 6:39) to describe short, proverbial examples that lack narrative. While the writer of Matthew spreads several of these same examples throughout his Gospel, the writer of Luke concentrates such material in this short passage. Jesus explains kingdom of God behavior in one short parable after another, with the hope, it seems, that everyone will understand at least one of the lessons in one of the proverbial examples. A modern-day preacher would do well to heed this pattern of providing a variety of examples so that hearers, diverse in their experiences and understanding, might connect with one or more.

Form follows function for Jesus, the preacher. The first rapid sequence of three short examples includes a blind person, a disciple, a teacher, and a brother. Just as a hearer will find some connection with one or

Homiletical Perspective

Every preacher should love to proclaim this text! Is there a church where these issues do not exist, where members live in harmonious, blissful peace unmarred by petty disputes? What Jesus says here is hardly exceptional; this text is about the rule. Although his teaching is parabolic, Jesus has probably seen enough blind guides to know one when he sees one. He knows, as well, that the blind are destined to recover their sight in him.

Henry David Thoreau saw this irony of the blind leading the blind in how we act and live and said of the New Testament that people "favor it outwardly . . . defend it with bigotry . . . and (yet) I know of no book that has so few readers."[1] The truth is that reading texts like this one cause congregational discomfort. We do not read this text much because we have a reasonably good idea of what it says about us and what it asks of us. Some, however, will find comfort in hearing this text as an indictment of their rascally neighbor. This hard news as good news is surely about "them" and not "me," we are sometimes tempted to believe. Yet the truth is that the proclamation on this day is really about both "them" and "us." Jesus says to all of his followers, then and now,

1. Henry David Thoreau, *A Week on the Concord and Merrimack Rivers* (Boston: James R. Osgood & Co., 1873), 80.

Theological Perspective

Pastoral Perspective

understanding. Otherwise, he is the blind person of verse 39, attempting to lead others who are blind. Only when the teacher has discovered his own faults can he assist others in seeing their own (v. 42). If the teacher's faults remain, the disciple will also share those faults (v. 40). The removal of the "log" from one's eye allows the listener to see the (spiritual) path clearly and lead others along it.

The language of these verses suggests action directed at oneself. The sight metaphor implies that the main goal is the disciple's understanding. Action is taken in order to clarify one's own vision. While the context suggests that the disciple is involved in the activity of leading others, the overall effect of the parable is to emphasize that the disciple's self-correction must precede the instruction of others. Thus the first parable clarifies the disciple's ongoing need for self-inspection. As the recipients of the blessings of verses 20–23, followers may be tempted to understand themselves as having already achieved spiritual perfection—after all, "[theirs] is the kingdom of God" (v. 20). By contrast, the parable assumes that followers of Jesus do in fact have logs in their eyes. They are still called to teach and lead others, but will not see to do so without recognition of their own faults.

The second parable (vv. 43–45) gives the idea that fruit is the natural product of the "good tree." This imagery contrasts with the previous verses, where the actions taken appeared to involve some attention and perhaps effort (in the removal of the "log"). The focus was on the disciple's own ability to correct her vision. Here, the good deeds or "fruits" come naturally. Just as it seems unnatural that a thorn bush would bear figs, so also the fig tree bears figs without apparent effort. The thorn bush does not choose to bear thorns, nor the fig tree figs, but each produces that which is natural to it. Metaphorically, the disciple's yield comes not through her own hard work but through her identity as a "good person" (v. 45).

Following on the heels of verses 39–42, the good tree metaphor may serve as reassurance that the good-hearted disciple can and will act in a good way. The former verses can appear to initiate a never-ending process. Who has removed every spot from her eye? Given on the heels of some of Jesus' more difficult teachings (vv. 27–38), the instructions of the first parable could lead to constant self-obsession. If the disciple cannot act until she sees perfectly (and therefore until she loves perfectly, and gives perfectly), perhaps she will never act at all. The metaphorical terms of the second parable provide a

experience with God. Going from church to church, they search for excitement, certainty, and an experience with God that seems clear and powerful.

Obviously, nothing is wrong with the desire for an experience of God or even with a need for excitement. A church where everything is dull is not necessarily more faithful to the message of Christ than a church where there is energy in worship and in the life of the members. Granted, there is excess in the worship of some churches where the buzz word is entertainment; but to move to the other side and say, "We will make this as boring as possible in the name of Jesus," is hardly the right response.

The experience of God is important, but for Jesus, experience without action is dead. How do we live our faith as changed, compassionate, caring Christians?

While Jesus is explicit about our both hearing and acting on his words, he couches much of this passage in what may be termed "subversive parables," or at least "confusing parables." For example, the parable of the log and the speck is confusing. Is Jesus saying that one aspect of following him is not to be judgmental? Or is Jesus saying that once we remove the log, we then can speak about the specks in other people's lives? Besides, what constitutes a "log," and what qualifies as a "speck"? Why are the followers of Jesus labeled as being ones with "logs" and others have "specks"?

What about Jesus' statement that the disciple is not above the teacher and that anyone who is fully qualified will be like the teacher? Don't we have to interpret these words?

Granted, in the first century, Jewish teachers were respected for their knowledge and for their insights into the Torah. They were called to interpret the law. Followers listened closely to their rabbis as those teachers explained, for example, what it meant to observe the Sabbath.

However, in much of our world today, words such as "above" or "below" have nuances that most of us have come to reject. Even in leadership circles, there is a democratization and collaboration of people who work together. The old chain-of-command approach to leadership has been largely replaced by the recognition that everyone in a corporation, a church, or an institution can make valuable contributions.

Besides, Jesus makes no distinction between good and bad teachers. Frankly, the history of religion, including our day, presents a frightening array of teachers whose ability to articulate their ideas has led

more of the sorts of people mentioned, so the hearer is called to behavior that respects all sorts of people, all the time, one right after another. The NRSV translates the Greek word for brother (*adelphos*) as "neighbor." While this is an effort to be gender-inclusive, it is probably not a necessary substitution. It is clear that Jesus is giving many examples of many different kinds of people, but does not seem compelled to try to list all possible examples, or even to use an inclusive, general word that includes all people. The writer of Luke consistently lifts up the lowly, bringing all people to equal footing before God. Not only should the blind not be left to lead the blind; sighted hearers are called by this sentence-long example to lead the blind themselves. The preacher calls the teacher to lift up the disciple to equal status. The preacher calls the hearers to consider their brothers as no greater sinners than themselves, but to remove the log of sin from their own eye, in order to see clearly, before removing the speck of sin from another's eye.

Matthew's theme of righteousness seems to creep into Luke's Gospel in verses 43–45. Both writers have used material from a common source to divide good tree from bad tree, good fruit from bad fruit, figs and grapes from thorns, good people from evil people, good treasure of the heart from evil treasure (see Matt. 7:15–20 and 12:33–35). Even here, though, Luke's kinder, gentler Jesus does not condemn, as Matthew's Jesus does; the bad fruit tree is not cut down and thrown into the fire, and he does not declare his hearers a brood of vipers.

Before the final example concerning foundations, Matthew's Jesus declares that the Lord will deny evildoers, and cast them away. Luke's Jesus makes no such declaration, indicating that the man who does evil will suffer as a direct result of his own behavior, not because of the Lord's wrath. In Matthew, the one who builds on rock, a firm foundation, is prudent; the one who builds on sand, a weak foundation, is foolish. Luke does not attribute the builder's choice of a foundation to his wisdom, but describes those who come to Jesus, hear, and act on his words, as the ones who build on a firm foundation that will stand in time of trouble. This example may preach well to those who, because of their economic status, can imagine or actually build a house upon a firm foundation. It will preach well, but differently, to those who live in huts made of pallets on the site of a former city dump or who build houses on flood plains where land is cheap, those who know from experience about precarious foundations and the danger of flooding. Helping hearers to understand

three things. First, it is hard to lead if you have no vision for where you are going (v. 39). Second, you cannot teach unless you have already learned (v. 40). Third, you are what you do, no matter what you believe (vv. 41–42, 46–47). One approach to the preaching of this text is a case by case consideration of these three things.

Jesus' thinking that the blind leading the blind is a recipe for disaster makes sense. Even if the church has not, corporate leaders have already figured out what Jesus saw coming long ago. Once, at the end of a parable, he said to his followers, "For the children of this age are more shrewd . . . than are the children of light" (Luke 16:8). For some reason, the church can be slow to learn these important lessons. Sadly, leaders with no vision for God's kingdom lead the church all the time on committees, boards, and even in pulpits. Leadership guru Peter Senge in his national bestseller *The Fifth Discipline* used the example of the movie *Spartacus* to portray the importance of vision. Senge retells the story of a Roman slave and gladiator who led an army of slaves in an uprising in 71 BCE. The slaves twice defeated the Roman legions but in the end were captured by the Roman general Marcus Crassus. Crassus wanted to execute Spartacus but had never seen him. So he said to the captured slaves: "You have been slaves. You will be slaves again. But you will be spared your rightful punishment of crucifixion by the mercy of the Roman legions . . . (if) you turn over to me the slave Spartacus." At that point, Spartacus rose to spare his troops and said to Crassus, "I am Spartacus." Then to everyone's surprise, the man next to him rose and said, "I am Spartacus."[2] So too the next, and the next man rose, each proclaiming in turn, "I am Spartacus." The slaves had a vision given to them by a guide who could see freedom.

Teaching is hard work, and Jesus knows it. Little wonder he admonishes his followers not to try until they have learned their own lessons. It seems that Jesus is unfamiliar with the "Those who cannot do, teach" mentality. What he was aware of was that most groups tend to look like their leaders and, more importantly, act like their leaders. In other words, before anyone attempts to teach or lead another, some self-evaluation is in order. Rabbi Jonathan Sacks tells the story of how philosopher Ludwig Wittgenstein once said that his aim in philosophy was to show the fly how to get out of the bottle. When a fly becomes trapped in a bottle, it

2. Peter Senge, *The Fifth Discipline: The Art and Practice of the Learning Organization* (New York: Currency Doubleday, 1990), 205.

Luke 6:39-49

Theological Perspective

corrective to the first. The disciple with good things stored in her heart will naturally act out of that storehouse and yield good fruit.

The third parable (vv. 46–49) returns to a metaphor of evident effort on the part of the disciples. Jesus points to the need not only to listen to his words but also to act. The one who hears and acts is the builder who digs out a strong foundation for his house. When the river floods, the high waters burst against the house but do not disturb it. Likewise, actions of the disciple that are based on Jesus' words provide strength in time of distress. The parable does not identify what happens in the process of acting out Jesus' words, only the results. It is not the teachings alone, but the act of following these instructions, that forms a firm foundation for the disciple.

The parable of the two foundations concludes the sermon (6:20–49) and leaves the reader with an emphasis on the need to act on Jesus' words. This segment of Jesus' teaching identifies a problem common to many Christians: one can hear Jesus' words and not act. The two actions of hearing and doing are not necessarily linked. The danger of hearing without action seems real, given the scope of Jesus' words in the Sermon on the Plain. "Love your enemies" and "Give to everyone who begs from you" sound like nice ideals, but putting them into practice strikes many disciples as a bit impractical. The third parable serves as a caution against such an approach to Jesus' teachings. His words are not to be viewed as out-of-reach idealism, but as a concrete foundation for the benefit of those who listen. In putting Jesus' words into practice, the listener gains the ability to withstand the storms that come.

SUSAN E. HYLEN

Pastoral Perspective

to disastrous results and uncritical responses. So-called leaders who exude personal charisma and magnetism can and do direct people to do violent things to others and to themselves.

Simply to say that the teacher is above the disciple is not enough. To respect the role of a teacher is one thing; but to follow without discernment someone who calls himself or herself a teacher, is to forfeit our own integrity.

Furthermore, what does Jesus mean when he says that "everyone who is fully qualified will be like the teacher" (v. 40)? Is Jesus talking about us as disciples being more like him? And what does it mean to be "fully qualified"? Can we list the qualities and decide for ourselves whether we are fully qualified?

Frankly, these parables remind us that faith is ultimately experienced but never fully explained. However, even experience is never enough. Does it make us more caring people? Does it sensitize us to the needs of our world? Does it prompt us to be "peacemakers" in a world filled with ethnic and religious hatred?

The fact is that most of us never get rid of our "blindness" or the "logs" in our eyes. If we wait to speak or act until we have our lives absolutely pristine, we will never speak or act.

Maybe Jesus is saying to his followers that they are more like other people than they even realize. That awareness allows us to preach and to act in a more compassionate, tolerant way. The problem is not other people; it is people, and I am one of those people. We may protest war, but we have to recognize how easy it is for us to divide people into friends and enemies.

In Epiphany, we see the gift of God. We return to wherever we call home. We act out of this grace we have received, but we act knowing that we are not just the answer. We too are part of the problem.

CHARLES BUGG

Exegetical Perspective

how the example works differently for those of various socioeconomic groups will enhance this Gospel writer's concern with those who live at the margins of society.

The Sermon on the Plain ends here. Jesus the preacher wraps up his sermon with a final admonition to heed the words of the Lord. A wise modern-day preacher learns by these concluding remarks to be quite purposeful in her final remarks to hearers.

The Gospel of Luke, written during a time of Roman oppression, a time when mercy, forgiveness, and grace did not exist in the public sphere, provides an essential understanding of God's love for all people in all times and places. In this Gospel, Jesus couches law in mercy, tempers judgment with forgiveness, usurps punishment with grace. The emphasis on the needs of the last, the least, and the lost is the particular gift of this Gospel to present-day preachers. In a world of violence and injustice, a world always at war, Lukan themes, as lifted up in these proverbial examples, are timeless. Themes of equality and respect for all people preach well, regardless of the particular nature of the suffering that might surround and invade the lives of hearers. The words of Luke's Jesus afflict the comfortable and comfort the afflicted in extraordinary ways. The examples, indeed, may preach most effectively in a manner that allows the "proverb" to speak for itself, with minimal interpretation. Carefully chosen parallel examples and well-told stories with contemporary themes may accompany the reading aloud of this text with little additional comment from the preacher, allowing hearers the opportunity to make creative connections with their own life stories.

DENA L. WILLIAMS

Homiletical Perspective

searches for a way out but repeatedly bangs its head against the sides until it dies of exhaustion. Had the fly the ability to reason, to learn, it could save itself fear, despair, and death by reasoning that if there is a way in, there is a way out. The fly cannot reason that it should look up. To learn, to have insight, is to see familiar things from an unfamiliar perspective.[3] It is difficult for any of us to see ourselves in any other way than from our own familiar perspectives. If we remove that log, however, we may be surprised with what we learn and therefore can teach.

Finally, Jesus uses two metaphors to teach one lesson. Bad trees will not bear good fruit, and bad foundations are not good support. In other words, because we are intended to be a new creation, transformed by grace, what we become in the process matters. We are what we do, what we practice. Perhaps the adage "Practice makes perfect" is correct. Not one of us will sit at the keyboard to play Beethoven's Piano Concerto no. 4 in G major, drive the court to slam a 360-degree dunk, or pass the state bar exam without significant practice along the way. What makes anyone think becoming a Christian, living the life of faith, even with the very grace of God, will not take work, practice, and dedication following Christ's call?

Preachers may well know they and their congregations need this text. In this text, Jesus bruises our egos in order to correct our vision, teach us lessons of the heart, and fine-tune our practices of faith. This sermon is not for the meek, mild, or squeamish, because it demands change. The result, however, of hearing these words and doing them, of putting them into practice, is a house that will withstand the winds of change, the tests of time, and the rising tides that will certainly come.

VAUGHN CROWE-TIPTON

3. Jonathan Sacks, *To Heal a Fractured World: The Ethics of Responsibility* (New York: Schocken Books, 2005), 134.

1 Kings 8:22-23, 41-43

²²Then Solomon stood before the altar of the Lᴏʀᴅ in the presence of all the assembly of Israel, and spread out his hands to heaven. ²³He said, "O Lᴏʀᴅ, God of Israel, there is no God like you in heaven above or on earth beneath, keeping covenant and steadfast love for your servants who walk before you with all their heart. . . .

⁴¹"Likewise when a foreigner, who is not of your people Israel, comes from a distant land because of your name ⁴²—for they shall hear of your great name, your mighty hand, and your outstretched arm—when a foreigner comes and prays toward this house, ⁴³then hear in heaven your dwelling place, and do according to all that the foreigner calls to you, so that all the peoples of the earth may know your name and fear you, as do your people Israel, and so that they may know that your name has been invoked on this house that I have built."

Theological Perspective

The prayer put into the mouth of Solomon in the account of the dedication of the temple in 1 Kings 8, especially in its latter portion (vv. 41–53), bears the marks of exilic reflection on the meaning of Israel for "the nations," and vice versa. Our lectionary text concentrates our attention on one of Solomon's petitions in this last part of the prayer: the one in which he asks God to grant the prayer of a stranger from a distant land, if that stranger should happen to hear of the God of Israel and come to pray to him, so that God may be known and honored by "all the peoples of the earth." Whether or not verses 41–43 constitute "the most marvelously universalistic passage in the OT," as one commentator suggests,[1] they clearly do express that motif. The temple is to be the dwelling place of the name of God, and a focus for the knowledge and worship of God; but God is not confined to that place, nor is the scope of God's concern and God's work to be confined to the people of Israel.

One way to construe this petition, and perhaps the most obvious way, would be this: it asks God to grant whatever the visiting stranger asks, simply as a demonstration of God's reality and power. This will

Pastoral Perspective

The delightful struggle of a person on a faith journey is to know in whom to believe. When a person says, "I don't believe in God," a good response is, "Tell me about the God in which you do not believe." Often the God revealed in such a conversation does not resemble the God in today's reading. When Solomon begins his dedicatory prayer over the temple in Israel, he stands with open arms, a posture of receptivity and supplication. His prayer is relational. The very action of openness is indicative of his relationship with the God of Israel whom Solomon has come to know.

His prayer acknowledges that the God to whom he is praying is not like the other gods who are conjectured in the heavens or even beneath the earth. This one God is unique and distinct. This God has made a covenant with the people of Israel. This God has made promises. This God is steadfast in love. This God is loyal. In relationship with this God, Solomon and the people of Israel are shaped as they walk with their whole heart and their whole selves in God's presence. The whole of Scripture is the drama of how people are shaped by their continuing understanding of and their unfolding realization of who this God is who has promised to be with them. This God guides them, loves them with steadfastness, is the source of life, and is even life in death.

1. Simon J. DeVries, *1 Kings*, Word Biblical Commentary (Nashville: Thomas Nelson Publishers, 2003), 126.

Exegetical Perspective

A God of Intimacy and Transcendence. The accomplishment of King Solomon in erecting a grand central temple redounds to his permanent legacy, but also raises profound theological questions. With one epochal push of the envelope, Solomon has linked a building on earth with the holy presence of God. A place to encounter a responsive God is a blessing for sure, but also a cause for anxiety! Heaven forbid that this new temple might lead us to presume upon the gift of God's nearness.

The sophisticated theology of 1 Kings 8 grapples with both the prospects and pitfalls of Solomon's erection of an official state shrine. This theology, associated with Deuteronomy and the Sinai covenant, upholds God's gift of intimacy with God's people but simultaneously insists on God's lofty independence from all parochial ties. With this theology understood, the symbolism of Solomon's temple becomes a blessing for us rather than a xenophobic curse.

The God of the Sinai covenant is *terrific* in the double sense of that word. God abounds in a *terrific* magnificence, which transfixes Israel and draws it into deep, personal relationship with the Divine. Simultaneously, God possesses an independence of Israel *terrific* in its frightful ramifications (cf. Lat. *terrificus,* "frightening"). In complete liberty over against all Israel's presumptions and prejudices, God

Homiletical Perspective

Our lection reveals for a moment the brilliant light of God's border-ignoring love. In it Solomon prays out his belief in a God who will listen not only to the chosen people, but also to the prayers of non-Israelites. The passage calls into question forms of political self-interest that would fortify their claims by appropriating divine authority. It can therefore speak, not only to nations, but also to any groups with a sense of their own special, divinely ordained status—like churches.

A Glint of Light. The history of Israel looks like the history of most nations in one important way: this people finds itself more than occasionally succumbing to the lure of nationalism and the dark underbelly of divinely sanctioned violence. Some of these moments appear in the story before nationhood has even begun, as when "the great work the LORD did against the Egyptians" involves killing off the soldiers who pursue Israel during the Red Sea crossing (Exod. 14:31); and when God promises Israel that through their military activity, God will be driving out each nation from the land (Josh. 3:9–11). The nationalist theology gains strength during the theocratic reign of Israel's and then Judah's kingdoms, when the new nations gather armies and conquer territories.

The preacher might help our congregations recognize this temptation in their homelands and in

1 Kings 8:22-23, 41-43

Theological Perspective

impress the stranger, who upon returning home will tell others, and thus God's reputation will spread. On this reading, no assessment of the merits or moral quality of the stranger's prayer is implied. It might be a prayer for wisdom, or for healing, or for victory in battle, or for success in trade, or for the slow and painful death of a rival. No matter what it is, Solomon asks God to grant it simply to show what God can do (and incidentally—thinks Solomon—to call attention to "this house that I have built" [v. 43]).

Another way to construe the petition involves more subtle considerations. On this reading, the stranger is not just someone who has happened to hear of the God of Israel and has decided to come to the temple to give this God a trial run with the desires of his heart. Instead, the stranger is someone who "fears God": a non-Israelite, to be sure, but one who seeks to be engaged in genuine worship, one who has been brought to the temple, in a sense, by the one whose name dwells there. This stranger's prayer will be a pious or righteous prayer, offered with an appropriate intention and informed by an awareness of the character of the one to whom it is offered.

The text itself may not offer sufficient resources to enable a decision between these two possibilities. The situation is somewhat like that in the Farewell Discourses in the Fourth Gospel, when Jesus promises, "I will do whatever you ask in my name, so that the Father may be glorified in the Son. If in my name you ask me for anything, I will do it" (John 14:13–14). In the case of John, however, the context makes it clearer that those who are addressed are "believers," with all that this implies. To pray "in Jesus' name" is not just to invoke his blessing on one's desires, or to use his name as a password or entry code—though, sad to say, this passage is commonly read and exploited superficially in just that way. Instead, it is to ask that the reality of God in Christ shape one's prayers and one's praying.

On the assumption that our second construal of Solomon's petition, along lines similar to the passage in John, is at least defensible and potentially fruitful, Solomon's prayer gives rise to some interesting issues. One that may be especially germane to the season and to our own times can be stated this way: how do you know when someone is praying to God?

The simple fact that someone is praying at the temple is evidently not a sufficient sign that God is the object of their prayers. Nor is physical presence at the temple a necessary condition of authentic prayer, as later passages in the Solomonic prayer already make clear. So how do you know?

Pastoral Perspective

Humanity's part in this covenantal relationship is to be faithful, which means to trust that God is trustworthy. Even as one looks at the tragedies littered throughout our history, there are also those events pointing to the divine presence that has always been working its purposes out. It is incumbent upon all who would live faithfully to choose to see God's mysterious ways woven into the fabric of life. In a cartoon, Stu and Mr. Lenny are arguing whether the glass in front of them is half full or half empty. They go back and forth—"Half full." "Half empty." "Half full." "Half empty"—until a third character, Bobo, comes upon this scene and is asked to tell them which one is right. Bobo picks up the glass, drinks it, and says, "Delicious." Solomon has chosen to see all as under the guidance of a providential power that is steady, loving, and loyal. That is delicious, joyful.

To explicate more what this God is like, our lectionary passage takes up the issue of "foreigners." These people are not of the people of Israel, yet they have heard of the name of God, have experienced God's mighty hand, have known God's outstretched arm, and therefore have come to worship in the temple. This was a distinctive note in Solomon's admonition. In 400 BCE, there was conflict between foreigners who were part of the worshiping community and those who were opposed to their participation. The continuum from exclusive to inclusive is a lens to use for all faith traditions. Solomon's words indicate that the foreigner who is faithfully seeking to worship God is to be heard by God. Therefore, all shall know the God who makes promises and whose love is steadfast. Isaiah writes, "And the foreigners who join themselves to the Lord . . . to love the name of the Lord . . . and hold fast my covenant—these I will bring to my holy mountain, and make them joyful in my house of prayer . . . for my house shall be called a house of prayer for all peoples" (Isa. 56:6–7).

Who would be a foreigner? Who would not be welcome? Who is in and who is out? Radical hospitality for all peoples is an earmark of how God would want people of faith to act. In her touching story "The Welcome Table," Alice Walker tells of an elderly African American woman who gets dressed in her Sunday meeting clothes and walks down the road to a nearby church in the South, being drawn by the "glittering cross that crowns the steeple." She enters the church, only to be met with hostile looks, and then hears words of rejection. The church is to be the welcome table where all are welcome, but this

Exegetical Perspective

reaches out beyond the boundaries of any single nation or culture, bursting the parameters of all human constructs and worldviews.

The Temple as a Portal to Intimacy. Solomon is dedicating a symbolic edifice intended to nurture the covenant. The edifice is a sacrament in stone and timber, tangibly connecting a vassal people to their covenantal lord, their suzerain. It concretely signifies the dominion and presence of a God who has singled out a peculiar people for favor and relationship.

The scandalous divine favoring of Israel is clear from the unique association of God's name with the temple. All peoples on earth can know that this house in Jerusalem built by Solomon is the unique, personal possession of God, "called by thy name" (v. 43 RSV; cf. vv. 17–20, 29; Deut. 12:5). God personally makes the Jerusalem temple what it is, a matchless place for knowing God.

With God's name present at the temple, the intimacy intended by the covenant is finally possible. As Solomon declares, the God of the temple is a deity reaching out toward Israel in loving loyalty (cf. Deut. 7:9). No God anywhere is as unswerving and relentless in this outreach as the Lord (1 Kgs. 8:23). The Lord's incomparable, enveloping love enraptures the beloved, drawing Israel ever more fully into the life of God. The people's response is wholehearted devotion (v. 23; cf. Deut. 6:5; Matt. 22:37). It is a costly but joyful response, in which God's servants learn to give of themselves ever more deeply to their suzerain and to their covassals (cf. Hos. 2:19).

God's people should know that their infatuation with God will draw notice. Their unique love relationship will mediate knowledge of the Divine to the world and draw outsiders into the community of faith (see v. 60; see Exod. 19:6). Seeing the ecstatic intimacy shared between God and God's people, what outsider would not want in?

God's Transcendence of the Temple. In the thinking of the Sinai covenant, access to God at the temple is always a privilege, never a "given." The divine presence is completely free and mysterious (see Exod. 33:15; Ps. 80:3, 7, 19), independent of all human conceit and manipulation. Thus carrying poles, symbolizing God's unfettered mobility, stand ready in the temple to speed the ark on its way (1 Kgs. 8:7–8; cf. Exod. 20:24). So too, when Solomon begins his prayer, he stands before an altar, not before God's self (v. 22). He addresses himself

Homiletical Perspective

their own souls. Nation-states, like untransformed persons, exist for their own ends. And when that self-serving bias comes armed with a confidence that the divine shares it, violence often ensues. The architects of the medieval Crusades, the Puritans who slaughtered Native Americans, and the Muslim attackers of September 11, 2001, share this theology. These are the very acts of "faith" that prompt the atheist manifestos of the early twenty-first century to make George Bailey's claim in *It's a Wonderful Life* about religion itself: "Better for humanity if it had never been born." Nationalism bolstered by a sense of divine support almost always leads to disaster.

Amid this pervasive theology of special claims and national prerogatives, Hebrew Scriptures occasionally imagine a wider scope for God's care. This internationalism shows up at the very inception of Israel's story, when God's call and promise to Abraham and Sarah includes the words "in you all the families of the earth will be blessed" (Gen. 12:3). It recurs powerfully in Mosaic injunctions for God's people to show hospitality to strangers because they themselves were strangers in Egypt (Exod. 22:21; Lev. 19:33–34; Deut. 10:19). It rings out in the prophetic visions of the nations streaming to God's holy mountain.

First Kings 8 provides one of those windows to the wide scope of God's care, and the preacher should consider throwing this window wide open. In that chapter, King Solomon stands reverently before the altar of YHWH in the brand-new temple and speaks out a prayer of dedication. The king clarifies in his prayer that neither that august building nor the city of Jerusalem nor the territory of Judah nor even the nation Israel corners the market on God's attention. This is a God not even the heavens can contain (v. 27), and Solomon expects God to answer the prayers of non-Israelites: "When a foreigner comes and prays toward this house, then hear in heaven your dwelling place, and do according to all that the foreigner calls to you" (vv. 42–43). The point is reach. God should answer the prayers so that word will get around and "all the peoples of the earth may know your name and fear you" (v. 43). Solomon believes in this moment that God will extend to all nations the kindness and attentiveness that he himself experiences from God. His is an unbounded theological hope.

Guarding the Light. Solomon's prayerful moment is a glorious epiphany, but does it inspire hope? Can an internationalist theology keep us from pasting the divine endorsement on our self-interested causes?

1 Kings 8:22-23, 41-43

Theological Perspective

Do Muslims and Christians pray to the same God? For that matter, do Christians pray to the same God? And what about those outside the Abrahamic religious traditions: is it safe to conclude that they don't pray to God at all?

The Catholic theologian Karl Rahner, whose thinking influenced much of the work of the Second Vatican Council, affirmed that God may be known and worshiped "implicitly" through the means provided by other religious traditions (even if those traditions make no use of the concept of God), as well as by avowedly nonreligious people. He suggested that some religious traditions and settings—and some nonreligious ways of life and thought—may offer better resources than others for this purpose, but that often this may have less to do with the amount of similarity they bear to Christianity in creed or practice than with the degree to which they foster or inhibit the transformative work of the Holy Spirit in human lives. Rahner was not asserting that God may be known apart from Christ and the Spirit. His view was that Christ and the Spirit can be present efficaciously in people's lives even when they are not recognized as such. What is going on in the heart is known only to God, though the "fruits of the Spirit" in the lives of those outside the Christian community offer at least provisional evidence of an affirmative response to the offer of grace.[2]

The idea that the stranger, the foreigner, may be called into relationship with God, and may in consequence offer a compelling witness to the reality and character of God, is perhaps no less radical now than it was in the time of the exile.

CHARLES M. WOOD

Pastoral Perspective

is a "whites only" church and she is thrown out of the church. All the while she is singing a spiritual in her head, "Shout my troubles over / Walk and talk with Jesus." She continues to walk down that road as she has heard Jesus' invitation to "Follow me." Peter Hawkins writes, "Her walk with God is her most profound act of resistance."[1]

Solomon's words would bless our resistance against any who would not welcome those who are drawn to walk and pray to this God of Israel. As congregations seek to be accessible to all, it is important that a congregation be reminded of those people who find it difficult to participate in a congregation. That might include those excluded by a language barrier, a physical challenge, hearing or visual impairment, persons with same-sex orientation, living with a brain disorder, persons with AIDS, or persons with any other situation that might cause one to be separated from the faith community. While there might be no perfect solution for every situation, it is imperative that congregations take to heart the words of Solomon about the God who is to hear the prayers of the foreigner in the house of prayer. Who is the foreigner for you and your congregation?

Recall the powerful story of Jesus turning over the money changers' tables in the temple. It was the "foreigners" who had come to worship and who needed to exchange their money. Jesus' assertive action challenges this practice. All people are to come to worship without such restrictions. Paul writes, "Welcome one another, therefore, just as Christ has welcomed you" (Rom. 15:7).

ALAN JOHNSON

---

2. See Karl Rahner, "The Teaching of Vatican II on the Church and the Future Reality of Christian Life," in *The Christian of the Future*, trans. W. J. O'Hara (New York: Herder & Herder, 1967), 77–101.

1. Peter Hawkins and Paula Carlson, *Listening for God* (Minneapolis: Augsburg Fortress, 1994), 109.

Exegetical Perspective

toward heaven, since it is from the beyond that God receives prayers (cf. vv. 30, 32, 34, 36, 39, 43, etc.).

God's transcendence of the temple renders all ethnocentric and chauvinistic attitudes on Israel's part inconceivable. Since even the cosmos is too confining for God's comfort (v. 27), how can any single people ever claim God as their special neighbor? An exclusive, gated community simply cannot house the Lord. Recognizing this, Solomon petitions God's responsiveness to foreigners' prayers (vv. 41–43). God is sovereign even over outsiders, Solomon recognizes, and they may come to see it if they observe God's wonder-working power and their prayers answered at the temple.

The healing and subsequent conversion of Naaman, a Syrian general, surely exemplifies the divine transcendence of all ethnic and geographic barriers (2 Kgs. 5). There is no denying that many Scriptures affirm this transcendence (Jer. 16:19–21; Zeph. 3:9–10; Mal. 1:11). At the same time, we must not overlook that even in God's outreach to this proud foreigner, the unique intimacy of God with Israel plays its part. We must pause at Naaman's peculiar transporting of Israelite soil back to Syria for use in worshiping the Lord (2 Kgs. 5:17). The act signifies God's scandalous use of God's particular, elected people, Israel, to reach out to all earth's nations.

In his odd little deed of carrying back soil, Naaman shows that the God to whom he has converted is no universal spirit, present everywhere under many guises. Perhaps better than anyone else, Jacques Ellul has realized the profound character of what Naaman actually does here, however primitive and off-putting it may initially appear to the modern reader. "It is to serve this true God that he acts in a way that seems ridiculous to us," Ellul writes. "It is in order to love exclusively, to make a rigorous demarcation, to affirm his break publicly, that, adopting the manners and ideas and customs of his day, he uses them to show that his [new] God is not the same as that of others."[1]

Naaman's new God is far from parochial, but nevertheless remains tightly bound up in earthly particularities, such as community, history, and geography. However much God proves elusive and transcendent, the Lord remains the God of Solomon's prayer in 1 Kings 8. The Lord remains the God of Solomon's people, the God of Solomon's land, and the God of Solomon's temple.

STEPHEN L. COOK

Homiletical Perspective

The preacher would do well to raise this question in such a time as this. Sadly, Solomon's prayer gives little hope that it can. One would think otherwise. When we invest the people who are not like us with the value of God's loving attention, it would seem that we are destined to value them ourselves; but immediately after speaking the enlightened hope that God will hear and answer the heartfelt prayers of any people from anywhere—just after an internationalist moment—Solomon turns his prayerful attention to Israel's military interests: "If your people go out to battle against their enemy . . . and they pray to the LORD, . . . then hear in heaven their prayer and their plea, and maintain their cause" (vv. 44–45). In other words, "Hear the foreigners' prayers, O God, and then help us to kill them." Maybe the praying ones are noncombatants?

We and our congregations cringe, not only at Solomon's contradiction but at our own. We have seen the clarity of justice and the fog of hatred stand side by side, in slave owners who testify "that all men are created equal"; in Christians who would no sooner turn the other cheek than they would soil their Bibles; in preachers of tolerance who refuse to tolerate the intolerant. We cringe because we not only know the people who isolate our epiphanies from other parts of our lives. We are those people.

One lesson we can learn from Solomon's chilling juxtaposition of internationalist hope and nationalist warfare is that even our dearest and clearest epiphanies are fleeting. We give thanks for light where it can be found, but we had better act on that light before it goes away. In C. S. Lewis's Narnia chronicle *The Silver Chair*, Prince Rilian lives twenty-three hours of each day in a spell-induced fog, but there is one waking hour when he sees clearly his predicament and understands its solution. The witch who cast the spell keeps him tied to the silver chair during such moments of clarity, so that he may not act. Our congregations face similar paralyses and so squander light. They will rightly aspire to large gestures and significant acts, but in a war-torn world marred by violent nationalism and tribalism, it seems a very good start for us to remember with them Solomon's insight that God answers the prayers of all peoples . . . and then immediately to act that epiphany out into worship and life.

ALLEN HILTON

---

1. Jacques Ellul, *The Politics of God and the Politics of Man* (Grand Rapids: Eerdmans, 1972), 36.

Psalm 96:1-9

¹O sing to the Lᴏʀᴅ a new song;
  sing to the Lᴏʀᴅ, all the earth.
²Sing to the Lᴏʀᴅ, bless his name;
  tell of his salvation from day to day.
³Declare his glory among the nations,
  his marvelous works among all the peoples.
⁴For great is the Lᴏʀᴅ, and greatly to be praised;
  he is to be revered above all gods.
⁵For all the gods of the peoples are idols,
  but the Lᴏʀᴅ made the heavens.
⁶Honor and majesty are before him;
  strength and beauty are in his sanctuary.

⁷Ascribe to the Lᴏʀᴅ, O families of the peoples,
  ascribe to the Lᴏʀᴅ glory and strength.
⁸Ascribe to the Lᴏʀᴅ the glory due his name;
  bring an offering, and come into his courts.
⁹Worship the Lᴏʀᴅ in holy splendor;
  tremble before him, all the earth.

Theological Perspective

Introduction. Psalm 96 offers an almost inexhaustible fund of theological topics for the preacher's sermonic work. Its very basic focus on worshiping the one true God provides the *basso continuo* for any other themes on which the preacher might wish to linger. It is a psalm that can orient the preacher and listeners to basic perspectives on the nature, acts, and worship of God.

First, it speaks *theologically* in describing the reasons for worshiping God. Second, it speaks *universally* in contextualizing God among the gods of other nations and peoples. Finally, it speaks *anthropologically.* It describes humanity as called to worship and notes the worship responses to which all people are invited.

This psalm, part of a collection of enthronement psalms, contains praise, reflection, and worshipful response. In a significantly secularized global context, this psalm brings to the fore such questions as, What is the nature of the God we worship? Which gods do we worship (if we can face that question honestly)? Does the presence of a transcendent God have any meaning for us? How might we respond to the call to "tremble" before God, to acknowledge that God is holy?

Singing, Telling, Declaring! (vv. 1–3). Here we have, in these first three verses, the *theological* reflections

Pastoral Perspective

In Islam the term *adhan* means "announcement." It is the call to the divine service on Friday and the five daily prayers (*salats*). According to Muslim tradition, Muhammad deliberated with his companions on the most effective way to call the faithful to prayer. Informed in a dream, one of the Prophet's friends envisioned a man delivering such an announcement from the roof of a mosque. The Prophet consented and appointed Bilal to perform such a service. To this day, in predominantly Muslim cities and towns, the seven formulas of the *adhan* are called out from mosques at the time of the *salat.*[1]

Several years ago, a young Christian couple from New England lived in Cairo. From their home and offices they heard the *adhan* calling their neighbors to prayer. Five times a day, the loudly amplified announcements resonated throughout the city. The couple's first impression of the *adhan* remains with them; in their words, it was a sound of "great persuasion and persistence," as if something important was about to happen.

The author of Psalm 96 delivers an announcement worthy of a most extensive broadcast. With voice raised in praise, the psalmist's message is clear:

1. H. A. R. Gibb and J. H. Kramers, eds., *Shorter Encyclopedia of Islam* (Leiden, Netherlands: E. J. Brill, 1974), 16.

Exegetical Perspective

Psalm 96 is a kingship hymn that calls on all people to celebrate God's power, glory, and faithfulness (vv. 1–6), declares the Lord's kingship (v. 10), and proclaims God's eschatological judgment (vv. 11–13). The same psalm almost in its entirety appears in a catena of psalms in 1 Chronicles 16:23–33 between quotations of Psalm 105:1–15 (= 1 Chr. 16:8–22) and Psalm 106:1, 47–48 (= 1 Chr. 16:34–36). The psalm has no heading in Hebrew, but the Septuagint introduces it with the heading "When the temple (house) was built after the exile: A psalm to David."

Setting this psalm in the worship of ancient Judah is arguably the most difficult problem for its interpretation. Sigmund Mowinckel proposed that a set of enthronement psalms belonged to a new year's ritual for the enthronement of the Lord as king in ancient Jerusalem. He based this theory on the decipherment of the new year's liturgy from ancient Babylon in which Marduk became the god-king. In reference to Psalm 96, Hermann Gunkel in his 1929 commentary made only perfunctory reference to Mowinckel and the enthronement psalms.[1] Four

<hr>

1. Sigmund Mowinckel, *Psalmenstudien II: Das Thronbesteigungsfest Jahwäs und die Ursprung der Eschatologie* (Amsterdam: Schippers, 1961). This volume was first published in Kristiania (Oslo) in 1922. Hermann Gunkel, *Die Psalmen* (Göttingen: Vandenhoeck & Ruprecht, 1929), 140. Psalm 10:16, despite the fact that it contained the phrase "The Lord is king forever and ever" (*YHWH malakh 'olam wa'ed*) could not be counted because it was part of an acrostic lament.

Homiletical Perspective

Psalm 96 offers a feast of possibilities for the preacher. For some odd reason, the Psalter lection of the day covers only the first nine verses of this short psalm. The first decision of the preacher is whether to attend to the psalm in its entirety or simply to this truncated version. I will deal with all of Psalm 96 as a rich preaching field.

In response to ancient questions about the sovereignty of Israel's God, the psalmist provides this singing lesson: "Say among the nations, 'The Lord is king!'" (vv. 10). Opening with the joyful theme of celebration at the enthronement of God, the psalmist calls not just the people of God, but "all the earth" to sing.

Centuries later, John of Patmos would describe heaven as awash in song as well, "Then I heard every creature in heaven and on earth and under the earth and in the sea, and all that is in them, singing, 'To the one seated on the throne and to the Lamb be blessing and honor and glory and might forever and ever!' And the four living creatures said, 'Amen!' And the elders fell down and worshiped" (Rev. 5:13–14). To recognize God's glory makes the believer want—and need—to sing. The Westminster Shorter Catechism begins with this theological assumption (author's paraphrase): "What is the chief end of human life?" "To glorify God and enjoy God forever."

Psalm 96:1-9

Theological Perspective

on and rationale for the call to worship the one true God. These verses have a venerable biblical lineage. With the festival of the ark's entrance into Jerusalem at David's command, this psalm was quoted as part of that joyous occasion (see 1 Chr. 16:22–33). Whether read on its own or appreciated for its part in one of Israel's most splendid events, the power and majesty of God are central. Worshipers are called to do three things in verses 1–3: to sing in the process of blessing God's name, to speak out of God's salvation to them, and to reflect on God's glory through God's " marvelous works."

There Is No Other! (vv. 4–6). These verses point to the *universality* of the God we worship. By doing so, they attend to the issue of what constitutes true worship and what makes up its antithesis—idolatry. The fact that "god" and "idols" are mentioned indicates the psalmist's awareness of the competing claims among which humanity must choose in deciding who their God is. It further demonstrates a keen awareness of the competing "gods" within and outside Israel's boundaries at the time. Certainly that situation has not changed for us today. Many "gods," some known and others more subtle, continue to compete for attention with the God of Jesus Christ.

Additionally, anyone preaching verses such as these is faced with the radical impact of today's global and high-speed communication networks as these affect people's awareness of differing interpretations of God.

In speaking of God's attributes and deeds, the preacher may choose to address the role of God's names. Naming God is central liturgically and doctrinally to all the world's religions. In Judaism there are traditions emphasizing a devotional focus on God's name. In Islam there is a meditative focus on what are called the ninety-nine beautiful names of God. For Christians there are many ways of naming the God of Jesus Christ, all of which strive to be faithful to Jesus' question, "Who do you say that I am?"

Verse 6 names four attributes of God: honor, majesty, strength, and beauty. These characterize the one true God who actually and dynamically lives, as compared to the dead idols with which God is contrasted previously. Any of these terms alone could serve as a preaching focus, or they could be preached as an overview of what constitutes God's identity and agency. While the first three are more familiar in the repeated lists of God's attributes biblically, that of beauty is a startling reality. What

Pastoral Perspective

God reigns supremely over all of creation. Declare the greatness of God to the ends of the earth!

With God eternally enthroned above the heavens and the earth, the psalmist offers a "new song" of adoration. The song, understood to be this psalm, bears the spirit of evangelism. The psalmist urges the congregation of Israel to raise its voices in praise. As heirs to God's saving acts in Israel's past, as witnesses to God's "strength" and "beauty" in the present, and as subjects of a king who holds eschatological justice in his hand (v. 13), Israel has reason (and the responsibility) to sing, to declare God's sovereignty to all the nations. Indeed, a universal recognition of God's reign depends on it.

As scholar James Mays notes, the Hebrew root of the verb "tell" (v. 2, *bissar*) came into Greek as the word often translated "good news" or "gospel."[2] In this light the psalmist's song calls to mind the gospel refrain to "go and tell," to be messengers of God's healing and salvific work in and through the person of Jesus Christ. Likewise, the psalmist's song anticipates an old spiritual our congregations sing in this season of Epiphany: "Go, tell it on the mountain, over the hills and everywhere." The pulse of that spiritual echoes the psalmist's invitation to share the good news of God's kingdom far and wide.

Psalm 96 also raises questions for careful consideration in our congregations. Do we "tell of his salvation from day to day"? If so, how do we go and tell this good news? Do we "ascribe to the LORD the glory due his name"? If so, how far do our songs carry beyond the walls of the church? How do we express reverence for a world "charged with the grandeur of God" (Gerard Manley Hopkins)? And, in the end, to whom is our highest allegiance given?

Within the church universal, the "new song" of appreciation and witness is sung to many tunes. How vast are our responses to the "holy splendor" of God's "marvelous works" in the world and in our lives! We testify. We speak bold declarations of holy love in the face of human violence. We sing hymns of praise in times of trial. We observe quiet acts of compassion. We meet a street-corner preacher who urges us to return to God. We behold the Christ, who announces that "the kingdom of God has come near" (Mark 1:15). In the season of Epiphany, we glimpse the new things God has done—and continues to do—in Jesus Christ.

2. James L. Mays, *Psalms*, Interpretation Series (Louisville, KY: John Knox Press, 1994), 308.

Exegetical Perspective

years later Gunkel and Joachim Begrich adopted Mowinckel's views with modifications, distinguishing between enthronement psalms (Pss. 93, 97, 99) that begin with the pronouncement *YHWH malakh* and those "comparable" psalms (Pss. 47, 96) where the declaration occurs elsewhere (47:9, 96:10). They even found echoes of the enthronement formula in Revelation 11:17, 19:6.[2] Contemporary scholars, however, have come to doubt the existence of an annual enthronement festival entirely, while sometimes continuing to use the expression "enthronement psalm," or something like it, to designate those hymns where the phrase *YHWH malakh* occurs (Pss. 47, 93, 96–99). Kraus's observation that the meaning of the phrase in question derives from its reversed word order in Hebrew (subject-verb instead of verb-subject) and means "the Lord is king," rather than "the Lord has become king," is correct. This shows us that the phrase points to God's kingly position, not a coronation ceremony.[3]

The call to sing a "new song" in verse 1 also occurs in Psalms 33:3; 98:1; 149:1 and Isaiah 42:10. Within the context of Second Isaiah (42:10), the "new song" refers to the dramatic intervention of God to save Israel. It may also be the case that the phrase indicates that the poet literally composed a "new song" for a liturgical celebration. A liturgical setting for the psalm finds further support in verse 2 by the call to bless God's name and announce God's salvation "from day to day," a clear reference to the ongoing temple services and, perhaps, an argument against the idea that the new song was for a specific festival rather than daily worship.

God's "name" in verse 2 refers to God's public reputation, most especially God's reputation for salvation (v. 2) and wonders (v. 3). These serve both as warnings to the nations and inducements to those same nations to join Israel in calling upon the Lord for salvation. Indeed, it is the Lord, not the gods of the nations, who is great and deserves praise (v. 4a). The Lord is "frightful/awesome" (*nora'*) in comparison with all the other gods (v. 4b). The reason for this superiority is that the nations' gods are worthless while the Lord created the vast heavens (v. 5).

In verse 5, the NRSV's translation "the gods of the peoples" as "idols" is incorrect. Here, as in so many other places (e.g., Lev. 19:4; 26:1 and esp. Isa. 2:8, 18,

Homiletical Perspective

The preacher may well note that the choristers envisioned in Psalm 96 are not just humans, but "the sea," "the field," and "all the trees" (vv. 11–12). "All the earth" sings God's praise. Clinton McCann provides this key preaching perspective when he comments on the diversity of the psalmist's choir, "The ecumenical and interfaith implications are profound; we are somehow partners with all the 'families of the peoples' (v. 7). The ecological implications are staggering; we humans are somehow partners with oceans and trees and soil and air in glorifying God. The destiny of humankind and the destiny of the earth are inseparable. We—people, plants, and even inanimate entities—are all in this together."[1] Read in this way, this psalm recalls a response that Jesus would make to religious leaders when asked to keep his followers quiet, "I tell you, if these were silent, the stones would shout out" (Luke 19:40). For the psalmist and Jesus, even stones sing the glorious praise of God.

As people live more distant and separate from the land that grows their food, stores their oil, and contains their water, what would it be like to preach a "new song" that celebrates the sovereign reign of God and the global interdependence of "all the earth"? What would it mean for the preacher to call the people not to sing the same old song of consumptive excess, ecological neglect, and environmental arrogance, but a "new song" that recognizes our responsibility to live in harmony with our partners in praise? What would it be like to both learn that song and live it?

Psalm 96 also gives the preacher a poignant opportunity to contrast the audacious claims of God's sovereignty ("For great is the Lord, and greatly to be praised; God is to be revered above all gods," v. 4) with the meager theological claims of postmodernity. Psalm 96 does not sit easily with a postmodern worldview that eschews authority, particularly any claims to ultimate authority. The authority of the God that we meet in Psalm 96 is not in doubt. God reigns now, even if we catch only glimpses of God's reign amid our feeble attempts to subvert that reign. To sing Psalm 96 is also a great occasion to pray the prayer that Jesus taught his disciples, to pray for the day when God's reign in heaven and on earth would be known with confident certainty, to pray, "Thy kingdom come; thy will be done." In a world that looks to political leaders or the marketplace or celebrities or sports stars for

2. Hermann Gunkel and Joachim Begrich, *Introduction to Psalms*, ed. J. D. Nogalski (Macon, GA: Mercer University Press, 1998), 66–81.

3. Hans-Joachim Kraus, *Psalms 1–59: A Commentary*, trans. H. C. Oswald (Minneapolis: Augsburg Publishing House, 1988), 86–89, and *Psalms 60–150: A Commentary*, trans. H. C. Oswald (Minneapolis: Augsburg Publishing House, 1993), 251–52.

1. J. Clinton McCann Jr., "Psalms," in *The New Interpreter's Bible*, vol. 4 (Nashville: Abingdon Press, 2001), 1066.

Psalm 96:1-9

Theological Perspective

does it mean to say that the God we worship is possessed of *beauty*?

Worship in the Presence (vv. 7–9). This section of the pericope focuses on the *anthropological* responses elicited by the psalm's call to worship. This call contains a number of invitations to respond in specific ways. First, the call is extended to "families of the peoples," meaning all are welcome. It is a call to focus on the content, power, and majesty of "the glory due his name." This worship is also a call to place—"come into his courts"—and to resources, which means "bring an offering." The impact of this worship is so profound that the psalmist notes that the reaction of the worshipers will be to "tremble before him." In fact, the worship directly affects "all the earth."

Conclusion. This magnificent psalm looks back to Israel's long historical lineage and forward to its many appearances in the unfolding of Christianity as well. It is used throughout the church year in a number of ways, including not only in the season of Epiphany but as the psalm appointed for Christmas Day, the feast of the incarnation.

In proclaiming Jesus as the Son of God, within the context of this psalm in any season, preachers may indeed "tell of God's salvation . . . declare God's glory . . . [and] God's marvelous works." This preserves proclamation of the gospel from any risk of describing Jesus as only a "good person" or a "teacher of great moral precepts," common messages today in many non-Christian venues. What is at stake is the divinity of Jesus, and the psalm's use in preaching can effectively assist the proclaimer in charting a history for listeners that points to this conclusion.

There is both tension and the joy of worship in this psalm, and thus it invites us to do two things. First, all are welcome to the worship of the God of our Lord Jesus Christ. Second, it also asks the listeners to consider how inclusive their view of God is, something Jesus prodded others to do on many occasions. In effect, the psalm asks what it means to sing to the Lord "a new song." Preachers may powerfully proclaim that "new song" in speaking of the salvation offered to all in the epiphany of Jesus, Son of God, and Savior of all!

SUSAN K. HEDAHL

Pastoral Perspective

A deacon of a local church regularly serves dinner at a soup kitchen. His commitment to feeding his hungry neighbors is inspired by the life and teachings of Christ. If you ask him why he returns weekly to serve the poorest of the city's poor, he will tell you about a "regular" at the soup kitchen. She is a recovering addict, burdened with mental illness. She knows Scripture; she can quote long passages of the Gospels; and like the psalmist she shares the conviction that God's greatness is worth sharing: *Sing to the Lord. Tell of his salvation. Declare his glory.*

Without prompting, she will tell those gathered in the dining hall about God's saving power. She will tell them with great passion about the surpassing love of Jesus. Her streetwise and faithful witness reaches kitchen staff and clients alike. Her "new song" resonates with the deacon long after the tables are cleared and the floor is swept. Broom in hand, he reflects on another evening at the soup kitchen. He says, "When she speaks of God, my faith grows. I feel a great Amen swell in me. I don't normally feel that way." Such is the power of her song sung with the compelling urgency of Psalm 96.

The following afternoon at church, a new church member sits in your office. Having returned to the church after decades away, she wants to know why her friends, husband, and children do not see what she sees. She wants to know how anyone could deny the "strength" and "beauty" of God. She wants to know how something so vitally important to her could be dismissed so easily. You could ask her what veiled and unveiled such a revelation in her own life, but instead you open today's psalm. You respond to her questions with an ancient invitation: *Sing to the Lord. Tell of his salvation. Declare his glory.* Exactly how she will lift her voice is yet unknown, but she knows now—as the psalmist knew then—that it is time to let her life sing.

ANDREW NAGY-BENSON

Exegetical Perspective

20; 19:1–3; 31:7; Hab. 2:18), the word *'ellil* refers to the nullity, the worthlessness, of these supposed divinities, not their physical representations.

In verse 6, the Lord appears in power and splendor with hosts in splendid dress, suggesting the splendor of a royal court and its retainers, such as we find in Psalm 21:5. This allusion reminds us of other "theophanic" texts such as Psalms 50:2 and 89:14, where the poets imagine the glorious retinue of the Lord. The royal associations of this imagery fit well with the celebration of God's kingship in Psalm 96:10.

The sequence in verses 7–8a matches the wording of Psalm 29:1–2a, with the interesting difference that Psalm 96:7 reads "families of [the] peoples" where Psalm 29:1 reads "sons of [the] gods" (my trans.). It is difficult to say which way the dependence lies or whether both texts derive from a common tradition. The working and reworking of hymnic phrases in the Psalter could certainly create such parallels without literary dependence. In keeping with the announced purpose of recounting God's honor to the nations in an effort to maintain/increase the divine reputation (name), it is no surprise that Psalm 96:7 would use the expression "families of [the] peoples," calling upon all nations to bring their honors to the Lord.

The reference to doing obeisance to the Lord in "holy adornment" (v. 9, my trans.) is the identical expression we find in Psalm 29:2; but in 96:9 the reference is to the peoples, not the gods, who, as we have learned in verse 5, are "nullities." The eschatological portion of the psalm, verses 10–13, finds anticipation in the command that all the peoples, not just Israel, should "do obeisance" and "tremble" before the Lord. The kingship of the Lord announced in verse10 will be an everlasting kingship over the whole earth, not an annual kingship in Jerusalem.

FRED L. HORTON

Homiletical Perspective

inspiration and leadership, Psalm 96 invites people to look to God for leadership and inspiration that will never fail them.

If read during the season of Epiphany, this psalm may inspire the preacher to explore the evangelical claims of this text. Good news of God's loving reign is revealed in Psalm 96 and the psalmist implores the reader to sing this good news. This psalm could well be coupled with a later chorus in Revelation that declares, "The kingdom of the world has become the kingdom of our Lord and of his Christ, and he will reign for ever and ever" (Rev. 11:15 NIV). What would it mean to sing this song in church contexts that cordon off "outsiders" and define who belongs in the company of God in narrow ways? This psalm invites the preacher to delve deeply into the profound questions that arise when we are asked to sing and live out this "new song."

This psalm argues not only for the sovereign rule of God, but for the "just" rule of God. In the closing verses of this psalm, we learn to sing a "new song" that refuses to settle for a world of inequities and injustice in which wars persist, cancer resists a cure, tyrants deprive their people of the most basic needs, and evil dances unrestrained. According to the psalmist, writes James Luther Mays, "History and society are not left to the capriciousness of fickle gods or the arbitrary decisions of human rulers. Instead, the Lord will rule with righteousness and faithfulness. There is a power that sets things right, a might that can be trusted."[2] The preacher cannot sing this "new song" or teach it to her congregation without recognizing that to do so is to oblige a people to act in ways that demonstrate God's just ways through "all the earth."

For the preacher of Psalm 96, the field is ripe with possibilities to learn and then to teach others to "sing to the LORD a new song" (v. 1).

GARY W. CHARLES

---

2. James Luther Mays, *Psalms*, Interpretation Series (Louisville, KY: Westminster John Knox Press, 1994), 308.

Galatians 1:1‑12

¹Paul an apostle—sent neither by human commission nor from human authorities, but through Jesus Christ and God the Father, who raised him from the dead—²and all the members of God's family who are with me,

To the churches of Galatia:

³Grace to you and peace from God our Father and the Lord Jesus Christ, ⁴who gave himself for our sins to set us free from the present evil age, according to the will of our God and Father, ⁵to whom be the glory forever and ever. Amen.

⁶I am astonished that you are so quickly deserting the one who called you in the grace of Christ and are turning to a different gospel—⁷not that there is another gospel, but there are some who are confusing you and want to pervert the gospel of Christ. ⁸But even if we or an angel from heaven should proclaim to you a gospel contrary to what we proclaimed to you, let that one be accursed! ⁹As we have said before, so now I repeat, if anyone proclaims to you a gospel contrary to what you received, let that one be accursed!

¹⁰Am I now seeking human approval, or God's approval? Or am I trying to please people? If I were still pleasing people, I would not be a servant of Christ.

¹¹For I want you to know, brothers and sisters, that the gospel that was proclaimed by me is not of human origin; ¹²for I did not receive it from a human source, nor was I taught it, but I received it through a revelation of Jesus Christ.

Theological Perspective

Grace and Paul's apostleship go hand in hand. This is the central message of the opening words of Paul's Epistle to the Galatians. The source of the message and the content of the message are completely intertwined. Justification by grace is no more of human origin than Paul's call. The good news of grace falls upon humanity from heaven like a light on the road to Damascus: foreign, unbidden, blinding, and causing a complete reversal of expectations.

Paul spends nearly a third of his Letter to the Galatians defending his authority, despite the risk that he appears to be boasting. In the opening verses Paul makes clear that he was "sent neither by human commission nor from human authorities, but through Jesus Christ and God the Father." In the main body of the letter, Paul's seeks to shore up his own authority against those who apparently are coming into the Galatian churches and questioning his authority to preach. Paul might easily have claimed that the legitimacy of an argument is independent of its origin—but he does not. Paul, like his accusers, argues that the message, the messenger, and the origin of the message are inextricably bound. Let us turn our attention to the way in which justification by grace and Paul's direct commission from Christ are connected.

Pastoral Perspective

In his seminal commentary on Romans, Karl Barth maintains that the purpose of biblical interpretation is to engage the received texts until the walls between the first century and our century disappear. Paul does not speak *only* to his contemporaries, in other words—no adequate doctrine of inspiration will allow such a chronologically compartmentalized notion. "What was of grave importance, is so still,"[1] Barth writes. That is to say the word once delivered is an eternal word, efficacious for all believers who in any time and place submit themselves in faith to the authority of Scripture.

That hermeneutical conviction—relevant again with the failure of reductionistic approaches to Holy Scripture—seems apt pastoral counsel for preachers endeavoring to engage the Epistle lection for the day. In Galatia there is a ferocious battle raging for the hearts and minds of believers. If Paul's doctrine of grace is not at war with the law per se, it is at the very least in a fierce firefight with legalism. The combatant's weapons are high-caliber credentials and representative authority. At stake is the lofty ground of apostolic credibility and along with it both the reliability of the gospel once delivered and

1. Karl Barth, *The Epistle to the Romans* (London: Oxford University Press, 1933), 1.

Exegetical Perspective

For twenty-first-century readers of a first-century letter, some reminders of ancient letter-writing protocols help us see key features in the opening of Galatians. Even more importantly, noting Paul's core argument in this letter helps us appreciate how carefully he has crafted its beginning and how passionately he writes.

In Galatians, Paul writes to Gentile congregations in central Asia Minor, churches he had established. (Scholars debate whether "Galatia" designates an ethnic territory in northern Asia Minor, inhabited by Celts, or the Roman province extending farther south, where Acts 13–14 says Paul evangelized.) Now other missionaries have come behind Paul, persuading these Gentile Christians that to be fully righteous, they must also follow elements of the Jewish law. In particular, male Christians must be circumcised, the sign of full admission into God's covenant with Israel. These rival missionaries evidently made a plausible case: having accepted the Jewish God through a Jewish messiah, Gentiles might be expected now to adopt Jewish practices. For Paul, however, requiring Gentiles to be law observant violated the gospel of Jesus Christ. Deeply engaged in cross-cultural ministry, Paul here works strenuously to separate pressures for religious and cultural conformity from the proclamation of God's liberating acts through Christ.

Homiletical Perspective

Imagine this: A small congregation, new in their Christian faith and enthusiastic in the way that longer-term believers are seldom enthusiastic, have discovered a set of strict requirements that some are insisting true believers must follow. It does not really matter what these new conditions are. In the case of the Christians in Galatia, the new Christians, previously pagans, have encountered the Jewish law that demands circumcision for all men seeking covenantal relationship with God. For most adult men in most settings, this would be a laughably unacceptable requirement.

But new believers can be a different breed altogether. Turning to their Jewish-Christian neighbors as guides, the little church in Galatia seems willing, even eager to take on the more strict conditions for holy relationship that have long guided God's people, the Jews. The apostle Paul, a Jew himself, had founded this community of believers by sharing with them the gospel of Jesus Christ that he had received in a revelation from God. No stranger to Jewish law, Paul's encounter with the risen Christ revealed One whose fulfillment of the law nullified what had been the requirements of the law for Israel. With all Christians who would come after them, the believers in Galatia had been freed from adherence to the law by the grace of Jesus Christ.

Galatians 1:1-12

Theological Perspective

Despite the common portrait of Paul as hard-nosed and doctrinaire, he is often very flexible in matters that are causing divisions in the churches. For example, when it comes to eating food sacrificed to idols, Paul says that it is not inherently sinful to do so, but we should be careful lest we cause a weaker believer to sin (1 Cor. 8:1–13). Paul is equally flexible about marriage. While it is better to remain unmarried, it is not an absolute rule (1 Cor. 7:25ff.). On such matters of *adiaphora* (things indifferent) Paul gives guidance but not mandates. This makes his absolute inflexibility in Galatians all the more striking.

The overarching motif of Paul's Letter to the Galatians is a defense of justification by grace against the "different gospel" that is confusing believers and perverting the gospel of Christ. On this matter, Paul uses the strongest possible language. Anyone who disagrees with Paul (human, angel, or even a hypothetical latter Paul) should be "accursed."

Later in the church's history, controversies arose over the human role in justification. Medieval theologians like Scotus and Occam talked about grace "cooperating" with human nature, a notion repudiated by Luther and Calvin. Further controversies arose between Calvinists, who claimed that even faith was a gift selectively bestowed by God, and Arminians, who held that all humans are offered the gift of salvation but must freely accept the offer of forgiveness.

Paul is not directly addressing these controversies. It is enough that he refutes any concept of human worthiness through acts of the law. *God* saves. *God* is the actor. This is kerygma: core preaching that cannot be compromised without losing the essence of the faith. Whatever form Christianity might take in our changing world—from Korea to Africa to emerging church movements in America—this part of the message cannot be compromised. While there are many other important theological truths, all other Christian doctrines appear as mere *adiaphora* to this, the kerygma of Christianity: we who were once enemies of God have been made right with God through an act of pure, unmerited grace on God's part. Paul is rebutting those Judaizers of the "circumcision faction" (Gal. 2:12) who are calling Gentile believers to become circumcised and follow Torah, thus questioning the sufficiency of Christ's death and resurrection (Gal. 2:21) for setting us "free from the present evil age" (v. 4) and saving us from our sins.

This message is so radical, so scandalous, that it could not have originated from Paul. It is not born

Pastoral Perspective

the efficacy of the gospel once received. This is our battle too.

Historically, the *what* of the so-called "Galatian problem" (quite unlike its where and when) is not so much in question. Jewish-Christian teachers from Jerusalem, the Judaizers, have boldly come to this Gentile church, determined both to rein in the self-contradictory teachings of Paul and, simultaneously, to fetter the Galatians' antinomian faith by means of the Mosaic traditions. Steeped in deep reverence for the salvation history of Israel and its given traditions—as well as for the Jewish underpinnings of the embryonic Christian gospel—the Judaizers are on a mission to circumscribe both Paul's theology and the Gentiles' discipleship with the jots and tittles of Jewish legal observance.

For these Judaizers, Paul's "gospel" is demonstrably erroneous (and therefore incomplete) by virtue of the fact that he, a Jew, has set aside the patterns of Jewish faithfulness that Jesus himself observed. The Galatians' faith, therefore, lacking as it is in traditional cultic requirements or expressions, is correspondingly deficient. And so the Judaizers' call for (at least) a minimal observance of the Mosaic law—circumcision, dietary observance, and rituals associated with Sabbath. Acceding to these "correctives" would, they seem to say, complete the Galatians' conversion.

Paul sees this "new" teaching of the "old-time religion" as no less than an insult to God (1:6), to Jesus (3:13), and to the Holy Spirit (3:3). To embrace the law of Moses after being embraced by the grace of God was a radical perversion of the one true gospel, the gospel Paul preached (1:9). Grace qualified, Paul contended, was grace nullified. The proof of "his" gospel's truth was the reality of Gentile faith itself, continually confirmed by the gifts of the Spirit. The law was not the problem; it was in fact still valuable. The *use* of the law against those who are already believers was the problem—as was the Galatians' willingness to abandon the Spirit in favor of "works."

Many interpreters map this "crisis of authority" ethnically—that is, the battle lines are drawn between Jew and Gentile. In this interpretation the Judaizers attack with the same "hermeneutic of power" that can be found in all forms of legalism (not least in the colonializing impulses of some recent missionary movements). Perhaps.

A deeper sounding of the tectonics, however, might locate a sharper fault: the fault where the *pneumatic* and *magisterial* (or *administrative*) plates converge. The work of the Holy Spirit shakes the

Exegetical Perspective

That work begins in the letter's first line. Whereas contemporary letters first greet the recipient (Dear Cindy) and end with the sender's expressed sincerity and name (Yours truly, Diane), in ancient letters, both names came in the opening formula: sender (sometimes with descriptive elaboration) to recipient (sometimes with descriptive elaboration), salutation. For example, a Greek letter begins, "Ammonius to Apollonius his brother, greetings."[1] A surviving Hebrew letter begins, "From Simeon b. Gamaliel and from Yohanan b. Zakkai to our brothers in the Upper and Lower Galilee and to Simonia and to Obed Bet Hillel: Shalom!"[2] Where Greek salutations commonly expressed "greetings" (*chairein*) and Hebrew letters "peace" (*shalōm*), Paul consistently extends "grace and peace" (*charis kai eirēnē*). In Paul's letters and other early Christian letters, thanksgiving for the recipients usually follows, expressed as a prayer.

Against this general template and Paul's practices in his other letters, Galatians 1:1–12 shows distinctive features. First, Paul's self-description as "an apostle" (also in 1 and 2 Cor. and Rom.) is particularly emphatic. Early Christians used the term "apostle" for one sent out as authorized delegate or representative of a group or person, whether Jesus' twelve closest disciples (Acts 1:26) or others (Acts 14:14; 1 Cor. 15:7, 9). Paul here insists that his apostolic authority derives not from a human group or source, but directly from Jesus and God (v. 1). That emphasis may explain Paul's naming no specific cosenders of this letter (no Timothy, Sosthenes, or Silvanus, as in other letters), though "all the brothers and sisters with me" join in this letter (v. 2a, my trans.). Unlike Paul's other salutations, he offers no descriptive, commendatory phrases for the Galatians, increasing the abrupt tone of the opening (v. 2b).

Yet in expressing "grace and peace" to these churches, Paul's abruptness gives way to a fuller-than-usual expression of Christ's self-giving according to God's will (vv. 3–5). Paul stresses parental language for "our" God, and emphasizes Christ's purpose to rescue "us" from sin and evil. While doxologies are sprinkled throughout Paul's letters (Rom. 11:36; Phil. 4:20), only in Galatians does one appear so early. With "to whom be the glory forever and ever. Amen" (v. 5), Paul turns a compressed doctrinal summary into the church's celebration, inviting worship and a concise reproclamation of the gospel before the argument proper begins.

1. Stanley Stowers, *Letter Writing in Greco-Roman Antiquity* (Philadelphia: Westminster Press, 1989), 98–99.
2. David Aune, *The New Testament in Its Literary Environment* (Philadelphia: Westminster Press, 1987), 176.

Homiletical Perspective

Paul was no resident pastor who would stick around to encourage the congregation. He was an evangelist, planting churches and moving on. During his absence from Galatia, new voices entered the community, preaching a gospel with a different slant and a very different set of priorities. These new preachers, Jewish Christians, insisted as part of their conversion practices that a believer needed first to become a Jew, and only then a Christian.

The young Christians of Galatia had not forgotten Paul. If he had been there, they would have known that he disapproved of this new obsession with rules and with laws, but they were doing only what so many believers have been drawn to do when trying to live a gospel faith. They were abandoning what they knew to be true, compromising their beliefs, in favor of a new set of standards that somehow seemed more compelling, and that were at any rate far easier to embrace and enact. A gospel about the redeeming love of God can be hard to accept, after all, just as good news about God's activity on behalf of the poor is hard to accept when we ourselves are relatively rich, and good news about a Jesus who repeatedly fed the poor and sat at the table with sinners can be hard to hear when our own cupboards are full and when we do not care much for inviting the unworthy into our dining rooms.

How much more satisfying to please others in place of God by our tangible obedience of a specific law. How much more satisfying to respond to the certain direction of those who seem convinced about their own moral integrity. The feedback is immediate! Paul is far away, and God's critique is seldom heard directly in our ears. Besides, who does not seek human approval? Who does not long to be included in an exclusive group? It seems only natural, this striving to gain favor.

Paul will have none of it, so he opens his letter to his Galatian friends by reminding them of the challenging and wonderful truth that our salvation, indeed the world's salvation, will not be accomplished by our own doing, by the forms of worship we employ or the words we use to describe God's transcendence.

God comes in Jesus Christ not because of circumcisions performed, not because of laws followed, not because of right action or holy living. God comes to the Galatians, and to all of those who follow, because God chooses to do so. God's grace is a gift offered in love and in mercy by God to all who receive it by faith in Jesus Christ.

Would we who seek to follow Christ in this the twenty-first century be willing to turn away from

Galatians 1:1-12

Theological Perspective

of natural theology or "of human origin" (v. 11). It shatters earthly wisdom, falling on human efforts at divine appeasement or self-justification like a bombshell. It breaks into their (and our) comfortable world of incremental approximation of the Divine and declares that the distance between humans and God is not merely quantitative but infinitely qualitative. No orthodoxy, no orthopraxy, no orthopathy will bridge the chasm between the holy and righteous Father of Jesus Christ and us creatures. There is no meeting God halfway or even preparing for such a message; it comes unbidden and unexpected, like a light on the road to Damascus, like a virgin birth, like a dead man rising. As Karl Barth observes, "The gospel is not a religious message to inform mankind of their divinity or to tell them how they may become divine. The gospel proclaims a God utterly distinct from men. Salvation comes to them from Him, because they are, as men, incapable of knowing Him, and because they have no right to claim anything from him."[1] This message, its content, and the messenger go hand in hand. Just like Paul's apostleship, grace is not from a "human source" but from Jesus Christ (v. 12). Like Paul, the message itself and the content of this message of forgiveness are sent from God (v. 1).

This message was so scandalously theocentric that many of Paul's listeners could not hear it; they wanted to justify themselves, just as many moderns do, refusing to accept forgiveness from God but turning rather to the supposed comfort of legalism. Grace saves, moderns might say, as long as one also adheres to the new Torah in its many dimensions: orthodoxy of belief on abortion, biblical inerrancy, or the timing of the rapture; right social witness; a discernible conversion experience, and so on. All such claims are an effort to domesticate the message of justification by giving us control over it, but "grace is the incomprehensible fact that God is well pleased with a man . . . Only when grace is recognized to be incomprehensible is it grace."[2]

So in these opening verses, everything points to God. Paul's authority comes not from himself but *from God*. The message he preaches is not his; it is *from God*. And sinners do not save themselves through adherence to the law; they are saved *by God*.

KYLE FEDLER

Pastoral Perspective

foundations of deeply held cultural assumptions, produces constant tremors, and thereby creates theological tensions and uncertainty. It is not only a "Galatian (or Corinthian!) problem" that enthusiastic new converts, unaware of and often oblivious to the traditions of the elders, report ecstatic experience as proof of God's doing a new thing.

Meanwhile, older generations of believers are wont to "test the spirits to see whether they are from God" (1 John 4:1). These maintain that the "new" faithfulness cannot be divorced from the old, fear the erosion or dissolution of the rock from whence their faith was hewn. One camp will point to what they consider the spiritual proof of their position over against the other—most often attendance and energy—while the other camp will talk of tradition and stability, the faithfulness of prior generations, order and the need for continuity. And so congregations go to war over styles of worship, types of music, the gender of clergy, and the like.

For his part, Paul tried to hold the middle. He eschewed tradition for tradition's sake but continued to honor and practice the particular forms of his heritage. At the same time he said that such forms were not binding for new converts. His via media left him vulnerable to both camps.

Even more troubling to him was that, in Galatia at least—and this *was* a Galatian problem—the magisterial Judaizers had convinced new believers that they must discount their experience and "back up" to become Jewish before they could really be Christian (Gal. 3:3). For Paul this was an outrage at two levels—both that the Jewish teachers would teach such a thing (and doubly so if this letter was written after the events of Acts 15), and that those who had believed *him* would now believe *this*.

Galatians reads like a dispatch from the fronts of the doctrinal wars, a field guide for contemporary strategy. Our congregations too are caught in the DMZ between TV screens and pulpits, ministry mailings and denominational newspapers. This teacher is eager to correct that one, each questioning the credentials and positions of the other. The faithful wonder, Whose word is the reliable word? What saves souls and pleases God? What ground is expendable? What ground must we hold?

Beneath these question is the question of truth: Who has the understanding and authority to correct whom, and by what source? If good theology is the only real answer to bad theology, where do we find it? Paul and Barth would point us back to the texts.

THOMAS R. STEAGALD

---

1. Karl Barth, *Epistle to the Romans* (New York: Oxford University Press, 1968), 28.
2. Ibid., 31.

Exegetical Perspective

But begin it does. Precisely at the point where Paul would customarily offer prayerful thanks for the recipients, he expresses shock and rebuke: not "I give thanks," but "I am astonished" (*thaumazō*, v. 6). Interestingly, all the verb forms expressing what is going wrong are in the present tense; he pictures the Galatians in the very act of "deserting" and "turning," and his rivals, "who are confusing you and want to pervert the gospel of Christ" (vv. 6–7). An audience stopped midturn might more easily turn back. With a dense concentration of the noun "gospel" (*euangelion)* and the verb "proclaim" (*euangelein*) (vv. 7–11), Paul insists on a singular and unitary gospel. "Another gospel" can only be a perverted gospel (v. 7).

In sharp contrast to his grace and peace blessing, Paul twice calls down a formal curse on anyone— including himself or a divine messenger—who would proclaim a contrary gospel (vv. 8–9). The term *anathema* is used for things set aside for God, whether consecrated offerings or, as here, things accursed. Paul's language is polarizing and extreme as he works to shift identifications and to insist that there are extreme risks to accepting the views of his rivals.

Verses 10–12, then, conclude the letter's opening, suggest themes of the entire letter, and make a transition to the autobiographical section that follows. As Paul disavows human authority for his apostleship (v. 1), so he refuses human approval or endorsement (v. 10), and rejects a human source for the gospel he proclaims (vv. 11–12). Rather, his gospel came, he insists, "through a revelation [*apokalypsis*] of Jesus Christ" (v. 12b). Paul's confidence in his experience of Christ is startling, yet consistent with his later exhortation to the Galatians to trust their own experience of Christ and the Spirit (Gal. 3:4). The ambiguity of the expression "*apokalypsis* of Jesus Christ" in both Greek and English elegantly conveys that Christ is both the revealer of the gospel and the content it reveals.

From one perspective, Paul's closing assertions seem paradoxical. If his lawfree gospel was not "people pleasing," does he imply that the rigorist insistence on circumcision was? Yet perhaps their conviction—"to have our God you must adopt our religiocultural practices"—can be understood as self-reinforcing and pleasing to a social group protecting its identity. Paul seeks to proclaim the work of God in Jesus Christ, including its ethical consequences (Gal. 5:13–6:10), but without making corollary demands for religious, cultural, or ethnic conformity. In our increasingly pluralistic and global society, perhaps Paul's vehemence on this score deserves a fresh hearing.

B. DIANE LIPSETT

Homiletical Perspective

some of the laws of faith that cause us such struggle in our day, if such laws were diverting us from truly living faithful lives? How would we even determine which laws were worthy of being overturned and which are necessary in order to live in covenantal relationship with one another and with God?

I sometimes wonder if my own denomination, the Presbyterian Church (U.S.A.), has been overtaken by imposters when I hear repeated arguments about ordination standards. I wonder what happened to Christ's commandment that we "love our neighbors as we love ourselves," or of our theological tradition's premise that "people of good conscience may differ." I worry that some among us are trying to confuse the faithful, introducing new versions of truth, versions that I find to be fundamentally misguided.

In light of Paul's own struggle to relinquish one law, finding it both unnecessary for the propagation of the faith and cruel to the humanity of the individual professing faith in Jesus Christ, I wonder what he might think of the church's ongoing and painful struggle over the ordination of gays and lesbians and of their role in the church, both in leadership positions and as members of the church of Jesus Christ. It might be interesting to wrestle with Paul's own beliefs about the law and his willingness, at least in this letter, to set aside strict adherence to the law for the sake of the gospel and for the salvation of Christ's new believers. That would mean putting Paul's broad Christian inclusiveness face to face with his previously stated opinions about homosexuality. Preachers today, given the incredible amount of scholarship done on homosexuality and on Paul, might be able to enjoy a good debate, surprising themselves, even surprising Paul about how God continues to do a new thing in the midst of a church in love with its laws and its order.

Whatever the particular issue facing the preacher in a denomination or a congregation, the question of salvation by grace over against salvation by the works of the law is at the heart of the gospel this text leads us to proclaim.

MARIA LASALA

Luke 7:1-10

¹After Jesus had finished all his sayings in the hearing of the people, he entered Capernaum. ²A centurion there had a slave whom he valued highly, and who was ill and close to death. ³When he heard about Jesus, he sent some Jewish elders to him, asking him to come and heal his slave. ⁴When they came to Jesus, they appealed to him earnestly, saying, "He is worthy of having you do this for him, ⁵for he loves our people, and it is he who built our synagogue for us." ⁶And Jesus went with them, but when he was not far from the house, the centurion sent friends to say to him, "Lord, do not trouble yourself, for I am not worthy to have you come under my roof; ⁷therefore I did not presume to come to you. But only speak the word, and let my servant be healed. ⁸For I also am a man set under authority, with soldiers under me; and I say to one, 'Go,' and he goes, and to another, 'Come,' and he comes, and to my slave, 'Do this,' and the slave does it." ⁹When Jesus heard this he was amazed at him, and turning to the crowd that followed him, he said, "I tell you, not even in Israel have I found such faith." ¹⁰When those who had been sent returned to the house, they found the slave in good health.

Theological Perspective

In some NT stories, Jesus is depicted as reaching out to or accepting the lowly and outcast, regardless of their apparent "worthiness" to others (e.g., Luke 7:36–50; 18:9–14). Other stories depict the important role of faith for healing and forgiveness (e.g., Luke 7:50; 8:48; 17:19; 18:42). The story of Jesus healing the centurion's slave (Luke 7:1–10) fits neither of these categories exactly. Its narrative differences can be theologically fruitful. The story raises questions about the worth of those Jesus serves, for the centurion is presented as worthy of Jesus' action, not because of his faith but because of his virtue (v. 5). Yet the faith of the centurion is notable and becomes the climax of the story, even though the content of that faith may sound unusual to modern ears.

Luke presents the centurion as a humble man. He is clearly a person of authority (v. 8), yet one who acts with benevolence and even love toward the people of Israel (v. 5). While the Jewish elders deem his actions "worthy" (v. 4) of Jesus' actions toward his slave, the centurion considers himself unworthy of Jesus' presence in his home (v. 6). For someone of such authority, his humility toward the Jewish healer and teacher is striking. As he says in verse 8, he is accustomed to ordering people about, yet he does not presume to do so with Jesus. The centurion acts

Pastoral Perspective

Jesus concludes his Sermon on the Plain, leaves for Capernaum, and hears the news of a Roman centurion's slave who is ill and close to death. It is a fascinating encounter, but how do we understand the text?

Do we emphasize the centurion's faith in Jesus? Given his Roman background and his task as a soldier of the empire, he seems an unlikely candidate for faith in Jesus. The centurion is almost everything the Christ is not; yet he has a beloved slave who is deathly ill, and Jesus presents a possibility for healing.

Desperation and faith often walk the same road. When we are at the end of our own resources, we may look for strength in surprising places. While the centurion stays at home, he sends intermediaries to ask Jesus' help.

Whom does the Gentile centurion send to ask for Jesus' help? Here is where our preconceptions of Roman soldiers as characters always pitted against the Jews as adversaries is challenged. Is Rome not the adversary? Are we not supposed to dislike those who take our land?

The Gospel of Luke has a fascinating way of bringing the most unlikely people together. The Roman centurion sends his Jewish friends to ask for Jesus' help. In fact, the more we hear about the centurion, the more we like him. The Jewish elders

Exegetical Perspective

The preaching has ended. The service begins. Jesus concludes his Sermon on the Plain in chapter 6 with the admonition that his followers hear his words *and act on them*. Anyone who hears and does not act on the word builds a house without a foundation, one that will wash away in the next flood (6:49). The writer of Luke's Gospel, in chapter 7, puts the words of Jesus into action. Jesus proceeds from one town to the next, healing and raising the dead. The words of his own sermon call him to action. Such authenticity serves any preacher well.

A centurion has a slave whom he "value[s] highly" (*entimos*) according to the NRSV. This translation might imply that the owner highly regards the slave's commercial value as property. Another possible translation, "holds in honor," changes the nature of the owner's regard for his slave. It is impossible to know which is the better translation. It is also impossible to know whether an owner is likely to hold his slave in honor in the world of this Gospel, even though Luke shows great compassion for those who live on the fringe of society. An opportunity presents itself to consider unequal valuing of people in various times and places.

The centurion, who serves the Roman governing powers in some capacity, is a Gentile whose usual status among Jews is nearly as questionable as his

Homiletical Perspective

Most congregations will have no trouble with this text, at least not at hearing it read. No one in our day is surprised the centurion sought Jesus' help for his servant or that the religious leaders were impressed with the faith of the centurion. We would be too! No one in our day is surprised Jesus acted on behalf of this man's request or saw his faith as impressive. That is *so Jesus*. In fact, we would be troubled if Jesus had not acted on this man's behalf, if the religious leaders had scorned his faith, or if he had looked at Jesus and scoffed at how some prophet from Nazareth could help his servant.

What we have instead is a nice neat story about a good centurion, how everyone recognizes his goodness, and how Jesus rewards his good faith with his servant's life. That would be a great sermon if it were not so . . . wrong. According to that sermon, deserving people are supposed to garner divine support and favors. Right? The problem is that we can still remember a rich young ruler who came to Jesus with all the signs of a blessed life but whose heart ached for meaning and purpose and love. If ever there were someone who typified the "good and blessed life," it should have been him. The looks on the faces of the disciples as Jesus let him walk away empty hearted must have been awful. No wonder Peter essentially says, "If he cannot get into the

Luke 7:1-10

Theological Perspective

out the virtue of humility. His declaration that he is unworthy reinforces that he is worthy of Jesus' gift of life for his slave.

The modern reader may wonder why Luke takes care to portray the centurion as a "worthy" or virtuous man. Elsewhere Luke suggests that God's gifts are available even to those deemed unworthy by some (i.e., Luke 1:51–55; 23:39–43). While Luke emphasizes God's gifts to the lowly, he is also telling a story of the early church that will make sense to other first-century readers. Specifically, he seems concerned to explain why a Jewish Messiah was largely rejected by his people and yet accepted by Gentiles. The piety or virtue of the centurion and other Gentile converts sends a positive message about the kind of people to whom the Christian message would appeal (e.g., Acts 10:1–8; 13:43–48). By pointing out the virtue of the centurion, Luke does not contradict Jesus' mission to the poor and oppressed, but creates a picture of a virtuous man who responds to Jesus' mission with understanding and faith. Jesus' gifts are directed toward all, and especially the poor, but the righteous—no matter their ethnic or religious background—respond with faith.

The centurion's request provides an opportunity for a statement of faith in Jesus from a non-Jewish source. Jesus strongly affirms his faith: "Not even in Israel have I found such faith" (v. 9). Yet the centurion's faith itself creates a second theological question. He compares Jesus to himself—a Roman centurion: "For I also am a man set under authority, with soldiers under me; and I say to one, 'Go,' and he goes, and to another, 'Come,' and he comes, and to my slave, 'Do this,' and the slave does it" (v. 8). The opening words, "for I also," imply that the centurion thinks of Jesus in these terms as well. The comparison is not immediately appealing. It suggests that Jesus is also one who orders people around—free people of lower military rank as well as slaves. This image of a commanding officer does not fit with many people's imaginations of Jesus. The comparison may also appear striking because Romans were not necessarily well liked in Judea and Galilee. Their rule was often seen as an unwelcome foreign occupation. Jesus as a Roman centurion? It seems odd at first. Yet Jesus himself affirms this viewpoint and calls it "faith." What kind of faith is this?

The centurion's statement suggests that he understands Jesus to be "under authority." Just as the centurion had orders to complete a particular mission, so too did Jesus. The centurion does not directly name the authority under whom Jesus serves,

Pastoral Perspective

who came to Jesus cannot say enough good things about him. He has built the Jewish synagogue; he "has loved our people." There is no doubt in the minds of Jewish elders that Jesus should heal the slave.

Jesus is convinced. He leaves where he is and begins the journey to see the slave and the centurion. However, the trip is stopped by the words of another group of emissaries for the soldier. Through these friends, the centurion confesses how unworthy he feels and says that if Jesus simply speaks the words of healing, the slave will be well. The centurion understands the authority and the power of words. Words make things happen, and the words of Jesus, even spoken at a physical distance, will bring restored health to the slave.

Perhaps, more central to the story is the amazement at the faith of the centurion. "I tell you," Jesus says to the crowd around him, "not even in Israel have I found such faith" (v. 9).

This is a text about faith. It is not about the polished profession of faith that we often look for in our churches. In fact, we read this story not knowing just how much of a believer the centurion is. Does he know the right words to say about who Jesus is? Do his words qualify him for membership in one of our churches?

Those questions seem to be irrelevant. Here is a centurion who believes that the Christ has words that can bring wholeness even in the brokenness of his own life. In a way, this story reminds us not only about faith but also about how closely faith is connected to the grace of God. Do any of us ever fully understand who this one sent from God is? Are any of us gifted enough with understanding that can wrap our minds around all that Jesus reveals of God?

If the human connection with the Divine is dependent on the strength of our faith at any moment, then our relationship rises and falls with the shifting sands of circumstances and personal moods. Paul wrote to the Ephesians, "For by grace you have been saved through faith, and this is not your own doing; it is the gift of God" (Eph. 2:8).

It is a strange mix of God's unmerited favor (grace) and our response to the divine initiative (faith). It is never either/or. It is not all God or all us. It is both/and. The gift is offered by the Holy One, but like all gifts, the gift is received or rejected. The gift is never forced.

Those of us in the pastoral ministry do well to remember the message of this story. There are times when we so desperately want people to accept and appropriate what we believe is right for them. In

Exegetical Perspective

slave's. The writer of the Gospel of Luke was most probably a Gentile writing for Gentile hearers. This Gospel and its sequel, the book of Acts, tell the story of the inclusion of Gentiles among those to whom Jesus comes. The centurion is no ordinary Gentile. He has important Jewish friends who value him highly. He sends them to talk with Jesus. The Jews request the favor not on behalf of the slave, but on behalf of the centurion. They explain that he is a friend of Jews, that he built the synagogue in the village. Because he loves the Jews, they regard him as worthy to receive a favor from Jesus. This centurion, a Gentile, lives out Jesus' recent admonition in chapter 6 to love one's enemies, in this case, the Jews. The outsider models kingdom behavior. Luke's Jesus goes with the Jews, intending to visit the Gentile in his home.

The centurion intervenes before Jesus arrives at his house. He sends friends, once again. The text does not reveal for certain whether the friends are Jew or Gentile, but because they come from and return to his house, they are probably Gentile. The centurion sends the message that he is not worthy to have Jesus enter his house or to approach Jesus on the way. The centurion's motives may be mixed. Is he sparing Jesus from having to come to the house of a Gentile? Is he hesitant to have his Gentile friends witness a Jew visiting his house? The text is unclear. What is clear, however, is the centurion's respect for the power of Jesus' words. He has such confidence in the word of the prophet that he knows Jesus does not need to come to his house. He believes Jesus can heal his slave from a distance. The centurion equates the power, the authority, of Jesus' words with the power he wields over the soldiers under him.

Jesus speaks words of commendation, of high praise for the centurion. This Gentile has modeled kingdom behavior, faith, in ways Jesus has never witnessed in a Jew. Although the Gospel writer records no word of healing from Jesus, the friends find the slave in good health. Is it the power of the centurion's faith that heals the slave, and not, in this case, the power of Jesus' words? The faith that recognizes the power of the words may be so powerful in itself that the need for the words diminishes. The conclusion drawn by hearers and preachers in the present day, when the words of Jesus are not heard directly, is that deep faith is sufficient to bring the power of the Divine into our lives.

That Jesus declares the centurion to possess more faith than anyone he has found among the people of Israel calls for a more pointed word. Preachers must contextualize anti-Semitism, evidenced here in Luke.

Homiletical Perspective

kingdom, what about us?" According to the spiritual algebra of our day, being good should equal blessings: blessings should equal a good life. The problem is that equation does not always add up true. The problem is that every one of us knows some good and faithful servant whose life is a wreck, and we have seen too many people with lots of things but whose lives are empty in every way that matters.

Think about this text again. Only this time, look carefully beneath our modern readings and reconsider who this centurion is. This man is a Roman leader, a Gentile, and a powerful man. His place in society is set. The text is clear. This man cares for his servant and has been more than gracious to the religious leaders, even building their synagogue. Nevertheless, for Luke's first readers this man is an outsider. His presence creates an uneasy tension. If he were part of the religious establishment, one of "us," then there would be no issue. Too easily, we modern readers assume the centurion is one of "us," when the truth is he is one of "them." This story is about—and perhaps any sermon that comes from it should be too—the distance between "us" and "them."

To help modern listeners hear this text as ancient readers would have, you may have to change the characters. We have no context in which to place a "centurion." We are not an occupied people. We do not live under the authority of foreign rule. We do not know what it is have "them" begin to join "our" groups, our ranks, our faith. A sermon that takes the congregation on a historical survey will drown everyone in obscure detail. Instead, consider changing the characters and asking the right questions of the text with these new actors. The dissonance of moving from a comfortable place of familiarity to a place of discomfort will have a strong effect on a congregation.

For example, ask the congregation to imagine a scenario where a larger company buys out the place where they work. New bosses, new managers, new corporate schemes, new hierarchy all become status quo. Other scenarios will work. New political leaders come to town. A new school board takes charge. A new minister comes to your congregation. These scenarios may help a congregation feel this text, as well as "hear it again for the first time."

Another issue that lurks in this story is about authority. The centurion is a figure of authority. In nearly every respect, he is the one who can send others, care for others, and do for others—until the day a person he cares about faces a reality beyond his

Luke 7:1-10

Theological Perspective

yet he seems to understand Jesus as a Jewish healer (and thus sends Jewish elders to make the initial request in v. 3). This background suggests that he understands Jesus as one under the authority of the God of Israel. This view parallels Luke's presentation of Jesus as one sent by God "to proclaim release to the captives and recovery of sight to the blind" (4:18). The centurion understands the source of Jesus' healing power.

The centurion also thinks of Jesus as one who commands others. Like the centurion, he says to someone, "Go," and he goes. This language makes sense in a context in which Jesus' commands are largely directed toward the healing of others. He commands the paralytic, "Stand up and take your bed and go to your home" (Luke 5:24), and the man with the withered hand, "Stretch out your hand" (6:10). In each case, Jesus' commands produce results. The paralytic walks, the man's hand is restored. The centurion understands this power by relating it to his own. Jesus' words will be carried out because of the authority he embodies. Because of this, the centurion knows that Jesus need not come into his home where his slave lies sick. His orders will be executed even in his absence. So he requests healing for his slave without demanding Jesus' presence.

The metaphor of Jesus as a Roman centurion is fruitful for reflection because it is fresh to modern ears in a way that other NT language like "Son of God" or "Messiah" is not. The faith affirmed in this passage attributes the power and authority of Jesus to the one who sent him. It emphasizes the sureness with which Jesus' commands will be carried out on earth. Such faith is difficult to find.

SUSAN E. HYLEN

Pastoral Perspective

some ways, this desire to see folks make positive changes is understandable. After all, every pastor has some element of ego need. Regardless of how we present the choice to believe or not believe in the Christ, we still feel some sense of rejection because we have delivered the message. We ask ourselves, "Did I say it cogently or clearly enough?"

However, it is not just our egos that are involved. When we felt the call to ministry, we understood that we were called to be advocates for or witnesses to a message that carries ultimate significance for the lives of people.

As a young minister, I recall all of the well-meaning people who told me that the call to "full-time" ministry was the call to share a transformational message. How disappointed I was when I discovered that I could not convince everyone of what I saw as the "Holy Center" of life.

As a pastor of a church, I felt the pain of my own failure to receive the message of God's grace and goodness when I encountered people in the church for whom the faith we professed seemed to make little difference.

For me, the way to deal with this was "to reframe" my approach to ministry. What I was doing in preaching, teaching, leading worship, counseling, and the myriad other responsibilities was "offering." I was offering my presence, my words, and ultimately myself, but that meant what I had to offer could be accepted or rejected. Trying to force or manipulate people to do what I wanted was antithetical to the concept of offering. Furthermore, my own effort, even at its best, was an imperfect offering to God.

Was the centurion's faith response as clear or pristine as we may like? Probably not! But neither is the response of most of us as undiluted as we may like. We believe, but we ask God to love us at our places of unbelief. What matters, ultimately, is that somebody who was broken has been made whole. For that we give thanks to God!

CHARLES BUGG

Exegetical Perspective

In a post-Holocaust world, it is important to avoid emphasis on the anti-Semitism found in Gospel texts. The Evangelical Lutheran Church in America condemned Martin Luther's "Writings against the Jews" at National Assembly in 1991. These actions were too little, and much too late, for those who suffered and died as a result of the invasion into German culture of a murderous ideology, growing, at least in part, from Luther's writings.

That said, faith is nevertheless an important theme in Luke's Gospel. Everyone is able to hear the words spoken by Jesus on the plain, in the streets, and in the house, but it is only faith, as found in the centurion, that saves. Those who hear the words of Jesus may or may not be faithful followers of Jesus.

An acceptable synonym for the Gospel writer's word "faith" (*pistis*), one more easily understood by contemporary listeners, is "trust." Followers are called by Luke's Jesus, not just to hear and trust the word of God's love for all people, but to live out the word, to live out their faith, in deeds. Faith or trust is not a momentary experience, but precipitates a way of life that includes compassion for all people: friends, enemies, and especially those in need. Faith is clearly not the venue of a privileged set, but includes Gentiles, centurions, women, widows, and sinners. In Luke's Gospel, healing is available to all people through faith or trust in the compassion of the Most High.

DENA L. WILLIAMS

Homiletical Perspective

control. Nearly every congregant will understand authority. We like to be in authority but cringe when it looms over us. We have a love/hate relationship with power, but we do understand it. In this story a man of stature sets aside his place and power to ask of another what he cannot do for himself or for someone he loves. An ancient reader would have expected the centurion to use his position to coerce Jesus into helping this servant. Modern readers gloss over this act. In the ancient world, those of higher stature would never ask those of lower stature for assistance. An act like that would have enormous social consequences. Nevertheless, the centurion sets aside social convention because of his care for his servant and asks Jesus for assistance.

Also significant in this text is the theme of faith. The centurion stands among those who have not seen and yet believe. On the one hand, perhaps we could argue the centurion has nothing to lose. Why not try what Jesus has to offer? If it works, great, except even asking the favor has social consequences. To ask, to allow others to speak on his behalf, is an act of faith that places this centurion's position in the community on the line. Note in the story that very little is said about the healing itself. The bulk of the story is about the centurion and his ability to believe without seeing. Little wonder that Jesus commends the centurion.

Finally, note that Jesus does not say in this story that the faith of Israel is faulty, bad, or small. In fact, when Jesus praises the centurion, he uses the faith of Israel as an example of the highest kind. Jesus says to his followers, "This Roman, Gentile, politically advantaged military man, outsider has more faith than even the most faithful in our day." I can imagine the title of a sermon on this text might be "Jesus Said What?!"

VAUGHN CROWE-TIPTON

Exodus 34:29-35

²⁹Moses came down from Mount Sinai. As he came down from the mountain with the two tablets of the covenant in his hand, Moses did not know that the skin of his face shone because he had been talking with God. ³⁰When Aaron and all the Israelites saw Moses, the skin of his face was shining, and they were afraid to come near him. ³¹But Moses called to them; and Aaron and all the leaders of the congregation returned to him, and Moses spoke with them. ³²Afterward all the Israelites came near, and he gave them in commandment all that the Lᴏʀᴅ had spoken with him on Mount Sinai. ³³When Moses had finished speaking with them, he put a veil on his face; ³⁴but whenever Moses went in before the Lᴏʀᴅ to speak with him, he would take the veil off, until he came out; and when he came out, and told the Israelites what he had been commanded, ³⁵the Israelites would see the face of Moses, that the skin of his face was shining; and Moses would put the veil on his face again, until he went in to speak with him.

Theological Perspective

This text has to do with glory, a subject calculated to discomfit the self-consciously humble. Were it simply about Moses's bringing the law down from the mountain, we could understand the ethical significance with little effort. Were it simply about Moses's special stature before God, we could easily assimilate that to our notions of effective religious leadership. But this glory is strange. For one thing, Moses does not even perceive it. For another, the veil he chooses to put on is not for himself, but to protect the people from being overwhelmed. Finally, the glory that shines is, apparently, a splendor that is thrust on Moses in his role as the bearer of God's word, commissioned now to deliver to God's people the Ten Commandments.

Those of us who have been nurtured on a "theology of the cross" find ourselves feeling a bit ambivalent about the language of glory. To be sure, our creeds and confessions speak of "the glory of God" and of our duty to "glorify and enjoy God," but in truth glory has become something of an abstraction to us, who have left its definition largely to the Pentecostals and the lyrics of older hymns. Luther himself, and Calvin in his own way, have taught us to be suspicious of glory, comparing the theology of glory unfavorably to the theology of the cross, and emphasizing the virtues of self-denial and humility.

Pastoral Perspective

Moses as Leader. This passage of Scripture answers a deep thirst for leaders who are truthful and trusted. Moses was such a leader. As mediator between the people and the divine presence, he would announce God's covenant with the people. But Moses would also communicate something about himself as well.

We can learn something about pastoral and spiritual leadership from him. Moses was in God's presence forty days. He did not know that his face was aglow when he returned to the congregation. The divine presence was full of mercy and grace, slow to anger and rich in kindness and fidelity (Exod. 34:6). Moses could not see his own face, but others could see it. They were afraid, perhaps awestruck. Moses was carrying something that would mark his encounter and forever define the relationship between the Holy One at Sinai-Horeb and the people.

Time Alone with God. Preparing to be a faithful bearer of God's word involves time alone with God. God spoke to Moses "face to face, as one speaks to a friend" (Exod. 33:11). God is passionate about this relationship (Exod. 34:14). Talk between intimates or friends will normally include the language of endearment and trust as well as commiseration. Moses received instructions and prepared himself to

Exegetical Perspective

The literary context of this pericope is important. The paragraph stands as the conclusion of the significant events presented in Exodus 32–34: the golden calf idolatry and subsequent divine punishment (32:1–35); Moses's intercession and divine reconciliation (33:1–34:9); the renewal of the covenant (34:10–28). In today's short passage, Moses is portrayed as the one through whom God's presence would be most regularly and fully communicated.

Immediately preceding this unit—in fact the Hebrew and Greek texts combine verses 27–28 with verses 29–35—it is reported that Moses spent "forty days and forty nights" fasting in God's presence as "he" [God probably, but the text could mean Moses] wrote again "on the tablets the words of the covenant, the ten commandments" (34:28; see 24:15–18). Some commentators consider the phrase "the ten commandments" (v. 28) to be the work of the final redactor, seeking to smooth out the connection of chapters 32–34 with the report of the covenant fashioned in chapters 19–24.

It is clear that chapters 32–34 stand between chapters 25–31 (the instructions for constructing the tabernacle and establishing the priesthood) and chapters 35–40 (the execution of those plans). It is also clear that Moses, rather than Aaron, played the primary role in carrying out the work that was

Homiletical Perspective

Transfiguration Sunday marks the transition from the end of Epiphany to the beginning of Lent. This point on the church calendar celebrates God's remarkable embrace of Jesus, the climax of his earthly life, and the symbolic shift of his ministry from Galilee to Jerusalem. Jesus' transfiguration parallels Moses's encounter with YHWH on Mount Sinai (Exod. 34:29–35) and should not be considered apart from it. Both passages provide preachers a wonderful opportunity to explore what it means to be close to God.

The theme of the exodus narrative is the establishment of God's special relationship with the people of Israel. The Ten Commandments are the hallmark of that covenant, and in an unusual interaction YHWH establishes Moses as the unrivaled voice of interpretation of the covenant.[1] The nature of their unique relationship is explored in this passage and is symbolized dramatically in Moses's shining face.

Israel's apostasy confronts Moses on the return from Sinai and provokes him to destroy the stone tablets. YHWH's anger over the sins of the people brings into question whether YHWH is still with them. This sets up the unusual dialogue, where

1. Walter Brueggemann, *Theology of the Old Testament* (Minneapolis: Fortress Press, 1997), 186.

Exodus 34:29-35

Theological Perspective

But does God shine? What is one to make of the brightness of which this text speaks? This light, reflected in Moses's face and veiled to protect the people, seems to have something in common with that glory of the Lord that shone around those Bethlehem shepherds, leaving them "terrified" (Luke 2:9). Or perhaps one thinks of that transfiguring brightness that surrounded Jesus on another mountaintop (Luke 9:28–36). As the Old Testament lesson to be read on Transfiguration Sunday, this story of Moses suggests that God's glory does shine and that its beauty disconcerts. This glory silences our religious chatter and renders us blinking and confused in its light. Perhaps that is what holy ground feels like. In any case, that is how Peter and the disciples felt, at least as recorded in Mark's Gospel, for in speaking to Jesus, Peter, we are told, "did not know what to say, for they were terrified" (Mark 9:6). Far from being an abstraction this glory appears in Scripture to be something of a threat. What are we to make of it?

Perhaps its reflected nature is a clue. Moses does not shine as a result of his own charisma. In his role as bearer of the divine word to Israel, Moses is invited into conversation with God and given words to say and stamped with the glory those words evoke. In recent years we have been taught to think of God as vulnerable, so it comes as something of a surprise to hear that God is glorious and that proclaiming God's word brings with it a certain splendor. This text will not allow such splendor to be hidden under the bushel basket of some well-contrived modesty. These "ten words" (v. 28) are glorious precisely as they bear witness to the One whom heaven and earth cannot contain, and yet whose glory it is to be Israel's God. Aaron and the others are right to be afraid to come too near Moses or to look at his face. This splendor shines not with the polish of ethical insight or even brilliant analytical study, but with the terrible light of God's reflected presence, a light that illumines God's word and renders God's people conspicuous, marking them as witnesses to the Lord of life.

Often we do not think of God's word as all that glorious or God's people as shining all that conspicuously. Scripture is a text to be studied, a word to be proclaimed to a gathering of not even very ambitious sinners. There is nothing self-evidently glorious about most local congregations. Yet Moses's face shone. Jesus' figure became dazzling bright. This glory, Basil the Great observed, far from being an abstraction, brings us near to the disturbing events of Easter morning, where the disciples'

Pastoral Perspective

bring God's word to the people at Mount Sinai. The people were sometimes referred to as stiff-necked, unruly, and stubborn.

The Glow Comes from Time Alone with God. The aura on Moses's face comes from standing in the presence of the Divine. Others may notice the glow before it is seen by the one who bears it. This can happen when the spiritual leader's life is informed by life in the community and tradition and grounded in prayer and hope. In this way, one does not belong privately to one's self. Encounter with the Divine presupposes a self in relationship, open to promptings from the Divine, faithful to one's vows and sense of call to ministry, and available to the community where one serves. This always calls for pastoral presence *and* prophetic discernment.

Face Aglow in Worship. The idea of "face" presupposes a social relationship between two or more parties. In this case, it is between Moses and God. It is about the covenant and the chosen people. A certain level of faithfulness, spiritual and moral accountability, is expected. The idea of face work is implied. In ministry, face work is about how a people who share a common religious identity show their face to one another and strive to be faithful to God.

An Illustration. Typically, a black church worship service is a place where God's presence-in-community is experienced. It evokes an emotional response. A sense of God's presence may be reflected in the radiance or glow on people's faces. God's presence may be felt in terms of shared smiles and warm greetings, fervent prayer, soul-stirring gospel music, hand clapping, shouts of praise, and amens! At a relatively quiet point in a particular worship service, a young lad, perhaps six or seven years old and a child of the congregation, was sitting with his parents. He appeared to be restless. He turned around and saw all of the faces looking forward. His face was expressionless at first; then suddenly a big and broad glowing smile appeared. His smile called out smiles on the faces of others. Nothing was said, no words spoken, just a big broad grin spread across his face.

The child could not see his own face, but members of the congregation could. It was as if the entire congregation once again conveyed a sense of the presence of God in their midst with an emotional response, this time to the child, and the child was smiling back with a big glow on his face. The smile and glow were part of the meaning of

completed when "the glory of the Lord filled the tabernacle" (40:34). Beyond these broad strokes, there is no current consensus concerning whether the narrative of 34:29–35 is the work of J, E, JE, a final redactor, or some other source. The best one can do is to concentrate on the final form of the passage in its context, letting that guide the interpretation.

The language and style of this passage is basically clear. The description of Moses's function as a mediator between God and the people recalls his same role associated with the "tent of meeting" (33:7–11; see also 20:18–20). Great emphasis is placed on Moses's "speaking/talking" with God, and then with the people. Some form of the Hebrew root *dbr*, to speak/talk, is used seven times (34:29, 31, 32, 33, 34 [2x], 35; see also 33:11) in this brief passage. Moreover, as noted by the late Brevard S. Childs, Yale professor of Old Testament, in verses 29–33 the tense of the Hebrew verbs is that used basically to recount the historical past of Moses's meeting with God. In verses 34–35, however, the tense of the verbal forms is frequentative, emphasizing the ongoing work of Moses as mediator between God and the people.[1] Moses's main function was to convey to the people the "words" (commandments) that God had spoken to him (34:32, 34; see 34:27–28), in order that the people might acknowledge obediently the "covenant" (34:28) or the "testimony" (Heb.; but NRSV translates "covenant," 34:29).

While the basic message of 34:29–35 seems clear enough, an element of uncertainty is added by the use of two very unusual terms. The first is *qaran 'or panaw* (NRSV "the skin of his face shone"; NIV "his face was radiant," 34:29, 30, 35). The root of the term *qrn* is used as a noun in almost every context referring to some form of "horn." Once it appears as a *hif'il* describing an animal's budding horns (Ps. 69:31). Three times in Exodus 34 the root seems to be used in *qal* (34:29, 30, 35). There are no other verbal uses of the root. Translation of the term is problematic in Exodus 34. In the Septuagint, the Peshitta, and Targum, the term *qaran* was interpreted as "sending out rays" or "shining." Presumably this translation was suggested by the larger context where Moses entered the cloud of smoke and fire on Mount Sinai (19:18–20). That cloud was associated with the presence of God's "glory" (*kabod*). The divine *kabod* had a visually luminous quality (16:10; 24:16–17; 33:22). Thus, apparently, the early translators of this

1. Brevard W. Childs, *The Book of Exodus* (Philadelphia: Westminster Press, 1974), 617.

Moses attempts to intercede with YHWH, essentially saying, *"If we have this special relationship, Lord, and you won't go with us, how will anyone know we are special?"* Moses wants to be reassured. The interaction seems to reach its peak when YHWH agrees and says his countenance will indeed lead Israel—but Moses is not finished. With amazing brashness he goes on to ask one of the most remarkable questions in the Bible: he wants to see God's glory as proof!

The Scriptures say that those who look at God will die. The majesty of an omnipotent sovereign is so great that a direct human encounter will be lethal. Yet this is exactly what Moses is asking: he wants to be "up close and personal"! There are many stories of contact with God through dreams, messengers, and angels. There are countless prayers and conversations with God, but a direct encounter with God is rare indeed.

The concept of the glory of God is an abstraction that tries to encompass the power and majesty of God. In Hebrew the word is *kabod*, literally, "to be loaded down with riches." It refers to God's awesome power and a bright—even blinding—clouded aura. This aura dramatically indicates God's nearness, while still concealing God's awesomeness. The Hebrew translation is helpful here. While the glory of God may be an elusive concept, a blessing of riches is something most of us can understand. We have recognized it in some of the people we most admire. Every now and then we encounter people who have a depth, or joy, or even a kind of charisma that, as we get to know them, we discover grows from a deep personal relationship to God. These folks commonly talk about their relationship to God as one filled with great abundance. And how often have we heard the phrase "Her face just glows," as others try to describe the aura they see in these people?

As Moses returns from Sinai, one expects the focus of the text to be on the tablets, but it is not. Moses's face steals the show and shifts the focus of the entire story. Verse 29 says that Moses's face "shone" because he had been talking with God. The translation has seen some debate, but it is clear that he has been visually transformed by his divine encounter (cf. Matt. 17:2 and image of Jesus' face). Thus the story that began with a discussion of God's face has now turned to a discussion of Moses's face. Ironically Moses, who once hid from the face of God (Exod. 3:6), now has others hiding from his.

Moses's relationship to YHWH—especially as it lays the foundation for a covenanted people from

Exodus 34:29-35

Theological Perspective

bafflement and joy and even terror come face to face with the risen Lord, whose splendor dispels the gloom of death itself.[1] The unbearable brightness of Moses's face is the residue of God's steadfast love for Israel, his faithfulness to them in the face of betrayal and even death, and his gift to them of a dignity and honor they did not choose and would never have chosen for themselves. They are meant for shining, and they shine, unaware of the weight of glory that is theirs in the God who makes his face to shine upon them (Num. 6:25).

Vincent van Gogh painted a number of ordinary objects: a yellow chair, a vase of sunflowers, a collection of small sailboats beached by the sea. Among his compositions is a painting of a pair of old work boots, almost worn out, each boot leaning against the other. At first glance, nothing could appear more ordinary or unglorious. But as one looks at the painting, one notices that the boots are illumined from beyond the painting and that they describe a life not just of labor and toil, but of vast human dignity, even beauty. The boots are glorious, not because their style is chic, but because it is their peculiar splendor to reflect the humanity that has labored so long and so hard in their use. These boots cry out that their owner was made for the glory of God, that to be a human being is to be a glory-bearing, glory-reflecting, glory-bound creature. That is surely the meaning of such transfiguring glory: to see in its brightness an anticipation of the glory of the risen Lord and to find in him the destiny of every "ordinary" life. For he is, as Karl Barth reminds us, "the one who makes us radiant. We ourselves cannot put on bright faces. But neither can we prevent them from shining. Looking up to him, our faces shine."[2]

THOMAS W. CURRIE

Pastoral Perspective

God's felt presence in the worshiping community. The glow on the child's face was in response to a congregation expressing their experience of God's presence.

Moses encountered the presence of God at Sinai-Horeb, and the child encountered the presence/spirit of God through the community that surrounds him.

Leadership in the Community of Faith. This passage of Scripture, then, gives certain clues about spiritual leadership. Moses shows us that faithful spiritual leadership grows from intimate encounters with the Divine. It entails bringing again the word of God to the people. They may sometimes be referred to as "a stiff-necked people" (Exod. 34:9). Leadership that develops from time spent with God may mean that one's face is aglow. There are dangers. The spiritual leader is sometimes feared, as was Moses. A challenge for religious leadership may arise when people become fearful, angry, resistant, or speak against their leaders. This can become a problem if the spiritual leader fears conflict or has a high need to be liked. If so, then the spiritual leader may be vulnerable to a sense of failure and depression when she does not find favor in the sight of the people.

Moreover, we are never free from tendencies toward delusions of grandeur—for instance, listening only to our own inner voice, believing it to be God's voice, and shutting out others. Standing in the divine presence meant that others would notice the glow on the face of Moses before he became aware that he looked different to them. Moses recognized fear in their response to him. When Moses was able to understand that they were responding to a change in the way he looked to them, then he was able to adjust in appropriate ways. He asked Aaron and the community leaders to come and talk with him. He was able to interpret his experience in ways that brought understanding. The people in turn were able to let go of their fear and receive Moses's message.

Together, Moses and the people were able to change from fear and misunderstanding to acceptance and cooperation. Such communication and willingness to change informs and reforms the spiritual life of the congregation. It encourages trust and enables ways of being accountable to the Holy One and to one another.

ARCHIE SMITH JR.

---

1. Cf. Robert Jenson, *Systematic Theology*, vol. 1, *The Triune God* (New York: Oxford University Press, 1997), 143, n. 91.
2. Karl Barth, "Look Up to Him!" in *Deliverance to the Captives* (New York: Harper & Bros., 1961), 47.

unusual Hebrew form decided that Moses's skin "glowed" or "radiated" with the divine *kabod*, since Moses had been in God's presence for so long. It should be noted, however, that when Jerome made his Latin translation, the Vulgate, he read the term more literally (on the basis of the nearly unanimous meaning of the root elsewhere in the Old Testament) and represented Moses as being "horned." Hence, Michelangelo's famous sculpture of Moses with horns.

This leads to consideration of the second unusual term, *masweh* (NRSV and NIV "veil," 34:33–35). This term appears only here. The context makes it clear that Moses was putting on (34:33, 35) and taking off (34:34) something; hence the traditional translation "veil." The "veiling" of priests—Moses seems to be functioning in a priestly role here—was widely practiced in antiquity. The most common form was the use of masks that represented the Deity or some aspect of divine power being communicated. Thus, some have suggested that Moses was wearing some form of "horned mask." Obviously this cannot be proven, but it is an interesting possibility.

One thing remains puzzling, however. Usually priests put on their face coverings when they enter the presence of the Divine. In this text, the opposite is the case. Moses put on the *masweh* only after leaving the divine presence and after reporting to the people (34:33, 35). Moses did not need protection before God (see 33:11), but the people needed assurance that Moses was still the peoples' only direct source of communication with God. Thus they were allowed to see the radiance of Moses's face each time Moses returned from being in the presence of the divine *kabod*, and then they were guarded from it until Moses next conferred with God.

In the New Testament this tradition seems clearly reflected in the event Christians know as the transfiguration (Matt. 17:1–8; Mark 9:2–8; Luke 9:28–36). In the Gospels the emphasis, of course, is on Jesus who, as had Moses, reflected the divine glory. Indeed, Jesus was the source of that glory! Paul also remembered (and altered) the tradition when he proclaimed Jesus' superiority over Moses and interpreted the veil as blinding, rather than protecting, the Jews from the brilliance of Jesus' divine glory (2 Cor. 3:17–18; 4:3–4).

WALLACE EUGENE MARCH

whom we all draw inspiration—is a valuable place for preachers to focus. What we see is that the intimacy of faith—the closeness to God—is the defining factor in transfiguration. This is both personal and corporate. The story certainly ordains Moses as the undisputed leader and makes his relationship exemplary, but it also clearly portrays him as representative of the nation of Israel. The glory on his face represents the glorious promise that falls on all of Israel and the special relationship they have with YHWH.

Two critical points are definitive for the people of Israel and for all people of faith. The first is that this concept of proximity has at its base a moral and spiritual idea that shapes our very being.[2] *Our closeness to God molds who we are.* The second is that while one of the most defining obligations of all Jews is to do justice, the enduring message of Moses's encounter is that they are also called to be in the presence of God. The two are inextricably connected.

There is a popular trend in our contemporary culture to focus on "doing the right thing" and to be known for acts of compassion. Much is admirable about politicians, movie stars, and rock stars speaking out and offering great acts of charity, but the risk is that this leads us to figure backward: it reasons that if one does good things, one must therefore be good and close to God. The fundamental point of this lesson from Scripture is that proximity to God is the necessary and defining first step. It is the proximity that enables us to embody and radiate God's love in the world. It is the closeness that calls us and sustains us—especially when our work is no longer popular or personally advantageous.

Meister Eckhart, the fourteenth-century German theologian, once said, "We should not think that holiness is based on what we do but rather on what we are, for it is not our works that sanctify us, but who sanctifies our works."

NICK CARTER

---

2. R. W. L. Moberly, *Prophecy and Discernment*, Cambridge Studies in Christian Doctrine 14 (Cambridge: Cambridge University Press, 2006), 9.

Psalm 99

¹The LORD is king; let the peoples tremble!
  He sits enthroned upon the cherubim; let the earth quake!
²The LORD is great in Zion;
  he is exalted over all the peoples.
³Let them praise your great and awesome name.
  Holy is he!
⁴Mighty King, lover of justice,
  you have established equity;
  you have executed justice
  and righteousness in Jacob.
⁵Extol the LORD our God;
  worship at his footstool.
  Holy is he!

Theological Perspective

Christians are becoming more aware of the long history of conquest and colonial power that continues to influence global realities and relationships. In 2007, Jamestown commemorated its quadricentennial as a settlement of the British crown. Queen Elizabeth visited to give the event proper fanfare. The founding of the colony at Jamestown, however, was celebrated not only in light of early ties between Americans and the British but also with knowledge of a later successful battle for independence. Many countries did not have such successful revolts. Western nations plundered the natural resources and wealth of countries they colonized to build their own empires and left much devastation in their wake. Dominant colonial powers functioned to oppress indigenous communities. God's favor was confused with those who were victorious. Desmond Tutu was once quoted as saying, "They used to say that the missionaries came to Africa and they had the Bible and we had the land. And then they said, 'Let us pray.' And when we opened our eyes, we had the Bible and they had the land!"[1]

These stories make it difficult to proclaim enthusiastically with the psalmist that the "Holy One has become *king*!" Significant questions can be raised concerning the meaning of a monarchial title in the

1. Desmond Tutu, quoted in J. Milburn Thompson, *Justice and Peace: A Christian Primer* (Maryknoll, NY: Orbis Press, 2003), 14.

Pastoral Perspective

Psalm 99 is a song of exaltation, a psalm to be sung in praise of the holiness and majesty of God. God is extolled here as mighty king and lover of justice. The psalmist anticipates that the earth will quake and the people tremble at the great and awesome name of God. While a major focus of this psalm is the acknowledgment of God as king, there is clear recognition of other important aspects of God: God is a universal God (vv. 2–3); God is a lover of justice and an establisher of equity who acts in a just and righteous way (v. 4); God is a relational, living God who listens, responds, and guides the people (vv. 6–7).

The psalmist seems to have personal knowledge of and intimate experience with God. God is high and lifted up but also walks with the people on a daily basis. The psalmist knows a God of all people, who listens to, answers, provides guidance for, forgives, and holds people accountable for their actions. The psalmist has developed a trusting relationship with God based on this personal encounter.

What vision of the faithful life does this psalm hold for us today? How can this song of praise, written so many years ago, bring energy to us and enhance our relationship with the living, present God?

God Is a Universal God. God's kingdom is not tied to any location, religion, culture, material possession,

⁶Moses and Aaron were among his priests,
   Samuel also was among those who called on his name.
   They cried to the LORD, and he answered them.
⁷He spoke to them in the pillar of cloud;
   they kept his decrees,
   and the statutes that he gave them.

⁸O LORD our God, you answered them;
   you were a forgiving God to them,
   but an avenger of their wrongdoings.
⁹Extol the LORD our God,
   and worship at his holy mountain;
   for the LORD our God is holy.

Exegetical Perspective

Psalm 99 is usually thought of as the culmination of the enthronement psalms (Pss. 93, 95–99), a series of psalms that focus on God's kingship. In Psalm 99, God's immanence in manifesting the divine reign is a particular emphasis. While the literary form is hardly clear cut, the psalm can be broadly divided in three sections, each of which ends with an affirmation of God's holiness or otherness.

The first section opens with an unequivocal declaration of God's rule. This is followed by the declaration that God "sits enthroned upon the cherubim," a clear reference to the ark of the covenant (1 Sam. 4:4; 2 Sam. 6:2; 2 Kgs. 19:15; Ps. 80:1). Both the trembling of the people and the quaking of the earth are classic indications of a divine theophany (see Exod. 19:16–19; 1 Kgs. 19:11). The point being underscored is that God's reign is immanent and hence a manifestation to the world of God's presence. This presence becomes localized in verse 2: God is "great" in Zion, the place of worship in Jerusalem. God is considered exalted over "all peoples" in the Masoretic tradition (similar to Ps. 46:10), while some manuscripts of the Greek translation have "all gods." Reading with the Hebrew text, the psalmist links God's immanence with God's universality: because the Deity is present in this world, God is over all peoples, whether they acknowledge it or not. So the psalmist calls on the peoples to give due

Homiletical Perspective

Any time believers are inclined to define religion as "Do this" or "Don't do that," we need Psalm 99. It is a passage of Scripture that reminds us how a sense of wonder can be more important to a life of faith than an obsession over behavior. Ask a friend sometime what comes to mind when he or she hears the word "holiness." More than likely, you will catch an earful about morality, as if holiness and morality were the same thing. Psalm 99 has nothing to do with morality or niceness, and everything to do with holiness.

Have you ever felt awe-deficient? Or too analytical about matters of faith? Or tempted to enlist God as your personal genie? The author of Psalm 99 has already anticipated these sorts of misalignments. He has a word to reengage our reverence, and it is "holiness." More precisely, it is the *holiness of God*. A quick glance at Psalm 99, with its hymnlike refrain of "Holy is he!" brings to mind the popular Christian hymn often sung on Holy Trinity Sunday, or Isaiah's own words of "Holy, holy, holy is the LORD of hosts." Many translators decide that an exclamation point is in order after the "Holy is he!" This may be nothing more than an emphatic mark meant to discourage too much chumminess with God. We are pretty good domesticators, after all, especially when it comes to whittling God down to a size that fits us and our needs.

Psalm 99

Psalm 99

Theological Perspective

ancient world and how it translates into our contemporary context. What does the reign of God for which we are hoping look like? How can Christians today proclaim that the "Holy One has become king" without claiming power over others?

The use of monarchial imagery for God has not always been seen by theologians as problematic. However, Protestant theologians since the time of the Reformation have emphasized the psalmist's teaching about God's sovereignty in terms of justice and equity rather than domination over others. John Calvin observed that Psalm 99 did not allow one to "associate the ideas of tyranny with the government of God, because there is constant concord between [God's] power and justice."[2] In verse 4, the psalmist declares, "Mighty King, lover of justice, you have established equity; you have executed justice and righteousness in Jacob." According to Calvin, this verse could be interpreted as God's challenge to God's people to practice "perfect equity" or as a witness to God's own high regard for justice and equity. Calvin's interpretation was congruent with concern raised throughout the Hebrew Bible that kings not become abusive or idolatrous. Deuteronomy 17:14–20 laid down the law that human kings must read and observe the Torah and must not exalt themselves over God or other members of the community.

Contemporary theologians challenge us to find new ways to speak of God's reign when we know our global history is shaped by conquest and colonization. Feminist theologians have helped us think about social implications of language referring to God in exclusively masculine terms or by monarchial imagery. Sallie McFague indicated in *Metaphorical Theology* that religious language is dangerous when it becomes absolutized. This is consistent with Calvin's and other reformers' concerns about idolatry. All language for God is metaphorical. God-language should convey the richness and diversity of language used for God in the Hebrew Bible and throughout our Christian tradition to point us toward God's reign of justice and equity.

Some theologians suggest drawing upon postcolonial theory to inform theological conversations and biblical interpretation. This point bears significance for one's interpretation of Psalm 99, because God's justice and equity cannot be adequately defined in our multicultural, multireligious, and multinational context without a deeper understanding of the experience of those who have consistently been pushed to the social, economic, and political margins.

2. John Calvin, *Commentary on the Book of Psalms* (Grand Rapids: Eerdmans, 1949), 75.

Pastoral Perspective

racial or ethnic group. God's reign is continuous and everlasting for all people at all times. We are reminded on a daily basis that we live in a global society, one that is impacted by the beliefs, values, and actions of all people. The New Living Bible translation of Psalm 99:1 reads, "Let the nations tremble, let the whole earth quake." In her book *Psalms for Praying: An Invitation to Wholeness*, Nan C. Merrill reinterprets this verse in an even more definitive way: "For the Beloved reigns supreme; let all the earth give thanks!"[1]

Many of us today are reluctant to give up our limited vision of God as a God of a few select people. We associate God with a certain denomination, economic class, race, political party, or country. It is sometimes difficult for us to believe that God's Holy Spirit is at work throughout the world, even beyond the global Christian church. The writer of Psalm 99 encourages all people to experience the majesty and awesome name of God and to praise and worship the Holy One.

God Loves, Knows, and Practices Justice. The psalmist experienced God as a "lover of justice" who established equity and practiced justice and righteousness. It is important for us to understand God's justice today, as we struggle daily with an unjust world, sorely lacking in equality. We need to know and experience the depth and spaciousness of God's justice so that we can understand the puniness of our attempts to establish a world of equality and love. We should constantly ask for guidance from the Holy Spirit to help us love, know, and practice justice as God has loved and practiced justice throughout history.

Ruby Sales, a bold and courageous civil-rights activist for the past forty years, talks about experiencing the justice of God as an act of freedom. Sales says that God frees us from the smallness of our concept of justice learned through our social circumstances and cultural experiences. God teaches us how to rise above our own ignorance and love of judging others. We can learn to live beyond our love of titles and status, she says, our slavery to a system that may be outdated and unjust, and our willingness to be seduced by the false myths of race, culture, social status, wealth, and entitlement. As we open ourselves to God's knowledge and practice of justice, we are transformed into human beings who can practice true equality and fairness.[2]

1. Nan C. Merrill, *Psalms for Praying: An Invitation to Wholeness* (New York: Continuum, 2006), 203.
2. Ruby Sales, civil rights leader and director of Spirit House, Columbus, GA, in discussion with the author, July 2008.

recognition to God's majesty (v. 3), closing the section by declaring God's holiness.

The second section opens with a series of titles for God: "Mighty King" is the NRSV's rendering of an enigmatic Hebrew clause (other renderings: "Mightiest King" and "Might of the King"). "Lover of justice" continues the acclaim given to God (v. 4), and then the psalmist notes God has established "equity" (Hebrew *mesharim*), a term with a rich range of meanings. When the term is used to characterize God's application of justice, it carries the sense of "fairly." God's love of justice is what directs the establishment of fairness. The psalmist moves these qualities into the world of his audience by directly addressing God as the one who has done justice and righteousness "in Jacob," using the personal name to indicate the community (as in texts like Isa. 14:1). As in the first section, the recognition of the presence of God's work is cause for worship, and so the psalmist calls on the audience to "extol" the Lord, and to worship at his "footstool," a term often used to characterize the ark of the covenant (1 Chr. 28:2; Ps. 132:7). However, given the parallel call to worship at the temple in verse 8, here it is more likely a reference to the temple. The author concludes his call with the same declaration used to end the first section, bringing the audience's attention to God's holiness.

The third section offers a historical retrospective of the experiences of some of Israel's notable leaders as a way to illustrate God's past and continuing work of justice. The author's combination of "Moses and Aaron" as priests is unusual, since Moses is usually termed the "servant" of God, highlighting his prophetic role; in formal worship occasions he directs Aaron to perform the priestly rituals (such as Lev. 9:5–21). However, both Moses and Aaron were understood to have ancestry within the tribe of Levi (Exod. 2:1). Samuel, as well, was considered a priest (1 Sam. 3:1) and a prophet (1 Sam. 3:20–21), and the combination of these three seems to highlight their role as intercessors for the community ("called on his name," v. 6). The Hebrew appears to be deliberately ambiguous; as the NRSV has it, they "were among" the priests and those who called upon God. In other words, the psalmist is citing these examples from among a larger group. The verse ends by repeating their actions, and then using a redundant pronoun for emphasis: God personally "answered them." God's answer was given from a "pillar of cloud," possibly a reference to the pillar of cloud by day that led Israel out of Egypt (Exod. 13:21–22) but given the

Greg Jones of Duke Divinity School once struck up a conversation with a friend who had been visiting with a rabbi. The rabbi noted that when he asked Jews to identify the one word that came first to their mind when thinking of God, they invariably referenced the word "holy." Yet when the same question was asked of Christians, the typical reply was a mention of the word "love." Why the difference? Jones thinks it might be because Christians want an approachable God. We are interested in relationship. As an antidote to the perception that God might be too austere and too swift to judge, love suggests the possibility of a wonderfully close relationship. The problem is, we are often more interested in getting something from God than having God fill up that God-shaped hole in our hearts. One has to wonder if that tendency can allow for any meaningful relationship to develop at all.

Psalm 99 opens with enthronement language. "The LORD is king," and then . . . guess what? The people tremble. That is right. The whole earth quakes. Rudolph Otto is credited with giving us four words about God that seem to tremble and quake even as we speak them: *mysterium tremendum et fascinans*. God is *mysterium* or mystery, though less a puzzle and more a secret. The secret is so precious that it is beyond speech or hearing. God is also *fascinans*, which has to do with luring or drawing us in. God beckons us to be nearer.

Tremendum comes from a root word that gives us the idea of "tremendous." Stand at the top of any great mountain and the word "tremendous" often gets voiced. No wonder Mount Sinai, Mount Tabor, and Mount Hermon are sources of such spiritual power. *Tremendum* also suggests the word "tremble," as in the Negro spiritual: "Were you there when they crucified my Lord? Sometimes it causes me to tremble . . ." The people whom the psalmist sees trembling may be doing so not out of fear so much as out of wonder, or the wild anticipation that God will make life right with them in ways they cannot entirely fathom.

There are three directions that a preacher might pursue with this psalm for cracking open the meaning of God's holiness. All three point to different angles for defining divine holiness. First, God's holiness is anchored in justice and righteousness. In fact, these two commitments are described elsewhere in the Scriptures as the very foundation of the Lord's throne. God's credibility rests upon these two features, so crucial for human community to thrive. God executes justice because God is in love with the idea of people receiving justice. We ought to

Psalm 99

Theological Perspective

African biblical scholar Musa Dube argues that postcolonial theory encourages us to evaluate how the complex process of colonization has shaped the lives of postcolonial subjects. Distinctive native African traditions, beliefs, and practices were subordinated to Eurocentric ideas, traditions, and beliefs. By the time Africa won political independence, the leaders of African nations had already been educated, trained, and formed by colonial powers.[3]

Celebrating God's justice and equity means church and society must find more inclusive ways to consider the needs of all in the world. Letty Russell modeled better practices in theological conversations, intending to help communities discover God's justice and equity in today's context. She included voices of women from the Two-Thirds World in roundtable theological discussions and advocated for a more relational understanding of the church's mission. Space was created where everyone's voice would be heard. Mission in Christian communities is for being and doing *with* as opposed to being and doing *for* others.

Considering God's reign in terms of justice and equity has great relevance for Christian communities as they celebrate Transfiguration Sunday. Our world is still divided by patterns of individual and communal relationships formed long ago. Race, gender, and social and economic class create boundaries that are not easily overcome. In 2003, the United Nations' Human Development Report stated that "the richest 5% of the world's people receive 114 times the income of the poorest 5%. The richest 1% receive as much as the poorest 57%. And the richest 25 million Americans have as much income as almost 2 billion of the world's poorest people."[4] These statistics offer clear evidence that our world is in great need of transformation. The transfiguration story is as much about human transformation as it is about Jesus' transfiguration. In this liturgical context, Psalm 99 invites us to reflect on how God's own justice and equity challenge us to live in a new way. Congregations can be encouraged to celebrate God's transformative reign by moving the center of their concern from the local congregation itself to the congregation as it engages the world. To proclaim God's reign today means that we must reevaluate our own loyalties and practices and make decisions with the needs of all of God's people in mind.

ELIZABETH HINSON-HASTY

Pastoral Perspective

God Is a Relational God. Perhaps the most hopeful revelation in Psalm 99 is the psalmist's knowledge of God as a God in relationship with people, both as individuals and in community. The psalmist knows that Moses, Aaron, and Samuel have called on the name of the Lord and that the Lord has answered their call (v. 6). God has spoken to the community in the "pillar of cloud." He has provided guidance through the provision of "decrees" and "statutes" (v. 7).

God's relational activities include listening, answering, guiding, forgiving, and avenging wrongdoing (v. 8). Perhaps we can view the "avenging" activity of God as a means of holding us accountable for our behavior and actions. In God's just and righteous action, God helps us to be honest with ourselves and leads us into new, right living.

The powerful, living spirit of God is as available to us today as this spirit was available to the psalmist, to Moses, Aaron, Samuel, and the Hebrew people. Thomas Kelly, a Quaker missionary, educator, speaker, and writer, expresses a relationship with God in the following way:

> In this humanistic age we suppose man is the initiator and God is the responder. But the Living Christ within us is the initiator and we are the responders. God the Lover, the accuser, the revealer of light and darkness presses within us. . . . And all our apparent initiative is already a response, a testimonial to His secret presence and working within us. The basic response of the soul to the Light is internal adoration and joy, thanksgiving and worship, self-surrender and listening.[3]

KATHERINE E. AMOS

---

3. Musa Dube, "Postcoloniality, Feminist Spaces, and Religion," in *Postcolonialism, Feminism, and Religious Discourse*, ed. Laura E. Donaldson and Kwok Pui-lan (New York: Routledge, 2002), 101.

4. *Human Development Report 2003* (New York: Oxford University Press, 2003), 39.

3. Thomas R. Kelly, *A Testament of Devotion* (San Francisco: HarperSan-Francisco, 1992), 4.

Exegetical Perspective

phrasing, more likely a reference to the way God's presence was manifested as the deity spoke to Moses in the tent of meeting (Exod. 33:9–11). The psalmist is underscoring the immanence of God's response to those who called upon God. These intercessors were obedient to the legal strictures and statutes that God provided for them, perhaps implying they had called upon God for justice and God had provided the means for attaining and discerning justice.

Verse 8 once again offers a direct address to God, acknowledging that an answer was given. The psalmist goes on to declare, "You were a forgiving God," for those who called. The clause that follows is problematic: the NRSV renders it "an avenger of their wrongdoings," taking the Hebrew *noqem* as a participle from the root "avenge" (*nqm*). Others see this as the participle of the root "purify" (*nqh*) with a third person masculine plural suffix pronoun. This alternative understanding would provide a translation, "and the purifier of them from their wrongdoings."[1] Given the highly upbeat tone of the psalm as a whole, the alternative rendering is more coherent. The psalmist connects the recognition of this action of God with the need to worship, and now directly addresses the audience: "Extol" God's name (echoing vv. 3 and 5) and worship at God's "holy mountain," a frequent reference to the temple mount (for example, Isa 11:9). The reason worship is called for is also provided: because the Lord, "our God," is holy (repeating the refrain of vv. 3 and 5).

Psalm 99 provides a connection among several dominant characteristics of God: the divine rule is immanent, that is, accessible at the temple. A major concern of God's rule is justice, and justice includes in its domain such concerns as fairness and forgiveness. Finally, the appropriate human response to God's rule is worship: to "extol" God's essence (the name) and to come to the location of the divine presence and worship. All this expresses God's otherness, the divine holiness.

KENNETH G. HOGLUND

Homiletical Perspective

explore how much injustice really occurs in our communities because we do not quite love the idea of justice enough. It is a nice sounding word, but usually there are a few too many personal drawbacks or costs for us to love perfect justice too completely.

Second, we cannot speak about the holiness of God without understanding God's commitment to relationship. While the word for "holy" in Greek (*hagios*), or Latin (*sanctus*), connotes a set-apartness, the Hebrew term (*qadosh*) also suggests betrothal. God is dedicated to us as in a pledge of marriage, wanting us for God's exclusive use. Moses, Aaron, and Samuel come to life in this psalm as examples of ones in whom God is willing to invest time. God heard them praying and crying out. God answered them. It would be a good idea for us to spend more energy exploring how we can relate to God without making the awesome into something cuddly and adorable, or the divine into something cute and affable.

Third, there is a strange juxtaposition of judgment and grace in the character of God. Even though we can never fully comprehend this coexistence in the same being, it is our task to appreciate it. It is precisely what makes the Lord holy. The Lord holds us to account, and yet the Lord forgives. God takes sin just as seriously as God delivers the forgiveness of sin—but note the order of God's activity. God forgives Moses, Aaron, and Samuel. *Then* God avenges their wrongs. Forgiveness, in this psalmist's imagination, just as in the practice of Jesus' own ministry, precedes God's judgment.

No wonder we Christians keep uttering the same phrase each week: "Hallowed (or holy) be thy name." God's name reminds us of a wholeness of which we cannot get enough.

PETER W. MARTY

---

1. See the comments of Mitchell Dahood, *Psalms II: 51–100*, Anchor Bible (Garden City, NY: Doubleday & Co., 1968), 370.

2 Corinthians 3:12-4:2

[12]Since, then, we have such a hope, we act with great boldness, [13]not like Moses, who put a veil over his face to keep the people of Israel from gazing at the end of the glory that was being set aside. [14]But their minds were hardened. Indeed, to this very day, when they hear the reading of the old covenant, that same veil is still there, since only in Christ is it set aside. [15]Indeed, to this very day whenever Moses is read, a veil lies over their minds; [16]but when one turns to the Lord, the veil is removed. [17]Now the Lord is the Spirit, and where the Spirit of the Lord is, there is freedom. [18]And all of us, with unveiled faces, seeing the glory of the Lord as though reflected in a mirror, are being transformed into the same image from one degree of glory to another; for this comes from the Lord, the Spirit.

[4:1]Therefore, since it is by God's mercy that we are engaged in this ministry, we do not lose heart. [2]We have renounced the shameful things that one hides; we refuse to practice cunning or to falsify God's word; but by the open statement of the truth we commend ourselves to the conscience of everyone in the sight of God.

Theological Perspective

Despite knotty textual uncertainties, the strained midrashic interpretation of Moses's "veil" in Exodus 34:29–35, and Paul's ire over challenges to his apostolic standing, few passages in his letters contain a more vivid picture of the core of his theology. His readers are called from lives of spiritual bondage and intellectual blindness to a new freedom, hope, and boldness as a result of the transfiguring encounter with "the Spirit of the Lord" (3:17–18) that releases them from bondage and brings sight to their eyes. Hardened hearts are softened and blind eyes become sighted as the glory of God is revealed and lives are transformed (3:18) into God's image.

The preacher may probe one or more of the narrative impulses that provide the deep structures for this passage: the references to the giving of the Mosaic law; Paul's autobiographical allusions to being struck blind on the road to Damascus and the subsequent restoration of his sight as a symbol of his personal transformation; the Gospel narrative of Jesus' transfiguration on the mountain with Peter, James, and John; and, ultimately, the parallels in the passage to the listeners' experiences.

Bridging the passage to the present will not be difficult, because pastors will have experienced its themes for themselves or with parishioners. From this writer's experience, for example, I might recall a

Pastoral Perspective

On Transfiguration Sunday, the glorious mountaintop is a tempting place to set up camp. Our experience of life's ups and downs tells us that the trek back down from the mountaintop is often the hardest part. The descent is hard on the knees; we stumble on loose rock. We leave a powerful retreat weekend or return from vacation, surprised to find that reentry is a lot harder than we expected.

Paul's Second Letter to the Corinthians is a guide for the trip back down the mountain and into the foothills of daily life, but it is not without its demands. In 2 Corinthians 3:12, Paul commends this community to act with great boldness, especially in regard to speech. One obstacle to speaking boldly is the desire to avoid offending anyone. Crowds will gather around a heated debate between political candidates, and from a safe distance we like to eavesdrop on our neighbors' arguments; but what about those less dramatic conversations in which we are called to speak the truth boldly? What about the backstage moments when we find ourselves afraid to speak a gospel word boldly? While Martin Luther proclaimed, "Sin boldly," Paul declares, "Speak boldly!" (perhaps equally scandalous for us today).

As Christians in a secular age and an age of religious pluralism, how are we to act with boldness? Paul does not prescribe a certain speech to be

Exegetical Perspective

Both the weekly Bible study group and the Sunday lectors find passages like 2 Corinthians 3:12–4:2 difficult to understand. Even though translations like the NRSV have smoothed out ambiguities in the Greek, readers are dropped in the middle of a complicated, rhetorical argument. Even scholars disagree over exactly what is at stake here. Second Corinthians provides some clues. Paul faces accusations of having been less than honest and straightforward in dealing with the church. A visit sometime after writing 1 Corinthians involved the apostle's embarrassing humiliation, cancellation of a follow-up trip, and dispatch of a "letter of tears." Now Paul, the offender, and the Corinthians are becoming reconciled. Paul hopes that they will contribute generously to the collection for poor Christians in Jerusalem, which he had initiated earlier (1 Cor. 16:1–4). Paul's apostleship remains under attack by others from outside the church, who employ letters of recommendation and perhaps sophisticated preaching based on Hebrew Scripture to advance their claim of superiority to Paul (2 Cor. 3:1–6; 10:1–13:13).

Who the intruders were and even whether those mentioned in 2 Corinthians 3:1–6 are identical with the false apostles of chapters 10–13 remain debated. Some scholars even propose that the treatment of Exodus 34 in 2 Corinthians 3:7–18 is the result of

Homiletical Perspective

People hunger for authenticity from the pulpit. Part of what authenticity may mean for a preacher is a frank acknowledgment that he or she finds a passage difficult to understand, or, more problematic for proclamation, difficult to embrace or to believe.

The Problem. It is a big one for preaching in the twenty-first century. Paul frames his proclamation to the people of Corinth by comparing Moses to the Christ. From Paul's perspective this is arguing from the lesser (Moses and the Law) to the greater (the Lord and the Spirit). This is an authentic proclamation and tactic for Paul the Pharisee who became Paul the apostle of Jesus Christ. Paul, however, was in a very different situation from preachers today. This text and Paul's argument from the lesser to the greater raise the question: Is it faithful *now* for Christian preachers to make points in sermons or anywhere else by claiming the superiority of the Christian faith over and against other faith traditions—Judaism, for example?

If a preacher is hesitant to make such claims of superiority of Christianity over Judaism, then this text presents problems for interpretation. Paul is saying that Jesus is better than Moses, that the Spirit of Christ is greater than the gift of the Law. In fact, Paul takes the biblical tradition of Moses's veiled face after

2 Corinthians 3:12-4:2

Theological Perspective

very successful substance-abuse rehabilitation center in Daytona Beach, Florida. The center is named for two recovering alcoholics: Leon Stewart, an attorney; and Hal Marchman, a pastor. Released from the shackles of addiction, they teamed with others to witness boldly to the hope of freedom from addiction for others. Marchman became the Walter Rauschenbusch of the city, reaching out to substance abusers in the Hell's Kitchen of the community. Myriads of people became unchained and enabled to reclaim their lives because of his bold but loving intervention into their lives. With tough love and the message of a transfiguring gospel, Marchman became a catalyst for lights turning on, for shackles breaking, for habits overcome, and for lives converted (3:16).[1]

A concrete illustration such as the one above is important. Laity often imagine the transfiguration of Jesus as something singular (only for him) or mysterious and mystical (only for a few chosen "holy" persons on a sacred mountain far away and long ago). Paul, however, emphasizes the theophany of God to Moses—and tacitly perhaps, the transfiguration of Jesus—as a vehicle for bearing witness to life-changing experiences for any and every believer who encounters God.

Now a theological caveat must be made in keeping with the narrative before us. For, like the Jews who could not or would not see Jesus as the Christ (3:14–15), we also may be victim to our own bondage and darkness. An examination of the use of Moses's veil as a mask that hides what is glorious and good may be a fruitful move in the message at this juncture. Today's sermon can reference persons like those who had the law revealed in the theophany of Sinai but could not fathom ("see") its depth—who have access to truth but do not act upon it or incorporate it in their lives. Rather, many congregants are "blind" or obstinate of heart, having never "gotten it." Like the Corinthians (parallel references to the hearers of Isa. 6:9–10 and Rom. 12:2), they are veiled (2 Cor. 3:14) from the transforming truth by "carnal" concerns (Rom. 12:2). Illustrations of this abound. In order to concretize this point, the preacher might brainstorm with the congregation. Ask worshipers, for example, to fill in the blank: "He/she was blinded by _____." This interactive occasion can lead to a revelatory moment in the message. In all likelihood, the laity will ably fill in the blank with real-world illustrations.

Pastoral Perspective

delivered from the top step of the town hall, nor does he provide the text of a flyer we must hand out door to door. What Paul does encourage is a boldness that comes from being vulnerable. One of the boldest things we can do as believers is to be transparent with others about the faith to which we cling. For some, this transparency may involve mentioning the word "church" in a conversation with someone who is skeptical of all things religious. For others, it may mean rearranging their lives, releasing the grip on earthly illusions of security, and engaging in conversations about these choices. The bold act of being transparent is by its very nature a two-way vulnerability. The same vulnerability that prompts us to open our mouths and boldly share our stories also prompts us to open our ears. In the hearing of another—bold listening—we may be changed. Listening is a bold act, just as speaking truth is a bold act.

What would it mean for those in the pews on Sundays to speak boldly? How might preachers convey the urgency of using one's voice today? We can name the perils of our time, but when it comes right down to it, what power do most of us have in the realms of politics, social justice, even church policy? That feeling of helplessness or voicelessness comes up every election day when large numbers of people choose not to vote. Just as Paul named bold actions the Corinthians could take in response to their life-changing faith, Christians today need reminders of the agency they have in this world, speaking in a variety of ways and contexts, listening to a variety of voices. To act with boldness is to approach the Christian life with open ears and eyes. To act with boldness is to peek out from the security blankets to which we have been clinging in order to see the world as God created it.

For Paul, to act with boldness is also to remove a veil from one's face. In preaching on this text, it will be important to remember that Paul uses "veil" as a metaphor for what prevents us from seeing the full truth about God. This is a complicated metaphor. Many Muslim women choose to wear the *hijab*, or traditional Islamic headdress. Krista Tippett, host of National Public Radio's *Speaking of Faith*, writes, "Westerners have long had an impossible time seeing beyond the *hijab* to the human life behind it."[1] Paul's admonition to throw off our veils has not likely helped Western blindness to those who choose to wear veils.

1. On addictive behaviors, see Amy Frykholm, "Addictive Behavior," *Christian Century* 124 (Sept. 4, 2007): 20–22.

1. Krista Tippett, *Speaking of Faith* (New York: Viking Penguin, 2007), 145.

Exegetical Perspective

Paul's attempts to revise a homily by the opponents. However, it is more likely Paul's own theological vindication for the gospel he preaches. He not only denies the personal accusations made against him (2 Cor 2:17–3:6; 4:1–6); he insists that the opponents fail to comprehend the new covenant in Christ. Second Corinthians 3:7–11 interprets Exodus 34:29–30 as evidence that the glory accompanying the ministry of the new covenant is greater than that witnessed when the law was given to Moses. Paul appeals to the fact that the Israelites could not look on Moses's glorified face as evidence that divine glory was present at Sinai. However, he insists, in light of the new covenant, that the glory of Sinai was to fade away. The glory of the new covenant in the Spirit remains forever.

Second Corinthians 3:12–18 develops these points by contrasting the apostles' ministry with that of Moses (vv. 12–13), explaining Jewish opposition to the gospel as a continuation of the ancient "hardening" that made it impossible for the Israelites to look upon God's glory (vv. 14–16), and celebrating the vision of God's glory in Christ as a process of transformation by which the image of Christ is being realized in us (vv. 17–18). After the theological exposition, Paul returns to defending his ministry. He is not engaged in some rhetorical contest for followers that would lead him to distort the gospel or take advantage of an audience. Paul's ministry reflects the mercy he has received from God (4:1–2).

Paul employs a clipped, allusive style of argument that requires the reader to fill in missing references, based on the earlier section of the letter or a general familiarity with Paul's preaching. Although Paul often uses "the Lord" for Jesus, in a discussion based on an OT passage, "the Lord" refers to God, and "glory [or Spirit] of the Lord" refers to God's glory or Spirit rather than the risen Jesus. The expression "old covenant" (v. 14) occurs nowhere else in the NT. Paul likely created it in parallel with "new covenant" (v. 6). It refers to the Torah, not the Hebrew Scriptures as they would be in the 2nd century CE.

Paul makes two major modifications as he adapts Exodus 34. Instead of Moses "entering" the tent of meeting, Paul has him "turn to" the Lord (v. 16). Then Paul can suggest that believers have the same experience of looking upon God's glory with "unveiled face" as Moses did (v. 18a). Paul also attributes to Moses a motive that is lacking in Exodus, preventing the Israelites from viewing the "end" (Gk., *telos*) of what is perishing (v. 13b). What does Paul mean by "end"? It could refer to "end" as

Homiletical Perspective

encounters with God and offers an interpretation that is not found in the story itself, namely, the idea that Moses put the veil on his face to hide the fact that the glory would fade or be set aside. The text from Exodus 34 does not support Paul's interpretation, and, in fact, speaks of Moses veiling his face to abate the fears of the Israelites over the intensity of Moses's shining skin. Paul uses the text to make his own point about the superiority of Christ over Moses. There are many preachers today who would maintain that to make such an argument in the twenty-first century perpetuates a veil of blindness and hostility between people of different faiths. There are many interpreters of the Christian faith today who would rather lift this veil of exclusivity and separation, bringing more light into churches that exist alongside synagogue, mosque, and temple.

One option for an authentic proclamation of this text from Paul is for the preacher to bring his or her community of faith into the conflicts and issues of interfaith relations. A preacher might begin a sermon on this text by acknowledging her or his own difficulties with Paul's way of framing his proclamation to the church at Corinth. The God of the Bible can handle any such authentic wrestling with the text. Congregations can handle the honesty. And the world needs greater sensitivity and respect for all the great faith traditions by which God's people are nurtured.

Paul's Point. It is impossible to know all the problems Paul was facing in the church at Corinth. One problem, however, seems to be that Paul's authority was being questioned by the congregation because of other teachers who were proclaiming a gospel different from Paul's preaching. This text (2 Cor. 3:12–4:2) seems to indicate that one such "new" teaching was a form of Christianity based on the laws of Moses. Paul wrote to remind the church of his boldness in preaching the gospel of Christ as the one who lifts the veil of death and offers the Spirit of life and freedom. Paul wanted the Corinthian church to hold fast to the permanent glory (v. 11) and to the freedom that comes in Christ (v. 17).

Transformed. Paul admonishes the church at Corinth to take a look at their own life in Christ and to see in their own unveiled faces how they are being "transformed . . . from one degree of glory to another" (v. 18). A preacher could build a sermon around this theme of *transformation*. Paul had enough experiences in ministry with this particular

2 Corinthians 3:12-4:2

Theological Perspective

As with the Israelites in Moses's time, idolatry continues to consume people. Sensual pleasure, material lust, and absorption in nature are some of the "veils" that prevent us from hearing, seeing, and acting in gospel ways, replacing the Pauline virtues of life, love, and spiritual freedom. This is the "hardness of heart" that makes it so difficult to change our ways, right our paths, and trek the road less traveled.

Paul Tillich, in his sermon on Romans 5:20, "You Are Accepted,"[2] suggests that our personal and societal idolatries often manifest themselves in a kind of "moral reversal." Rather than seeing the state of our own sin (addictions), we project onto the external objects of our addiction. We blame the alcohol, the drugs, the temptress, the temptor, "the system," the cops, or religion. Other people—parents, spouses, friends, or children—receive the venom of our projections. Returning to the text, Paul claims that even today, in spite of everything (3:14), the blind do not see, and even though they "know," they cannot fathom they are the problem.

The good that they would do, they cannot. And, quite the reverse, they do evil against their own judgment and will (Rom. 7:14–23). For Paul, only the transformative and reconciling power of the Ground of Good from whom they are separated can change them.

During this worship service, perhaps as a climax to the sermon, a viewing of a compelling video of the song "Some People Change,"[3] performed by the duo of Eddie Montgomery and Troy Gentry, might make a powerful and transforming impact. In one verse a young man, fated to hate by the racism of his family environment, was

On the road to nowhere fast,
Till the Grace of God got in the way.

Then the man "saw the Light" and became a "brand new man" (2 Cor. 5:17).

Here is a bold enactment of the gospel of love, hope, and deliverance for Transfiguration Sunday. Bondage and blindness, coupled with self-contempt and hopelessness, are overcome by the transforming power of God.

DONALD W. MUSSER

Pastoral Perspective

A balanced perspective can include a positive view of veils and those who choose to wear them today. Today veils are often worn as marks of identity, modesty, or faithfulness. To speak out against actual veils in contemporary society can be damaging both to the Christian understanding of others' spiritual practice and identity, as well as to others' willingness to engage Christians in interfaith dialogue. While it will be important to name the positive role of veils for many, we would also do well to turn the focus back to ourselves and what hinders our full understanding of God. It is far easier to focus on a neighbor's silk head covering than it is to acknowledge our own spiritual blindness. What might veils mean to those in the local community? How can we use this metaphor in a helpful way? Drawing on Paul's metaphor, preachers may dare to look at the ways they shield themselves from the real needs of the world and the real callings of God.

Acknowledging a metaphorical veil is itself an act of boldness. We practice this in worship. Liturgical practices vary, of course, but in most Christian churches today people are invited to confess their sins before God and one another. Confessing one's sins is bold speech, and hearing sweet words of forgiveness constitutes bold listening. Preachers help to lift off whatever cloud may have settled on the text that prevents us from seeing God fully revealed. Liturgical music, dance, and other forms of art can also help us see the presence of God in our worship and in our lives.

As we acknowledge our spiritual blindness and turn toward God, Paul assures us that God is present in this very turning (2 Cor. 3:16). This turning also leads us to experience the freedom and transformation of the Christian life. The trip down from the mountaintop is not all sweat, aching muscles, and disappointment. For Paul and for Christians throughout the ages, the trip down includes clearer vision, glimpses of God's glory more fully revealed, and the freedom to speak boldly.

CALLISTA S. ISABELLE

---

2. Paul Tillich, "You Are Accepted," in *The Shaking of the Foundations* (New York: Charles Scribner's Sons, 1948), 153–63. Available online at www.religion-online.org.
3. From the audio CD *Some People Change* (Sony Records), Oct. 24, 2006.

Exegetical Perspective

termination or to "end" as goal. The NRSV "end of the glory that was being set aside" has chosen the former and specified that the "what," namely, glory, is coming to an end, from 2 Corinthians 3:7. That reading implies that Moses concealed a fading glory so that the Israelites would not recognize that the Torah was as time-bound as the laws of other nations. If one adopts the more common meaning of *telos* as goal or result, then the purpose of Moses's ministry or the temporal limits of the Torah (cf. Rom. 5:12–14) could not be perceived until they culminated in Christ.

In either reading, one should not infer that Paul attributes the deceitful behavior to Moses that Paul is being accused of (4:1–2). By introducing "hardening" into the Exodus 34 story, Paul implies that the "veiled minds" of the Israelites belong to God's plan of salvation (cf. Rom. 9–11). However, the Torah does not convey God's Spirit, freedom (cf. Gal. 4:21–31), or the transforming vision of God's glory. By contrasting the way in which Jews of his day "hear Moses read" with his own reading of Exodus 34, Paul indicates that Christians will have a very different interpretation of the Hebrew Scriptures from Jews. Some scholars think that objections raised by Jews in Corinth may have elicited this complicated description of Moses's ministry. Jews may have been arguing that God's glory on Sinai far eclipsed any revelation Christians might claim.

Paul takes the logical form "if the old covenant had glory . . . , how much more the new" to a crescendo in verses 17–18. The "we" who gaze upon God's glory are no longer only special servants of God, but all believers. Paul's terse references to the Lord and the Spirit could suggest identification of Jesus and the Spirit (cf. Rom. 8:9), but given the OT context, Paul presumably means God's Spirit (so 3:3). The image into which believers are transformed must be the risen Christ (cf. Rom. 8:29; 12:2; Gal. 4:19). Thus Paul affirms the integrity of his apostolic ministry within a theological vision that invites us to reflect on both the relationship between the church and Israel and the goal of all religious practice, transformation into the image of God.

PHEME PERKINS

Homiletical Perspective

church and others to know that no one falls head first into the pool of God's transforming love and emerges fully formed as a perfect reflection of Christ. The work of God's justifying and redemptive Spirit moves in human lives *from one degree of glory to another.*

This is wonderfully good news! No one sails through life without setbacks, without rough seas, without hardships and doubts. Paul is a prime example of this obvious truth. Yet for the follower of Christ, the setbacks or hardships are not the defining events of life. For the followers of Christ, the defining event is the freedom offered through the life, death, and resurrection of Jesus Christ. The true identity of the Christian is found in the love of God that has been written upon hearts. No outward circumstances or worldly appearances can change the inward and spiritual reality of God's justifying and redemptive grace. The work of the Christian believer, then, is to allow the love of Christ and the freedom of the Spirit to be manifest in daily living. The work of the Christian believer, with Paul, is not to lose heart but to continue to act—no matter what the circumstances of life—with boldness in the direction of God's redeeming work of love and mercy.

There is a beautiful statue on the campus of Tuskegee University in Tuskegee, Alabama, entitled *Lifting the Veil of Ignorance.* The statue is of Booker T. Washington, who founded Tuskegee University in 1881, standing over a slave and lifting a veil so that the light of education can strike his face. The slave, crouched down, has a book in one hand and is using the other hand to help lift the veil. His feet are poised to stand and move forward. The slave is looking out into the world with wide-eyed hope. The caption under the statue reads: "He lifted the veil of ignorance from his people and pointed the way to progress through education and industry."

In Christ the veil of ignorance and death is being lifted so that humanity might live in the truth of God's redeeming love and in the work of God's transforming Spirit.

ROBERT WARDEN PRIM

Luke 9:28-36 (37-43)

[28]Now about eight days after these sayings Jesus took with him Peter and John and James, and went up on the mountain to pray. [29]And while he was praying, the appearance of his face changed, and his clothes became dazzling white. [30]Suddenly they saw two men, Moses and Elijah, talking to him. [31]They appeared in glory and were speaking of his departure, which he was about to accomplish at Jerusalem. [32]Now Peter and his companions were weighed down with sleep; but since they had stayed awake, they saw his glory and the two men who stood with him. [33]Just as they were leaving him, Peter said to Jesus, "Master, it is good for us to be here; let us make three dwellings, one for you, one for Moses, and one for Elijah"—not knowing what he said. [34]While he was saying this, a cloud came and overshadowed them; and they were terrified as they entered the cloud. [35]Then from the cloud came a voice that said, "This is

Theological Perspective

Sifting through the various scholarly and theological views of the transfiguration of Jesus can be a daunting task. Is it a misplaced resurrection narrative, as some say? Is it a tale arising from the Hellenistic mystery tradition, as others claim? Perhaps, as Donald Luther thinks, no words or phrases—epiphany, theophany, christophany, or even revelation of the Divine—are adequate to the task of describing what happened on that mountaintop.[1] He prefers, rather, the idea that the narrative in Luke's Gospel conveys to contemporary readers—just as the original experience conveyed to Peter, James, and John—a great sense of mystery. And mystery is alluring; it draws us in at that same time that it always just eludes our full comprehension. The transfiguration of Jesus *is* such a story, but one that has much to say, nevertheless, about the divinity and glory of Jesus, his (pending) death and resurrection, his relationship with the law and prophets of Israel, as well as the way in which contemporary readers of this text are to live their lives, here and now, transfigured.

The text in Luke says that Jesus took three of his disciples to a mountaintop to pray. "While he was praying, the appearance of his face changed, and his

1. Donald Luther, "The Mystery of the Transfiguration: Luke 9:28–36 (37–43)," *Word and World* 21, no. 1 (Winter 2001): 92.

Pastoral Perspective

What does the transfiguration event mean to those who seek to embody glimpses of the kingdom of God in congregations? How is this transfiguration relevant to church leaders' efforts to discern and participate in the mission of God? What does this passage mean as we cooperate with God's will of love and freedom, peace and justice, wholeness and fullness of life for all? Following Jesus, I believe that we must be clear about our identity, resolute in our mission, and intentional in our spiritual formation.

The transfiguration bears witness to the identity of Jesus Christ. By God's action in the transformation itself and in the words of the voice from heaven, a theological statement is made. Jesus Christ is declared to be the Chosen Son of God. The disciples heard the declaration: "Listen to him!" The Christ event—his incarnation, passion, death, resurrection, ascension, gift of the Holy Spirit, and promised second coming—is the defining script for our local performances of the gospel.

Following Jesus, congregations must be clear about their christological identity. Congregations fashion distinctive identities and cultures that are a blend of ingredients from broader religious traditions of which they are a part and local traditions shaped by communal secular forces. Though we are undeniably shaped by social, cultural,

my Son, my Chosen; listen to him!" ³⁶When the voice had spoken, Jesus was found alone. And they kept silent and in those days told no one any of the things they had seen.

³⁷On the next day, when they had come down from the mountain, a great crowd met him. ³⁸Just then a man from the crowd shouted, "Teacher, I beg you to look at my son; he is my only child. ³⁹Suddenly a spirit seizes him, and all at once he shrieks. It convulses him until he foams at the mouth; it mauls him and will scarcely leave him. ⁴⁰I begged your disciples to cast it out, but they could not." ⁴¹Jesus answered, "You faithless and perverse generation, how much longer must I be with you and bear with you? Bring your son here." ⁴²While he was coming, the demon dashed him to the ground in convulsions. But Jesus rebuked the unclean spirit, healed the boy, and gave him back to his father. ⁴³And all were astounded at the greatness of God.

Exegetical Perspective

A Glimpse of Glory. The principal reading for today (vv. 28–36) is Luke's account of Jesus' transfiguration, for which this Sunday in the church year is named. It occurs in the Gospel as a moment when Jesus' identity is revealed to the inner circle of Jesus' disciples (Peter, John, and James). Luke's community realized that the resurrection of all the dead, a harvest of which Jesus' resurrection was seen as the firstfruits, was not going to come as speedily as his followers had once thought and hoped. They were struggling to come to terms with the church as an institution with a future as well as a past, and to find effective ways to put into words their enduring faith. The account of Jesus' transfiguration is the climax of a section of the Gospel dealing with Jesus' identity (9:7–50). The optional reading (vv. 37–43a) takes us from the glimpse of Jesus' glory to some hard words about Jesus' continuing ministry, and especially about implications for the work of his followers. This section is followed by Luke's long journey narrative (9:51–19:28), which begins when Jesus has "set his face to go to Jerusalem" (9:51) and ends at the gates of the city (19:28).

God's voice pronounces the definitive word about Jesus' identity in the account of the transfiguration: "This is my Son, my Chosen" (v. 35). This word interprets the visual splendor of Jesus' appearance,

Homiletical Perspective

One common homiletical approach to the transfiguration focuses Peter's awkward response to the vision of glory and our similar desire to capture the holy. Although this a time-honored way of preaching the text, Luke's account of the transfiguration teases the preacher with many more thematic possibilities. Glory and light, clouds and voices, sleepy disciples and their proposed construction projects, and appearances of ancient prophets—any one of these images could fund a single sermon. Here we will concentrate on three possible themes: the vision of glory, the meaning of Jesus' "exodus" (v. 31), and listening to the Son.

The Vision of Glory. Raphael's exquisite painting *The Transfiguration* presents a chaotic scene at the bottom of the canvas. Stuck at the foot of the mountain, the disciples cannot cure the sick boy. Frustration is palpable in the outstretched arms and panicked faces of the crowd. In their midst, however, two figures point in the direction of the mountain, toward the sky, in which the transfigured Jesus shines, arrayed in white. This is the Jesus who will come down the mountain, bringing life and healing to the boy.

A sermon that focuses on the vision of Jesus will try to do what those two figures do: point to the one in whom there is healing, resurrecting, and

Luke 9:28-36 (37-43)

Theological Perspective

clothes became dazzling white" (v. 29). The glory of Jesus shines through this story, illuminating and highlighting his divine nature. It is one of the points of the story, though certainly not the only point of the story. Yet Peter, James, and John almost missed it—the dazzling white as well as the point. They had already failed to take seriously (or at least understand) Jesus' proclamation that he would suffer, be rejected, be killed, and be raised on the third day (v. 22), and they were sleepy on the mountain (perhaps prefiguring Gethsemane).

As Jesus was transformed, he was joined by Moses and Elijah, also in great splendor. They talked with him; specifically, they spoke of the coming death of Jesus in Jerusalem. The heavy-lidded Peter, John, and James (again) failed to grasp the meaning of the conversation, with its veiled terms of departure and fulfillment. (Still, while the transfiguration texts in Matthew and Mark foreshadow the death of Christ, the text in Luke is downright explicit about it.) Peter, James, and John failed to see the presence of Moses and Elijah and their conversation with Jesus as evidence that the Christ had come in fulfillment of Israel's laws and prophecies. But that was what it was; it was and is one of the main points of the story.

When the three disciples finally and fully awoke, they were amazed at the sight before them. Peter, scrambling to his feet (as it were), offered to build booths in the tradition of the Jewish feast of Tabernacles for each of them. It reads now as a comical moment, heightened only by the quick rebuke that comes from the clouds: "This is my Son, whom I have chosen; listen to him" (v. 35 NIV). All that is missing is the cosmic hand, reaching down to give Peter a good "you-are-missing-the-point" slap upside the head. When the cloud lifts, Moses and Elijah are gone, Jesus stands alone, and the writer of the Gospel—in a clear, but understated way—reasserts Jesus as the one who has come to fulfill the law.

The transfiguration of Jesus offers a glimpse of what is possible, not only for Jesus, but for all humanity. For this reason, the last verse in this narrative is somewhat disappointing, or maybe just puzzling. The reader might presume, or at least hope, the disciples finally comprehended the import of the transfiguration; but whatever they understood, they did not act on it. They kept to themselves and told no one (v. 36). So the significance of Jesus' very public healing of the boy with an unclean spirit in the verses just after Luke's transfiguration narrative is heightened.

The lectionary includes verses 37–43 only parenthetically, but these verses are critical to unpacking

Pastoral Perspective

and economic pressures, we are to "listen to him!" We are called to be faithful to the unique revelation of Jesus Christ. A theological statement is made about our identity as we embody our theological understanding of Christ in all of our congregational practices.

The transfiguration bears witness to the redemptive mission of Jesus Christ. In the face of suffering, rejection, and death, Jesus is resolute in fulfilling his redemptive mission. He is prayerful and bold as he moves toward his destiny in Jerusalem. As Jesus converses with Moses and Elijah, our redemptive mission is seen in continuity with the Christian church's Hebrew past as well as with the promised future of all of creation. Moses is a figure that reminds us of the past: the exodus event and the communal responsibility to teach the statutes and ordinances given to Moses at Horeb (Mal. 4:4). Horeb is also known as Mount Sinai, where God appeared to both Moses and Elijah (1 Kgs. 19:8–18). Elijah is the prophet who will one day turn people's hearts back to the covenant (Mal. 4:5–6). Thus, in Jewish thought Elijah is associated with the end times. Both of these revered leaders talk with Jesus about his "departure, which he was about to accomplish at Jerusalem" (v. 31). So we might say that in the transfiguration event Jesus is clear about his mission, which continues the redemptive work of God from the exodus through the end times.

Following Jesus, congregations must be resolute in bearing witness to the redemptive mission of Jesus Christ. Jesus takes Peter, James, and John to pray with him on the mountain. Later, these disciples would find it hard to stay awake in prayer; but throughout his ministry Jesus was faithful in spiritual disciplines that would bring him into the presence of his Father. We must likewise be people of prayer and resolute in our mission. Carlos F. Cardoza-Orlandi, a professor of world Christianity and ordained minister of the Christian Church (Disciples of Christ), says that "the church needs to develop a spirituality of mission learning to discern, discover, participate, be patient, and be dependent on God's grace."[1] As we exercise spiritual discernment and social analysis of our present situations, our theology of mission must be informed by our historic traditions. It must also be informed by visions of the future reign of God. The transfiguration might be framed in context as a case of the disciple's spiritual formation in process. Jesus'

---

1. Carlos Cardoza-Orlandi, *Mission: An Essential Guide* (Nashville: Abingdon Press, 2002), 44.

which was transformed from that of an ordinary person into angelic glory. If the sound and lights were not enough to underline the importance of this story, Luke also gives us other clues to the seriousness with which it should be taken. First, the witnesses are the same three disciples who accompanied Jesus to Jairus's home when Jesus restored Jairus's daughter to life (8:51). The note that the transfiguration took place about a week after the account of Peter's confession of Jesus as "the Messiah of God" (9:20) links the two episodes, but the focus on the three witnesses instead of all of the disciples again underlines the greater importance of this one. Second, the transfiguration is set on a mountain, which is a traditional site for encounters with God (v. 28). Finally, Jesus has gone there to pray, as he often is said to do at key moments in Luke's Gospel.

The account of the transfiguration is often interpreted as a story of an appearance by the resurrected Jesus that has been read back into his earthly ministry, but that interpretation seems unwarranted. In this account, Jesus and the disciples go up the mountain together, while in the appearance narratives Jesus suddenly appears or is revealed to the others who have gathered without him. Furthermore, the resurrection accounts include a commission to the disciples (e.g., 24:46–48), and not words from heaven about Jesus. Finally, the change in Jesus' appearance in this account is only temporary; once back at the base of the mountain, he returns to his usual self.

The story of Jesus' baptism (3:21–22) also tells of a heavenly voice that declares Jesus' identity. There the voice is addressed to Jesus ("You are my Son") as a call into his ministry. Here the voice speaks about Jesus to those who will have to carry on his ministry. They are told to listen to him while they can. It is an ominous conclusion to the Galilean ministry!

Numerous details in this account evoke memories of Israel's founding stories, which anchor and interpret Jesus' transfiguration. Jesus' face and clothes become dazzling, like the face of Moses on Sinai (Exod. 34:29–35). The two figures who "appear in glory" with Jesus are Moses and Elijah—figures in Israel's past, in whose likeness the prophet of the end time was expected to come. In the summary of Jesus' conversation with the heavenly visitors, the word translated as "departure" is *exodos*. It is usually interpreted in this passage to refer to Jesus' death—or perhaps to the complete event of death, resurrection, and ascension in which he "departs" to heaven—that will take place in Jerusalem. While

sustaining power. For the author of Luke's Gospel, Jesus is the savior not only of this young boy, but of the whole world. Yet it is often tempting to imagine that our world is beyond saving. Disaster persists. Brokenness, sin, and injustice threaten human life. Hope wanes even among faithful people. We need sermons that point to the God who is at work transfiguring the creation now marked by suffering and death. Shown in glory with Moses and Elijah, two great figures of Israel's past, Jesus is revealed as the culmination of the story of a God who comes, again and again, to rescue God's people. Preachers might explicitly name ways in which the transfigured Jesus becomes present to a community not fully awake to the promises of God. Through the gifts of worship and sacraments, prayer and fellowship, service and work for justice and peace, the cloud of Jesus' glory envelops weary disciples. Look, the preacher proclaims: *here* shines the one in whom there is power to overcome death. Good news!

The Meaning of Jesus' Exodus. A second theme closely related to the transfigured glory of Jesus is the "exodus" that he is to "accomplish" (v. 31). Only Luke reports this particular detail of Jesus' conversation with Moses and Elijah, which would make it an interesting preaching topic for transfiguration in this Year C. A preacher, however, would have to be creative in introducing the theme to the congregation, because the NIV and NRSV translate "departure" for "exodus," and because the Old Testament resonance of the term might not be immediately accessible to many churchgoers. Still, it would be worth the effort, for Jesus' conversation points to this reality: though we see him now in glory, we will soon see him on the cross.

How could a preacher develop the idea of Jesus' exodus into a sermon? One way would be to recall the meaning of the Israelite exodus and compare and contrast the meaning of the cross. For the Jews, the exodus from Egypt is the supreme story of salvation, the rescue of God's chosen people "with a strong hand and an outstretched arm" (Ps. 136:12). In the first exodus, all the people of Israel were to remain awake and alert, and all the people made the passage through the Red Sea into freedom. Similarly, the cross is, for Christians, God's supreme act of salvation. The same God who once brought Israel through the Red Sea now brings those who have faith out of slavery to sin and death and into the freedom of resurrection life. This time, the mighty hand and outstretched arm that accomplishes this

Luke 9:28-36 (37-43)

Theological Perspective

the transfiguration story. Heidi Neumark uses these verses as she tells a powerful story of transfiguration. In her memoir *Breathing Space: A Spiritual Journey in the South Bronx* she details the transformation of the church she served for almost twenty years. Aptly named Transfiguration Lutheran Church, the community was struggling, barely surviving, when she arrived. Standing amid poverty and the myriad problems that can accompany such a demon—crime, drug abuse, lack of education and opportunity, lack of hope—Transfiguration mostly kept its doors shut tight to the world around it.

The work of Jesus rebuking the unclean spirit was example enough for Neumark. "When Peter and the others came down from the mountain," she writes, "they found a father and a child gasping for life. But Jesus rebuked the unclean spirit, healed the boy, and gave him back to his father. And they found transfiguration. And so it is. When the disciples of this Bronx church unlocked the doors of their private shelter and stepped out into the neighborhood, they did meet the distress of the community convulsed and mauled by poverty. . . . But they also discovered transfiguration as a congregation in connection with others."[2]

The story of the transfiguration of Jesus loses its power if it does not include that moment when Jesus and the disciples come down from the mountain. The transfigured Jesus is changed, not in essence, but in the way he is seen; he acts in and for the world accordingly. Seeing Jesus differently means seeing oneself and others differently too. The congregation at Transfiguration Church understood: "But living high up in the rarefied air isn't the point of transfiguration. . . . [It was] never meant as a private experience of spirituality removed from the public square. It was a vision to carry us down, a glimpse of unimagined possibility at ground level."[3]

LORI BRANDT HALE

Pastoral Perspective

identity has been revealed and even proclaimed by Peter (vv. 18–27), but it is clear that even those disciples in his inner circle had important gaps in their "Christian religious education." Professing faith in Christ is one thing, but living our Christian faith requires greater depth and breadth in our spiritual formation. Thomas Groome, a Christian religious educator in the Roman Catholic tradition, reminds us that "lived Christian faith" involves believing, trusting, and doing God's will.[2] There is a mental dimension of Christian faith that undergirds belief. There is a relational dimension of Christian faith that forms us to have a trusting relationship with Jesus Christ, nurturing relationships in a Christian faith community, and relationships of kindness and justice toward the whole human family. There is also a behavioral dimension to Christian faith, an activity of doing God's will in the world.[3]

Though the disciples saw the transfiguration, their translation of this experience provided less than satisfactory results. They failed miserably in their efforts to bring healing and wholeness to a child. They could not bring reconciliation and peace between an anguished father and his only son (vv. 37–43). Did they simply fail to grasp who Jesus is? Did they lack requisite trust in the power of God? Was their difficulty one of embodying the gospel of word, deed, and sign? We could despair at the disciples' lack of "success," even as we feel pressured by cultural measures of success such as membership size, church budget, breadth of programs, expansiveness of church property, as well as by the church's status and influence in the public arena. Instead, we can be encouraged by the disciples' faithfulness to be present with Jesus. While being formed in the presence of Christ at the glorious transfiguration event and thereafter, they became one with him and his mission in the world. We should go and do likewise.

JEFFERY L. TRIBBLE SR.

---

2. Heidi Neumark, *Breathing Space: A Spiritual Journey in the South Bronx* (Boston: Beacon Press, 2003), 269.
3. Ibid., 268.

2. Thomas H. Groome, *Sharing Faith: A Comprehensive Approach to Religious Education and Pastoral Ministry, the Way of Shared Praxis* (New York: HarperCollins Publishers, 1991), 18.
3. Ibid., 18–21.

such interpretations are possible, in the accounts of Israel's history the *exodos* marked the beginning of the long journey into the promised land, and this episode comes at the outset of Jesus' long journey that will be "accomplished" only in Jerusalem. Peter's plan to build three "dwellings" for Jesus, Moses, and Elijah also evokes Israel's wanderings, for the Greek word translated as "dwellings" is used for the "booths" symbolizing the feast of Tabernacles (Lev. 23:33–43) that by the first century CE was a pilgrimage festival celebrating Israel's journey to freedom. On another level, Peter's plan to build booths expresses the human longing both to honor those persons who are important to us and to preserve in some way our glimpses of divine transcendence. The mystery of this experience is highlighted by the overshadowing cloud, by the disciples' terror (vv. 34–35), and by the awed silence in which they kept their memories (v. 36).

Glory Meets Suffering. In the optional verses for the day (vv. 37–43), the four leave the mountaintop for everyday reality. The time reference ("on the next day") tightly links the two accounts: The glory of God's presence and the pain of a broken world cannot be separated. The detailed description of the man's son underlines his suffering, and the stark statement of the disciples' failure to help (despite the statement in 9:1 that they had been given power to do so) evokes what in Luke is a rare outburst of frustration and anger from Jesus (v. 41). When Jesus accomplishes what the disciples have been unable to do, the obedience of the "demon" said to have caused the boy's suffering echoes from below the endorsement of Jesus by the voice from the cloud.

The crowd was described as "astounded at the greatness of God" (v. 43a). Luke would say that they got it right. Just as God was at work in leading Israel through the wilderness after the *exodos*, God is present in and working through Jesus—Chosen and Anointed (Messiah)—to whom we must listen.

SHARON H. RINGE

salvation is, paradoxically, wounded and stretched out in suffering. This time, one person, Jesus Christ, will make the journey on behalf of all. How can we, like the disciples who managed to stay awake despite being "weighed down with sleep" (v. 32), remain alert to this particular glory? How can we remain confident that God is at work accomplishing an "exodus" on our behalf?

A second and very different way to develop the exodus theme would be to draw out for the congregation the paradox between glory and crucifixion, and to preach a sermon contrasting the world's approach to glory and that of God. God's glory is peculiar because it deliberately undergoes suffering and death—something the world does not easily understand or accept. Do we dare preach that the *true* God, in whom the power of life and death resides, actually chooses the way of the cross? Can we confidently and boldly proclaim that this alone is good news?

Listening to the Son. Finally, a preacher might concentrate on the voice that comes from the cloud: "This is my Son, my Chosen; listen to him!" This voice was heard at Jesus' baptism, and it resonates again in the desperate plea of the father in verse 38, "Teacher, I beg you to look at my son, he is my only child." These exhortations beg for hortatory sermons that plead for the congregation to listen to God's voice.

What does it mean to listen to the Son? In my congregation, the weeks before one Transfiguration Sunday brought the deaths of beloved members. Numb with grief, the congregation needed to hear Jesus' words of healing and mercy. Other communities may need to hear the words of challenge and judgment. For Luke, the voice of the chosen Son stands our dominant values on their heads. What voices do we need to block out if we are to listen to the Son? To what voices should we listen instead? What about the voices of those in trouble or distress, voices that challenge the status quo of comfort and familiarity? If we listen to those voices, what grace might we encounter that we cannot now imagine?

KIMBERLY MILLER VAN DRIEL

Contributors

Paul J. Achtemeier, Jackson Professor of Biblical Interpretation Emeritus, Union Theological Seminary, Richmond, Virginia

Katherine E. Amos, Resident Professor of Spirituality and the Arts, Wake Forest University Divinity School, Winston-Salem, North Carolina

Dale P. Andrews, Professor of Homiletics and Pastoral Theology, Boston University School of Theology, Boston, Massachusetts

Harold W. Attridge, Dean and Lillian Claus Professor of New Testament, Yale Divinity School, New Haven, Connecticut

Wesley D. Avram, Pastor, Bryn Mawr Presbyterian Church, Bryn Mawr, Pennsylvania

Jennifer Ryan Ayres, Assistant Professor of Christian Ethics, McCormick Theological Seminary, Chicago, Illinois

Samuel E. Balentine, Professor of Old Testament, Union Theological Seminary–Presbyterian School of Christian Education, Richmond, Virginia

Lee C. Barrett, Mary B. and Henry P. Stager Professor of Theology, Lancaster Theological Seminary, Lancaster, Pennsylvania

David L. Bartlett, Professor of New Testament, Columbia Theological Seminary, Decatur, Georgia

Angela Bauer-Levesque, Associate Professor of Hebrew Bible, Episcopal Divinity School, Cambridge, Massachusetts

Stephen Bauman, Senior Minister, Christ Church, New York, New York

Kathy Beach-Verhey, Co-Pastor, Faison Presbyterian Church, Faison, North Carolina

Michael S. Bennett, Senior Pastor, First Church of Christ UCC, Longmeadow, Massachusetts

April Berends, Rector, St. Mark's Episcopal Church, Milwaukee, Wisconsin

Deborah A. Block, Pastor, Immanuel Presbyterian Church, Milwaukee, Wisconsin

Stephen B. Boyd, Chair and Professor of Religion, Wake Forest University, Winston-Salem, North Carolina

Robin Gallaher Branch, Associate Professor of Biblical Studies, Crichton College, Memphis, Tennessee

Robert M. Brearley, Pastor, St. Simons Presbyterian Church, St. Simons Island, Georgia

Linda McKinnish Bridges, Associate Dean of the College and Adjunct Professor of Religion, Wake Forest University, Winston-Salem, North Carolina

William P. Brown, Professor of Old Testament, Columbia Theological Seminary, Decatur, Georgia

Charles Bugg, Professor of Church Ministry and Leadership, M. Christopher White School of Divinity, Gardner-Webb University, Boiling Springs, North Carolina

Drew Bunting, Associate Rector, St. Columba's Episcopal Church, Washington, D.C.

Gay L. Byron, Professor of New Testament and Christian Origins, Colgate Rochester Crozer Divinity School, Rochester, New York

Charles L. Campbell, Professor of Homiletics, Duke Divinity School, Durham, North Carolina

Philip E. Campbell, Director of Ministry Studies, Iliff School of Theology, Denver, Colorado

Nick Carter, President, Andover Newton Theological School, Newton Centre, Massachusetts

Gary W. Charles, Pastor, Central Presbyterian Church, Atlanta, Georgia

W. Michael Chittum, Pastor, First Congregational Church, Salt Lake City, Utah

John W. Coakley, Professor of Church History, New Brunswick Theological Seminary, New Brunswick, New Jersey

Stephen L. Cook, Catherine N. McBurney Professor of Old Testament, Virginia Theological Seminary, Alexandria, Virginia

Stephen A. Cooper, Associate Professor of Religious Studies, Franklin and Marshall College, Lancaster, Pennsylvania

Vaughn Crowe-Tipton, University Chaplain and Associate Professor of Religion, Furman University, Greenville, South Carolina

Thomas W. Currie, Dean, Union Theological Seminary–Presbyterian School of Christian Education at Charlotte, North Carolina

William J. Danaher Jr., Dean of Theology, Huron University College, the University of Western Ontario, London, Ontario, Canada

James Calvin Davis, Associate Professor of Hebrew Bible and Homiletics, Memphis Theological Seminary, Memphis, Tennessee

Valerie Bridgeman Davis, Associate Professor, Memphis Theological Seminary, Memphis, Tennessee

Steven P. Eason, Senior Pastor, Myers Park Presbyterian Church, Charlotte, North Carolina

Peter Eaton, Dean, St. John's Cathedral, Denver, Colorado

James H. Evans Jr., Robert K. Davies Professor of Systematic Theology, Colgate Rochester Crozer Divinity School, Rochester, New York

Kyle Fedler, Chair of Religion Department, Ashland University, Ashland, Ohio

Lewis F. Galloway, Senior Pastor, Second Presbyterian Church, Indianapolis, Indiana

Roger J. Gench, Senior Pastor, New York Avenue Presbyterian Church, Washington, D.C.

Howard K. Gregory, Suffragan Bishop of Montego Bay, Jamaica, West Indies

Jack Haberer, Editor, *Presbyterian Outlook*, Richmond, Virginia

Lori Brandt Hale, Associate Professor and Director of General Education, Augsburg College, Minneapolis, Minnesota

Walter J. Harrelson, Professor Emeritus, Vanderbilt Divinity School, and Adjunct University Professor, Wake Forest University Divinity School, Winston-Salem, North Carolina

Susan K. Hedahl, Professor of Homiletics, Lutheran Theological Seminary at Gettysburg, Gettysburg, Pennsylvania

Carol Lakey Hess, Associate Professor of Religious Education, Candler School of Theology, Atlanta, Georgia

Ernest Hess, Senior Pastor, Covenant Presbyterian Church, Atlanta, Georgia

Allen Hilton, Minister of Faith and Learning, Wayzata Community Church, United Church of Christ, Wayzata, Minnesota

Elizabeth Hinson-Hasty, Associate Professor of Theology, Bellarmine University, Louisville, Kentucky

Kenneth G. Hoglund, Professor of Religion, Wake Forest University, Winston-Salem, North Carolina

Fred L. Horton, J. T. Albritton Professor of Religion, Wake Forest University, Winston-Salem, North Carolina

Kendra G. Hotz, Assistant Professor of Religious Studies, Rhodes College, Memphis, Tennessee

James C. Howell, Pastor, Myers Park United Methodist Church, Charlotte, North Carolina

Christopher R. Hutson, Associate Professor of New Testament, Hood Theological Seminary, Salisbury, North Carolina

Susan E. Hylen, Mellon Assistant Professor of New Testament, Vanderbilt University, Nashville, Tennessee

Jerry Irish, McLean Professor of Religion and Religious Studies, Pomona College, Claremont, California

Callista S. Isabelle, Associate University Chaplain, Yale University, New Haven, Connecticut

Joseph R. Jeter, Walker Professor of Homiletics, Brite Divinity School, Texas Christian University, Fort Worth, Texas

Alan Johnson, Ordained Clergy, United Church of Christ, Boulder, Colorado

Jeffrey D. Jones, Pastor, First Baptist Church, Plymouth, Massachusetts

Mariam J. Kamell, University of St. Andrews, St. Andrews, Fife, United Kingdom

Veli-Matti Kärkkäinen, Professor of Systematic Theology, School of Theology, Fuller Theological Seminary, Pasadena, California

Maria LaSala, Co-Pastor, First Presbyterian Church, New Haven, Connecticut

Robert M. Leach, Pastor, Ogden Dunes Community Church, Ogden Dunes, Indiana

W. Carter Lester, Co-Pastor, First Presbyterian Church, Pottstown, Pennsylvania

B. Diane Lipsett, Assistant Professor of New Testament and Christian Origins, Wake Forest University Divinity School, Winston-Salem, North Carolina

Larry L. Lyke, Religion Department, Mount Holyoke College, South Hadley, Massachusetts

Stephens G. Lytch, Pastor, Philadelphia, Pennsylvania

Wallace Eugene March, A. B. Rhodes Professor Emeritus of Old Testament, Louisville Presbyterian Seminary, Louisville, Kentucky

George H. Martin, Retired Episcopal Pastor, Rosemount, Minnesota

Peter W. Marty, Senior Pastor, St. Paul Lutheran Church, and Host, *Grace Matters* Radio, Davenport, Iowa

J. Clinton McCann Jr., Evangelical Professor of Biblical Interpretation, Eden Theological Seminary, Webster Groves, Missouri

Kathleen McManus, Associate Professor of Theology, University of Portland, Portland, Oregon

Charles M. Mendenhall, Executive Director, Care and Counseling Center of Georgia, Decatur, Georgia

Calvin Miller, Writer in Residence, Research Professor, Beeson Divinity School, Samford University, Birmingham, Alabama

Troy Miller, Associate Professor of Bible and Theology, Crichton College, Memphis, Tennessee

Randle R. Mixon, Pastor, First Baptist Church, Palo Alto, California

Seth Moland-Kovash, Pastor, All Saints Lutheran Church, Palatine, Illinois

Shawnthea Monroe, Senior Minister, Plymouth Church of Shaker Heights, United Church of Christ, Shaker Heights, Ohio

D. Cameron Murchison, Dean of Faculty, Executive Vice President, and Professor of Ministry, Columbia Theological Seminary, Decatur, Georgia

Donald W. Musser, Senior Professor, Stetson University, DeLand, Florida

Andrew Nagy-Benson, Senior Minister, Spring Glen United Church of Christ, Hamden, Connecticut

Rick Nutt, Professor of Religion, Muskingum College, New Concord, Ohio

Kathleen M. O'Connor, William Marcellus McPheeters Professor of Old Testament, Columbia Theological Seminary, Decatur, Georgia

David L. Ostendorf, Executive Director, Center for New Community, Ellsworth, Wisconsin

Pheme Perkins, Professor of New Testament, Boston College, Chestnut Hill, Massachusetts

Karen Pidcock-Lester, Co-Pastor, First Presbyterian Church, Pottstown, Pennsylvania

Robert Warden Prim, Pastor, Nacoochee Presbyterian Church, Sautee-Nacoochee, Georgia

Rollin A. Ramsaran, Professor of New Testament, Emmanuel School of Religion, Johnson City, Tennessee

Stephen G. Ray Jr., Neal F. and Ila A. Fisher Professor of Theology, Garrett-Evangelical Theological Seminary, Evanston, Illinois

Robert Redman, Dean and Associate Professor of Theology and Ministry, Multnomah University, Portland, Oregon

Sharon H. Ringe, Professor of New Testament, Wesley Theological Seminary, Washington, D.C.

Rosetta E. Ross, Associate Professor of Religion, Spelman College, Atlanta, Georgia

Kenneth L. Sehested, Pastor, Circle of Mercy Congregation, Asheville, North Carolina

Archie Smith Jr., James and Clarice Foster Professor of Pastoral Psychology and Counseling, Pacific School of Religion, Berkeley, California

Thomas R. Steagald, Pastor, First United Methodist Church, Stanley, North Carolina

Karen Stokes, Pastor, Montclair Presbyterian Church, Oakland, California

Frederick J. Streets, Professor of Pastoral Counseling, Wurzweiler School of Social Work, Yeshiva University, New York, New York

Barbara Brown Taylor, Harry R. Butman Professor of Religion, Piedmont College, Demorest, Georgia

Nancy S. Taylor, Senior Minister, Old South Church, Boston, Massachusetts

Jeffery L. Tribble Sr., Assistant Professor of Ministry, Columbia Theological Seminary, Decatur, Georgia

Gene M. Tucker, Professor Emeritus of Old Testament, Emory University, Candler School of Theology, Atlanta, Georgia

Kimberly Miller van Driel, Pastor, Immanuel Evangelical Lutheran Church, Naugatuck, Connecticut

Neal Walls, Associate Professor of Old Testament Interpretation, Wake Forest University Divinity School, Winston-Salem, North Carolina

Raewynne J. Whiteley, St. James Episcopal Church, St. James, New York

Dena L. Williams, Senior Pastor, King of Glory Lutheran Church, Arvada, Colorado

Charles M. Wood, Lehman Professor of Christian Doctrine; Director, Graduate Program in Religious Studies, Perkins School of Theology, Southern Methodist University, Dallas, Texas

Rebecca Blair Young, Professor of Systematic Theology, Jakarta Theological Seminary, Jakarta, Indonesia

Scripture Index

Author Index

Numerals indicate numbered Sundays of a season; for example, "Advent 1" represents the first Sunday of Advent, and "Christmas 1" the first Sunday after Christmas.

Donald W. Musser	Transfiguration E TP	Karen Stokes	Epiphany 1 NT PP, Epiphany 2 E PP, Epiphany 3 E PP
Andrew Nagy-Benson	Epiphany 7 PS PP, Epiphany 8 PS PP, Epiphany 9 PS PP	Frederick J. Streets	Epiphany 1 PS PP, Epiphany 2 PS PP, Epiphany 3 PS PP
Rick Nutt	Epiphany 1 OT TP, Epiphany 2 OT TP, Epiphany 3 OT TP	Barbara Brown Taylor	Advent 4 PS HP, Christmas Eve PS HP, Christmas Day PS HP, Christmas 1 G HP, Christmas 2 G HP, Epiphany G HP
Kathleen M. O'Connor	Epiphany 1 OT EP, Epiphany 2 OT EP, Epiphany 3 OT EP		
David L. Ostendorf	Epiphany 4 G TP, Epiphany 5 G TP, Epiphany 6 G TP	Nancy S. Taylor	Advent 4 OT PP, Christmas Eve OT PP, Christmas Day OT PP
Pheme Perkins	Transfiguration E EP	Jeffery L. Tribble Sr.	Transfiguration G PP
Karen Pidcock-Lester	Christmas 1 OT PP, Christmas 2 A PP, Epiphany OT PP	Gene M. Tucker	Epiphany 4 OT EP, Epiphany 5 OT EP, Epiphany 6 OT EP
Robert Warden Prim	Transfiguration E HP	Kimberly Miller van Driel	Transfiguration G HP
Rollin A. Ramsaran	Christmas 1 E EP, Christmas 2 E EP, Epiphany E EP	Neal Walls	Advent 4 OT EP, Christmas Eve OT EP, Christmas Day OT EP
Stephen G. Ray Jr.	Epiphany 1 PS TP, Epiphany 2 PS TP, Epiphany 3 PS TP	Raewynne J. Whiteley	Epiphany 1 NT HP, Epiphany 2 E HP, Epiphany 3 E HP
Robert Redman	Advent 4 G TP, Christmas Eve G TP, Christmas Day G TP	Dena L. Williams	Epiphany 7 G EP, Epiphany 8 G EP, Epiphany 9 G EP
Sharon H. Ringe	Transfiguration G EP		
Rosetta E. Ross	Advent 1 PS TP, Advent 2 G TP, Advent 3 OT TP	Charles M. Wood	Epiphany 7 OT TP, Epiphany 8 OT TP, Epiphany 9 OT TP
Kenneth L. Sehested	Christmas 1 E PP, Christmas 2 E PP, Epiphany E PP	Rebecca Blair Young	Epiphany 4 PS TP, Epiphany 5 PS TP, Epiphany 6 PS TP
Archie Smith Jr.	Transfiguration OT PP		
Thomas R. Steagald	Epiphany 7 E PP, Epiphany 8 E PP, Epiphany 9 E PP